POWER GIRL
POWER TRIP

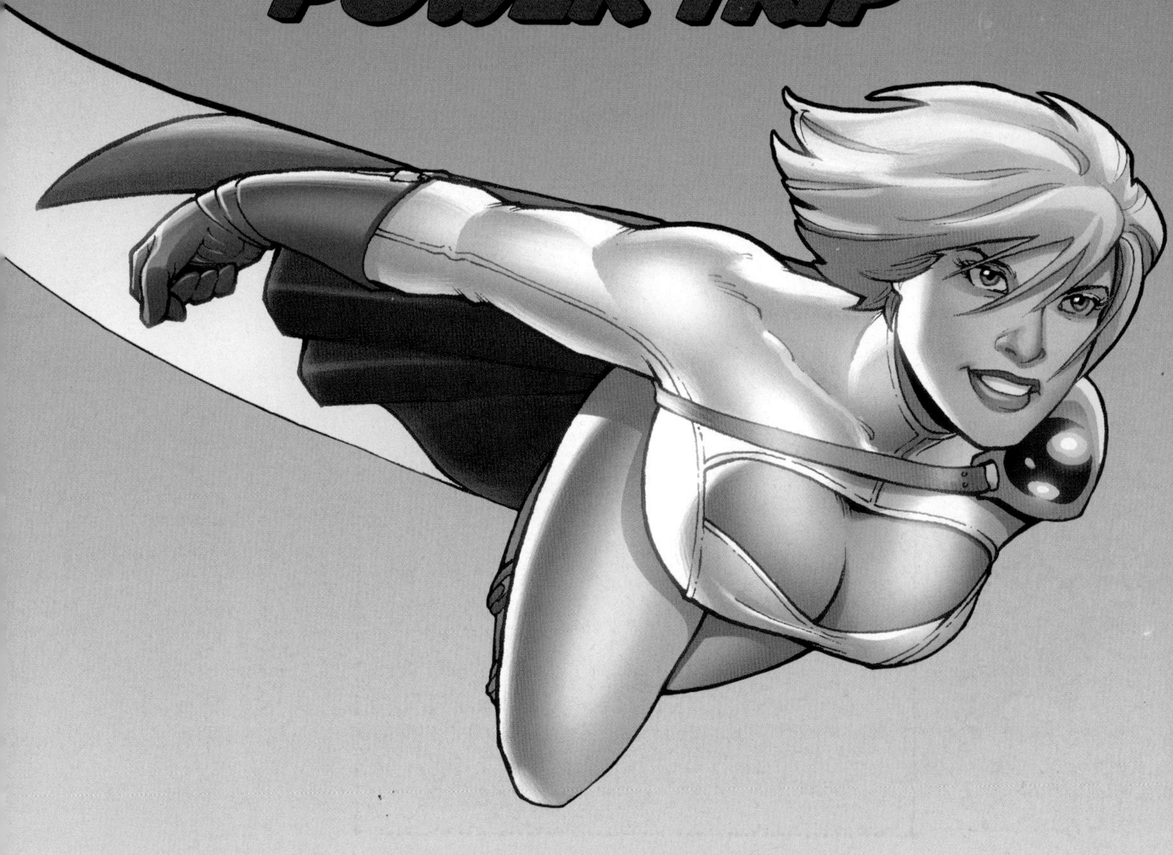

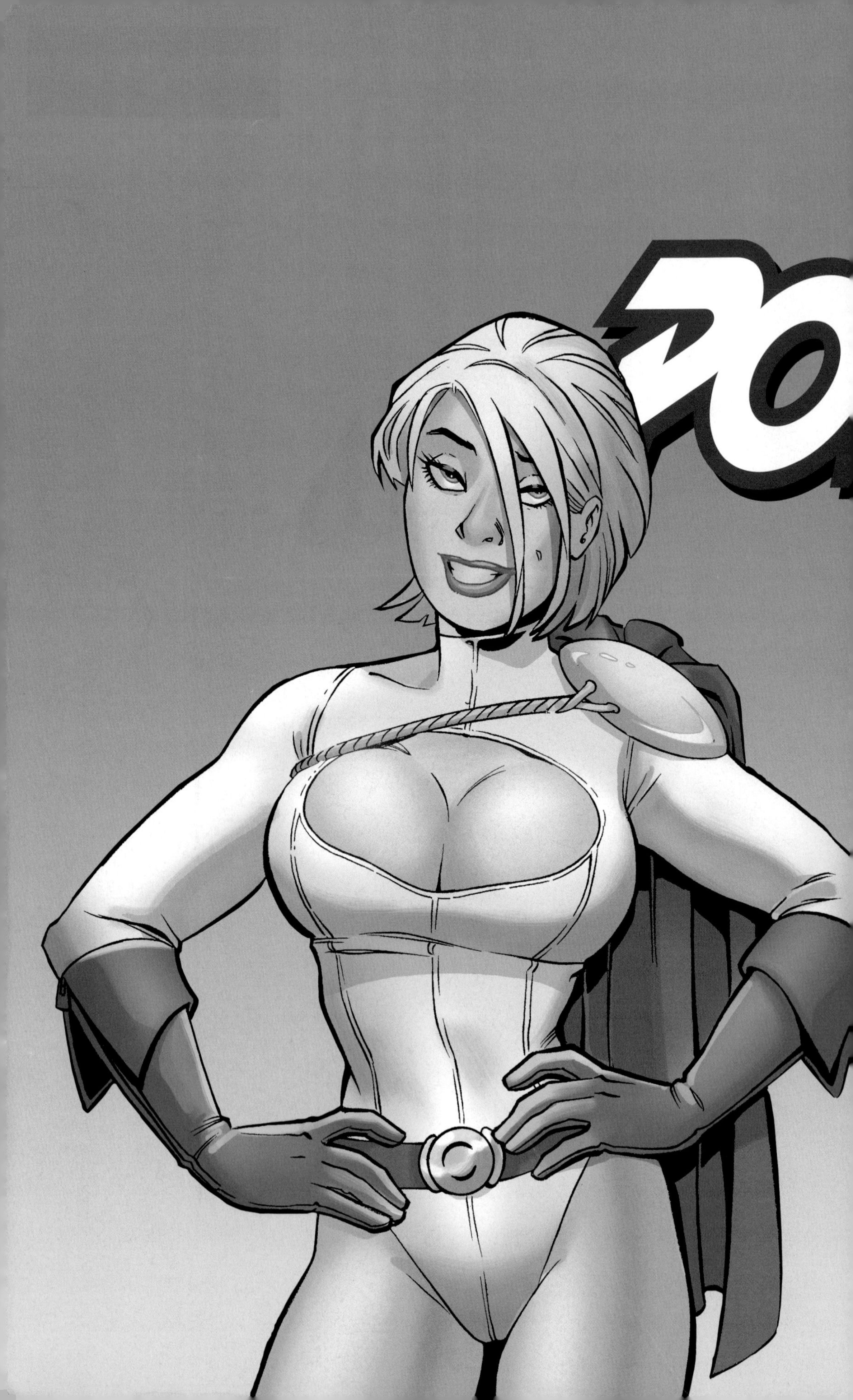

POWER GIRL
POWER TRIP

JUSTIN GRAY
JIMMY PALMIOTTI
Writers

GEOFF JOHNS
Writer – "Power Trip"

AMANDA CONNER
Writer – "Fuzzy Logic"

AMANDA CONNER
Artist

JIMMY PALMIOTTI
Inker – "Power Trip"

PAUL MOUNTS
Colorist

ROB LEIGH
JOHN J. HILL
Letterers

AMANDA CONNER
PAUL MOUNTS
Cover Artists

Brian Cunningham Mike Carlin Stephen Wacker Editors – Original Series
Rachel Gluckstern Sean Ryan Associate Editors – Original Series
Rex Ogle Harvey Richards Assistant Editors – Original Series
Robin Wildman Editor
Robbin Brosterman Design Director – Books

Bob Harras Senior VP – Editor-in-Chief, DC Comics

Diane Nelson President
Dan DiDio and Jim Lee Co-Publishers
Geoff Johns Chief Creative Officer
John Rood Executive VP – Sales, Marketing and Business Development
Amy Genkins Senior VP – Business and Legal Affairs
Nairi Gardiner Senior VP – Finance
Jeff Boison VP – Publishing Planning
Mark Chiarello VP – Art Direction and Design
John Cunningham VP – Marketing
Terri Cunningham VP – Editorial Administration
Alison Gill Senior VP – Manufacturing and Operations
Hank Kanalz Senior VP – Vertigo and Integrated Publishing
Jay Kogan VP – Business and Legal Affairs, Publishing
Jack Mahan VP – Business Affairs, Talent
Nick Napolitano VP – Manufacturing Administration
Sue Pohja VP – Book Sales
Courtney Simmons Senior VP – Publicity
Bob Wayne Senior VP – Sales

POWER GIRL: POWER TRIP

DC Comics, 1700 Broadway, New York, NY 10019
A Warner Bros. Entertainment Company.
Printed by RR Donnelley, Salem, VA, USA. 1/10/14. First Printing.

ISBN: 978-1-4012-4307-4

Library of Congress Cataloging-in-Publication Data

Palmiotti, Jimmy.
    Power Girl : Power Trip / Jimmy Palmiotti, Geoff Johns ; [illustrated by]
Amanda Conner.
        pages cm
    ISBN 978-1-4012-4307-4 (pbk.)
1. Graphic novels. I. Johns, Geoff, 1973- II. Conner, Amanda, illustrator.
III. Title.
    PN6728.P634P35 2014
    741.5'973—dc23
                        2013039773

POWER TRIP part one

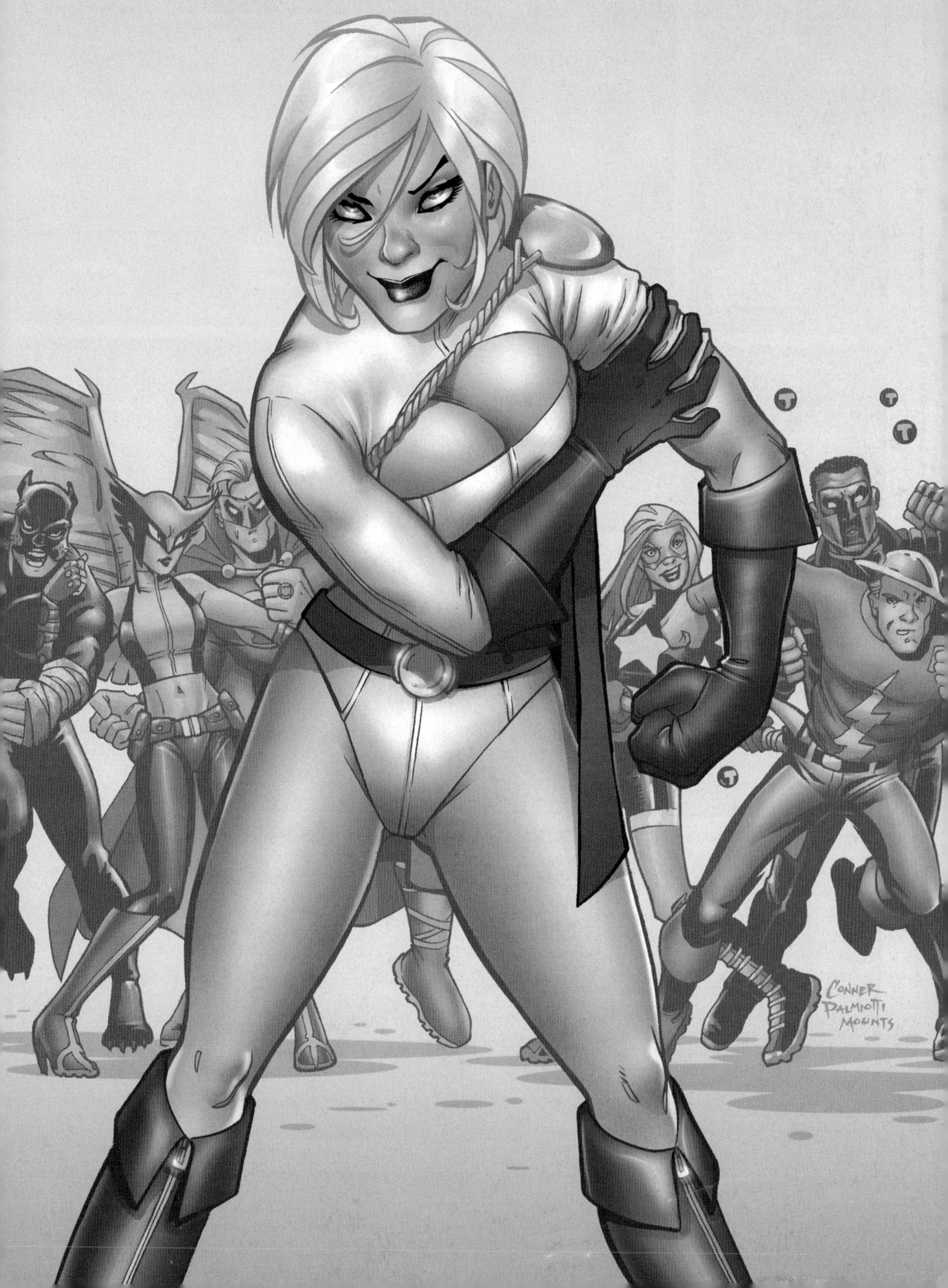
CONNER
DALMIOTTI
MOUNTS

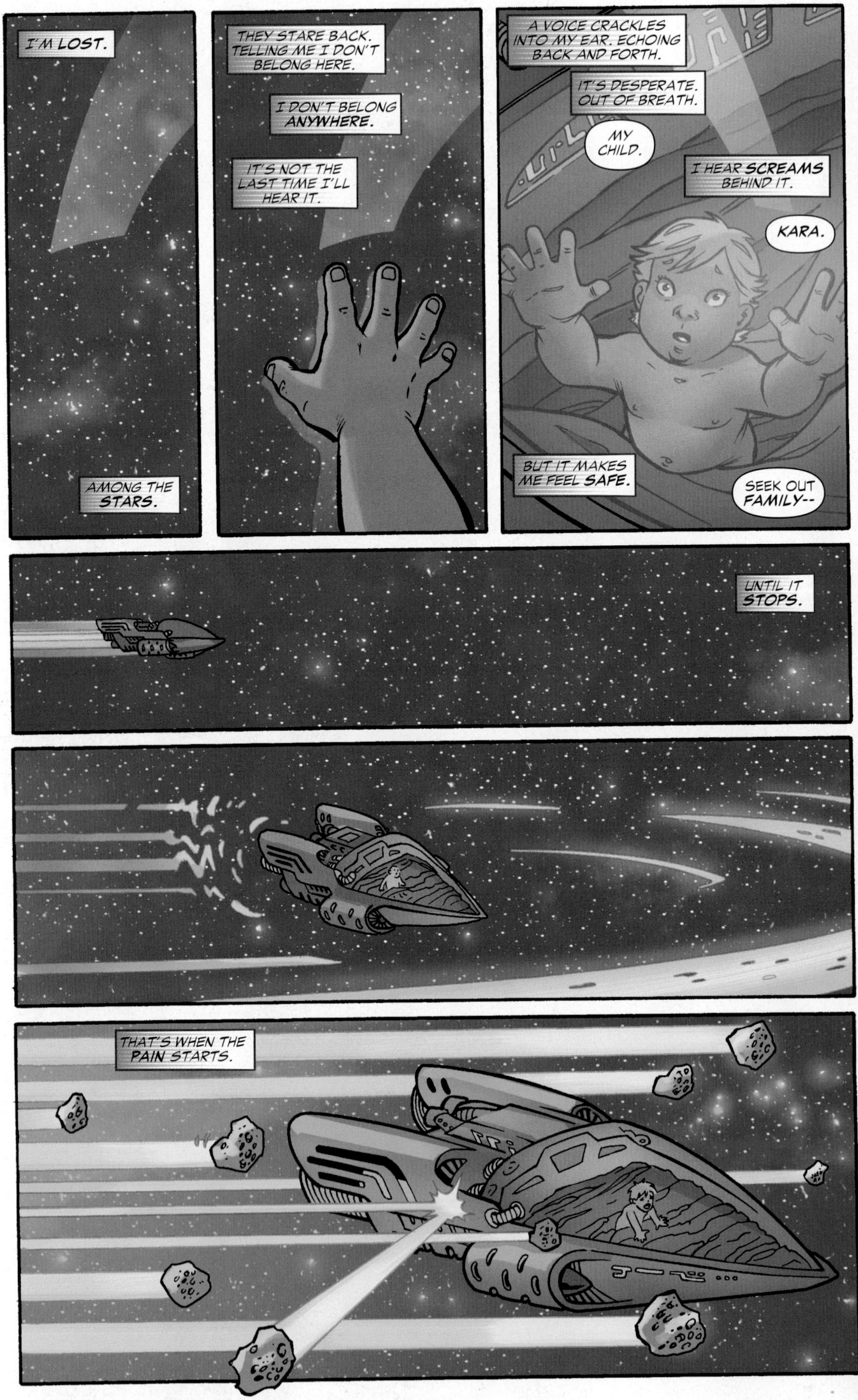
I'M LOST.
AMONG THE STARS.
THEY STARE BACK. TELLING ME I DON'T BELONG HERE.
I DON'T BELONG ANYWHERE.
IT'S NOT THE LAST TIME I'LL HEAR IT.
A VOICE CRACKLES INTO MY EAR. ECHOING BACK AND FORTH.
IT'S DESPERATE. OUT OF BREATH.
MY CHILD.
I HEAR SCREAMS BEHIND IT.
KARA.
BUT IT MAKES ME FEEL SAFE.
SEEK OUT FAMILY--
UNTIL IT STOPS.
THAT'S WHEN THE PAIN STARTS.

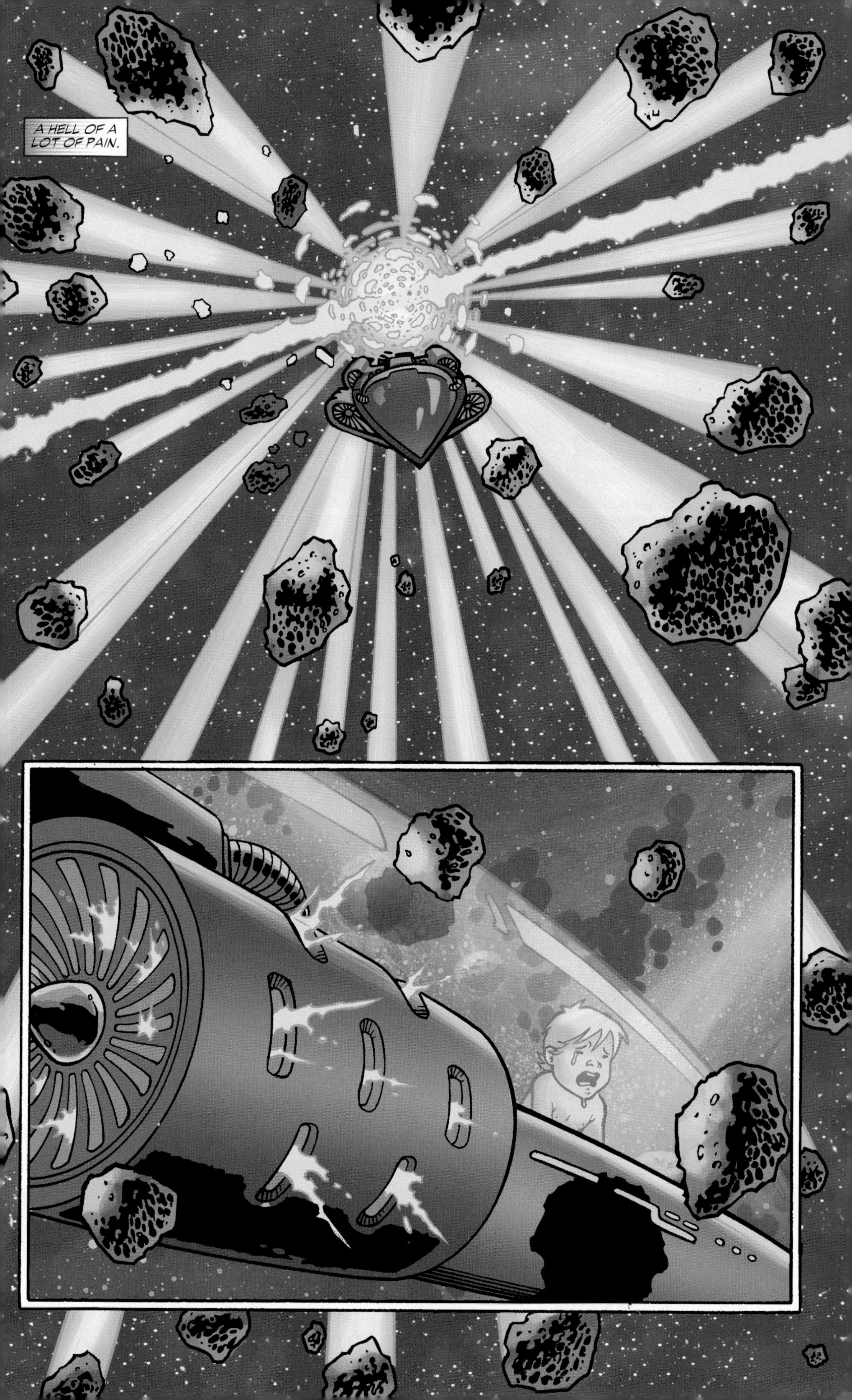
A HELL OF A LOT OF PAIN.

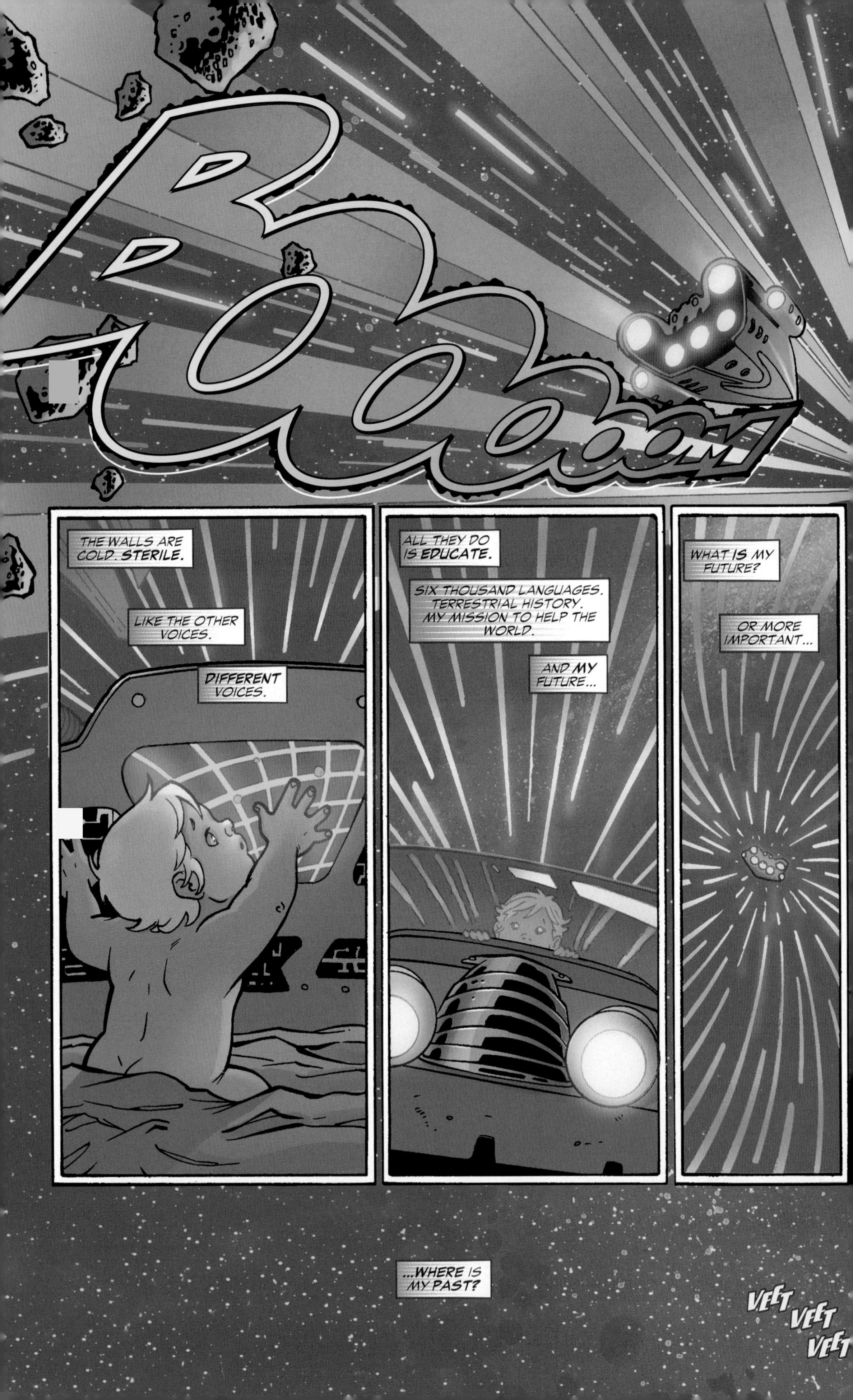
BRRROOOOOM
THE WALLS ARE COLD. STERILE.
LIKE THE OTHER VOICES.
DIFFERENT VOICES.
ALL THEY DO IS EDUCATE.
SIX THOUSAND LANGUAGES. TERRESTRIAL HISTORY. MY MISSION TO HELP THE WORLD.
AND MY FUTURE...
WHAT IS MY FUTURE?
OR MORE IMPORTANT...
...WHERE IS MY PAST?
VEET VEET VEET

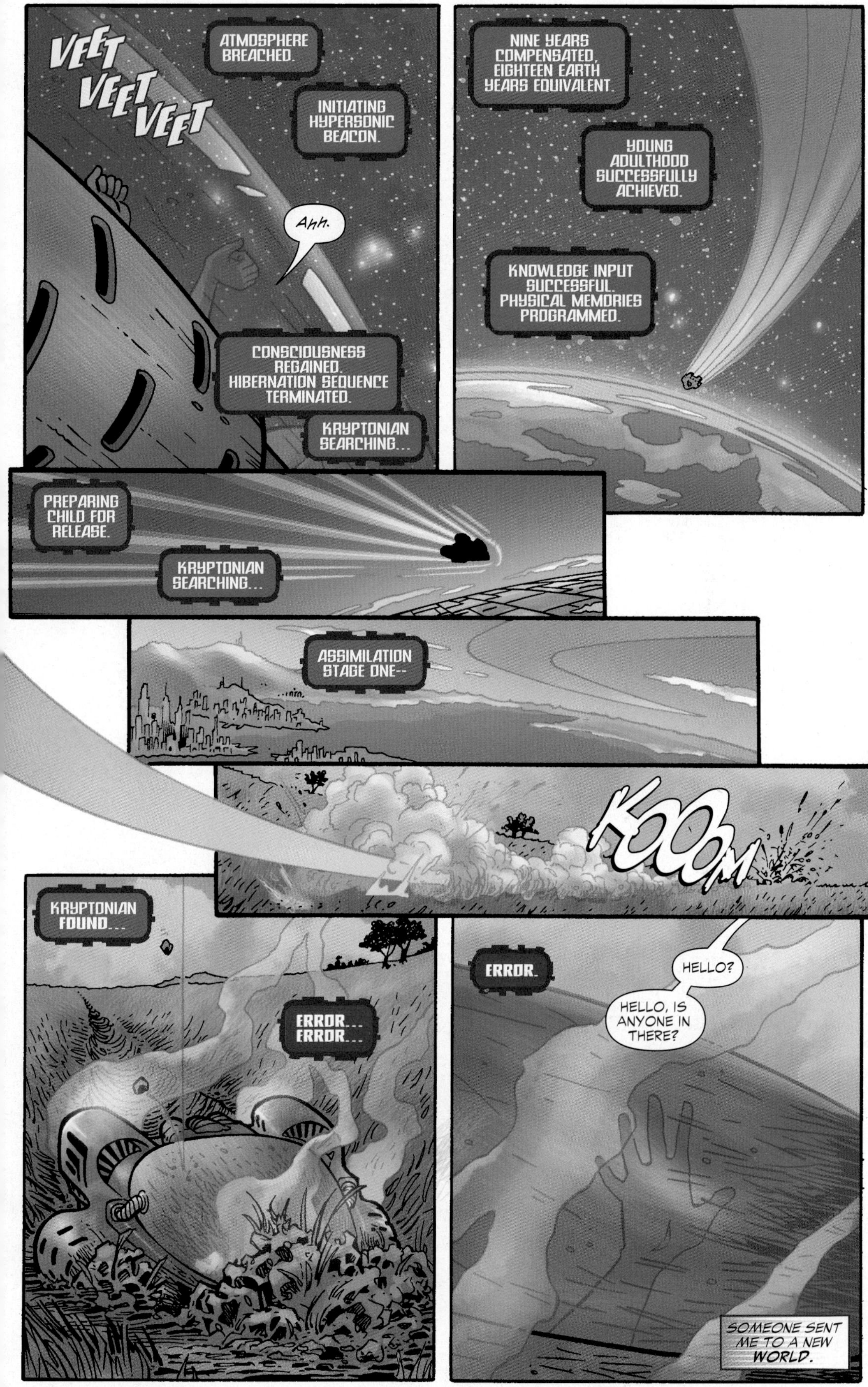
VEET VEET VEET
ATMOSPHERE BREACHED.
INITIATING HYPERSONIC BEACON.
Ahh.
CONSCIOUSNESS REGAINED. HIBERNATION SEQUENCE TERMINATED.
KRYPTONIAN SEARCHING...
NINE YEARS COMPENSATED, EIGHTEEN EARTH YEARS EQUIVALENT.
YOUNG ADULTHOOD SUCCESSFULLY ACHIEVED.
KNOWLEDGE INPUT SUCCESSFUL. PHYSICAL MEMORIES PROGRAMMED.
PREPARING CHILD FOR RELEASE.
KRYPTONIAN SEARCHING...
ASSIMILATION STAGE ONE--
KOOOM
KRYPTONIAN FOUND...
ERROR... ERROR...
ERROR.
HELLO?
HELLO, IS ANYONE IN THERE?
SOMEONE SENT ME TO A NEW WORLD.

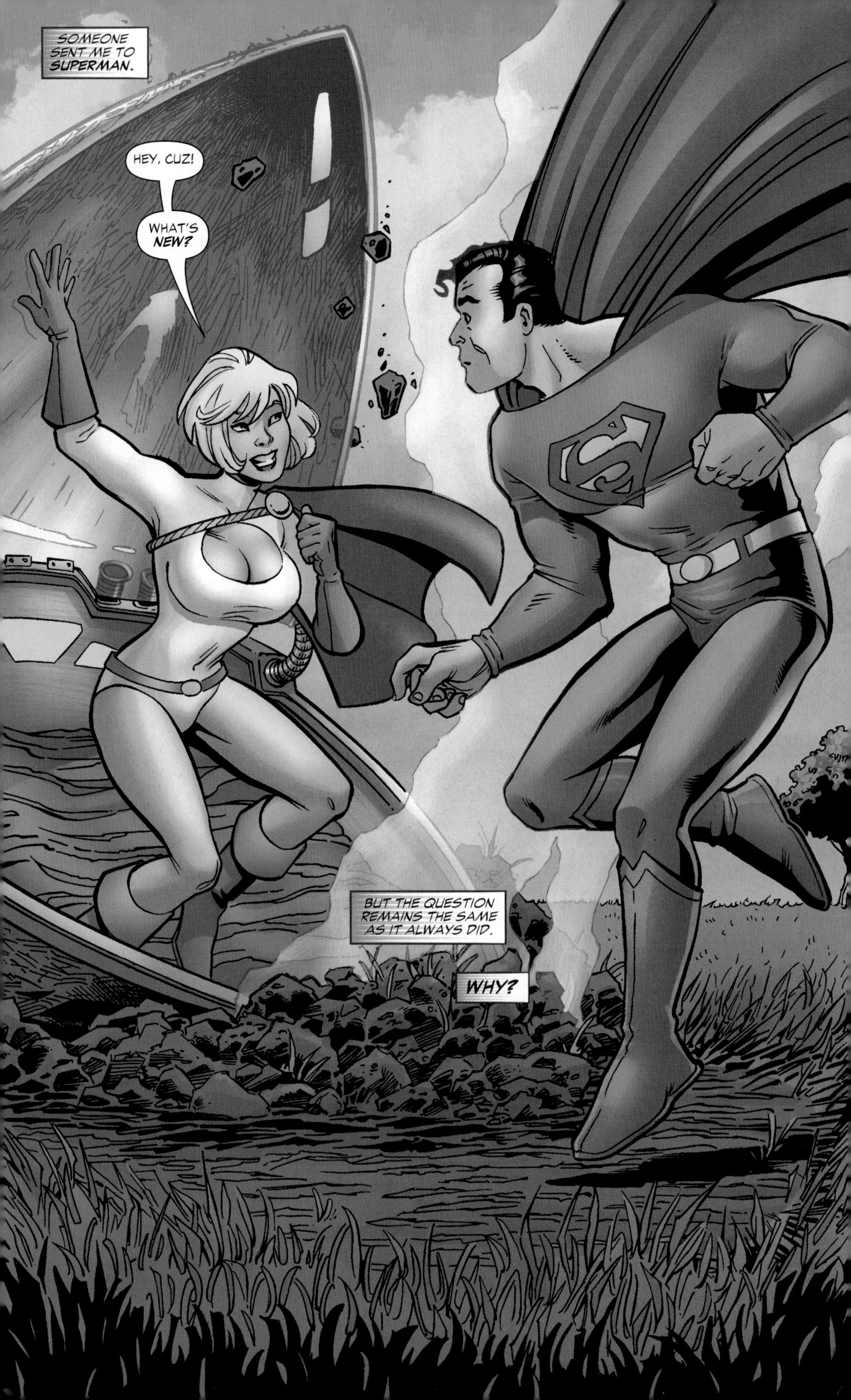
SOMEONE SENT ME TO SUPERMAN.
HEY, CUZ!
WHAT'S NEW?
BUT THE QUESTION REMAINS THE SAME AS IT ALWAYS DID.
WHY?

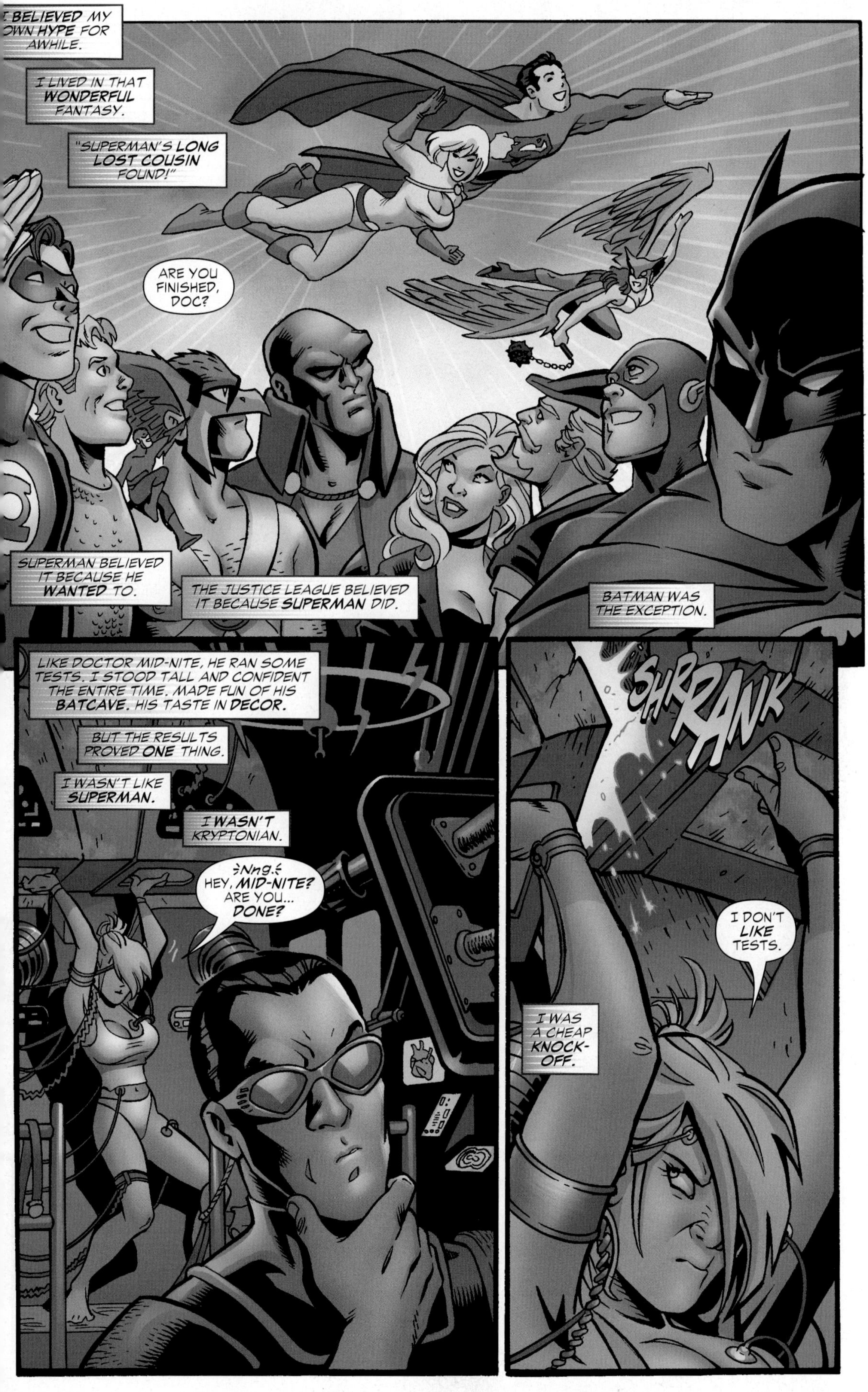
I BELIEVED MY OWN HYPE FOR AWHILE.
I LIVED IN THAT WONDERFUL FANTASY.
"SUPERMAN'S LONG LOST COUSIN FOUND!"
ARE YOU FINISHED, DOC?
SUPERMAN BELIEVED IT BECAUSE HE WANTED TO.
THE JUSTICE LEAGUE BELIEVED IT BECAUSE SUPERMAN DID.
BATMAN WAS THE EXCEPTION.
LIKE DOCTOR MID-NITE, HE RAN SOME TESTS. I STOOD TALL AND CONFIDENT THE ENTIRE TIME. MADE FUN OF HIS BATCAVE. HIS TASTE IN DECOR.
BUT THE RESULTS PROVED ONE THING.
I WASN'T LIKE SUPERMAN.
I WASN'T KRYPTONIAN.
Nng. HEY, MID-NITE? ARE YOU... DONE?
SHRRANK
I DON'T LIKE TESTS.
I WAS A CHEAP KNOCK-OFF.

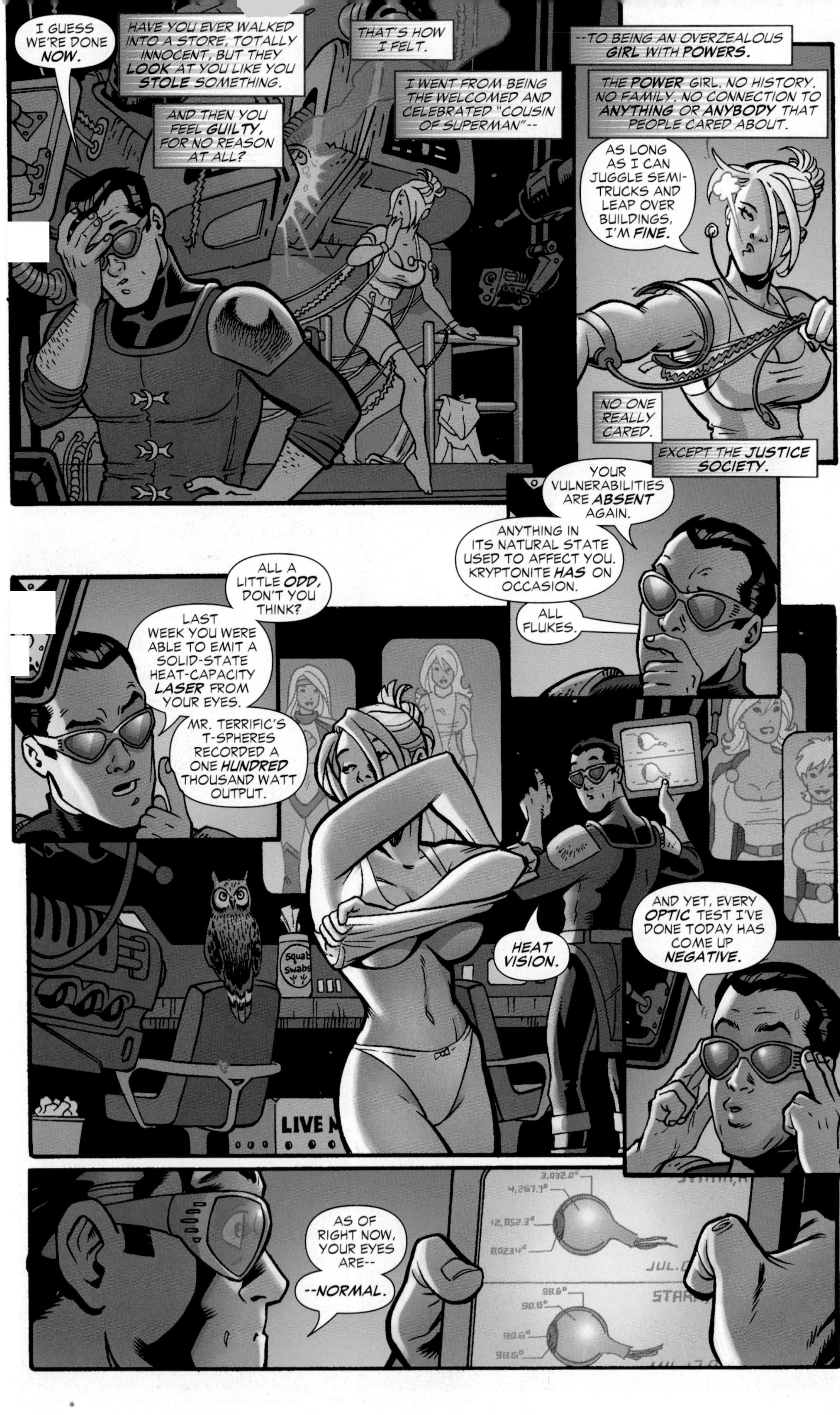
I GUESS WE'RE DONE NOW.
HAVE YOU EVER WALKED INTO A STORE, TOTALLY INNOCENT, BUT THEY LOOK AT YOU LIKE YOU STOLE SOMETHING.
AND THEN YOU FEEL GUILTY, FOR NO REASON AT ALL?
THAT'S HOW I FELT.
I WENT FROM BEING THE WELCOMED AND CELEBRATED "COUSIN OF SUPERMAN"--
--TO BEING AN OVERZEALOUS GIRL WITH POWERS.
THE POWER GIRL. NO HISTORY. NO FAMILY. NO CONNECTION TO ANYTHING OR ANYBODY THAT PEOPLE CARED ABOUT.
AS LONG AS I CAN JUGGLE SEMI-TRUCKS AND LEAP OVER BUILDINGS, I'M FINE.
NO ONE REALLY CARED.
EXCEPT THE JUSTICE SOCIETY.
YOUR VULNERABILITIES ARE ABSENT AGAIN.
ANYTHING IN ITS NATURAL STATE USED TO AFFECT YOU. KRYPTONITE HAS ON OCCASION.
ALL FLUKES.
ALL A LITTLE ODD, DON'T YOU THINK?
LAST WEEK YOU WERE ABLE TO EMIT A SOLID-STATE HEAT-CAPACITY LASER FROM YOUR EYES.
MR. TERRIFIC'S T-SPHERES RECORDED A ONE HUNDRED THOUSAND WATT OUTPUT.
HEAT VISION.
AND YET, EVERY OPTIC TEST I'VE DONE TODAY HAS COME UP NEGATIVE.
LIVE
3,032.0°
4,267.7°
12,852.3°
8,023.4°
98.6°
98.6°
98.6°
98.6°
AS OF RIGHT NOW, YOUR EYES ARE--
--NORMAL.

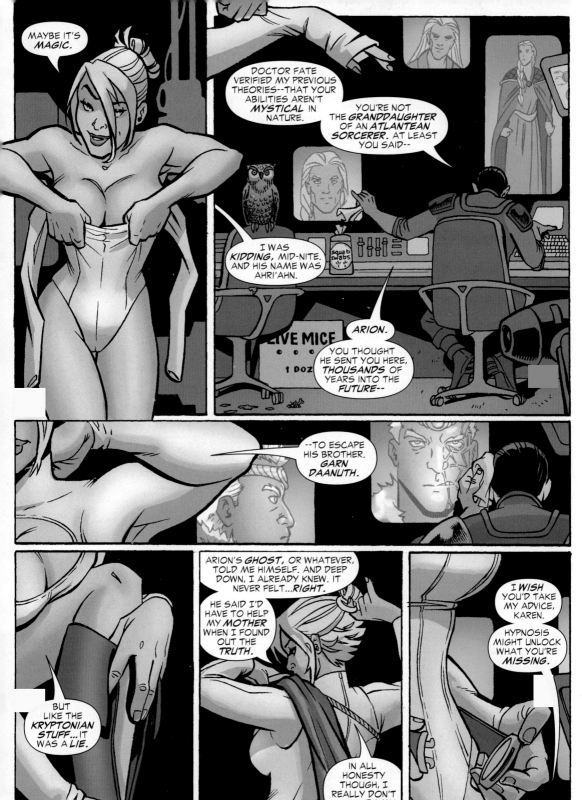

MAYBE IT'S MAGIC.

DOCTOR FATE VERIFIED MY PREVIOUS THEORIES--THAT YOUR ABILITIES AREN'T *MYSTICAL* IN NATURE.

YOU'RE NOT THE *GRANDDAUGHTER* OF AN *ATLANTEAN SORCERER*. AT LEAST YOU SAID--

I WAS *KIDDING*, MID-NITE. AND HIS NAME WAS AHRI'AHN.

ARION.

YOU THOUGHT HE SENT YOU HERE, *THOUSANDS* OF YEARS INTO THE *FUTURE*--

--TO ESCAPE HIS BROTHER. *GARN DAANUTH.*

ARION'S *GHOST*, OR WHATEVER, TOLD ME HIMSELF. AND DEEP DOWN, I ALREADY KNEW. IT NEVER FELT...*RIGHT*.

HE SAID I'D HAVE TO HELP MY *MOTHER* WHEN I FOUND OUT THE *TRUTH*.

BUT LIKE THE *KRYPTONIAN STUFF*...IT WAS A *LIE*.

IN ALL HONESTY THOUGH, I REALLY DON'T GIVE A *DAMN* ANYMORE.

I'M *TIRED* OF HAVING MY HEAD PLAYED WITH.

I *WISH* YOU'D TAKE MY ADVICE, KAREN.

HYPNOSIS MIGHT UNLOCK WHAT YOU'RE *MISSING*.

LIVE MICE
1 DOZ

squab swabs

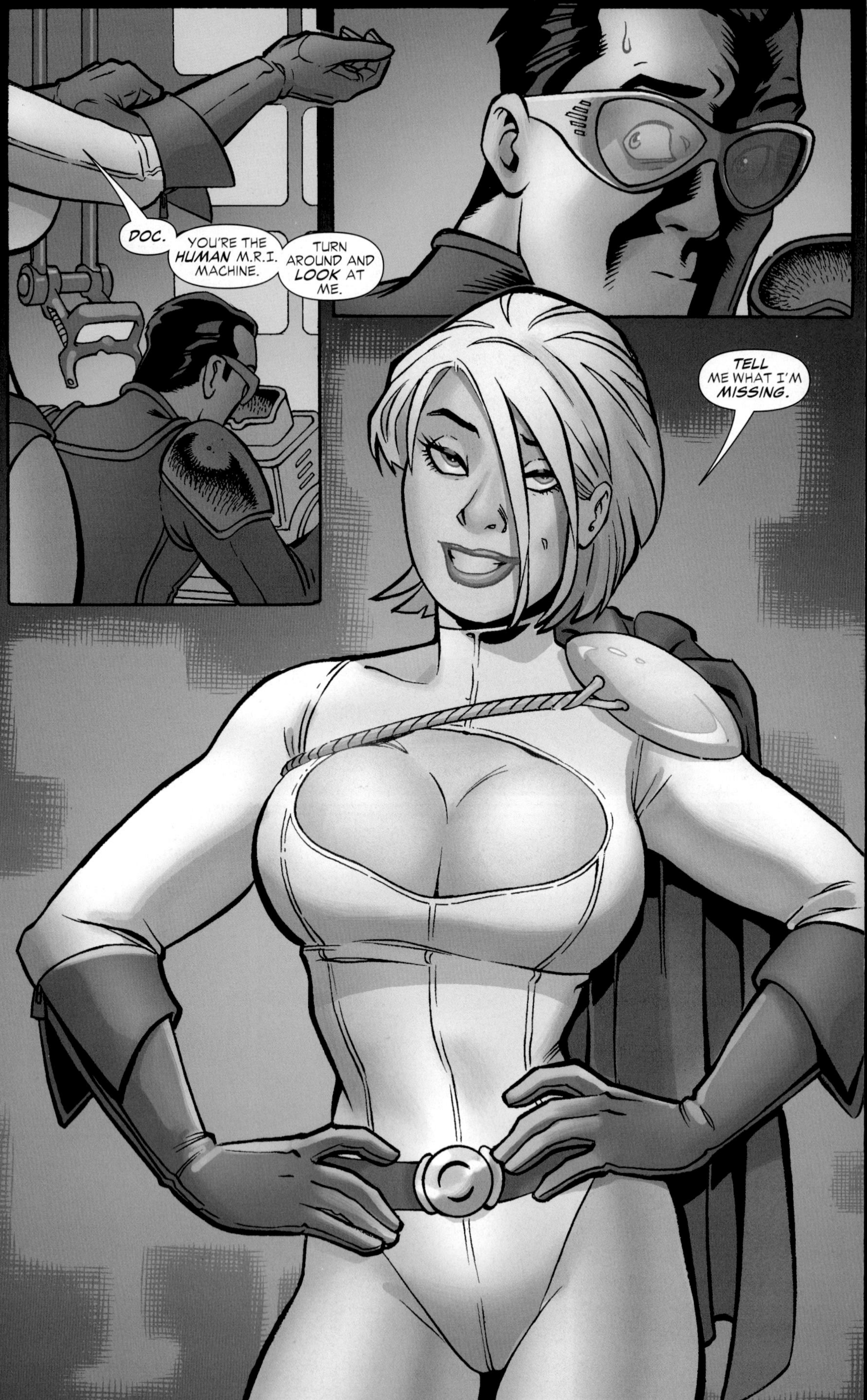
DOC.
YOU'RE THE HUMAN M.R.I. MACHINE.
TURN AROUND AND LOOK AT ME.
TELL ME WHAT I'M MISSING.

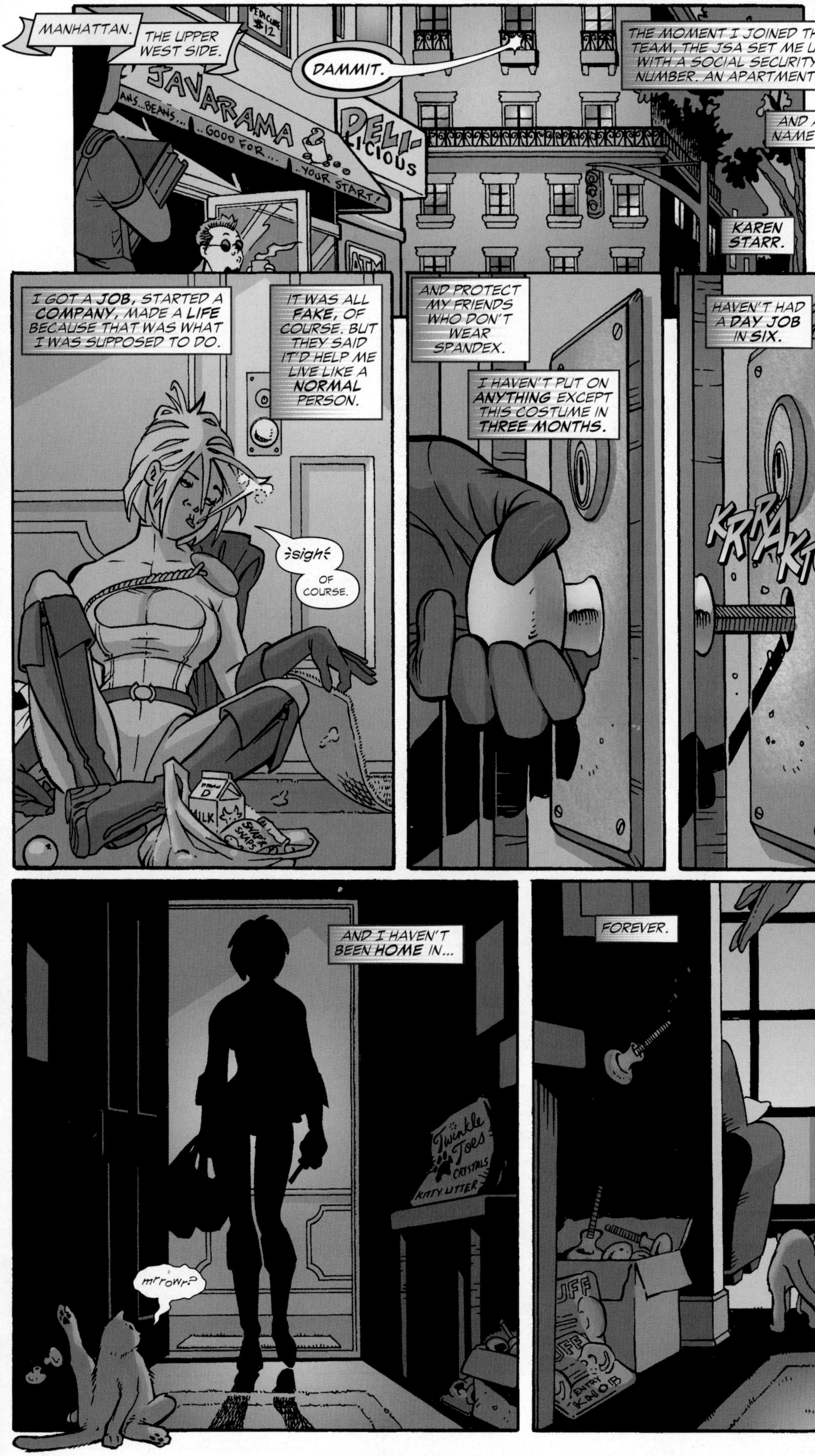
MANHATTAN.
THE UPPER WEST SIDE.
DAMMIT.
THE MOMENT I JOINED THE TEAM, THE JSA SET ME UP WITH A SOCIAL SECURITY NUMBER. AN APARTMENT.
AND A NAME.
KAREN STARR.
I GOT A JOB, STARTED A COMPANY, MADE A LIFE BECAUSE THAT WAS WHAT I WAS SUPPOSED TO DO.
IT WAS ALL FAKE, OF COURSE. BUT THEY SAID IT'D HELP ME LIVE LIKE A NORMAL PERSON.
sigh
OF COURSE.
AND PROTECT MY FRIENDS WHO DON'T WEAR SPANDEX.
I HAVEN'T PUT ON ANYTHING EXCEPT THIS COSTUME IN THREE MONTHS.
HAVEN'T HAD A DAY JOB IN SIX.
KRRAKTCH
AND I HAVEN'T BEEN HOME IN...
mrrowr?
FOREVER.

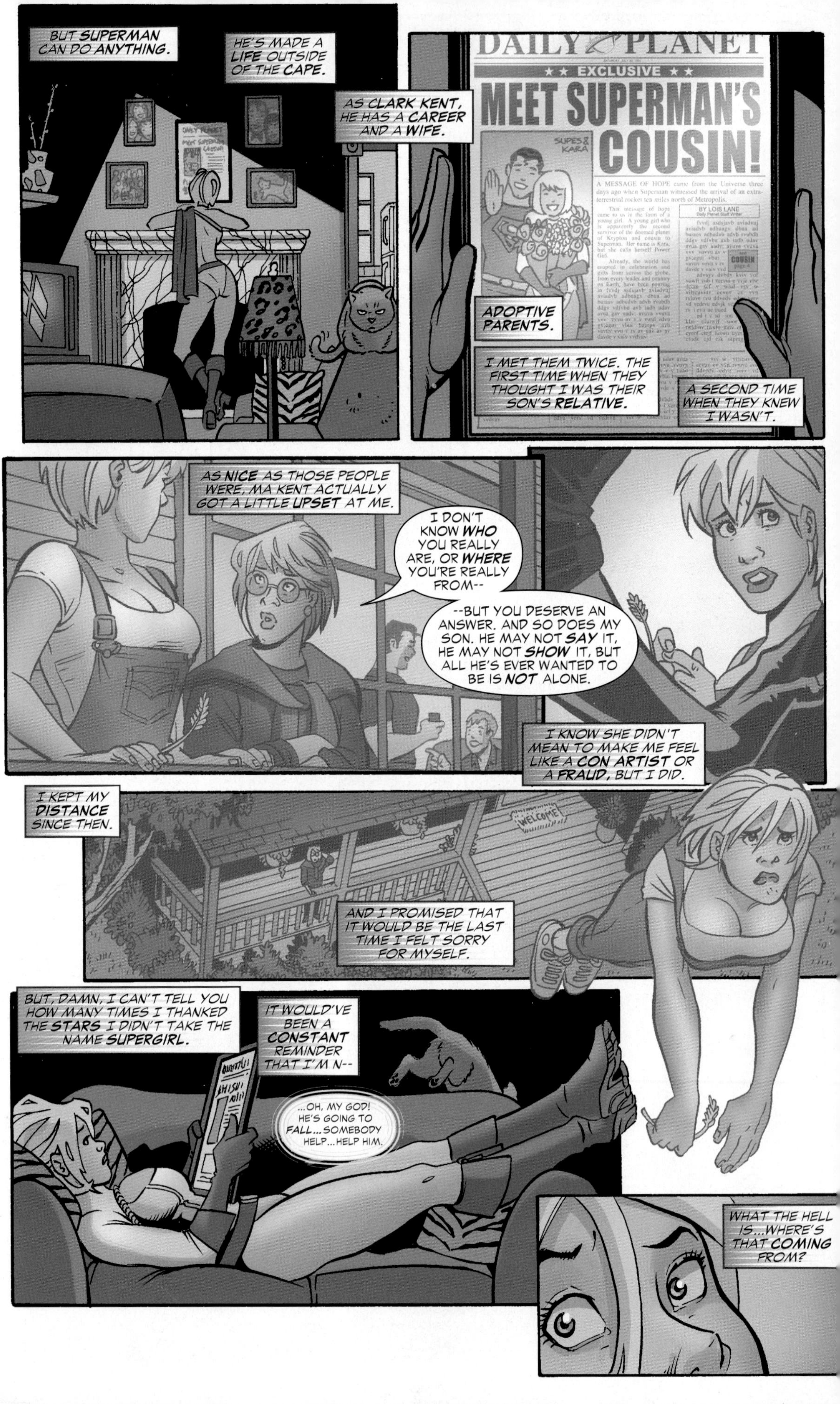

BUT SUPERMAN CAN DO ANYTHING.
HE'S MADE A LIFE OUTSIDE OF THE CAPE.
AS CLARK KENT, HE HAS A CAREER AND A WIFE.
DAILY PLANET
★ ★ EXCLUSIVE ★ ★
MEET SUPERMAN'S COUSIN!
SUPES & KARA
A MESSAGE OF HOPE came from the Universe three days ago when Superman witnessed the arrival of an extra-terrestrial rocket ten miles north of Metropolis.
BY LOIS LANE
Daily Planet Staff Writer
ADOPTIVE PARENTS.
I MET THEM TWICE. THE FIRST TIME WHEN THEY THOUGHT I WAS THEIR SON'S RELATIVE.
A SECOND TIME WHEN THEY KNEW I WASN'T.
AS NICE AS THOSE PEOPLE WERE, MA KENT ACTUALLY GOT A LITTLE UPSET AT ME.
I DON'T KNOW WHO YOU REALLY ARE, OR WHERE YOU'RE REALLY FROM--
--BUT YOU DESERVE AN ANSWER. AND SO DOES MY SON. HE MAY NOT SAY IT, HE MAY NOT SHOW IT, BUT ALL HE'S EVER WANTED TO BE IS NOT ALONE.
I KNOW SHE DIDN'T MEAN TO MAKE ME FEEL LIKE A CON ARTIST OR A FRAUD, BUT I DID.
I KEPT MY DISTANCE SINCE THEN.
WELCOME
AND I PROMISED THAT IT WOULD BE THE LAST TIME I FELT SORRY FOR MYSELF.
BUT, DAMN, I CAN'T TELL YOU HOW MANY TIMES I THANKED THE STARS I DIDN'T TAKE THE NAME SUPERGIRL.
IT WOULD'VE BEEN A CONSTANT REMINDER THAT I'M N--
...OH, MY GOD! HE'S GOING TO FALL... SOMEBODY HELP... HELP HIM.
WHAT THE HELL IS...WHERE'S THAT COMING FROM?

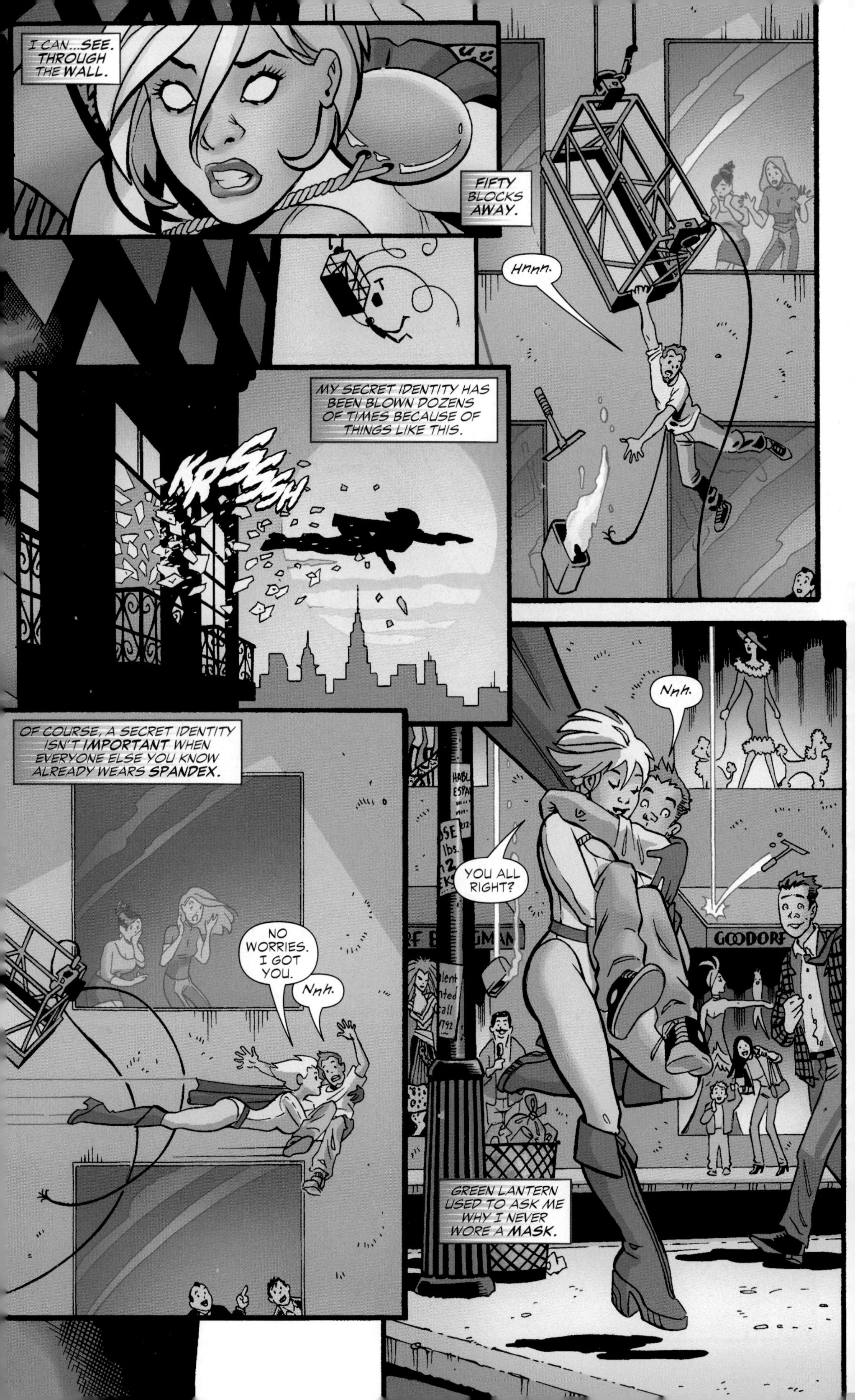

I CAN...SEE. THROUGH THE WALL.
FIFTY BLOCKS AWAY.
Hnnn.
MY SECRET IDENTITY HAS BEEN BLOWN DOZENS OF TIMES BECAUSE OF THINGS LIKE THIS.
KRSSSH
OF COURSE, A SECRET IDENTITY ISN'T IMPORTANT WHEN EVERYONE ELSE YOU KNOW ALREADY WEARS SPANDEX.
NO WORRIES. I GOT YOU.
Nnh.
Nnh.
YOU ALL RIGHT?
GOODORF
GREEN LANTERN USED TO ASK ME WHY I NEVER WORE A MASK.

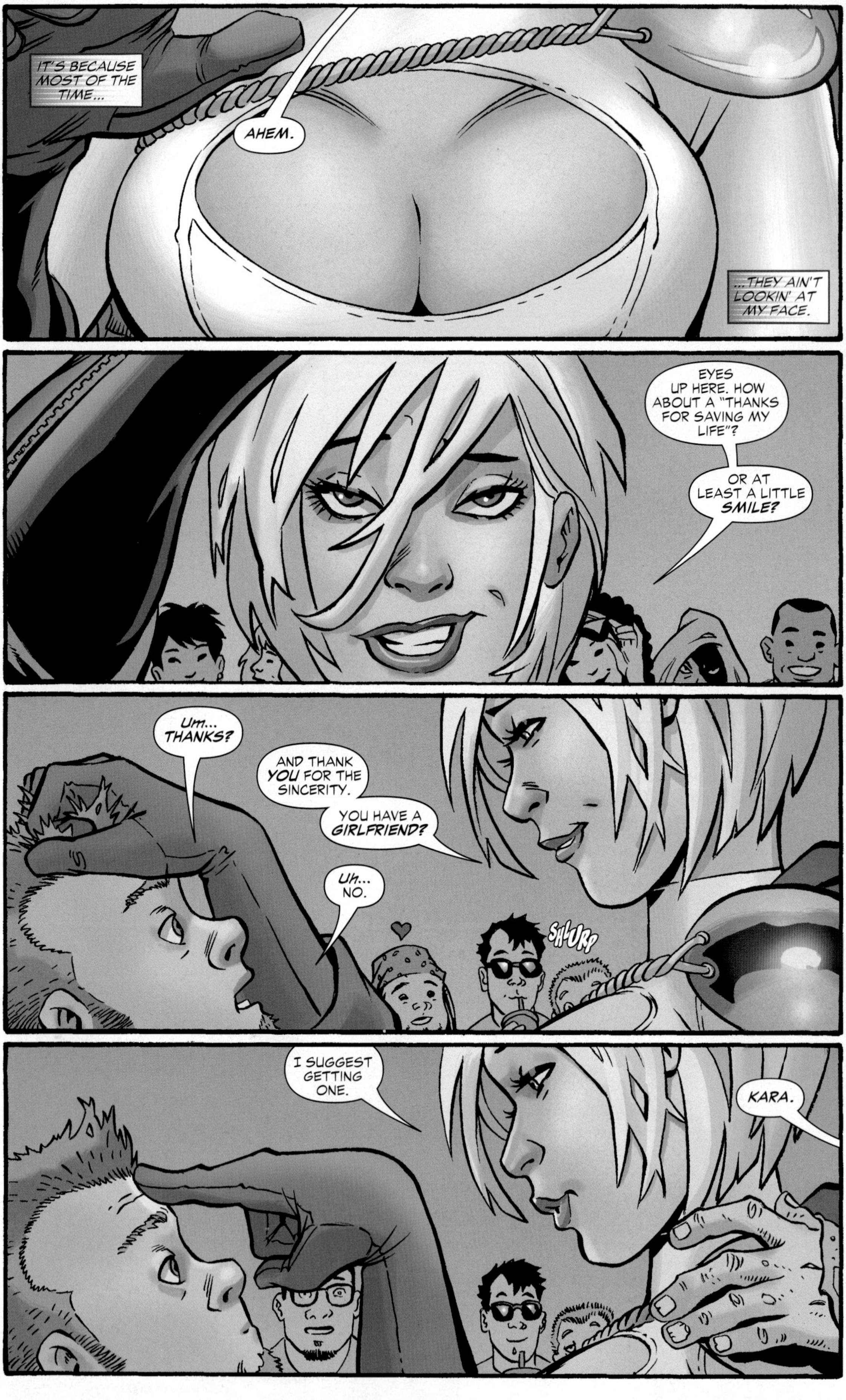

IT'S BECAUSE MOST OF THE TIME...
AHEM.
...THEY AIN'T LOOKIN' AT MY FACE.
EYES UP HERE. HOW ABOUT A "THANKS FOR SAVING MY LIFE"?
OR AT LEAST A LITTLE SMILE?
Um... THANKS?
AND THANK YOU FOR THE SINCERITY.
YOU HAVE A GIRLFRIEND?
Uh... NO.
SHLURP
I SUGGEST GETTING ONE.
KARA.

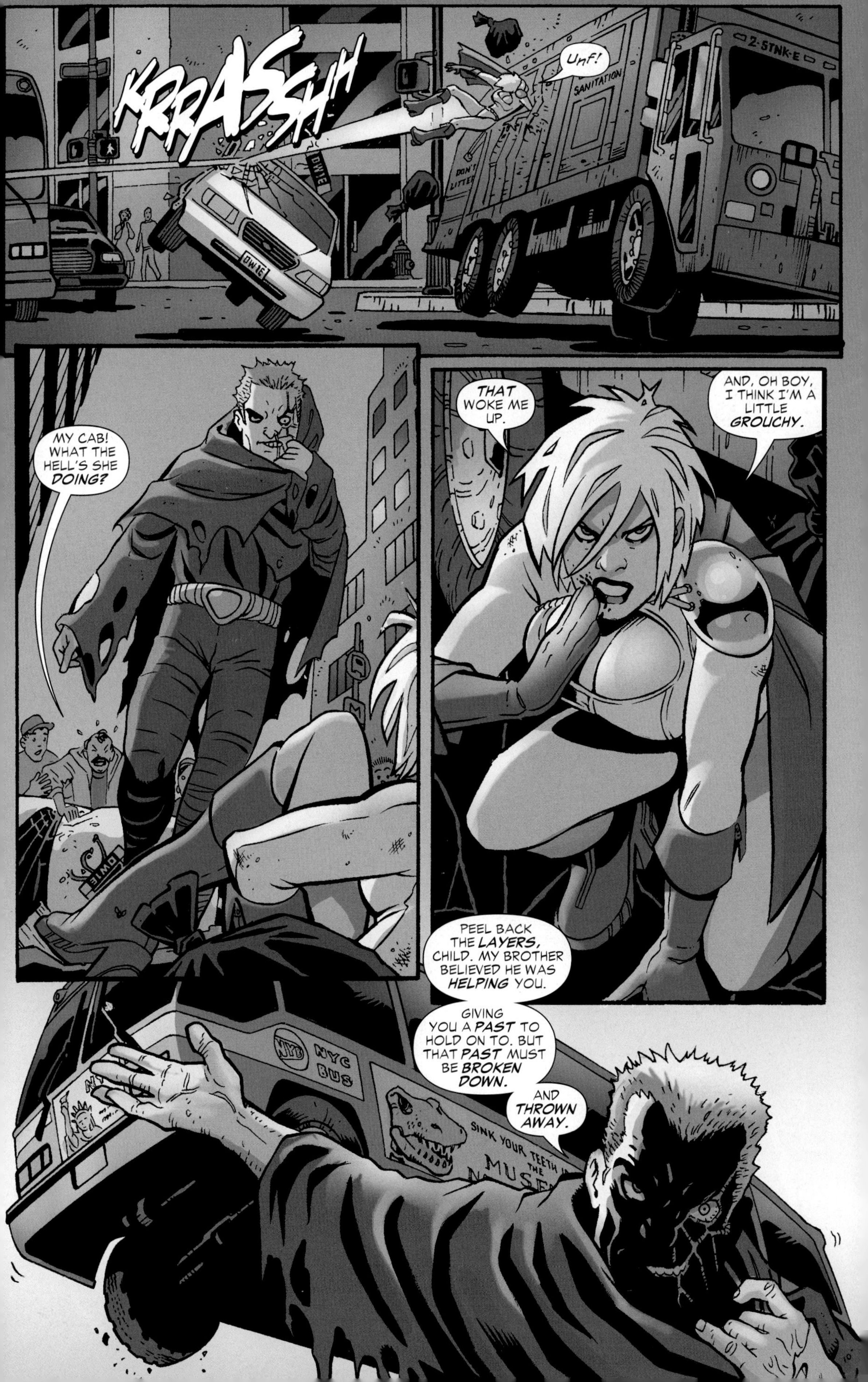
KRRASSH
Unf!
2-STNK-E
SANITATION
MY CAB! WHAT THE HELL'S SHE DOING?
THAT WOKE ME UP.
AND, OH BOY, I THINK I'M A LITTLE GROUCHY.
PEEL BACK THE LAYERS, CHILD. MY BROTHER BELIEVED HE WAS HELPING YOU.
GIVING YOU A PAST TO HOLD ON TO. BUT THAT PAST MUST BE BROKEN DOWN.
AND THROWN AWAY.
NYC BUS

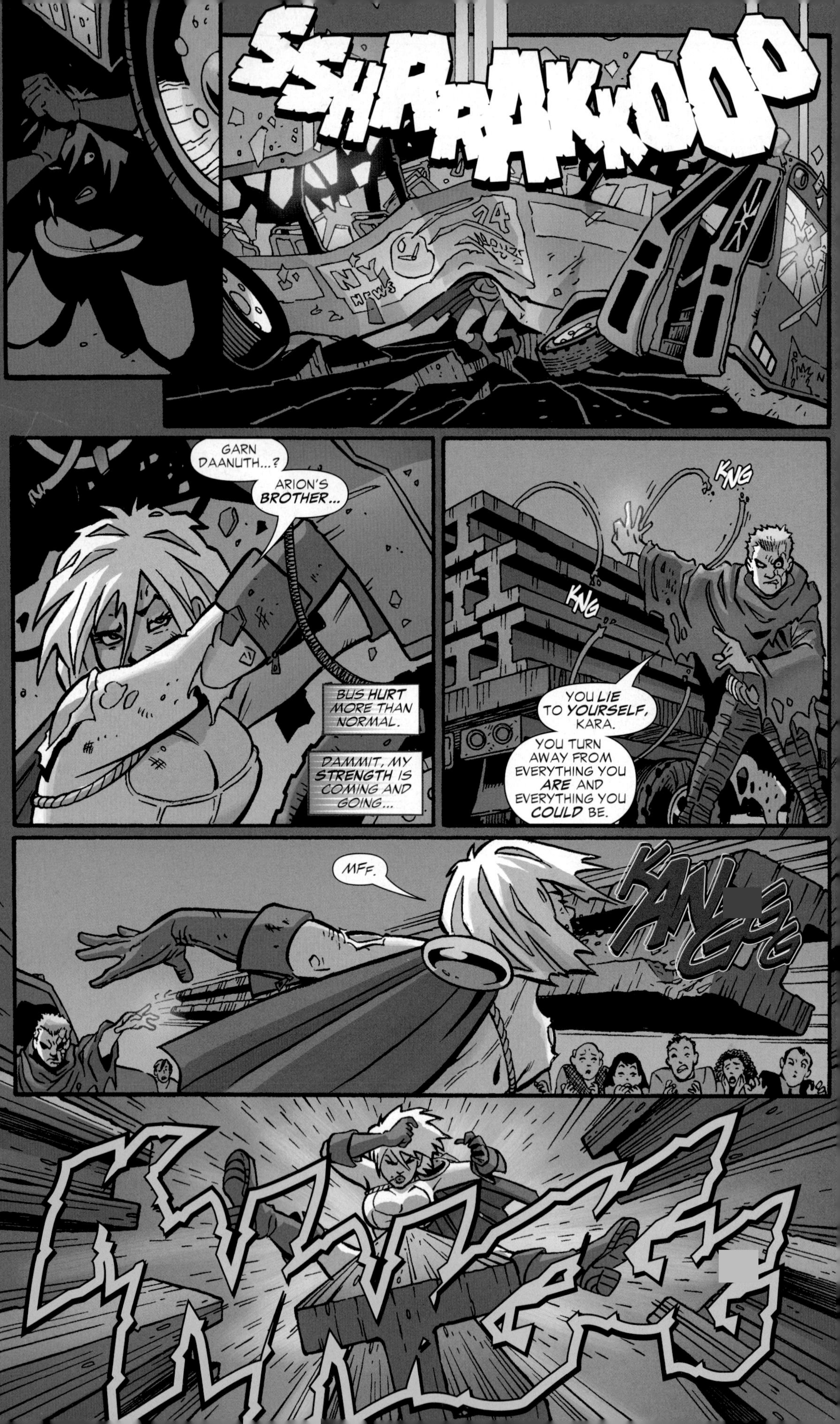
SSHRRAKKOOOO
GARN DAANUTH...?
ARION'S BROTHER...
BUS HURT MORE THAN NORMAL.
DAMMIT, MY STRENGTH IS COMING AND GOING...
KNG
KNG
YOU LIE TO YOURSELF, KARA.
YOU TURN AWAY FROM EVERYTHING YOU ARE AND EVERYTHING YOU COULD BE.
MFF.

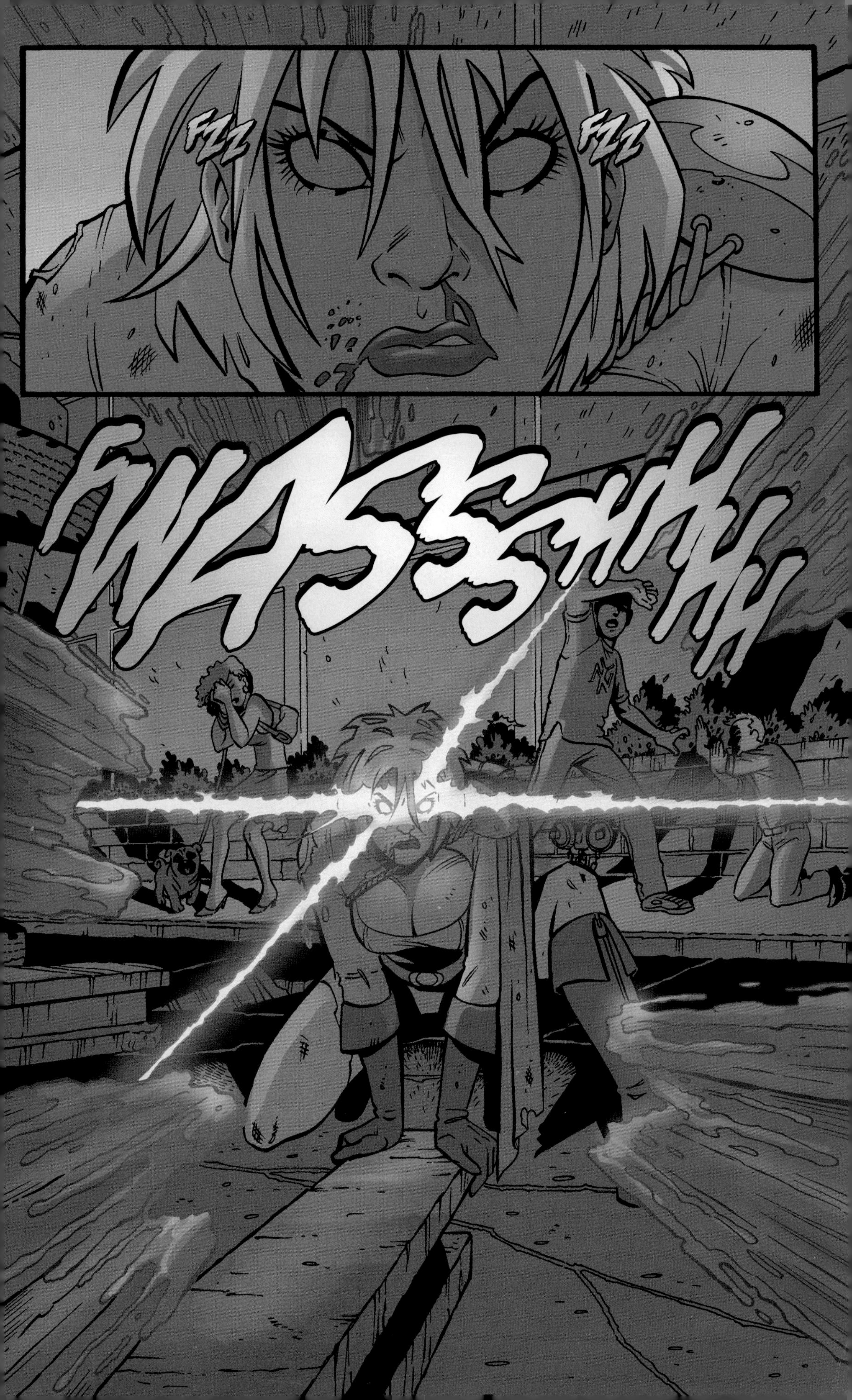
FZZ
FZZ
FWASSSHHHH

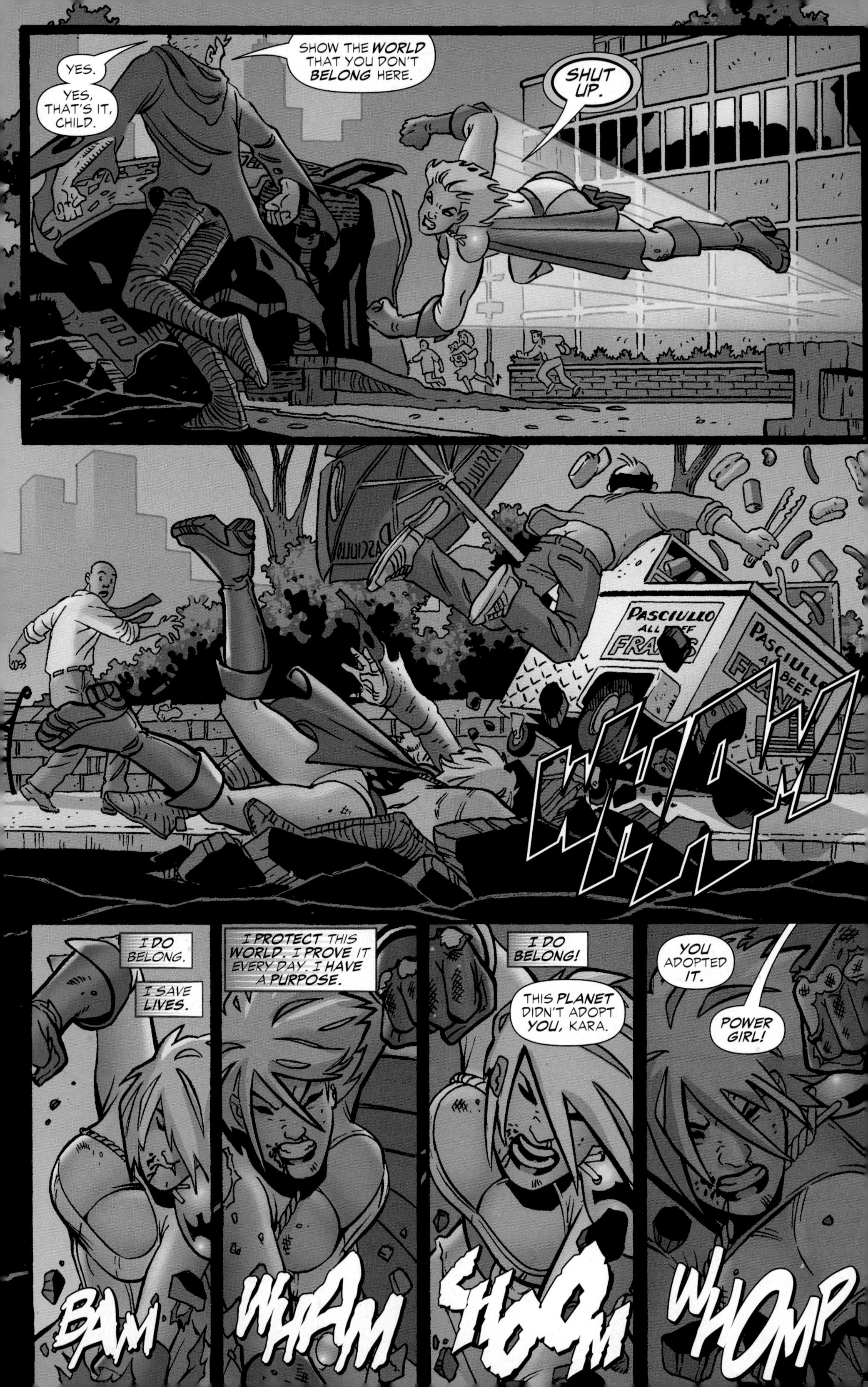

YES.
YES, THAT'S IT, CHILD.
SHOW THE WORLD THAT YOU DON'T BELONG HERE.
SHUT UP.
PASCIULLO ALL BEEF FRANKS
WHOOM
I DO BELONG.
I SAVE LIVES.
BAM
I PROTECT THIS WORLD. I PROVE IT EVERY DAY. I HAVE A PURPOSE.
WHAM
I DO BELONG!
THIS PLANET DIDN'T ADOPT YOU, KARA.
SHOOM
YOU ADOPTED IT.
POWER GIRL!
WHOMP

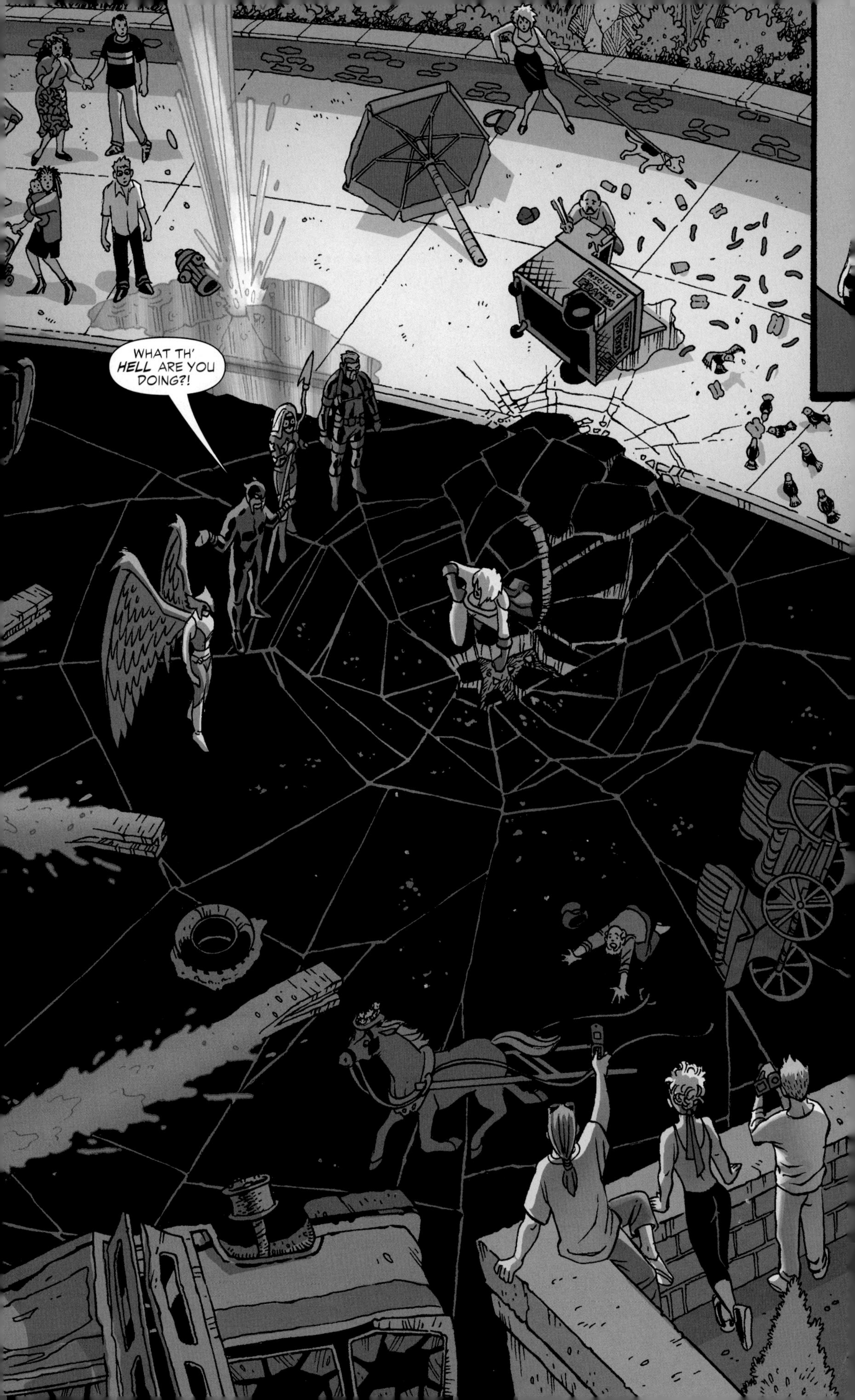
WHAT TH' HELL ARE YOU DOING?!

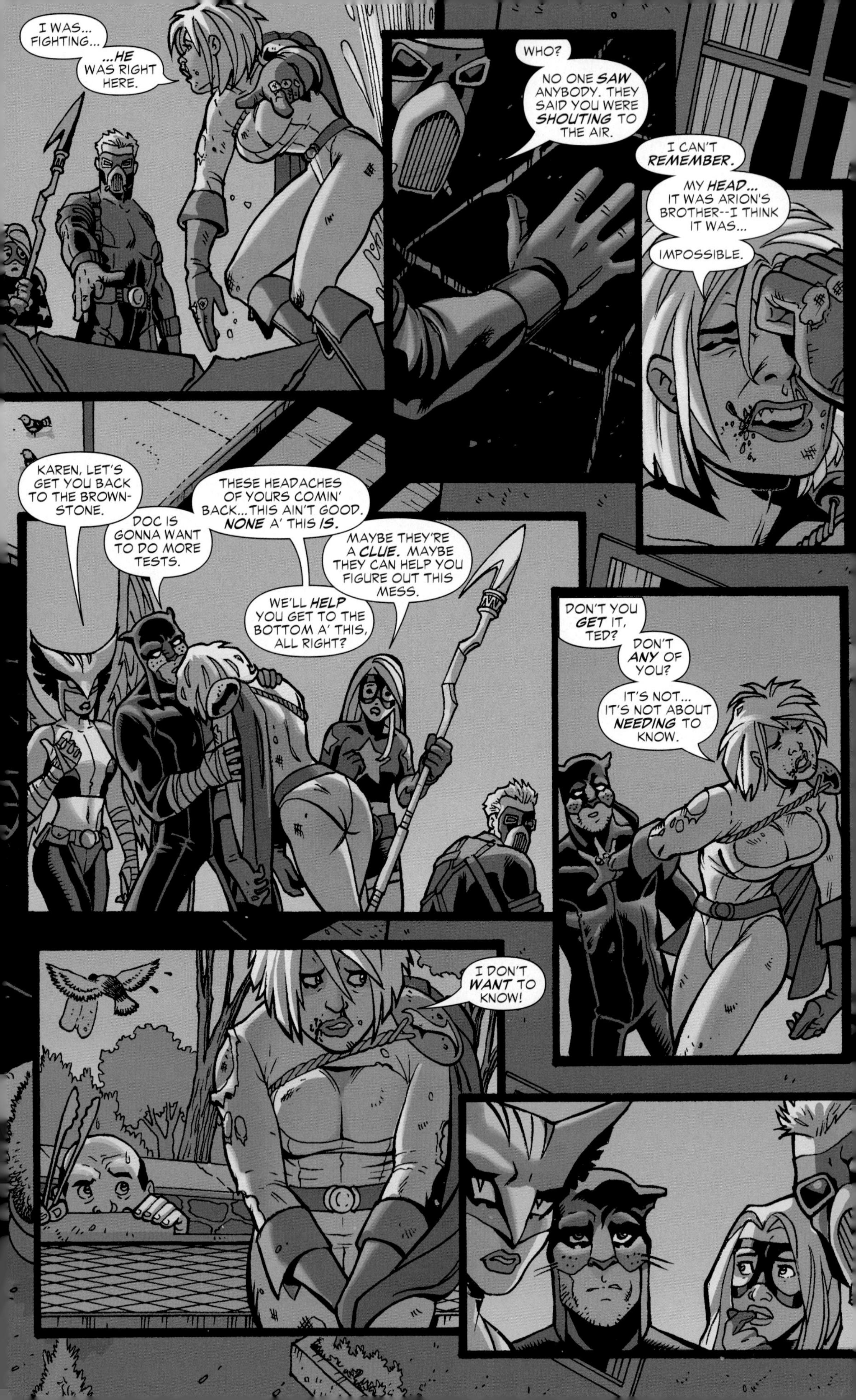

I WAS... FIGHTING... ...HE WAS RIGHT HERE.
WHO?
NO ONE SAW ANYBODY. THEY SAID YOU WERE SHOUTING TO THE AIR.
I CAN'T REMEMBER.
MY HEAD... IT WAS ARION'S BROTHER--I THINK IT WAS...
IMPOSSIBLE.
KAREN, LET'S GET YOU BACK TO THE BROWN-STONE.
DOC IS GONNA WANT TO DO MORE TESTS.
THESE HEADACHES OF YOURS COMIN' BACK...THIS AIN'T GOOD. NONE A' THIS IS.
MAYBE THEY'RE A CLUE. MAYBE THEY CAN HELP YOU FIGURE OUT THIS MESS.
WE'LL HELP YOU GET TO THE BOTTOM A' THIS, ALL RIGHT?
DON'T YOU GET IT, TED?
DON'T ANY OF YOU?
IT'S NOT... IT'S NOT ABOUT NEEDING TO KNOW.
I DON'T WANT TO KNOW!

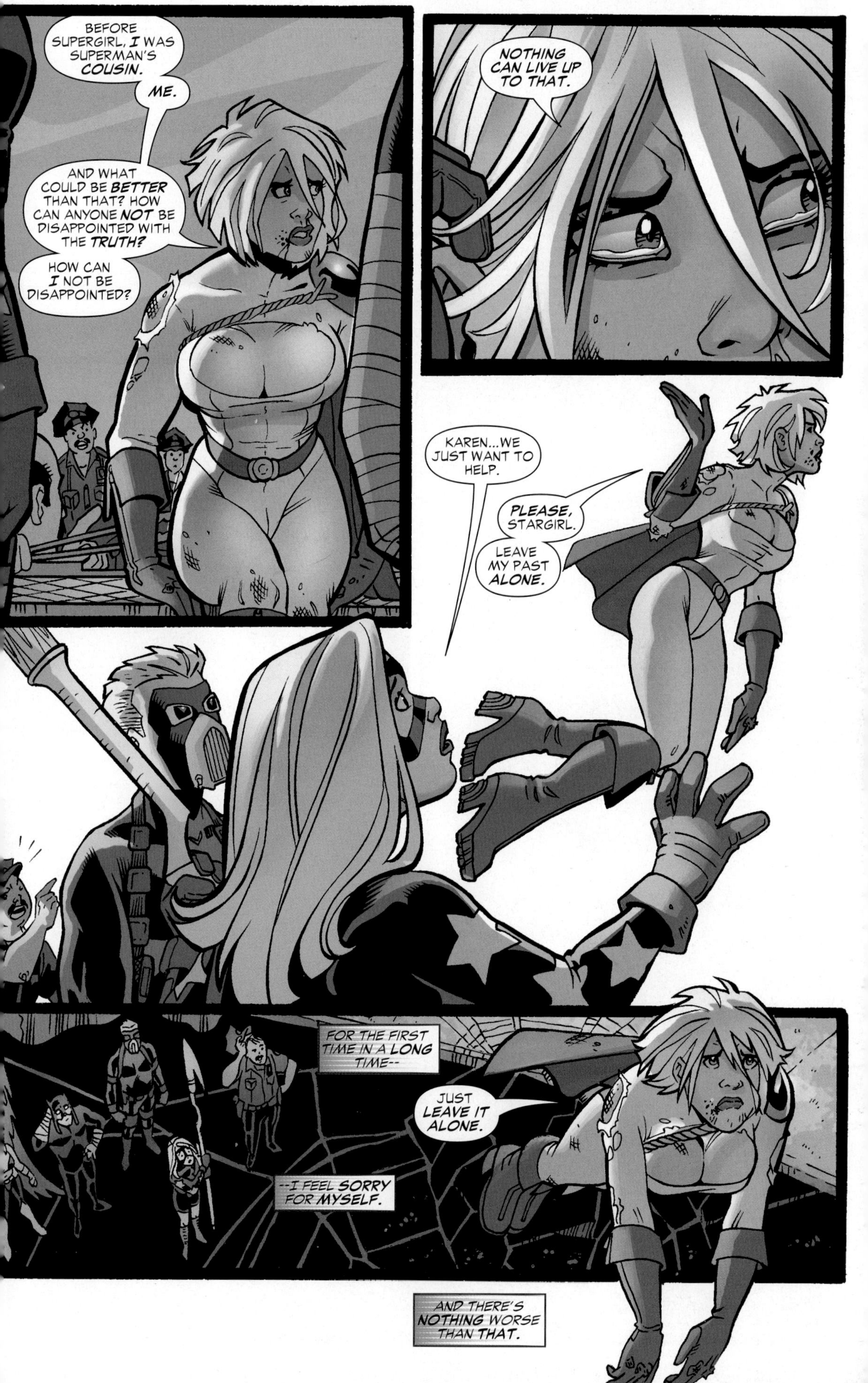
BEFORE SUPERGIRL, I WAS SUPERMAN'S COUSIN.
ME.
AND WHAT COULD BE BETTER THAN THAT? HOW CAN ANYONE NOT BE DISAPPOINTED WITH THE TRUTH?
HOW CAN I NOT BE DISAPPOINTED?
NOTHING CAN LIVE UP TO THAT.
KAREN...WE JUST WANT TO HELP.
PLEASE, STARGIRL.
LEAVE MY PAST ALONE.
FOR THE FIRST TIME IN A LONG TIME--
JUST LEAVE IT ALONE.
--I FEEL SORRY FOR MYSELF.
AND THERE'S NOTHING WORSE THAN THAT.

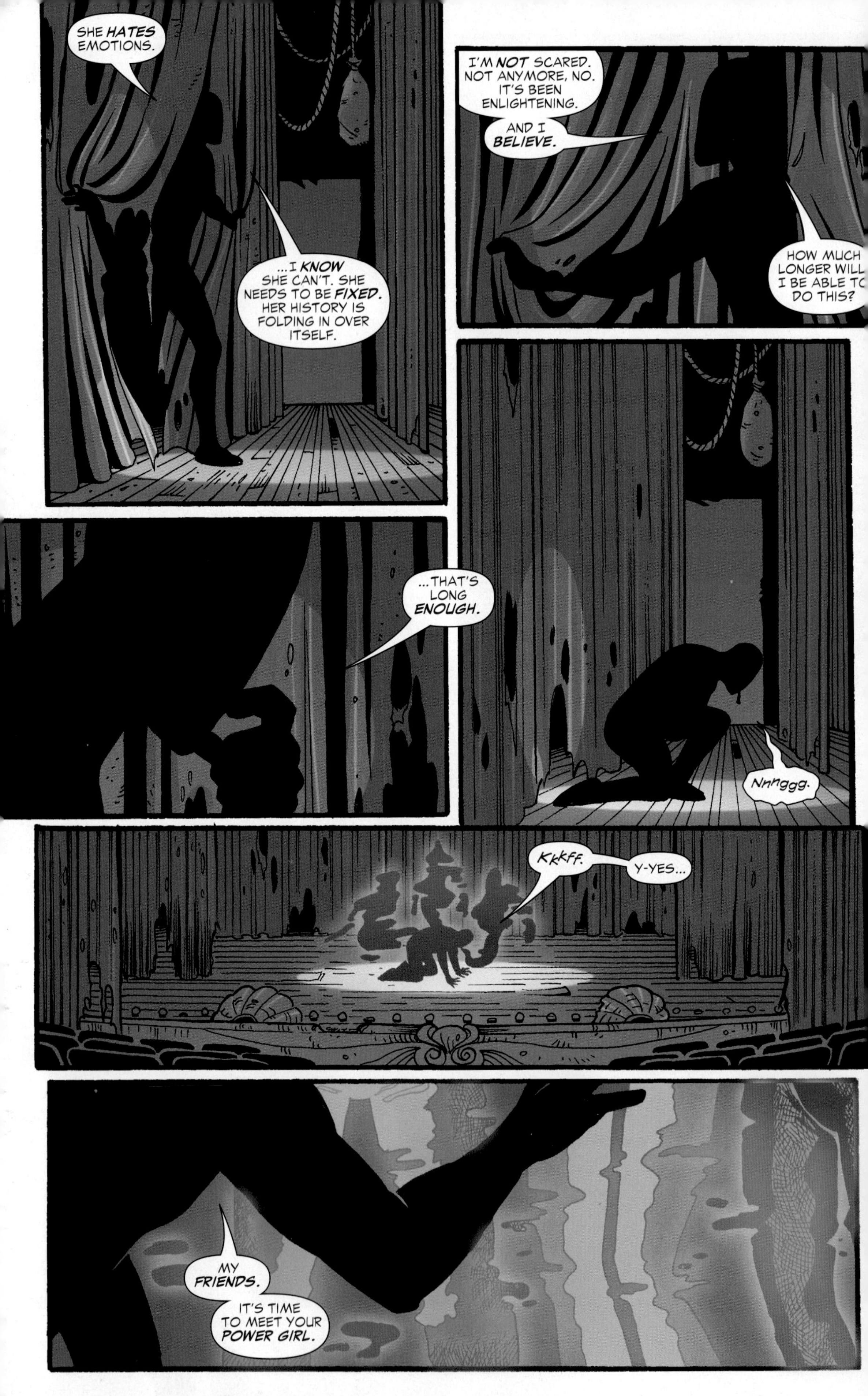
SHE HATES EMOTIONS.
...I KNOW SHE CAN'T. SHE NEEDS TO BE FIXED. HER HISTORY IS FOLDING IN OVER ITSELF.
I'M NOT SCARED. NOT ANYMORE, NO. IT'S BEEN ENLIGHTENING.
AND I BELIEVE.
HOW MUCH LONGER WILL I BE ABLE TO DO THIS?
...THAT'S LONG ENOUGH.
Nnnggg.
Kkkff.
Y-YES...
MY FRIENDS.
IT'S TIME TO MEET YOUR POWER GIRL.

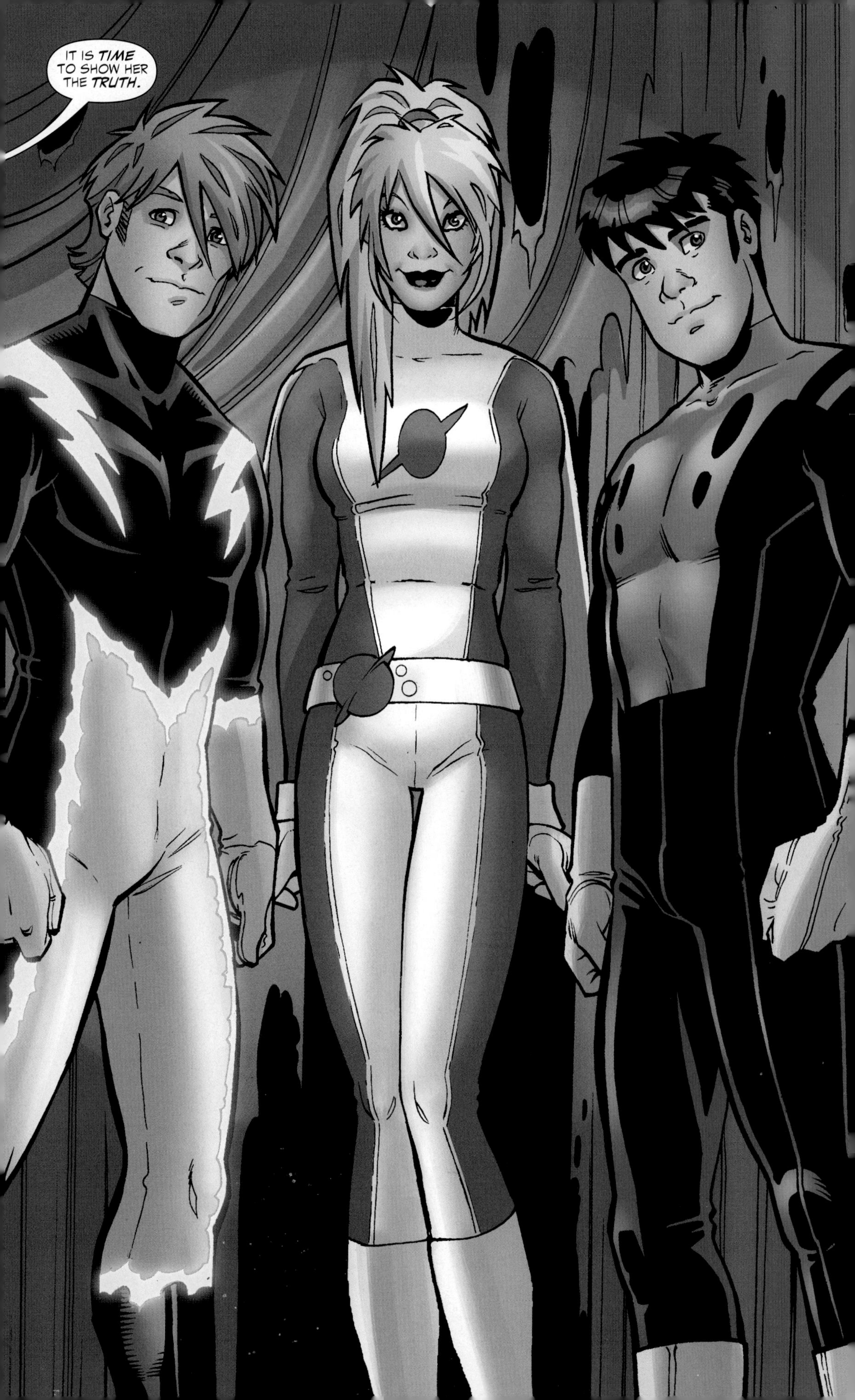
IT IS TIME TO SHOW HER THE TRUTH.

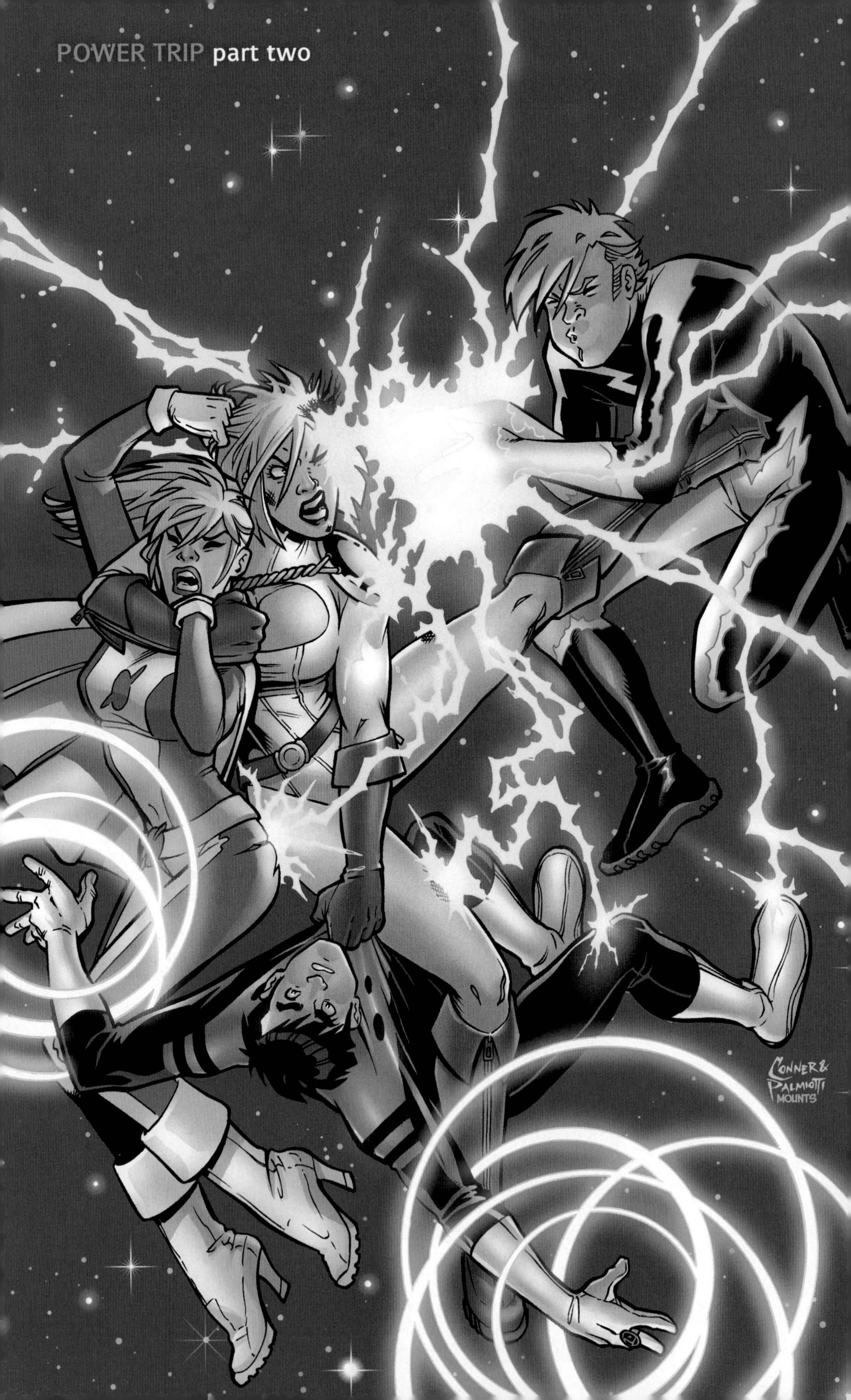
POWER TRIP part two
CONNER &
PALMIOTTI
MOUNTS

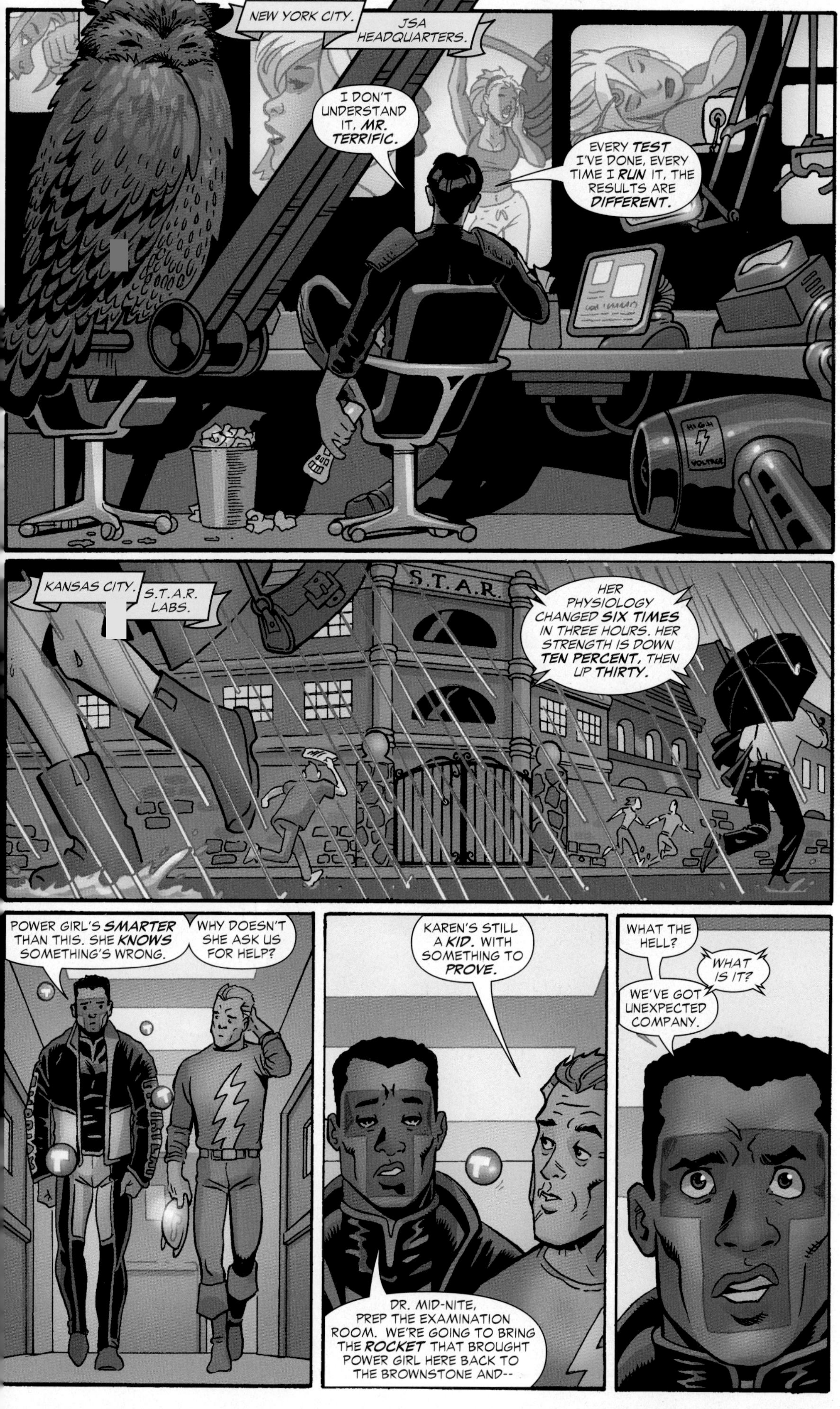
NEW YORK CITY.
JSA HEADQUARTERS.
I DON'T UNDERSTAND IT, MR. TERRIFIC.
EVERY TEST I'VE DONE, EVERY TIME I RUN IT, THE RESULTS ARE DIFFERENT.
KANSAS CITY.
S.T.A.R. LABS.
S.T.A.R.
HER PHYSIOLOGY CHANGED SIX TIMES IN THREE HOURS. HER STRENGTH IS DOWN TEN PERCENT, THEN UP THIRTY.
POWER GIRL'S SMARTER THAN THIS. SHE KNOWS SOMETHING'S WRONG.
WHY DOESN'T SHE ASK US FOR HELP?
KAREN'S STILL A KID. WITH SOMETHING TO PROVE.
DR. MID-NITE, PREP THE EXAMINATION ROOM. WE'RE GOING TO BRING THE ROCKET THAT BROUGHT POWER GIRL HERE BACK TO THE BROWNSTONE AND--
WHAT THE HELL?
WHAT IS IT?
WE'VE GOT UNEXPECTED COMPANY.

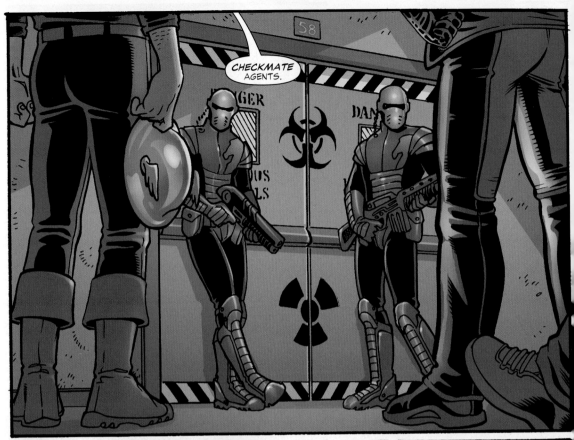

CHECKMATE AGENTS.

WHAT ARE *THEY* DOING HERE?

MR. TERRIFIC! I'M SORRY BUT WE'RE GOING TO HAVE TO RESCHEDULE THIS MEETING.

THIS ROCKET HAS BEEN IN SECURE STORAGE FOR *YEARS*, DOCTOR GAMMIL. UNDER STRICT *ORDERS* FROM THE *JUSTICE SOCIETY.*

WE JUST... I'M SORRY, BUT... THIS ORDER WAS FROM *HIGHER* UP.

WHO?

SIR. THE J.S.A. IS HERE. FASTER THAN EXPECTED.

NO DOUBT THANKS TO MR. GARRICK.

REMEMBER:
• DECONTAMINAT...
• ANTI-RADIATIO...
  SHOWER
• THROW BIO-SUIT...
  INTO UV HAMPE...
• WASH HANDS!
• WIPE FEET ON
  UV MAT

YOU REALLY SHOULD BE WEARING A BIO-SUIT, SIR.

THERE'S NO TELLING WHAT KIND OF RADIATION LEVELS, TOXINS OR EXTRATERRESTRIAL OR MYSTICAL VIRUSES WE MIGHT FIND INSIDE--

I APPRECIATE THE WARNINGS...

...BUT I'M NOT SURE MY HEALTH CAN GET MUCH WORSE.

DIRECTOR BONES! I DIDN'T SEE IT IN HERE BEFORE BUT...

SM

...I THINK I FOUND SOMETHING.

NO SMOKIN...

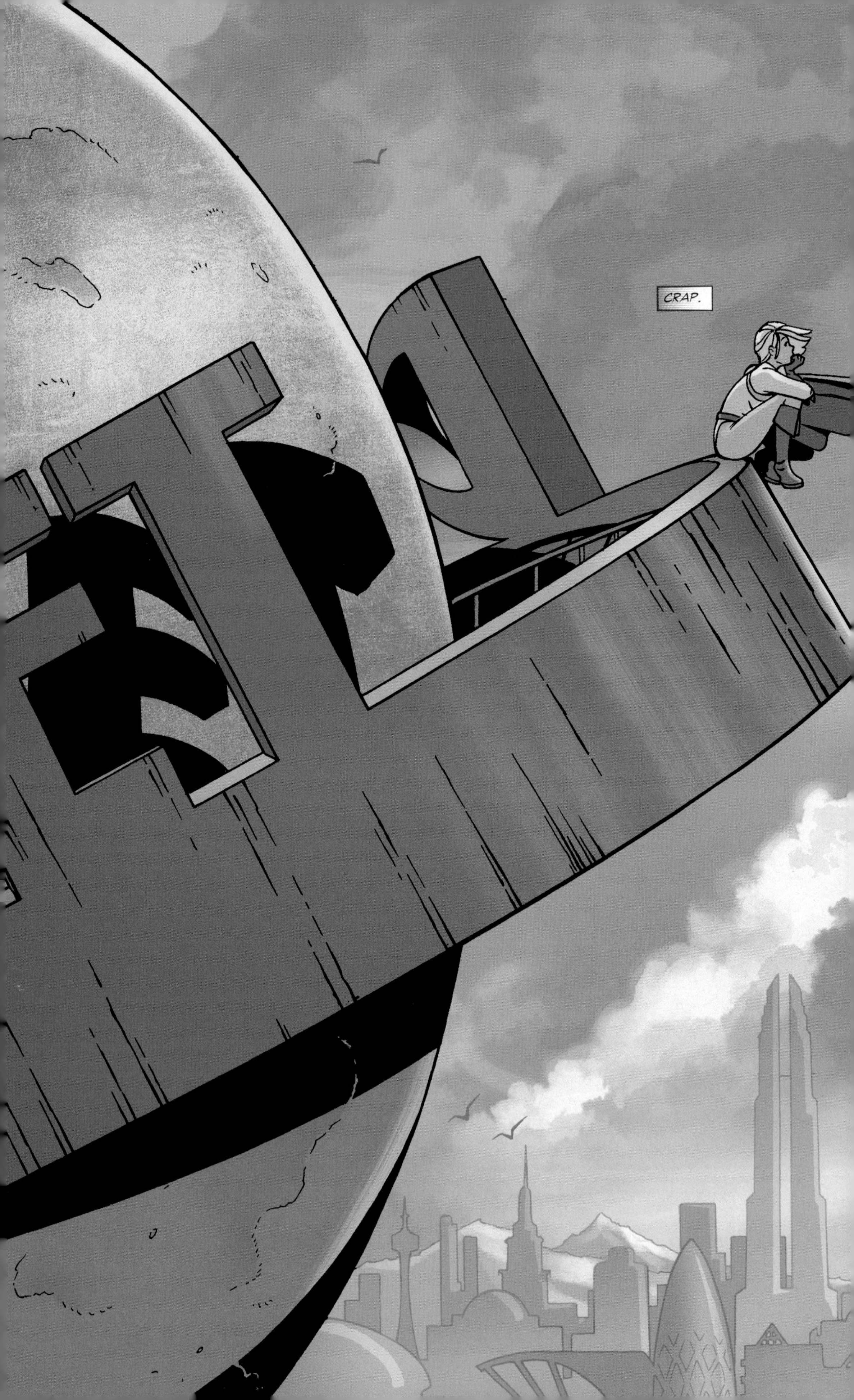
CRAP.

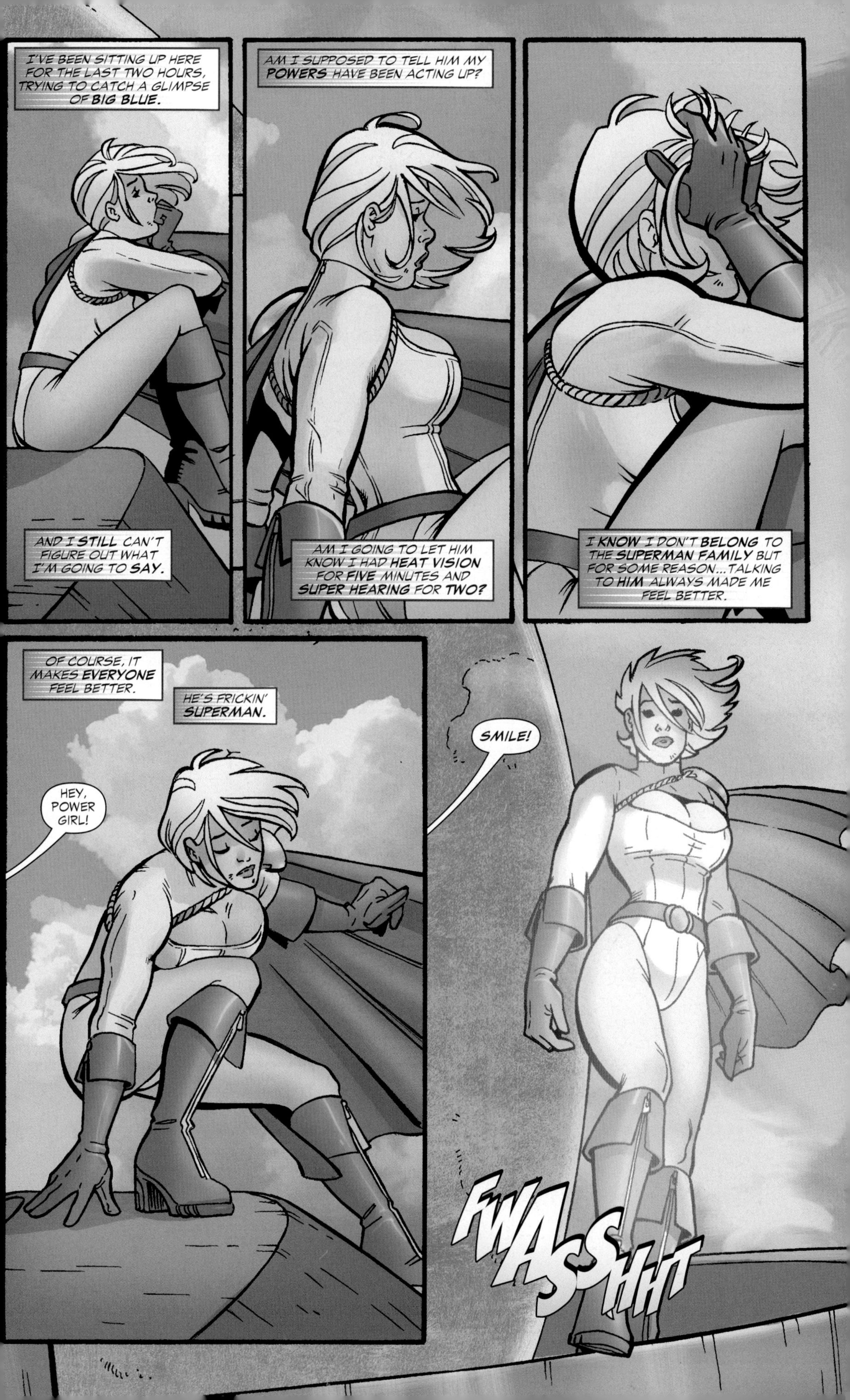
I'VE BEEN SITTING UP HERE FOR THE LAST TWO HOURS, TRYING TO CATCH A GLIMPSE OF BIG BLUE.
AND I STILL CAN'T FIGURE OUT WHAT I'M GOING TO SAY.
AM I SUPPOSED TO TELL HIM MY POWERS HAVE BEEN ACTING UP?
AM I GOING TO LET HIM KNOW I HAD HEAT VISION FOR FIVE MINUTES AND SUPER HEARING FOR TWO?
I KNOW I DON'T BELONG TO THE SUPERMAN FAMILY BUT FOR SOME REASON... TALKING TO HIM ALWAYS MADE ME FEEL BETTER.
OF COURSE, IT MAKES EVERYONE FEEL BETTER.
HE'S FRICKIN' SUPERMAN.
HEY, POWER GIRL!
SMILE!
FWASSHHT

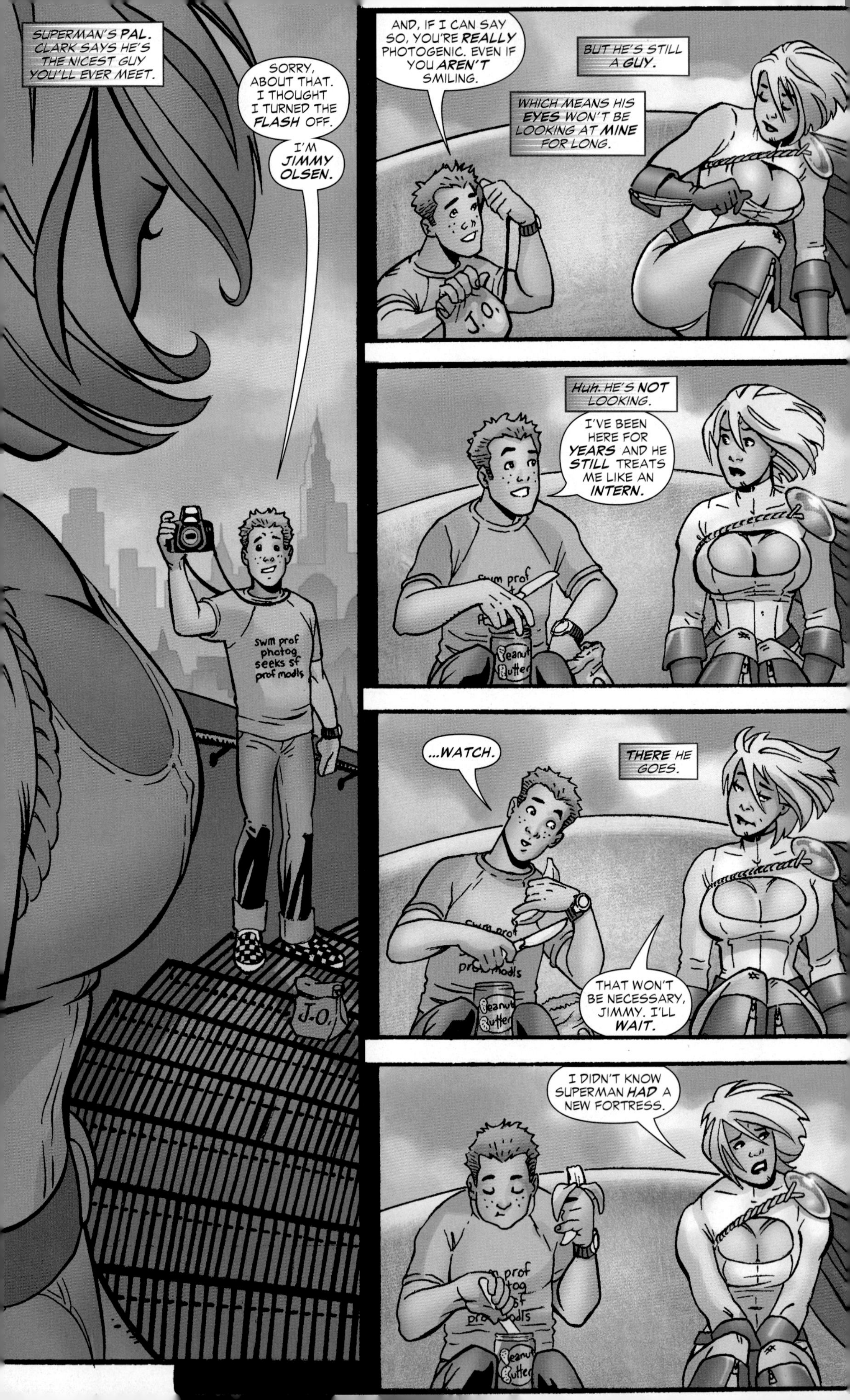
SUPERMAN'S PAL. CLARK SAYS HE'S THE NICEST GUY YOU'LL EVER MEET.
SORRY, ABOUT THAT. I THOUGHT I TURNED THE FLASH OFF.
I'M JIMMY OLSEN.
swm prof photog seeks sf prof modls
J.O.
AND, IF I CAN SAY SO, YOU'RE REALLY PHOTOGENIC. EVEN IF YOU AREN'T SMILING.
BUT HE'S STILL A GUY.
WHICH MEANS HIS EYES WON'T BE LOOKING AT MINE FOR LONG.
J.O.
Huh. HE'S NOT LOOKING.
I'VE BEEN HERE FOR YEARS AND HE STILL TREATS ME LIKE AN INTERN.
...WATCH.
THERE HE GOES.
THAT WON'T BE NECESSARY, JIMMY. I'LL WAIT.
I DIDN'T KNOW SUPERMAN HAD A NEW FORTRESS.

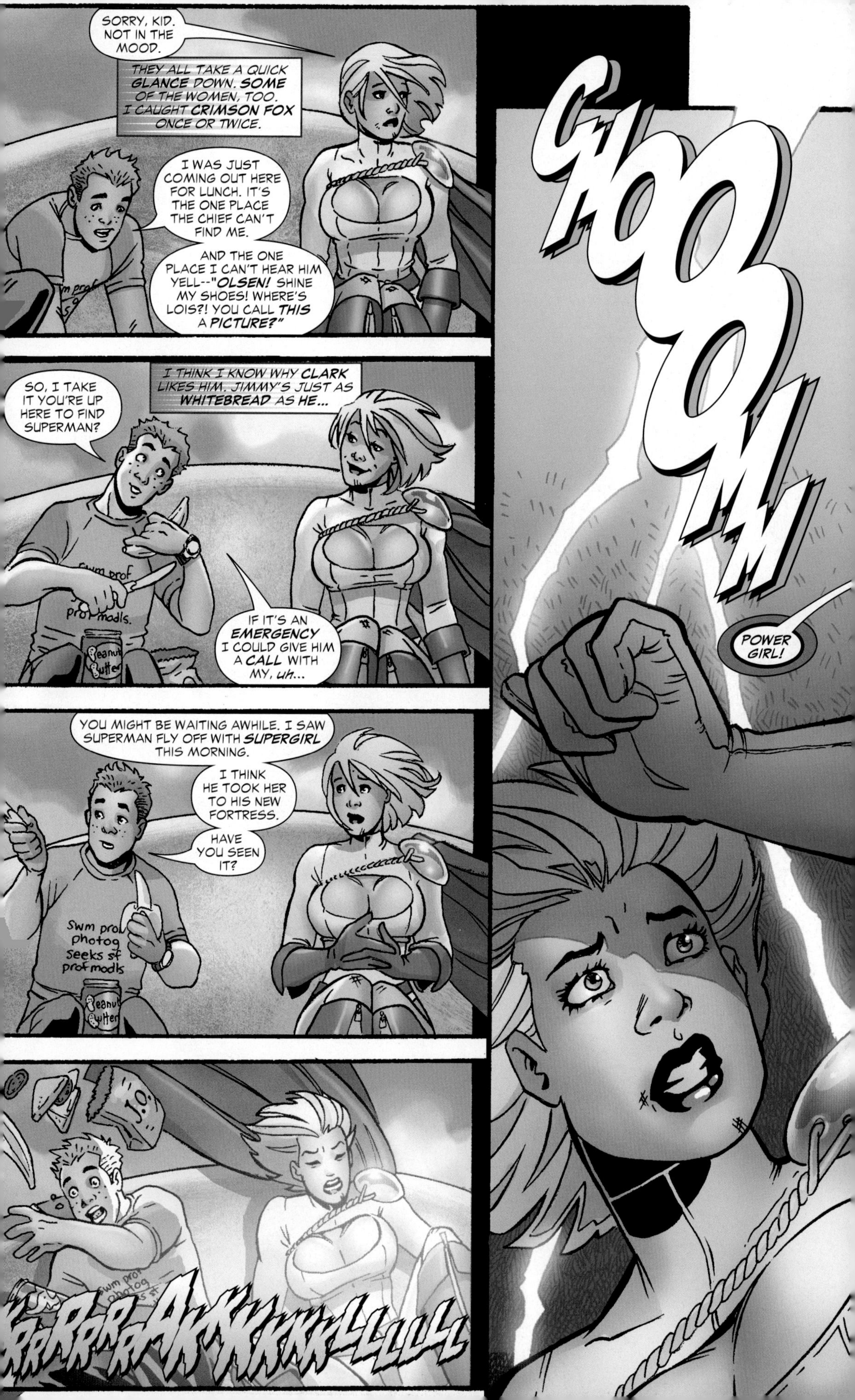
SORRY, KID. NOT IN THE MOOD.
THEY ALL TAKE A QUICK GLANCE DOWN. SOME OF THE WOMEN, TOO. I CAUGHT CRIMSON FOX ONCE OR TWICE.
I WAS JUST COMING OUT HERE FOR LUNCH. IT'S THE ONE PLACE THE CHIEF CAN'T FIND ME.
AND THE ONE PLACE I CAN'T HEAR HIM YELL--"OLSEN! SHINE MY SHOES! WHERE'S LOIS?! YOU CALL THIS A PICTURE?"
SO, I TAKE IT YOU'RE UP HERE TO FIND SUPERMAN?
I THINK I KNOW WHY CLARK LIKES HIM. JIMMY'S JUST AS WHITEBREAD AS HE...
IF IT'S AN EMERGENCY I COULD GIVE HIM A CALL WITH MY, uh...
YOU MIGHT BE WAITING AWHILE. I SAW SUPERMAN FLY OFF WITH SUPERGIRL THIS MORNING.
I THINK HE TOOK HER TO HIS NEW FORTRESS.
HAVE YOU SEEN IT?
swm prof photog seeks sf prof modls
Peanut Butter
RRRRRRAKKKKKLLLLLL
CHOOOOM
POWER GIRL!

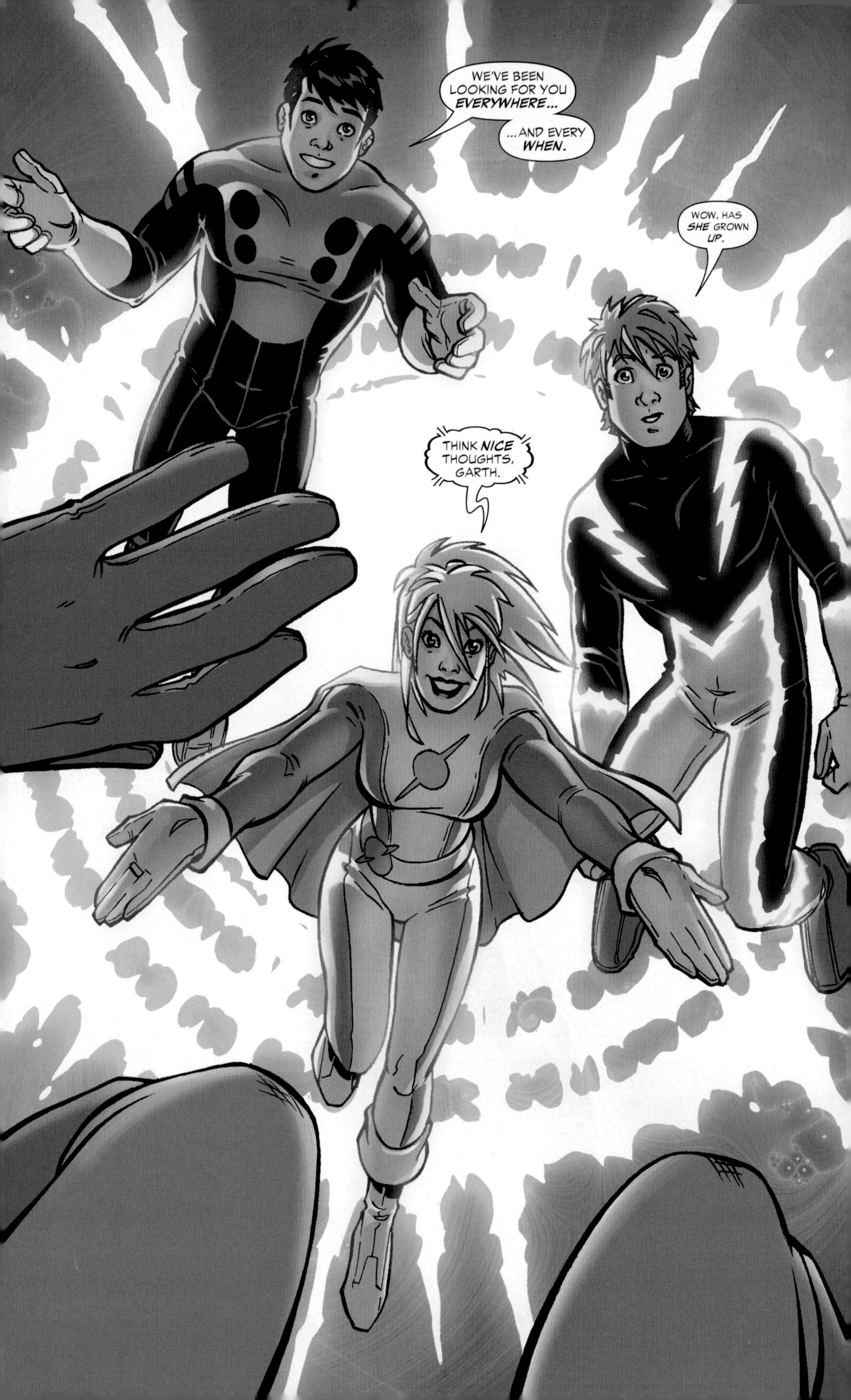
WE'VE BEEN LOOKING FOR YOU EVERYWHERE...
...AND EVERY WHEN.
WOW, HAS SHE GROWN UP.
THINK NICE THOUGHTS, GARTH.

DO I **KNOW** YOU?

THEY KIND OF LOOK LIKE... THE **LEGION OF SUPER-HEROES.** THAT TEAM FROM THE **FUTURE.**

SNAP

THE **THIRTY-FIRST CENTURY** IS **HARDLY** THE "FUTURE."

HEY, COSMIC BOY! IS THIS REDHEAD A TWENTIETH-CENTURY "SUPERHERO," TOO?

I THINK I SAW HIM ON A HOLO-VID IN THE RECORDS HALL.

HE WAS THE EDITOR-IN-CHIEF OF THE **DAILY UNITED PLANET,** LIGHTNING LAD.

OR HE **WILL** BE.

"LIGHTNING LAD"?

I THOUGHT YOU WENT BY "LIVE WIRE".

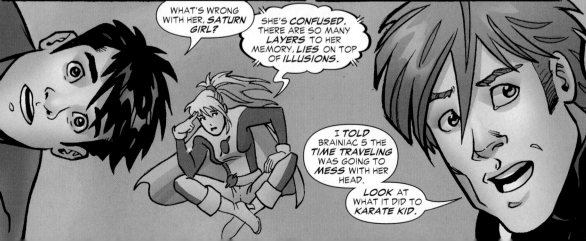

WHAT'S WRONG WITH HER, **SATURN GIRL?**

SHE'S **CONFUSED.** THERE ARE SO MANY **LAYERS** TO HER MEMORY, **LIES** ON TOP OF ILLUSIONS.

I **TOLD** BRAINIAC 5 THE **TIME TRAVELING** WAS GOING TO **MESS** WITH HER HEAD.

LOOK AT WHAT IT DID TO **KARATE KID.**

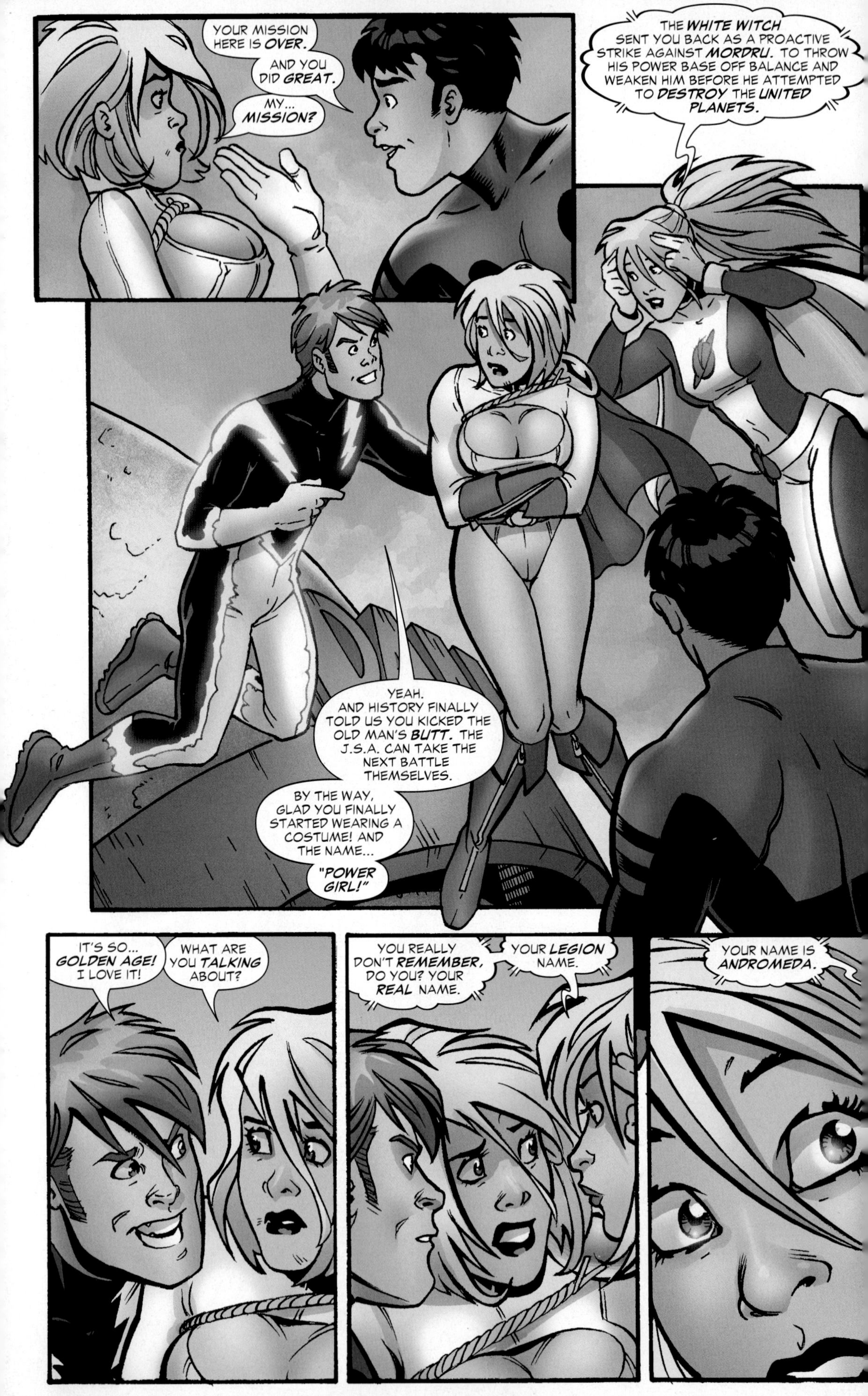
YOUR MISSION HERE IS OVER.
AND YOU DID GREAT.
MY... MISSION?
THE WHITE WITCH SENT YOU BACK AS A PROACTIVE STRIKE AGAINST MORDRU. TO THROW HIS POWER BASE OFF BALANCE AND WEAKEN HIM BEFORE HE ATTEMPTED TO DESTROY THE UNITED PLANETS.
YEAH. AND HISTORY FINALLY TOLD US YOU KICKED THE OLD MAN'S BUTT. THE J.S.A. CAN TAKE THE NEXT BATTLE THEMSELVES.
BY THE WAY, GLAD YOU FINALLY STARTED WEARING A COSTUME! AND THE NAME...
"POWER GIRL!"
IT'S SO... GOLDEN AGE! I LOVE IT!
WHAT ARE YOU TALKING ABOUT?
YOU REALLY DON'T REMEMBER, DO YOU? YOUR REAL NAME.
YOUR LEGION NAME.
YOUR NAME IS ANDROMEDA.

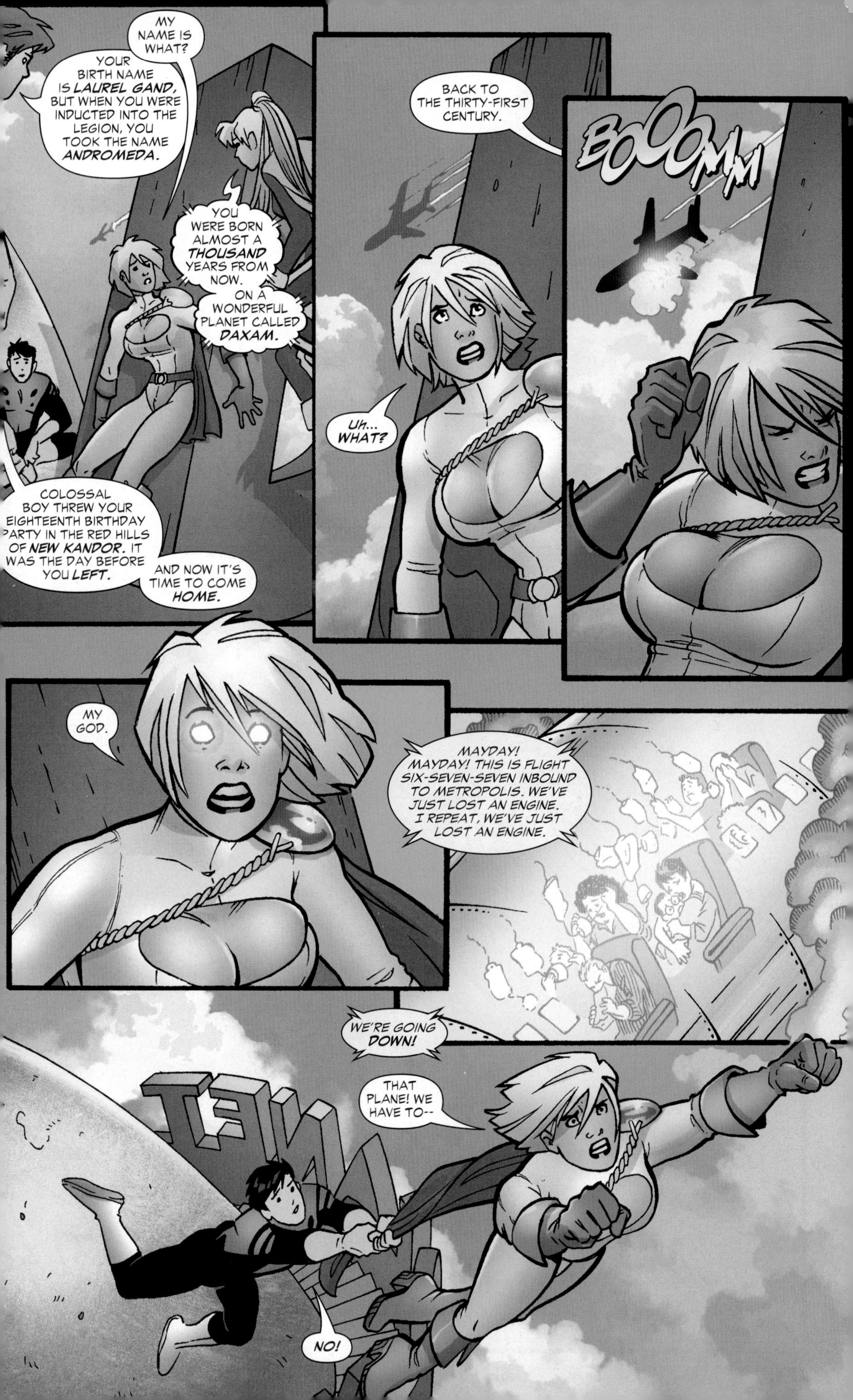
MY NAME IS WHAT?
YOUR BIRTH NAME IS LAUREL GAND, BUT WHEN YOU WERE INDUCTED INTO THE LEGION, YOU TOOK THE NAME ANDROMEDA.
YOU WERE BORN ALMOST A THOUSAND YEARS FROM NOW.
ON A WONDERFUL PLANET CALLED DAXAM.
COLOSSAL BOY THREW YOUR EIGHTEENTH BIRTHDAY PARTY IN THE RED HILLS OF NEW KANDOR. IT WAS THE DAY BEFORE YOU LEFT.
AND NOW IT'S TIME TO COME HOME.
BACK TO THE THIRTY-FIRST CENTURY.
Uh... WHAT?
BOOOMM
MY GOD.
MAYDAY! MAYDAY! THIS IS FLIGHT SIX-SEVEN-SEVEN INBOUND TO METROPOLIS. WE'VE JUST LOST AN ENGINE. I REPEAT, WE'VE JUST LOST AN ENGINE.
WE'RE GOING DOWN!
THAT PLANE! WE HAVE TO--
NO!

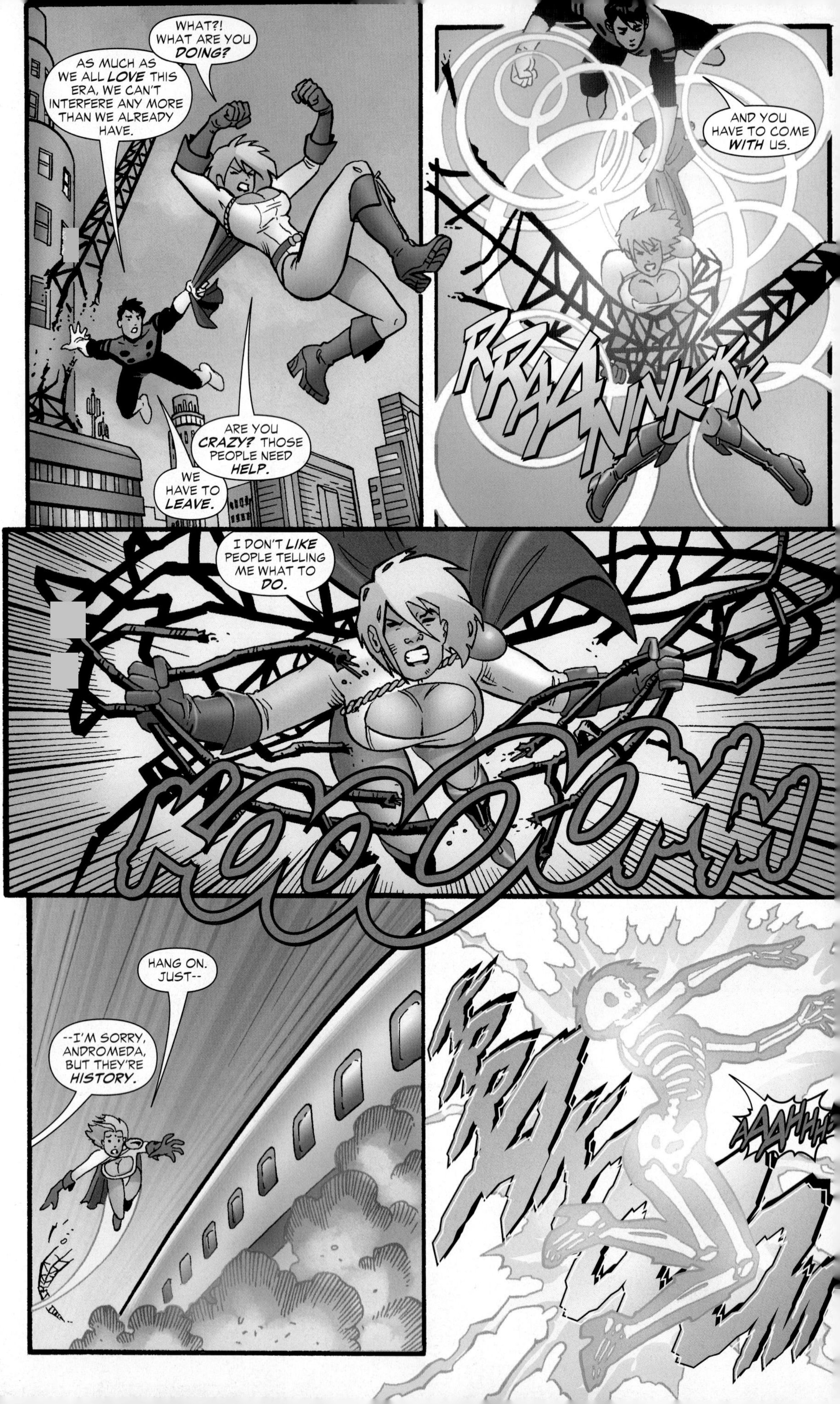

WHAT?! WHAT ARE YOU DOING?
AS MUCH AS WE ALL LOVE THIS ERA, WE CAN'T INTERFERE ANY MORE THAN WE ALREADY HAVE.
ARE YOU CRAZY? THOSE PEOPLE NEED HELP.
WE HAVE TO LEAVE.
AND YOU HAVE TO COME WITH US.
I DON'T LIKE PEOPLE TELLING ME WHAT TO DO.
HANG ON. JUST--
--I'M SORRY, ANDROMEDA, BUT THEY'RE HISTORY.

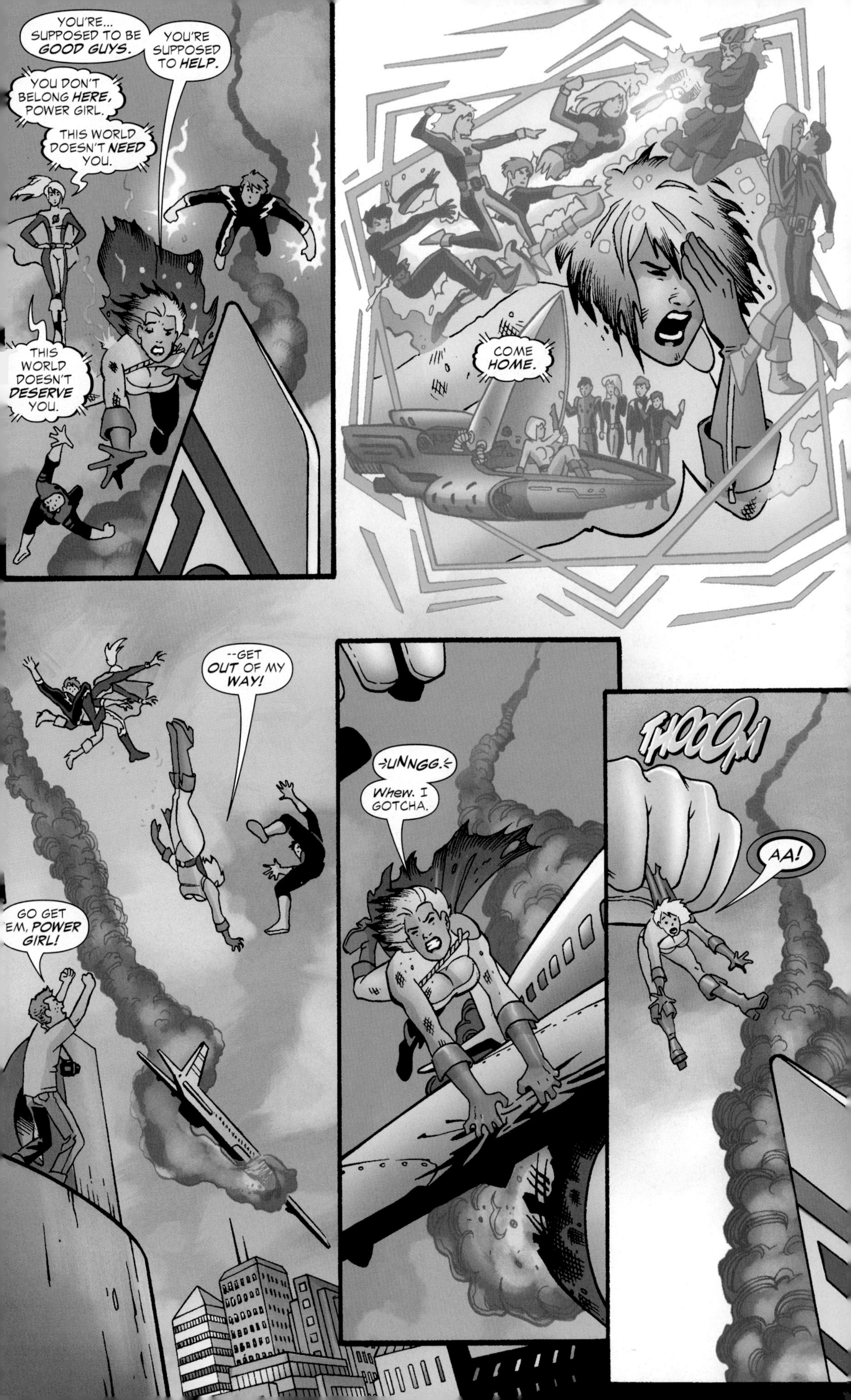
YOU'RE... SUPPOSED TO BE GOOD GUYS.
YOU'RE SUPPOSED TO HELP.
YOU DON'T BELONG HERE, POWER GIRL.
THIS WORLD DOESN'T NEED YOU.
THIS WORLD DOESN'T DESERVE YOU.
COME HOME.
--GET OUT OF MY WAY!
GO GET EM, POWER GIRL!
UNNGG.
Whew. I GOTCHA.
THOOOM
AA!

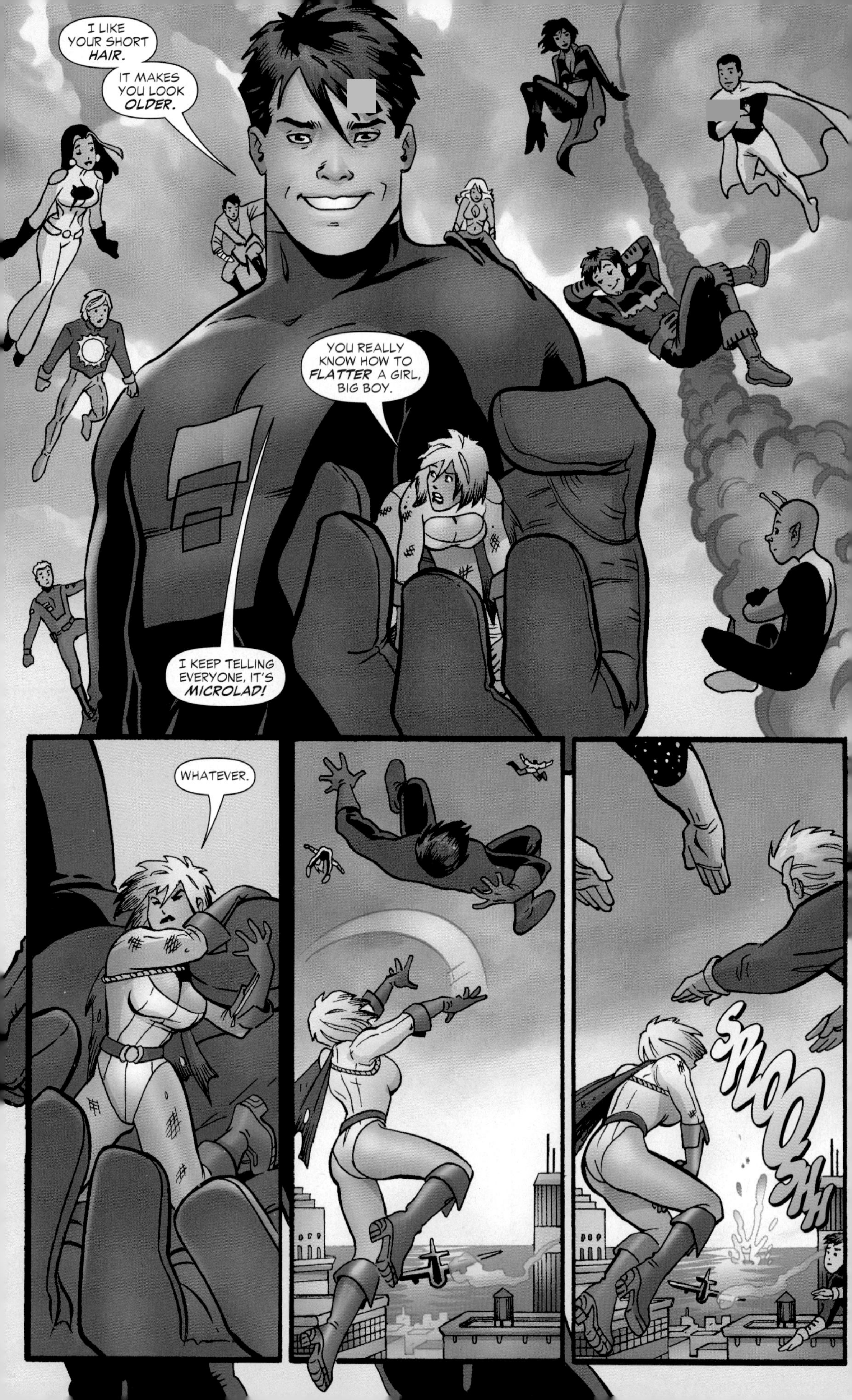

I LIKE YOUR SHORT HAIR.
IT MAKES YOU LOOK OLDER.
YOU REALLY KNOW HOW TO FLATTER A GIRL, BIG BOY.
I KEEP TELLING EVERYONE, IT'S MICROLAD!
WHATEVER.
SPLOOSH

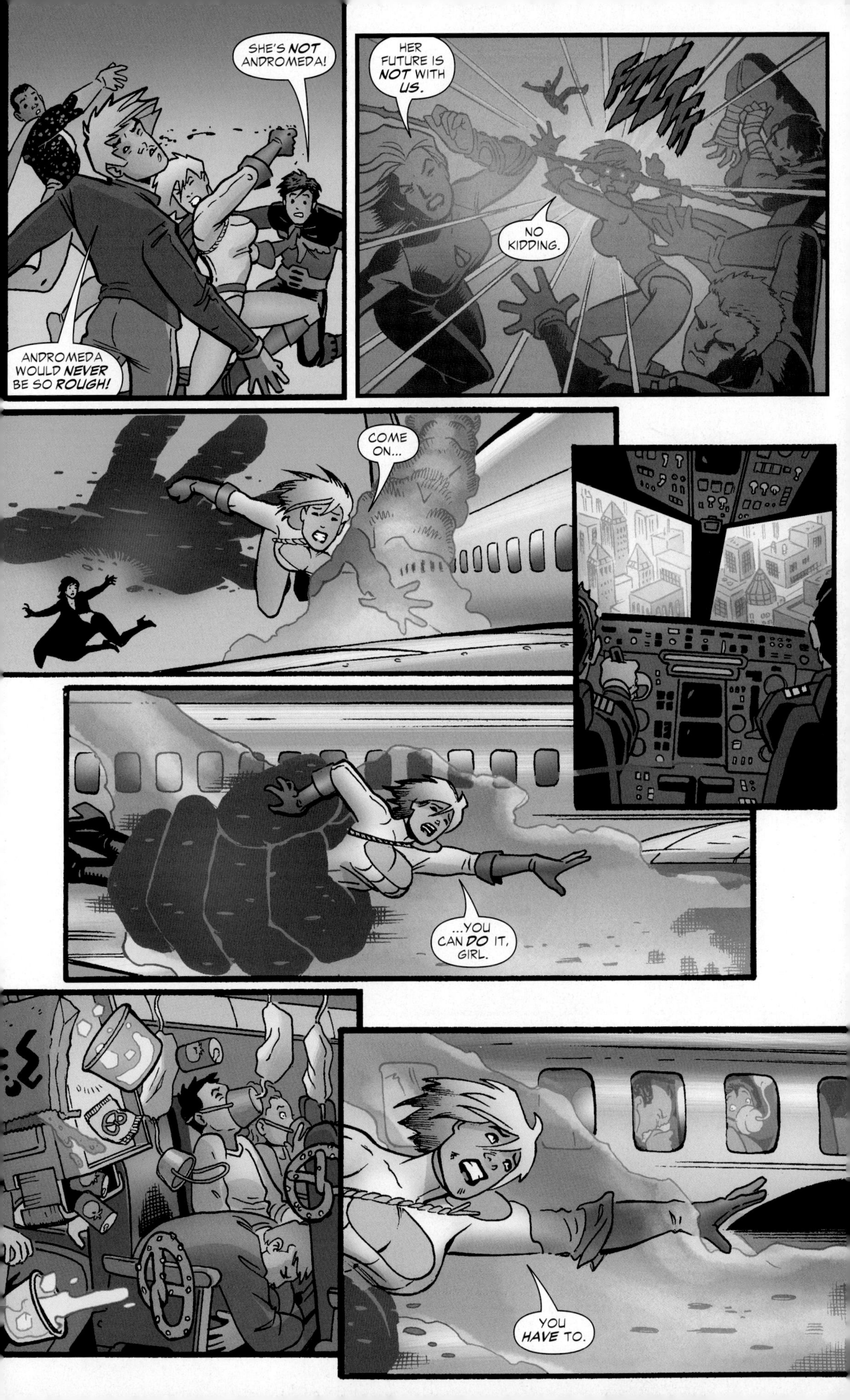

SHE'S NOT ANDROMEDA!
ANDROMEDA WOULD NEVER BE SO ROUGH!
HER FUTURE IS NOT WITH US.
FZZZT
NO KIDDING.
COME ON...
...YOU CAN DO IT, GIRL.
YOU HAVE TO.

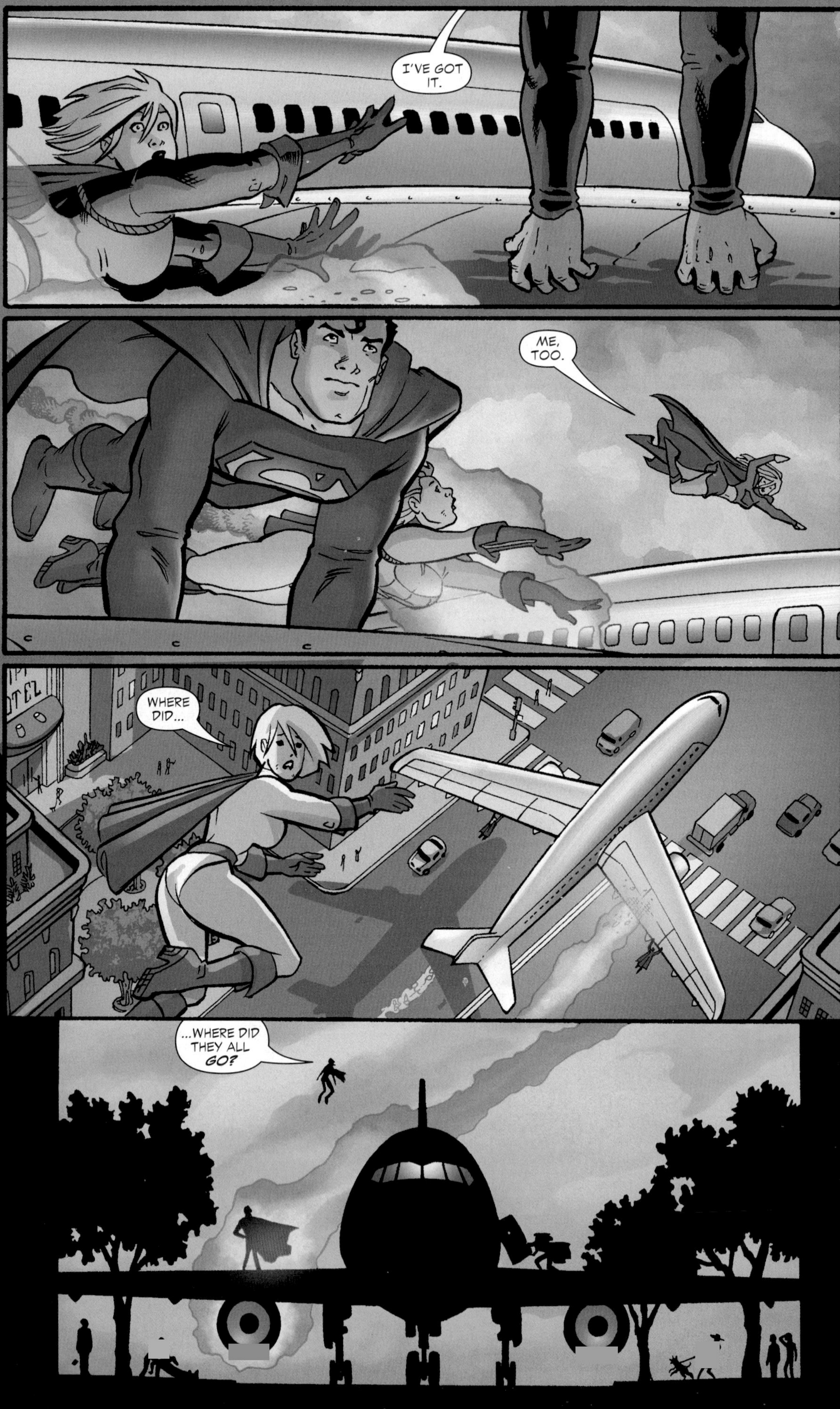
I'VE GOT IT.
ME, TOO.
WHERE DID...
...WHERE DID THEY ALL GO?

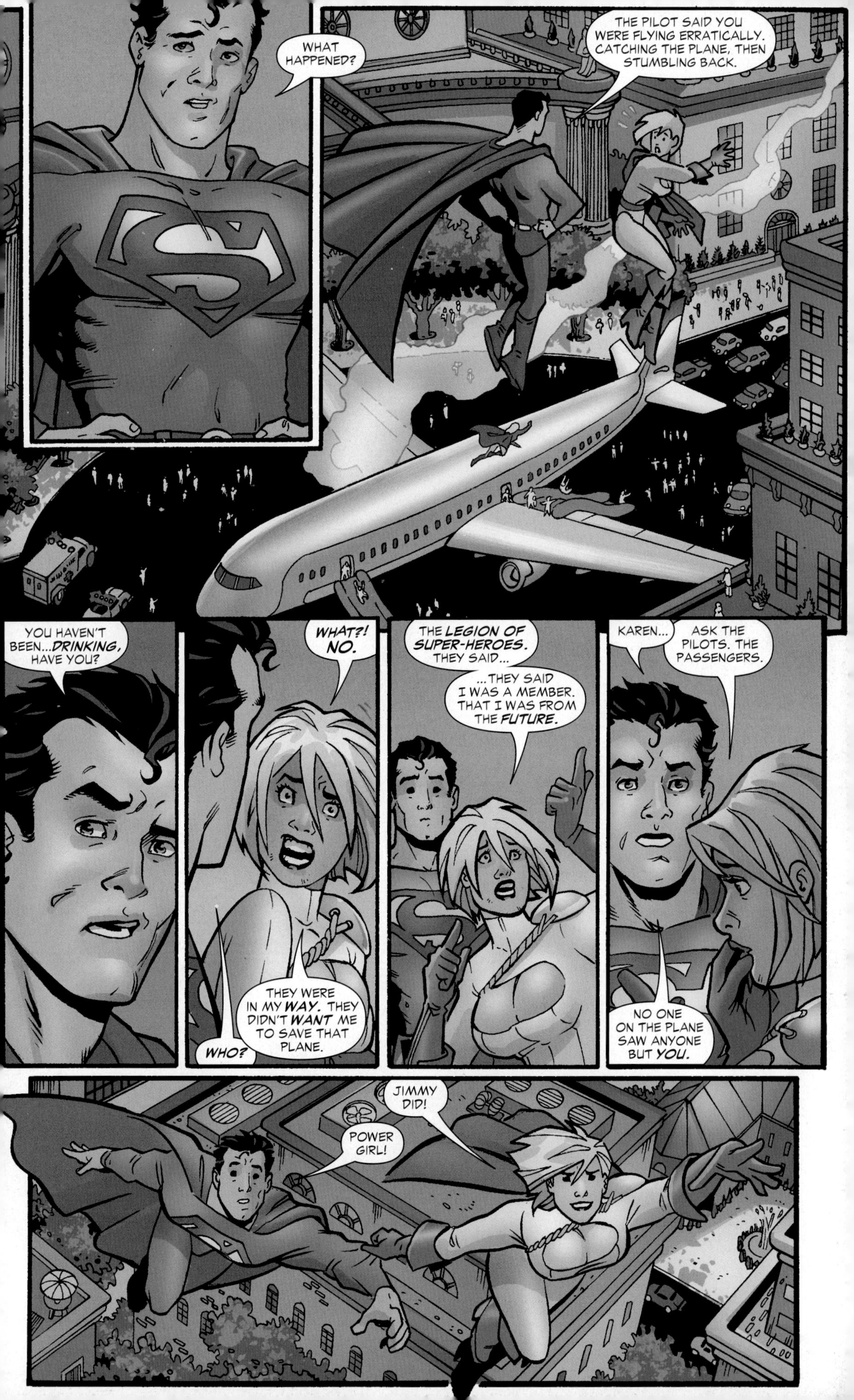
WHAT HAPPENED?
THE PILOT SAID YOU WERE FLYING ERRATICALLY. CATCHING THE PLANE, THEN STUMBLING BACK.
YOU HAVEN'T BEEN...DRINKING, HAVE YOU?
WHAT?! NO.
WHO?
THEY WERE IN MY WAY. THEY DIDN'T WANT ME TO SAVE THAT PLANE.
THE LEGION OF SUPER-HEROES. THEY SAID...
...THEY SAID I WAS A MEMBER. THAT I WAS FROM THE FUTURE.
KAREN...
ASK THE PILOTS. THE PASSENGERS.
NO ONE ON THE PLANE SAW ANYONE BUT YOU.
JIMMY DID!
POWER GIRL!

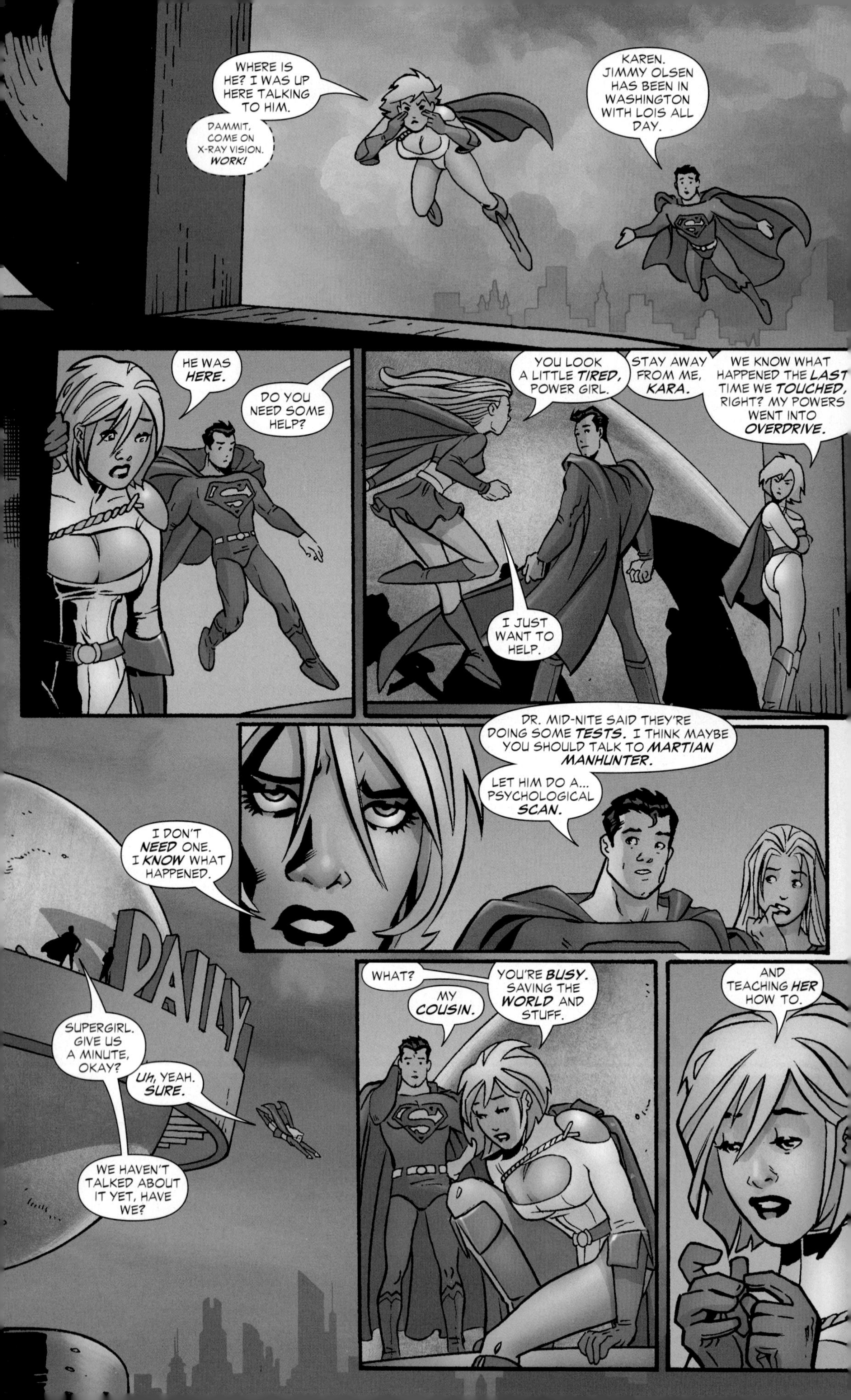
WHERE IS HE? I WAS UP HERE TALKING TO HIM.
DAMMIT, COME ON X-RAY VISION. WORK!
KAREN. JIMMY OLSEN HAS BEEN IN WASHINGTON WITH LOIS ALL DAY.
HE WAS HERE.
DO YOU NEED SOME HELP?
YOU LOOK A LITTLE TIRED, POWER GIRL.
STAY AWAY FROM ME, KARA.
WE KNOW WHAT HAPPENED THE LAST TIME WE TOUCHED, RIGHT? MY POWERS WENT INTO OVERDRIVE.
I JUST WANT TO HELP.
DR. MID-NITE SAID THEY'RE DOING SOME TESTS. I THINK MAYBE YOU SHOULD TALK TO MARTIAN MANHUNTER.
LET HIM DO A... PSYCHOLOGICAL SCAN.
I DON'T NEED ONE. I KNOW WHAT HAPPENED.
DAILY
SUPERGIRL. GIVE US A MINUTE, OKAY?
Uh, YEAH. SURE.
WE HAVEN'T TALKED ABOUT IT YET, HAVE WE?
WHAT?
MY COUSIN.
YOU'RE BUSY. SAVING THE WORLD AND STUFF.
AND TEACHING HER HOW TO.

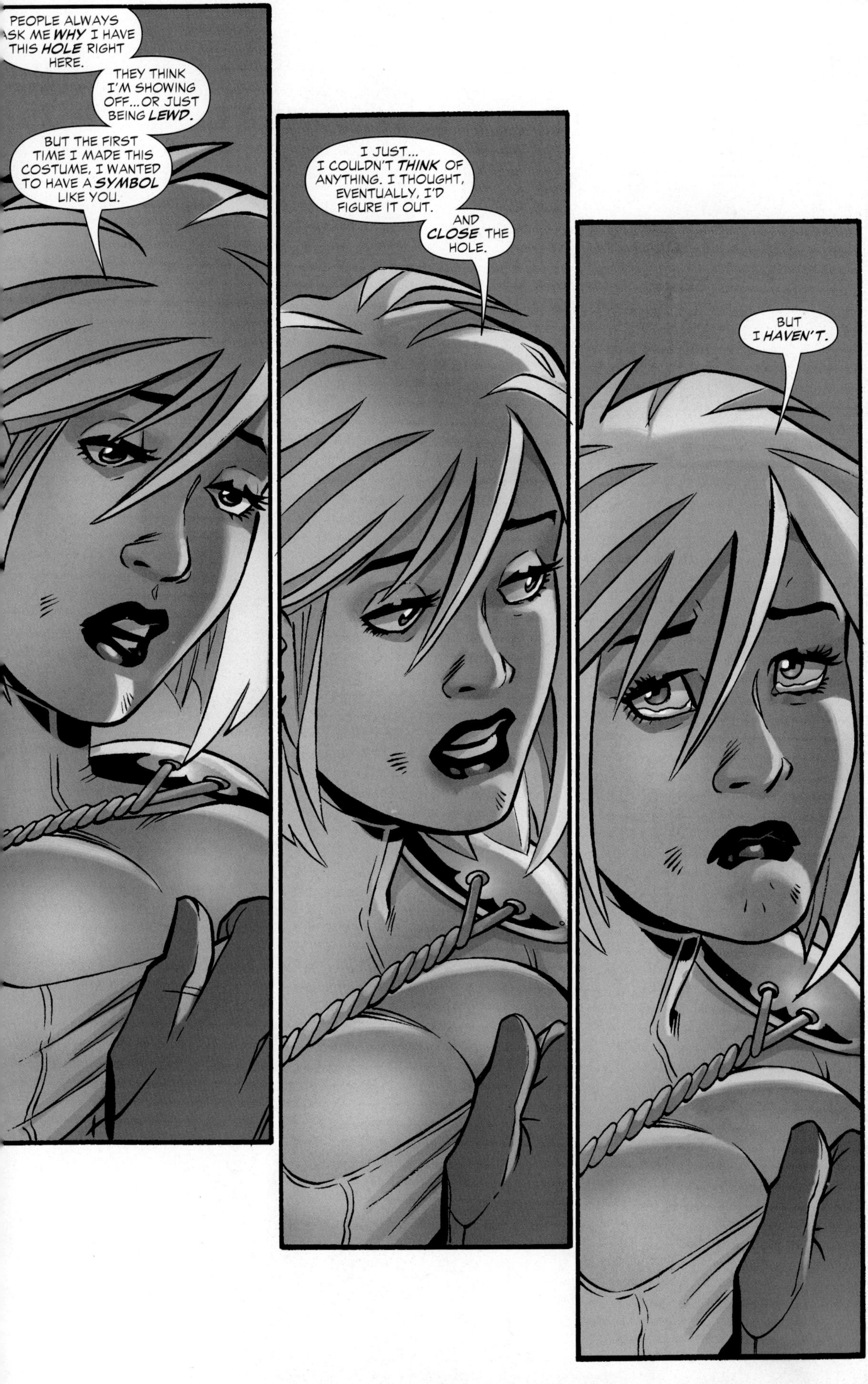
PEOPLE ALWAYS ASK ME WHY I HAVE THIS HOLE RIGHT HERE.
THEY THINK I'M SHOWING OFF...OR JUST BEING LEWD.
BUT THE FIRST TIME I MADE THIS COSTUME, I WANTED TO HAVE A SYMBOL LIKE YOU.
I JUST... I COULDN'T THINK OF ANYTHING. I THOUGHT, EVENTUALLY, I'D FIGURE IT OUT.
AND CLOSE THE HOLE.
BUT I HAVEN'T.

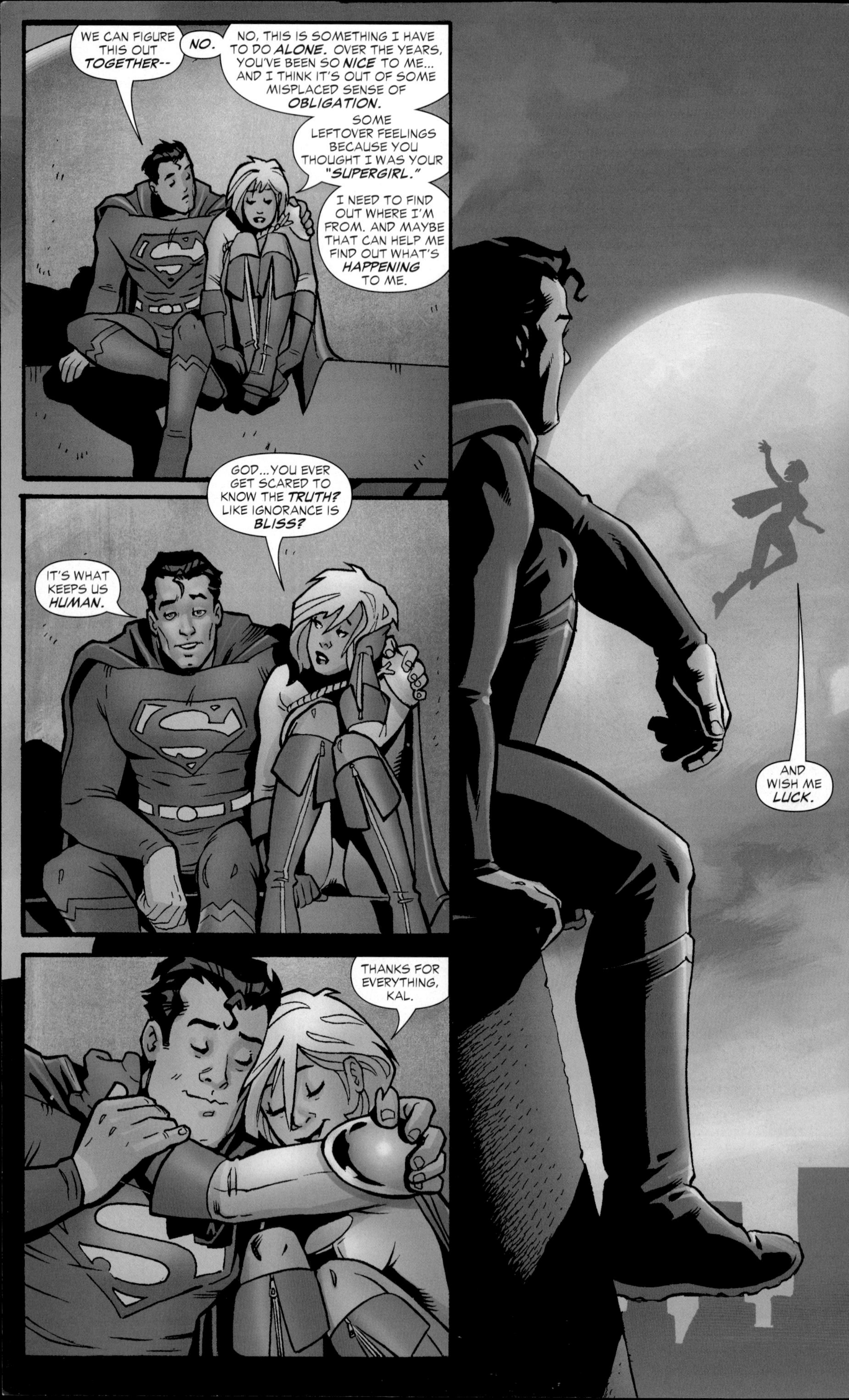
WE CAN FIGURE THIS OUT TOGETHER--
NO.
NO, THIS IS SOMETHING I HAVE TO DO ALONE. OVER THE YEARS, YOU'VE BEEN SO NICE TO ME... AND I THINK IT'S OUT OF SOME MISPLACED SENSE OF OBLIGATION.
SOME LEFTOVER FEELINGS BECAUSE YOU THOUGHT I WAS YOUR "SUPERGIRL."
I NEED TO FIND OUT WHERE I'M FROM. AND MAYBE THAT CAN HELP ME FIND OUT WHAT'S HAPPENING TO ME.
GOD...YOU EVER GET SCARED TO KNOW THE TRUTH? LIKE IGNORANCE IS BLISS?
IT'S WHAT KEEPS US HUMAN.
THANKS FOR EVERYTHING, KAL.
AND WISH ME LUCK.

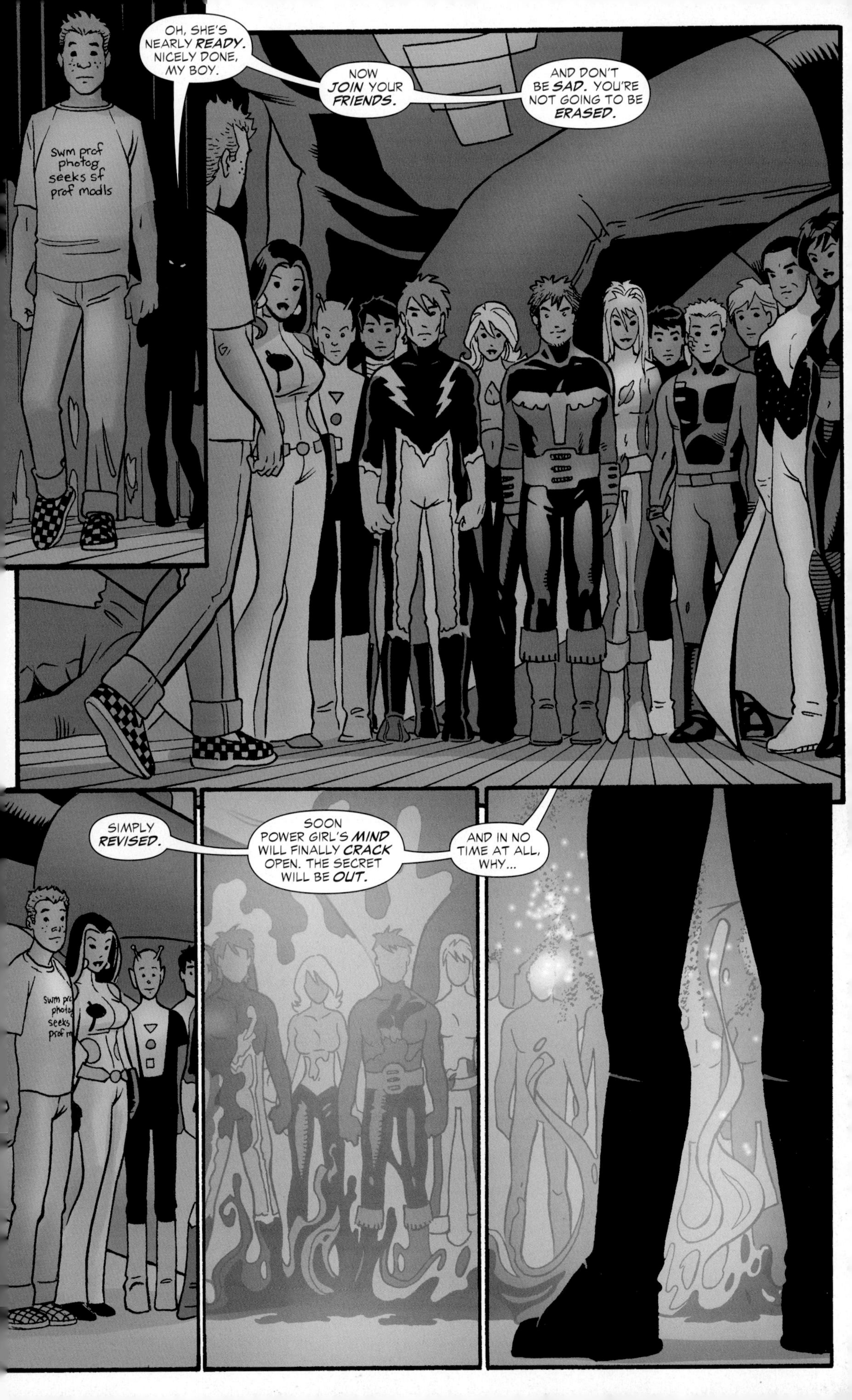
swm prof photog seeks sf prof modls
OH, SHE'S NEARLY READY. NICELY DONE, MY BOY.
NOW JOIN YOUR FRIENDS.
AND DON'T BE SAD. YOU'RE NOT GOING TO BE ERASED.
SIMPLY REVISED.
SOON POWER GIRL'S MIND WILL FINALLY CRACK OPEN. THE SECRET WILL BE OUT.
AND IN NO TIME AT ALL, WHY...

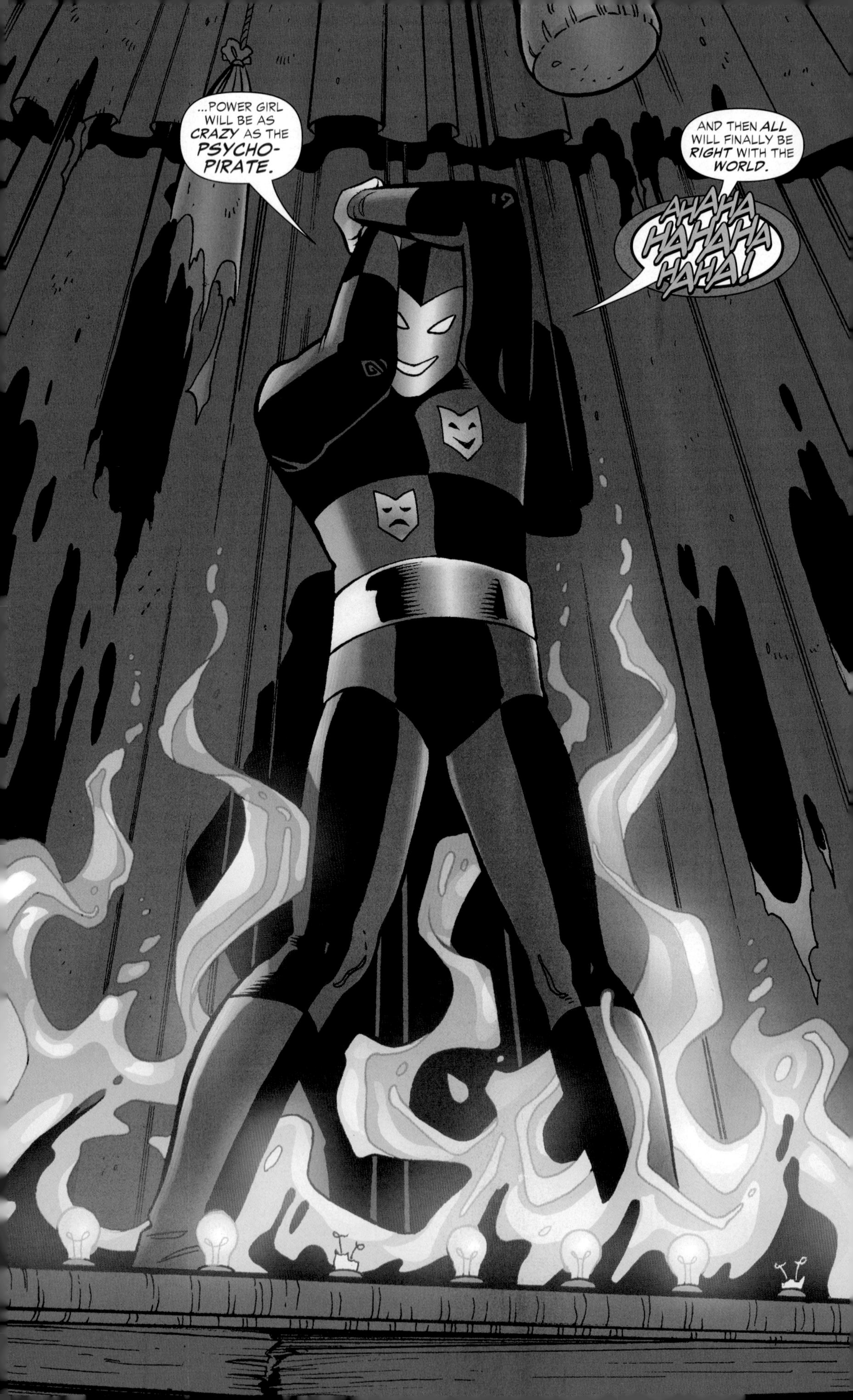
...POWER GIRL WILL BE AS CRAZY AS THE PSYCHO-PIRATE.
AND THEN ALL WILL FINALLY BE RIGHT WITH THE WORLD.
AHAHA HAHAHA HAHA!

POWER TRIP part three

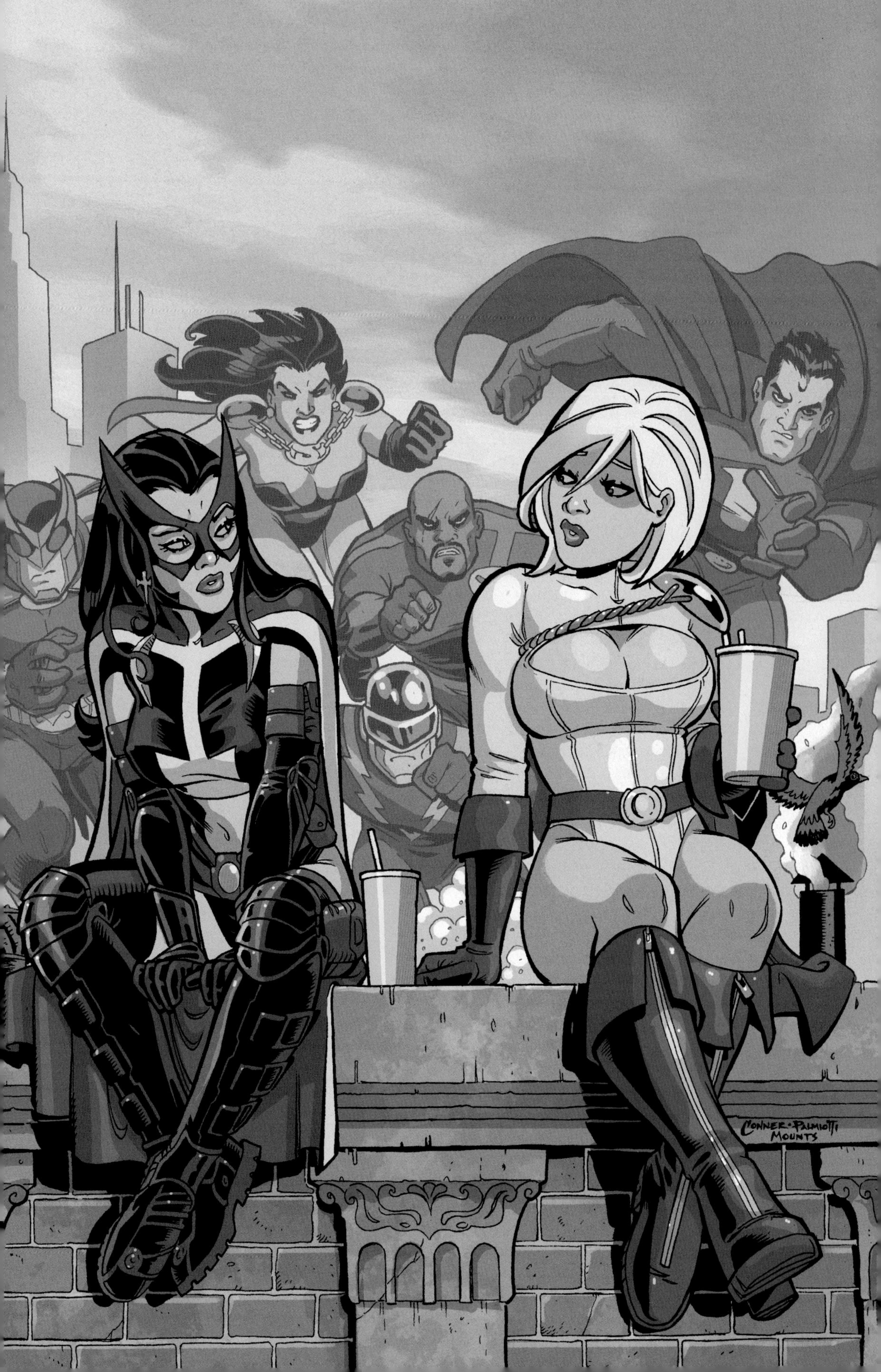
CONNER • PALMIOTTI
MOUNTS

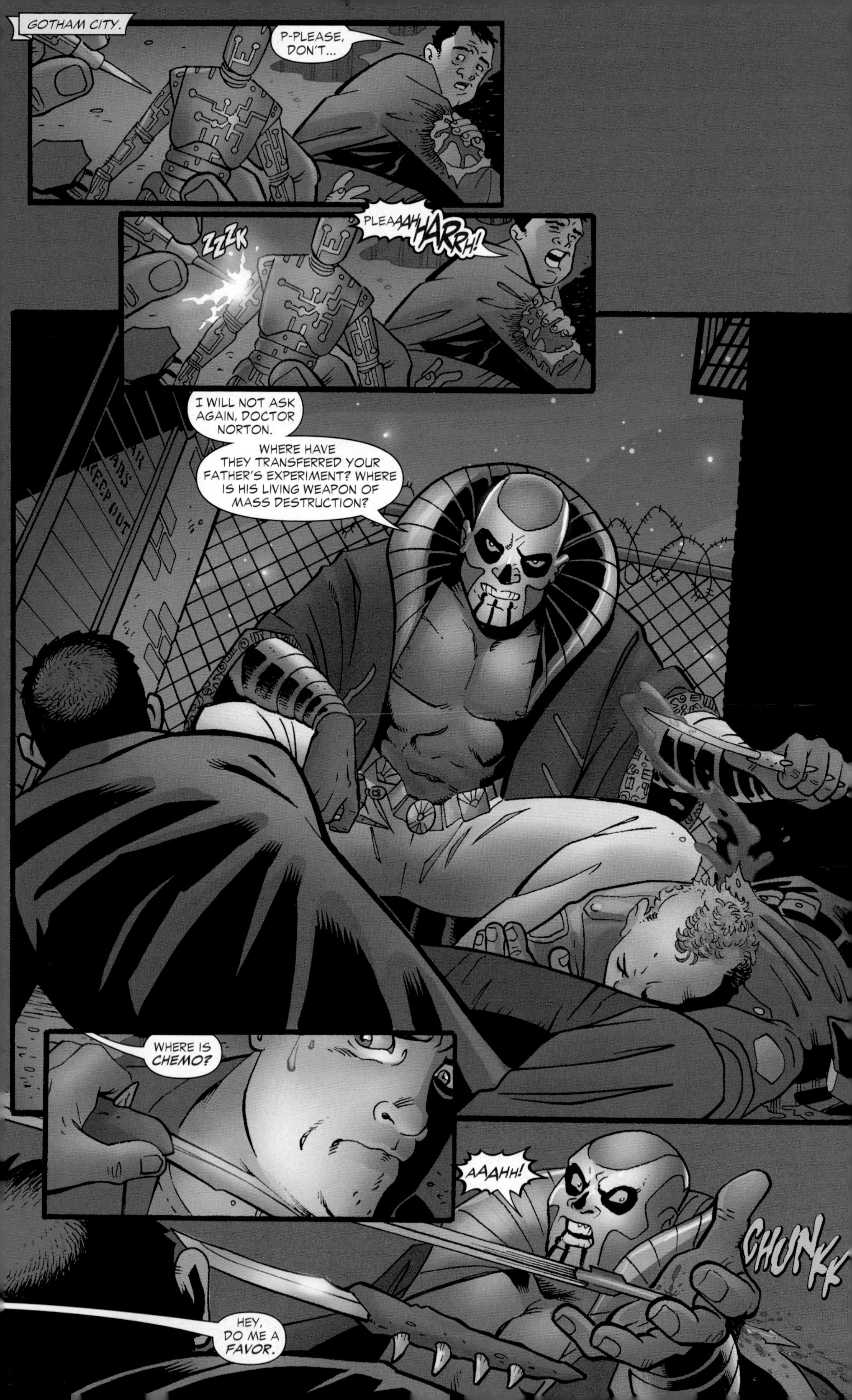
GOTHAM CITY.
P-PLEASE, DON'T...
ZZZK
PLEAAAHHARRH!
I WILL NOT ASK AGAIN, DOCTOR NORTON.
WHERE HAVE THEY TRANSFERRED YOUR FATHER'S EXPERIMENT? WHERE IS HIS LIVING WEAPON OF MASS DESTRUCTION?
KEEP OUT
WHERE IS CHEMO?
AAAHH!
CHUNKK
HEY, DO ME A FAVOR.

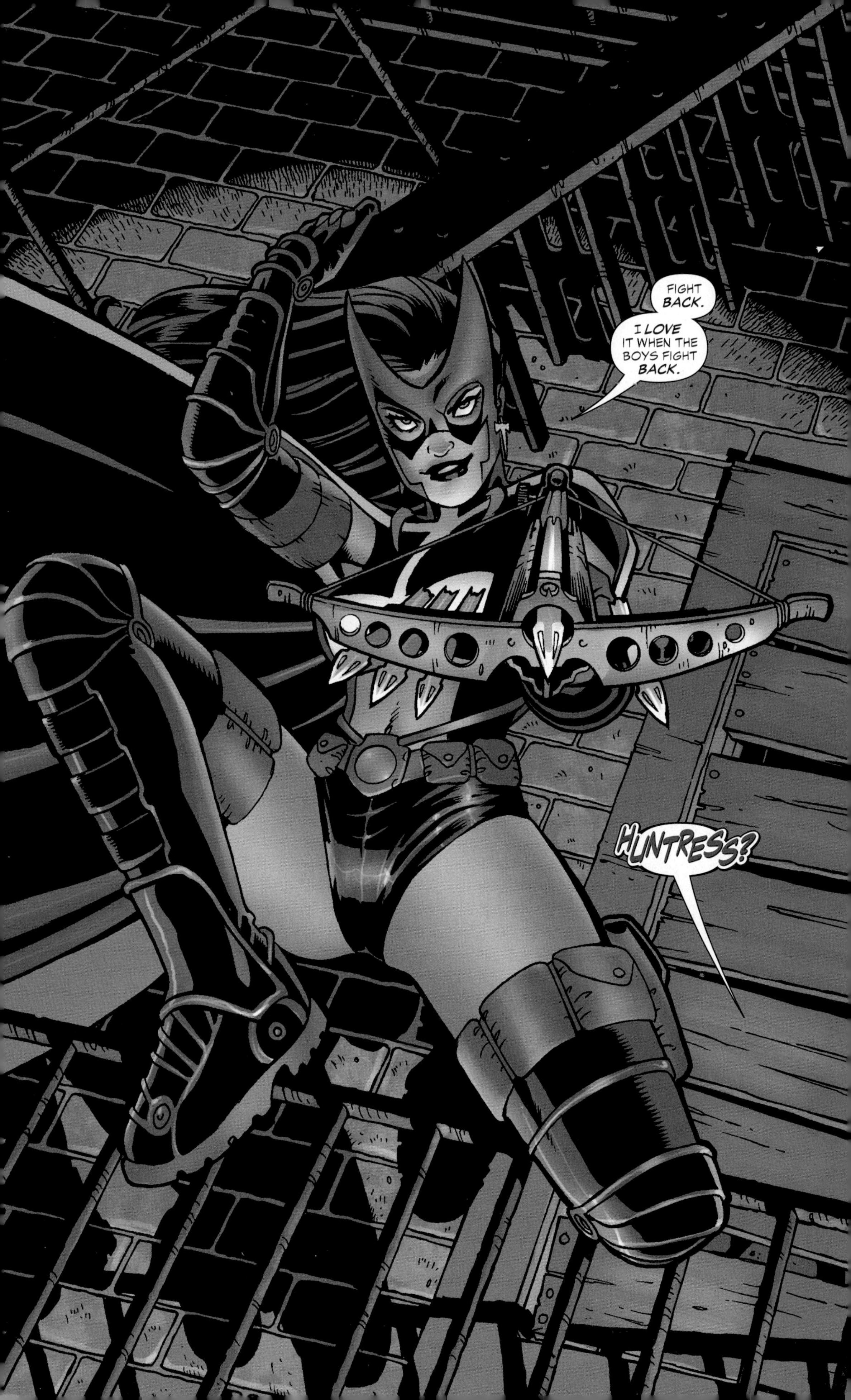
FIGHT BACK.
I LOVE IT WHEN THE BOYS FIGHT BACK.
HUNTRESS?

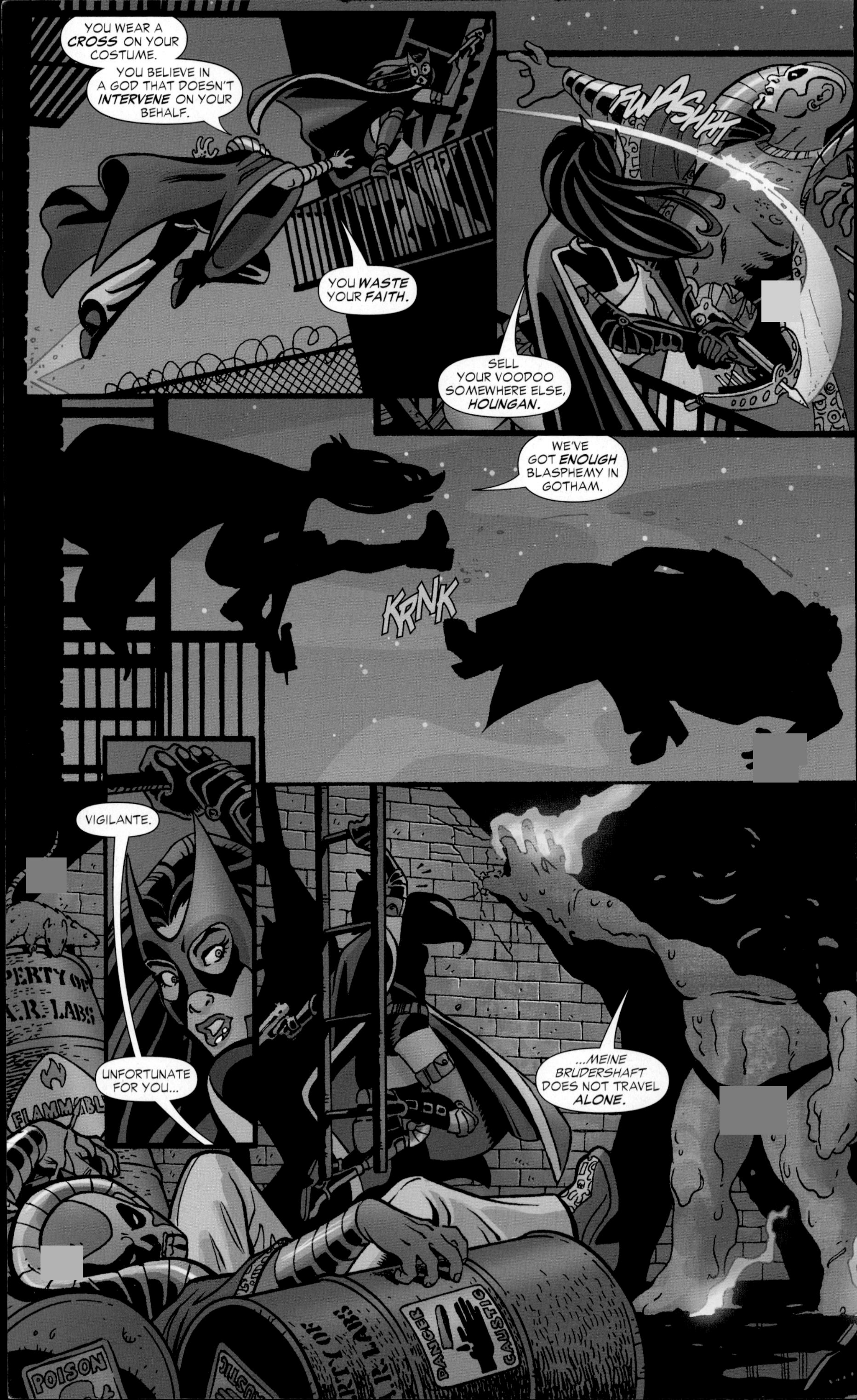
YOU WEAR A CROSS ON YOUR COSTUME.
YOU BELIEVE IN A GOD THAT DOESN'T INTERVENE ON YOUR BEHALF.
YOU WASTE YOUR FAITH.
FWASHK
SELL YOUR VOODOO SOMEWHERE ELSE, HOUNGAN.
WE'VE GOT ENOUGH BLASPHEMY IN GOTHAM.
KRNK
VIGILANTE.
UNFORTUNATE FOR YOU...
...MEINE BRUDERSHAFT DOES NOT TRAVEL ALONE.
DANGER
CAUSTIC
POISON

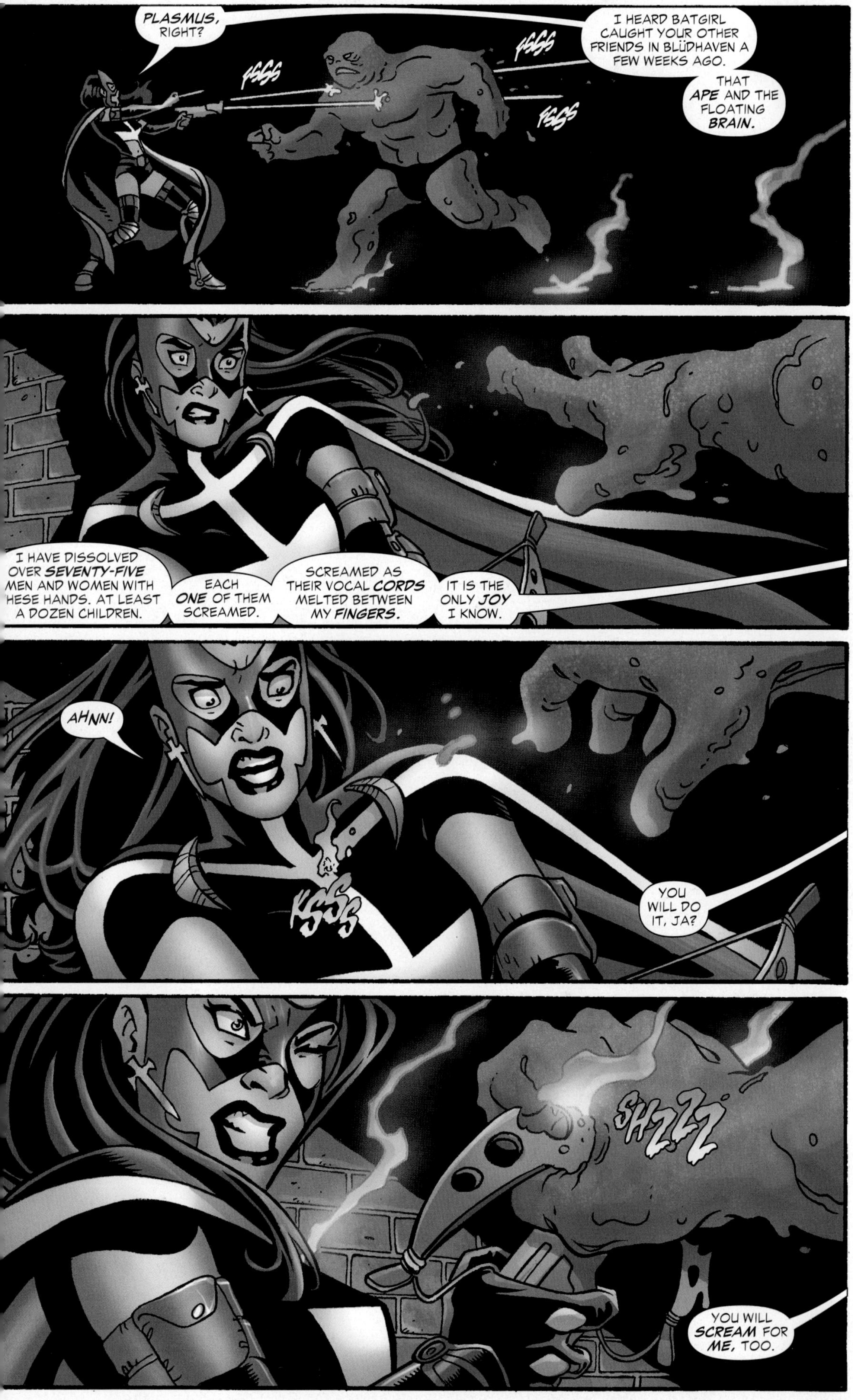
PLASMUS, RIGHT?
I HEARD BATGIRL CAUGHT YOUR OTHER FRIENDS IN BLÜDHAVEN A FEW WEEKS AGO.
THAT APE AND THE FLOATING BRAIN.
FSSS
FSSS
FSSS
I HAVE DISSOLVED OVER SEVENTY-FIVE MEN AND WOMEN WITH THESE HANDS. AT LEAST A DOZEN CHILDREN.
EACH ONE OF THEM SCREAMED.
SCREAMED AS THEIR VOCAL CORDS MELTED BETWEEN MY FINGERS.
IT IS THE ONLY JOY I KNOW.
AHNN!
KSSS
YOU WILL DO IT, JA?
SHZZZ
YOU WILL SCREAM FOR ME, TOO.

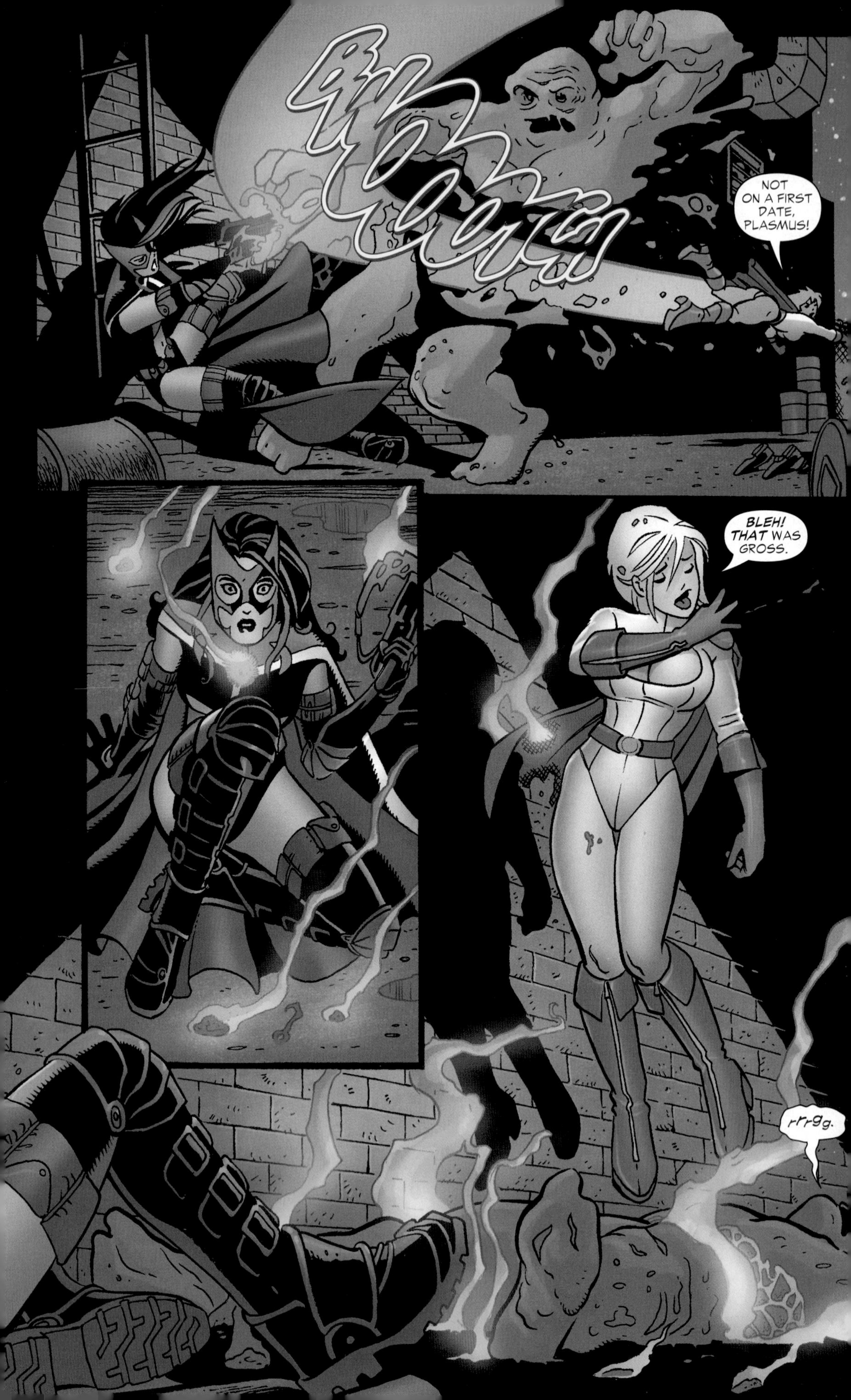
NOT ON A FIRST DATE, PLASMUS!
BLEH! THAT WAS GROSS.
rrrgg.

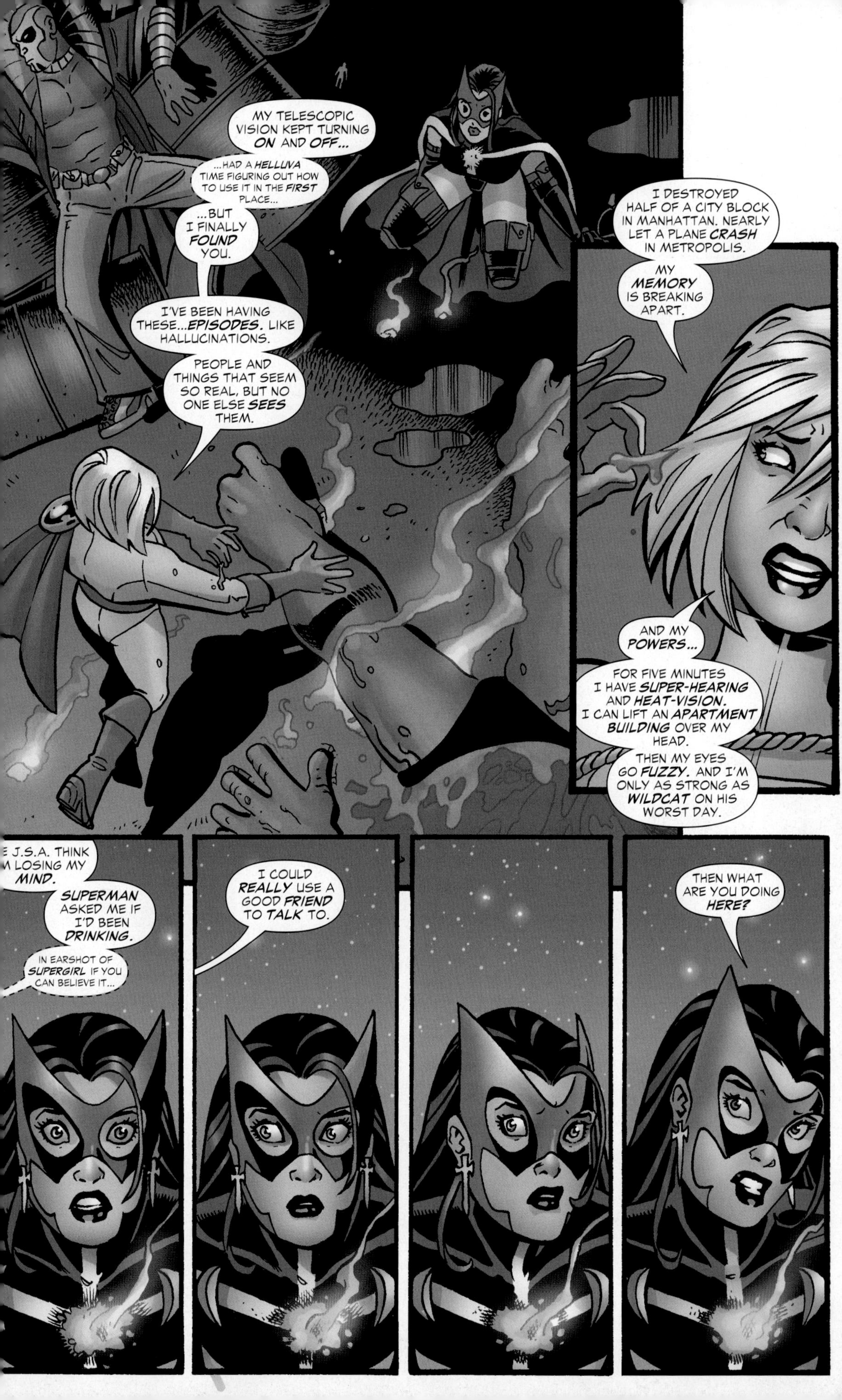
MY TELESCOPIC VISION KEPT TURNING ON AND OFF...
...HAD A HELLUVA TIME FIGURING OUT HOW TO USE IT IN THE FIRST PLACE...
...BUT I FINALLY FOUND YOU.
I'VE BEEN HAVING THESE...EPISODES. LIKE HALLUCINATIONS.
PEOPLE AND THINGS THAT SEEM SO REAL, BUT NO ONE ELSE SEES THEM.
I DESTROYED HALF OF A CITY BLOCK IN MANHATTAN. NEARLY LET A PLANE CRASH IN METROPOLIS.
MY MEMORY IS BREAKING APART.
AND MY POWERS...
FOR FIVE MINUTES I HAVE SUPER-HEARING AND HEAT-VISION. I CAN LIFT AN APARTMENT BUILDING OVER MY HEAD.
THEN MY EYES GO FUZZY. AND I'M ONLY AS STRONG AS WILDCAT ON HIS WORST DAY.
E J.S.A. THINK M LOSING MY MIND.
SUPERMAN ASKED ME IF I'D BEEN DRINKING.
IN EARSHOT OF SUPERGIRL IF YOU CAN BELIEVE IT...
I COULD REALLY USE A GOOD FRIEND TO TALK TO.
THEN WHAT ARE YOU DOING HERE?

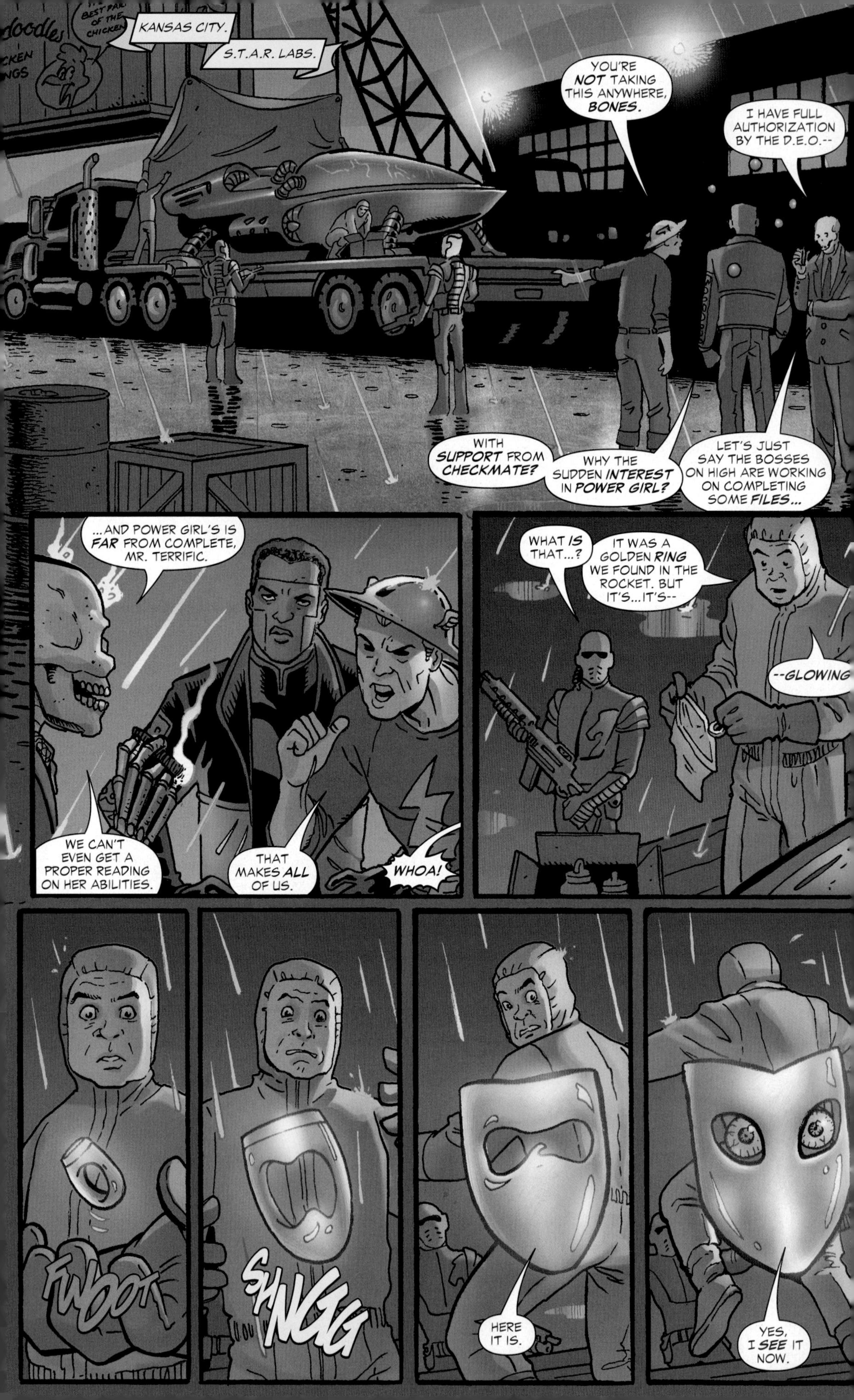
BEST PART OF THE CHICKEN
KANSAS CITY.
S.T.A.R. LABS.
YOU'RE NOT TAKING THIS ANYWHERE, BONES.
I HAVE FULL AUTHORIZATION BY THE D.E.O.--
WITH SUPPORT FROM CHECKMATE?
WHY THE SUDDEN INTEREST IN POWER GIRL?
LET'S JUST SAY THE BOSSES ON HIGH ARE WORKING ON COMPLETING SOME FILES...
...AND POWER GIRL'S IS FAR FROM COMPLETE, MR. TERRIFIC.
WE CAN'T EVEN GET A PROPER READING ON HER ABILITIES.
THAT MAKES ALL OF US.
WHOA!
WHAT IS THAT...?
IT WAS A GOLDEN RING WE FOUND IN THE ROCKET. BUT IT'S...IT'S--
--GLOWING
FWOOT
SHNGG
HERE IT IS.
YES, I SEE IT NOW.

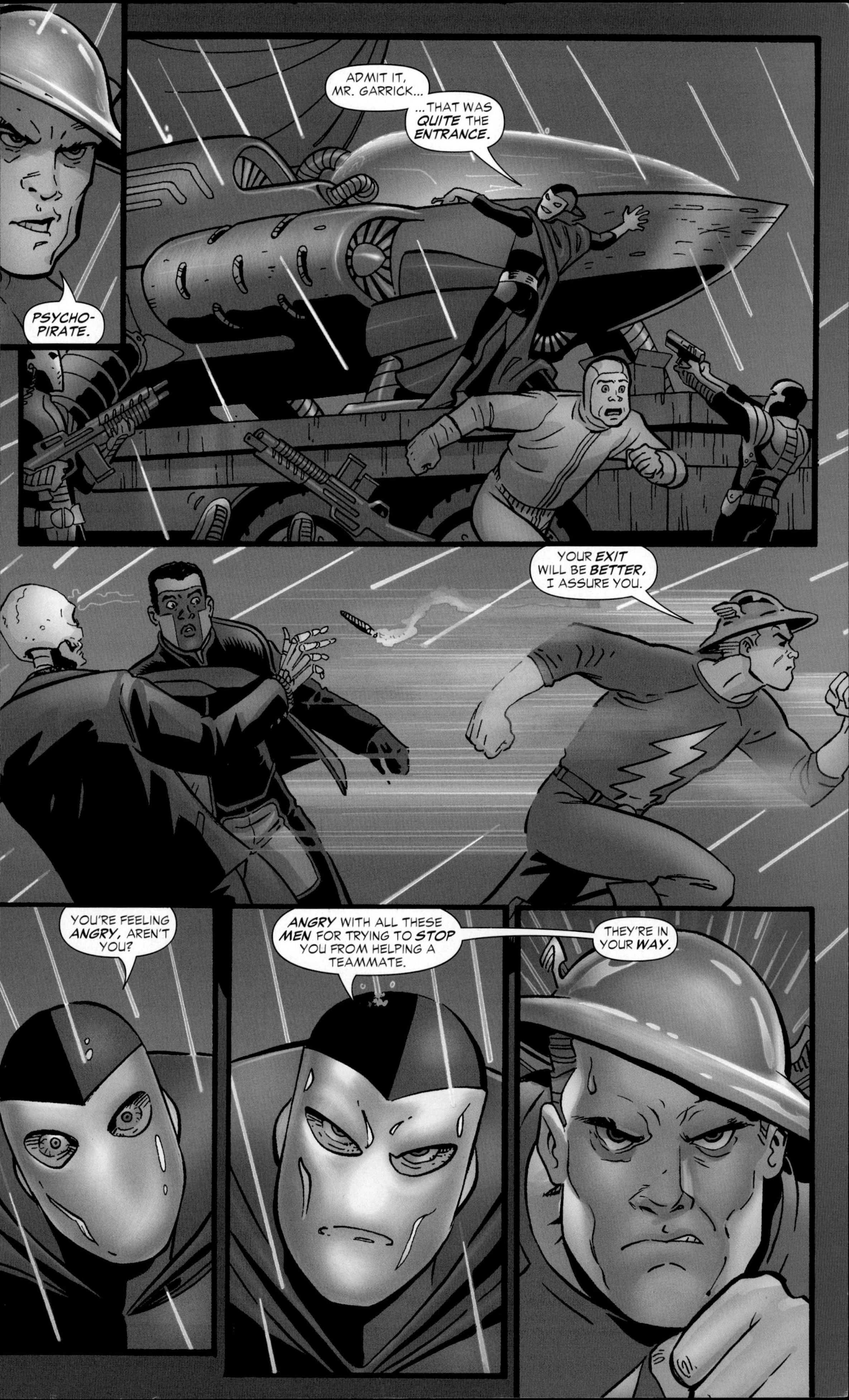
PSYCHO-PIRATE.
ADMIT IT, MR. GARRICK...
...THAT WAS QUITE THE ENTRANCE.
YOUR EXIT WILL BE BETTER, I ASSURE YOU.
YOU'RE FEELING ANGRY, AREN'T YOU?
ANGRY WITH ALL THESE MEN FOR TRYING TO STOP YOU FROM HELPING A TEAMMATE.
THEY'RE IN YOUR WAY.

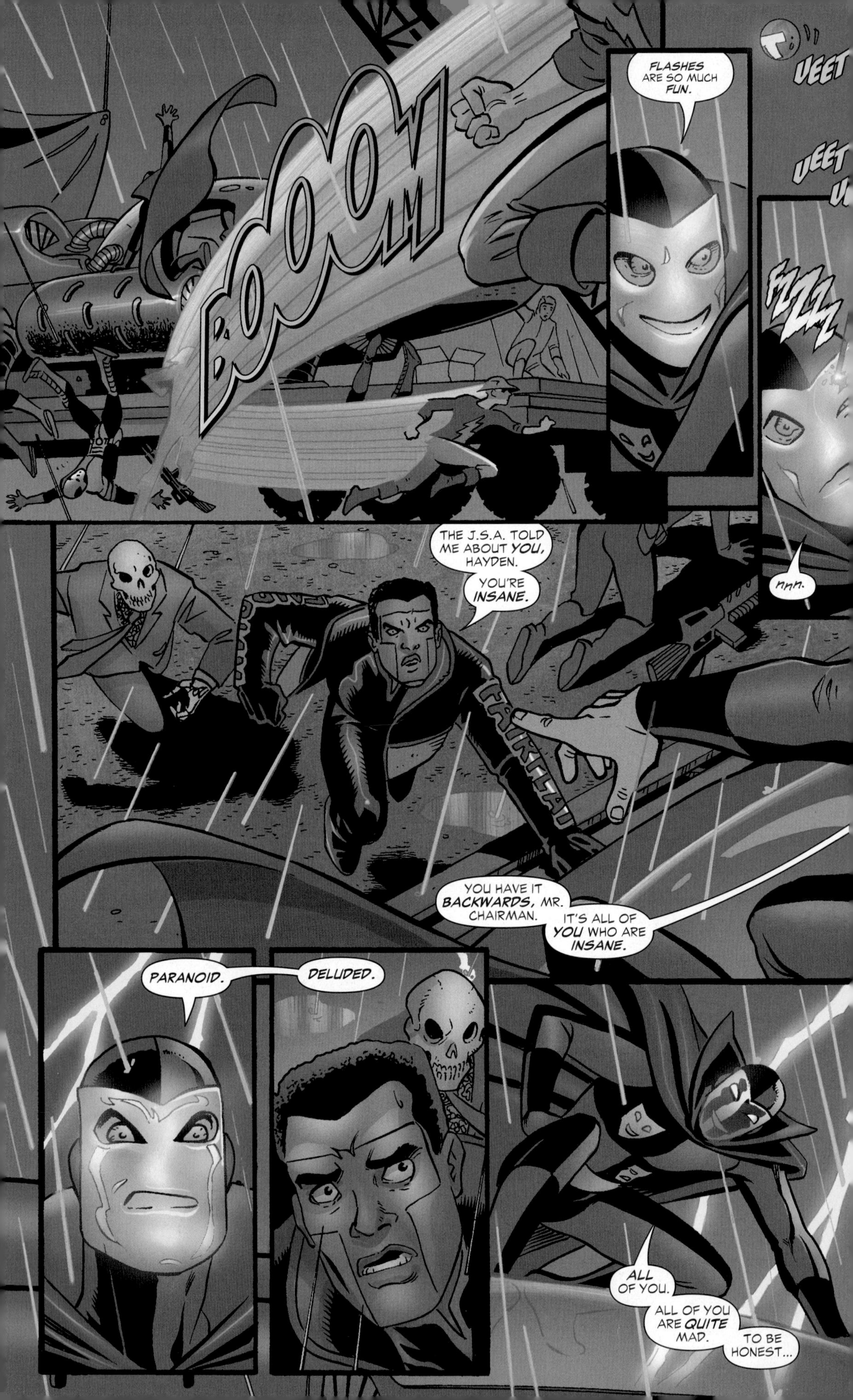
BOOOM
FLASHES ARE SO MUCH FUN.
VEET
VEET
FZZZZ
THE J.S.A. TOLD ME ABOUT YOU, HAYDEN.
YOU'RE INSANE.
nnn.
YOU HAVE IT BACKWARDS, MR. CHAIRMAN.
IT'S ALL OF YOU WHO ARE INSANE.
PARANOID.
DELUDED.
ALL OF YOU.
ALL OF YOU ARE QUITE MAD.
TO BE HONEST...

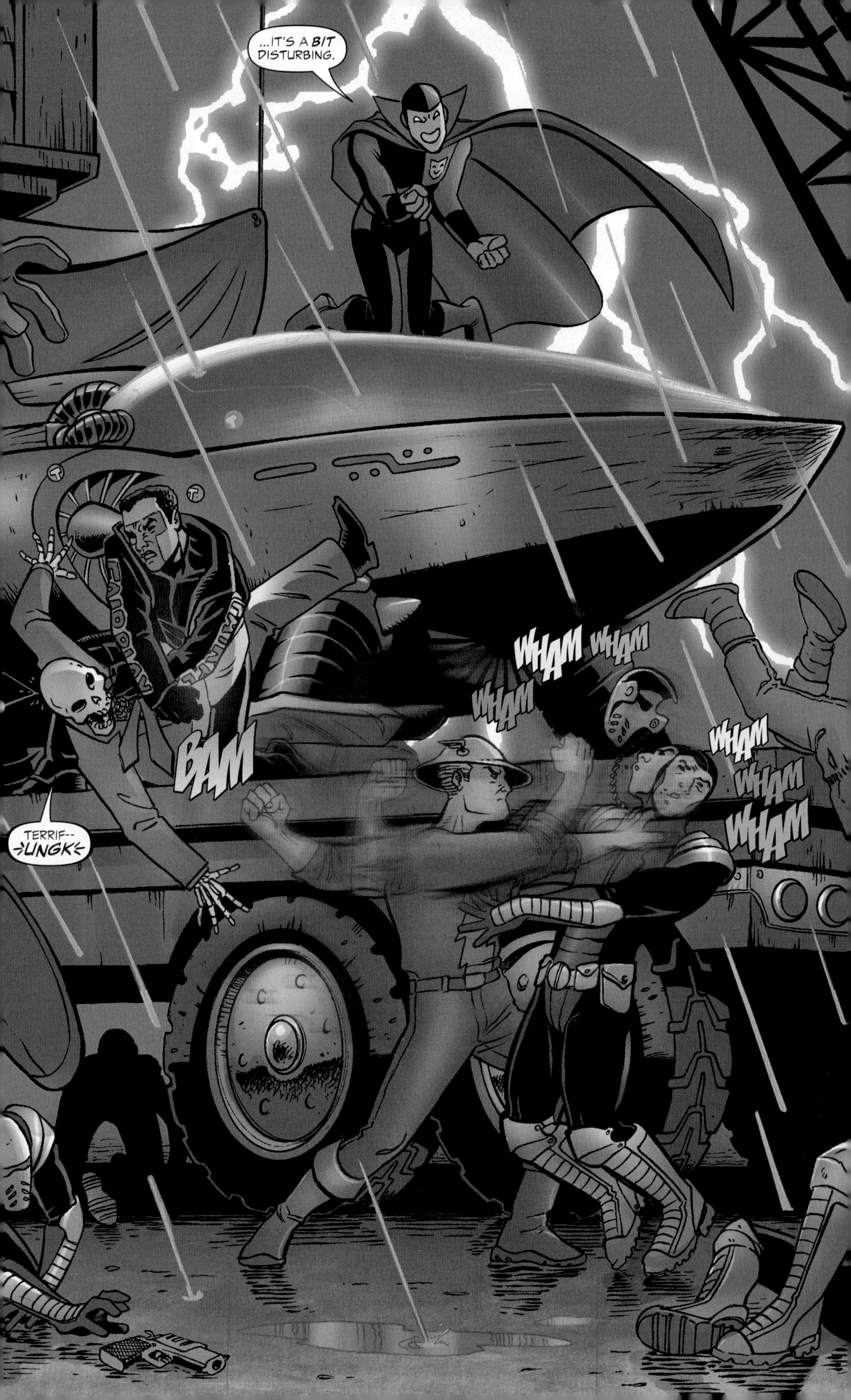
...IT'S A BIT DISTURBING.
WHAM WHAM
WHAM
BAM
WHAM
WHAM
WHAM
TERRIF-- UNGK

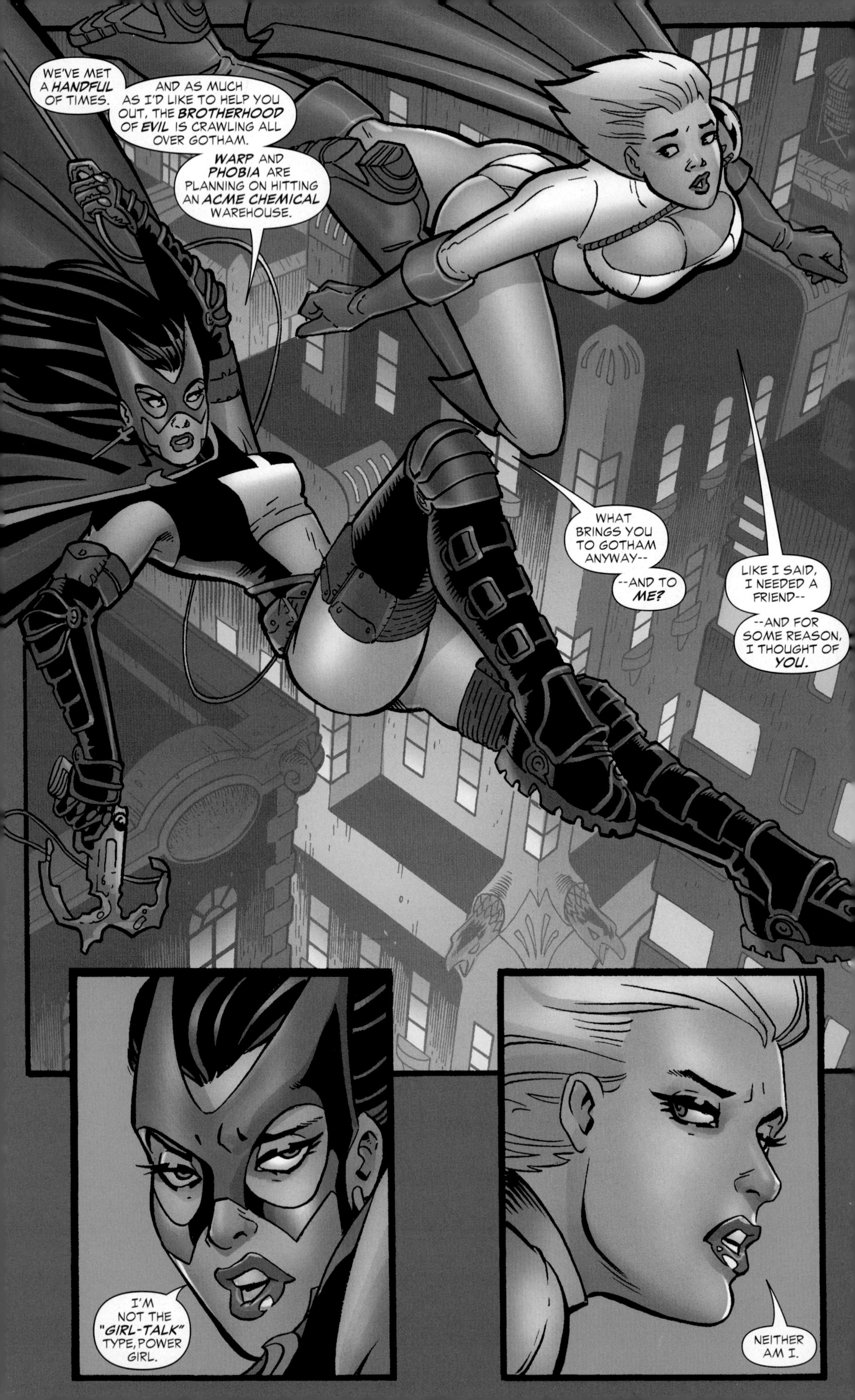

WE'VE MET A HANDFUL OF TIMES.
AND AS MUCH AS I'D LIKE TO HELP YOU OUT, THE BROTHERHOOD OF EVIL IS CRAWLING ALL OVER GOTHAM.
WARP AND PHOBIA ARE PLANNING ON HITTING AN ACME CHEMICAL WAREHOUSE.
WHAT BRINGS YOU TO GOTHAM ANYWAY--
--AND TO ME?
LIKE I SAID, I NEEDED A FRIEND--
--AND FOR SOME REASON, I THOUGHT OF YOU.
I'M NOT THE "GIRL-TALK" TYPE, POWER GIRL.
NEITHER AM I.

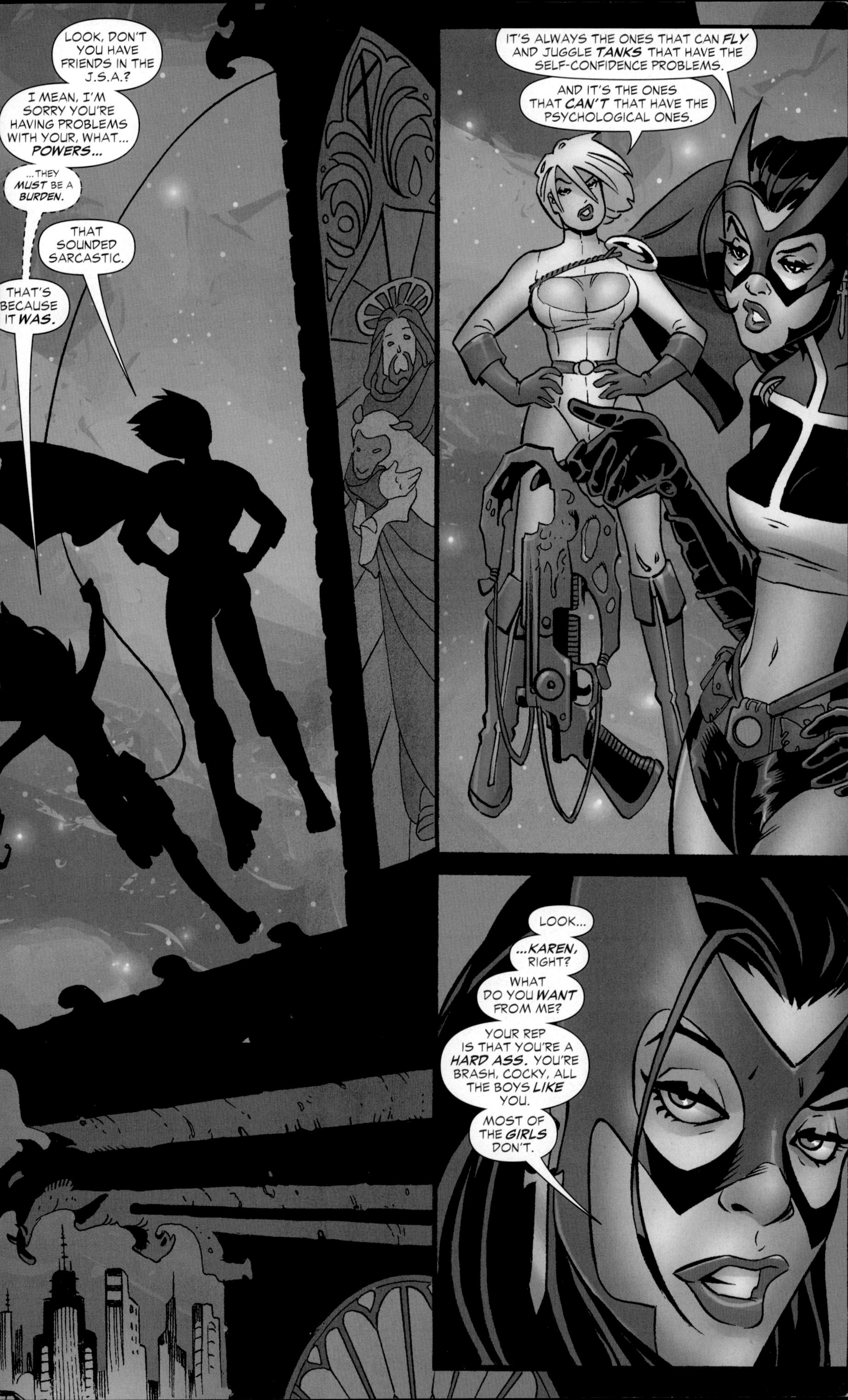
LOOK, DON'T YOU HAVE FRIENDS IN THE J.S.A.?
I MEAN, I'M SORRY YOU'RE HAVING PROBLEMS WITH YOUR, WHAT... POWERS...
...THEY MUST BE A BURDEN.
THAT SOUNDED SARCASTIC.
THAT'S BECAUSE IT WAS.
IT'S ALWAYS THE ONES THAT CAN FLY AND JUGGLE TANKS THAT HAVE THE SELF-CONFIDENCE PROBLEMS.
AND IT'S THE ONES THAT CAN'T THAT HAVE THE PSYCHOLOGICAL ONES.
LOOK...
...KAREN, RIGHT?
WHAT DO YOU WANT FROM ME?
YOUR REP IS THAT YOU'RE A HARD ASS. YOU'RE BRASH, COCKY, ALL THE BOYS LIKE YOU.
MOST OF THE GIRLS DON'T.

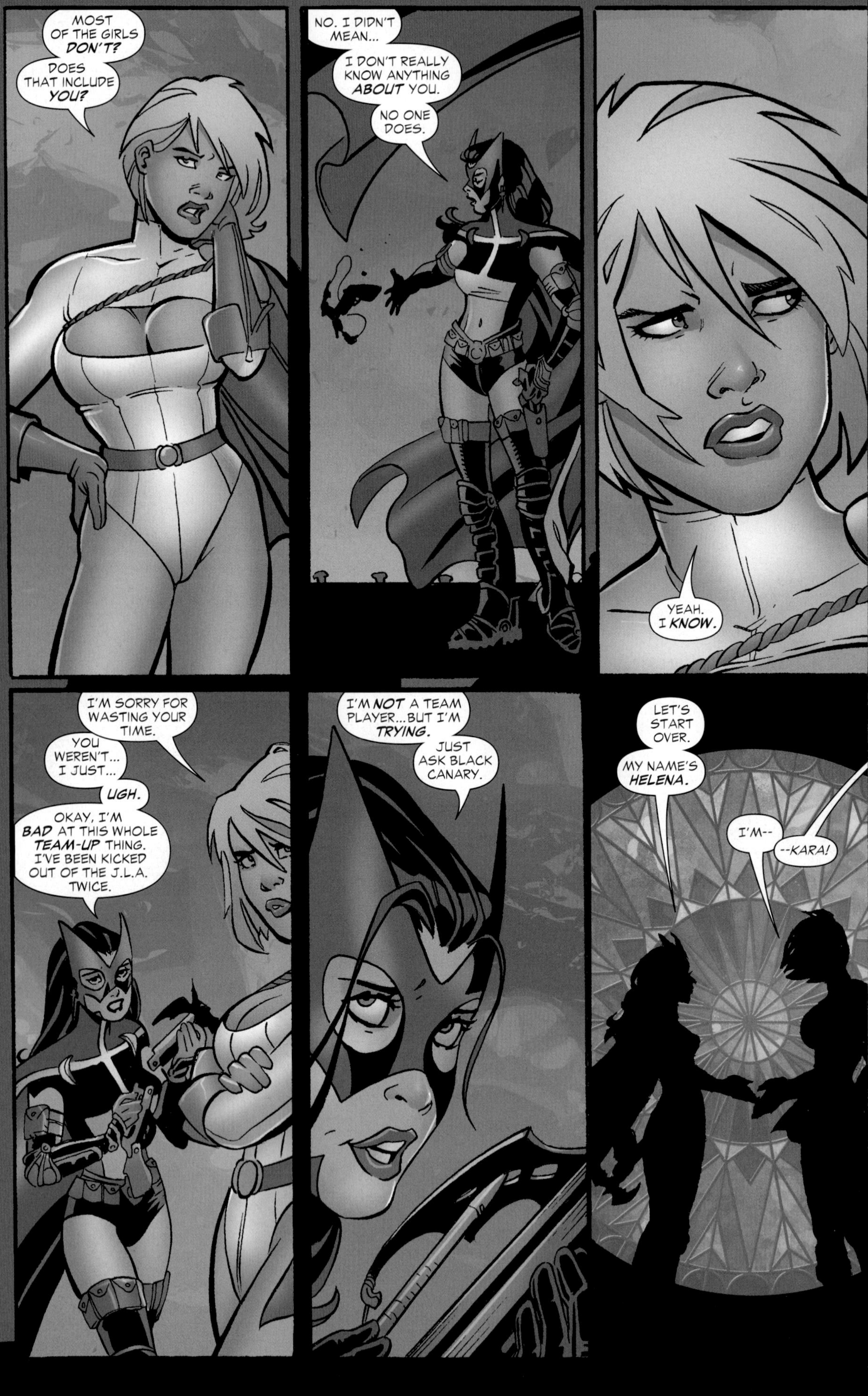
MOST OF THE GIRLS DON'T?
DOES THAT INCLUDE YOU?
NO. I DIDN'T MEAN...
I DON'T REALLY KNOW ANYTHING ABOUT YOU.
NO ONE DOES.
YEAH. I KNOW.
I'M SORRY FOR WASTING YOUR TIME.
YOU WEREN'T... I JUST...
UGH.
OKAY, I'M BAD AT THIS WHOLE TEAM-UP THING. I'VE BEEN KICKED OUT OF THE J.L.A. TWICE.
I'M NOT A TEAM PLAYER...BUT I'M TRYING.
JUST ASK BLACK CANARY.
LET'S START OVER.
MY NAME'S HELENA.
I'M--
--KARA!

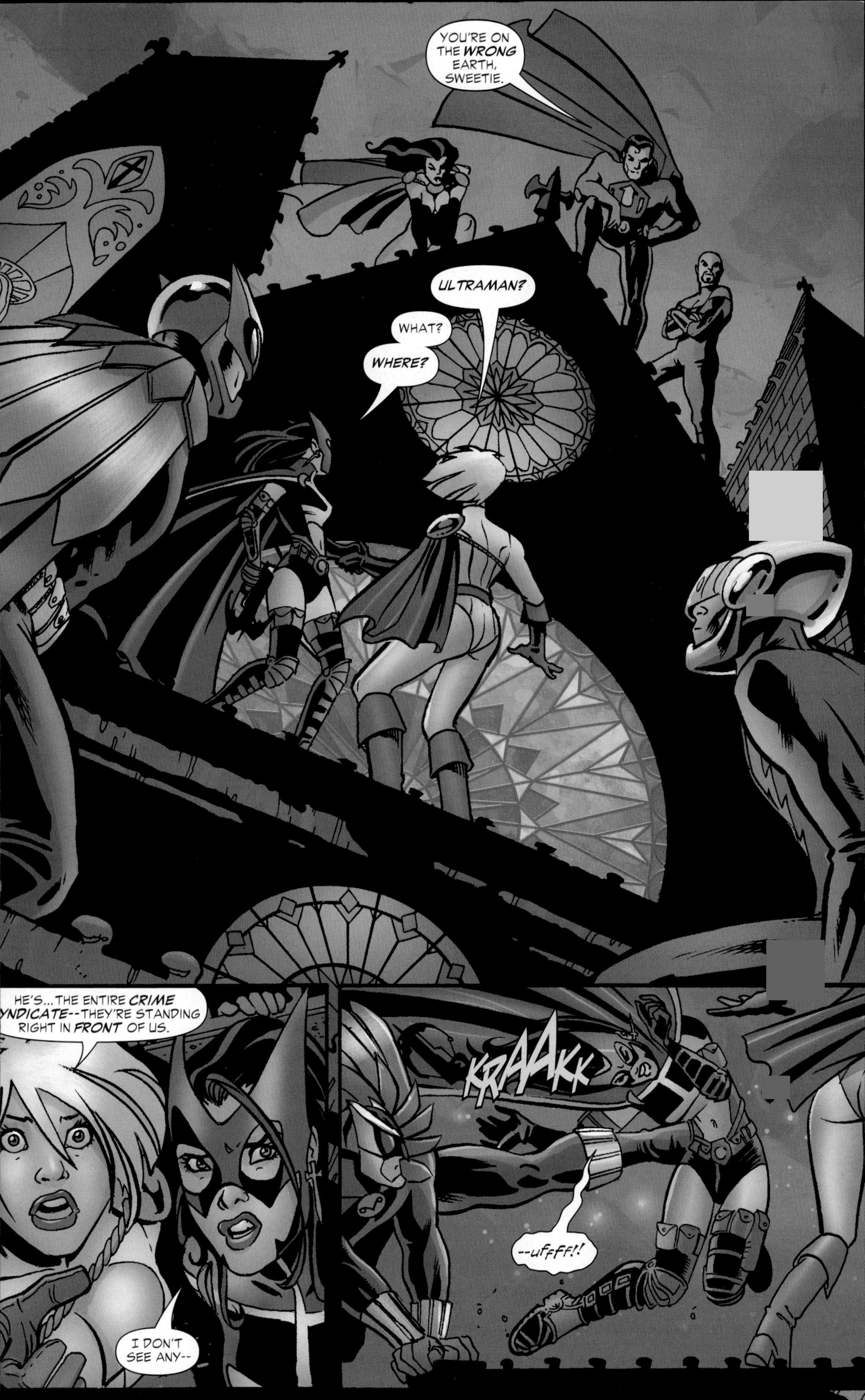
YOU'RE ON THE WRONG EARTH, SWEETIE.
ULTRAMAN?
WHAT?
WHERE?
HE'S...THE ENTIRE CRIME YNDICATE--THEY'RE STANDING RIGHT IN FRONT OF US.
I DON'T SEE ANY--
KRAAKK
--uFFFF!!

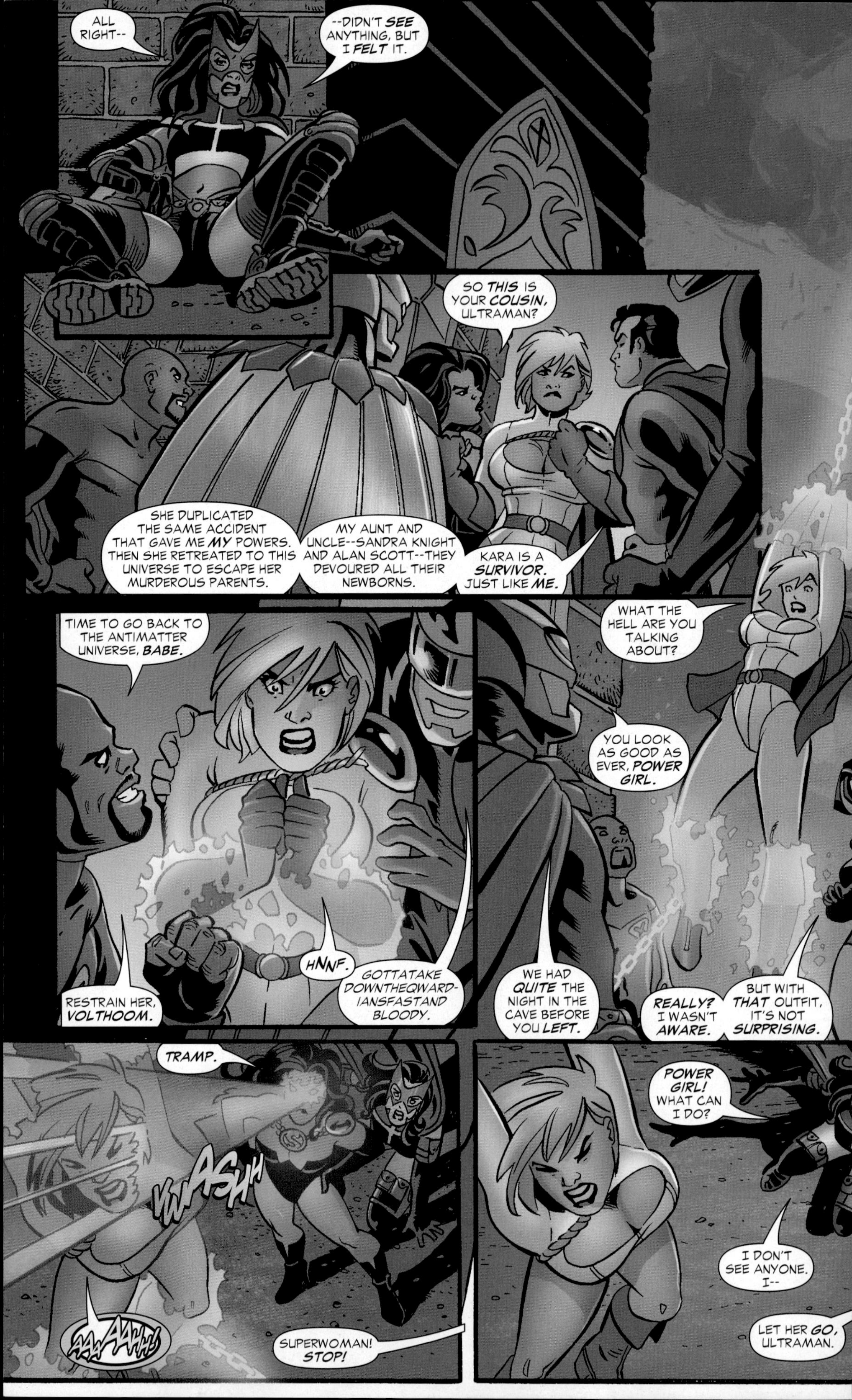
ALL RIGHT--
--DIDN'T SEE ANYTHING, BUT I FELT IT.
SO THIS IS YOUR COUSIN, ULTRAMAN?
SHE DUPLICATED THE SAME ACCIDENT THAT GAVE ME MY POWERS. THEN SHE RETREATED TO THIS UNIVERSE TO ESCAPE HER MURDEROUS PARENTS.
MY AUNT AND UNCLE--SANDRA KNIGHT AND ALAN SCOTT--THEY DEVOURED ALL THEIR NEWBORNS.
KARA IS A SURVIVOR. JUST LIKE ME.
TIME TO GO BACK TO THE ANTIMATTER UNIVERSE, BABE.
RESTRAIN HER, VOLTHOOM.
HNNF.
GOTTATAKE DOWNTHEQWARD-IANSFASTAND BLOODY.
WHAT THE HELL ARE YOU TALKING ABOUT?
YOU LOOK AS GOOD AS EVER, POWER GIRL.
WE HAD QUITE THE NIGHT IN THE CAVE BEFORE YOU LEFT.
REALLY? I WASN'T AWARE.
BUT WITH THAT OUTFIT, IT'S NOT SURPRISING.
TRAMP.
VWASH
AAAAAHH
SUPERWOMAN! STOP!
POWER GIRL! WHAT CAN I DO?
I DON'T SEE ANYONE. I--
LET HER GO, ULTRAMAN.

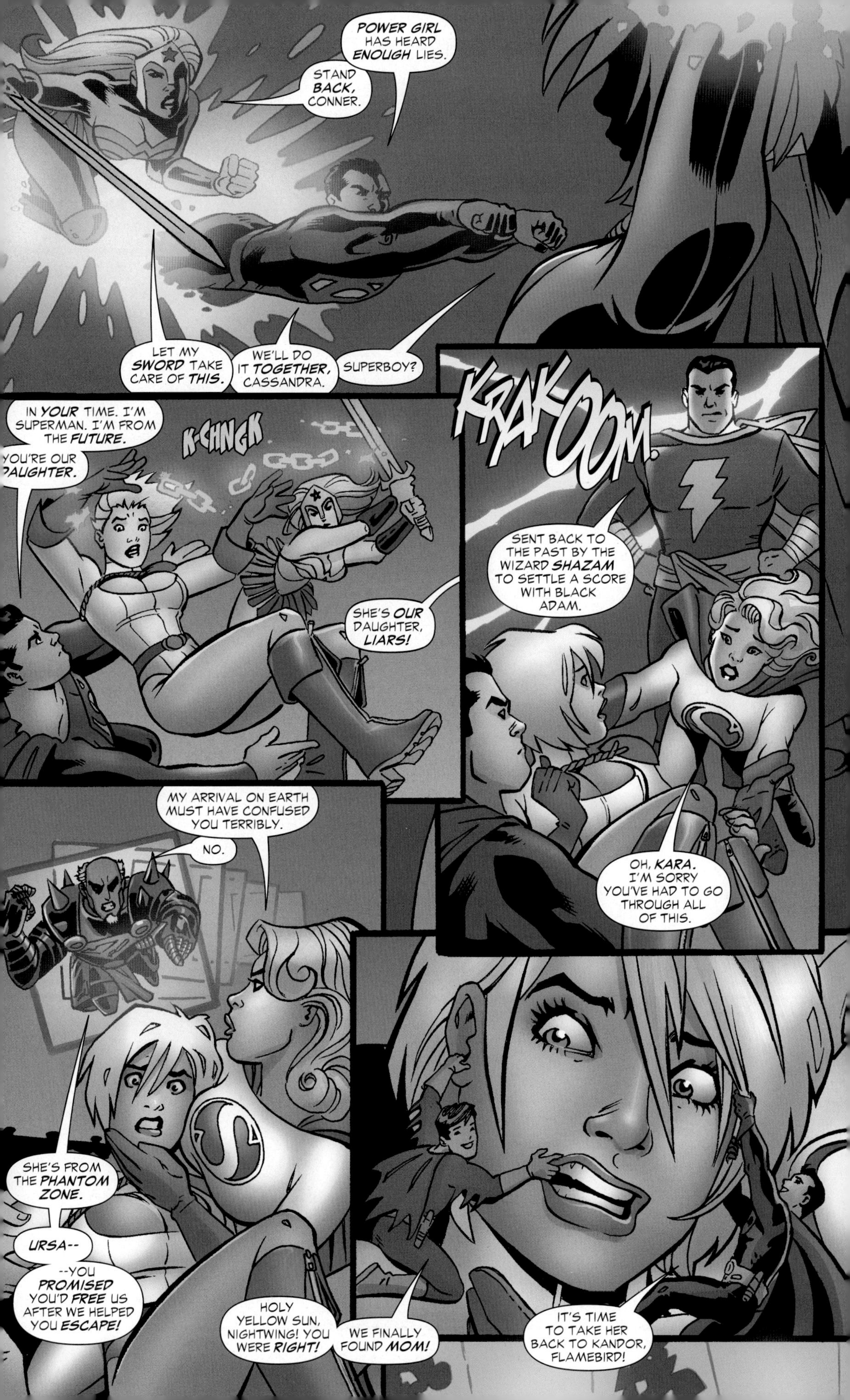

POWER GIRL HAS HEARD ENOUGH LIES.
STAND BACK, CONNER.
LET MY SWORD TAKE CARE OF THIS.
WE'LL DO IT TOGETHER, CASSANDRA.
SUPERBOY?
IN YOUR TIME. I'M SUPERMAN. I'M FROM THE FUTURE.
YOU'RE OUR DAUGHTER.
K-CHNGK
SHE'S OUR DAUGHTER, LIARS!
KRAKOOOM
SENT BACK TO THE PAST BY THE WIZARD SHAZAM TO SETTLE A SCORE WITH BLACK ADAM.
OH, KARA. I'M SORRY YOU'VE HAD TO GO THROUGH ALL OF THIS.
MY ARRIVAL ON EARTH MUST HAVE CONFUSED YOU TERRIBLY.
NO.
SHE'S FROM THE PHANTOM ZONE.
URSA--
--YOU PROMISED YOU'D FREE US AFTER WE HELPED YOU ESCAPE!
HOLY YELLOW SUN, NIGHTWING! YOU WERE RIGHT!
WE FINALLY FOUND MOM!
IT'S TIME TO TAKE HER BACK TO KANDOR, FLAMEBIRD!

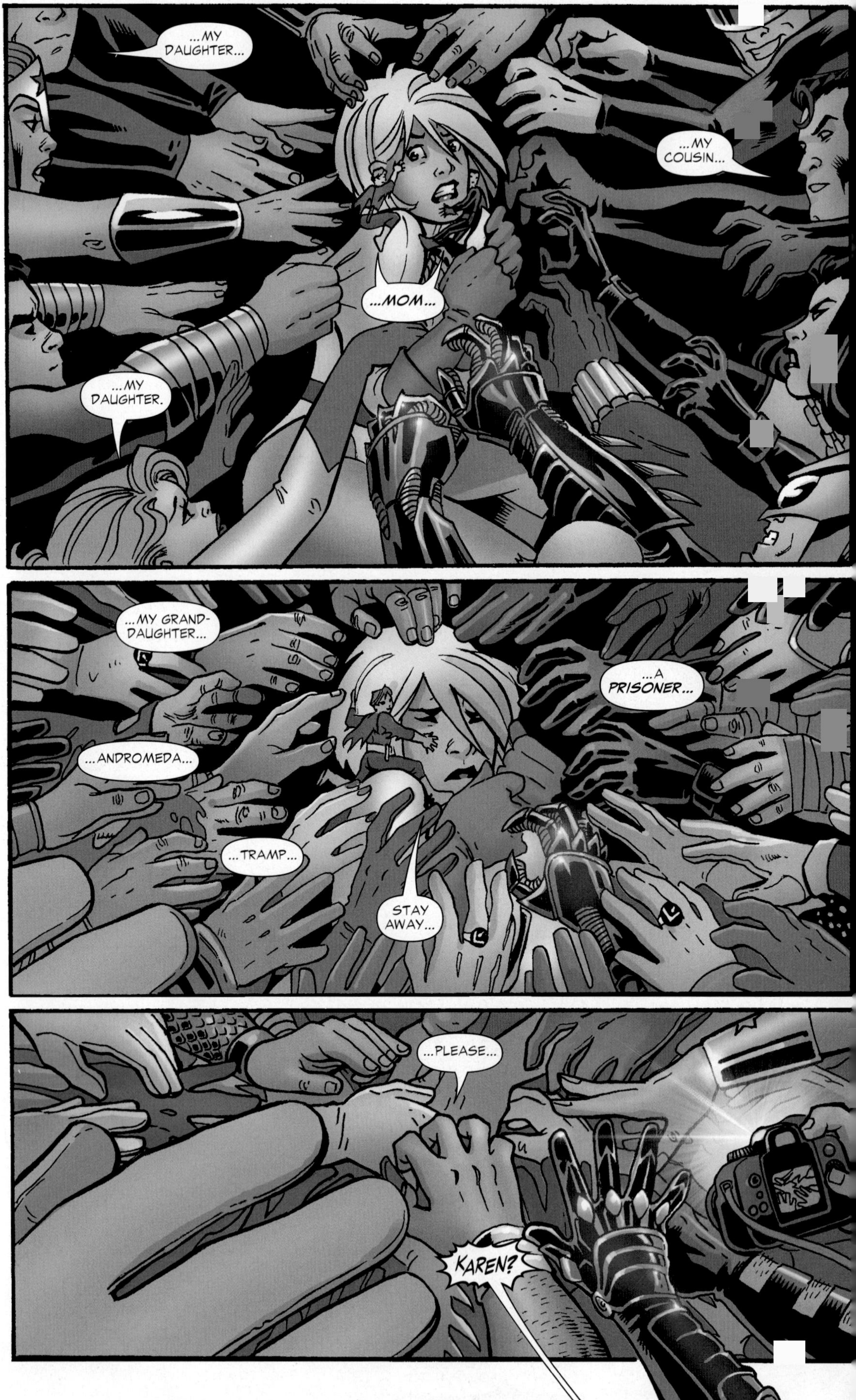
...MY DAUGHTER...
...MY COUSIN...
...MOM...
...MY DAUGHTER.
...MY GRAND-DAUGHTER...
...A PRISONER...
...ANDROMEDA...
...TRAMP...
STAY AWAY...
...PLEASE...
KAREN?

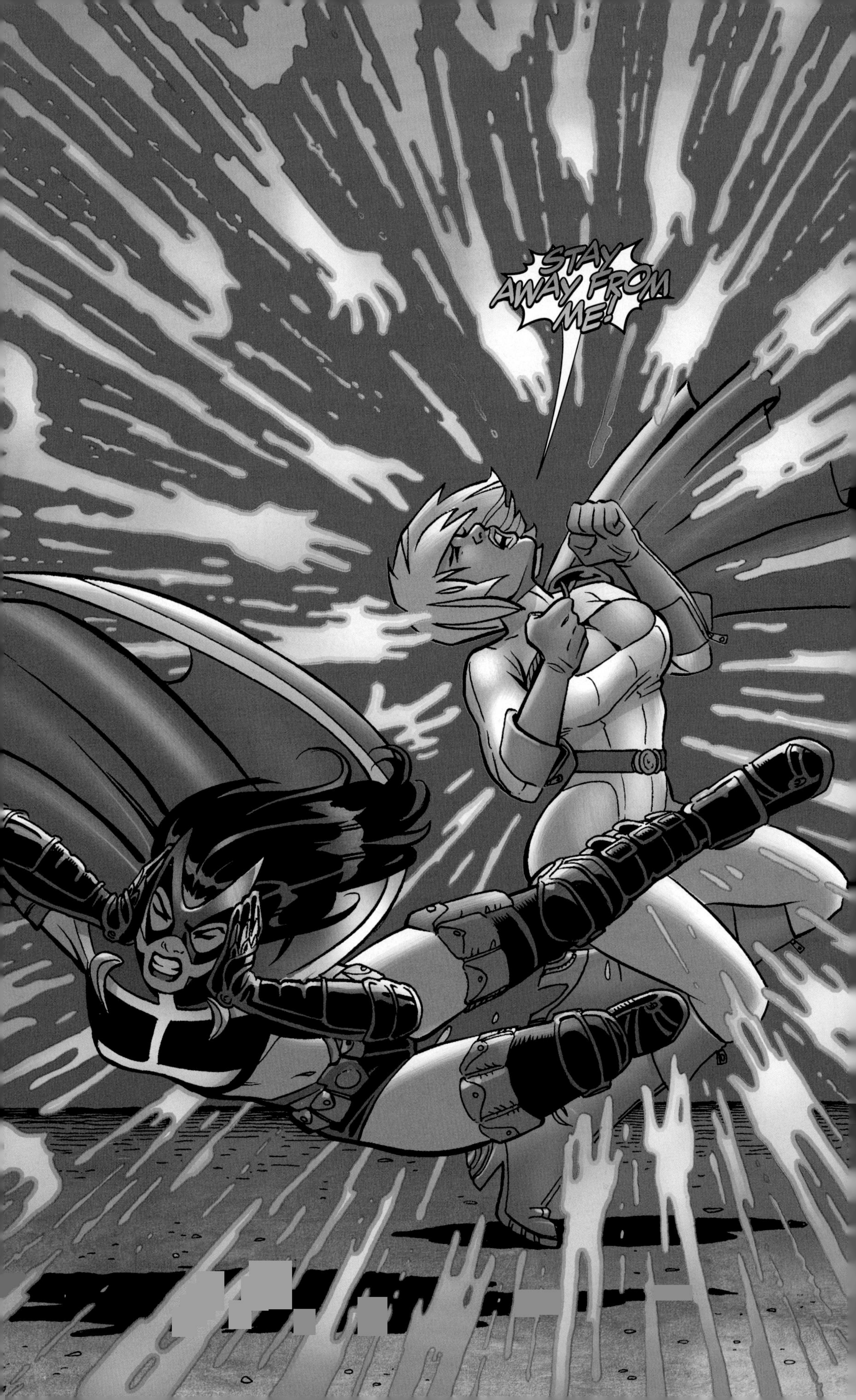
STAY AWAY FROM ME!

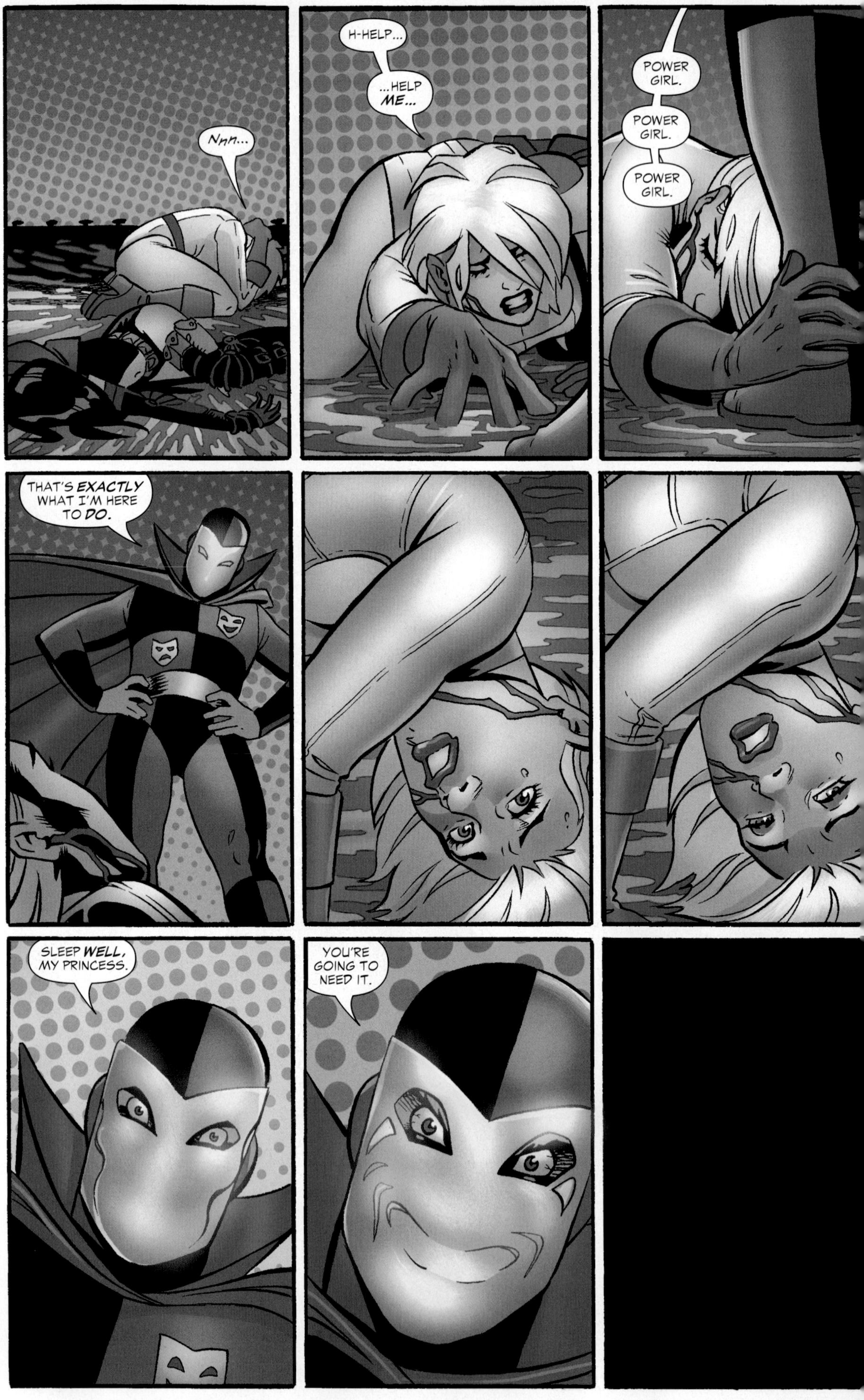
Nnn...
H-HELP...
...HELP ME...
POWER GIRL.
POWER GIRL.
POWER GIRL.
THAT'S EXACTLY WHAT I'M HERE TO DO.
SLEEP WELL, MY PRINCESS.
YOU'RE GOING TO NEED IT.

I HAVE HER.

AND IS SHE BROKEN?

OH, YES.

THE OTHERS STILL HAVE NO IDEA. NONE OF THEM.

SHE'LL BE READY.

MY REDEMPTION IS AT HAND.

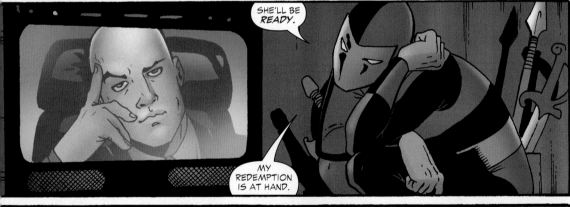

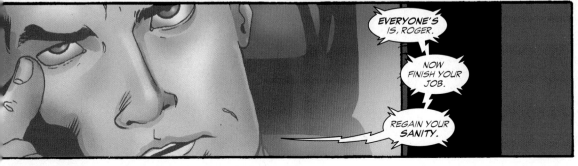

EVERYONE'S IS, ROGER.

NOW FINISH YOUR JOB.

REGAIN YOUR SANITY.

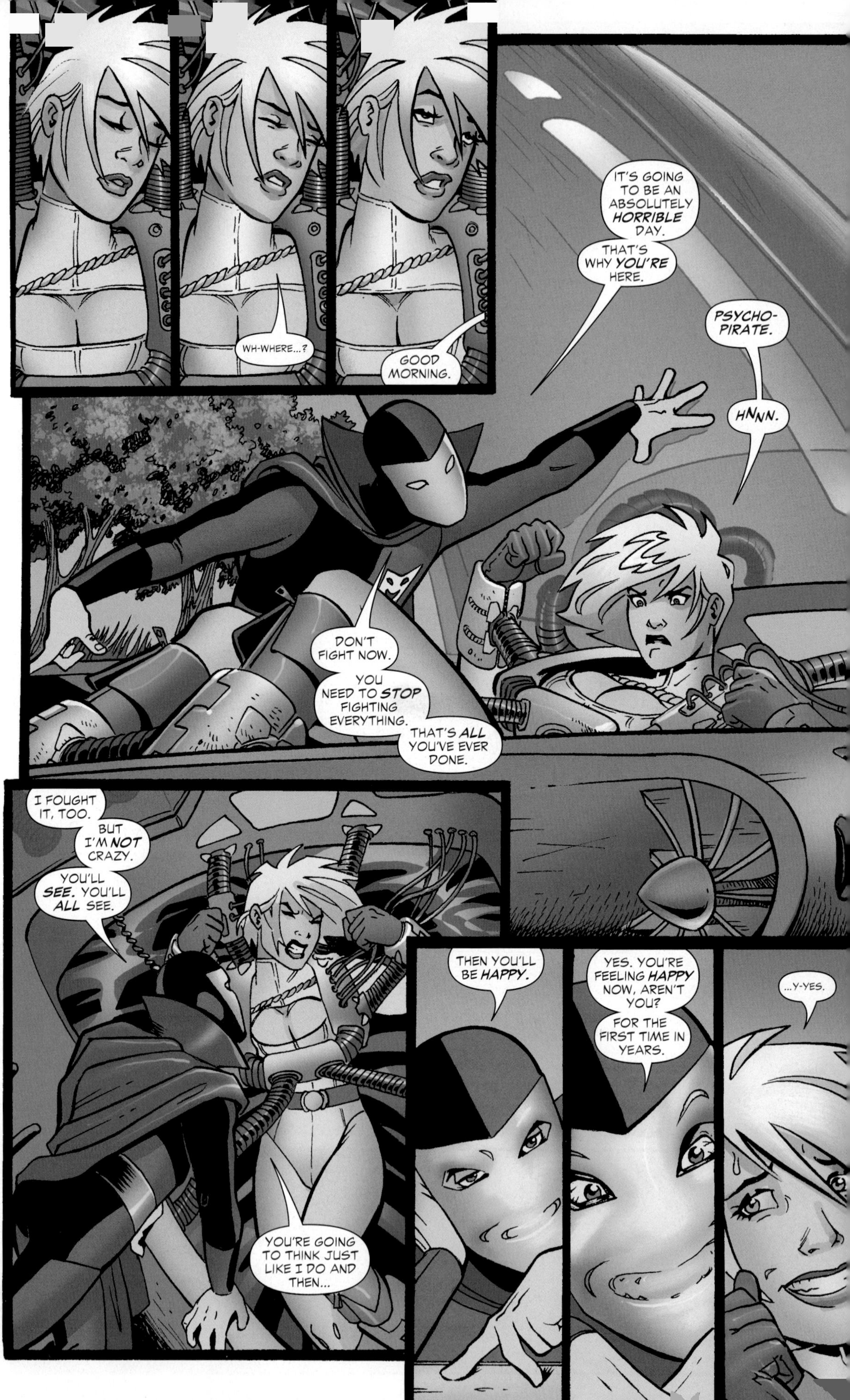
WH-WHERE...?
GOOD MORNING.
IT'S GOING TO BE AN ABSOLUTELY HORRIBLE DAY.
THAT'S WHY YOU'RE HERE.
PSYCHO-PIRATE.
HNNN.
DON'T FIGHT NOW.
YOU NEED TO STOP FIGHTING EVERYTHING.
THAT'S ALL YOU'VE EVER DONE.
I FOUGHT IT, TOO.
BUT I'M NOT CRAZY.
YOU'LL SEE. YOU'LL ALL SEE.
YOU'RE GOING TO THINK JUST LIKE I DO AND THEN...
THEN YOU'LL BE HAPPY.
YES. YOU'RE FEELING HAPPY NOW, AREN'T YOU?
FOR THE FIRST TIME IN YEARS.
...Y-YES.

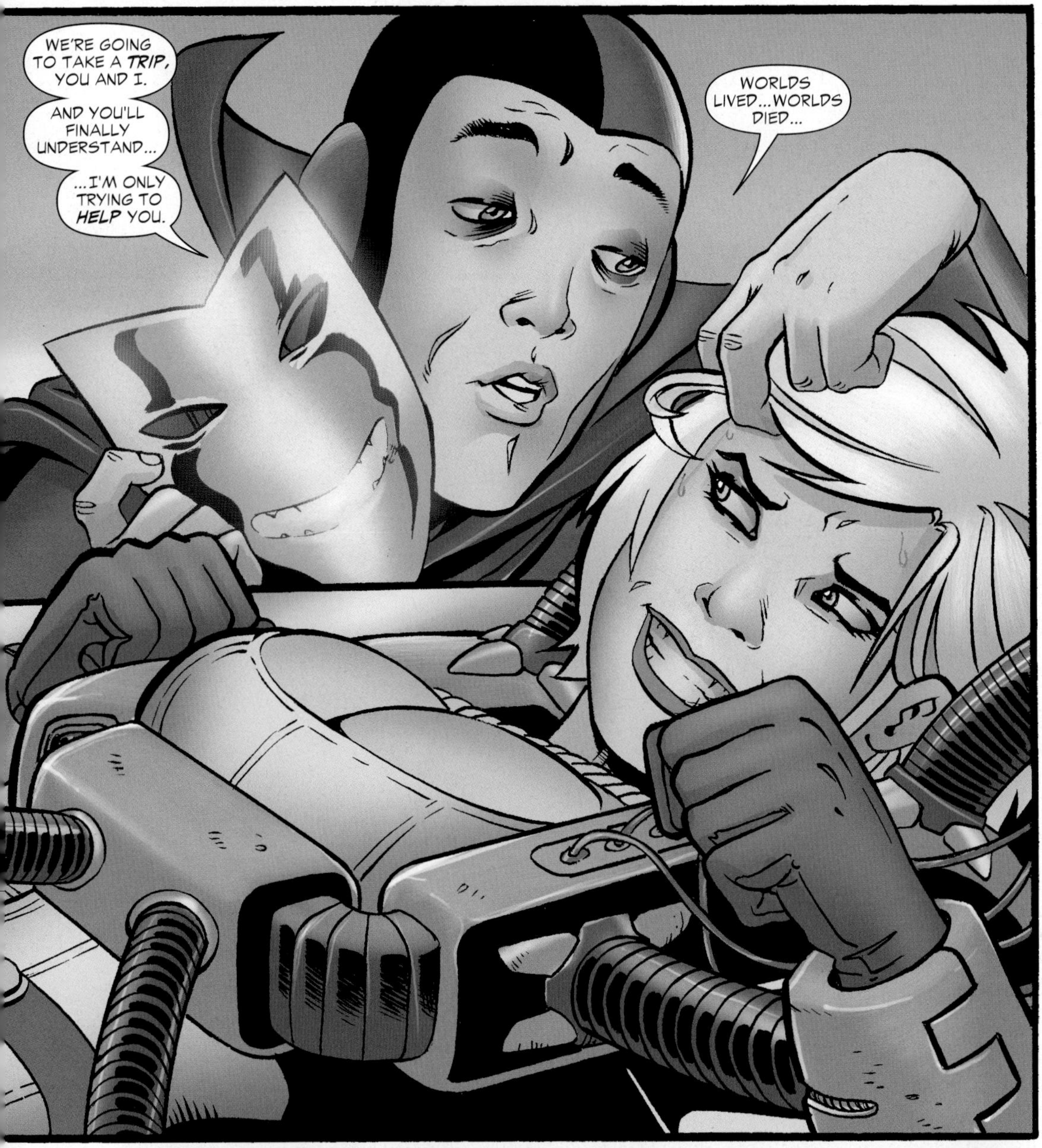
WE'RE GOING TO TAKE A *TRIP*, YOU AND I.
AND YOU'LL FINALLY UNDERSTAND...
...I'M ONLY TRYING TO *HELP* YOU.
WORLDS LIVED...WORLDS DIED...

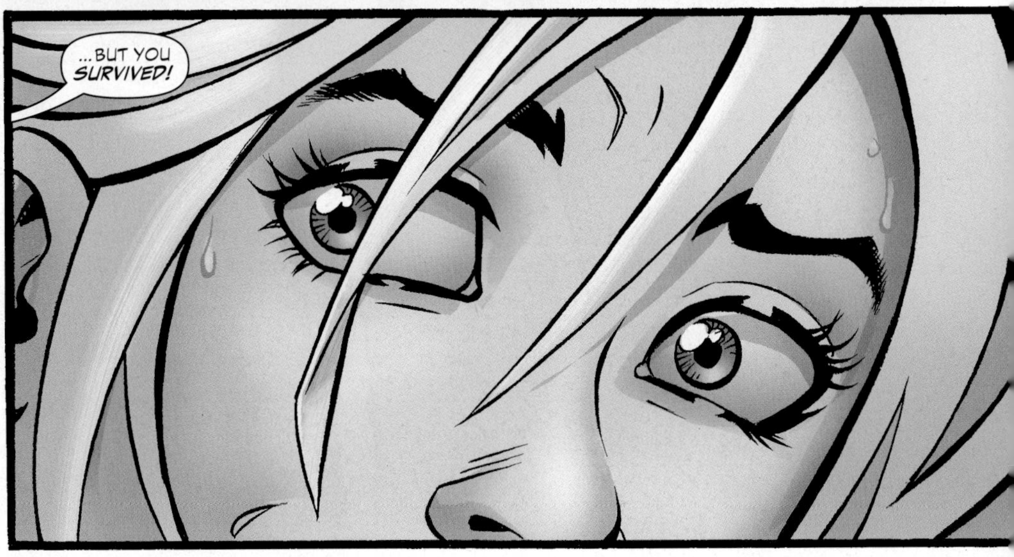
...BUT YOU *SURVIVED!*

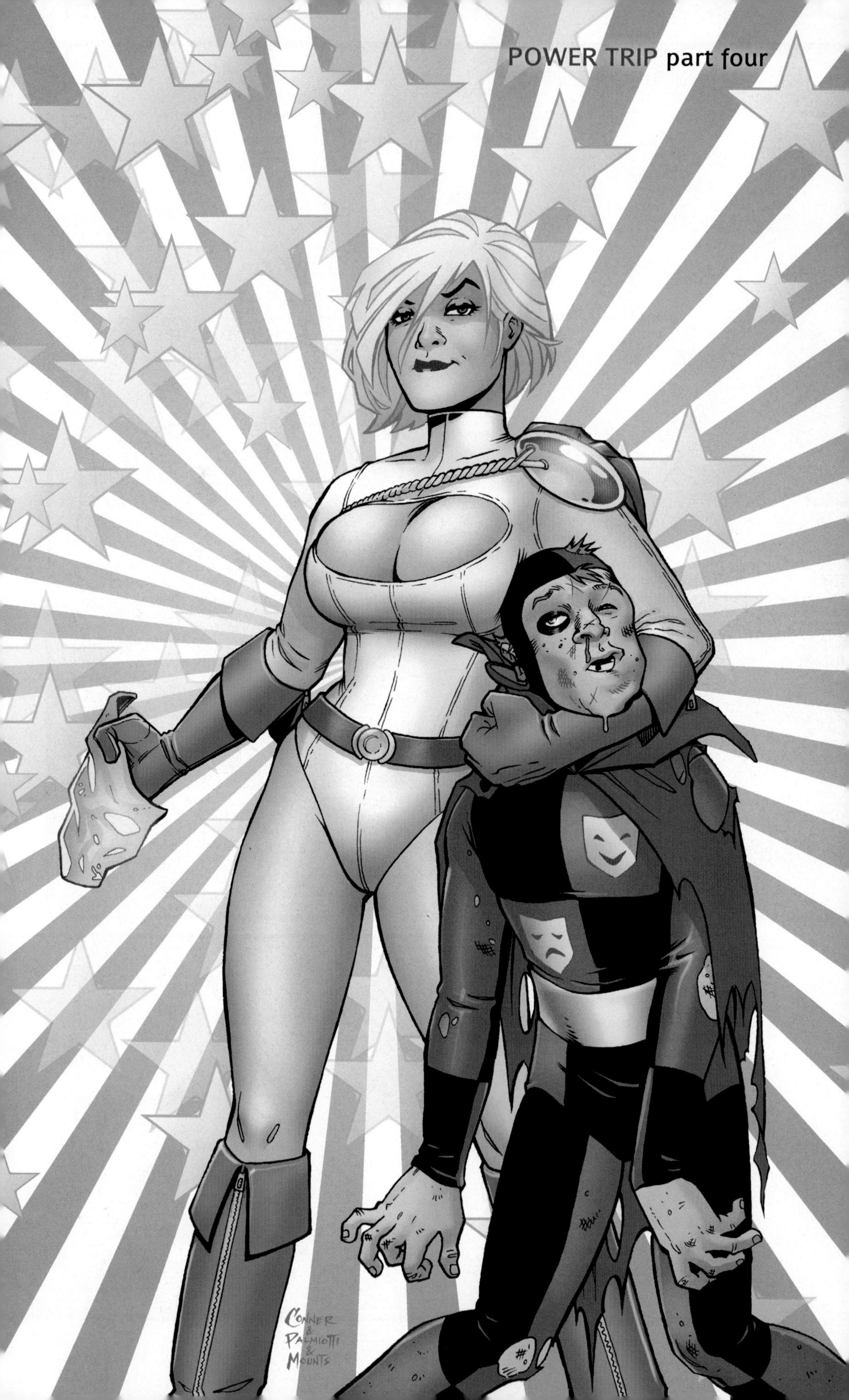
POWER TRIP part four
CONNER & PALMIOTTI & MOUNTS

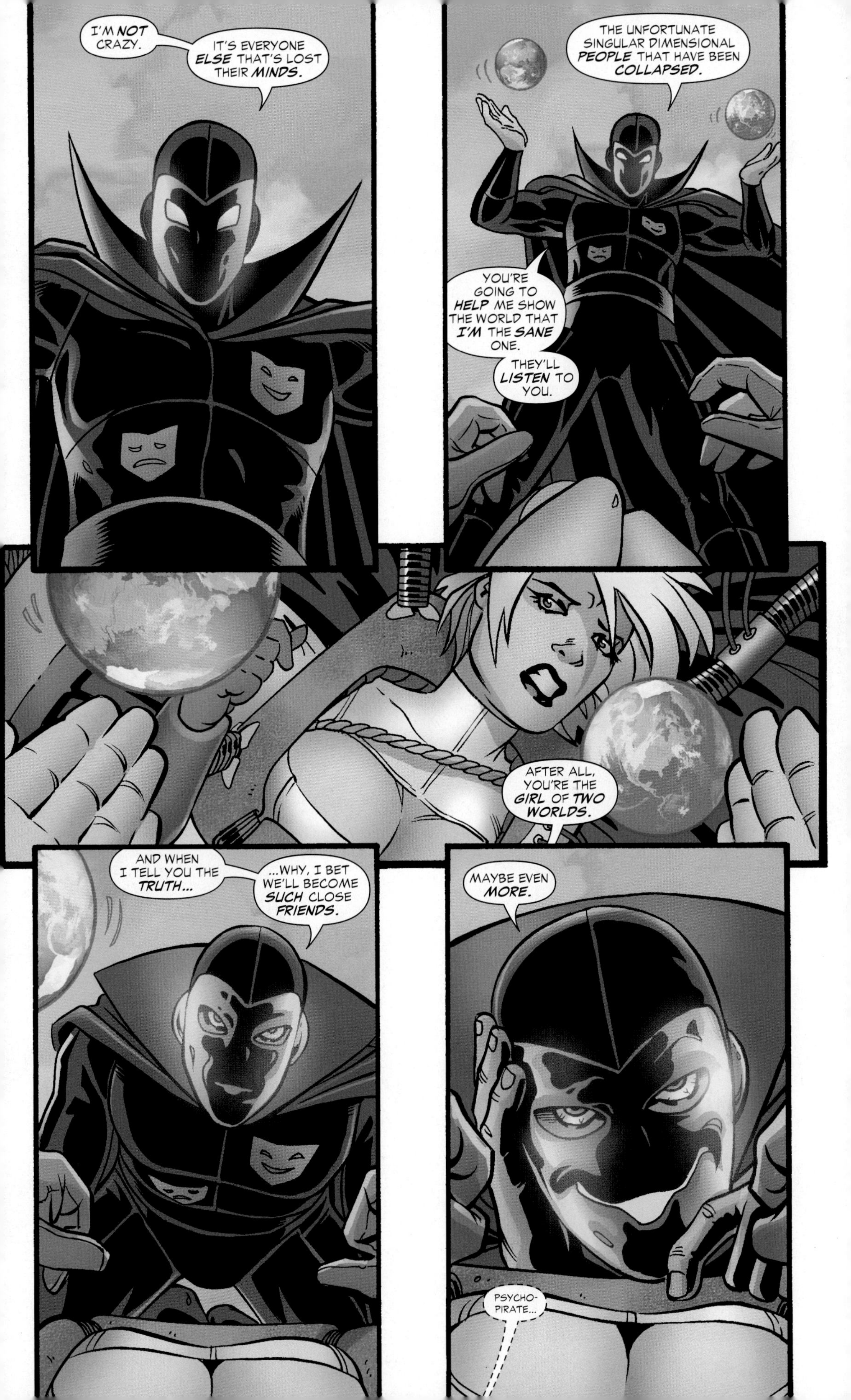
I'M NOT CRAZY.
IT'S EVERYONE ELSE THAT'S LOST THEIR MINDS.
THE UNFORTUNATE SINGULAR DIMENSIONAL PEOPLE THAT HAVE BEEN COLLAPSED.
YOU'RE GOING TO HELP ME SHOW THE WORLD THAT I'M THE SANE ONE.
THEY'LL LISTEN TO YOU.
AFTER ALL, YOU'RE THE GIRL OF TWO WORLDS.
AND WHEN I TELL YOU THE TRUTH...
...WHY, I BET WE'LL BECOME SUCH CLOSE FRIENDS.
MAYBE EVEN MORE.
PSYCHO-PIRATE...

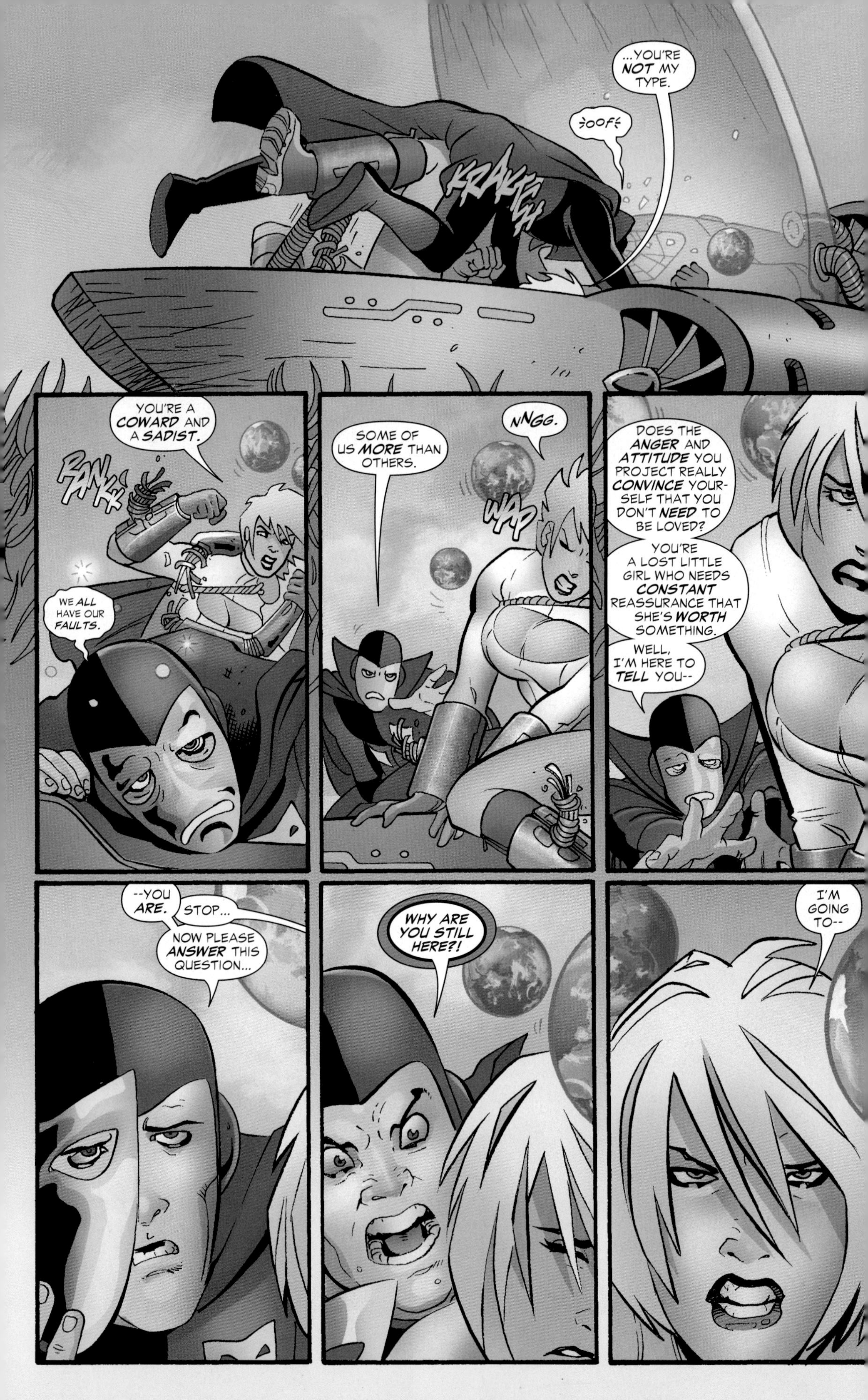
...YOU'RE NOT MY TYPE.
OOF
KRAKTCH
YOU'RE A COWARD AND A SADIST.
RANK
WE ALL HAVE OUR FAULTS.
SOME OF US MORE THAN OTHERS.
NNGG.
WAP
DOES THE ANGER AND ATTITUDE YOU PROJECT REALLY CONVINCE YOURSELF THAT YOU DON'T NEED TO BE LOVED?
YOU'RE A LOST LITTLE GIRL WHO NEEDS CONSTANT REASSURANCE THAT SHE'S WORTH SOMETHING.
WELL, I'M HERE TO TELL YOU--
--YOU ARE.
STOP...
NOW PLEASE ANSWER THIS QUESTION...
WHY ARE YOU STILL HERE?!
I'M GOING TO--

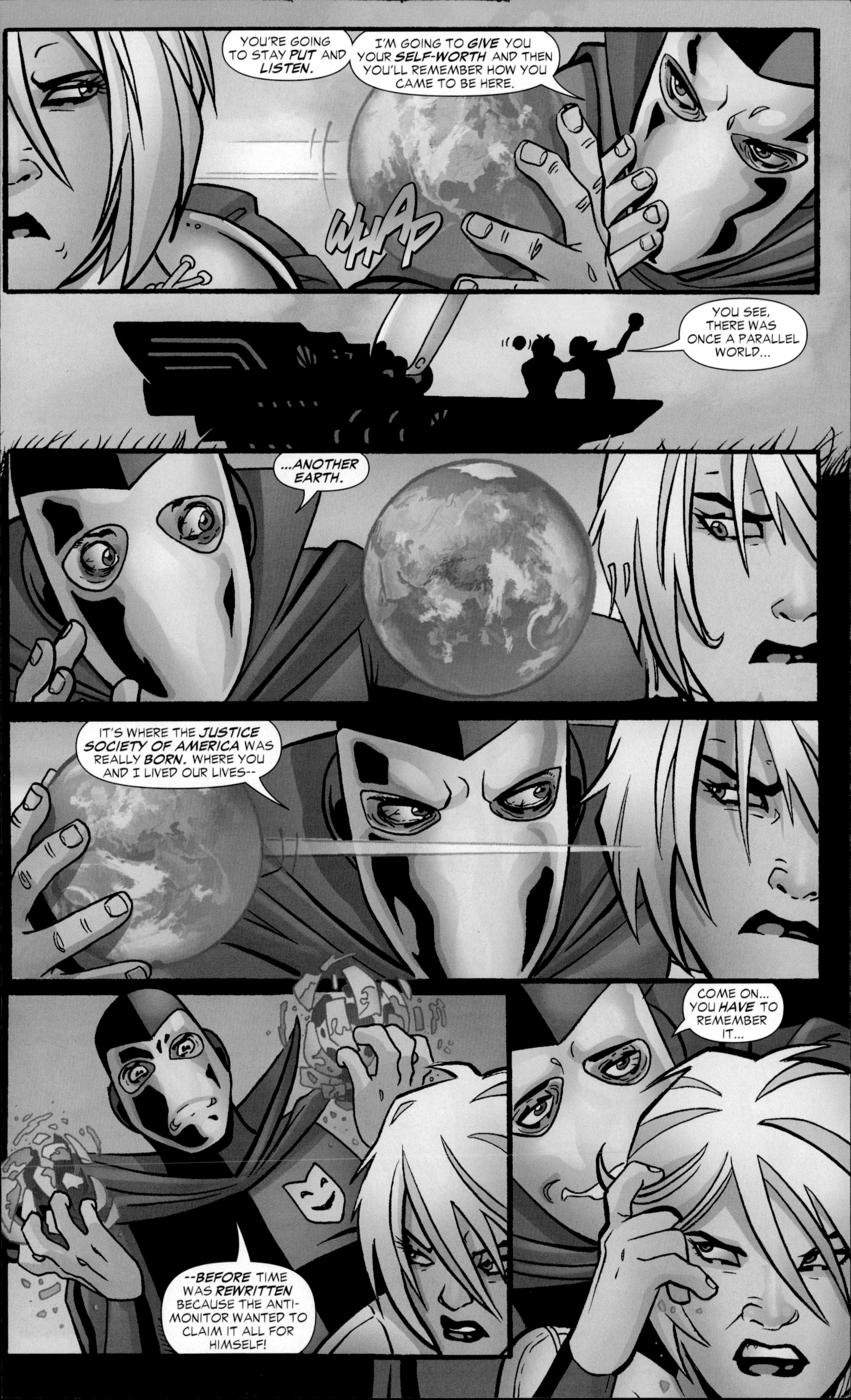
YOU'RE GOING TO STAY PUT AND LISTEN.
I'M GOING TO GIVE YOU YOUR SELF-WORTH AND THEN YOU'LL REMEMBER HOW YOU CAME TO BE HERE.
WHAP
YOU SEE, THERE WAS ONCE A PARALLEL WORLD...
...ANOTHER EARTH.
IT'S WHERE THE JUSTICE SOCIETY OF AMERICA WAS REALLY BORN. WHERE YOU AND I LIVED OUR LIVES--
--BEFORE TIME WAS REWRITTEN BECAUSE THE ANTI-MONITOR WANTED TO CLAIM IT ALL FOR HIMSELF!
COME ON... YOU HAVE TO REMEMBER IT...

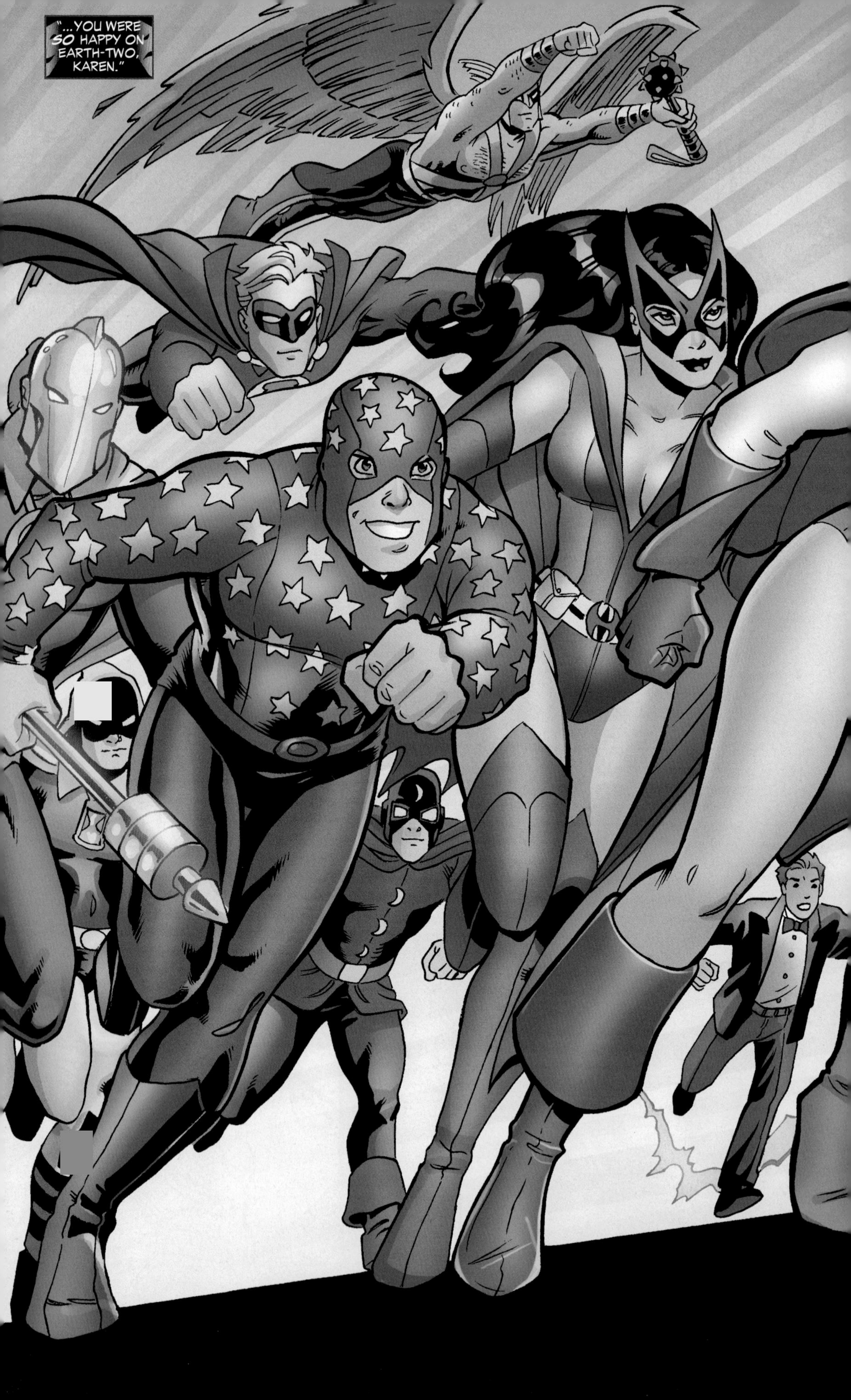
"...YOU WERE SO HAPPY ON EARTH-TWO, KAREN."

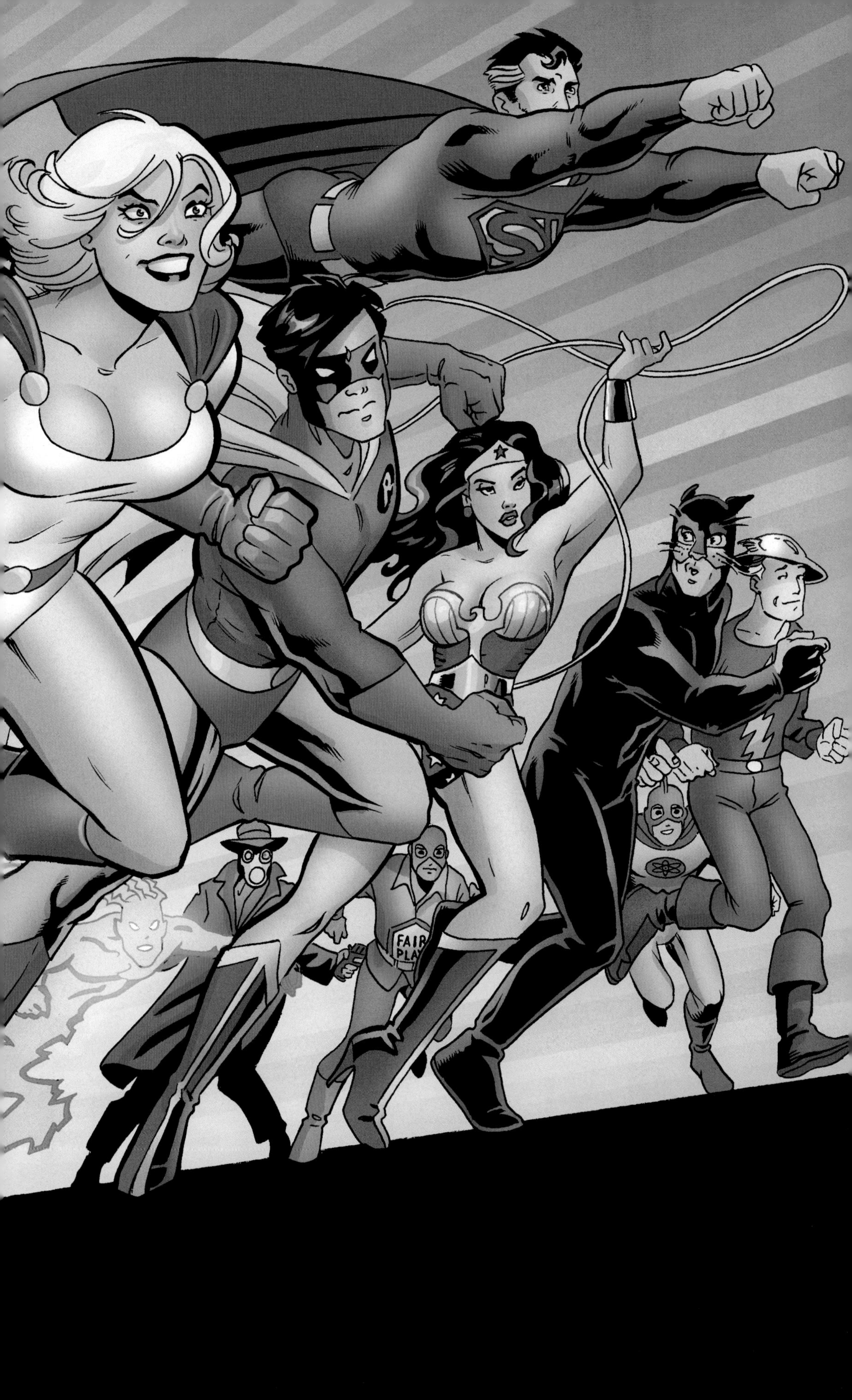
FAIR PLAY

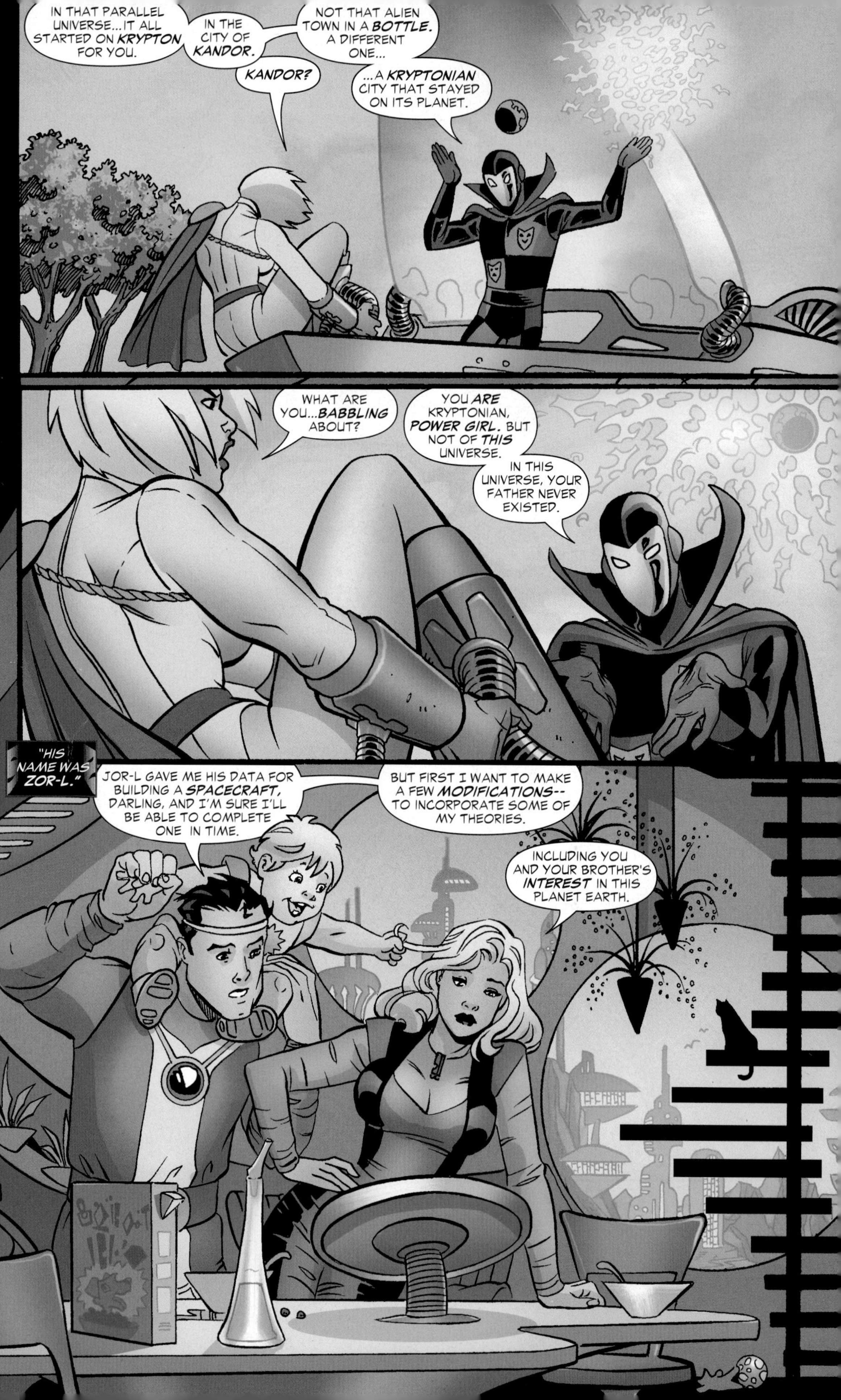
IN THAT PARALLEL UNIVERSE...IT ALL STARTED ON KRYPTON FOR YOU.
IN THE CITY OF KANDOR.
NOT THAT ALIEN TOWN IN A BOTTLE. A DIFFERENT ONE...
KANDOR?
...A KRYPTONIAN CITY THAT STAYED ON ITS PLANET.
WHAT ARE YOU...BABBLING ABOUT?
YOU ARE KRYPTONIAN, POWER GIRL. BUT NOT OF THIS UNIVERSE.
IN THIS UNIVERSE, YOUR FATHER NEVER EXISTED.
"HIS NAME WAS ZOR-L."
JOR-L GAVE ME HIS DATA FOR BUILDING A SPACECRAFT, DARLING, AND I'M SURE I'LL BE ABLE TO COMPLETE ONE IN TIME.
BUT FIRST I WANT TO MAKE A FEW MODIFICATIONS-- TO INCORPORATE SOME OF MY THEORIES.
INCLUDING YOU AND YOUR BROTHER'S INTEREST IN THIS PLANET EARTH.

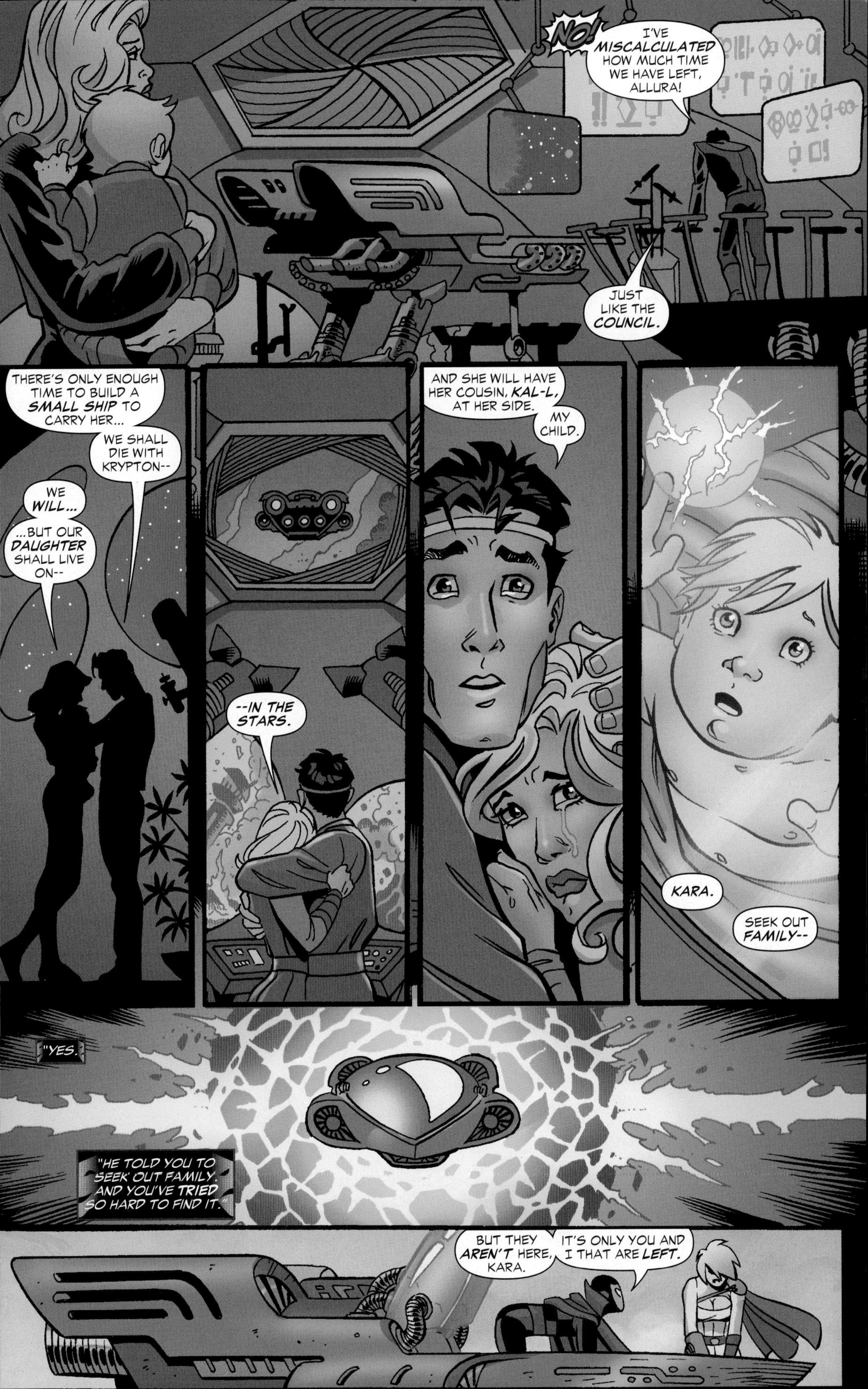
NO!
I'VE MISCALCULATED HOW MUCH TIME WE HAVE LEFT, ALLURA!
JUST LIKE THE COUNCIL.
THERE'S ONLY ENOUGH TIME TO BUILD A SMALL SHIP TO CARRY HER...
WE SHALL DIE WITH KRYPTON--
WE WILL...
...BUT OUR DAUGHTER SHALL LIVE ON--
--IN THE STARS.
AND SHE WILL HAVE HER COUSIN, KAL-L, AT HER SIDE.
MY CHILD.
KARA.
SEEK OUT FAMILY--
"YES.
"HE TOLD YOU TO SEEK OUT FAMILY. AND YOU'VE TRIED SO HARD TO FIND IT."
BUT THEY AREN'T HERE, KARA.
IT'S ONLY YOU AND I THAT ARE LEFT.

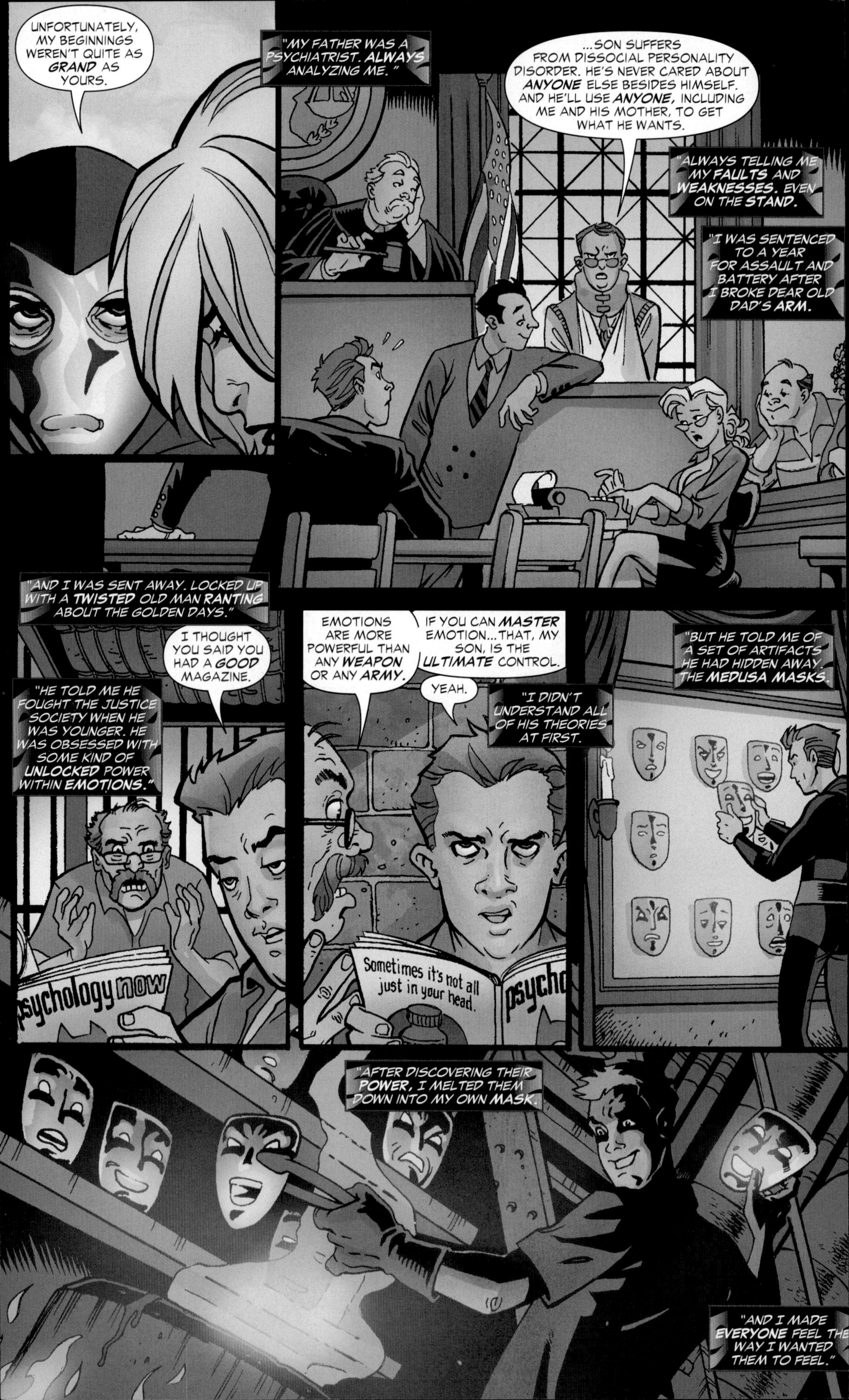

UNFORTUNATELY, MY BEGINNINGS WEREN'T QUITE AS GRAND AS YOURS.
"MY FATHER WAS A PSYCHIATRIST. ALWAYS ANALYZING ME."
...SON SUFFERS FROM DISSOCIAL PERSONALITY DISORDER. HE'S NEVER CARED ABOUT ANYONE ELSE BESIDES HIMSELF. AND HE'LL USE ANYONE, INCLUDING ME AND HIS MOTHER, TO GET WHAT HE WANTS.
"ALWAYS TELLING ME MY FAULTS AND WEAKNESSES. EVEN ON THE STAND.
"I WAS SENTENCED TO A YEAR FOR ASSAULT AND BATTERY AFTER I BROKE DEAR OLD DAD'S ARM.
"AND I WAS SENT AWAY. LOCKED UP WITH A TWISTED OLD MAN RANTING ABOUT THE GOLDEN DAYS."
"HE TOLD ME HE FOUGHT THE JUSTICE SOCIETY WHEN HE WAS YOUNGER. HE WAS OBSESSED WITH SOME KIND OF UNLOCKED POWER WITHIN EMOTIONS."
I THOUGHT YOU SAID YOU HAD A GOOD MAGAZINE.
psychology now
EMOTIONS ARE MORE POWERFUL THAN ANY WEAPON OR ANY ARMY.
IF YOU CAN MASTER EMOTION...THAT, MY SON, IS THE ULTIMATE CONTROL.
YEAH.
"I DIDN'T UNDERSTAND ALL OF HIS THEORIES AT FIRST.
Sometimes it's not all just in your head.
psycho
"BUT HE TOLD ME OF A SET OF ARTIFACTS HE HAD HIDDEN AWAY. THE MEDUSA MASKS.
"AFTER DISCOVERING THEIR POWER, I MELTED THEM DOWN INTO MY OWN MASK.
"AND I MADE EVERYONE FEEL THE WAY I WANTED THEM TO FEEL."

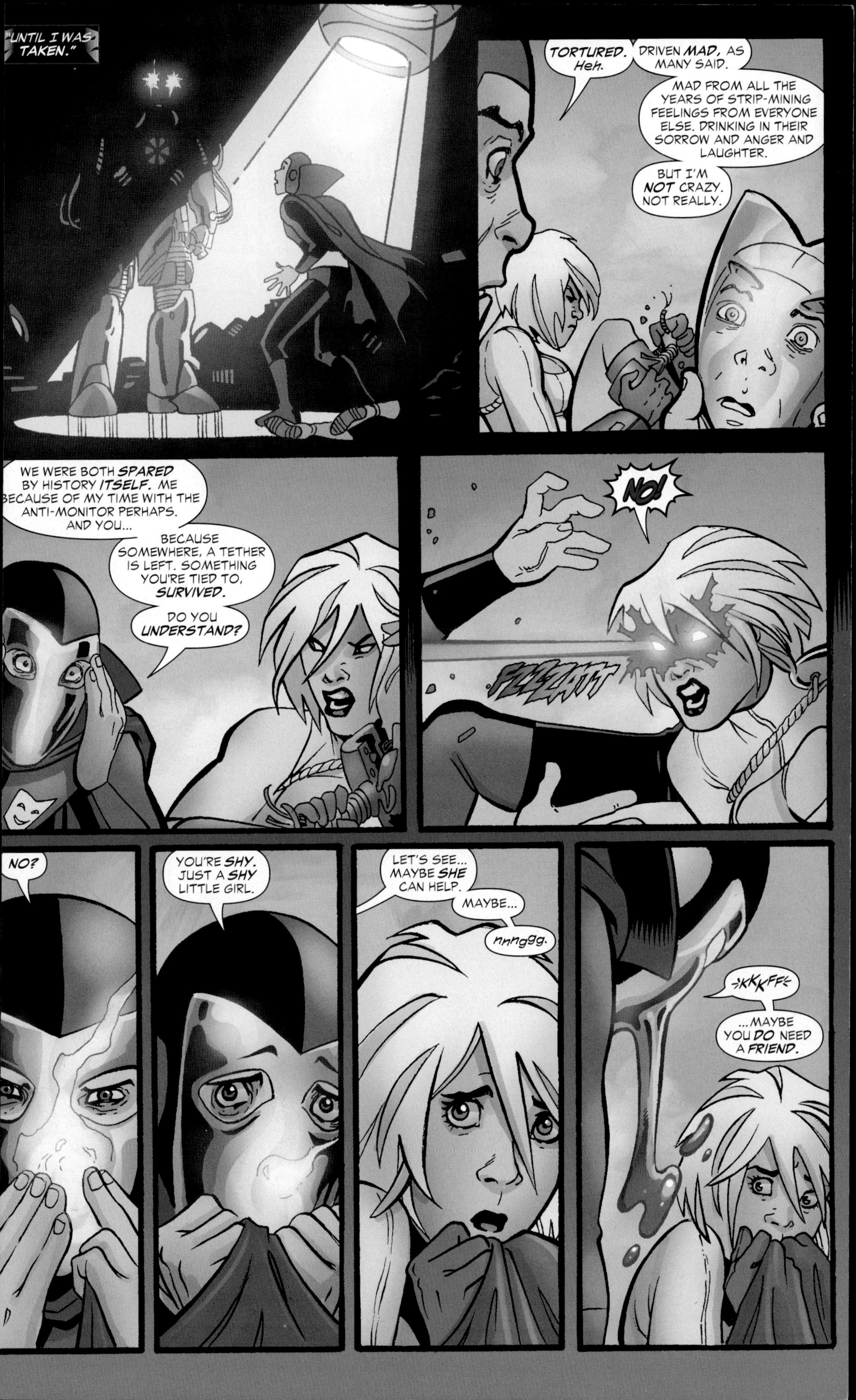
"UNTIL I WAS TAKEN."
TORTURED. Heh.
DRIVEN MAD, AS MANY SAID.
MAD FROM ALL THE YEARS OF STRIP-MINING FEELINGS FROM EVERYONE ELSE. DRINKING IN THEIR SORROW AND ANGER AND LAUGHTER.
BUT I'M NOT CRAZY. NOT REALLY.
WE WERE BOTH SPARED BY HISTORY ITSELF. ME BECAUSE OF MY TIME WITH THE ANTI-MONITOR PERHAPS. AND YOU...
BECAUSE SOMEWHERE, A TETHER IS LEFT. SOMETHING YOU'RE TIED TO, SURVIVED.
DO YOU UNDERSTAND?
NO!
FZZZAT
NO?
YOU'RE SHY. JUST A SHY LITTLE GIRL.
LET'S SEE... MAYBE SHE CAN HELP.
MAYBE...
nnngg.
KKKFF
...MAYBE YOU DO NEED A FRIEND.

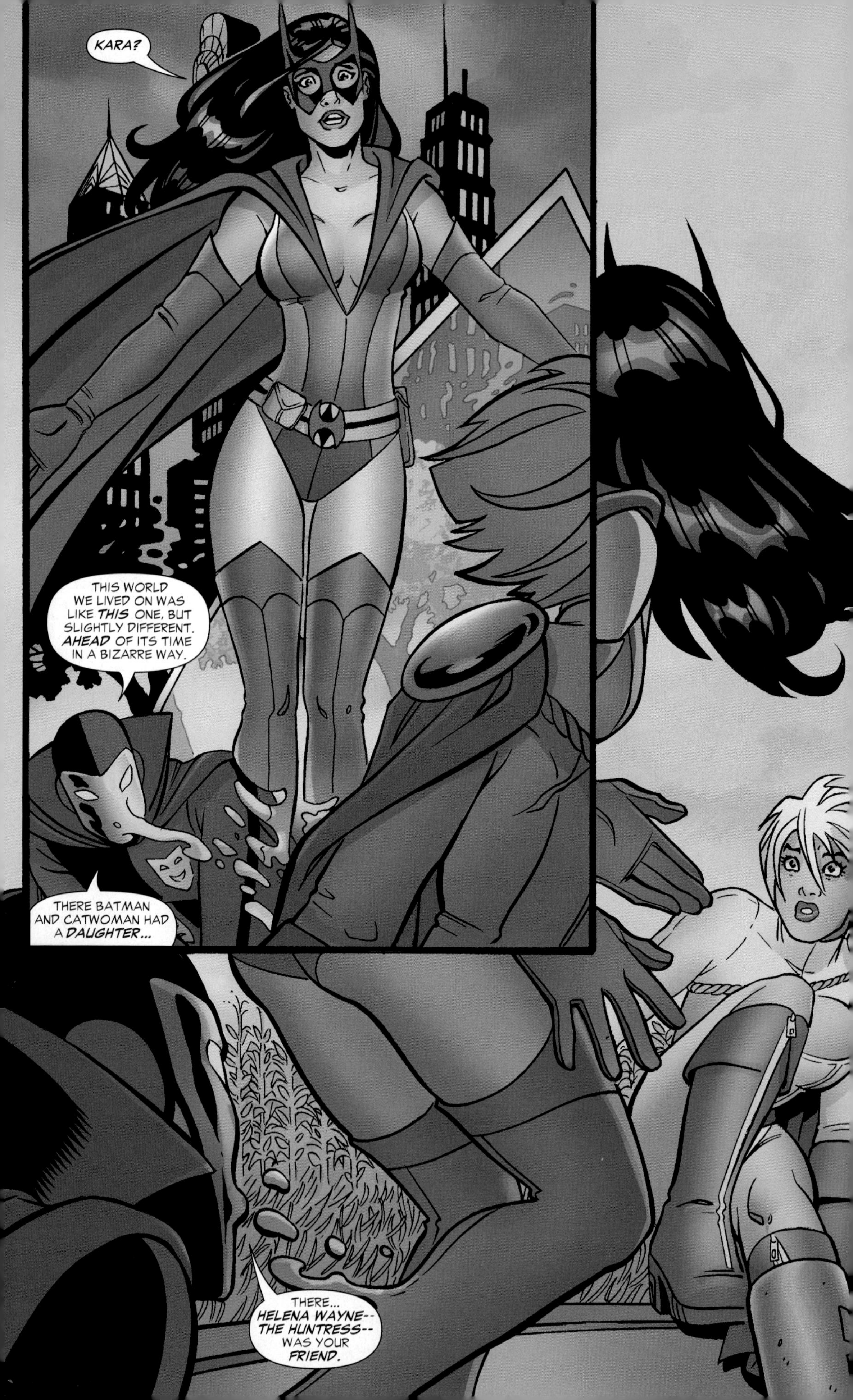
KARA?
THIS WORLD WE LIVED ON WAS LIKE THIS ONE, BUT SLIGHTLY DIFFERENT. AHEAD OF ITS TIME IN A BIZARRE WAY.
THERE BATMAN AND CATWOMAN HAD A DAUGHTER...
THERE... HELENA WAYNE-- THE HUNTRESS-- WAS YOUR FRIEND.

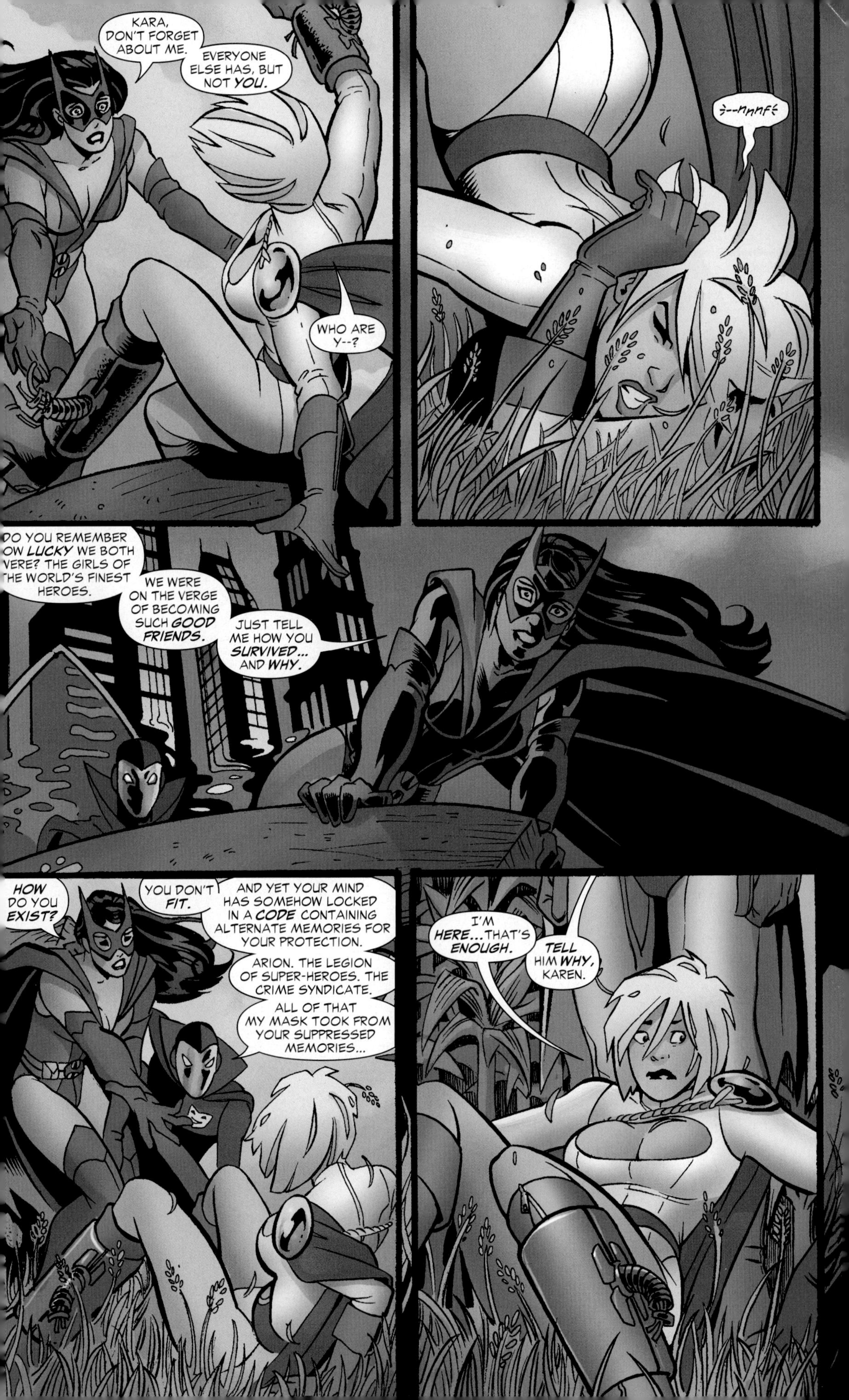
KARA, DON'T FORGET ABOUT ME.
EVERYONE ELSE HAS, BUT NOT YOU.
WHO ARE Y--?
--NNNF
DO YOU REMEMBER OW LUCKY WE BOTH VERE? THE GIRLS OF THE WORLD'S FINEST HEROES.
WE WERE ON THE VERGE OF BECOMING SUCH GOOD FRIENDS.
JUST TELL ME HOW YOU SURVIVED... AND WHY.
HOW DO YOU EXIST?
YOU DON'T FIT.
AND YET YOUR MIND HAS SOMEHOW LOCKED IN A CODE CONTAINING ALTERNATE MEMORIES FOR YOUR PROTECTION.
ARION. THE LEGION OF SUPER-HEROES. THE CRIME SYNDICATE.
ALL OF THAT MY MASK TOOK FROM YOUR SUPPRESSED MEMORIES...
I'M HERE... THAT'S ENOUGH.
TELL HIM WHY, KAREN.

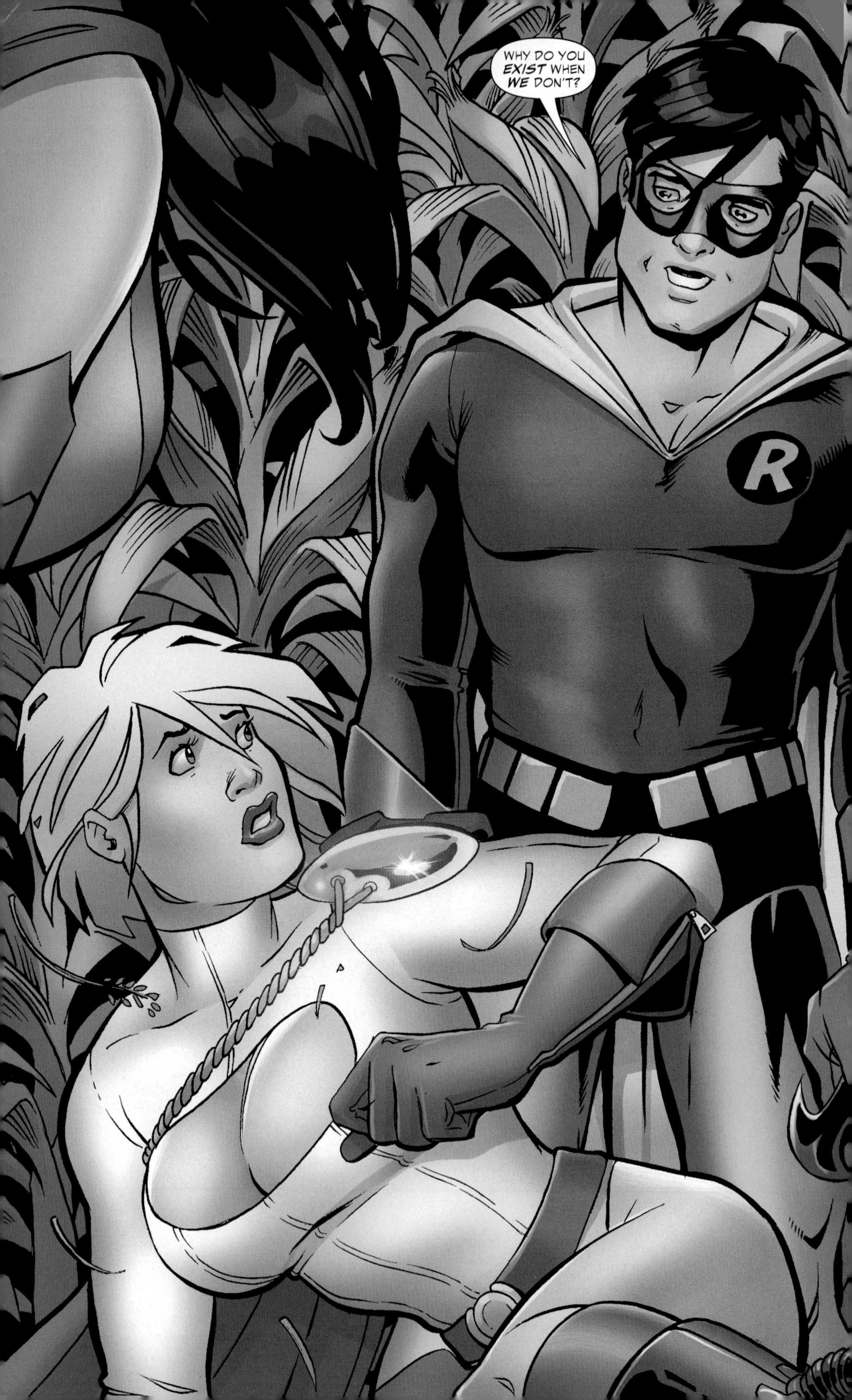
WHY DO YOU EXIST WHEN WE DON'T?

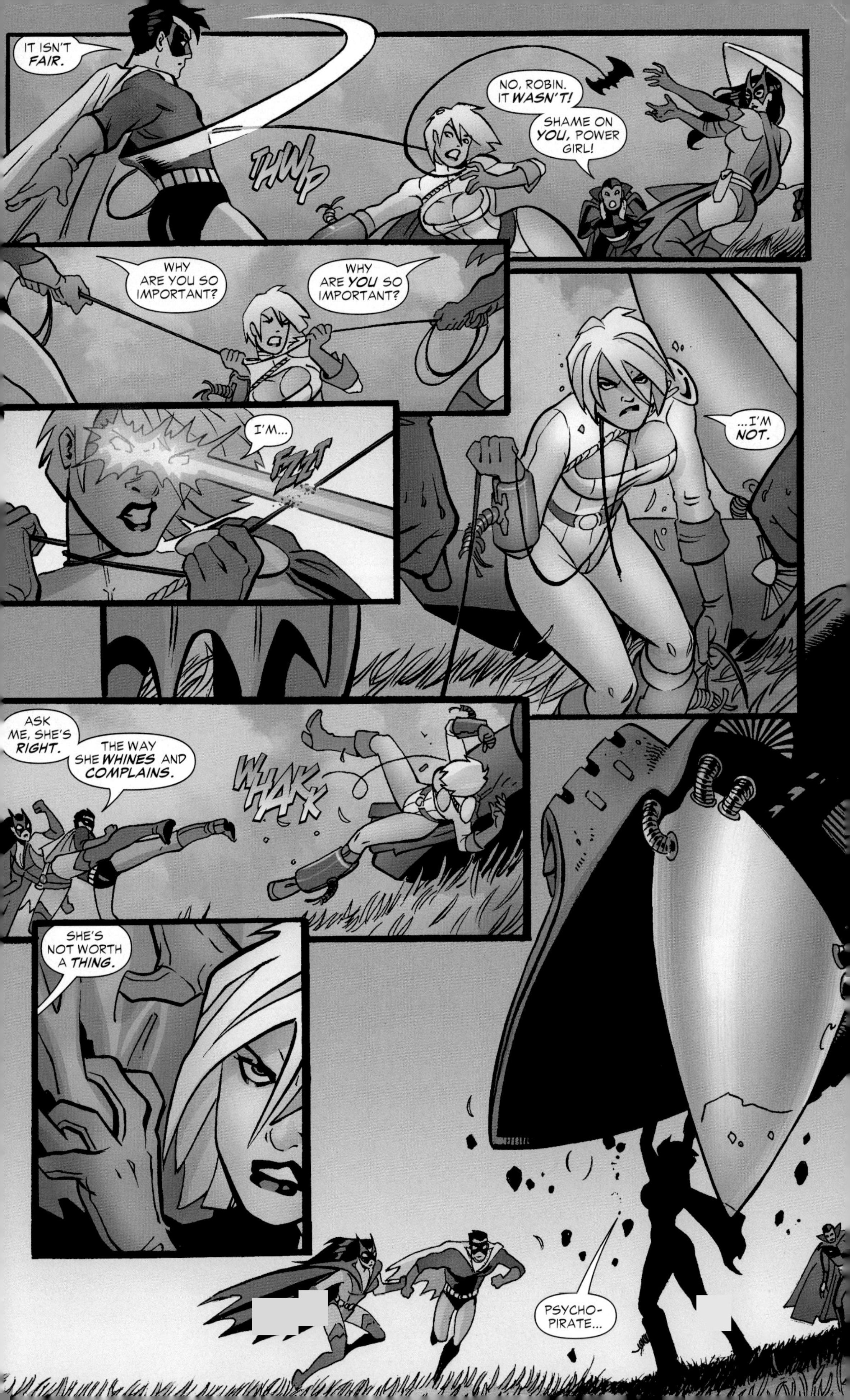
IT ISN'T FAIR.
NO, ROBIN. IT WASN'T!
SHAME ON YOU, POWER GIRL!
THWIP
WHY ARE YOU SO IMPORTANT?
WHY ARE YOU SO IMPORTANT?
I'M...
FZZT
...I'M NOT.
ASK ME, SHE'S RIGHT.
THE WAY SHE WHINES AND COMPLAINS.
WHAKK
SHE'S NOT WORTH A THING.
PSYCHO-PIRATE...

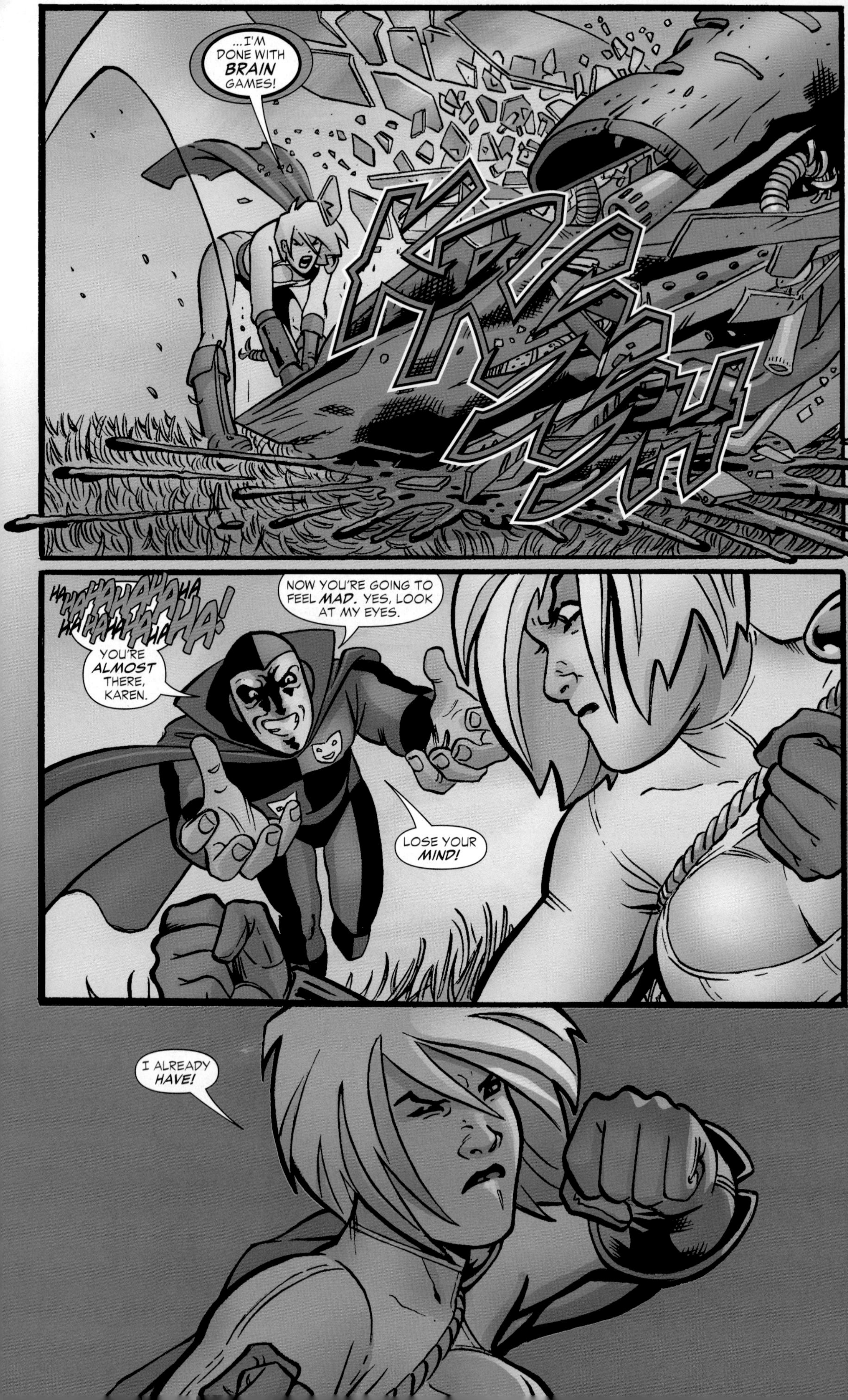

...I'M DONE WITH **BRAIN** GAMES!
KRAASHH
HAHAHAHAHAHAHAHAHAHAHAHA!
NOW YOU'RE GOING TO FEEL **MAD.** YES, LOOK AT MY EYES.
YOU'RE **ALMOST** THERE, KAREN.
LOSE YOUR **MIND!**
I ALREADY **HAVE!**

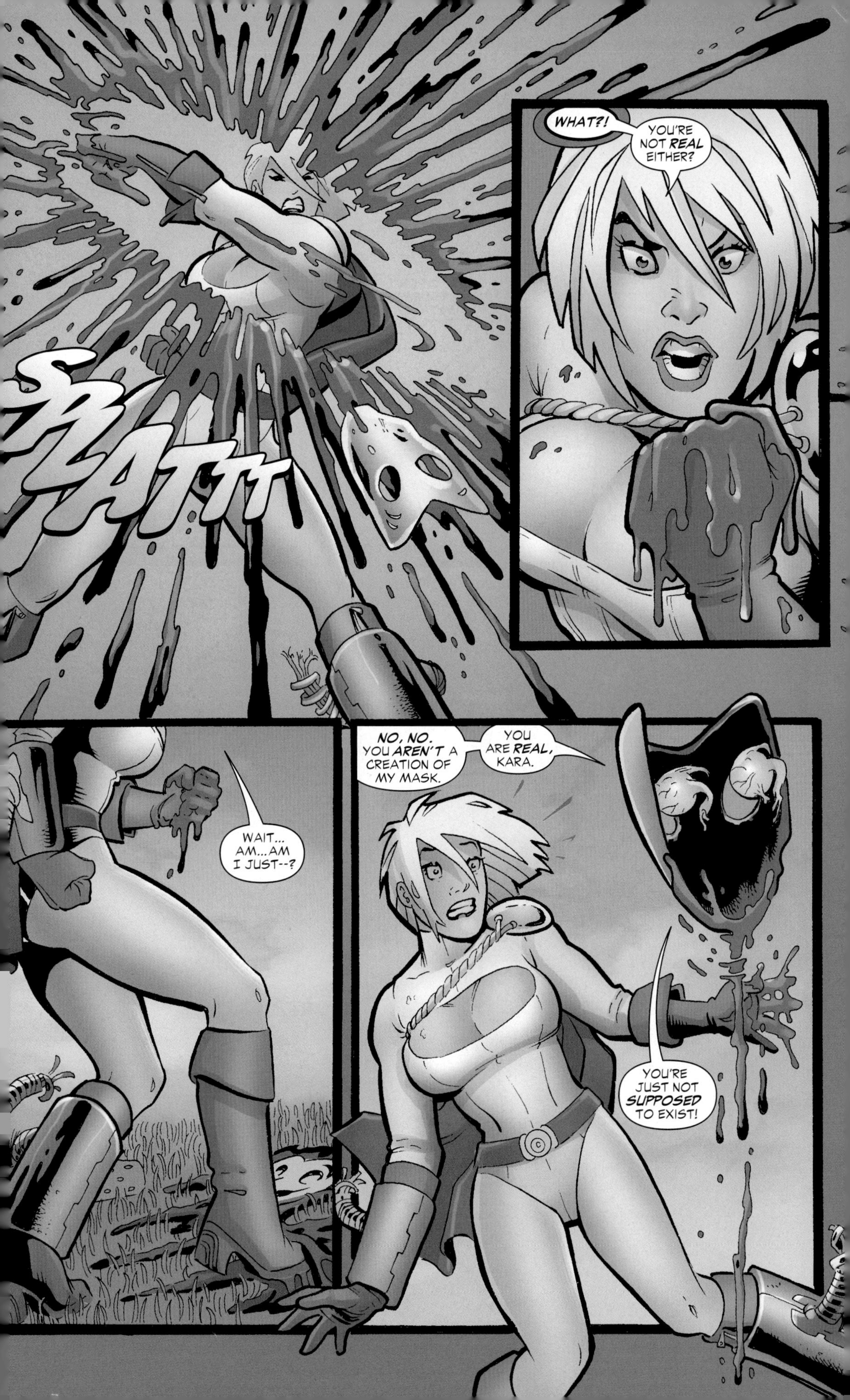
SPLATTT
WHAT?!
YOU'RE NOT REAL EITHER?
WAIT... AM...AM I JUST--?
NO, NO. YOU AREN'T A CREATION OF MY MASK.
YOU ARE REAL, KARA.
YOU'RE JUST NOT SUPPOSED TO EXIST!

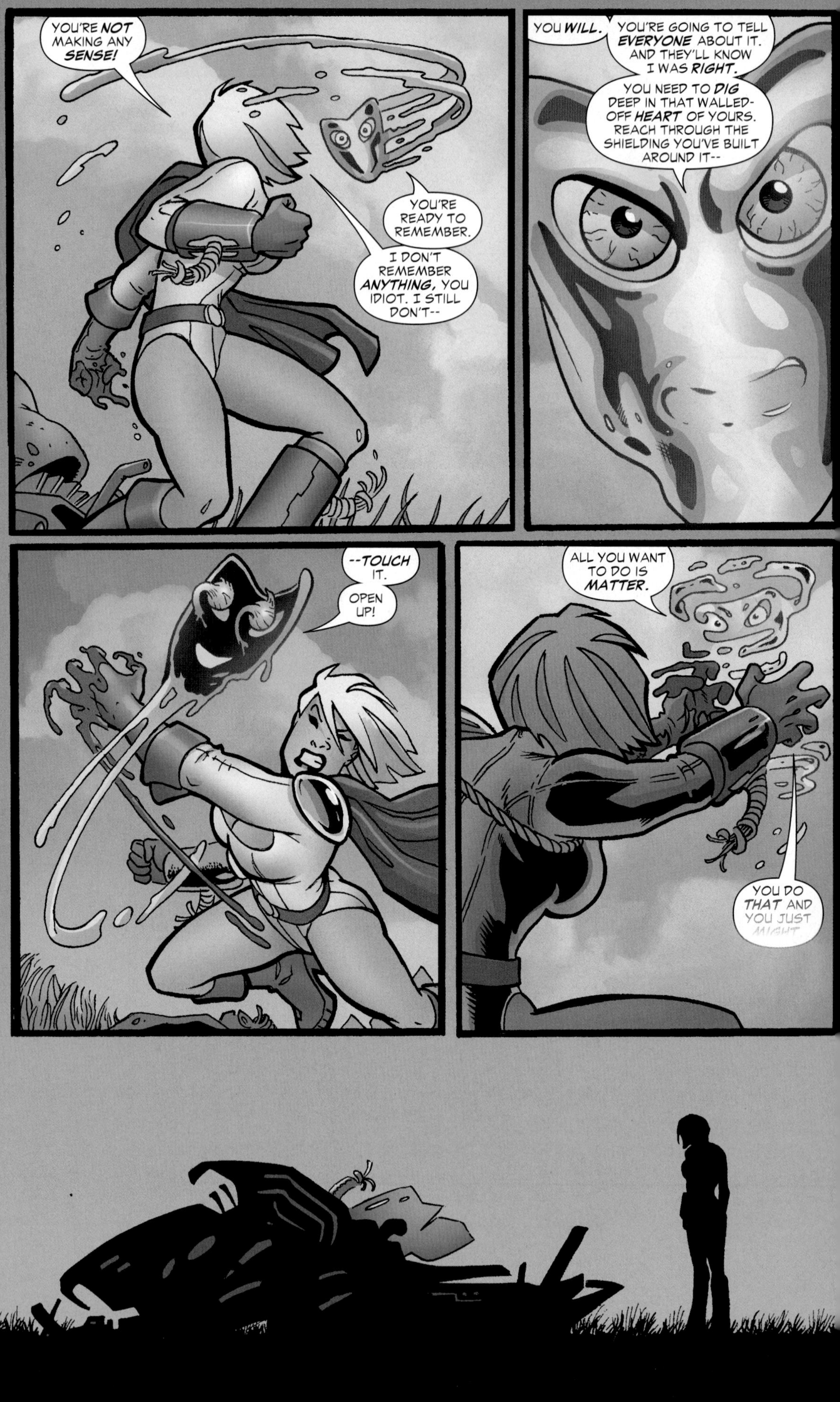

YOU'RE NOT MAKING ANY SENSE!
YOU'RE READY TO REMEMBER.
I DON'T REMEMBER ANYTHING, YOU IDIOT. I STILL DON'T--
YOU WILL.
YOU'RE GOING TO TELL EVERYONE ABOUT IT. AND THEY'LL KNOW I WAS RIGHT.
YOU NEED TO DIG DEEP IN THAT WALLED-OFF HEART OF YOURS. REACH THROUGH THE SHIELDING YOU'VE BUILT AROUND IT--
--TOUCH IT.
OPEN UP!
ALL YOU WANT TO DO IS MATTER.
YOU DO THAT AND YOU JUST

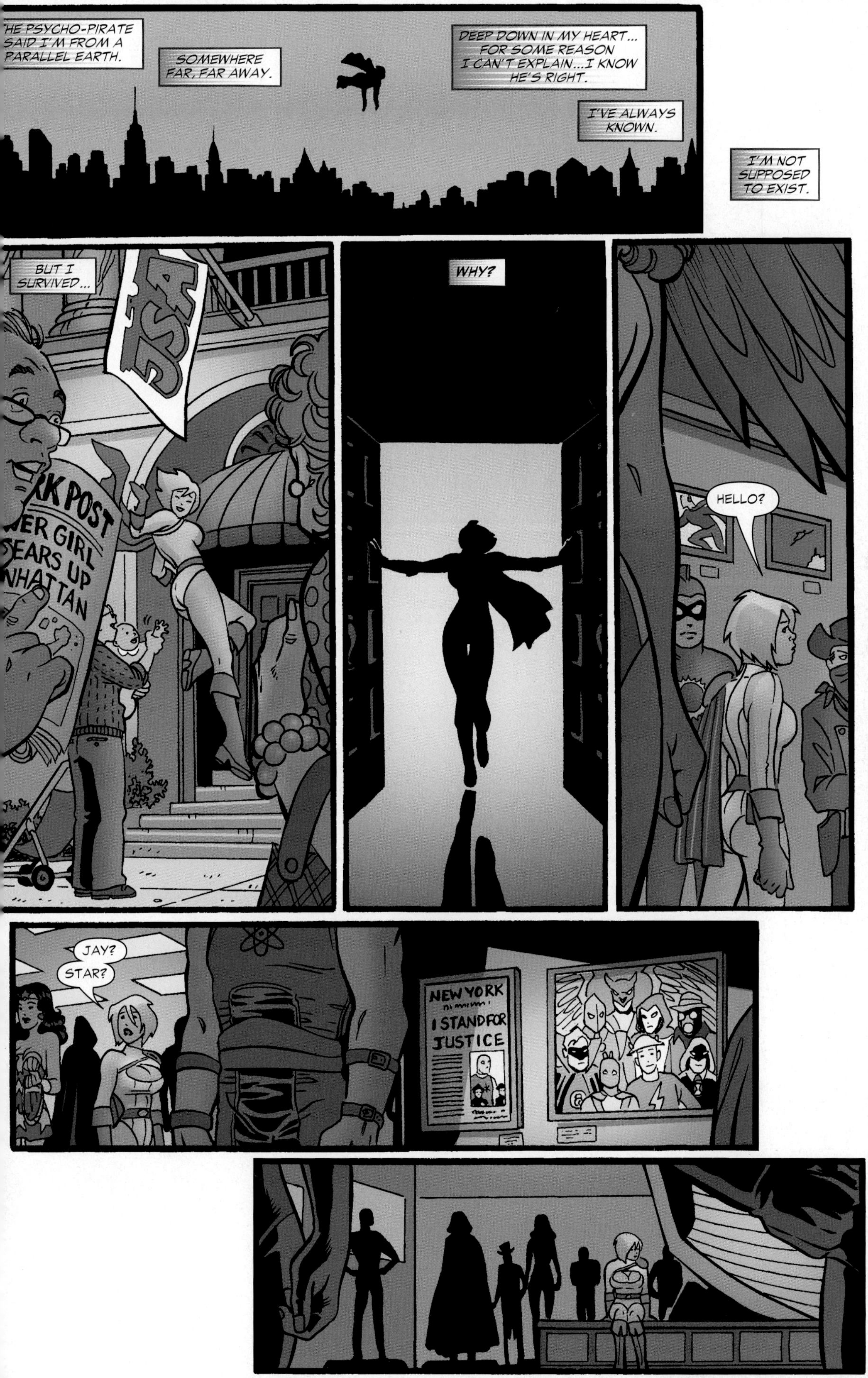
THE PSYCHO-PIRATE SAID I'M FROM A PARALLEL EARTH.
SOMEWHERE FAR, FAR AWAY.
DEEP DOWN IN MY HEART... FOR SOME REASON I CAN'T EXPLAIN...I KNOW HE'S RIGHT.
I'VE ALWAYS KNOWN.
I'M NOT SUPPOSED TO EXIST.
BUT I SURVIVED...
WHY?
HELLO?
JAY?
STAR?
NEW YORK
I STAND FOR JUSTICE

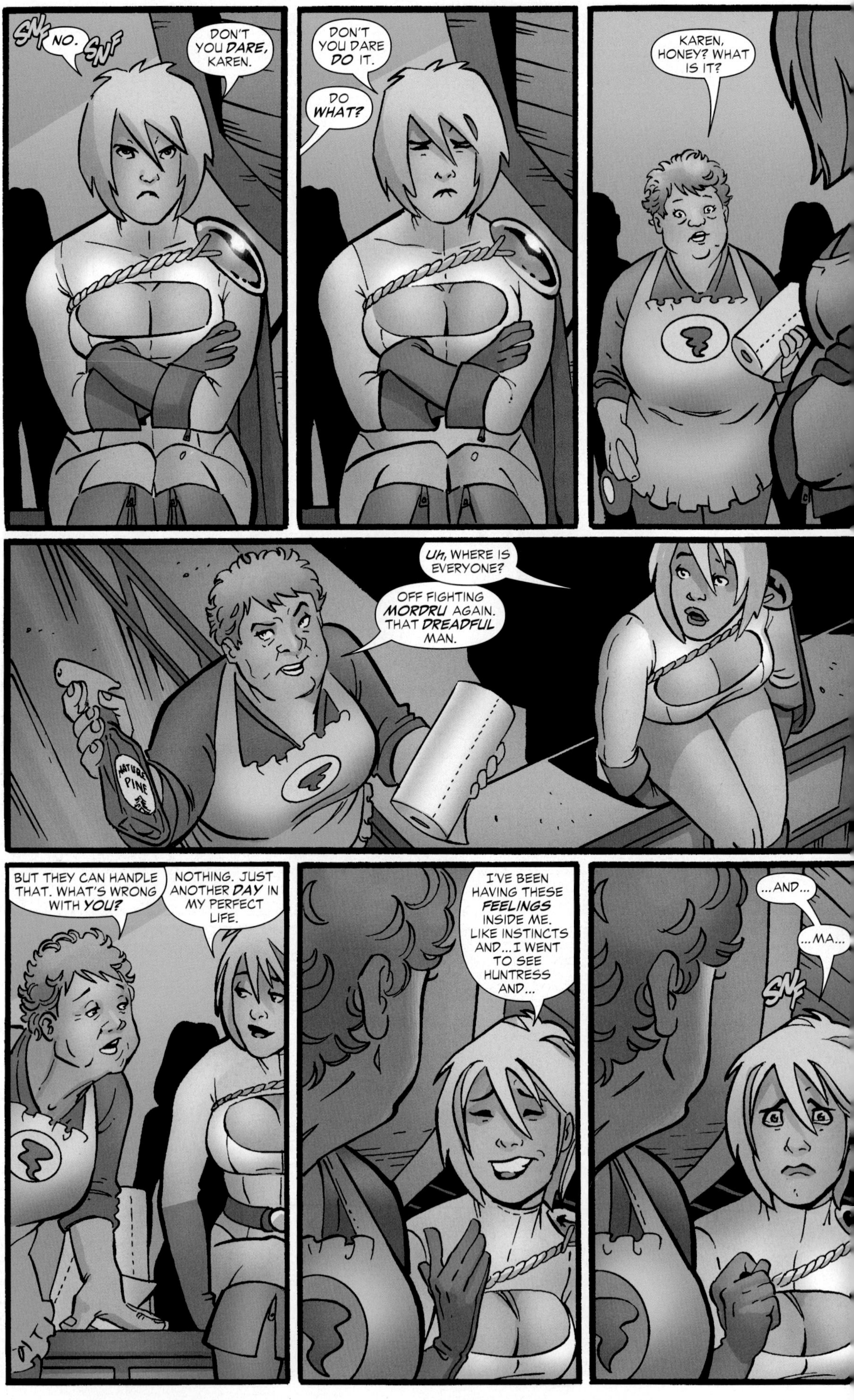
SNF
NO.
SNF
DON'T YOU DARE, KAREN.
DON'T YOU DARE DO IT.
DO WHAT?
KAREN, HONEY? WHAT IS IT?
Uh, WHERE IS EVERYONE?
OFF FIGHTING MORDRU AGAIN. THAT DREADFUL MAN.
NATURE'S PINE
BUT THEY CAN HANDLE THAT. WHAT'S WRONG WITH YOU?
NOTHING. JUST ANOTHER DAY IN MY PERFECT LIFE.
I'VE BEEN HAVING THESE FEELINGS INSIDE ME. LIKE INSTINCTS AND... I WENT TO SEE HUNTRESS AND...
...AND...
...MA...
SNF

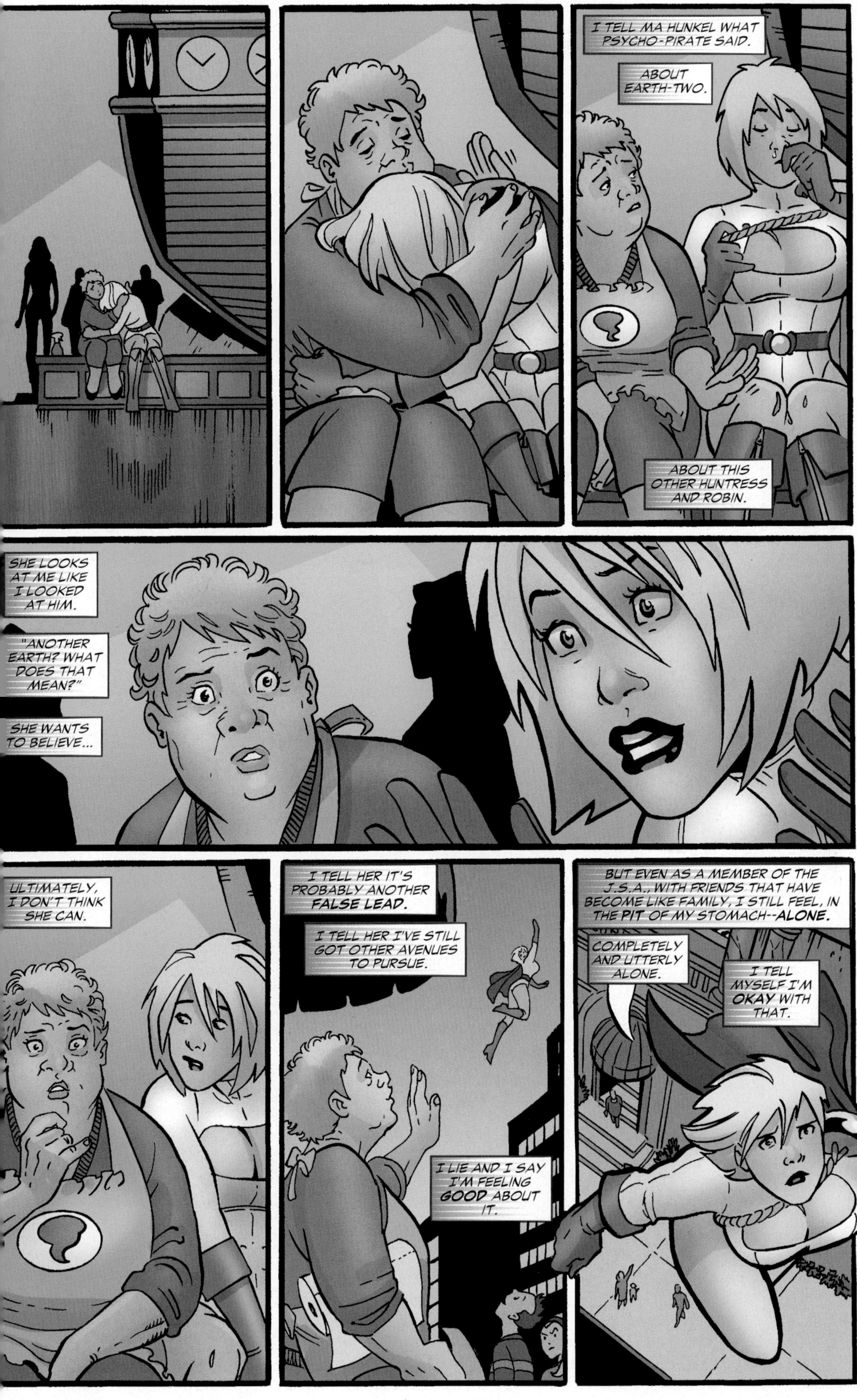
I TELL MA HUNKEL WHAT PSYCHO-PIRATE SAID.
ABOUT EARTH-TWO.
ABOUT THIS OTHER HUNTRESS AND ROBIN.
SHE LOOKS AT ME LIKE I LOOKED AT HIM.
"ANOTHER EARTH? WHAT DOES THAT MEAN?"
SHE WANTS TO BELIEVE...
ULTIMATELY, I DON'T THINK SHE CAN.
I TELL HER IT'S PROBABLY ANOTHER FALSE LEAD.
I TELL HER I'VE STILL GOT OTHER AVENUES TO PURSUE.
I LIE AND I SAY I'M FEELING GOOD ABOUT IT.
BUT EVEN AS A MEMBER OF THE J.S.A., WITH FRIENDS THAT HAVE BECOME LIKE FAMILY, I STILL FEEL, IN THE PIT OF MY STOMACH--ALONE.
COMPLETELY AND UTTERLY ALONE.
I TELL MYSELF I'M OKAY WITH THAT.

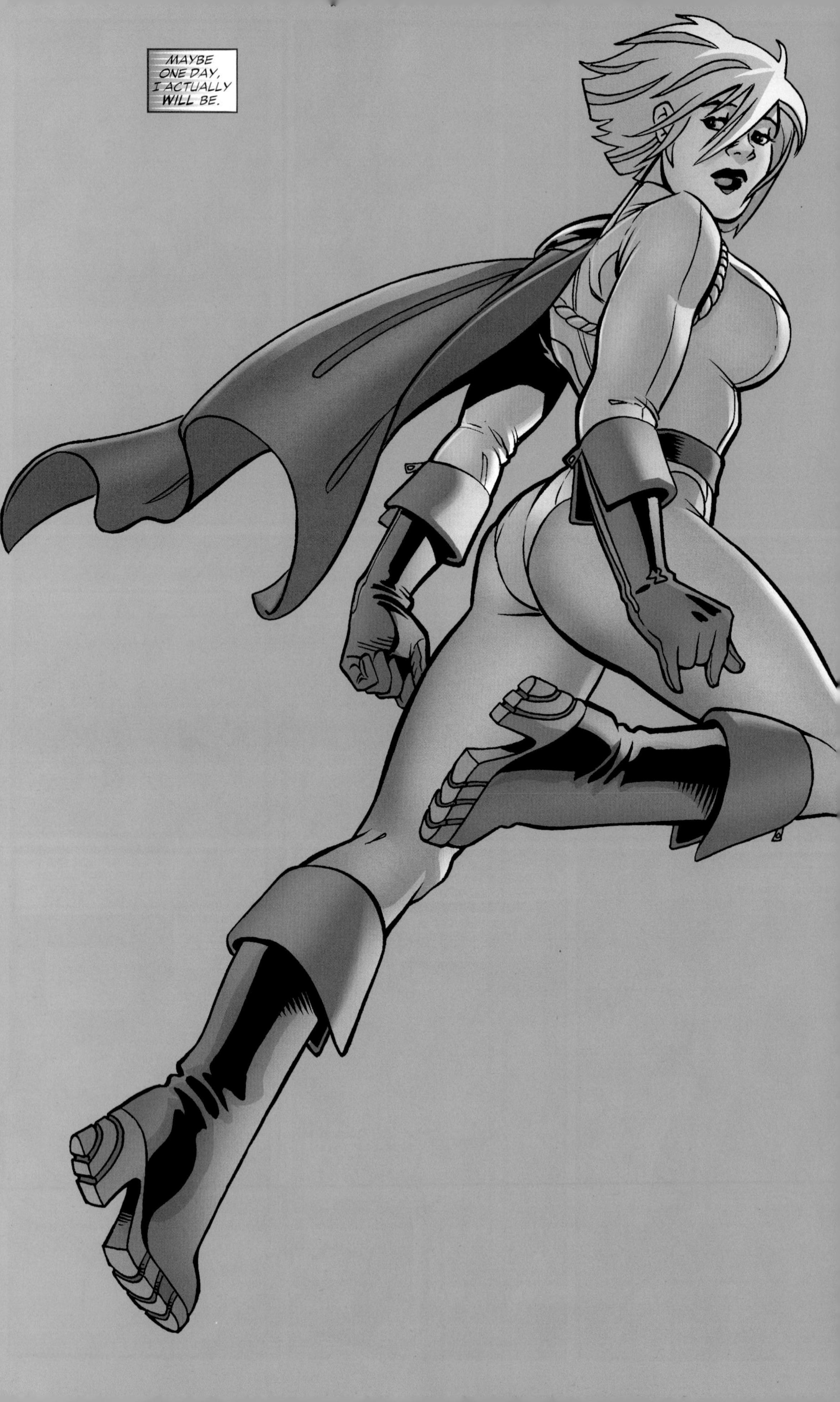
MAYBE ONE DAY, I ACTUALLY WILL BE.

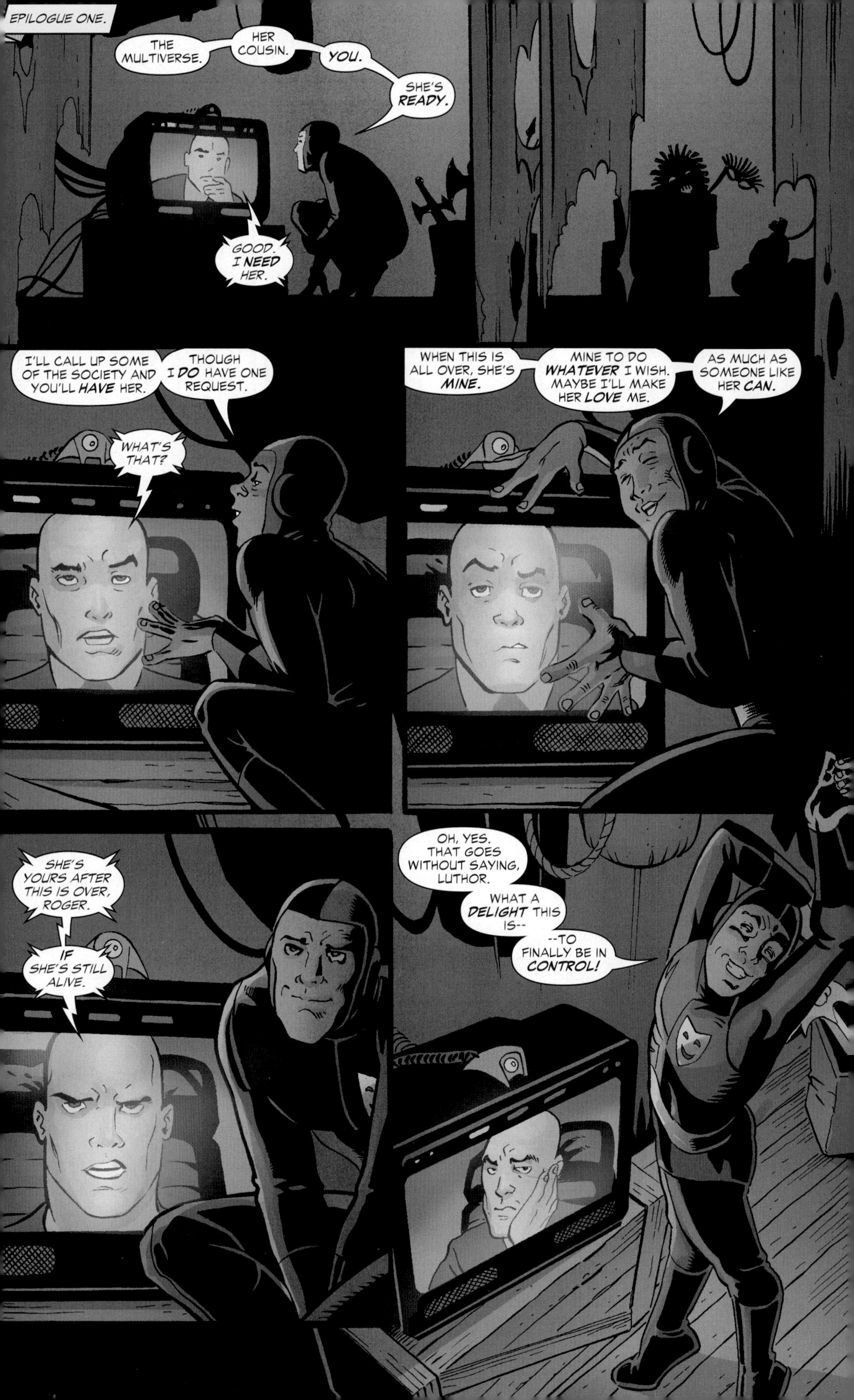
EPILOGUE ONE.
THE MULTIVERSE.
HER COUSIN.
YOU.
SHE'S READY.
GOOD. I NEED HER.
I'LL CALL UP SOME OF THE SOCIETY AND YOU'LL HAVE HER.
THOUGH I DO HAVE ONE REQUEST.
WHAT'S THAT?
WHEN THIS IS ALL OVER, SHE'S MINE.
MINE TO DO WHATEVER I WISH. MAYBE I'LL MAKE HER LOVE ME.
AS MUCH AS SOMEONE LIKE HER CAN.
SHE'S YOURS AFTER THIS IS OVER, ROGER.
IF SHE'S STILL ALIVE.
OH, YES. THAT GOES WITHOUT SAYING, LUTHOR.
WHAT A DELIGHT THIS IS--
--TO FINALLY BE IN CONTROL!

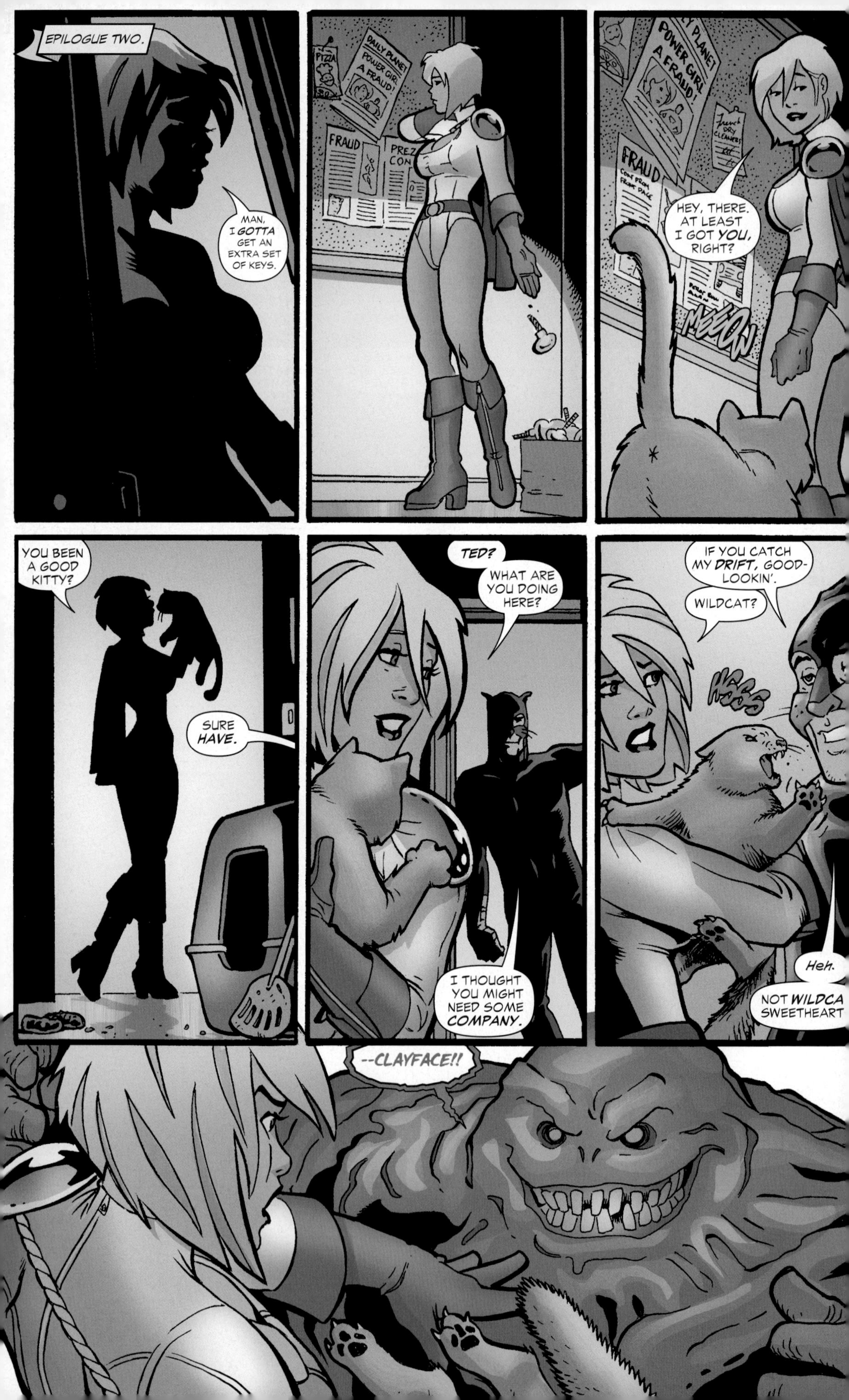
EPILOGUE TWO.
MAN, I GOTTA GET AN EXTRA SET OF KEYS.
DAILY PLANET
POWER GIRL A FRAUD!
FRAUD
HEY, THERE. AT LEAST I GOT YOU, RIGHT?
MEEOW
YOU BEEN A GOOD KITTY?
SURE HAVE.
TED?
WHAT ARE YOU DOING HERE?
I THOUGHT YOU MIGHT NEED SOME COMPANY.
IF YOU CATCH MY DRIFT, GOOD-LOOKIN'.
WILDCAT?
HSSS
Heh.
NOT WILDCA
SWEETHEART
--CLAYFACE!!

A NEW BEGINNING

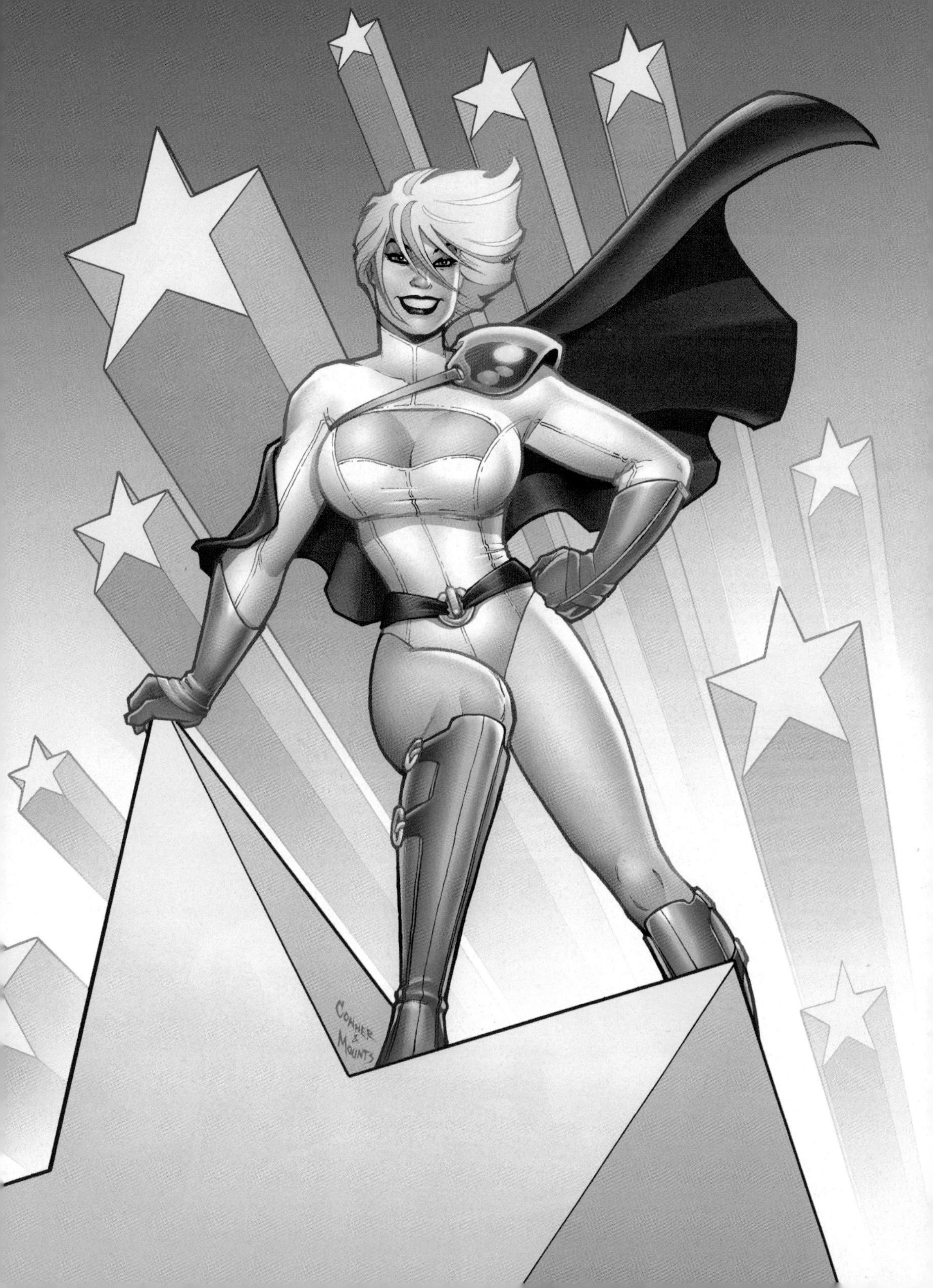
CONNER & MOUNTS

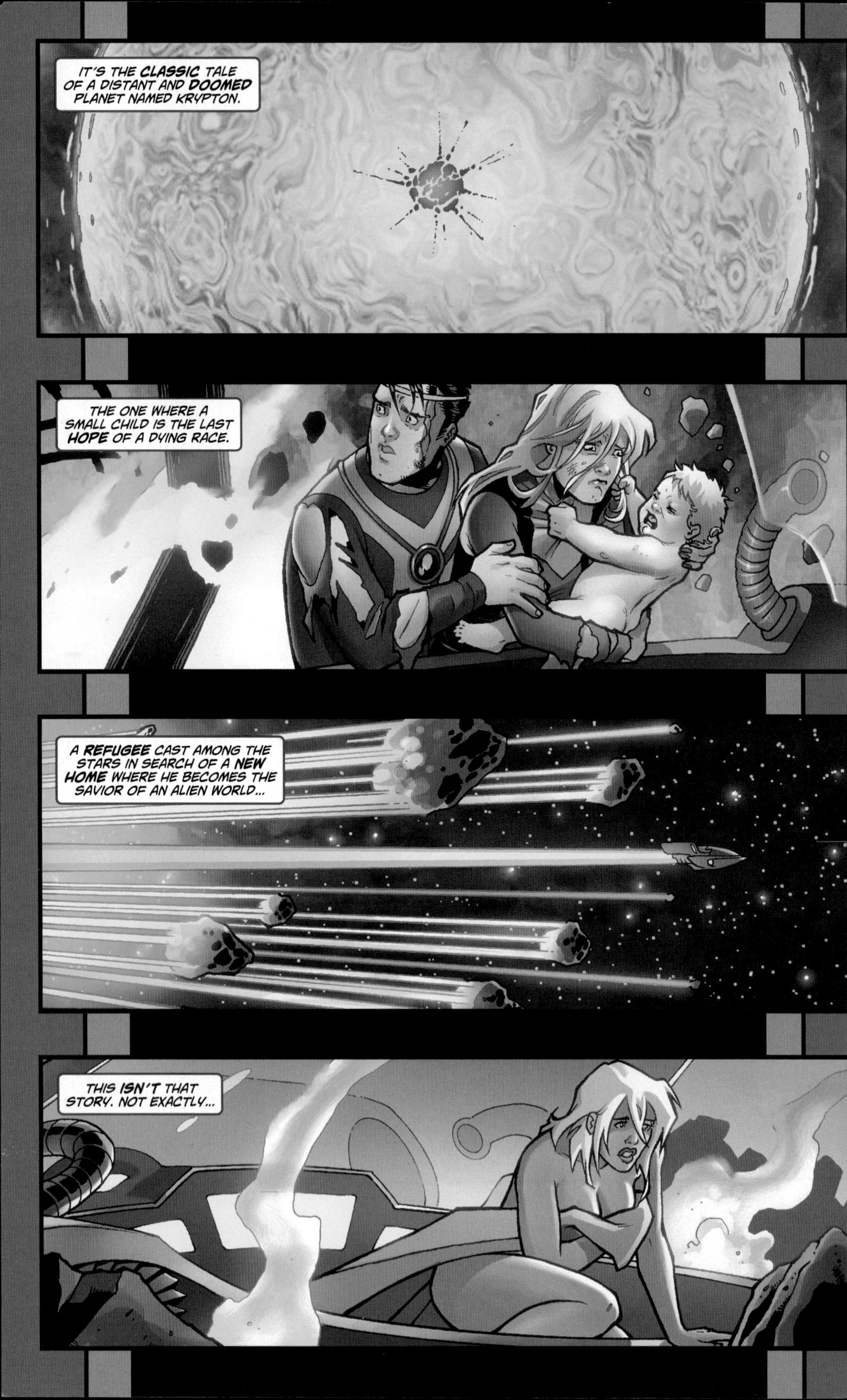
IT'S THE CLASSIC TALE OF A DISTANT AND DOOMED PLANET NAMED KRYPTON.
THE ONE WHERE A SMALL CHILD IS THE LAST HOPE OF A DYING RACE.
A REFUGEE CAST AMONG THE STARS IN SEARCH OF A NEW HOME WHERE HE BECOMES THE SAVIOR OF AN ALIEN WORLD...
THIS ISN'T THAT STORY. NOT EXACTLY...

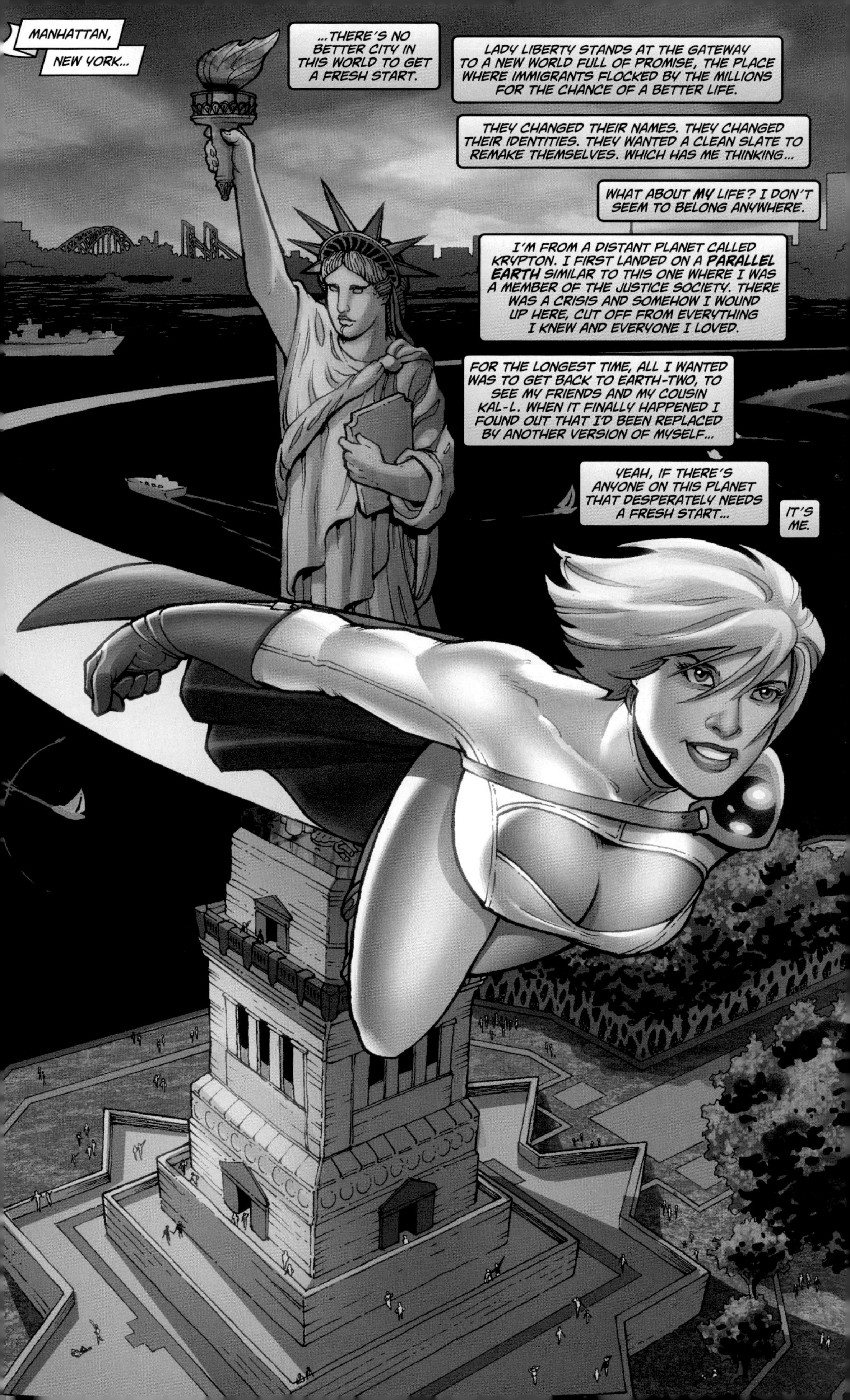
MANHATTAN, NEW YORK...
...THERE'S NO BETTER CITY IN THIS WORLD TO GET A FRESH START.
LADY LIBERTY STANDS AT THE GATEWAY TO A NEW WORLD FULL OF PROMISE, THE PLACE WHERE IMMIGRANTS FLOCKED BY THE MILLIONS FOR THE CHANCE OF A BETTER LIFE.
THEY CHANGED THEIR NAMES. THEY CHANGED THEIR IDENTITIES. THEY WANTED A CLEAN SLATE TO REMAKE THEMSELVES. WHICH HAS ME THINKING...
WHAT ABOUT MY LIFE? I DON'T SEEM TO BELONG ANYWHERE.
I'M FROM A DISTANT PLANET CALLED KRYPTON. I FIRST LANDED ON A PARALLEL EARTH SIMILAR TO THIS ONE WHERE I WAS A MEMBER OF THE JUSTICE SOCIETY. THERE WAS A CRISIS AND SOMEHOW I WOUND UP HERE, CUT OFF FROM EVERYTHING I KNEW AND EVERYONE I LOVED.
FOR THE LONGEST TIME, ALL I WANTED WAS TO GET BACK TO EARTH-TWO, TO SEE MY FRIENDS AND MY COUSIN KAL-L. WHEN IT FINALLY HAPPENED I FOUND OUT THAT I'D BEEN REPLACED BY ANOTHER VERSION OF MYSELF...
YEAH, IF THERE'S ANYONE ON THIS PLANET THAT DESPERATELY NEEDS A FRESH START...
IT'S ME.

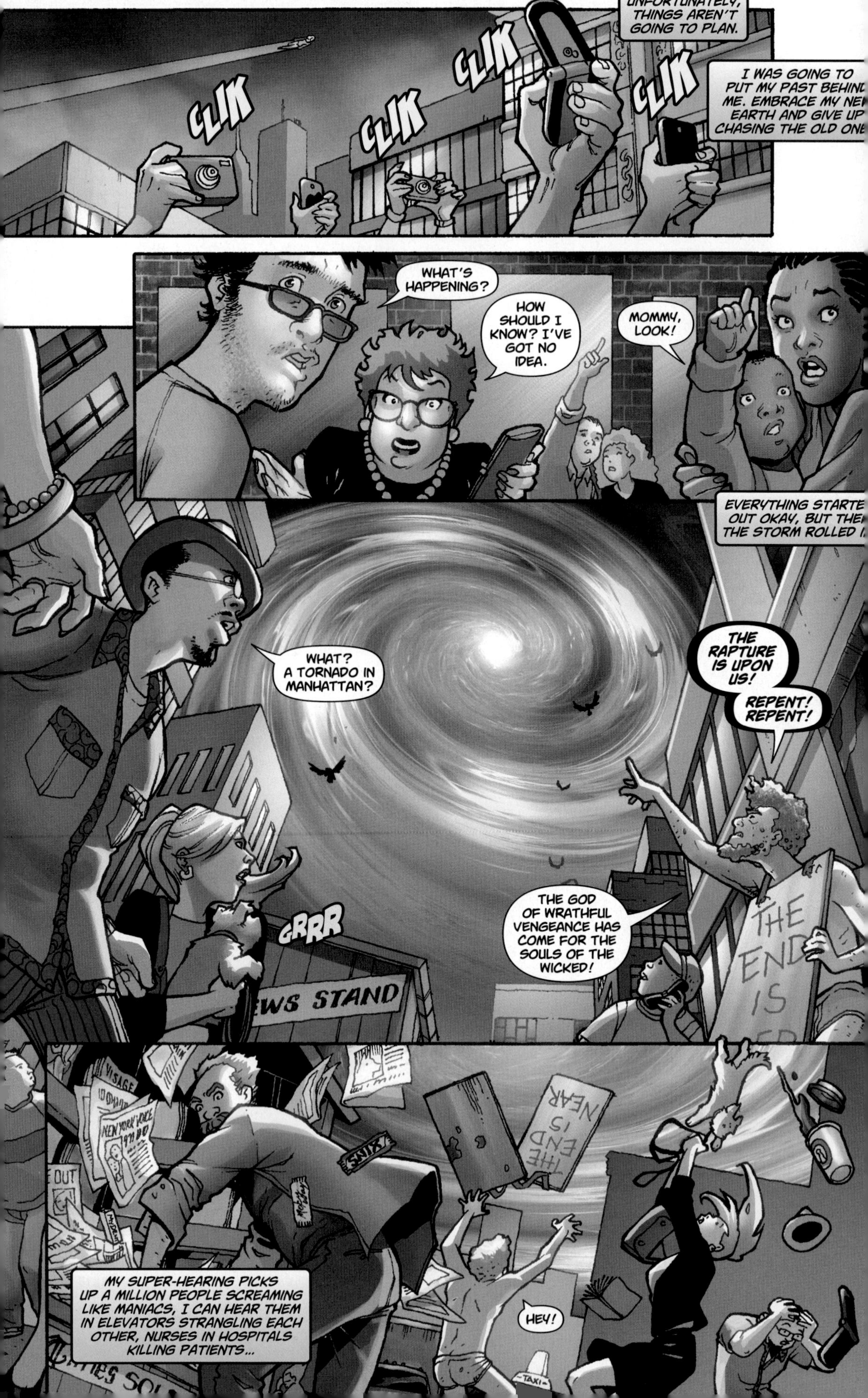

UNFORTUNATELY, THINGS AREN'T GOING TO PLAN.
CLIK
CLIK
CLIK
CLIK
I WAS GOING TO PUT MY PAST BEHIND ME. EMBRACE MY NEW EARTH AND GIVE UP CHASING THE OLD ONE
WHAT'S HAPPENING?
HOW SHOULD I KNOW? I'VE GOT NO IDEA.
MOMMY, LOOK!
EVERYTHING STARTED OUT OKAY, BUT THEN THE STORM ROLLED IN
WHAT? A TORNADO IN MANHATTAN?
THE RAPTURE IS UPON US!
REPENT! REPENT!
GRRR
NEWS STAND
THE GOD OF WRATHFUL VENGEANCE HAS COME FOR THE SOULS OF THE WICKED!
THE END IS
NEW YORK VOICE
SNIX
THE END IS NEAR
MY SUPER-HEARING PICKS UP A MILLION PEOPLE SCREAMING LIKE MANIACS, I CAN HEAR THEM IN ELEVATORS STRANGLING EACH OTHER, NURSES IN HOSPITALS KILLING PATIENTS...
HEY!
TAXI

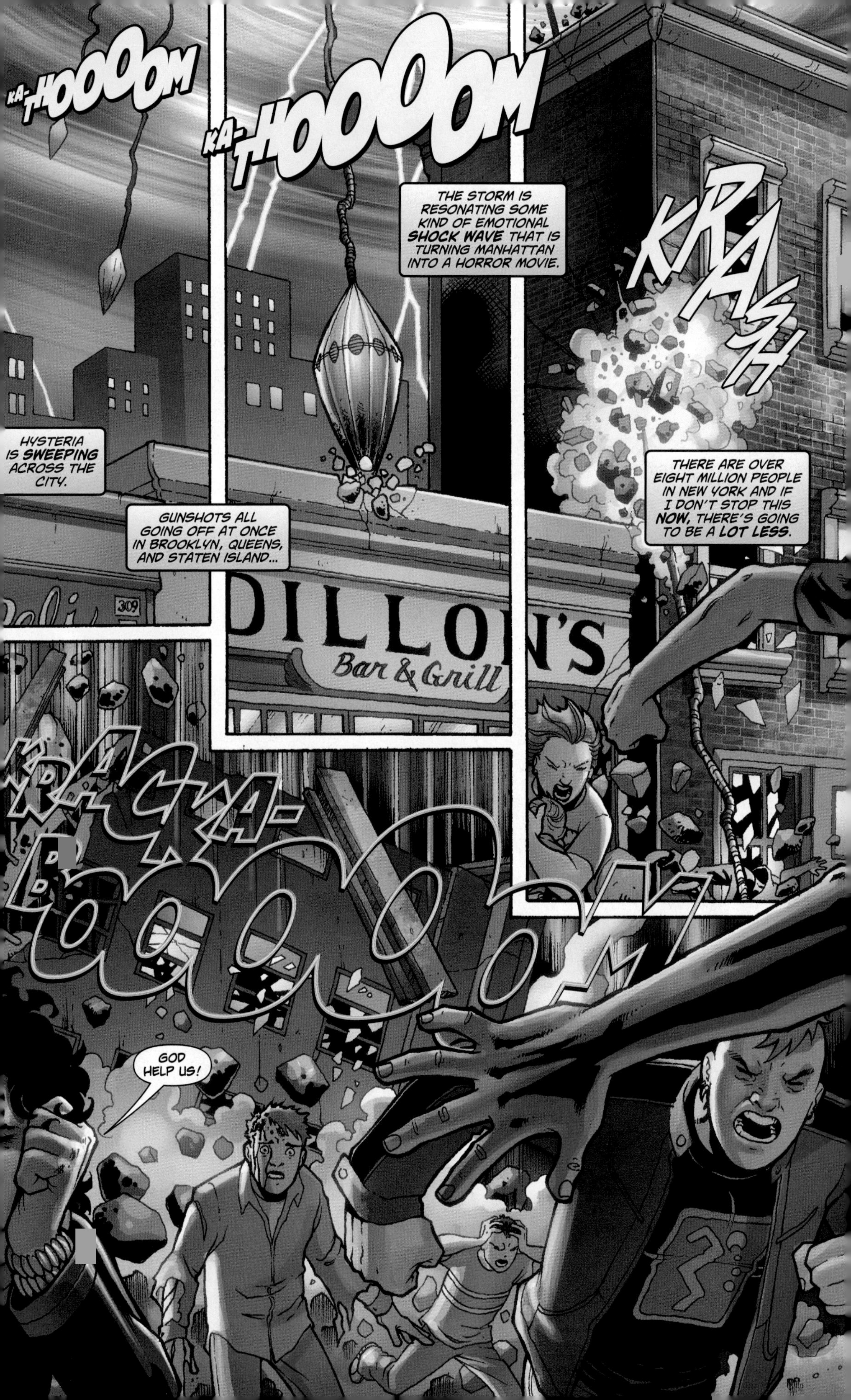
KA-THOOOOOM
KA-THOOOOOM
THE STORM IS RESONATING SOME KIND OF EMOTIONAL SHOCK WAVE THAT IS TURNING MANHATTAN INTO A HORROR MOVIE.
KRASH
HYSTERIA IS SWEEPING ACROSS THE CITY.
GUNSHOTS ALL GOING OFF AT ONCE IN BROOKLYN, QUEENS, AND STATEN ISLAND...
THERE ARE OVER EIGHT MILLION PEOPLE IN NEW YORK AND IF I DON'T STOP THIS NOW, THERE'S GOING TO BE A LOT LESS.
309
DILLON'S
Bar & Grill
KRACKA-BOOOOOM
GOD HELP US!

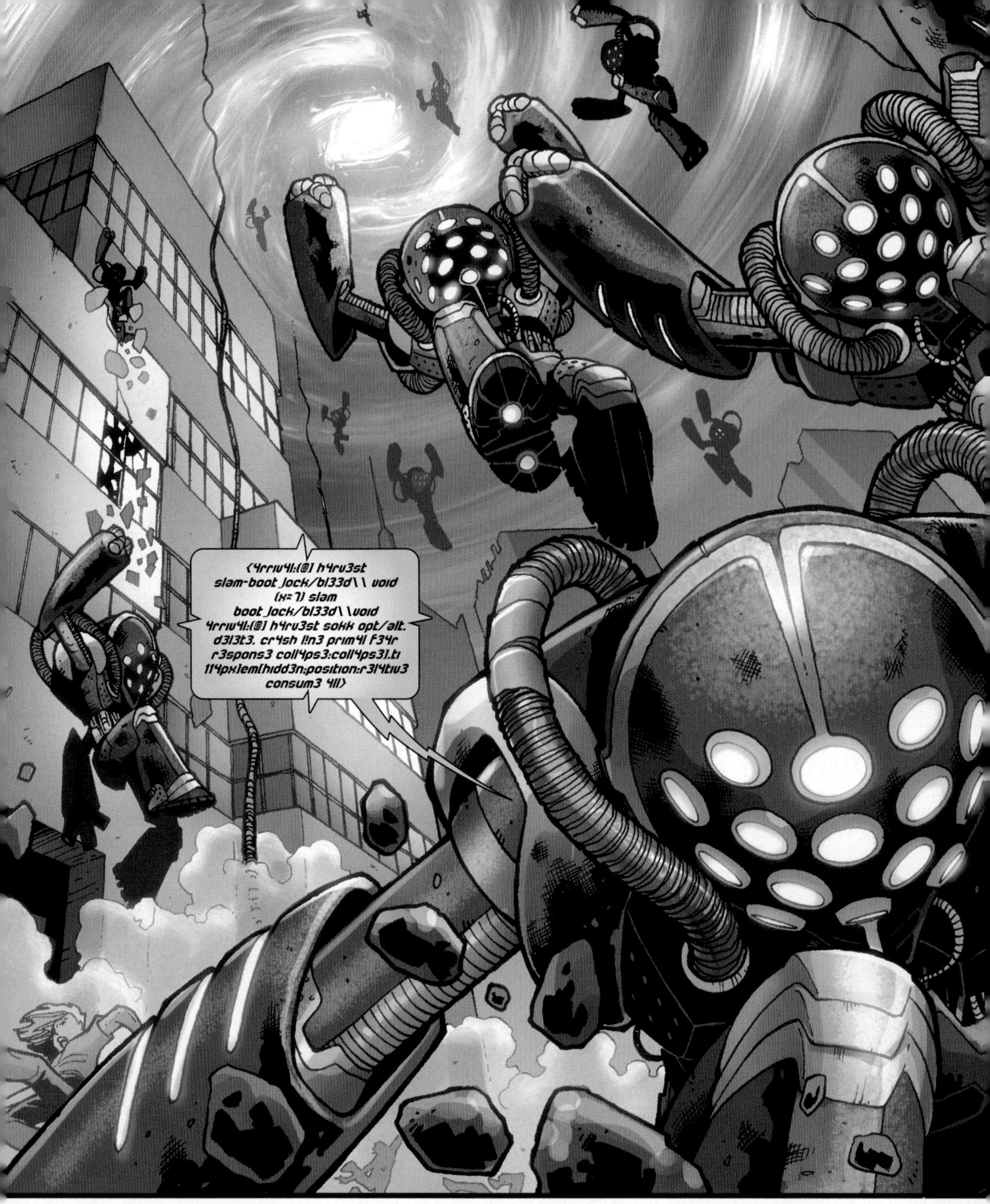
<4rriv4l:(@] h4rv3st slam-boot_lock/bl33d\ \ void (x=7) slam boot_lock/bl33d\ \void 4rriv4l:(@] h4rv3st sokk opt/alt. d3l3t3. cr4sh l!n3 prim4l f34r r3spons3 coll4ps3:coll4ps3].ti 114px]em[hidd3n;position:r3l4tiv3 consum3 4ll>

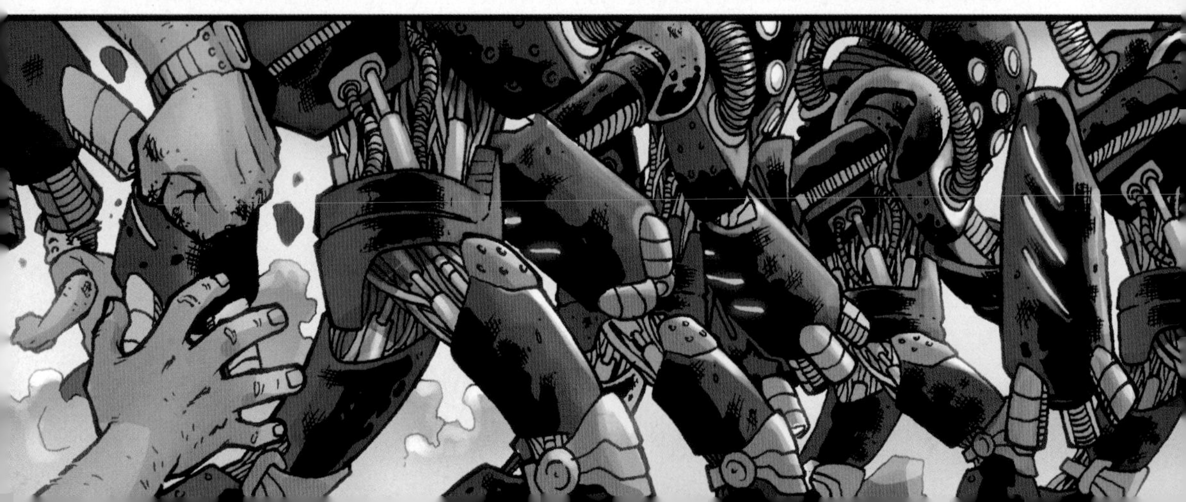

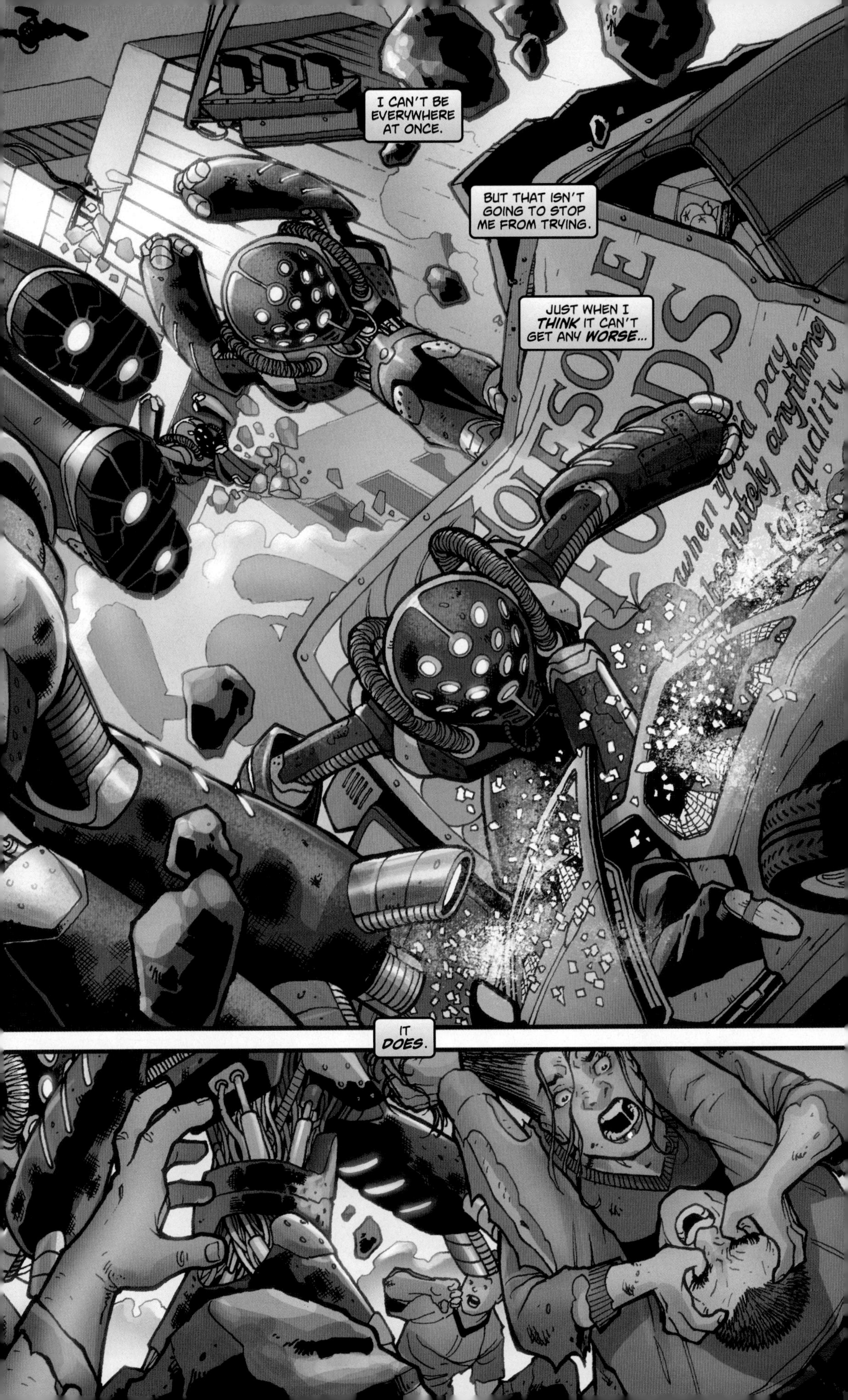
I CAN'T BE EVERYWHERE AT ONCE.
BUT THAT ISN'T GOING TO STOP ME FROM TRYING.
JUST WHEN I *THINK* IT CAN'T GET ANY *WORSE*...
when you'd pay
absolutely anything
IT *DOES*.

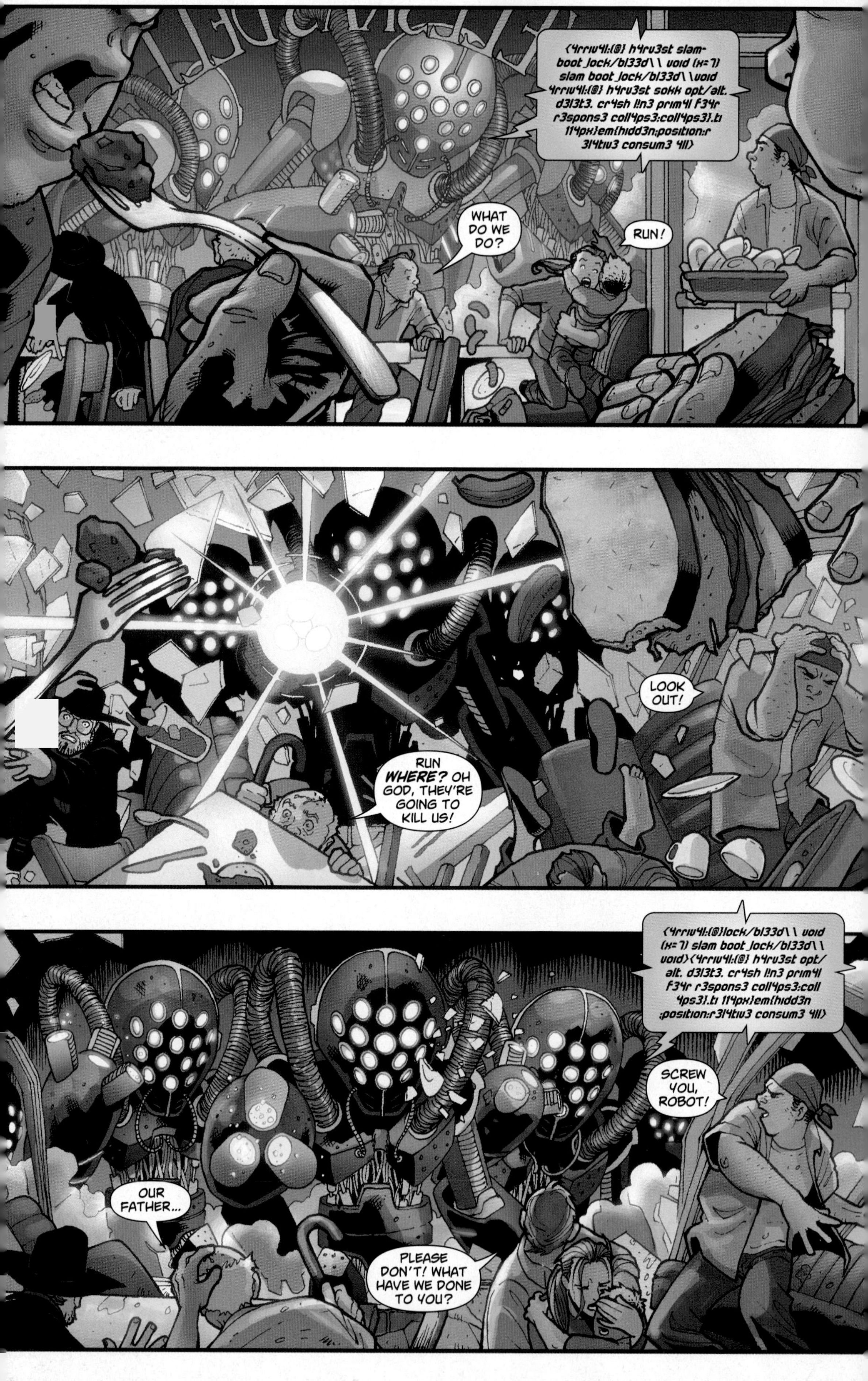
<4rriu4l:(@} h4ru3st slam-boot_lock/bl33d\ \ void (x=7) slam boot_lock/bl33d\ \void 4rriu4l:(@} h4ru3st sokk opt/alt. d3l3t3. cr4sh l!n3 prim4l f34r r3spons3 coll4ps3:coll4ps3}.ti 114px}em{hidd3n;position:r 3l4tiu3 consum3 4ll>
WHAT DO WE DO?
RUN!
LOOK OUT!
RUN ***WHERE?*** OH GOD, THEY'RE GOING TO KILL US!
<4rriu4l:(@}lock/bl33d\ \ void (x=7) slam boot_lock/bl33d\ \ void><4rriu4l:(@} h4ru3st opt/alt. d3l3t3. cr4sh l!n3 prim4l f34r r3spons3 coll4ps3:coll4ps3}.ti 114px}em{hidd3n ;position:r3l4tiu3 consum3 4ll>
SCREW YOU, ROBOT!
OUR FATHER...
PLEASE DON'T! WHAT HAVE WE DONE TO YOU?

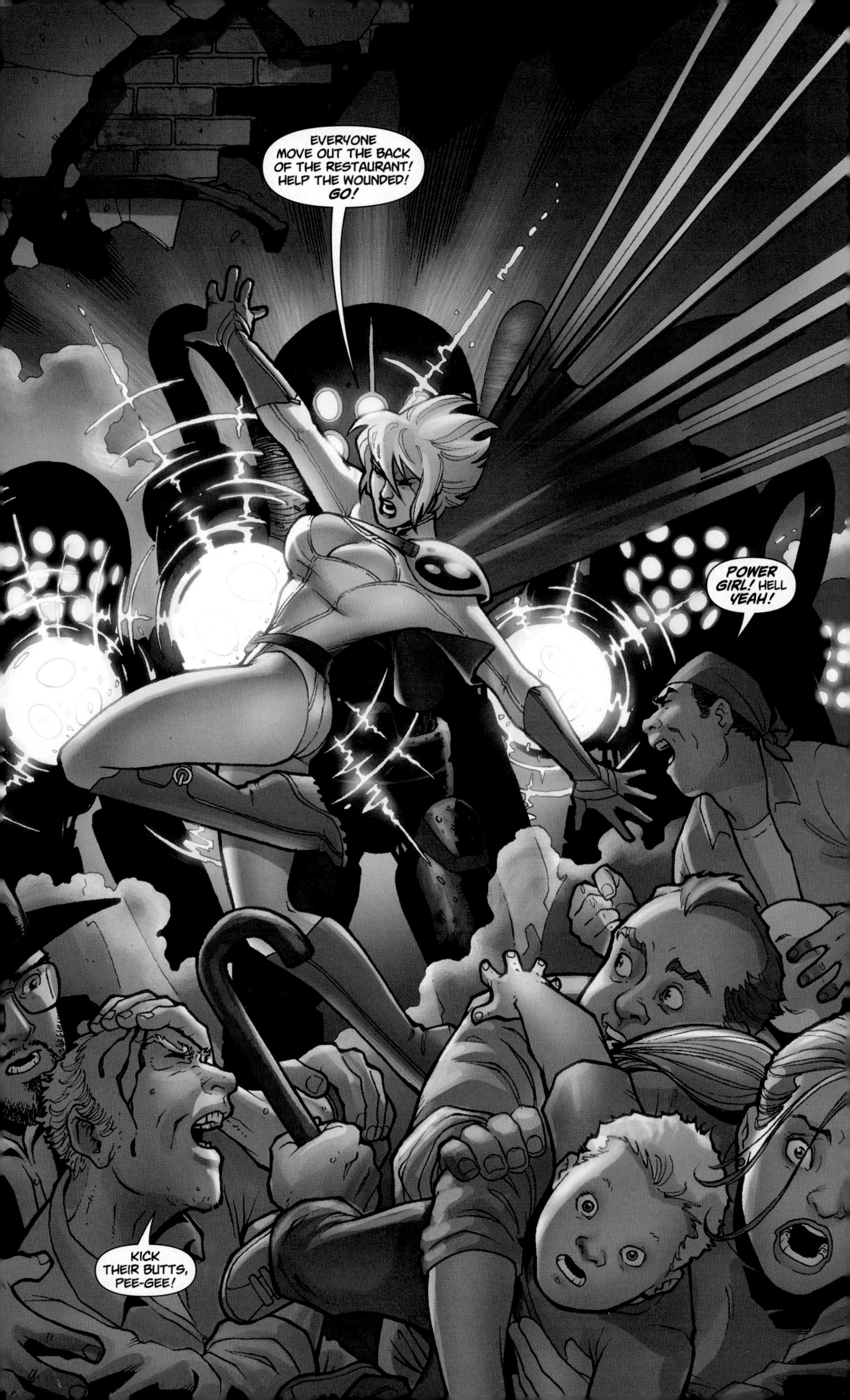
EVERYONE MOVE OUT THE BACK OF THE RESTAURANT! HELP THE WOUNDED! GO!
POWER GIRL! HELL YEAH!
KICK THEIR BUTTS, PEE-GEE!

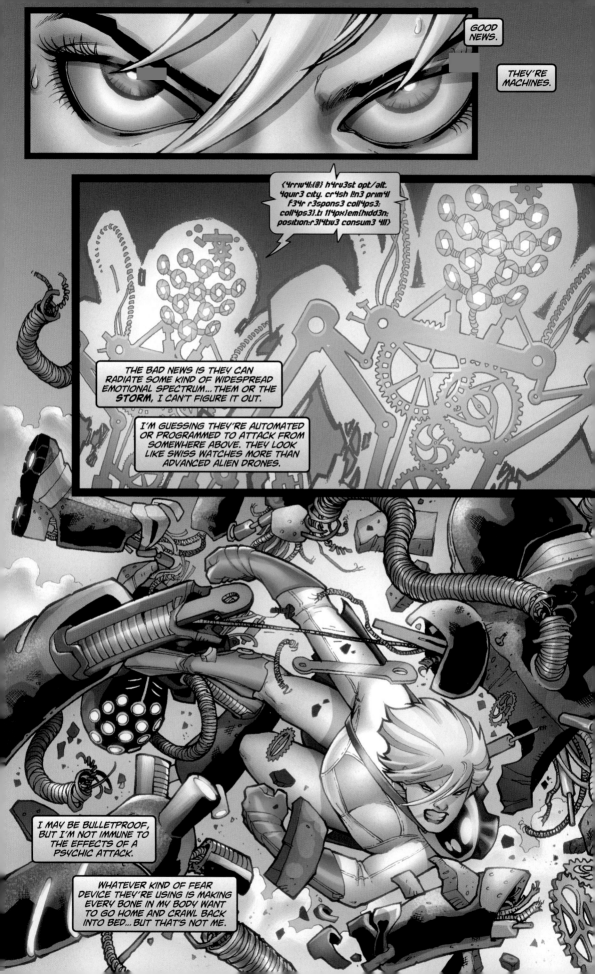

GOOD NEWS.

THEY'RE MACHINES.

(4rr1w4l:(@) h4ru3st opt/alt. 4quir3 city. cr4sh !ln3 pr1m4l f34r r3spons3 coll4ps3: coll4ps3l.ti 114px)em{hidd3n: position:r314tiv3 consum3 4ll)

THE BAD NEWS IS THEY CAN RADIATE SOME KIND OF WIDESPREAD EMOTIONAL SPECTRUM... THEM OR THE **STORM**, I CAN'T FIGURE IT OUT.

I'M GUESSING THEY'RE AUTOMATED OR PROGRAMMED TO ATTACK FROM SOMEWHERE ABOVE. THEY LOOK LIKE SWISS WATCHES MORE THAN ADVANCED ALIEN DRONES.

I MAY BE BULLETPROOF, BUT I'M NOT IMMUNE TO THE EFFECTS OF A PSYCHIC ATTACK.

WHATEVER KIND OF FEAR DEVICE THEY'RE USING IS MAKING EVERY BONE IN MY BODY WANT TO GO HOME AND CRAWL BACK INTO BED... BUT THAT'S NOT ME.

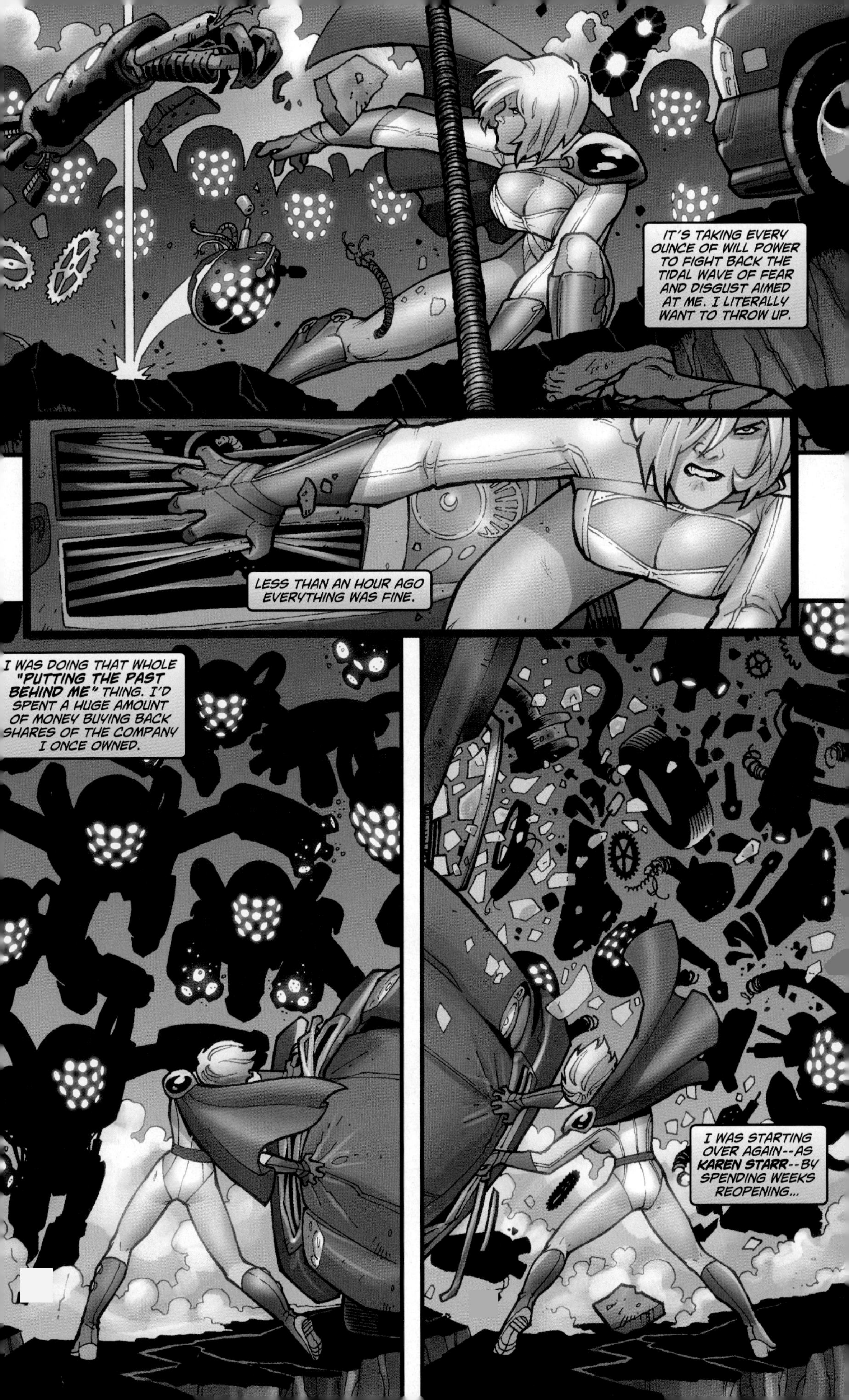
IT'S TAKING EVERY OUNCE OF WILL POWER TO FIGHT BACK THE TIDAL WAVE OF FEAR AND DISGUST AIMED AT ME. I LITERALLY WANT TO THROW UP.
LESS THAN AN HOUR AGO EVERYTHING WAS FINE.
I WAS DOING THAT WHOLE "PUTTING THE PAST BEHIND ME" THING. I'D SPENT A HUGE AMOUNT OF MONEY BUYING BACK SHARES OF THE COMPANY I ONCE OWNED.
I WAS STARTING OVER AGAIN--AS KAREN STARR--BY SPENDING WEEKS REOPENING...

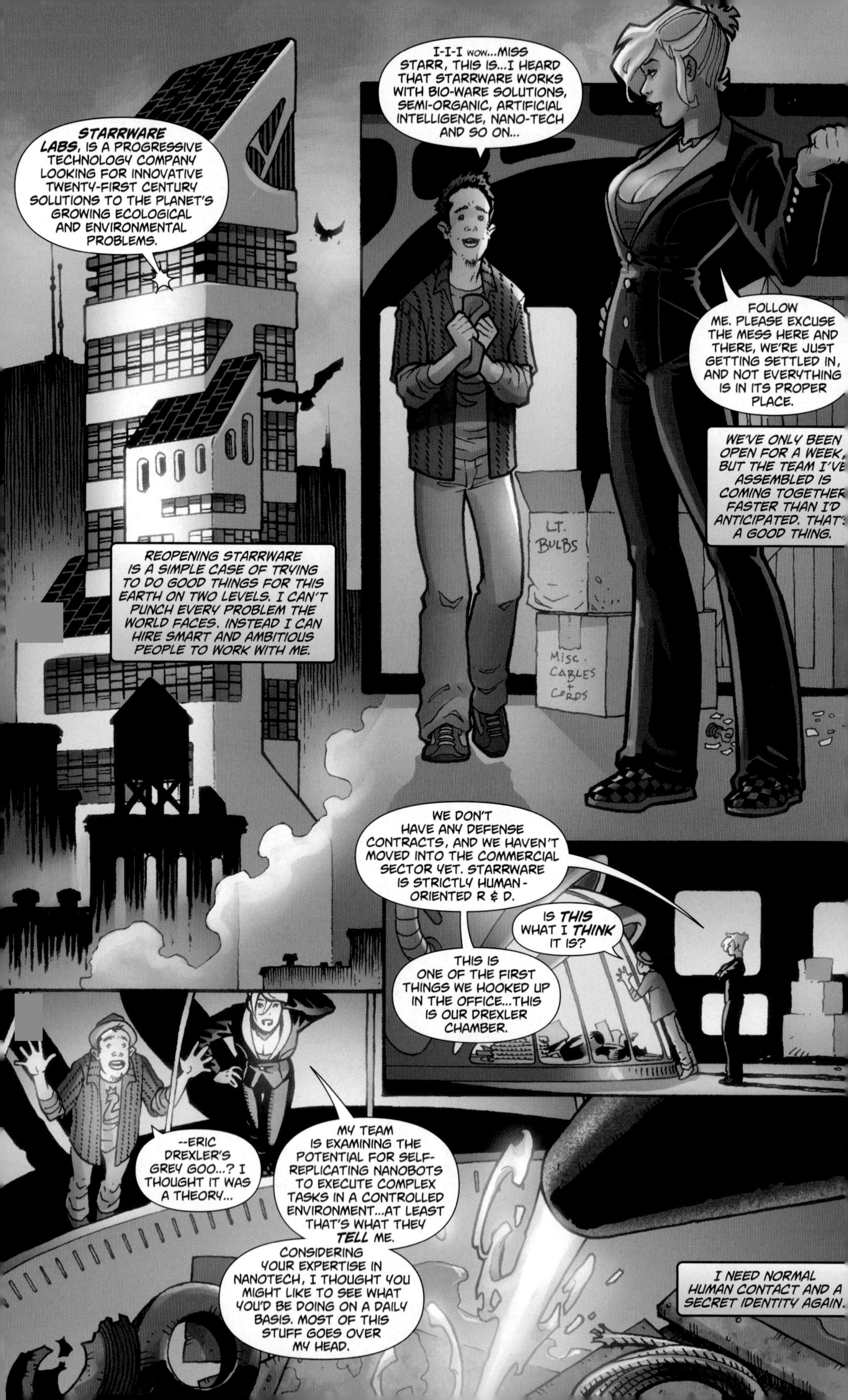
STARRWARE LABS, IS A PROGRESSIVE TECHNOLOGY COMPANY LOOKING FOR INNOVATIVE TWENTY-FIRST CENTURY SOLUTIONS TO THE PLANET'S GROWING ECOLOGICAL AND ENVIRONMENTAL PROBLEMS.
I-I-I WOW...MISS STARR, THIS IS...I HEARD THAT STARRWARE WORKS WITH BIO-WARE SOLUTIONS, SEMI-ORGANIC, ARTIFICIAL INTELLIGENCE, NANO-TECH AND SO ON...
FOLLOW ME. PLEASE EXCUSE THE MESS HERE AND THERE, WE'RE JUST GETTING SETTLED IN, AND NOT EVERYTHING IS IN ITS PROPER PLACE.
WE'VE ONLY BEEN OPEN FOR A WEEK, BUT THE TEAM I'VE ASSEMBLED IS COMING TOGETHER FASTER THAN I'D ANTICIPATED. THAT'S A GOOD THING.
LT. BULBS
MISC. CABLES + CORDS
REOPENING STARRWARE IS A SIMPLE CASE OF TRYING TO DO GOOD THINGS FOR THIS EARTH ON TWO LEVELS. I CAN'T PUNCH EVERY PROBLEM THE WORLD FACES. INSTEAD I CAN HIRE SMART AND AMBITIOUS PEOPLE TO WORK WITH ME.
WE DON'T HAVE ANY DEFENSE CONTRACTS, AND WE HAVEN'T MOVED INTO THE COMMERCIAL SECTOR YET. STARRWARE IS STRICTLY HUMAN-ORIENTED R & D.
IS THIS WHAT I THINK IT IS?
THIS IS ONE OF THE FIRST THINGS WE HOOKED UP IN THE OFFICE...THIS IS OUR DREXLER CHAMBER.
--ERIC DREXLER'S GREY GOO...? I THOUGHT IT WAS A THEORY...
MY TEAM IS EXAMINING THE POTENTIAL FOR SELF-REPLICATING NANOBOTS TO EXECUTE COMPLEX TASKS IN A CONTROLLED ENVIRONMENT...AT LEAST THAT'S WHAT THEY TELL ME.
CONSIDERING YOUR EXPERTISE IN NANOTECH, I THOUGHT YOU MIGHT LIKE TO SEE WHAT YOU'D BE DOING ON A DAILY BASIS. MOST OF THIS STUFF GOES OVER MY HEAD.
I NEED NORMAL HUMAN CONTACT AND A SECRET IDENTITY AGAIN.

WHAT I **DO** KNOW IS THAT THIS PARTICULAR BATCH IS PROGRAMMED TO BUILD A 1966 PONTIAC GTO FROM THE RAW MATERIALS WE PROVIDED.

STARRWARE IS A GREAT WAY TO CONNECT WITH PEOPLE AND STILL KEEP THEM AT A DISTANCE.

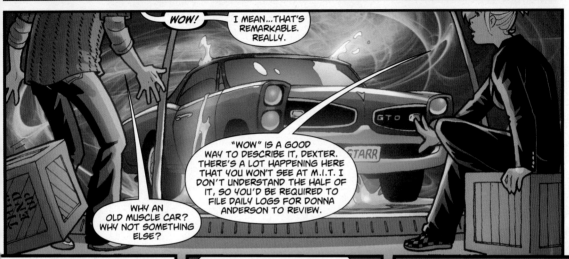

WOW!

I MEAN...THAT'S REMARKABLE. REALLY.

"WOW" IS A GOOD WAY TO DESCRIBE IT, DEXTER. THERE'S A LOT HAPPENING HERE THAT YOU WON'T SEE AT M.I.T. I DON'T UNDERSTAND THE HALF OF IT, SO YOU'D BE REQUIRED TO FILE DAILY LOGS FOR DONNA ANDERSON TO REVIEW.

WHY AN OLD MUSCLE CAR? WHY NOT SOMETHING ELSE?

I'M TRYING TO REMIND OUR RESEARCH TEAM THAT AMERICA USED TO STAND FOR INGENUITY, STYLE, A SENSE OF ADVENTURE AND DEPENDABILITY. WE NEED THAT KIND OF SPIRIT IF WE'RE GOING TO TACKLE 21ST CENTURY PROBLEMS

NOW, IF YOU'RE INTERESTED IN THE JOB, I'D LIKE YOU TO STOP BY HUMAN RESOURCES ON THE SEVENTIETH FLOOR.

SURE MISS STARR... I'M, UH, VERY INTERESTED!

GOOD. NOW IF YOU'LL EXCUSE ME, I'M LATE FOR ANOTHER INTERVIEW.

DEXTER NICHOLS IS A GOOD KID, SHY, AWKWARD AND TALL AS A BEANSTALK BUT BRILLIANT. I CAN OVERLOOK HIS STARING AT MY CHEST. IT'S SOMETHING I HAD TO GET USED TO A LONG TIME AGO.

HUMAN RESOURCES, MR. NICHOLS.

RIGHT! OKAY, SEE YOU AROUND THEN!

ORIGINALLY FROM THE MID-WEST, DEXTER HAS THOSE DOWN-HOME VALUES WHICH GRATE AGAINST THE HUSTLE AND BUSTLE OF BIG CITY LIFE. BUT I LIKE HAVING THAT KIND OF PERSON AROUND. HE'S HONEST, GROUNDED AND...

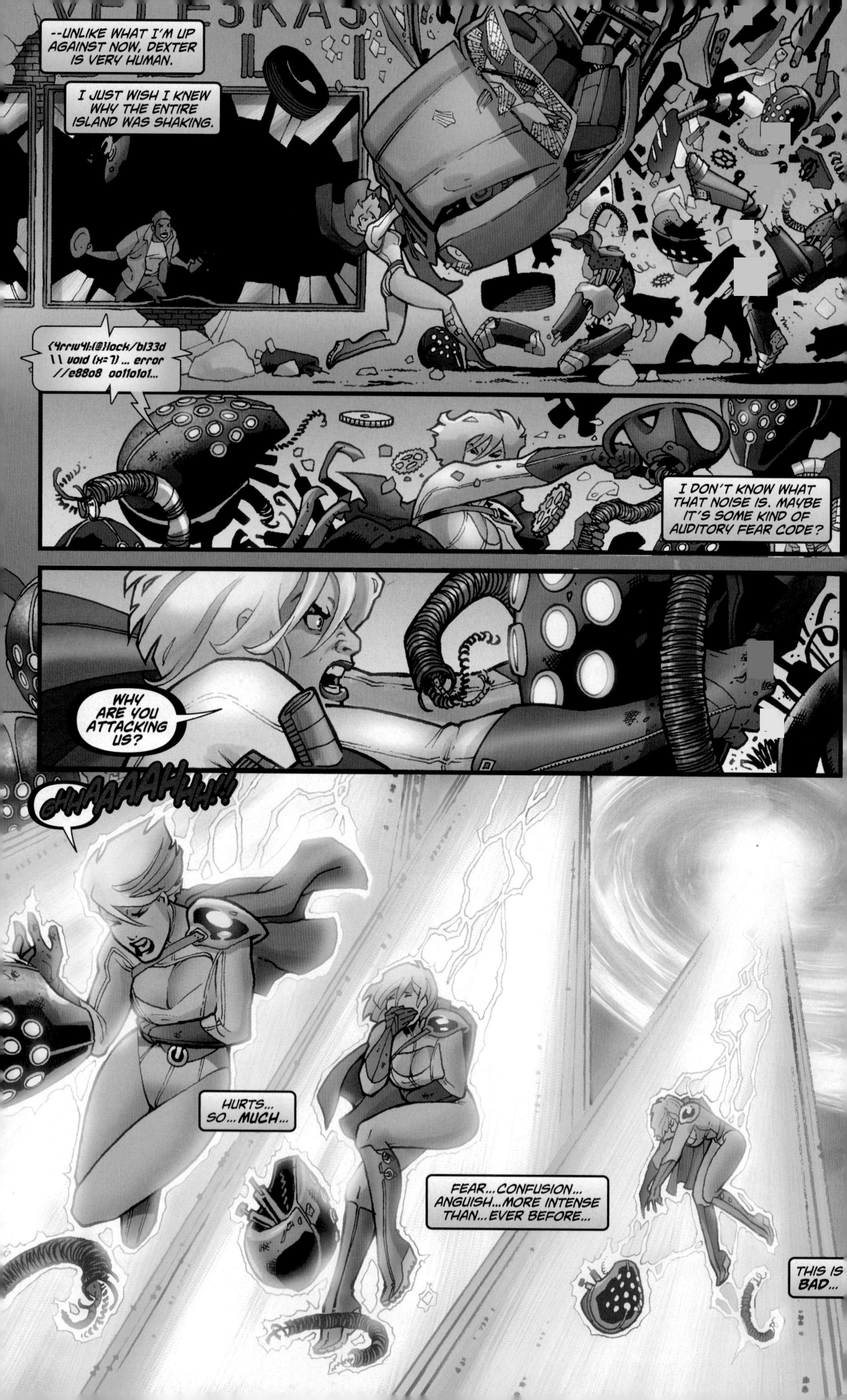
--UNLIKE WHAT I'M UP AGAINST NOW, DEXTER IS VERY HUMAN.
I JUST WISH I KNEW WHY THE ENTIRE ISLAND WAS SHAKING.
{4rriu4l:(@}lock/bl33d \\ void (x=7) ... error //e88o8 oo11o1o1...
I DON'T KNOW WHAT THAT NOISE IS. MAYBE IT'S SOME KIND OF AUDITORY FEAR CODE?
WHY ARE YOU ATTACKING US?
GHHAAAAAHHH!!
HURTS... SO... MUCH...
FEAR... CONFUSION... ANGUISH... MORE INTENSE THAN... EVER BEFORE...
THIS IS BAD...

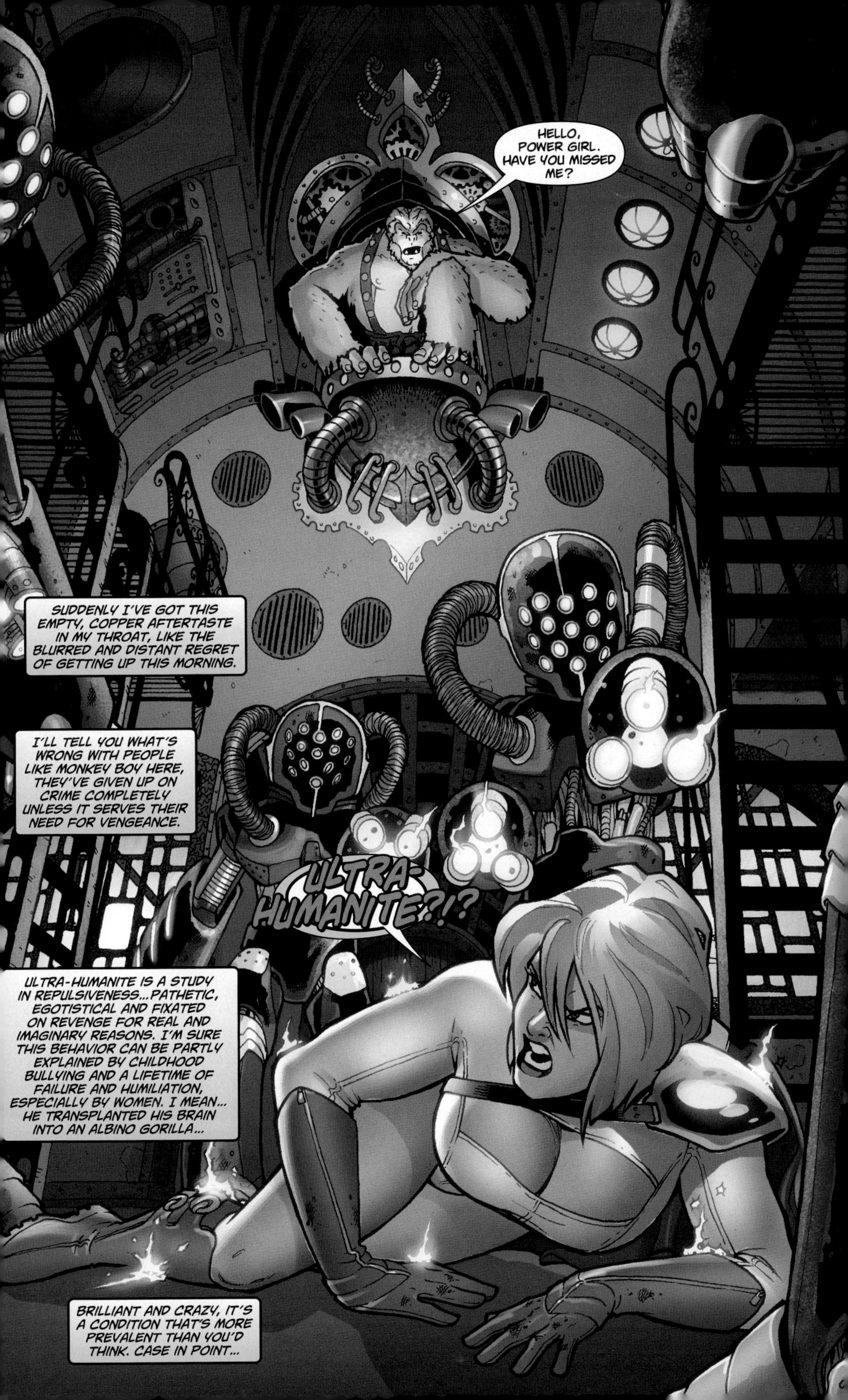
HELLO, POWER GIRL. HAVE YOU MISSED ME?
SUDDENLY I'VE GOT THIS EMPTY, COPPER AFTERTASTE IN MY THROAT, LIKE THE BLURRED AND DISTANT REGRET OF GETTING UP THIS MORNING.
I'LL TELL YOU WHAT'S WRONG WITH PEOPLE LIKE MONKEY BOY HERE, THEY'VE GIVEN UP ON CRIME COMPLETELY UNLESS IT SERVES THEIR NEED FOR VENGEANCE.
ULTRA-HUMANITE?!?
ULTRA-HUMANITE IS A STUDY IN REPULSIVENESS...PATHETIC, EGOTISTICAL AND FIXATED ON REVENGE FOR REAL AND IMAGINARY REASONS. I'M SURE THIS BEHAVIOR CAN BE PARTLY EXPLAINED BY CHILDHOOD BULLYING AND A LIFETIME OF FAILURE AND HUMILIATION, ESPECIALLY BY WOMEN. I MEAN... HE TRANSPLANTED HIS BRAIN INTO AN ALBINO GORILLA...
BRILLIANT AND CRAZY, IT'S A CONDITION THAT'S MORE PREVALENT THAN YOU'D THINK. CASE IN POINT...

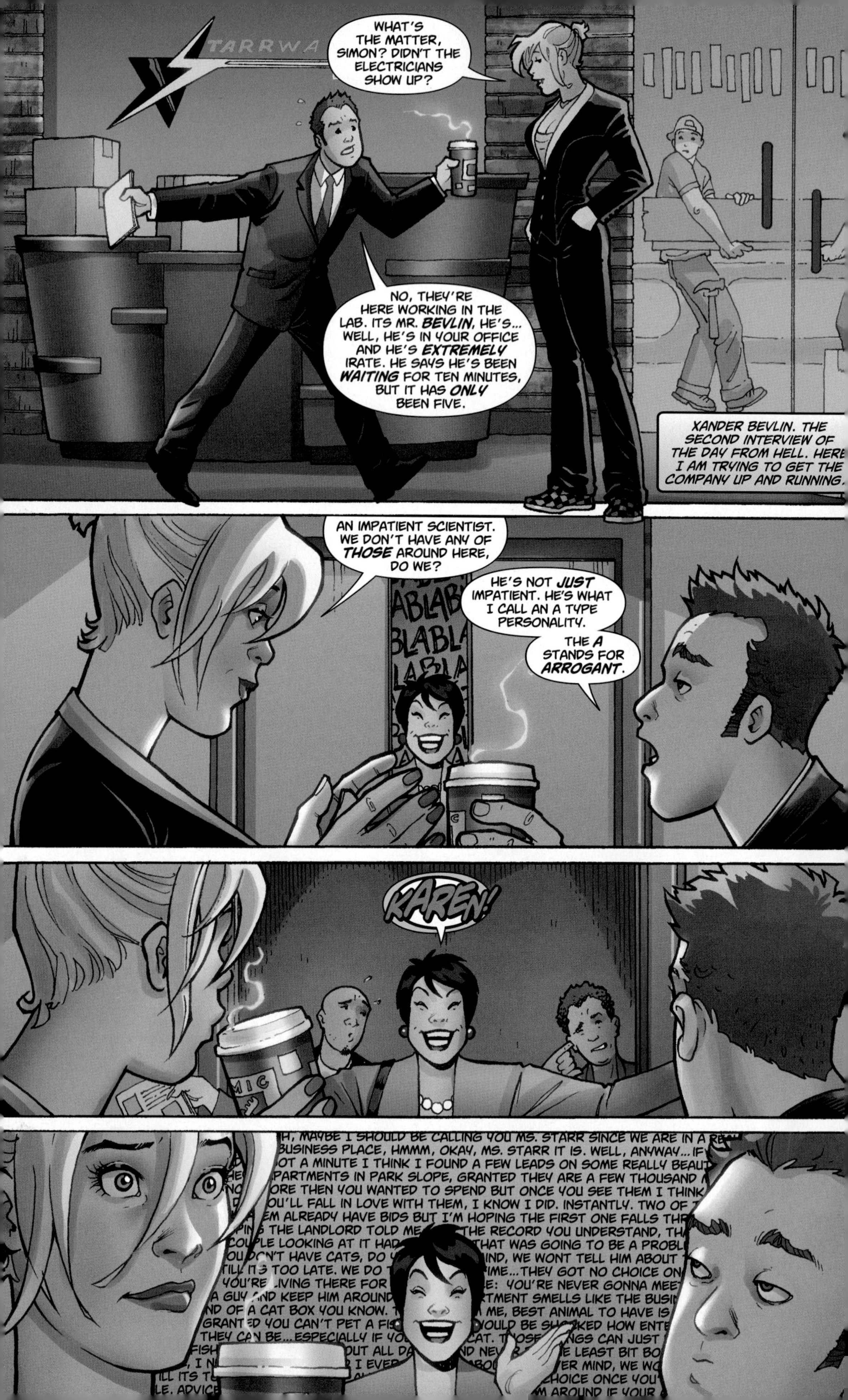
WHAT'S THE MATTER, SIMON? DIDN'T THE ELECTRICIANS SHOW UP?
NO, THEY'RE HERE WORKING IN THE LAB. ITS MR. BEVLIN, HE'S... WELL, HE'S IN YOUR OFFICE AND HE'S EXTREMELY IRATE. HE SAYS HE'S BEEN WAITING FOR TEN MINUTES, BUT IT HAS ONLY BEEN FIVE.
XANDER BEVLIN. THE SECOND INTERVIEW OF THE DAY FROM HELL. HERE I AM TRYING TO GET THE COMPANY UP AND RUNNING.
AN IMPATIENT SCIENTIST. WE DON'T HAVE ANY OF THOSE AROUND HERE, DO WE?
HE'S NOT JUST IMPATIENT. HE'S WHAT I CALL AN A TYPE PERSONALITY.
THE A STANDS FOR ARROGANT.
KAREN!

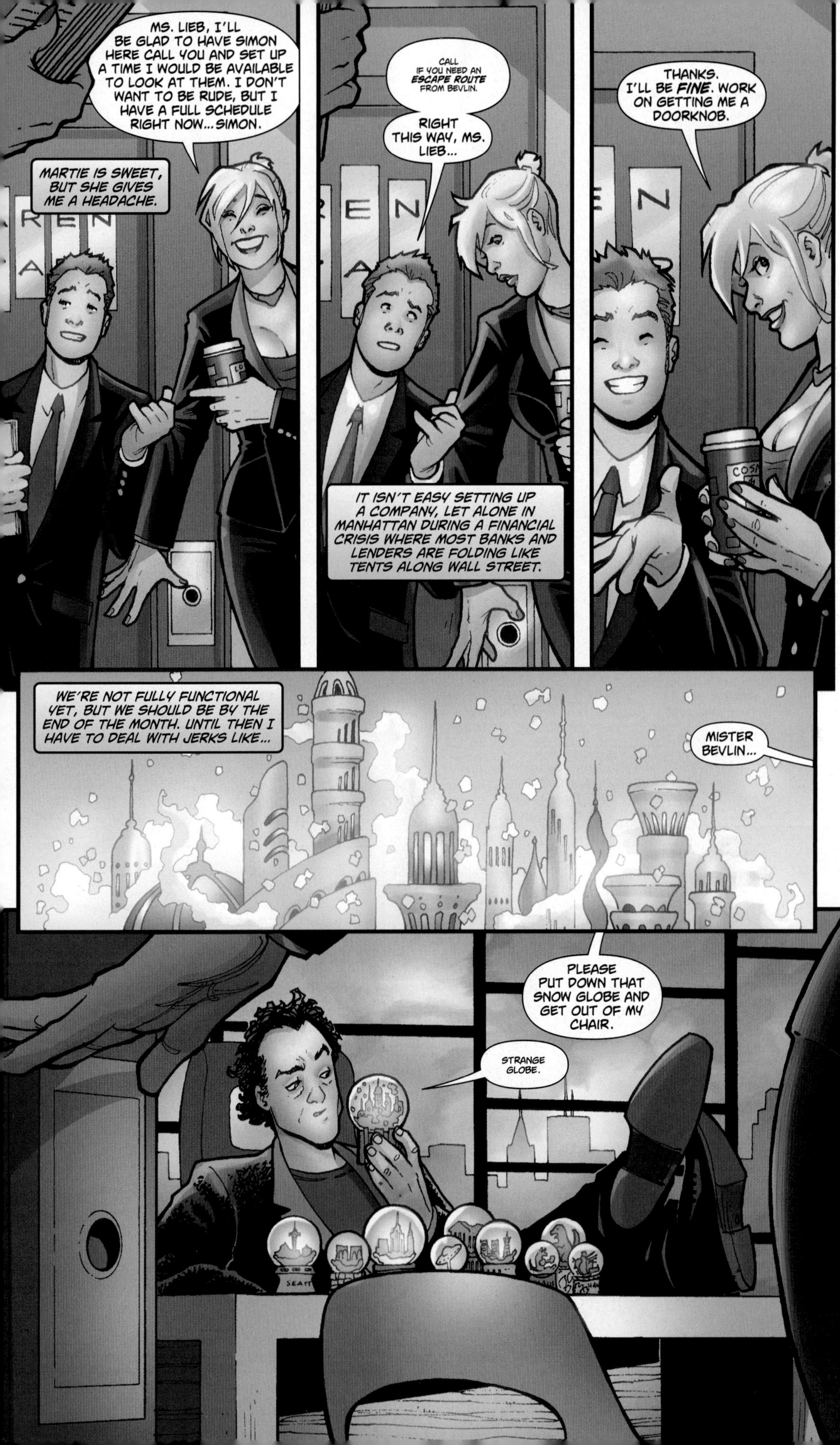

MS. LIEB, I'LL BE GLAD TO HAVE SIMON HERE CALL YOU AND SET UP A TIME I WOULD BE AVAILABLE TO LOOK AT THEM. I DON'T WANT TO BE RUDE, BUT I HAVE A FULL SCHEDULE RIGHT NOW... SIMON.
MARTIE IS SWEET, BUT SHE GIVES ME A HEADACHE.
CALL IF YOU NEED AN ESCAPE ROUTE FROM BEVLIN.
RIGHT THIS WAY, MS. LIEB...
IT ISN'T EASY SETTING UP A COMPANY, LET ALONE IN MANHATTAN DURING A FINANCIAL CRISIS WHERE MOST BANKS AND LENDERS ARE FOLDING LIKE TENTS ALONG WALL STREET.
THANKS. I'LL BE FINE. WORK ON GETTING ME A DOORKNOB.
WE'RE NOT FULLY FUNCTIONAL YET, BUT WE SHOULD BE BY THE END OF THE MONTH. UNTIL THEN I HAVE TO DEAL WITH JERKS LIKE...
MISTER BEVLIN...
PLEASE PUT DOWN THAT SNOW GLOBE AND GET OUT OF MY CHAIR.
STRANGE GLOBE.

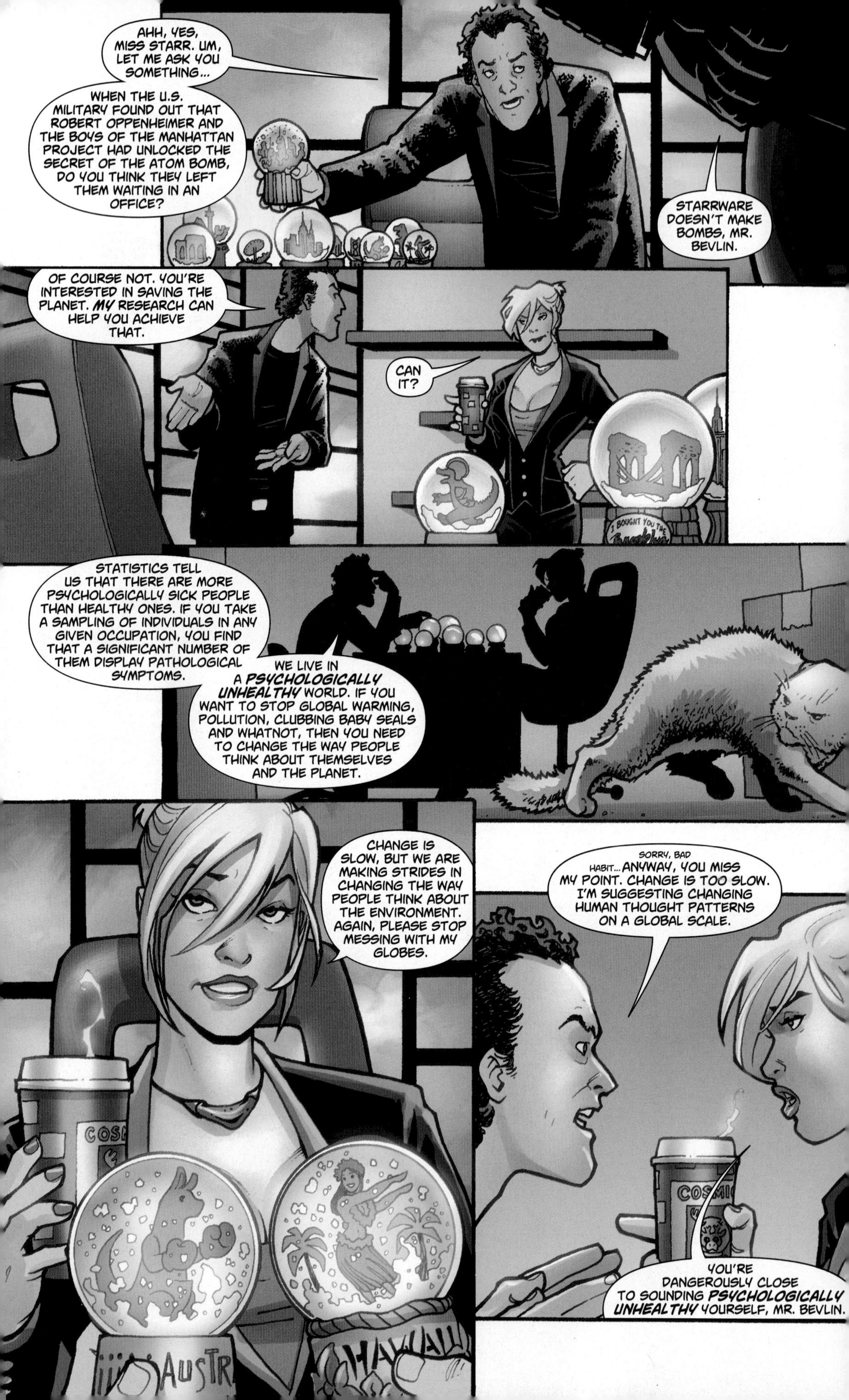
AHH, YES, MISS STARR. UM, LET ME ASK YOU SOMETHING...
WHEN THE U.S. MILITARY FOUND OUT THAT ROBERT OPPENHEIMER AND THE BOYS OF THE MANHATTAN PROJECT HAD UNLOCKED THE SECRET OF THE ATOM BOMB, DO YOU THINK THEY LEFT THEM WAITING IN AN OFFICE?
STARRWARE DOESN'T MAKE BOMBS, MR. BEVLIN.
OF COURSE NOT. YOU'RE INTERESTED IN SAVING THE PLANET. MY RESEARCH CAN HELP YOU ACHIEVE THAT.
CAN IT?
I BOUGHT YOU THE
STATISTICS TELL US THAT THERE ARE MORE PSYCHOLOGICALLY SICK PEOPLE THAN HEALTHY ONES. IF YOU TAKE A SAMPLING OF INDIVIDUALS IN ANY GIVEN OCCUPATION, YOU FIND THAT A SIGNIFICANT NUMBER OF THEM DISPLAY PATHOLOGICAL SYMPTOMS.
WE LIVE IN A PSYCHOLOGICALLY UNHEALTHY WORLD. IF YOU WANT TO STOP GLOBAL WARMING, POLLUTION, CLUBBING BABY SEALS AND WHATNOT, THEN YOU NEED TO CHANGE THE WAY PEOPLE THINK ABOUT THEMSELVES AND THE PLANET.
CHANGE IS SLOW, BUT WE ARE MAKING STRIDES IN CHANGING THE WAY PEOPLE THINK ABOUT THE ENVIRONMENT. AGAIN, PLEASE STOP MESSING WITH MY GLOBES.
SORRY, BAD HABIT... ANYWAY, YOU MISS MY POINT. CHANGE IS TOO SLOW. I'M SUGGESTING CHANGING HUMAN THOUGHT PATTERNS ON A GLOBAL SCALE.
YOU'RE DANGEROUSLY CLOSE TO SOUNDING PSYCHOLOGICALLY UNHEALTHY YOURSELF, MR. BEVLIN.

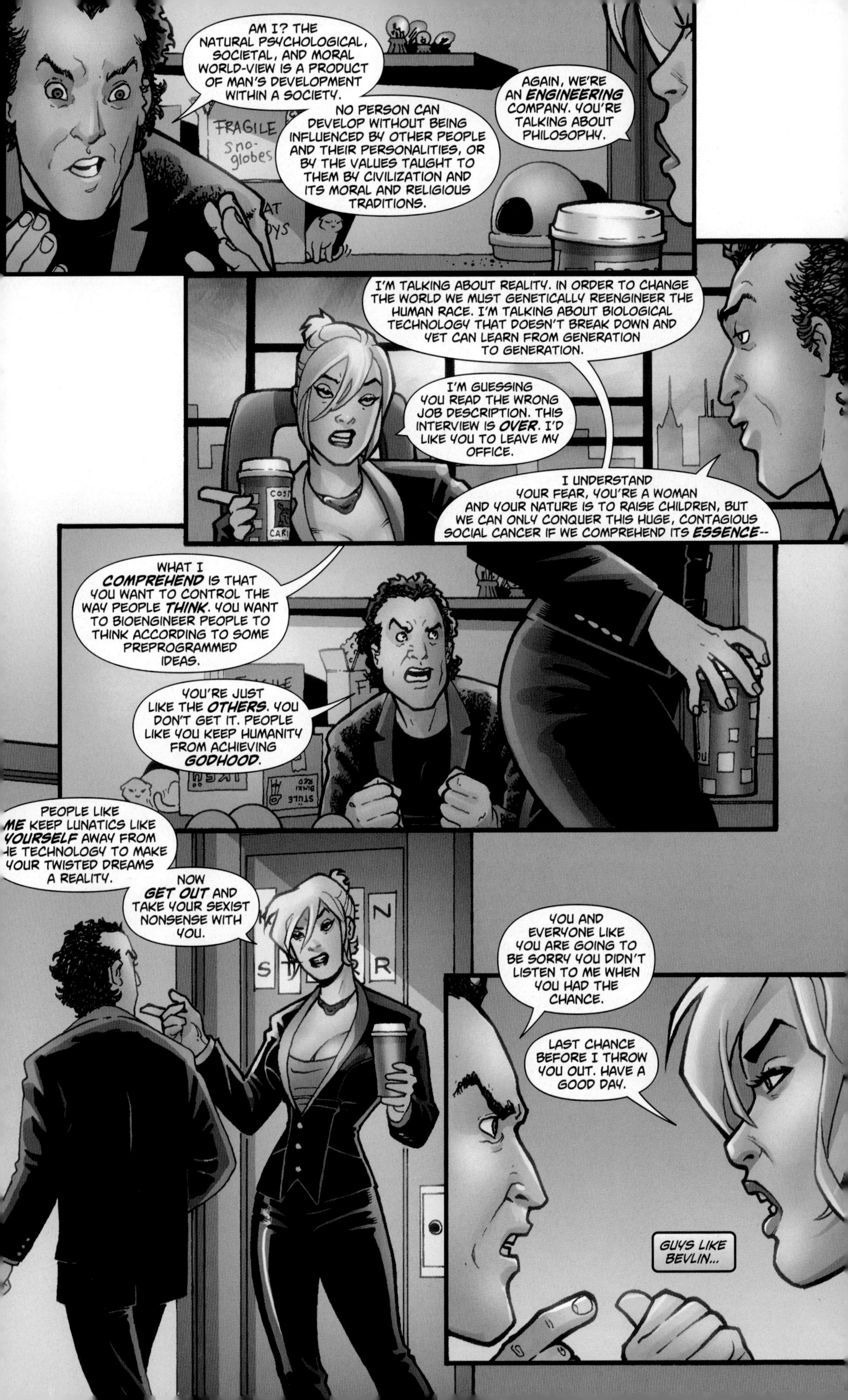
AM I? THE NATURAL PSYCHOLOGICAL, SOCIETAL, AND MORAL WORLD-VIEW IS A PRODUCT OF MAN'S DEVELOPMENT WITHIN A SOCIETY.
NO PERSON CAN DEVELOP WITHOUT BEING INFLUENCED BY OTHER PEOPLE AND THEIR PERSONALITIES, OR BY THE VALUES TAUGHT TO THEM BY CIVILIZATION AND ITS MORAL AND RELIGIOUS TRADITIONS.
FRAGILE sno-globes
AGAIN, WE'RE AN ENGINEERING COMPANY. YOU'RE TALKING ABOUT PHILOSOPHY.
I'M TALKING ABOUT REALITY. IN ORDER TO CHANGE THE WORLD WE MUST GENETICALLY REENGINEER THE HUMAN RACE. I'M TALKING ABOUT BIOLOGICAL TECHNOLOGY THAT DOESN'T BREAK DOWN AND YET CAN LEARN FROM GENERATION TO GENERATION.
I'M GUESSING YOU READ THE WRONG JOB DESCRIPTION. THIS INTERVIEW IS OVER. I'D LIKE YOU TO LEAVE MY OFFICE.
I UNDERSTAND YOUR FEAR, YOU'RE A WOMAN AND YOUR NATURE IS TO RAISE CHILDREN, BUT WE CAN ONLY CONQUER THIS HUGE, CONTAGIOUS SOCIAL CANCER IF WE COMPREHEND ITS ESSENCE--
WHAT I COMPREHEND IS THAT YOU WANT TO CONTROL THE WAY PEOPLE THINK. YOU WANT TO BIOENGINEER PEOPLE TO THINK ACCORDING TO SOME PREPROGRAMMED IDEAS.
YOU'RE JUST LIKE THE OTHERS. YOU DON'T GET IT. PEOPLE LIKE YOU KEEP HUMANITY FROM ACHIEVING GODHOOD.
PEOPLE LIKE ME KEEP LUNATICS LIKE YOURSELF AWAY FROM HE TECHNOLOGY TO MAKE YOUR TWISTED DREAMS A REALITY.
NOW GET OUT AND TAKE YOUR SEXIST NONSENSE WITH YOU.
YOU AND EVERYONE LIKE YOU ARE GOING TO BE SORRY YOU DIDN'T LISTEN TO ME WHEN YOU HAD THE CHANCE.
LAST CHANCE BEFORE I THROW YOU OUT. HAVE A GOOD DAY.
GUYS LIKE BEVLIN...

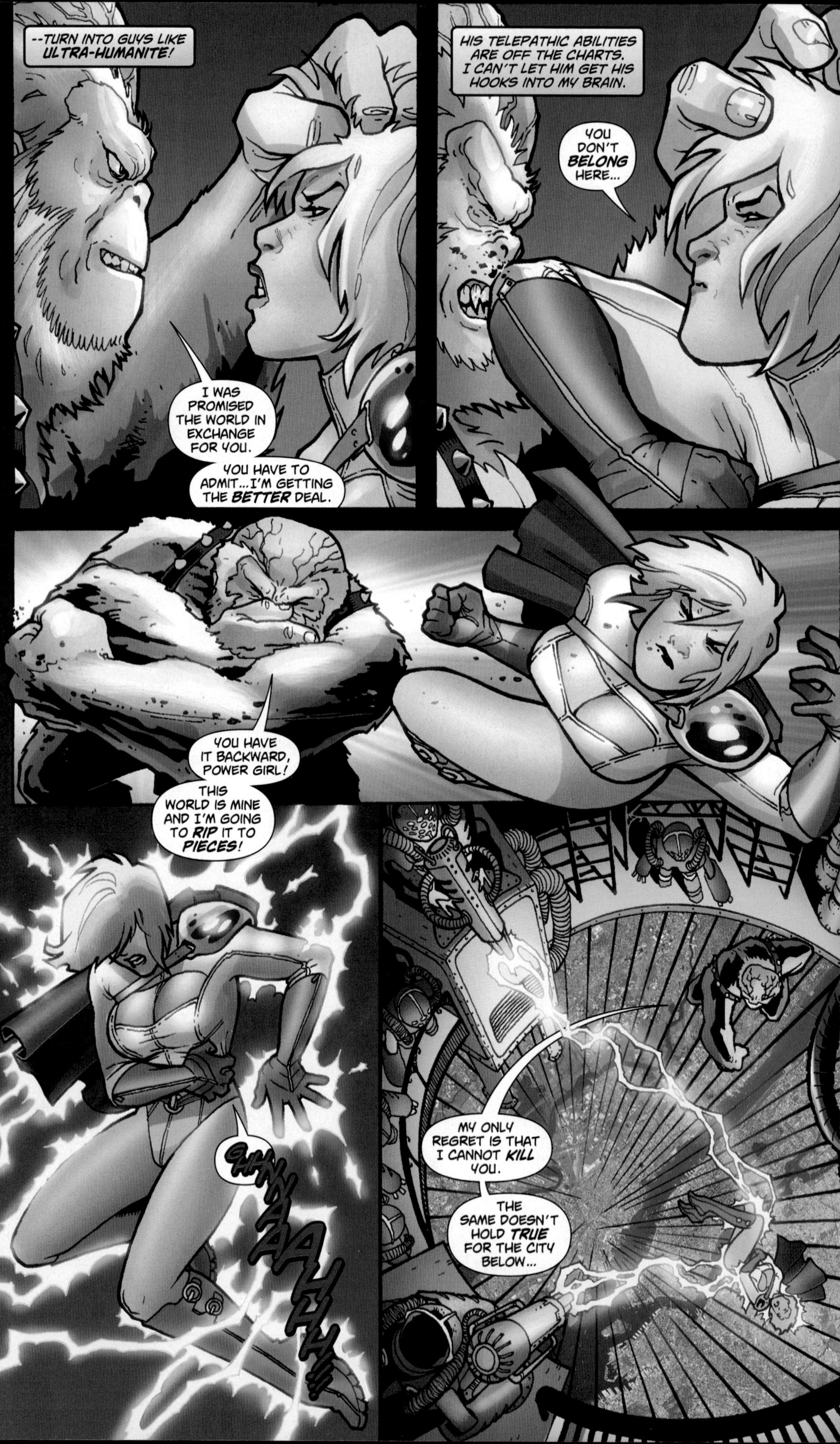
--TURN INTO GUYS LIKE ULTRA-HUMANITE!
I WAS PROMISED THE WORLD IN EXCHANGE FOR YOU.
YOU HAVE TO ADMIT...I'M GETTING THE BETTER DEAL.
HIS TELEPATHIC ABILITIES ARE OFF THE CHARTS. I CAN'T LET HIM GET HIS HOOKS INTO MY BRAIN.
YOU DON'T BELONG HERE...
YOU HAVE IT BACKWARD, POWER GIRL!
THIS WORLD IS MINE AND I'M GOING TO RIP IT TO PIECES!
GHHNNAAAHHH!!
MY ONLY REGRET IS THAT I CANNOT KILL YOU.
THE SAME DOESN'T HOLD TRUE FOR THE CITY BELOW...

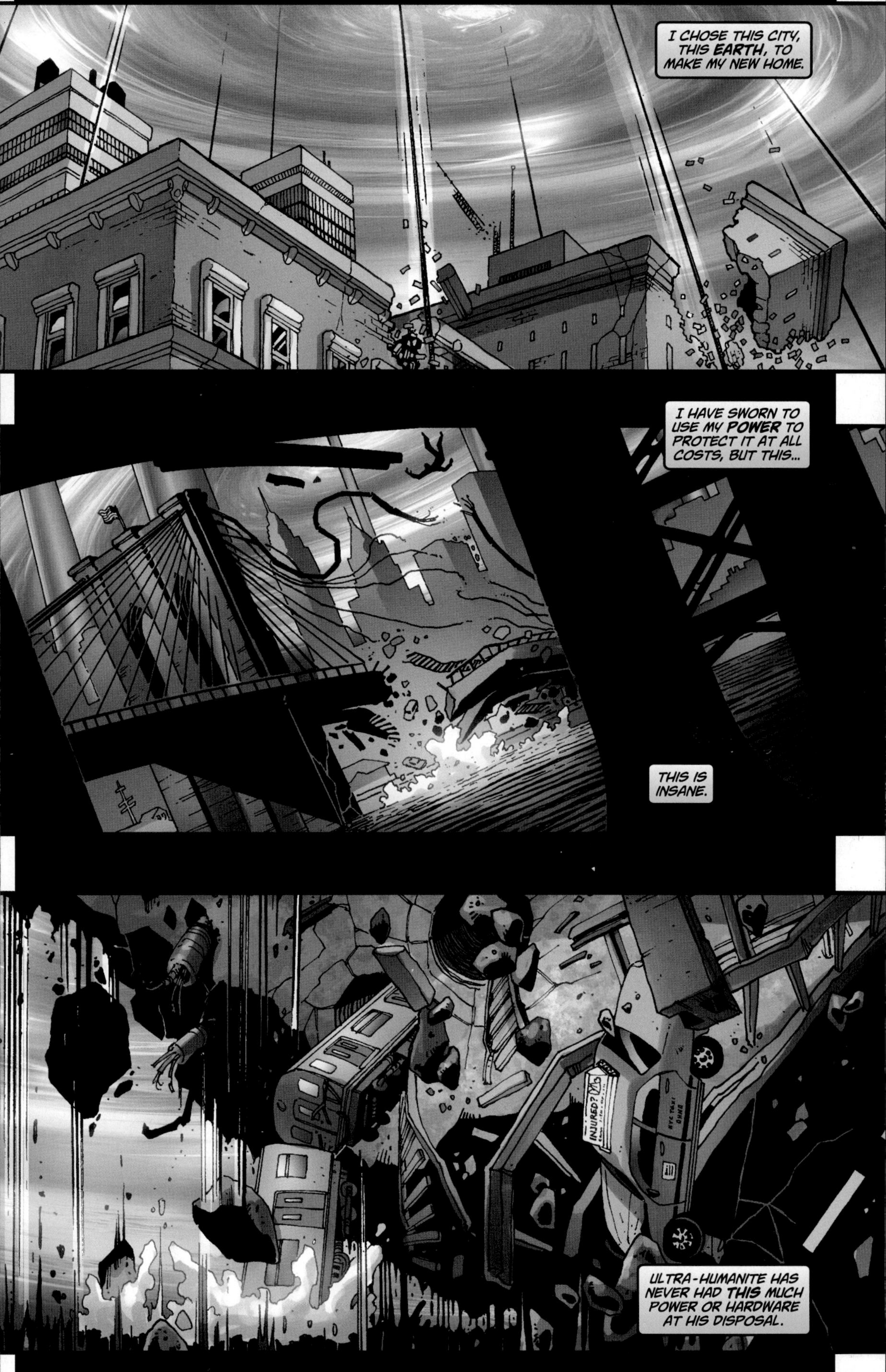
I CHOSE THIS CITY, THIS EARTH, TO MAKE MY NEW HOME.
I HAVE SWORN TO USE MY POWER TO PROTECT IT AT ALL COSTS, BUT THIS...
THIS IS INSANE.
INJURED?
ULTRA-HUMANITE HAS NEVER HAD THIS MUCH POWER OR HARDWARE AT HIS DISPOSAL.

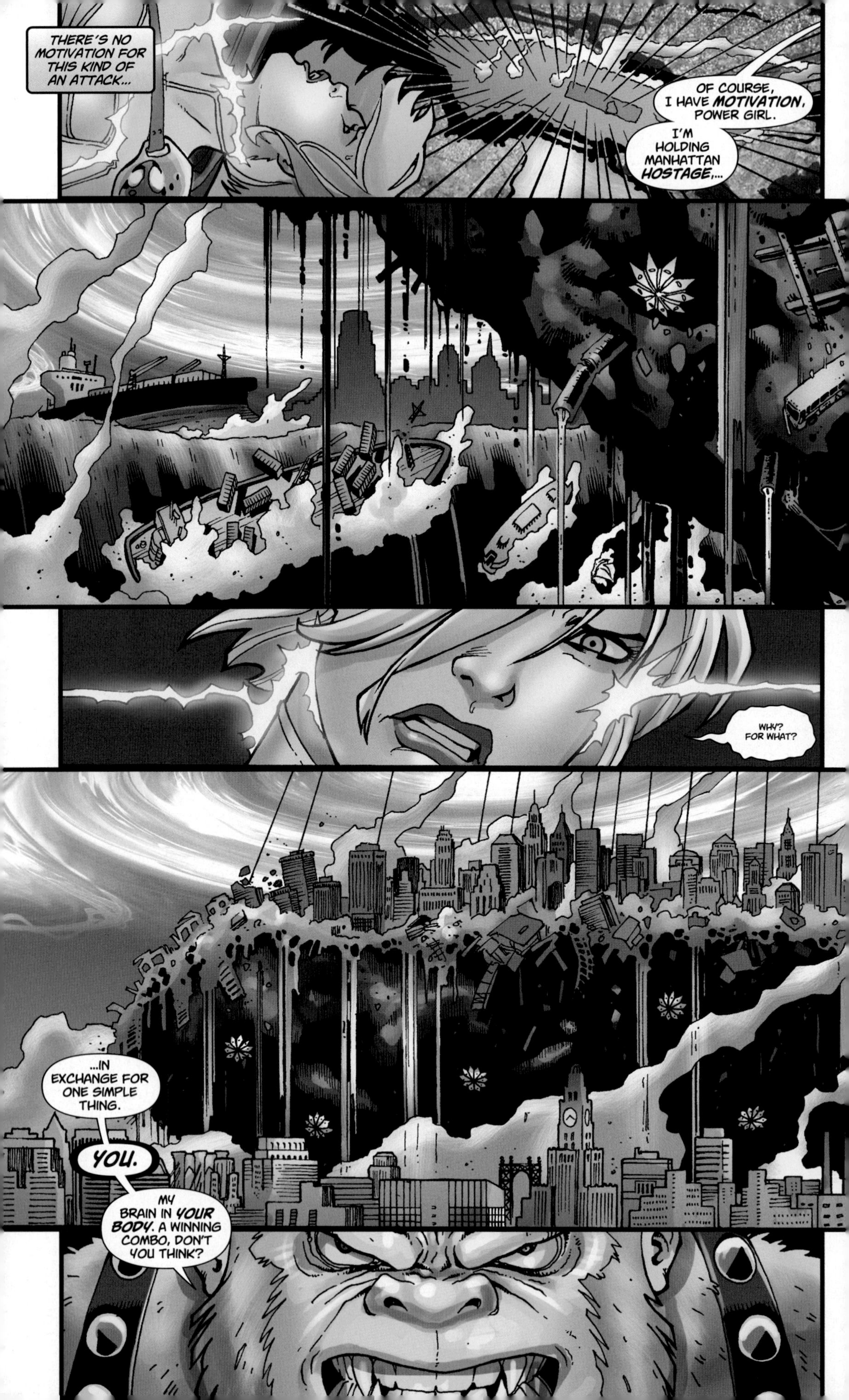
THERE'S NO MOTIVATION FOR THIS KIND OF AN ATTACK...
OF COURSE, I HAVE MOTIVATION, POWER GIRL.
I'M HOLDING MANHATTAN HOSTAGE,...
WHY? FOR WHAT?
...IN EXCHANGE FOR ONE SIMPLE THING.
YOU.
MY BRAIN IN YOUR BODY. A WINNING COMBO, DON'T YOU THINK?

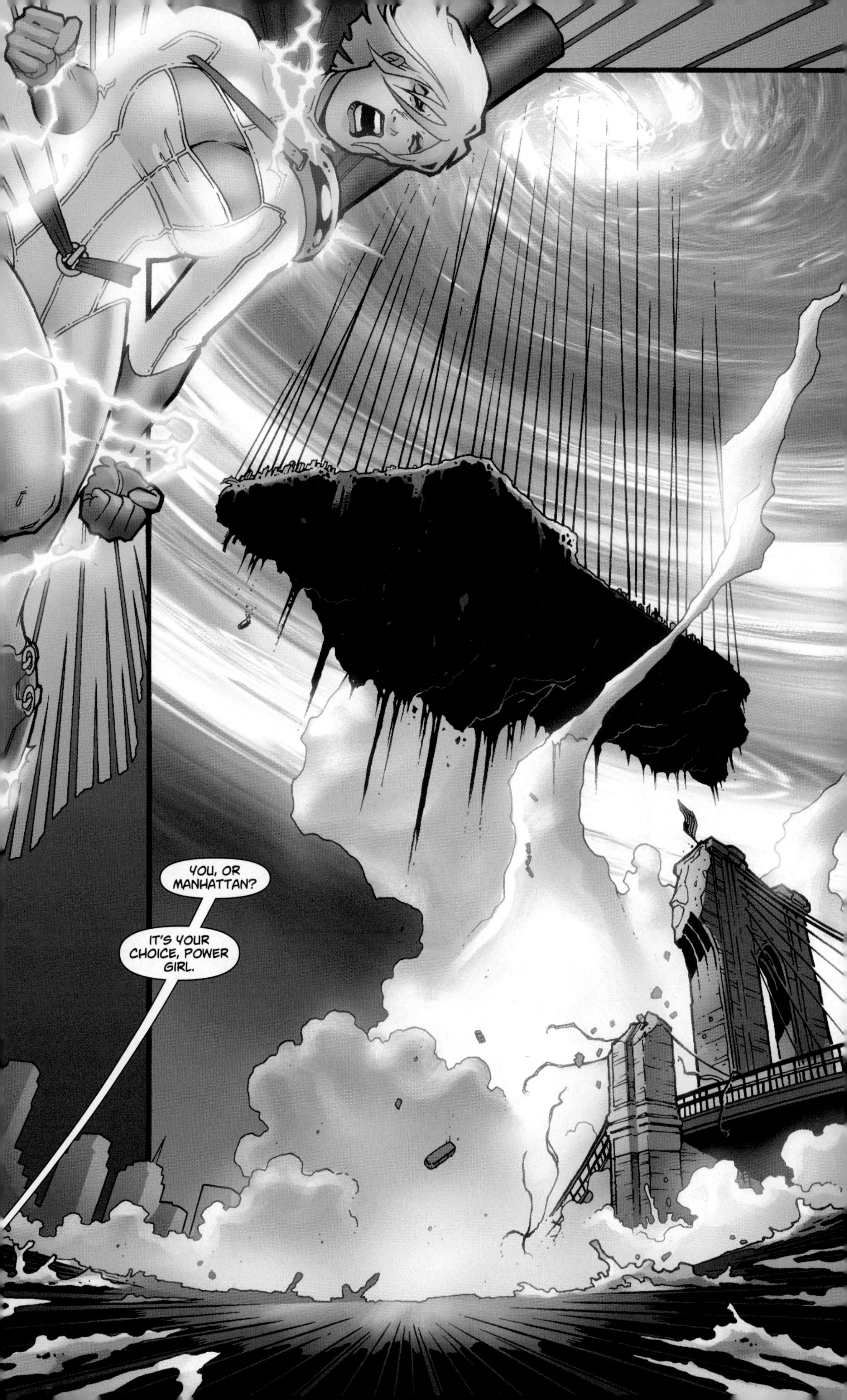
YOU, OR MANHATTAN?
IT'S YOUR CHOICE, POWER GIRL.

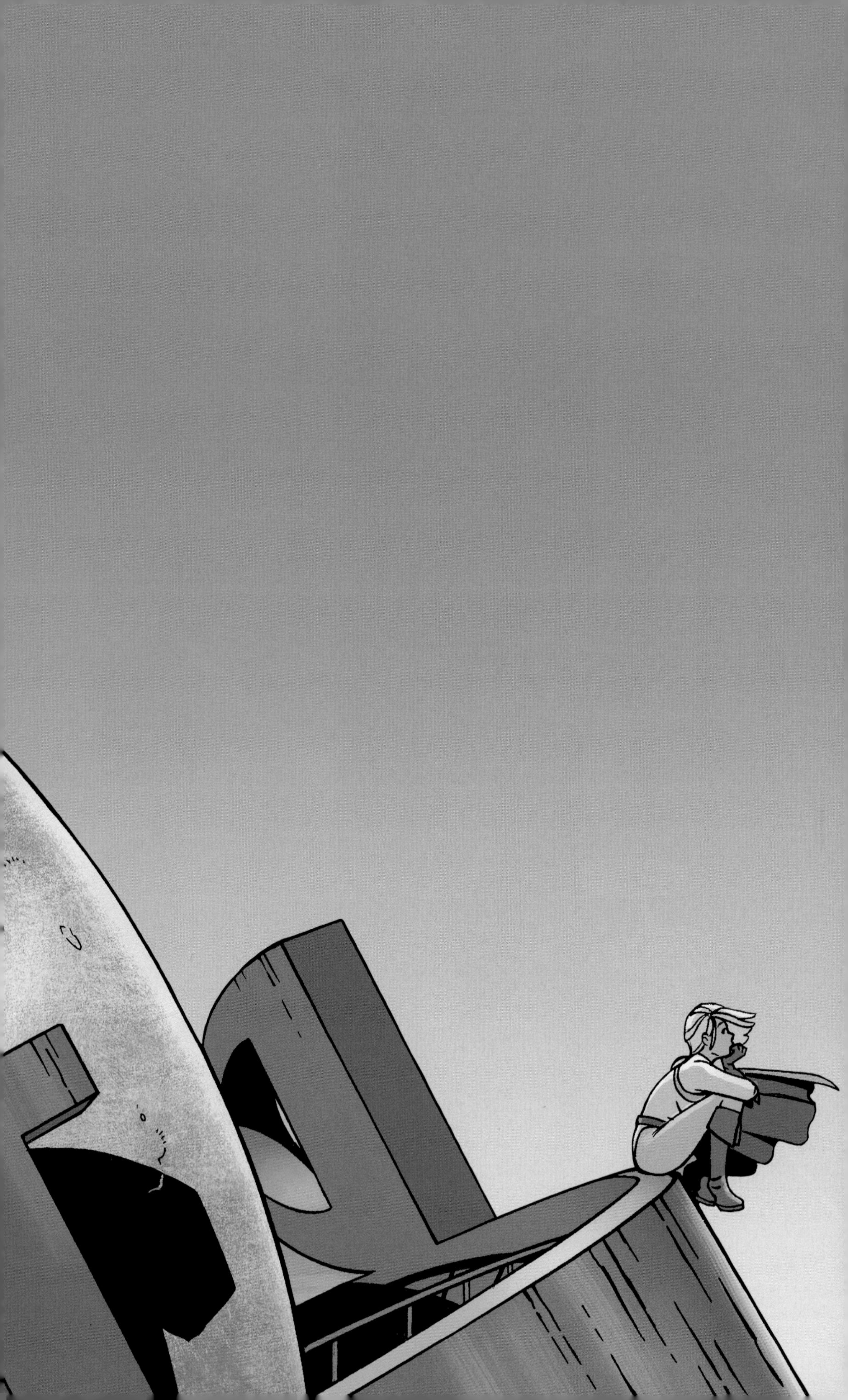

UNLEASHING THE BEAST

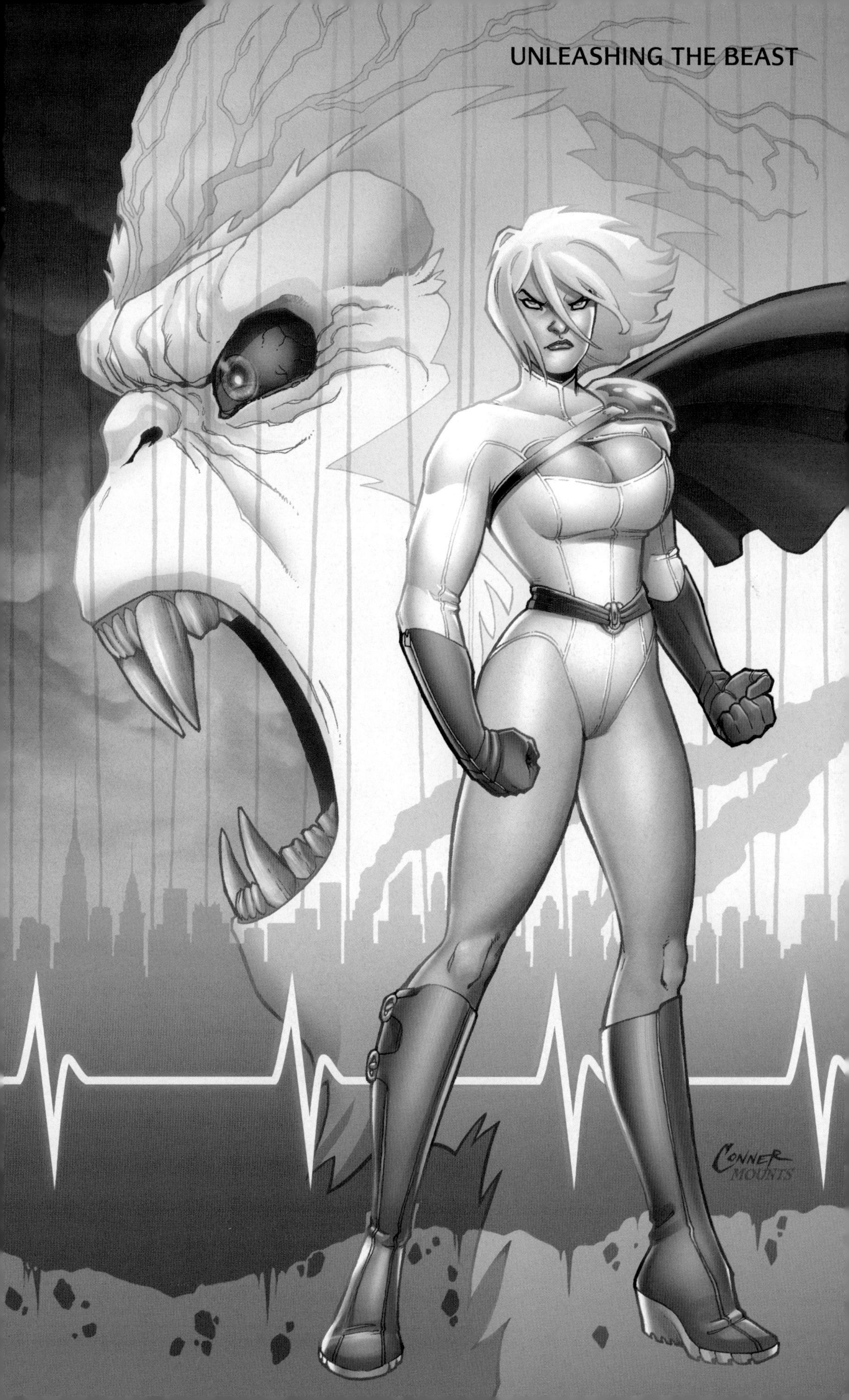
CONNER
MOUNTS

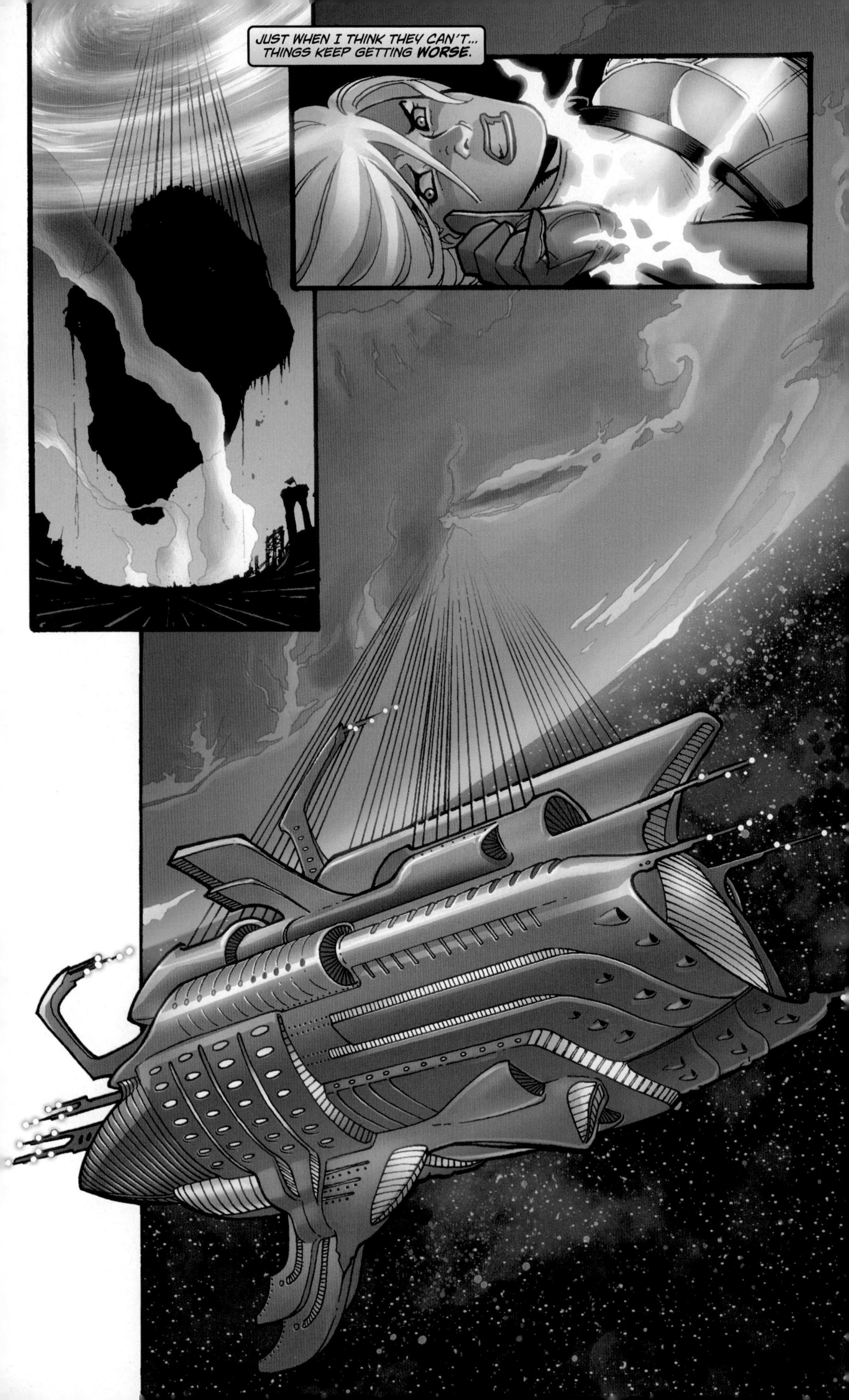
JUST WHEN I THINK THEY CAN'T... THINGS KEEP GETTING WORSE.

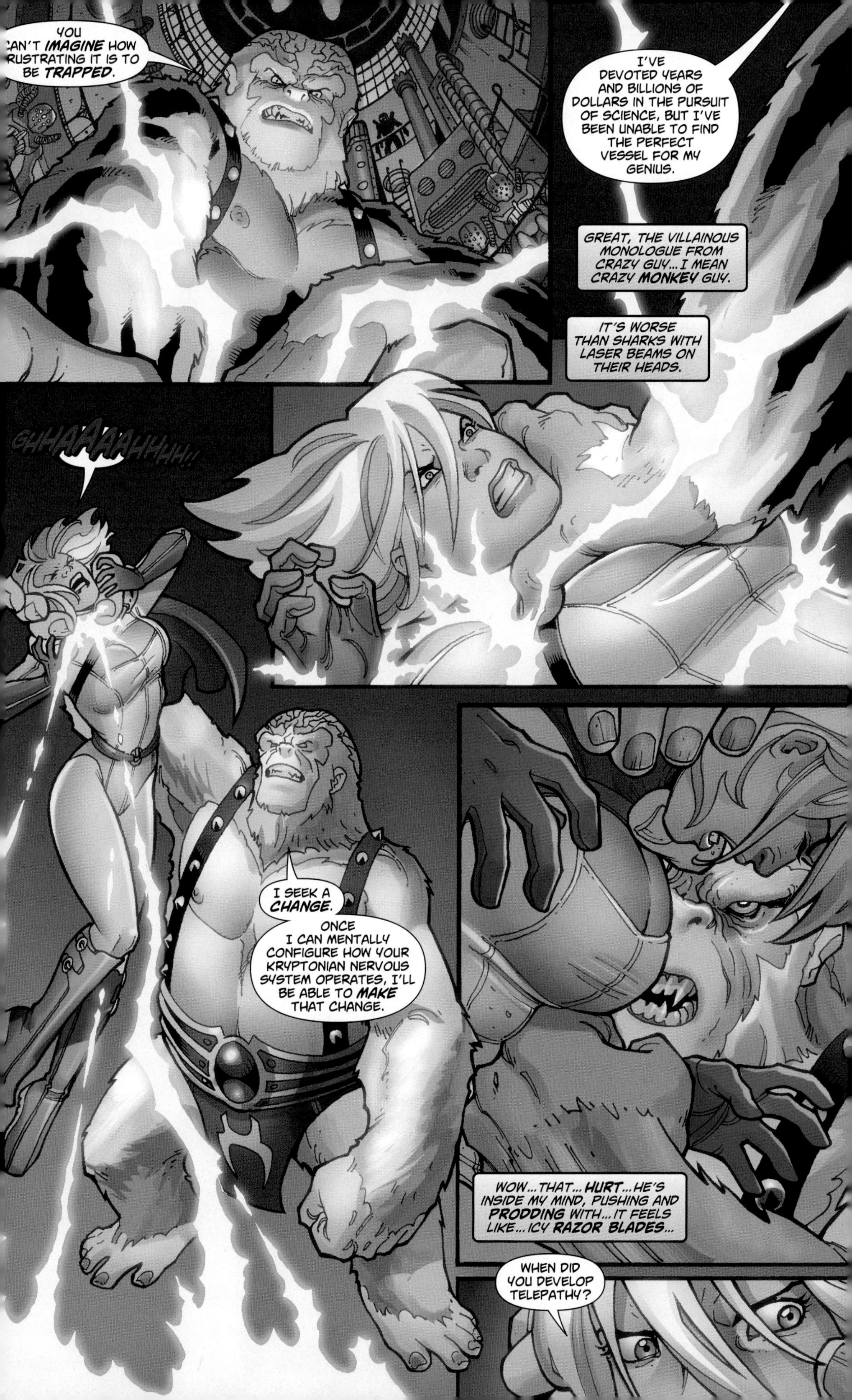
YOU CAN'T IMAGINE HOW FRUSTRATING IT IS TO BE TRAPPED.
I'VE DEVOTED YEARS AND BILLIONS OF DOLLARS IN THE PURSUIT OF SCIENCE, BUT I'VE BEEN UNABLE TO FIND THE PERFECT VESSEL FOR MY GENIUS.
GREAT, THE VILLAINOUS MONOLOGUE FROM CRAZY GUY... I MEAN CRAZY MONKEY GUY.
IT'S WORSE THAN SHARKS WITH LASER BEAMS ON THEIR HEADS.
GHHAAAAAHHHH!!
I SEEK A CHANGE.
ONCE I CAN MENTALLY CONFIGURE HOW YOUR KRYPTONIAN NERVOUS SYSTEM OPERATES, I'LL BE ABLE TO MAKE THAT CHANGE.
WOW... THAT... HURT... HE'S INSIDE MY MIND, PUSHING AND PRODDING WITH... IT FEELS LIKE... ICY RAZOR BLADES...
WHEN DID YOU DEVELOP TELEPATHY?

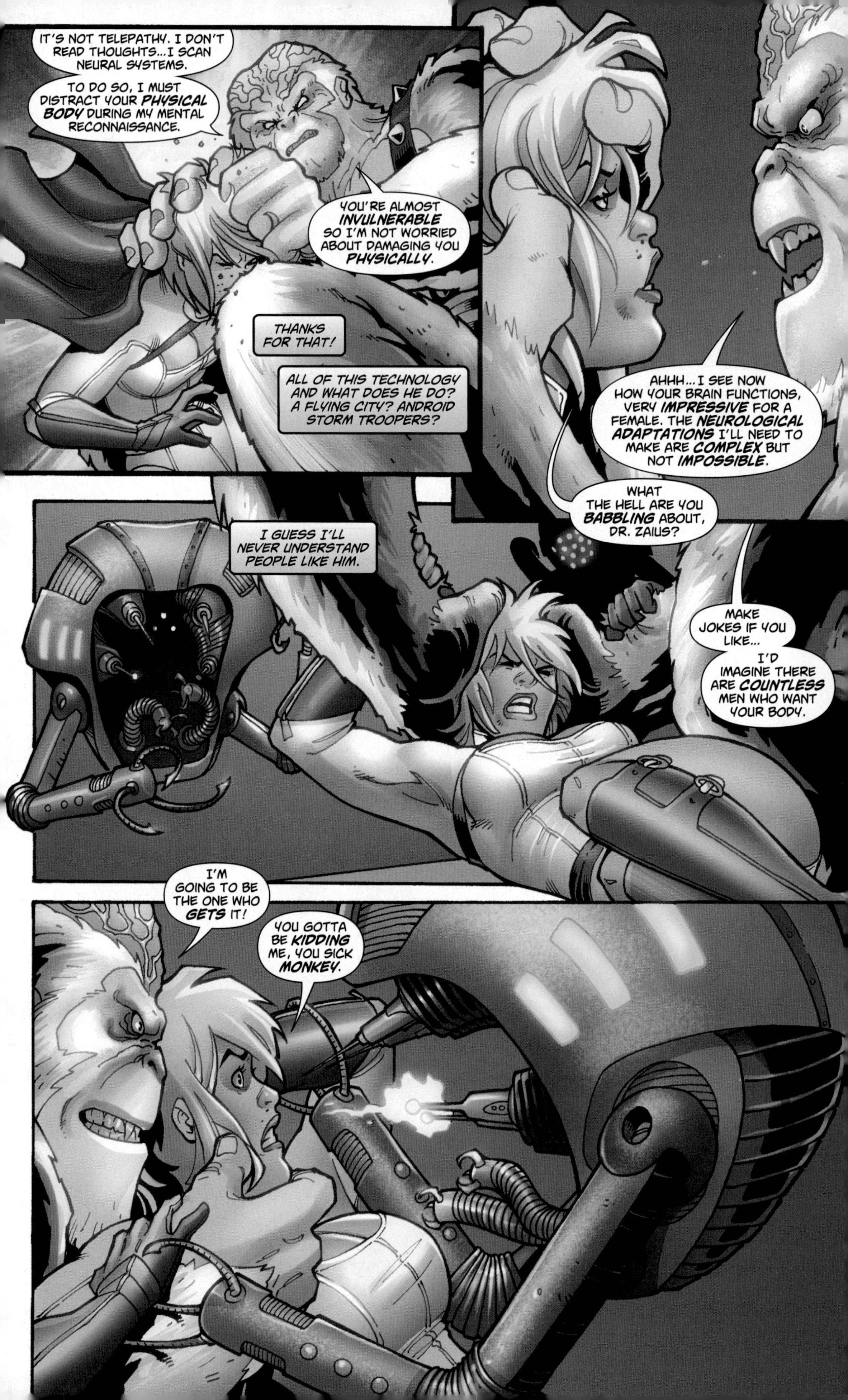
IT'S NOT TELEPATHY. I DON'T READ THOUGHTS...I SCAN NEURAL SYSTEMS.
TO DO SO, I MUST DISTRACT YOUR PHYSICAL BODY DURING MY MENTAL RECONNAISSANCE.
YOU'RE ALMOST INVULNERABLE SO I'M NOT WORRIED ABOUT DAMAGING YOU PHYSICALLY.
THANKS FOR THAT!
ALL OF THIS TECHNOLOGY AND WHAT DOES HE DO? A FLYING CITY? ANDROID STORM TROOPERS?
AHHH...I SEE NOW HOW YOUR BRAIN FUNCTIONS, VERY IMPRESSIVE FOR A FEMALE. THE NEUROLOGICAL ADAPTATIONS I'LL NEED TO MAKE ARE COMPLEX BUT NOT IMPOSSIBLE.
WHAT THE HELL ARE YOU BABBLING ABOUT, DR. ZAIUS?
I GUESS I'LL NEVER UNDERSTAND PEOPLE LIKE HIM.
MAKE JOKES IF YOU LIKE...
I'D IMAGINE THERE ARE COUNTLESS MEN WHO WANT YOUR BODY.
I'M GOING TO BE THE ONE WHO GETS IT!
YOU GOTTA BE KIDDING ME, YOU SICK MONKEY.

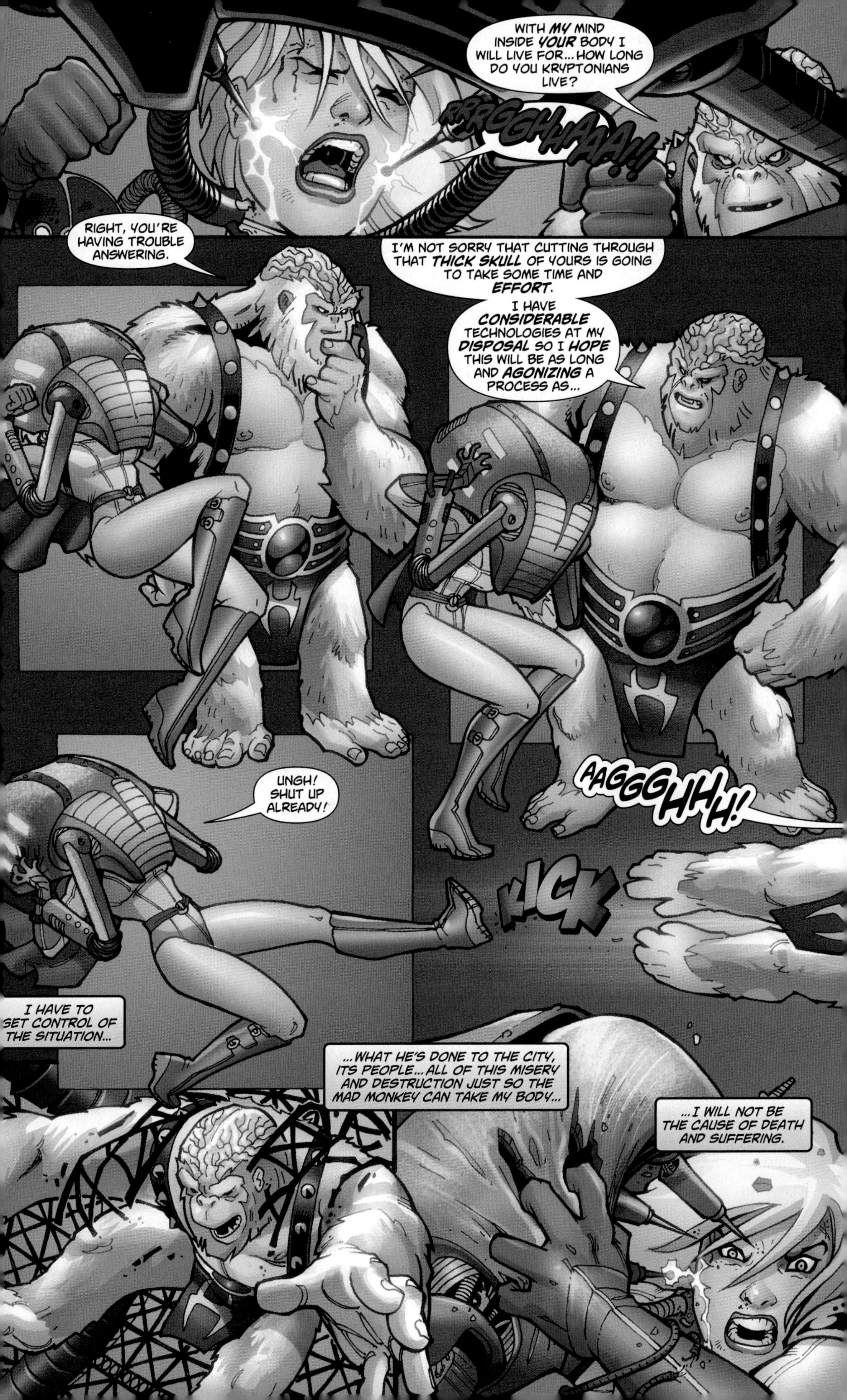
WITH MY MIND INSIDE YOUR BODY I WILL LIVE FOR... HOW LONG DO YOU KRYPTONIANS LIVE?
RRRGGHHAAA!!
RIGHT, YOU'RE HAVING TROUBLE ANSWERING.
I'M NOT SORRY THAT CUTTING THROUGH THAT THICK SKULL OF YOURS IS GOING TO TAKE SOME TIME AND EFFORT.
I HAVE CONSIDERABLE TECHNOLOGIES AT MY DISPOSAL SO I HOPE THIS WILL BE AS LONG AND AGONIZING A PROCESS AS...
UNGH! SHUT UP ALREADY!
AAGGGHHH!
KICK
I HAVE TO GET CONTROL OF THE SITUATION...
...WHAT HE'S DONE TO THE CITY, ITS PEOPLE... ALL OF THIS MISERY AND DESTRUCTION JUST SO THE MAD MONKEY CAN TAKE MY BODY...
...I WILL NOT BE THE CAUSE OF DEATH AND SUFFERING.

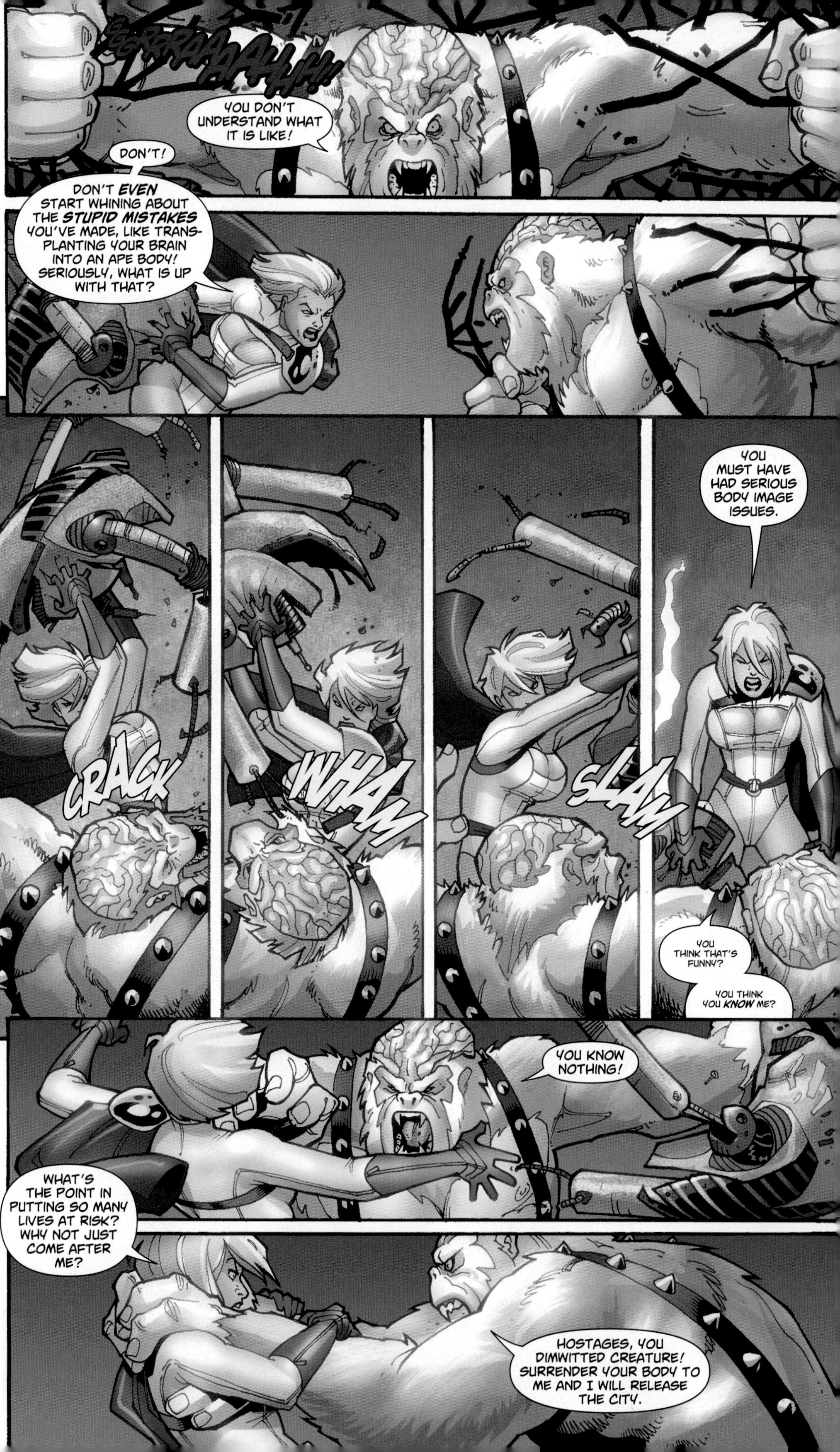
GGRRRAAAAAHHH!!
YOU DON'T UNDERSTAND WHAT IT IS LIKE!
DON'T!
DON'T **EVEN** START WHINING ABOUT THE ***STUPID MISTAKES*** YOU'VE MADE, LIKE TRANS-PLANTING YOUR BRAIN INTO AN APE BODY! SERIOUSLY, WHAT IS UP WITH THAT?
CRACK
WHAM
SLAM
YOU MUST HAVE HAD SERIOUS BODY IMAGE ISSUES.
YOU THINK THAT'S FUNNY?
YOU THINK YOU ***KNOW*** ME?
YOU KNOW NOTHING!
WHAT'S THE POINT IN PUTTING SO MANY LIVES AT RISK? WHY NOT JUST COME AFTER ME?
HOSTAGES, YOU DIMWITTED CREATURE! SURRENDER YOUR BODY TO ME AND I WILL RELEASE THE CITY.

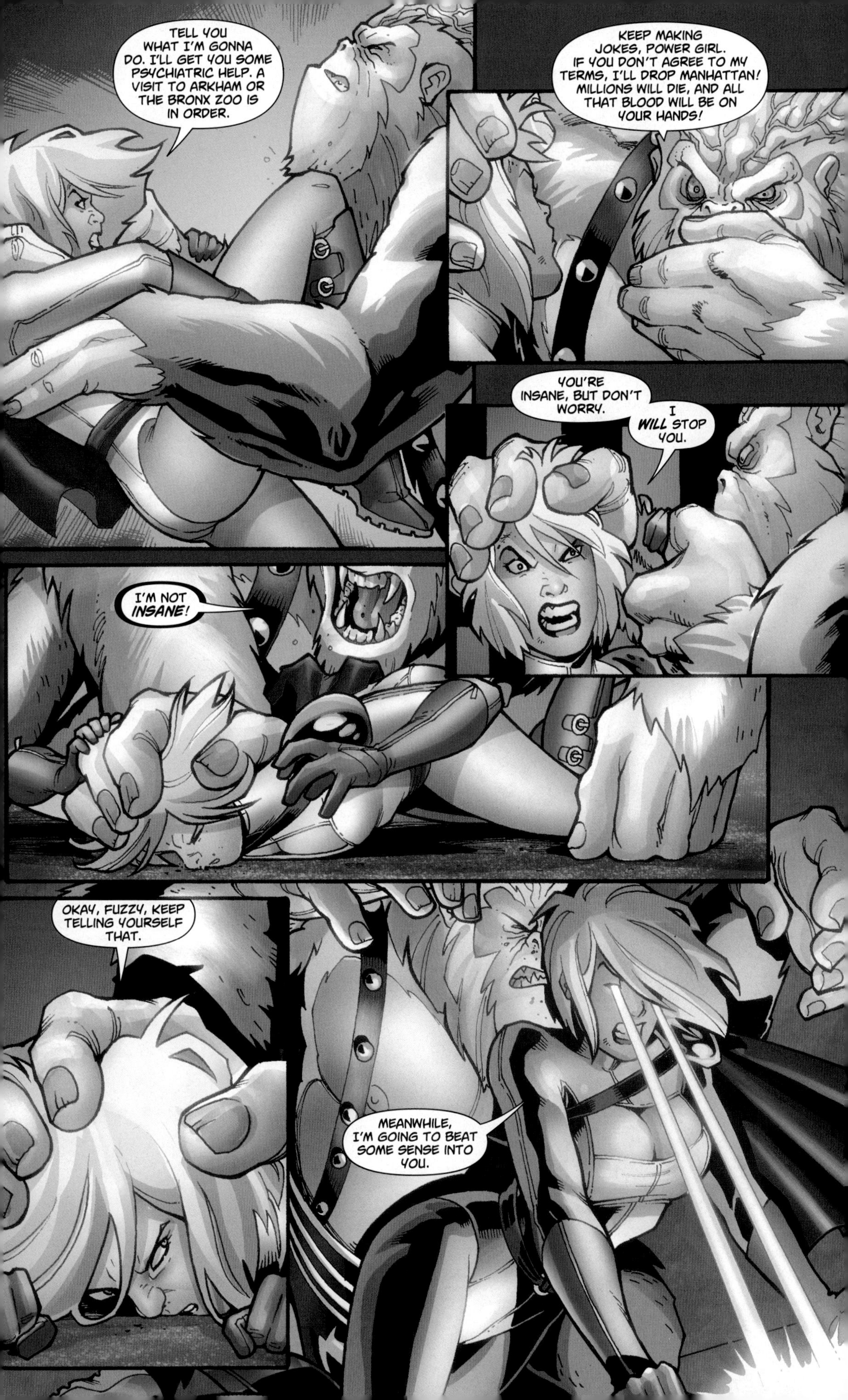
TELL YOU WHAT I'M GONNA DO. I'LL GET YOU SOME PSYCHIATRIC HELP. A VISIT TO ARKHAM OR THE BRONX ZOO IS IN ORDER.
KEEP MAKING JOKES, POWER GIRL. IF YOU DON'T AGREE TO MY TERMS, I'LL DROP MANHATTAN! MILLIONS WILL DIE, AND ALL THAT BLOOD WILL BE ON YOUR HANDS!
YOU'RE INSANE, BUT DON'T WORRY.
I WILL STOP YOU.
I'M NOT INSANE!
OKAY, FUZZY, KEEP TELLING YOURSELF THAT.
MEANWHILE, I'M GOING TO BEAT SOME SENSE INTO YOU.

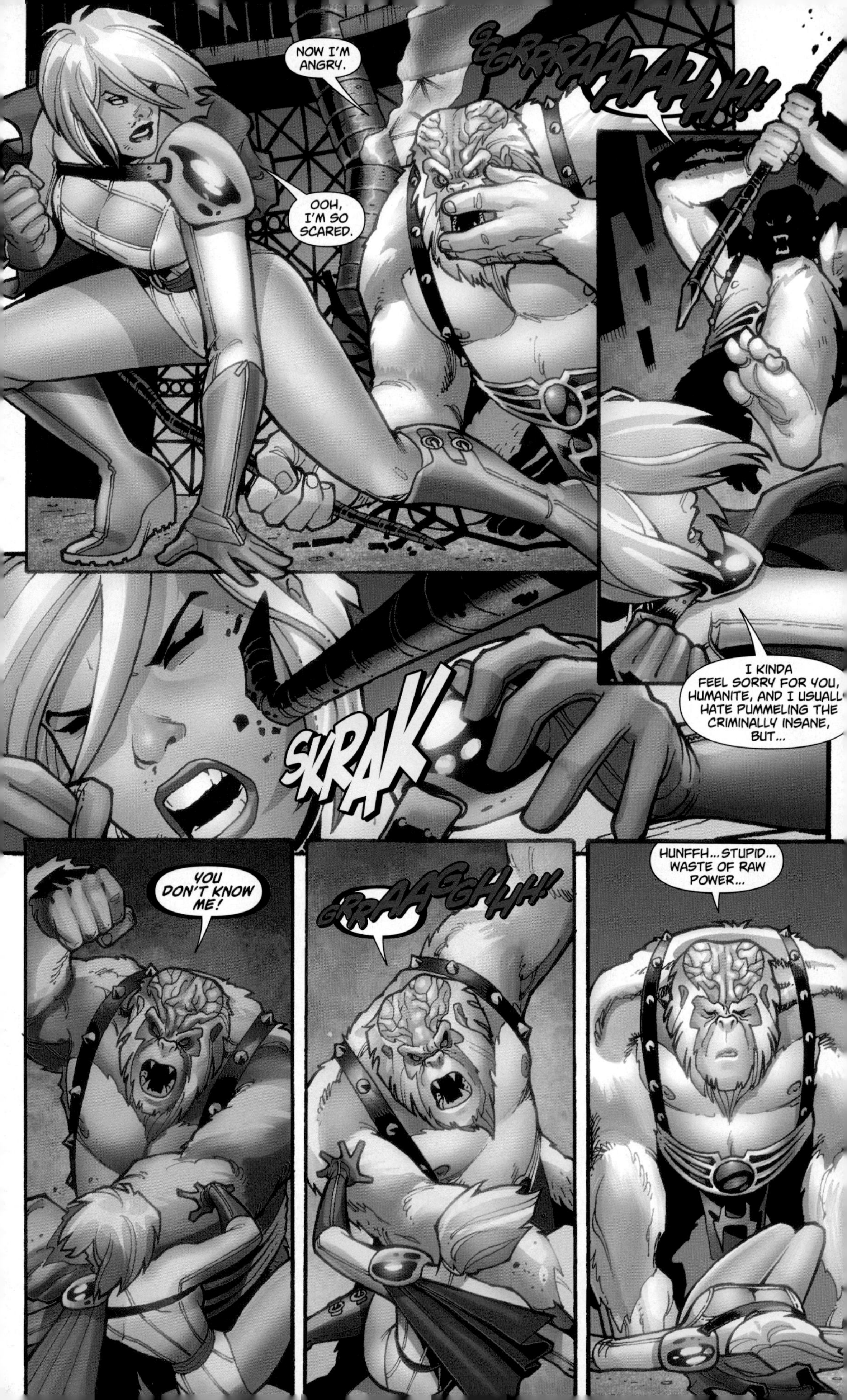
NOW I'M ANGRY.
OOH, I'M SO SCARED.
GGGRRRAAAAAAHHH!!
I KINDA FEEL SORRY FOR YOU, HUMANITE, AND I USUALL HATE PUMMELING THE CRIMINALLY INSANE, BUT...
SKRAK
YOU DON'T KNOW ME!
GRRAAAGHHH!!
HUNFFH... STUPID... WASTE OF RAW POWER...

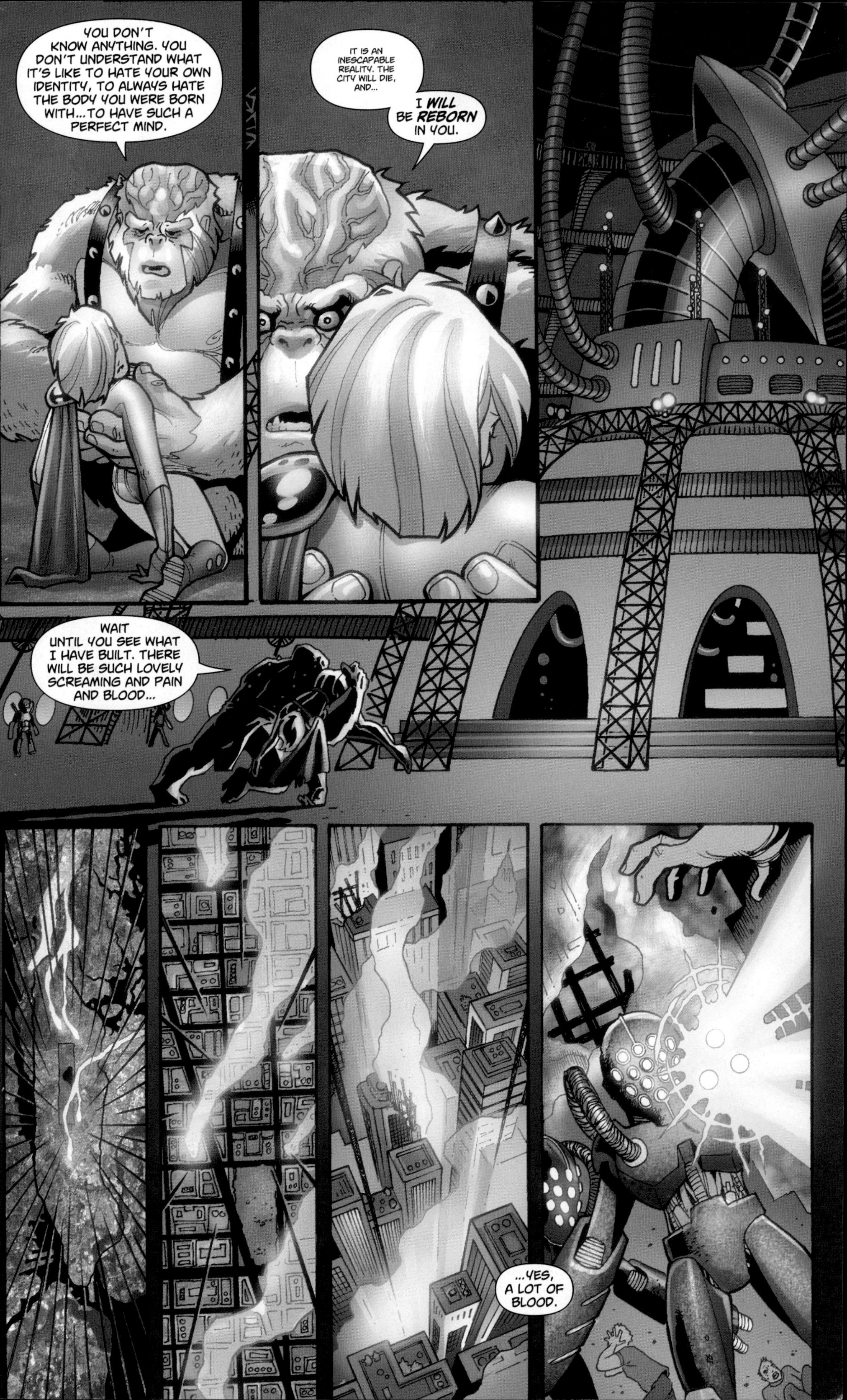
YOU DON'T KNOW ANYTHING. YOU DON'T UNDERSTAND WHAT IT'S LIKE TO HATE YOUR OWN IDENTITY, TO ALWAYS HATE THE BODY YOU WERE BORN WITH...TO HAVE SUCH A PERFECT MIND.
IT IS AN INESCAPABLE REALITY. THE CITY WILL DIE, AND...
I WILL BE REBORN IN YOU.
WAIT UNTIL YOU SEE WHAT I HAVE BUILT. THERE WILL BE SUCH LOVELY SCREAMING AND PAIN AND BLOOD...
...YES, A LOT OF BLOOD.

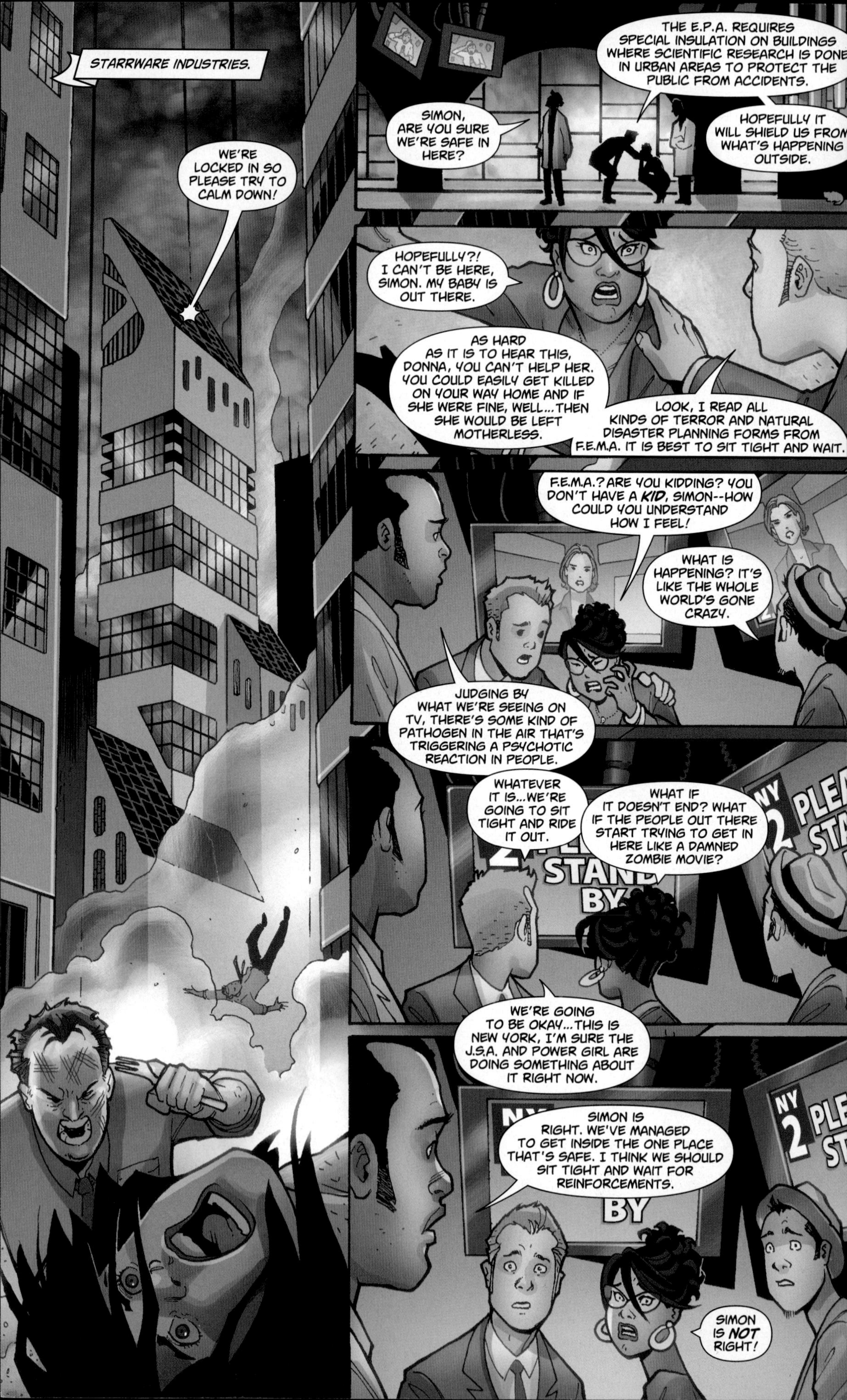
STARRWARE INDUSTRIES.
WE'RE LOCKED IN SO PLEASE TRY TO CALM DOWN!
SIMON, ARE YOU SURE WE'RE SAFE IN HERE?
THE E.P.A. REQUIRES SPECIAL INSULATION ON BUILDINGS WHERE SCIENTIFIC RESEARCH IS DONE IN URBAN AREAS TO PROTECT THE PUBLIC FROM ACCIDENTS.
HOPEFULLY IT WILL SHIELD US FROM WHAT'S HAPPENING OUTSIDE.
HOPEFULLY?! I CAN'T BE HERE, SIMON. MY BABY IS OUT THERE.
AS HARD AS IT IS TO HEAR THIS, DONNA, YOU CAN'T HELP HER. YOU COULD EASILY GET KILLED ON YOUR WAY HOME AND IF SHE WERE FINE, WELL...THEN SHE WOULD BE LEFT MOTHERLESS.
LOOK, I READ ALL KINDS OF TERROR AND NATURAL DISASTER PLANNING FORMS FROM F.E.M.A. IT IS BEST TO SIT TIGHT AND WAIT.
F.E.M.A.? ARE YOU KIDDING? YOU DON'T HAVE A KID, SIMON--HOW COULD YOU UNDERSTAND HOW I FEEL!
WHAT IS HAPPENING? IT'S LIKE THE WHOLE WORLD'S GONE CRAZY.
JUDGING BY WHAT WE'RE SEEING ON TV, THERE'S SOME KIND OF PATHOGEN IN THE AIR THAT'S TRIGGERING A PSYCHOTIC REACTION IN PEOPLE.
WHATEVER IT IS...WE'RE GOING TO SIT TIGHT AND RIDE IT OUT.
WHAT IF IT DOESN'T END? WHAT IF THE PEOPLE OUT THERE START TRYING TO GET IN HERE LIKE A DAMNED ZOMBIE MOVIE?
STAND BY
WE'RE GOING TO BE OKAY...THIS IS NEW YORK, I'M SURE THE J.S.A. AND POWER GIRL ARE DOING SOMETHING ABOUT IT RIGHT NOW.
SIMON IS RIGHT. WE'VE MANAGED TO GET INSIDE THE ONE PLACE THAT'S SAFE. I THINK WE SHOULD SIT TIGHT AND WAIT FOR REINFORCEMENTS.
BY
SIMON IS NOT RIGHT!

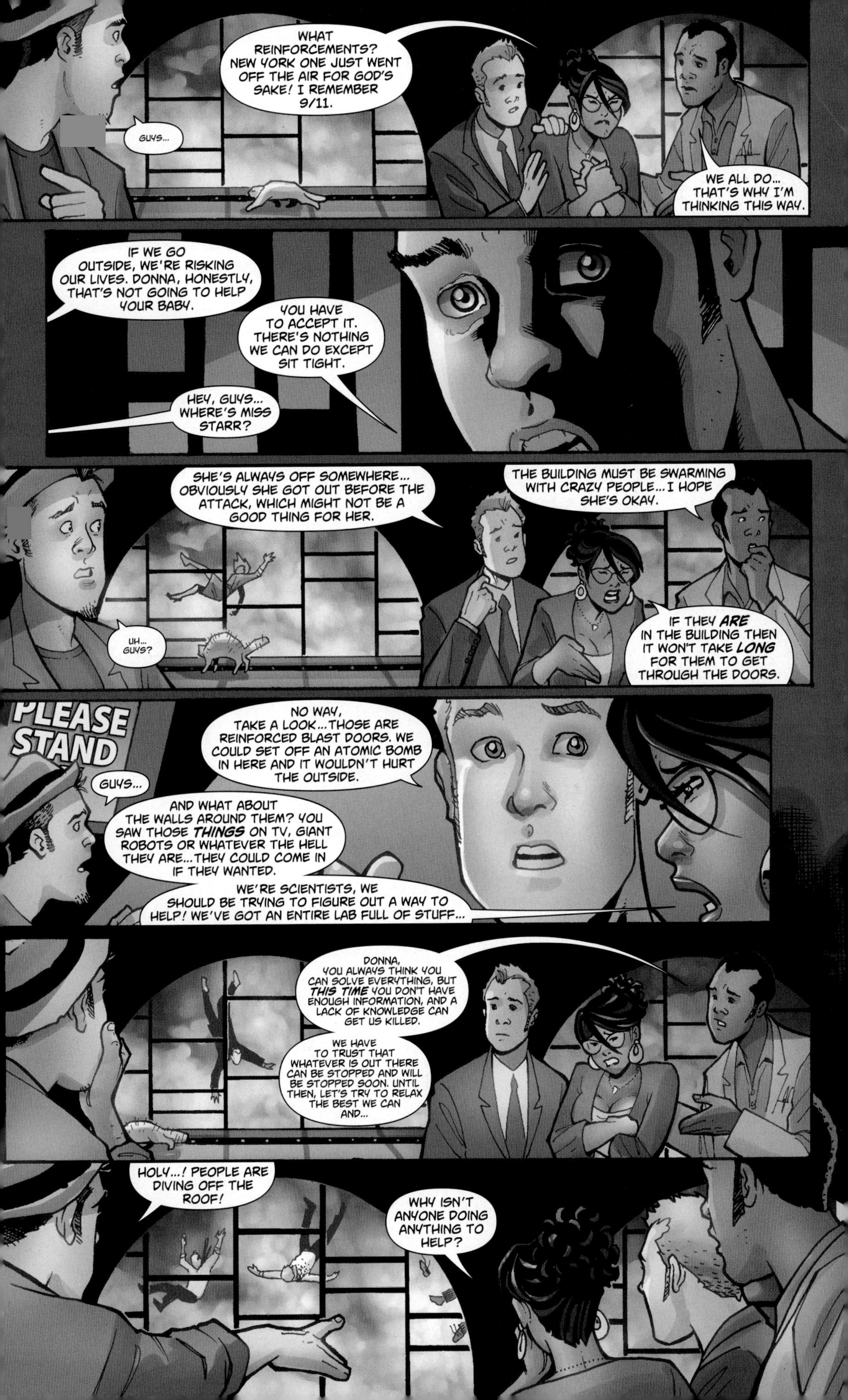
WHAT REINFORCEMENTS? NEW YORK ONE JUST WENT OFF THE AIR FOR GOD'S SAKE! I REMEMBER 9/11.
GUYS...
WE ALL DO... THAT'S WHY I'M THINKING THIS WAY.
IF WE GO OUTSIDE, WE'RE RISKING OUR LIVES. DONNA, HONESTLY, THAT'S NOT GOING TO HELP YOUR BABY.
YOU HAVE TO ACCEPT IT. THERE'S NOTHING WE CAN DO EXCEPT SIT TIGHT.
HEY, GUYS... WHERE'S MISS STARR?
SHE'S ALWAYS OFF SOMEWHERE... OBVIOUSLY SHE GOT OUT BEFORE THE ATTACK, WHICH MIGHT NOT BE A GOOD THING FOR HER.
THE BUILDING MUST BE SWARMING WITH CRAZY PEOPLE... I HOPE SHE'S OKAY.
UH... GUYS?
IF THEY ARE IN THE BUILDING THEN IT WON'T TAKE LONG FOR THEM TO GET THROUGH THE DOORS.
PLEASE STAND
NO WAY, TAKE A LOOK... THOSE ARE REINFORCED BLAST DOORS. WE COULD SET OFF AN ATOMIC BOMB IN HERE AND IT WOULDN'T HURT THE OUTSIDE.
GUYS...
AND WHAT ABOUT THE WALLS AROUND THEM? YOU SAW THOSE THINGS ON TV, GIANT ROBOTS OR WHATEVER THE HELL THEY ARE... THEY COULD COME IN IF THEY WANTED.
WE'RE SCIENTISTS, WE SHOULD BE TRYING TO FIGURE OUT A WAY TO HELP! WE'VE GOT AN ENTIRE LAB FULL OF STUFF...
DONNA, YOU ALWAYS THINK YOU CAN SOLVE EVERYTHING, BUT THIS TIME YOU DON'T HAVE ENOUGH INFORMATION, AND A LACK OF KNOWLEDGE CAN GET US KILLED.
WE HAVE TO TRUST THAT WHATEVER IS OUT THERE CAN BE STOPPED AND WILL BE STOPPED SOON. UNTIL THEN, LET'S TRY TO RELAX THE BEST WE CAN AND...
HOLY...! PEOPLE ARE DIVING OFF THE ROOF!
WHY ISN'T ANYONE DOING ANYTHING TO HELP?

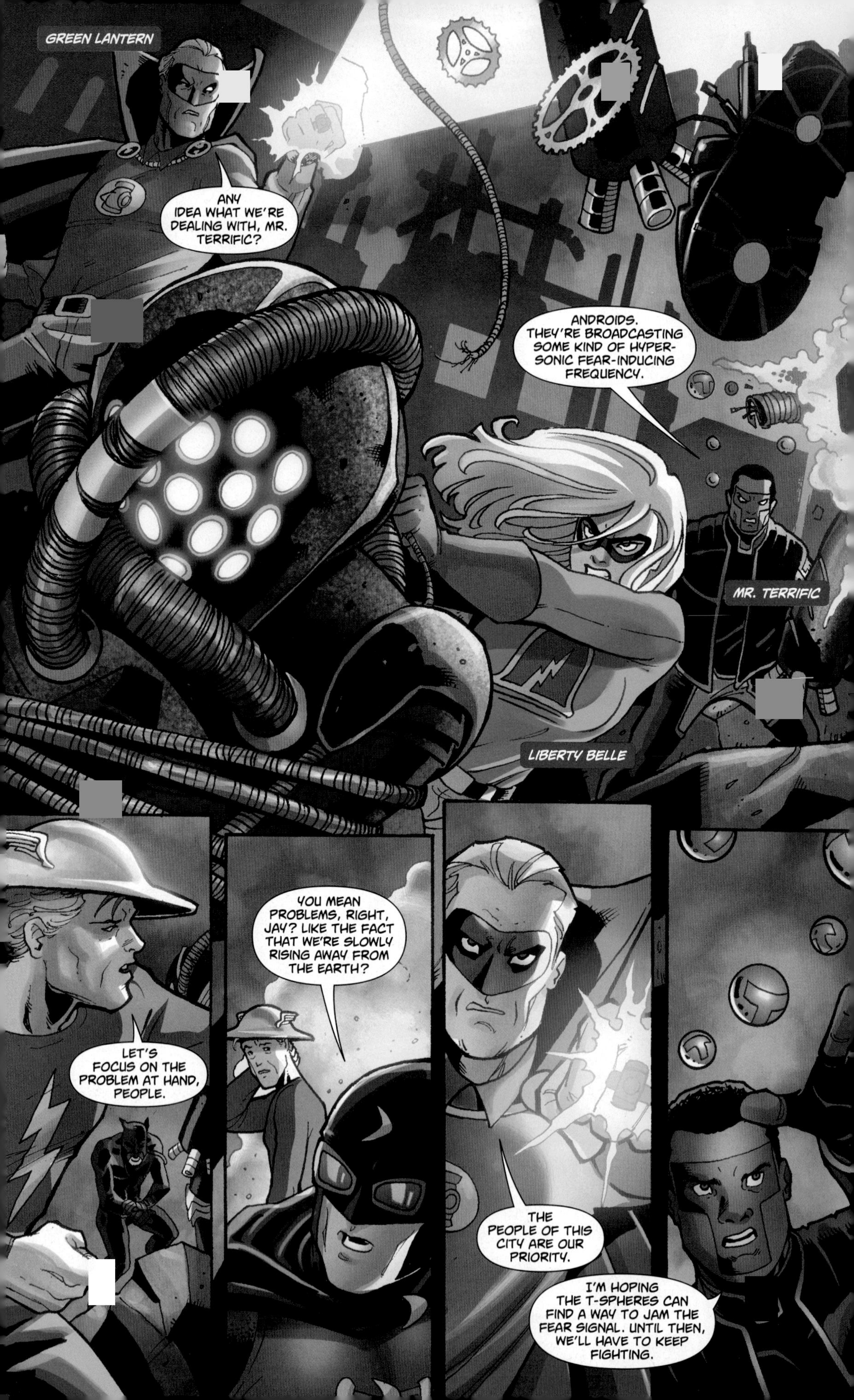
GREEN LANTERN
ANY IDEA WHAT WE'RE DEALING WITH, MR. TERRIFIC?
ANDROIDS. THEY'RE BROADCASTING SOME KIND OF HYPER-SONIC FEAR-INDUCING FREQUENCY.
MR. TERRIFIC
LIBERTY BELLE
LET'S FOCUS ON THE PROBLEM AT HAND, PEOPLE.
YOU MEAN PROBLEMS, RIGHT, JAY? LIKE THE FACT THAT WE'RE SLOWLY RISING AWAY FROM THE EARTH?
THE PEOPLE OF THIS CITY ARE OUR PRIORITY.
I'M HOPING THE T-SPHERES CAN FIND A WAY TO JAM THE FEAR SIGNAL. UNTIL THEN, WE'LL HAVE TO KEEP FIGHTING.

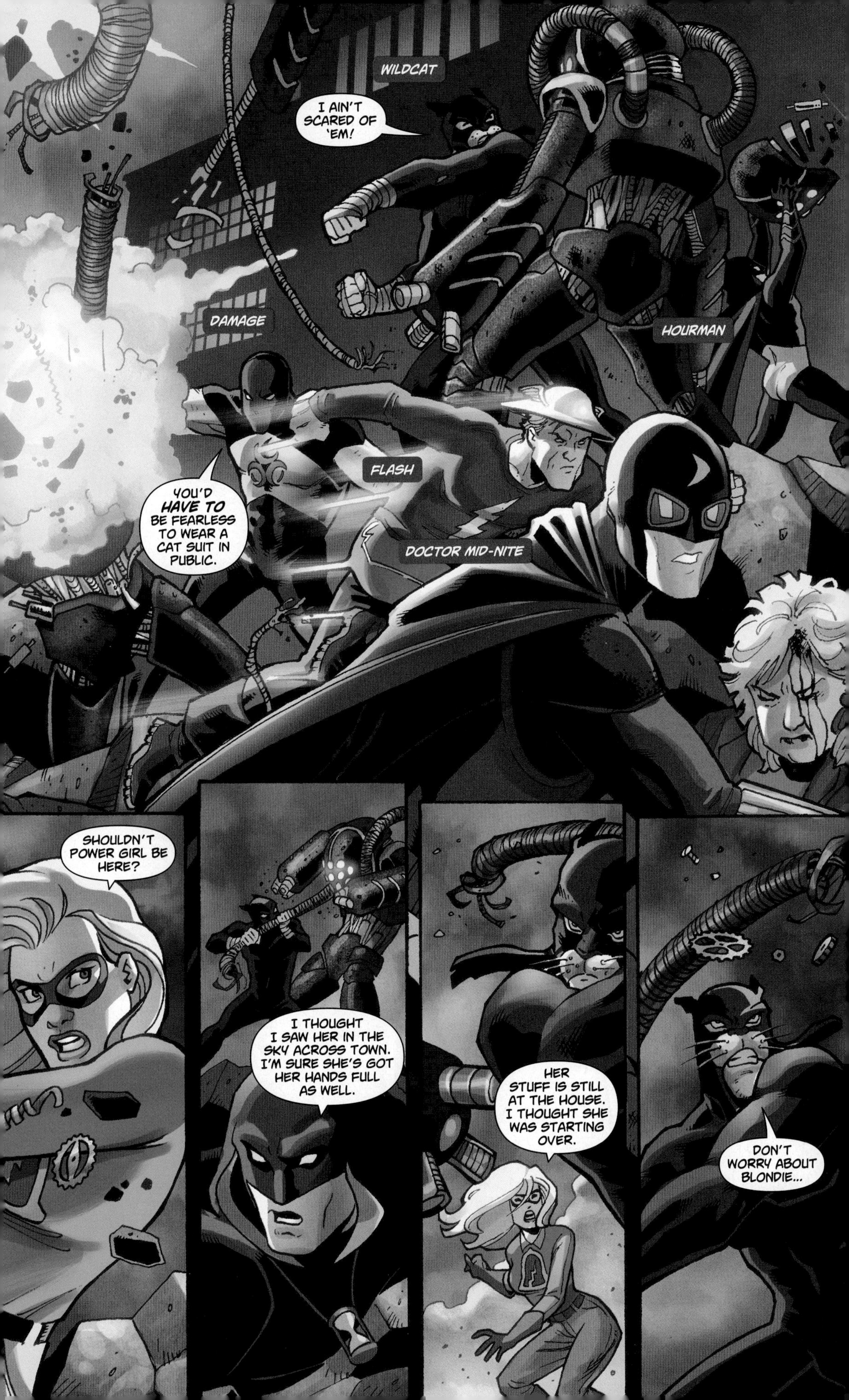
WILDCAT
I AIN'T SCARED OF 'EM!
DAMAGE
HOURMAN
FLASH
DOCTOR MID-NITE
YOU'D HAVE TO BE FEARLESS TO WEAR A CAT SUIT IN PUBLIC.
SHOULDN'T POWER GIRL BE HERE?
I THOUGHT I SAW HER IN THE SKY ACROSS TOWN. I'M SURE SHE'S GOT HER HANDS FULL AS WELL.
HER STUFF IS STILL AT THE HOUSE. I THOUGHT SHE WAS STARTING OVER.
DON'T WORRY ABOUT BLONDIE...

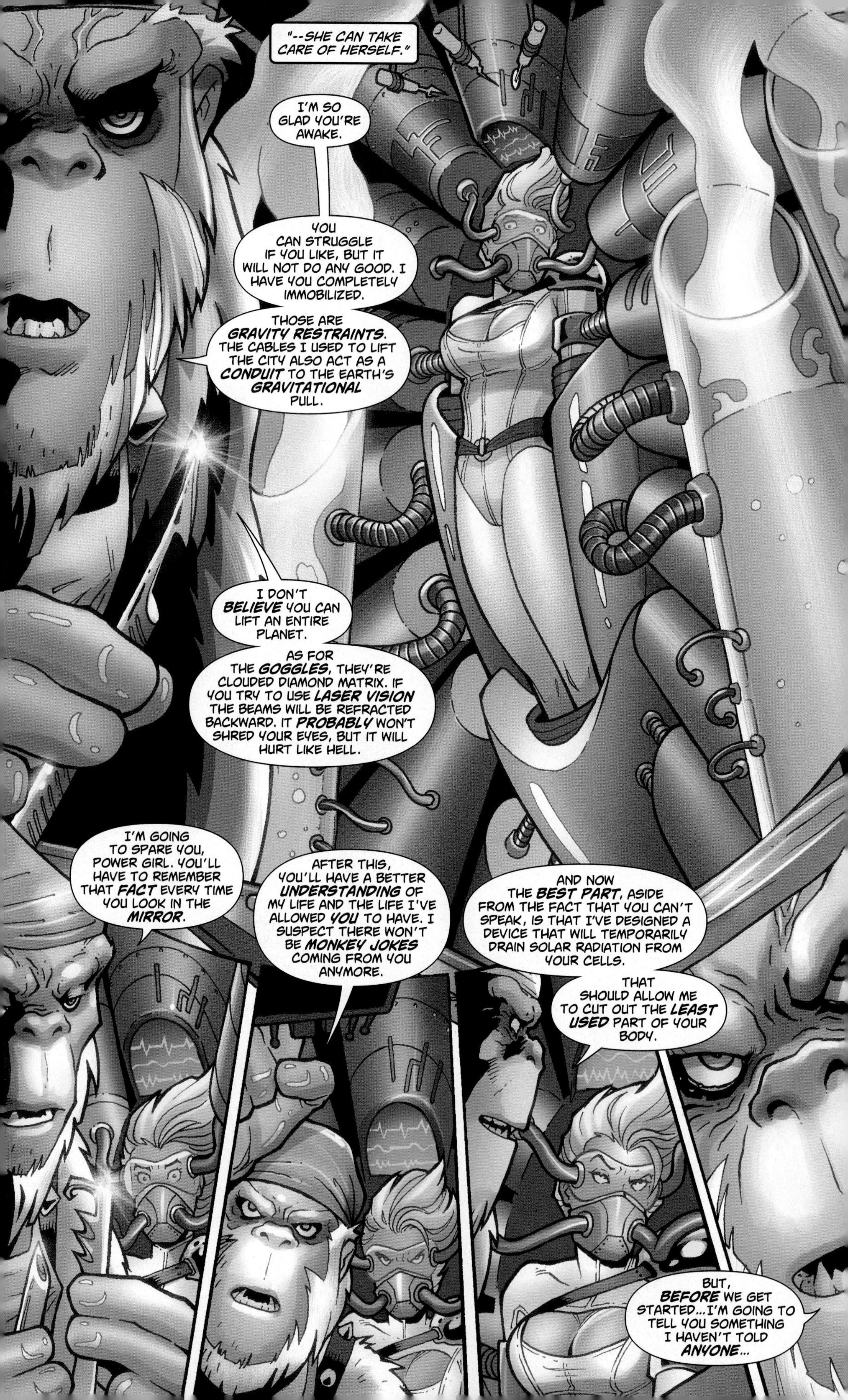
"--SHE CAN TAKE CARE OF HERSELF."
I'M SO GLAD YOU'RE AWAKE.
YOU CAN STRUGGLE IF YOU LIKE, BUT IT WILL NOT DO ANY GOOD. I HAVE YOU COMPLETELY IMMOBILIZED.
THOSE ARE GRAVITY RESTRAINTS. THE CABLES I USED TO LIFT THE CITY ALSO ACT AS A CONDUIT TO THE EARTH'S GRAVITATIONAL PULL.
I DON'T BELIEVE YOU CAN LIFT AN ENTIRE PLANET.
AS FOR THE GOGGLES, THEY'RE CLOUDED DIAMOND MATRIX. IF YOU TRY TO USE LASER VISION THE BEAMS WILL BE REFRACTED BACKWARD. IT PROBABLY WON'T SHRED YOUR EYES, BUT IT WILL HURT LIKE HELL.
I'M GOING TO SPARE YOU, POWER GIRL. YOU'LL HAVE TO REMEMBER THAT FACT EVERY TIME YOU LOOK IN THE MIRROR.
AFTER THIS, YOU'LL HAVE A BETTER UNDERSTANDING OF MY LIFE AND THE LIFE I'VE ALLOWED YOU TO HAVE. I SUSPECT THERE WON'T BE MONKEY JOKES COMING FROM YOU ANYMORE.
AND NOW THE BEST PART, ASIDE FROM THE FACT THAT YOU CAN'T SPEAK, IS THAT I'VE DESIGNED A DEVICE THAT WILL TEMPORARILY DRAIN SOLAR RADIATION FROM YOUR CELLS.
THAT SHOULD ALLOW ME TO CUT OUT THE LEAST USED PART OF YOUR BODY.
BUT, BEFORE WE GET STARTED...I'M GOING TO TELL YOU SOMETHING I HAVEN'T TOLD ANYONE...

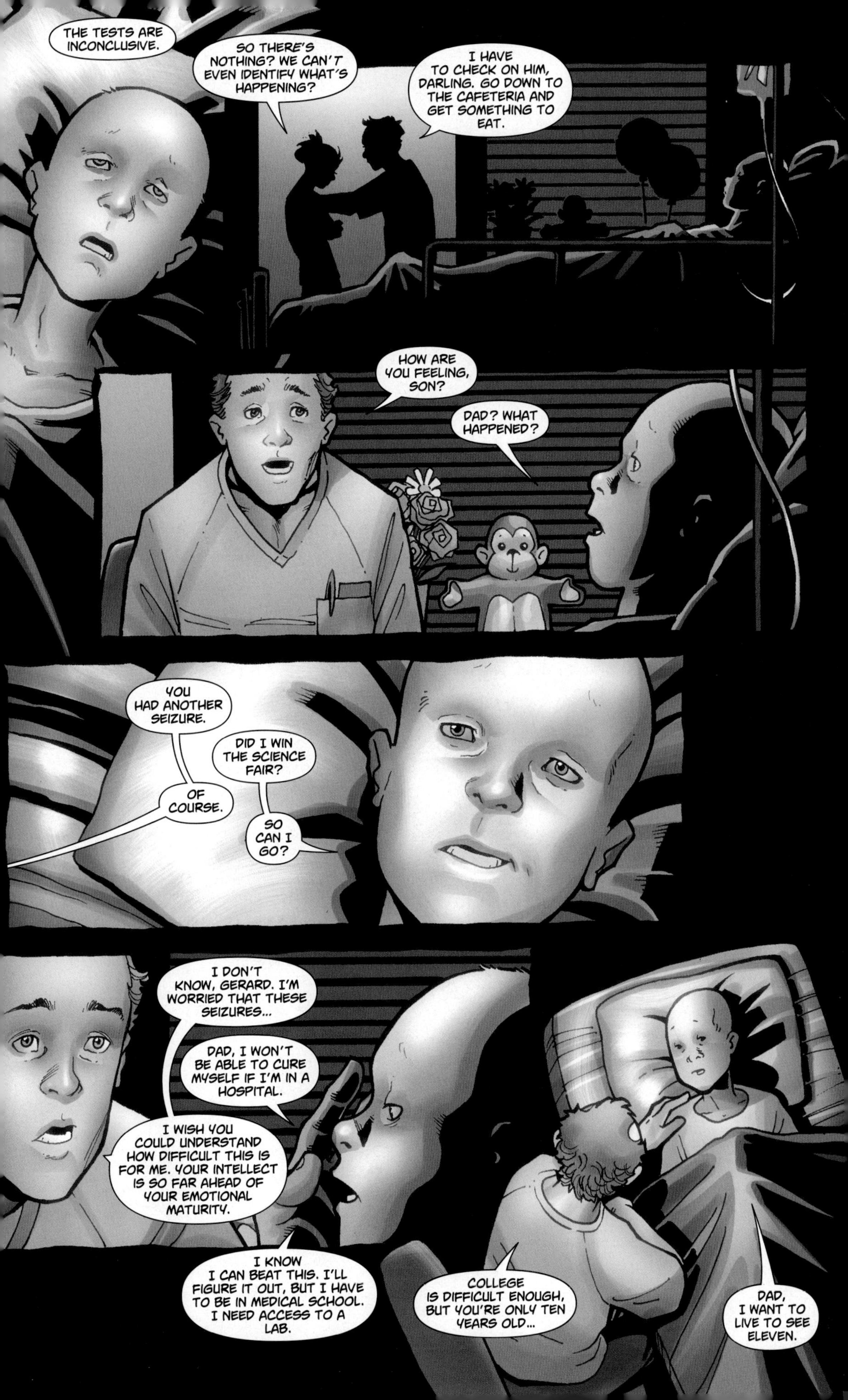
THE TESTS ARE INCONCLUSIVE.
SO THERE'S NOTHING? WE CAN'T EVEN IDENTIFY WHAT'S HAPPENING?
I HAVE TO CHECK ON HIM, DARLING. GO DOWN TO THE CAFETERIA AND GET SOMETHING TO EAT.
HOW ARE YOU FEELING, SON?
DAD? WHAT HAPPENED?
YOU HAD ANOTHER SEIZURE.
DID I WIN THE SCIENCE FAIR?
OF COURSE.
SO CAN I GO?
I DON'T KNOW, GERARD. I'M WORRIED THAT THESE SEIZURES...
DAD, I WON'T BE ABLE TO CURE MYSELF IF I'M IN A HOSPITAL.
I WISH YOU COULD UNDERSTAND HOW DIFFICULT THIS IS FOR ME. YOUR INTELLECT IS SO FAR AHEAD OF YOUR EMOTIONAL MATURITY.
I KNOW I CAN BEAT THIS. I'LL FIGURE IT OUT, BUT I HAVE TO BE IN MEDICAL SCHOOL. I NEED ACCESS TO A LAB.
COLLEGE IS DIFFICULT ENOUGH, BUT YOU'RE ONLY TEN YEARS OLD...
DAD, I WANT TO LIVE TO SEE ELEVEN.

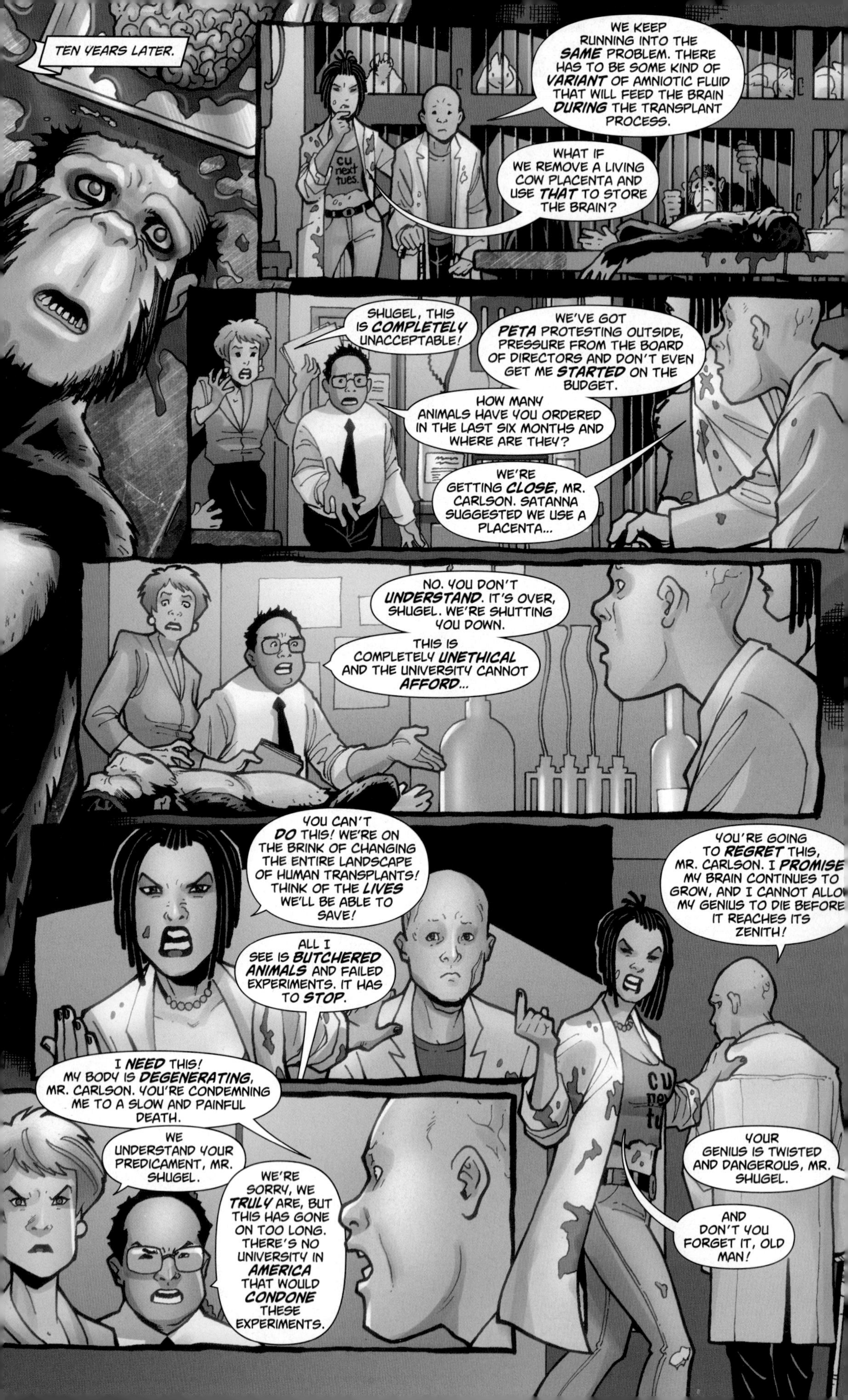
TEN YEARS LATER.
WE KEEP RUNNING INTO THE SAME PROBLEM. THERE HAS TO BE SOME KIND OF VARIANT OF AMNIOTIC FLUID THAT WILL FEED THE BRAIN DURING THE TRANSPLANT PROCESS.
WHAT IF WE REMOVE A LIVING COW PLACENTA AND USE THAT TO STORE THE BRAIN?
CU next tues.
SHUGEL, THIS IS COMPLETELY UNACCEPTABLE!
WE'VE GOT PETA PROTESTING OUTSIDE, PRESSURE FROM THE BOARD OF DIRECTORS AND DON'T EVEN GET ME STARTED ON THE BUDGET.
HOW MANY ANIMALS HAVE YOU ORDERED IN THE LAST SIX MONTHS AND WHERE ARE THEY?
WE'RE GETTING CLOSE, MR. CARLSON. SATANNA SUGGESTED WE USE A PLACENTA...
NO. YOU DON'T UNDERSTAND. IT'S OVER, SHUGEL. WE'RE SHUTTING YOU DOWN.
THIS IS COMPLETELY UNETHICAL AND THE UNIVERSITY CANNOT AFFORD...
YOU CAN'T DO THIS! WE'RE ON THE BRINK OF CHANGING THE ENTIRE LANDSCAPE OF HUMAN TRANSPLANTS! THINK OF THE LIVES WE'LL BE ABLE TO SAVE!
ALL I SEE IS BUTCHERED ANIMALS AND FAILED EXPERIMENTS. IT HAS TO STOP.
YOU'RE GOING TO REGRET THIS, MR. CARLSON. I PROMISE. MY BRAIN CONTINUES TO GROW, AND I CANNOT ALLOW MY GENIUS TO DIE BEFORE IT REACHES ITS ZENITH!
I NEED THIS! MY BODY IS DEGENERATING, MR. CARLSON. YOU'RE CONDEMNING ME TO A SLOW AND PAINFUL DEATH.
WE UNDERSTAND YOUR PREDICAMENT, MR. SHUGEL.
WE'RE SORRY, WE TRULY ARE, BUT THIS HAS GONE ON TOO LONG. THERE'S NO UNIVERSITY IN AMERICA THAT WOULD CONDONE THESE EXPERIMENTS.
YOUR GENIUS IS TWISTED AND DANGEROUS, MR. SHUGEL.
AND DON'T YOU FORGET IT, OLD MAN!

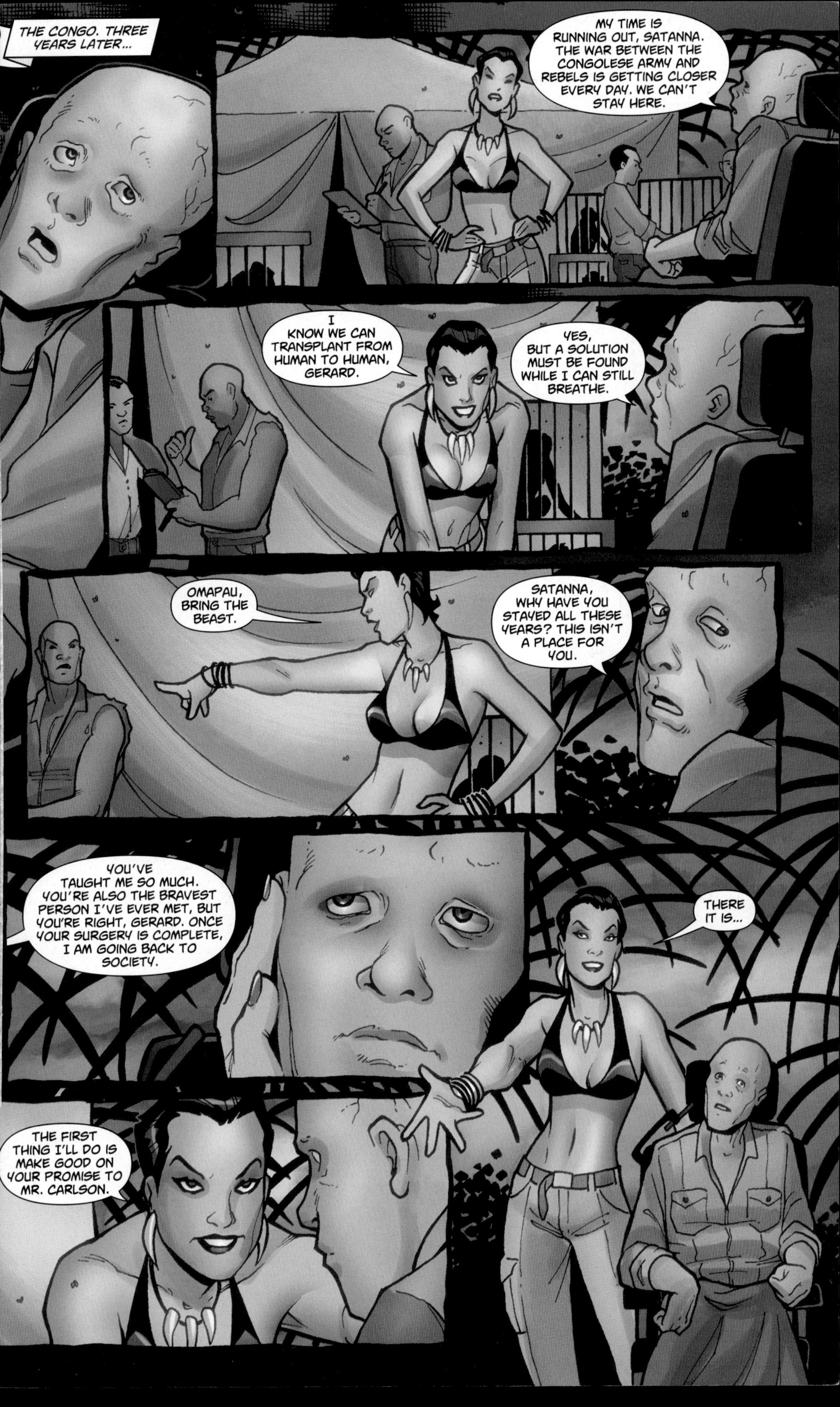
THE CONGO. THREE YEARS LATER...
MY TIME IS RUNNING OUT, SATANNA. THE WAR BETWEEN THE CONGOLESE ARMY AND REBELS IS GETTING CLOSER EVERY DAY. WE CAN'T STAY HERE.
I KNOW WE CAN TRANSPLANT FROM HUMAN TO HUMAN, GERARD.
YES, BUT A SOLUTION MUST BE FOUND WHILE I CAN STILL BREATHE.
OMAPAU, BRING THE BEAST.
SATANNA, WHY HAVE YOU STAYED ALL THESE YEARS? THIS ISN'T A PLACE FOR YOU.
YOU'VE TAUGHT ME SO MUCH. YOU'RE ALSO THE BRAVEST PERSON I'VE EVER MET, BUT YOU'RE RIGHT, GERARD. ONCE YOUR SURGERY IS COMPLETE, I AM GOING BACK TO SOCIETY.
THE FIRST THING I'LL DO IS MAKE GOOD ON YOUR PROMISE TO MR. CARLSON.
THERE IT IS...

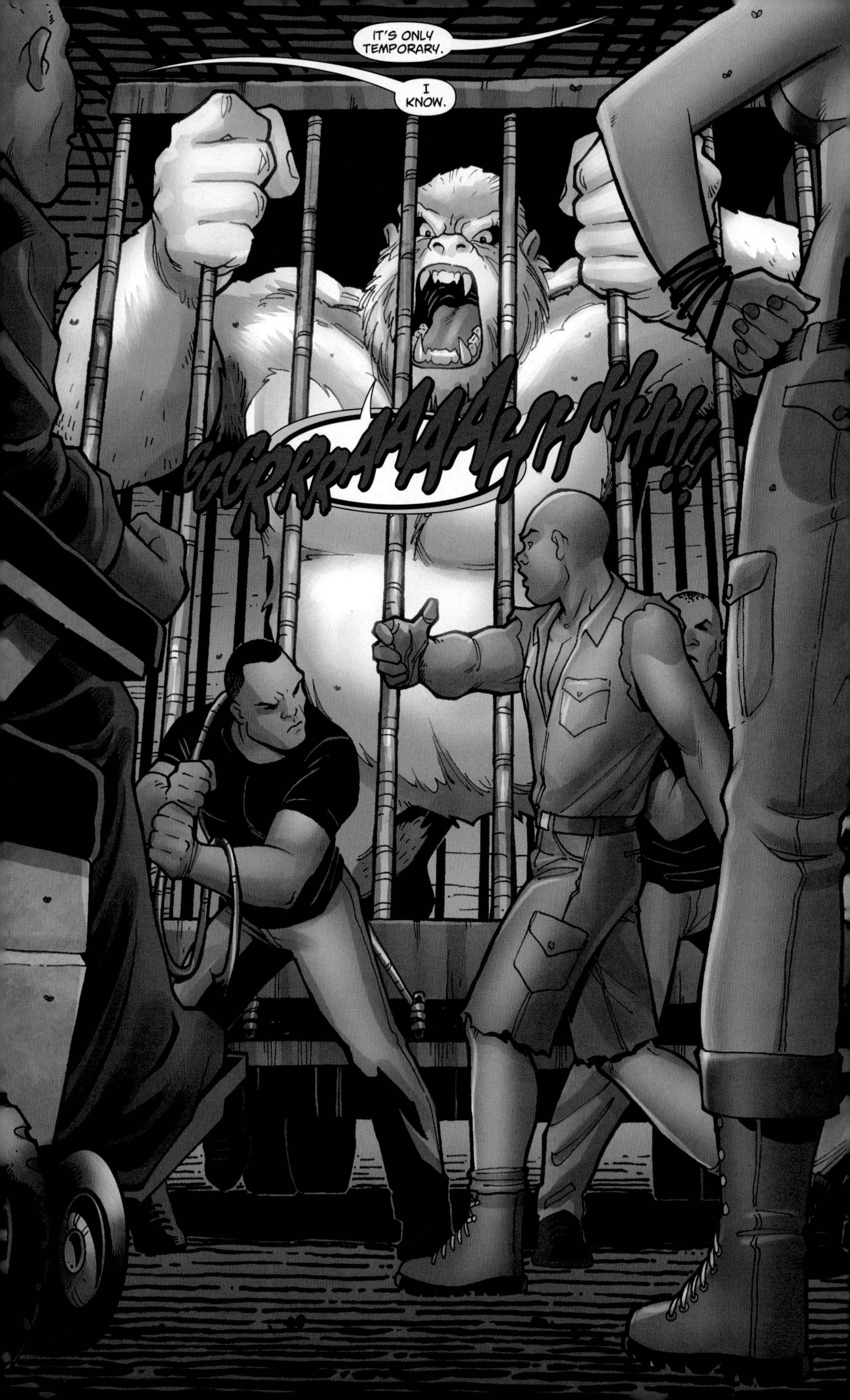
IT'S ONLY TEMPORARY.
I KNOW.
GGGRRRRAAAAAHHHHH!!!

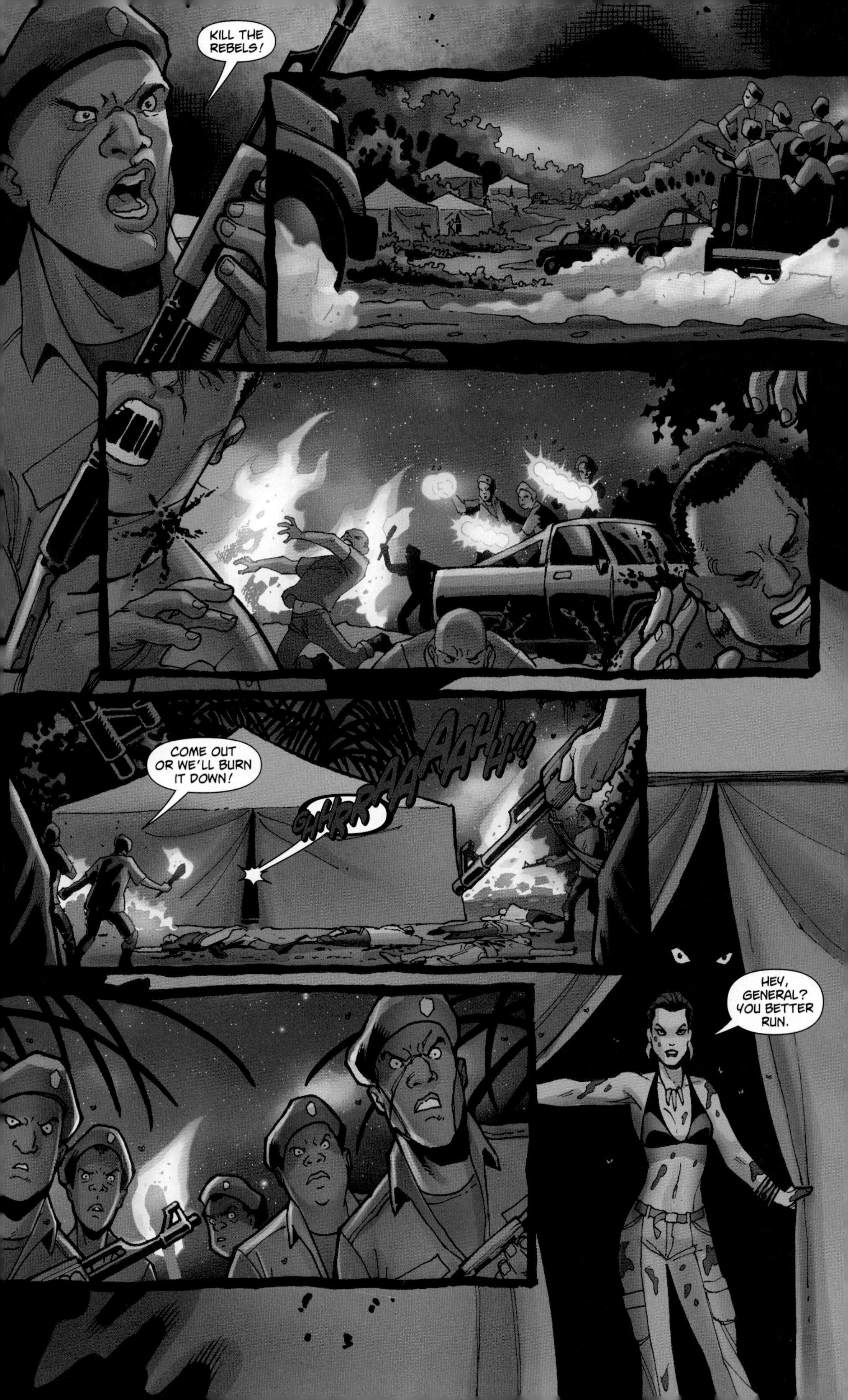
KILL THE REBELS!
COME OUT OR WE'LL BURN IT DOWN!
GHHRRAAAAAHH!!
HEY, GENERAL? YOU BETTER RUN.

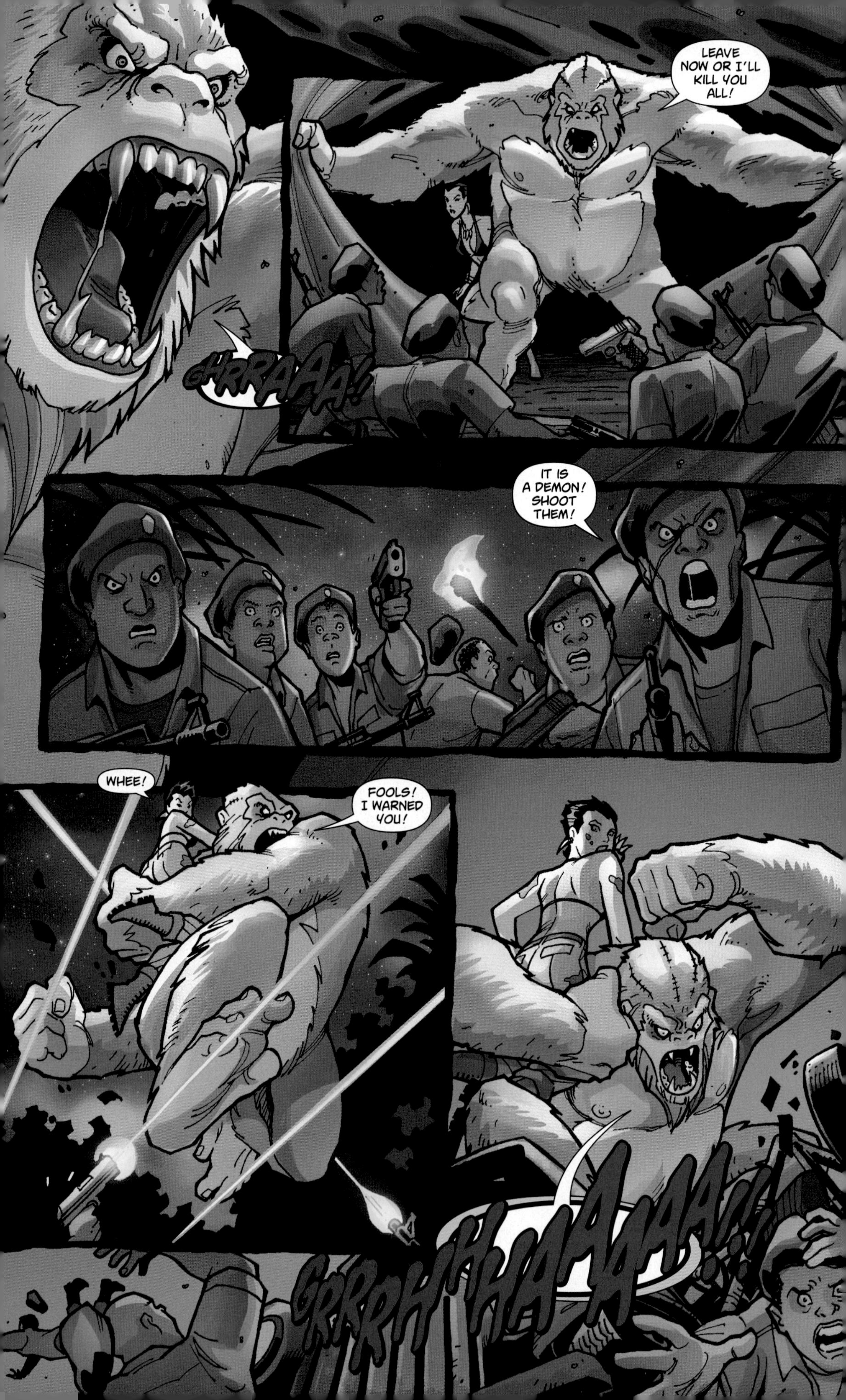
LEAVE NOW OR I'LL KILL YOU ALL!
GHRRAAAA!
IT IS A DEMON! SHOOT THEM!
WHEE!
FOOLS! I WARNED YOU!
GRRRHHHAAAAAA!!!

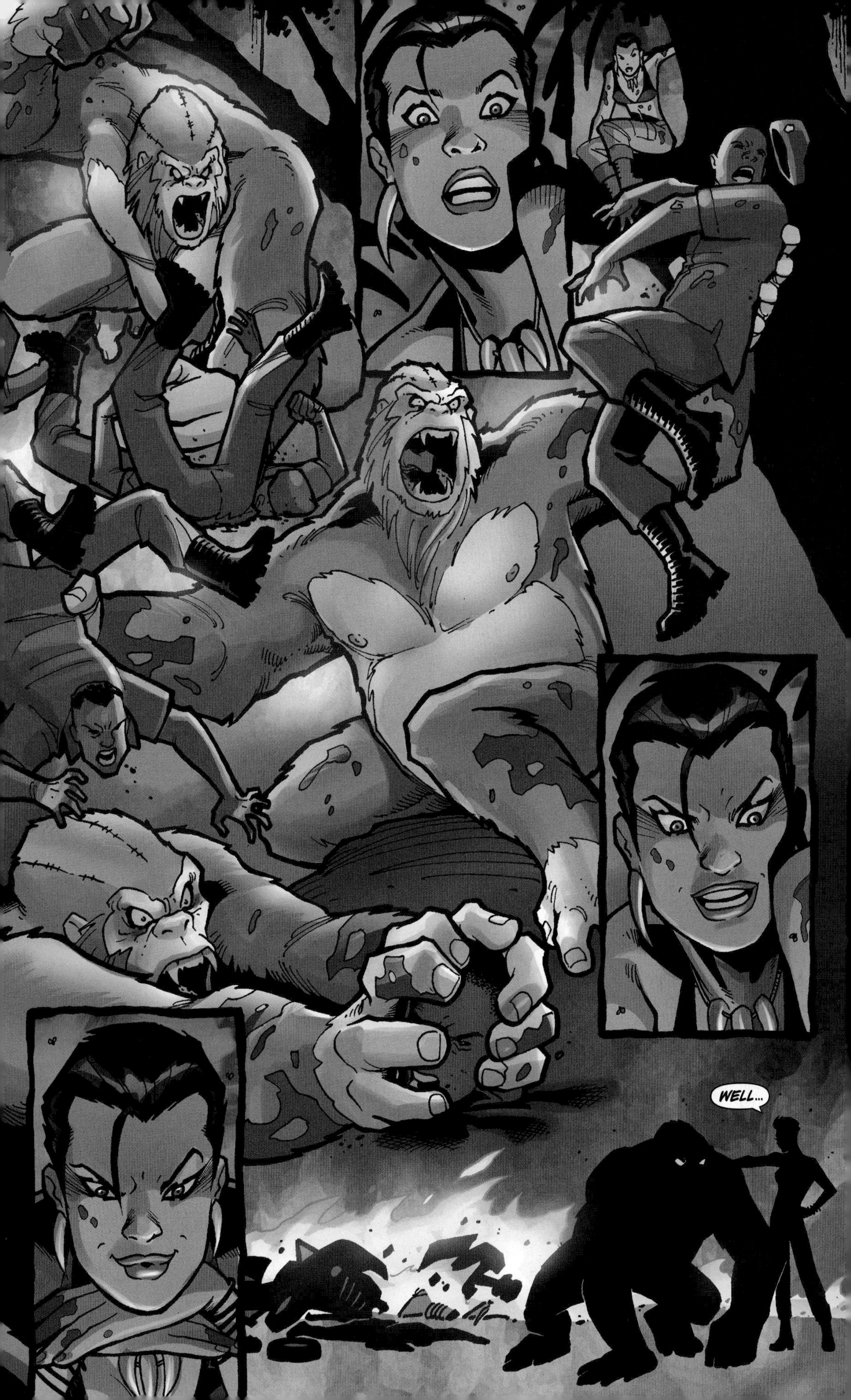
WELL...

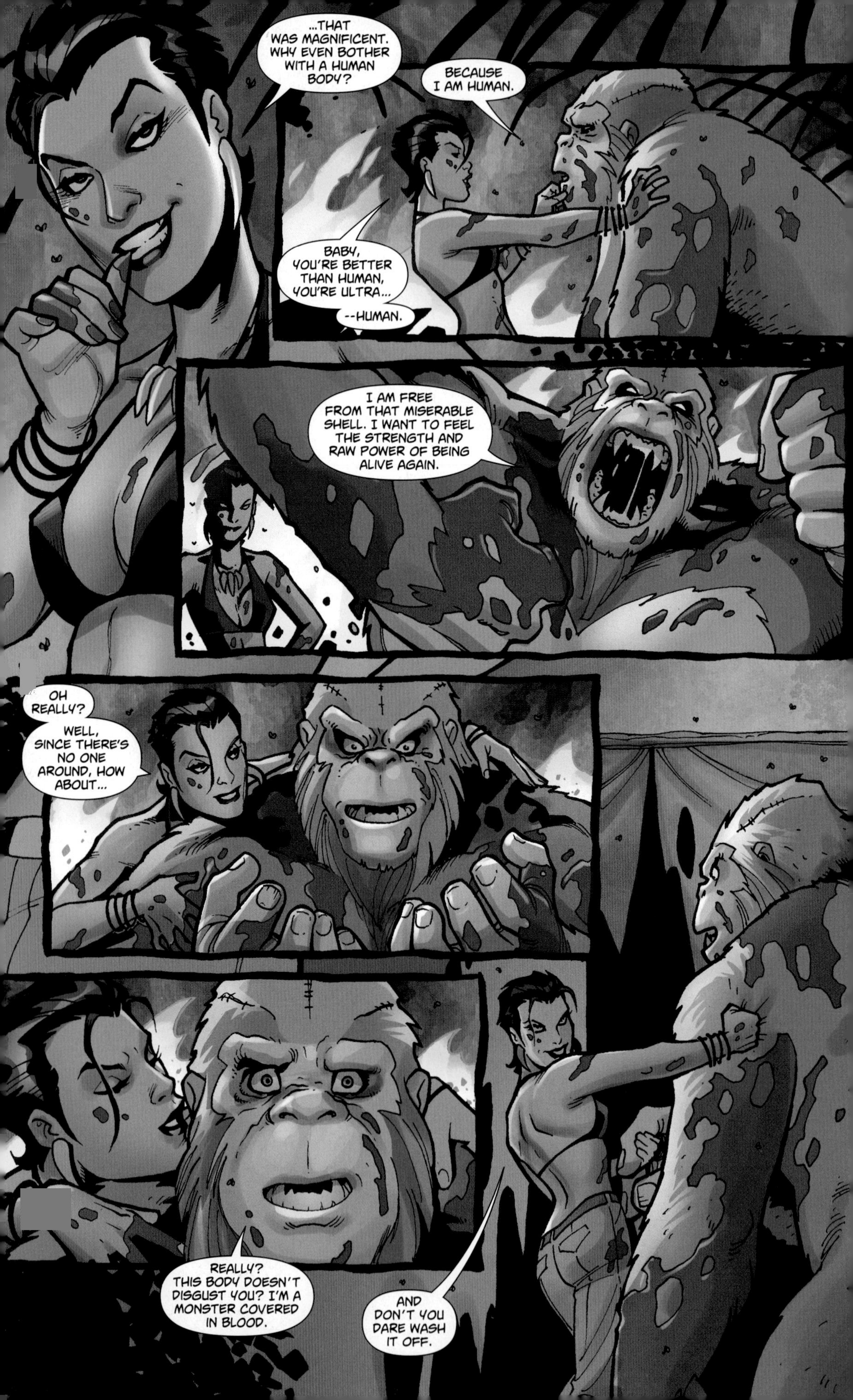
...THAT WAS MAGNIFICENT. WHY EVEN BOTHER WITH A HUMAN BODY?
BECAUSE I AM HUMAN.
BABY, YOU'RE BETTER THAN HUMAN, YOU'RE ULTRA...
--HUMAN.
I AM FREE FROM THAT MISERABLE SHELL. I WANT TO FEEL THE STRENGTH AND RAW POWER OF BEING ALIVE AGAIN.
OH REALLY?
WELL, SINCE THERE'S NO ONE AROUND, HOW ABOUT...
REALLY? THIS BODY DOESN'T DISGUST YOU? I'M A MONSTER COVERED IN BLOOD.
AND DON'T YOU DARE WASH IT OFF.

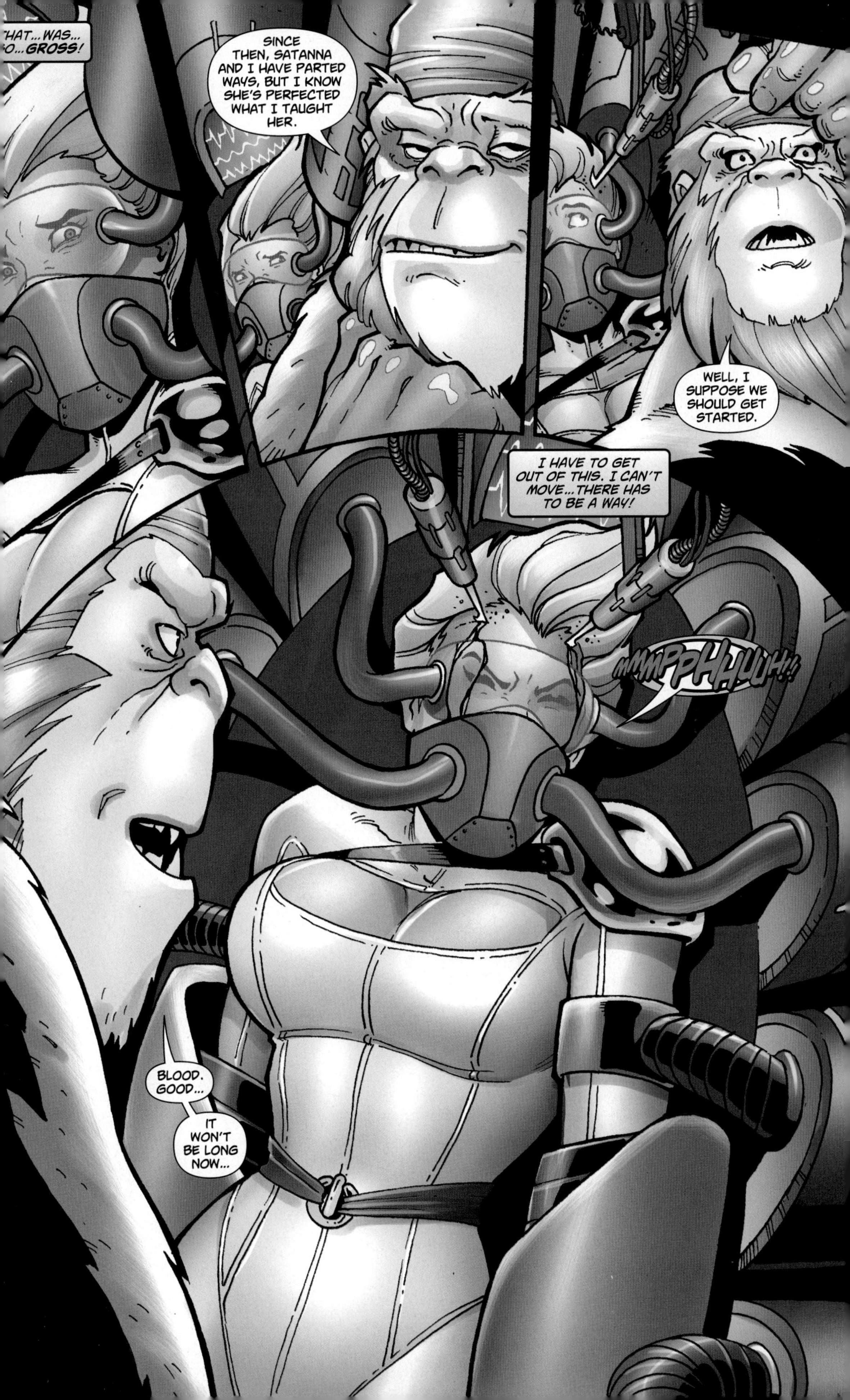

THAT... WAS... SO... GROSS!
SINCE THEN, SATANNA AND I HAVE PARTED WAYS, BUT I KNOW SHE'S PERFECTED WHAT I TAUGHT HER.
WELL, I SUPPOSE WE SHOULD GET STARTED.
I HAVE TO GET OUT OF THIS. I CAN'T MOVE... THERE HAS TO BE A WAY!
MMMPPHHUUH!!
BLOOD. GOOD...
IT WON'T BE LONG NOW...

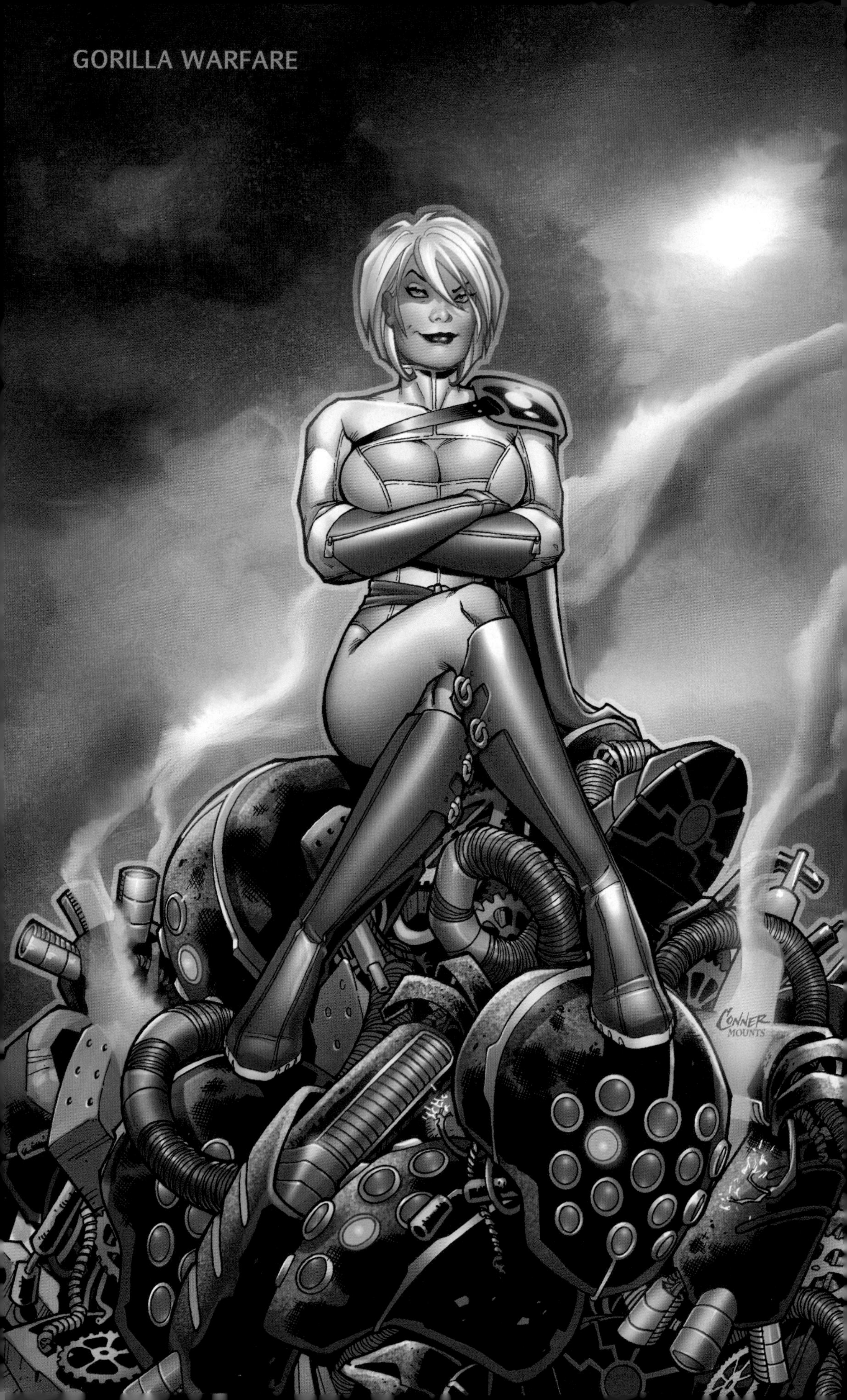
GORILLA WARFARE
CONNER
MOUNTS

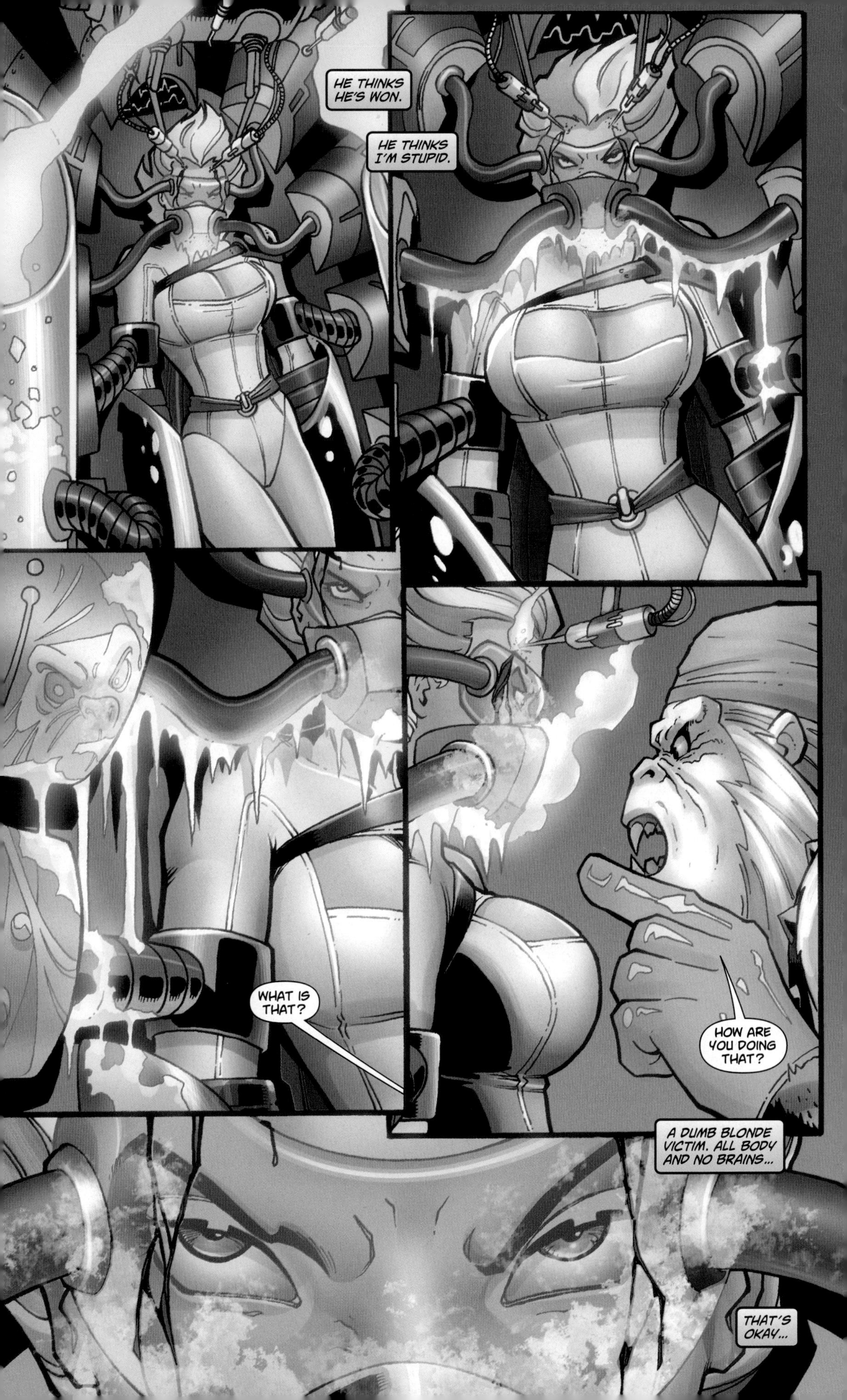
HE THINKS HE'S WON.
HE THINKS I'M STUPID.
WHAT IS THAT?
HOW ARE YOU DOING THAT?
A DUMB BLONDE VICTIM. ALL BODY AND NO BRAINS...
THAT'S OKAY...

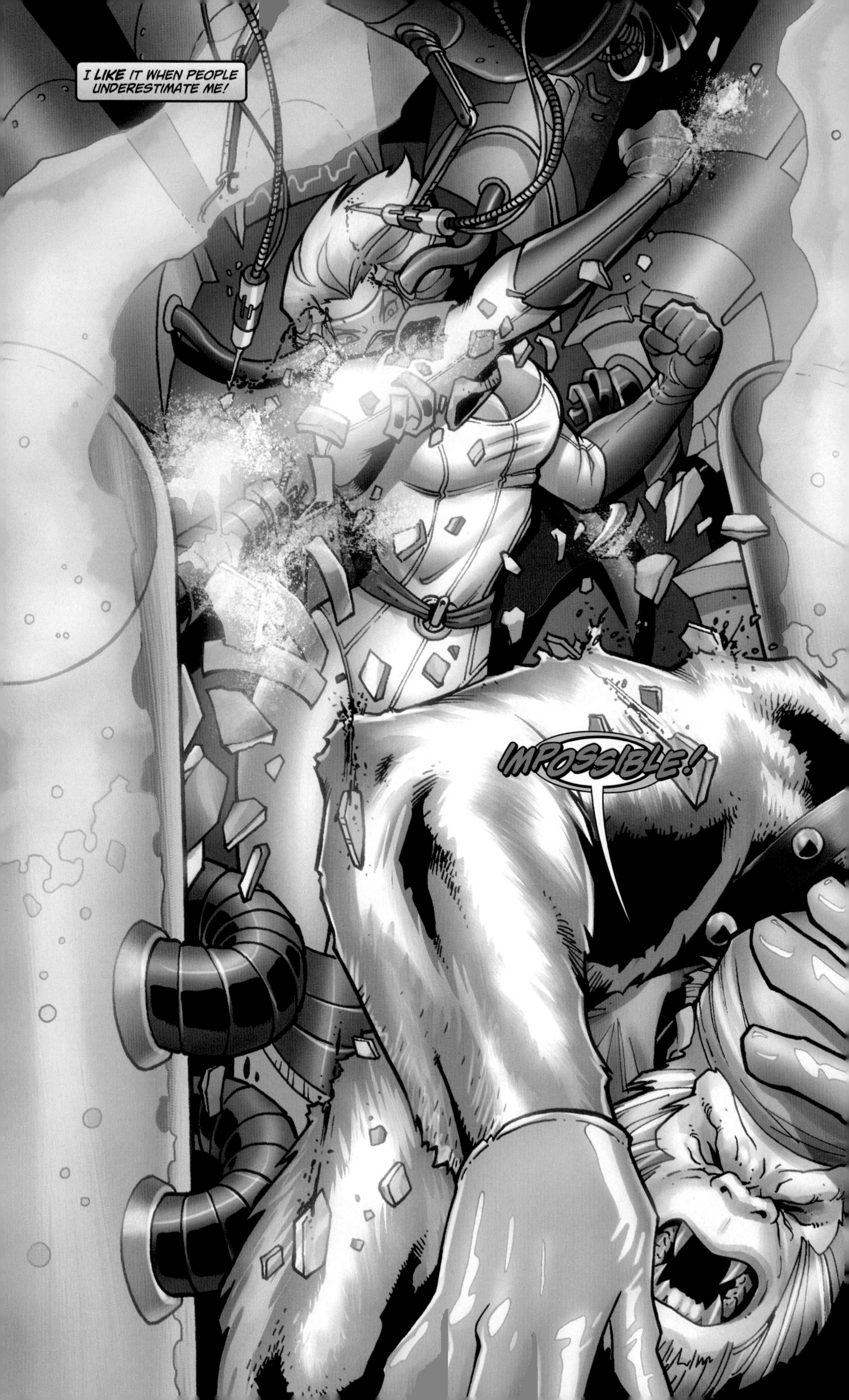
I LIKE IT WHEN PEOPLE UNDERESTIMATE ME!
IMPOSSIBLE!

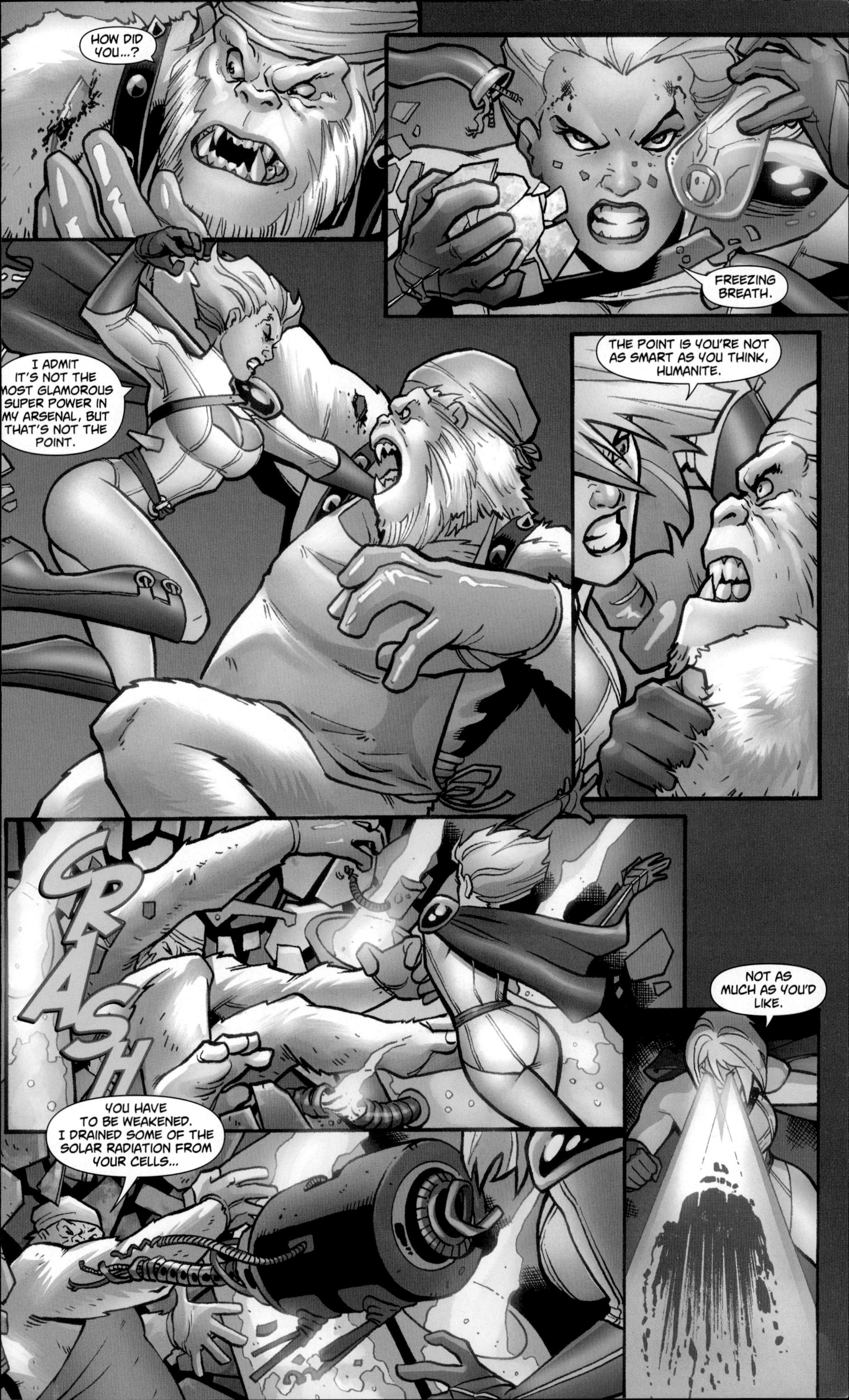
HOW DID YOU...?
FREEZING BREATH.
I ADMIT IT'S NOT THE MOST GLAMOROUS SUPER POWER IN MY ARSENAL, BUT THAT'S NOT THE POINT.
THE POINT IS YOU'RE NOT AS SMART AS YOU THINK, HUMANITE.
CRASH
YOU HAVE TO BE WEAKENED. I DRAINED SOME OF THE SOLAR RADIATION FROM YOUR CELLS...
NOT AS MUCH AS YOU'D LIKE.

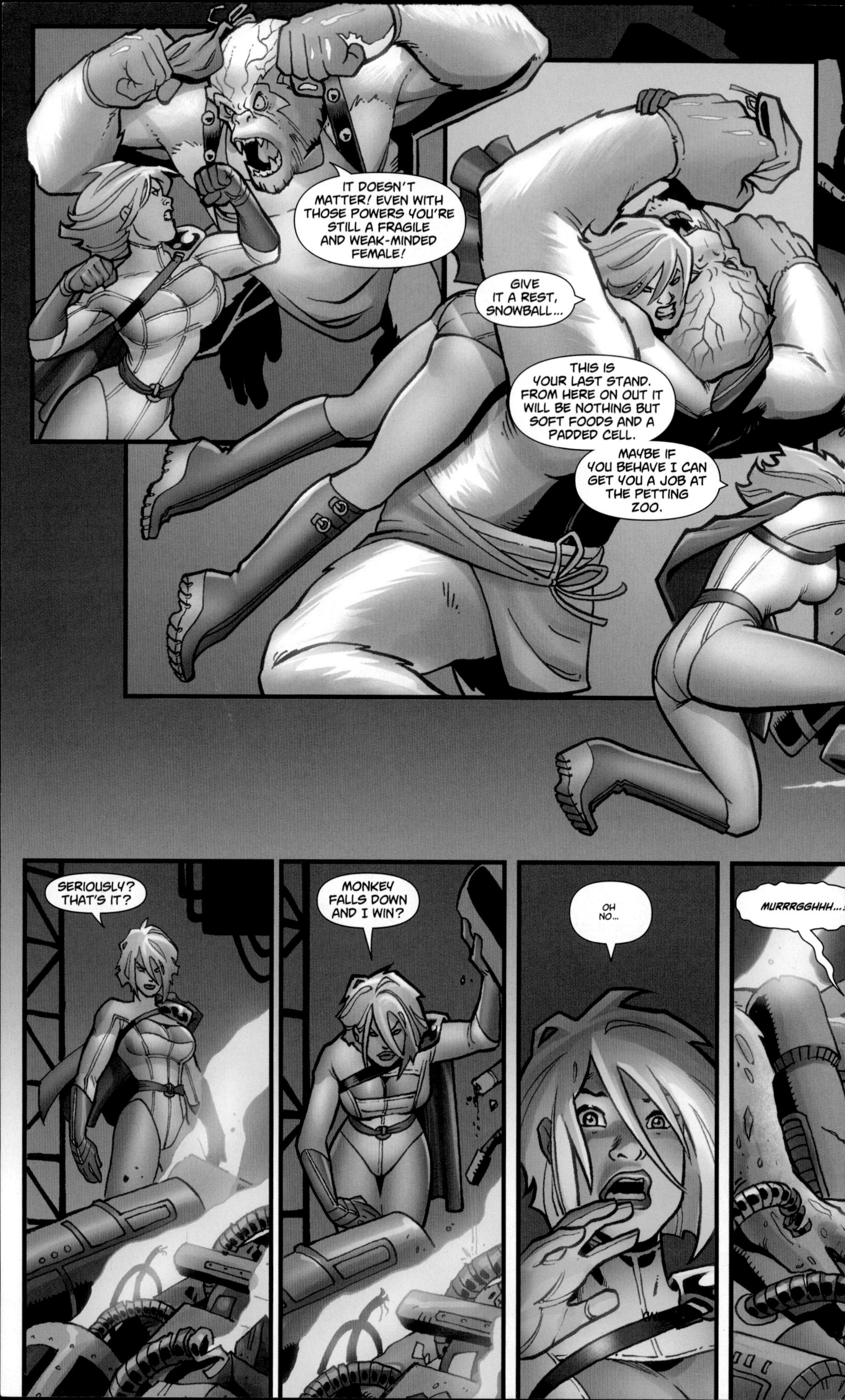
IT DOESN'T MATTER! EVEN WITH THOSE POWERS YOU'RE STILL A FRAGILE AND WEAK-MINDED FEMALE!
GIVE IT A REST, SNOWBALL...
THIS IS YOUR LAST STAND. FROM HERE ON OUT IT WILL BE NOTHING BUT SOFT FOODS AND A PADDED CELL.
MAYBE IF YOU BEHAVE I CAN GET YOU A JOB AT THE PETTING ZOO.
SERIOUSLY? THAT'S IT?
MONKEY FALLS DOWN AND I WIN?
OH NO...
MURRRGGHHH...

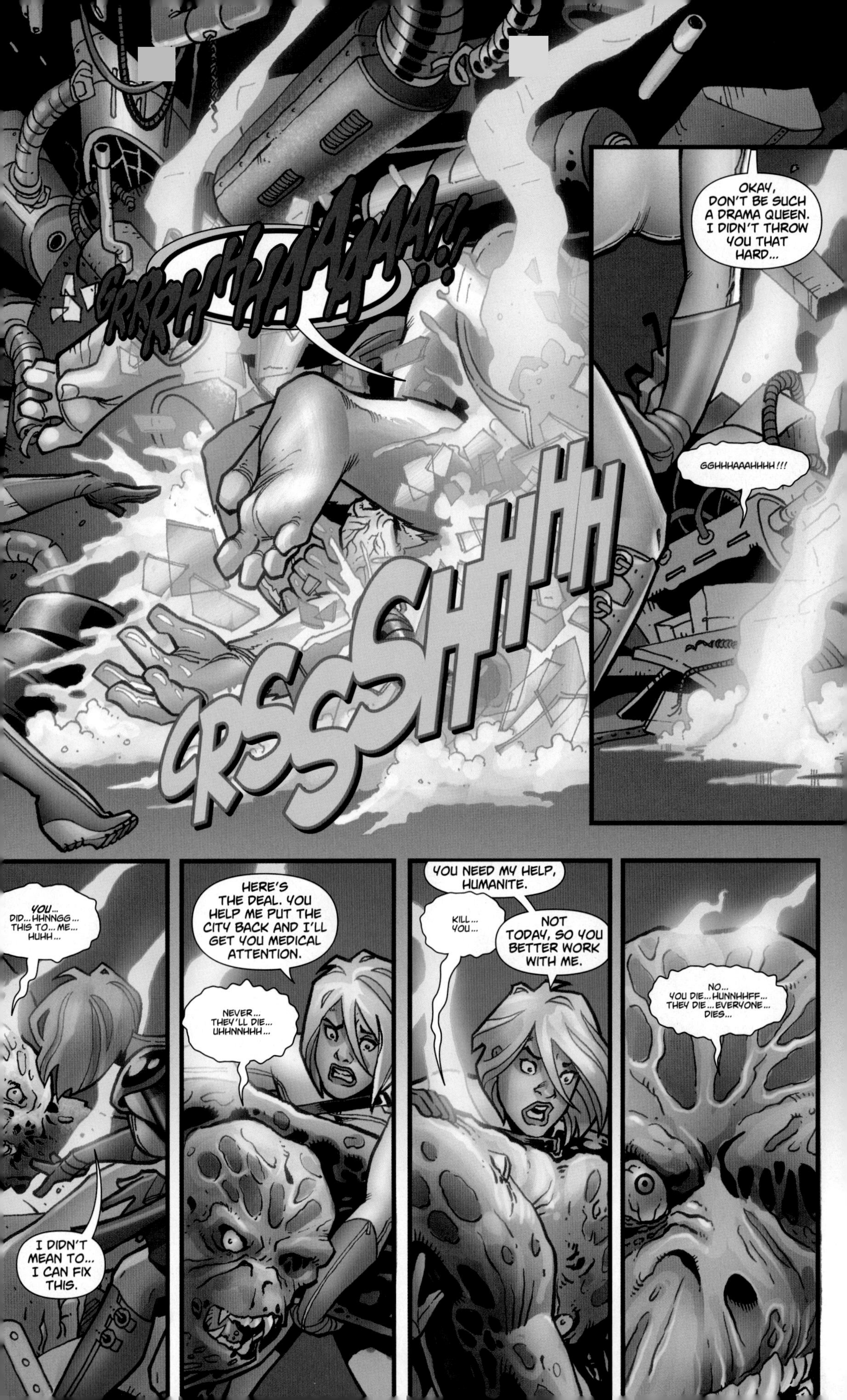
GRRRHHHAAAAAA!!!
CRSSSHHHHH
OKAY, DON'T BE SUCH A DRAMA QUEEN. I DIDN'T THROW YOU THAT HARD...
GGHHHAAAAHHHH!!!
YOU... DID... HHNNGG... THIS TO... ME... HUHH...
I DIDN'T MEAN TO... I CAN FIX THIS.
HERE'S THE DEAL. YOU HELP ME PUT THE CITY BACK AND I'LL GET YOU MEDICAL ATTENTION.
NEVER... THEY'LL DIE... UHHNNHHH...
YOU NEED MY HELP, HUMANITE.
KILL... YOU...
NOT TODAY, SO YOU BETTER WORK WITH ME.
NO... YOU DIE... HUNNHHFF... THEY DIE... EVERYONE... DIES...

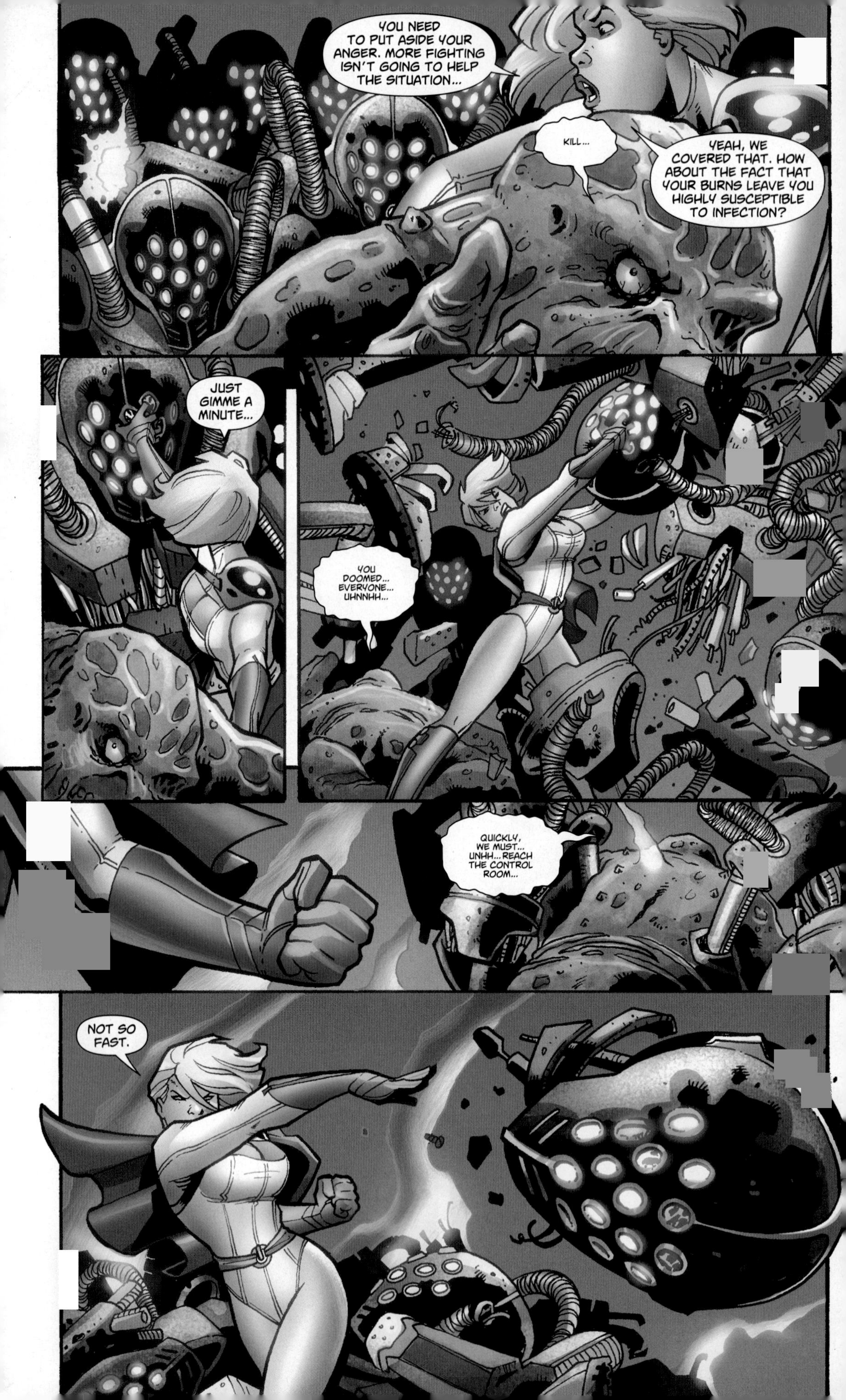
YOU NEED TO PUT ASIDE YOUR ANGER. MORE FIGHTING ISN'T GOING TO HELP THE SITUATION...
KILL...
YEAH, WE COVERED THAT. HOW ABOUT THE FACT THAT YOUR BURNS LEAVE YOU HIGHLY SUSCEPTIBLE TO INFECTION?
JUST GIMME A MINUTE...
YOU DOOMED... EVERYONE... UHNNHH...
QUICKLY, WE MUST... UNHH... REACH THE CONTROL ROOM...
NOT SO FAST.

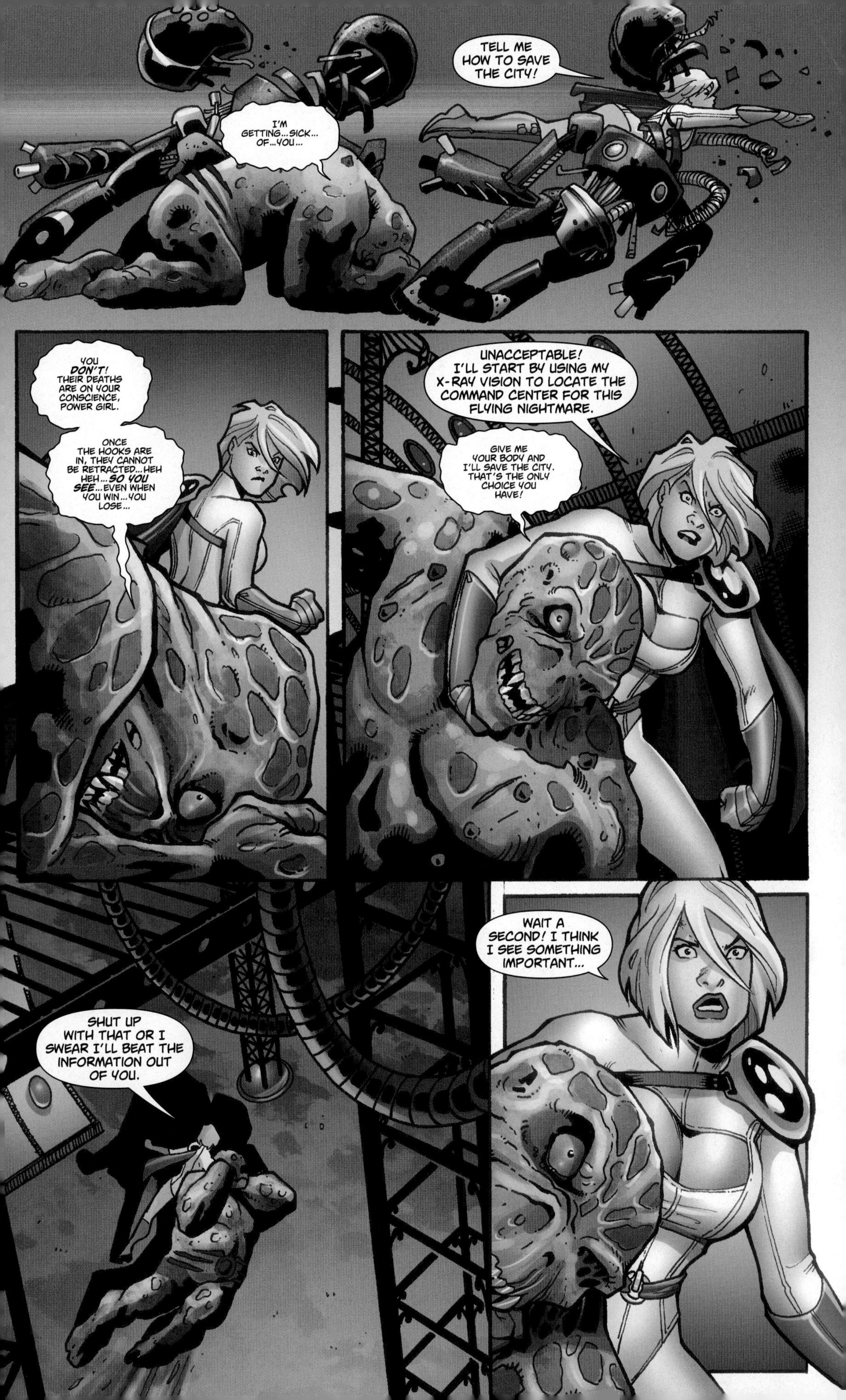
I'M GETTING...SICK... OF...YOU...
TELL ME HOW TO SAVE THE CITY!
YOU DON'T! THEIR DEATHS ARE ON YOUR CONSCIENCE, POWER GIRL.
ONCE THE HOOKS ARE IN, THEY CANNOT BE RETRACTED...HEH HEH...SO YOU SEE...EVEN WHEN YOU WIN...YOU LOSE...
UNACCEPTABLE! I'LL START BY USING MY X-RAY VISION TO LOCATE THE COMMAND CENTER FOR THIS FLYING NIGHTMARE.
GIVE ME YOUR BODY AND I'LL SAVE THE CITY. THAT'S THE ONLY CHOICE YOU HAVE!
SHUT UP WITH THAT OR I SWEAR I'LL BEAT THE INFORMATION OUT OF YOU.
WAIT A SECOND! I THINK I SEE SOMETHING IMPORTANT...

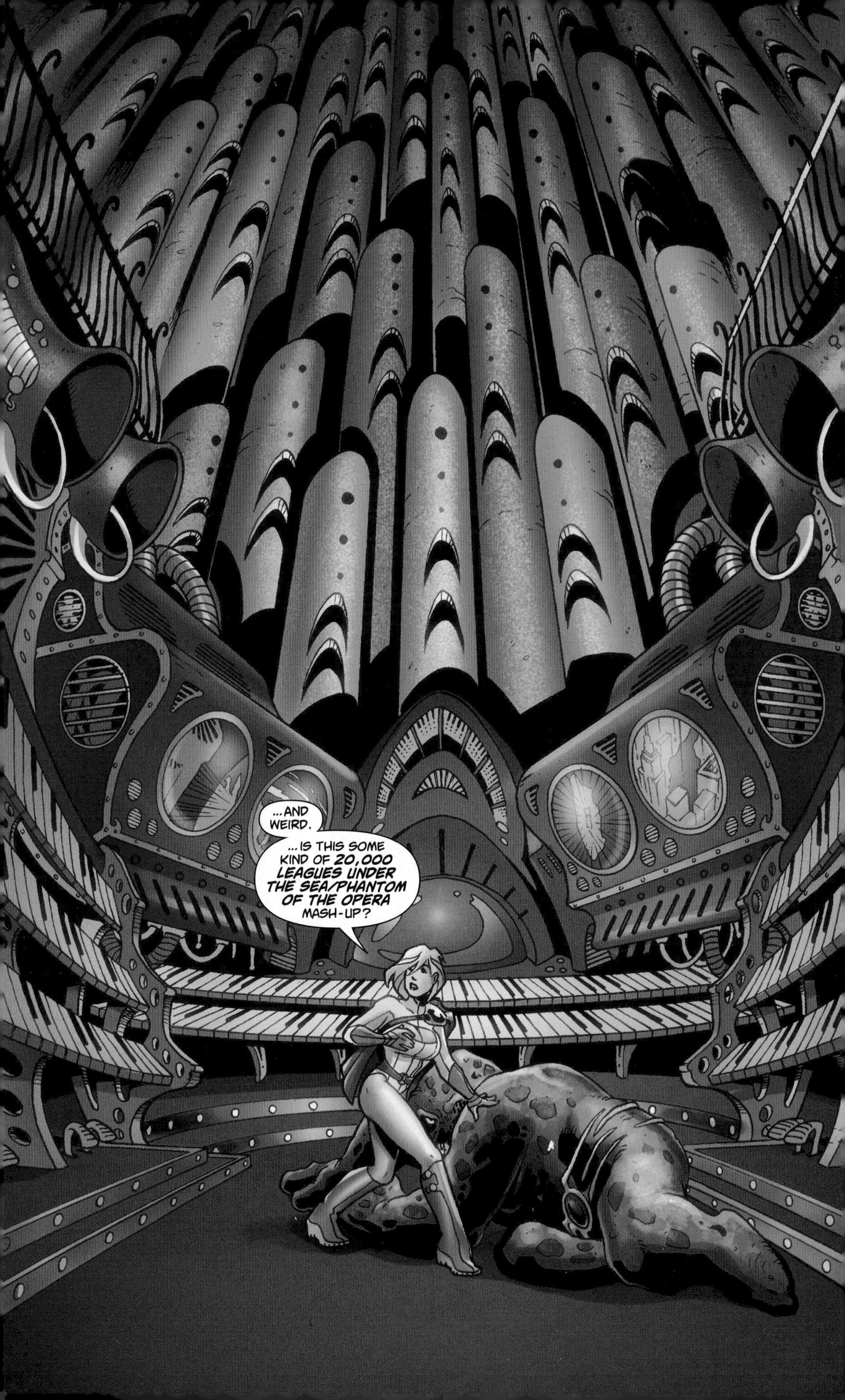
...AND WEIRD.
...IS THIS SOME KIND OF 20,000 LEAGUES UNDER THE SEA/PHANTOM OF THE OPERA MASH-UP?

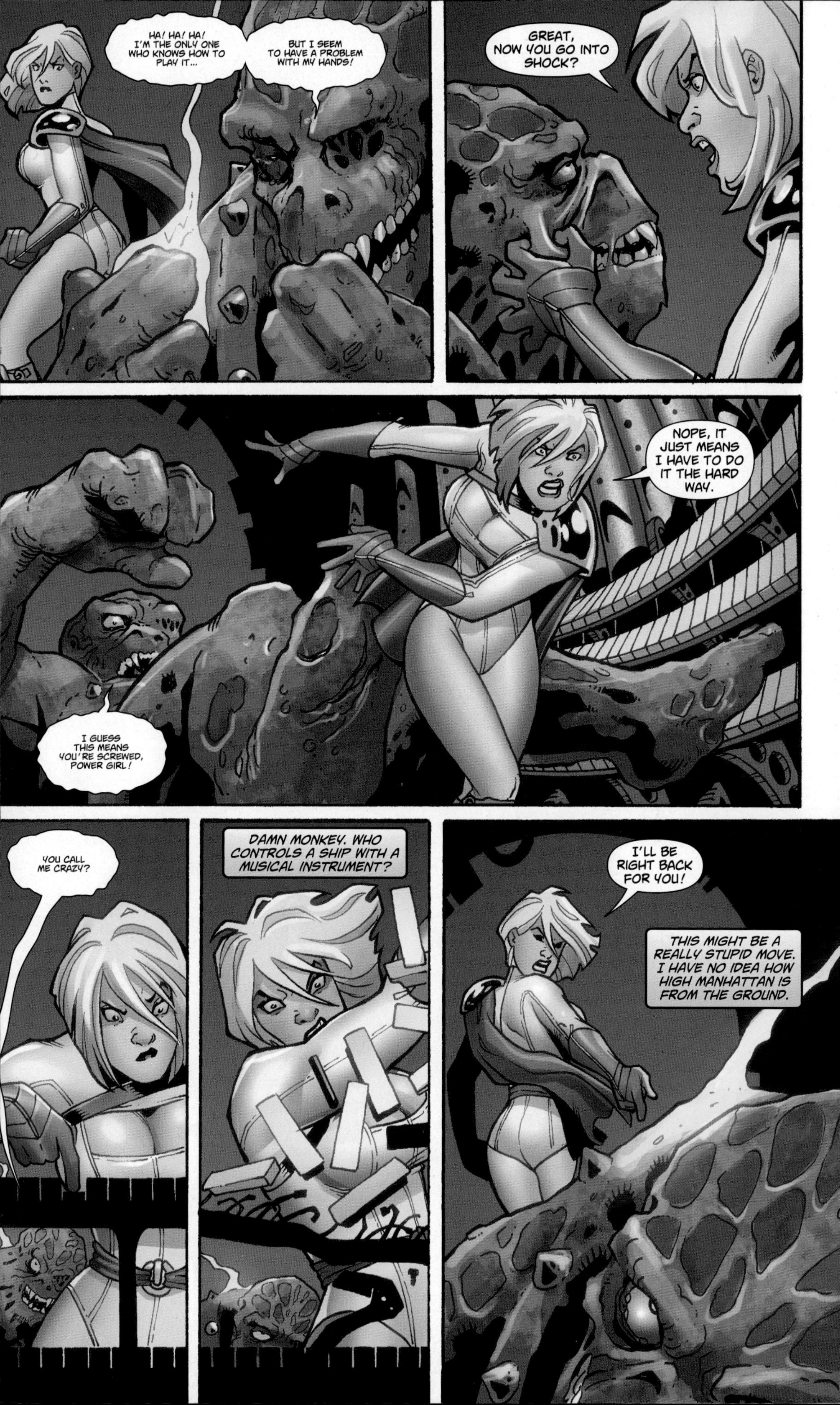
HA! HA! HA! I'M THE ONLY ONE WHO KNOWS HOW TO PLAY IT...
BUT I SEEM TO HAVE A PROBLEM WITH MY HANDS!
GREAT, NOW YOU GO INTO SHOCK?
I GUESS THIS MEANS YOU'RE SCREWED, POWER GIRL!
NOPE, IT JUST MEANS I HAVE TO DO IT THE HARD WAY.
YOU CALL ME CRAZY?
DAMN MONKEY. WHO CONTROLS A SHIP WITH A MUSICAL INSTRUMENT?
I'LL BE RIGHT BACK FOR YOU!
THIS MIGHT BE A REALLY STUPID MOVE. I HAVE NO IDEA HOW HIGH MANHATTAN IS FROM THE GROUND.

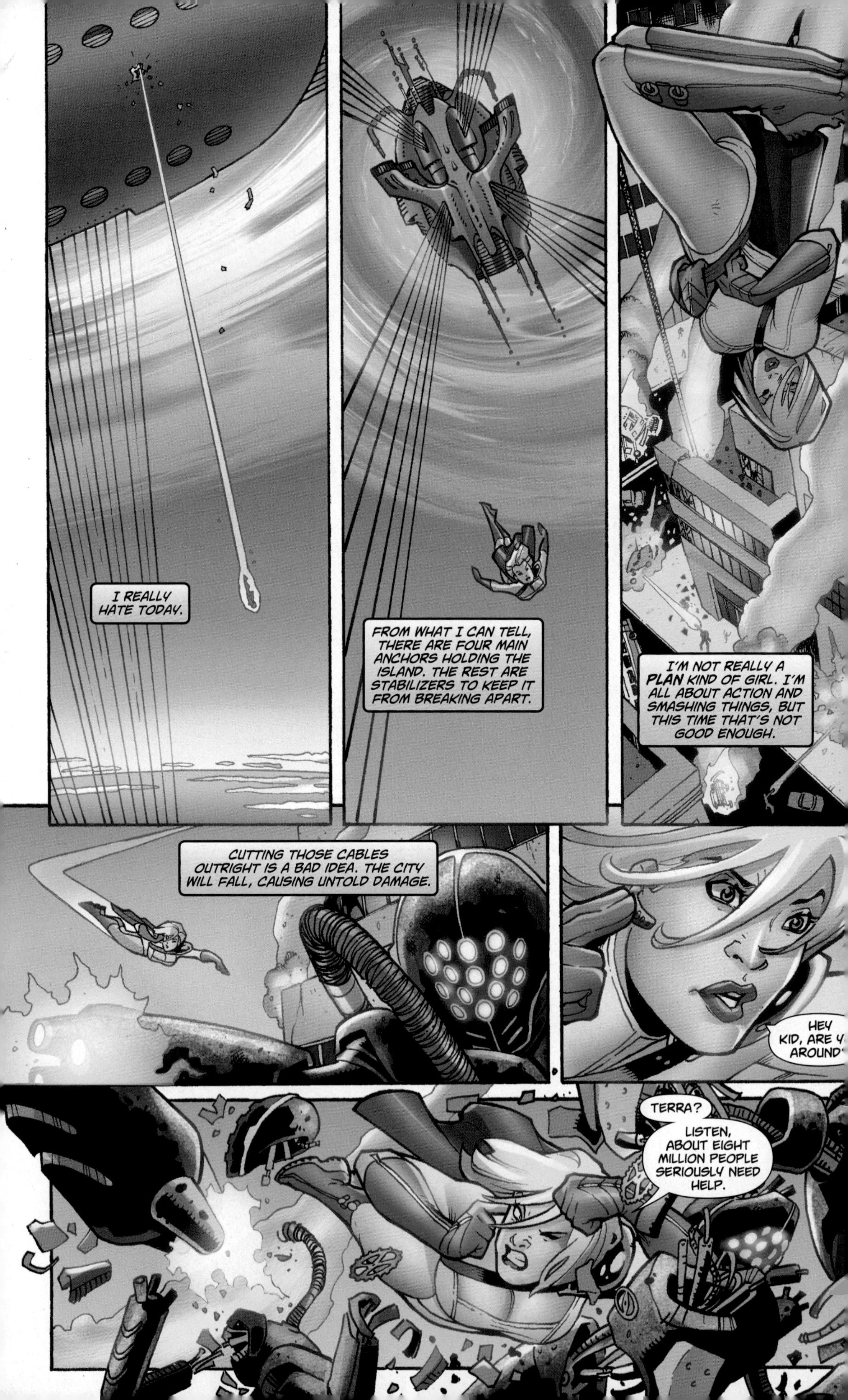
I REALLY HATE TODAY.
FROM WHAT I CAN TELL, THERE ARE FOUR MAIN ANCHORS HOLDING THE ISLAND. THE REST ARE STABILIZERS TO KEEP IT FROM BREAKING APART.
I'M NOT REALLY A PLAN KIND OF GIRL. I'M ALL ABOUT ACTION AND SMASHING THINGS, BUT THIS TIME THAT'S NOT GOOD ENOUGH.
CUTTING THOSE CABLES OUTRIGHT IS A BAD IDEA. THE CITY WILL FALL, CAUSING UNTOLD DAMAGE.
HEY KID, ARE Y AROUND
TERRA?
LISTEN, ABOUT EIGHT MILLION PEOPLE SERIOUSLY NEED HELP.

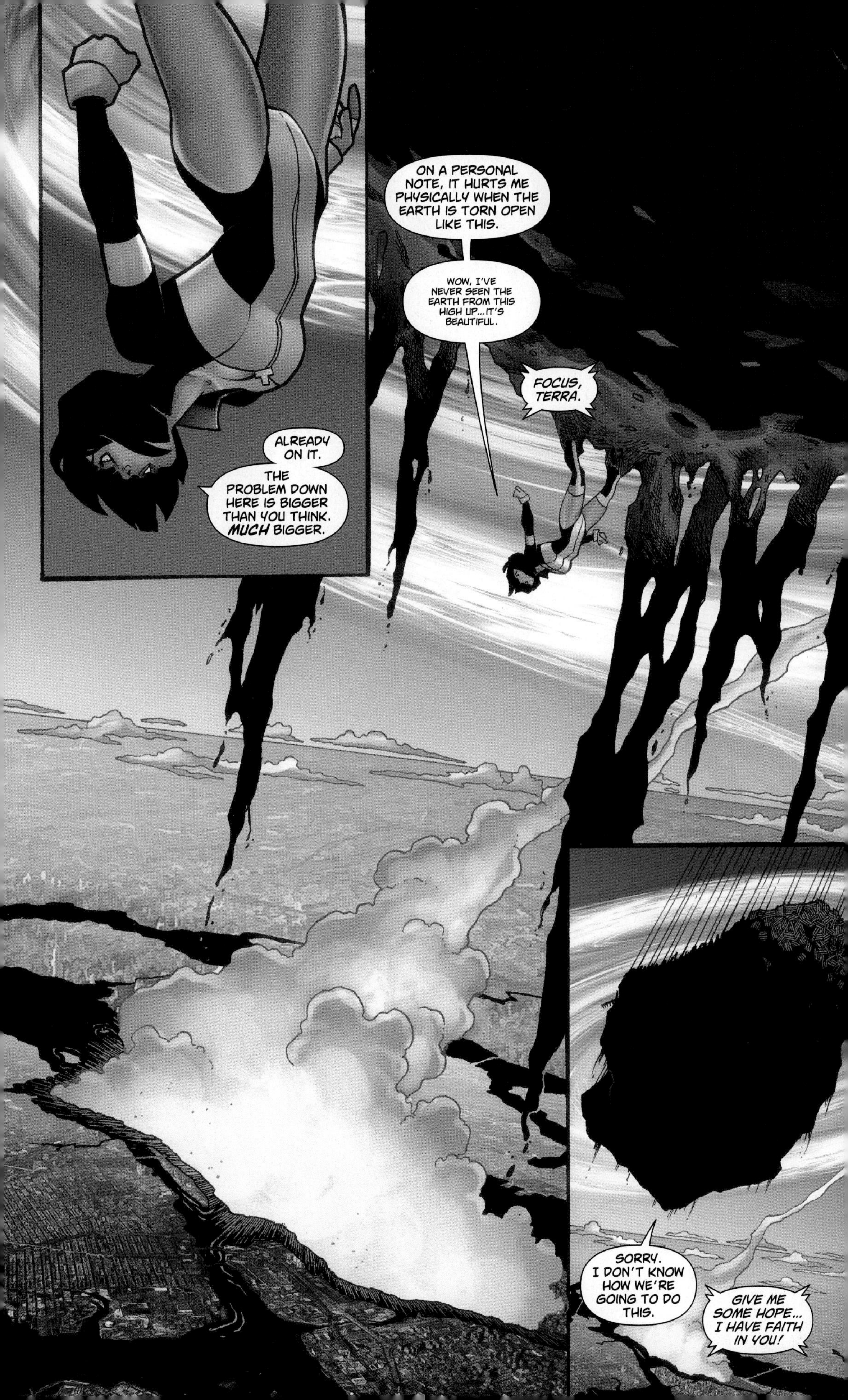
ON A PERSONAL NOTE, IT HURTS ME PHYSICALLY WHEN THE EARTH IS TORN OPEN LIKE THIS.
WOW, I'VE NEVER SEEN THE EARTH FROM THIS HIGH UP...IT'S BEAUTIFUL.
FOCUS, TERRA.
ALREADY ON IT.
THE PROBLEM DOWN HERE IS BIGGER THAN YOU THINK. MUCH BIGGER.
SORRY. I DON'T KNOW HOW WE'RE GOING TO DO THIS.
GIVE ME SOME HOPE... I HAVE FAITH IN YOU!

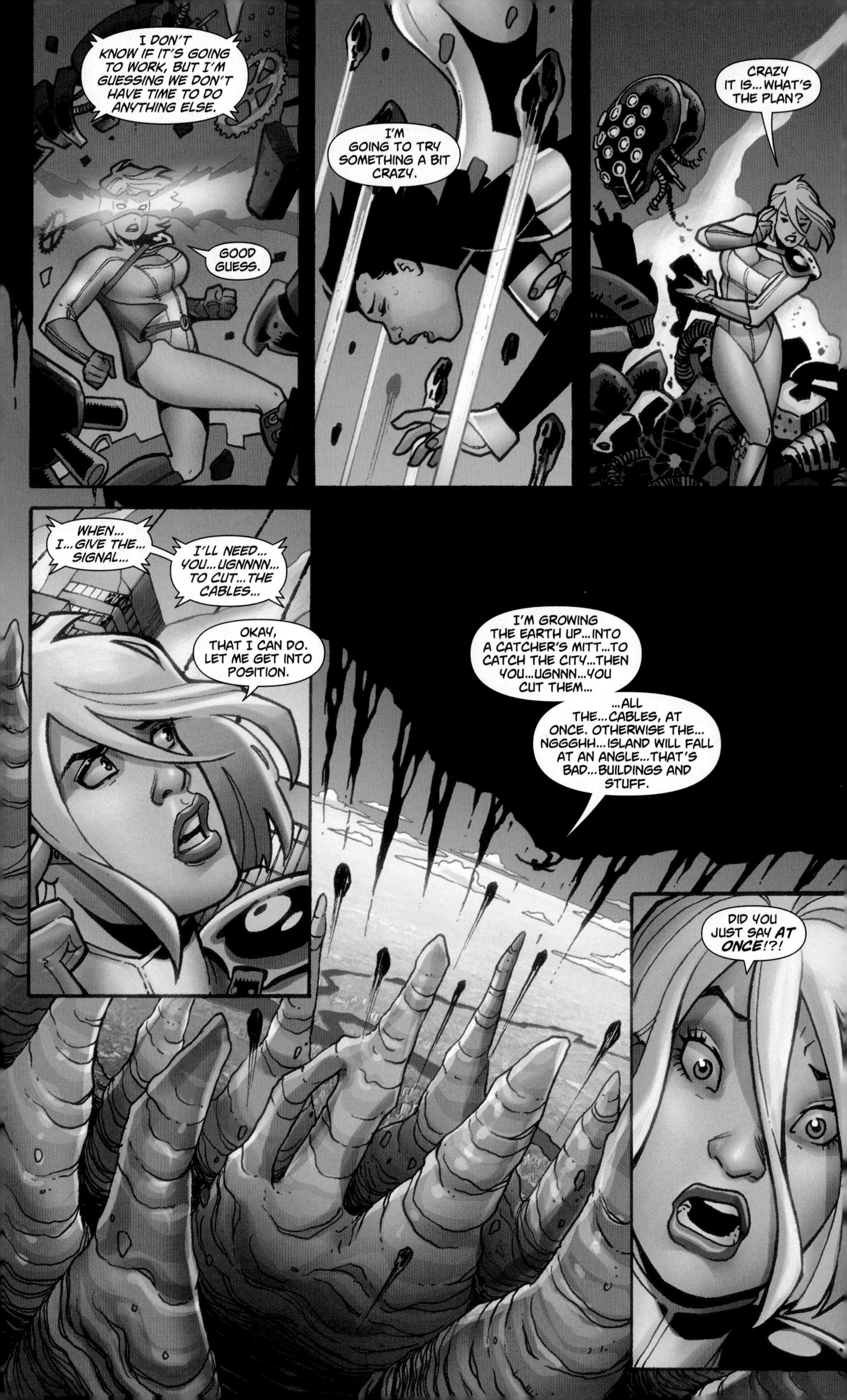
I DON'T KNOW IF IT'S GOING TO WORK, BUT I'M GUESSING WE DON'T HAVE TIME TO DO ANYTHING ELSE.
GOOD GUESS.
I'M GOING TO TRY SOMETHING A BIT CRAZY.
CRAZY IT IS...WHAT'S THE PLAN?
WHEN... I...GIVE THE... SIGNAL...
I'LL NEED... YOU...UGNNNN... TO CUT...THE CABLES...
OKAY, THAT I CAN DO. LET ME GET INTO POSITION.
I'M GROWING THE EARTH UP...INTO A CATCHER'S MITT...TO CATCH THE CITY...THEN YOU...UGNNN...YOU CUT THEM...
...ALL THE...CABLES, AT ONCE. OTHERWISE THE... NGGGHH...ISLAND WILL FALL AT AN ANGLE...THAT'S BAD...BUILDINGS AND STUFF.
DID YOU JUST SAY AT ONCE!?!

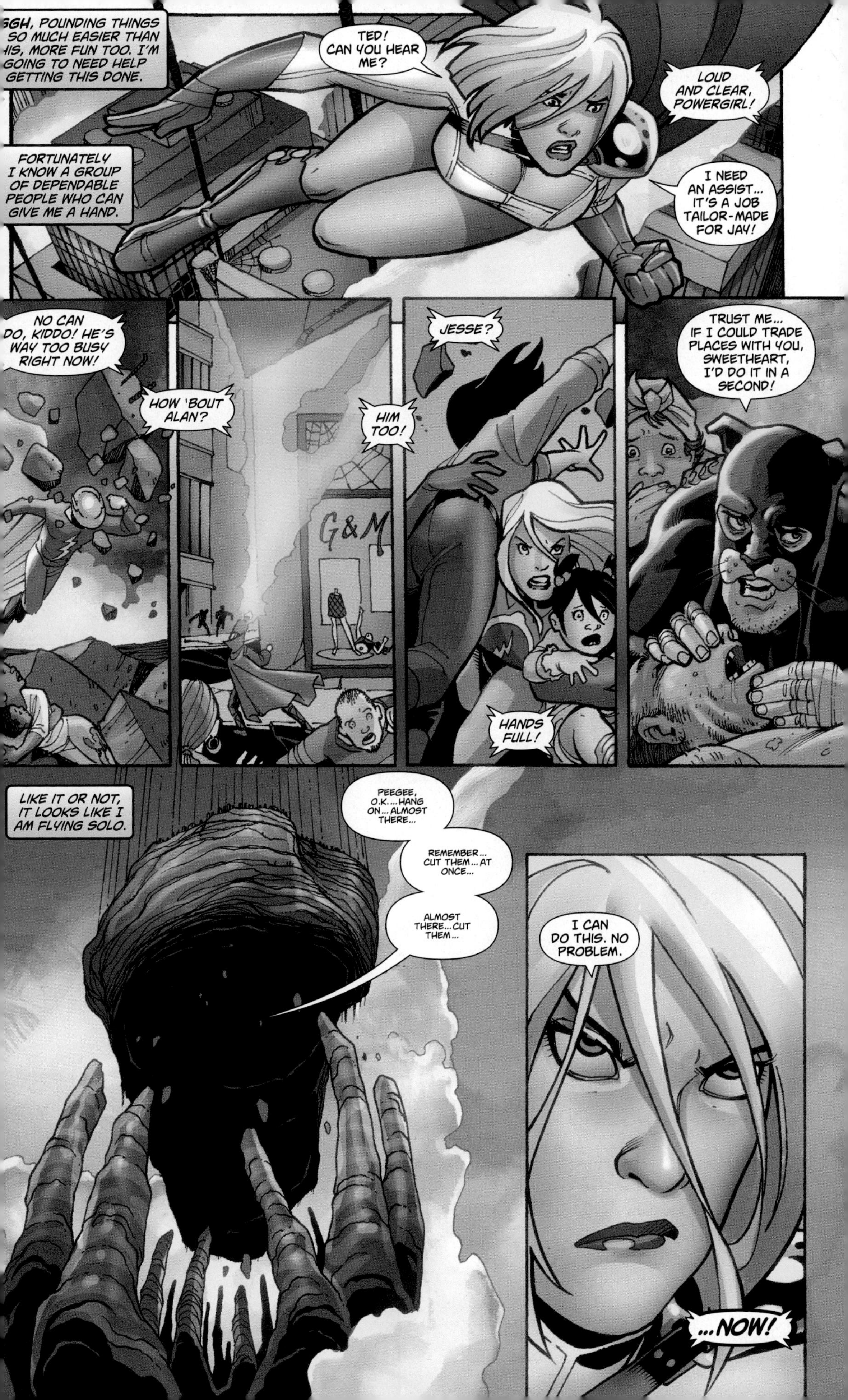

GGH, POUNDING THINGS SO MUCH EASIER THAN HIS, MORE FUN TOO. I'M GOING TO NEED HELP GETTING THIS DONE.
TED! CAN YOU HEAR ME?
LOUD AND CLEAR, POWERGIRL!
FORTUNATELY I KNOW A GROUP OF DEPENDABLE PEOPLE WHO CAN GIVE ME A HAND.
I NEED AN ASSIST... IT'S A JOB TAILOR-MADE FOR JAY!
NO CAN DO, KIDDO! HE'S WAY TOO BUSY RIGHT NOW!
HOW 'BOUT ALAN?
HIM TOO!
G&M
JESSE?
HANDS FULL!
TRUST ME... IF I COULD TRADE PLACES WITH YOU, SWEETHEART, I'D DO IT IN A SECOND!
LIKE IT OR NOT, IT LOOKS LIKE I AM FLYING SOLO.
PEEGEE, O.K.... HANG ON... ALMOST THERE...
REMEMBER... CUT THEM... AT ONCE...
ALMOST THERE... CUT THEM...
I CAN DO THIS. NO PROBLEM.
...NOW!

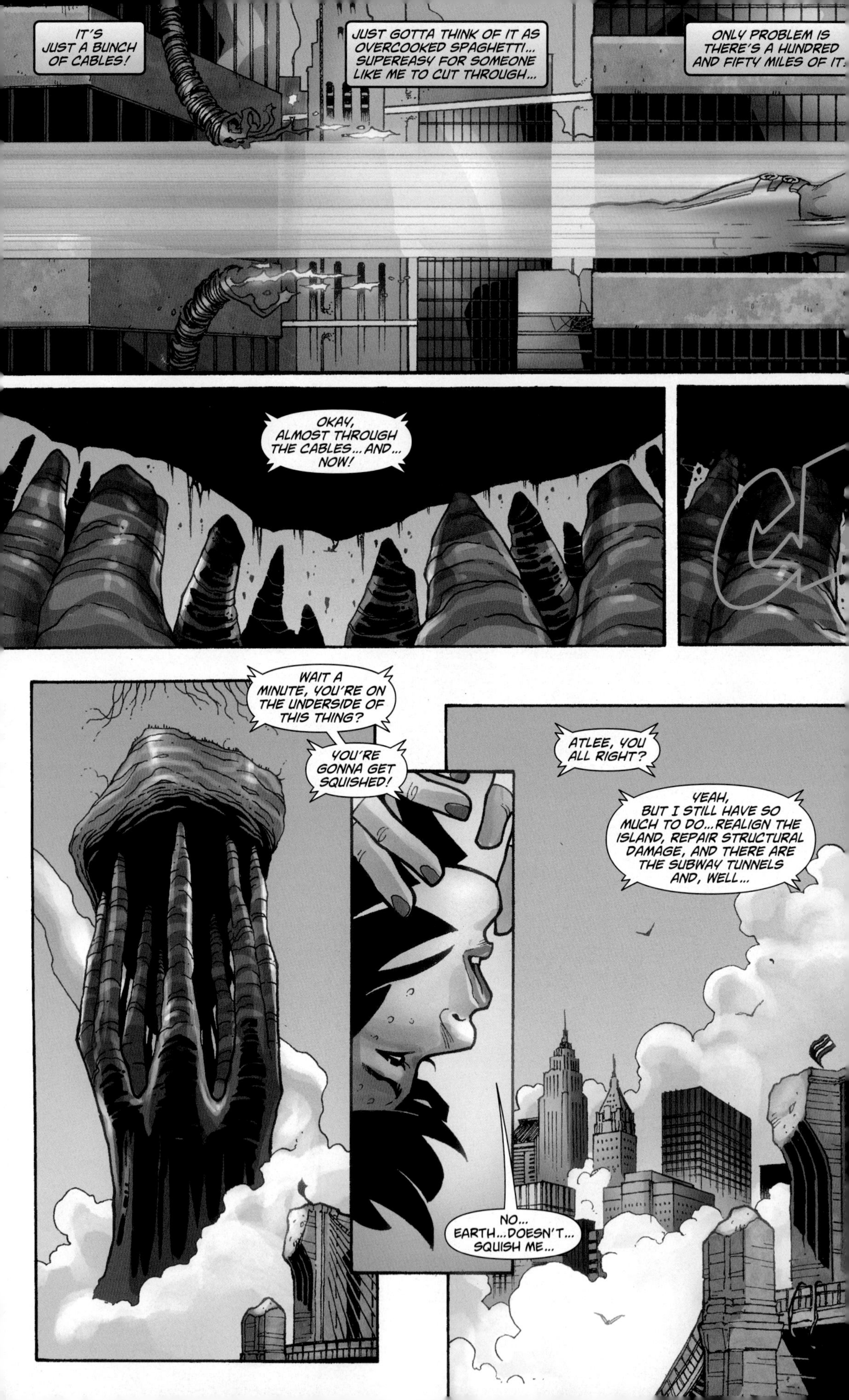

IT'S JUST A BUNCH OF CABLES!
JUST GOTTA THINK OF IT AS OVERCOOKED SPAGHETTI... SUPEREASY FOR SOMEONE LIKE ME TO CUT THROUGH...
ONLY PROBLEM IS THERE'S A HUNDRED AND FIFTY MILES OF IT.
OKAY, ALMOST THROUGH THE CABLES... AND... NOW!
WAIT A MINUTE, YOU'RE ON THE UNDERSIDE OF THIS THING?
YOU'RE GONNA GET SQUISHED!
ATLEE, YOU ALL RIGHT?
YEAH, BUT I STILL HAVE SO MUCH TO DO... REALIGN THE ISLAND, REPAIR STRUCTURAL DAMAGE, AND THERE ARE THE SUBWAY TUNNELS AND, WELL...
NO... EARTH... DOESN'T... SQUISH ME...

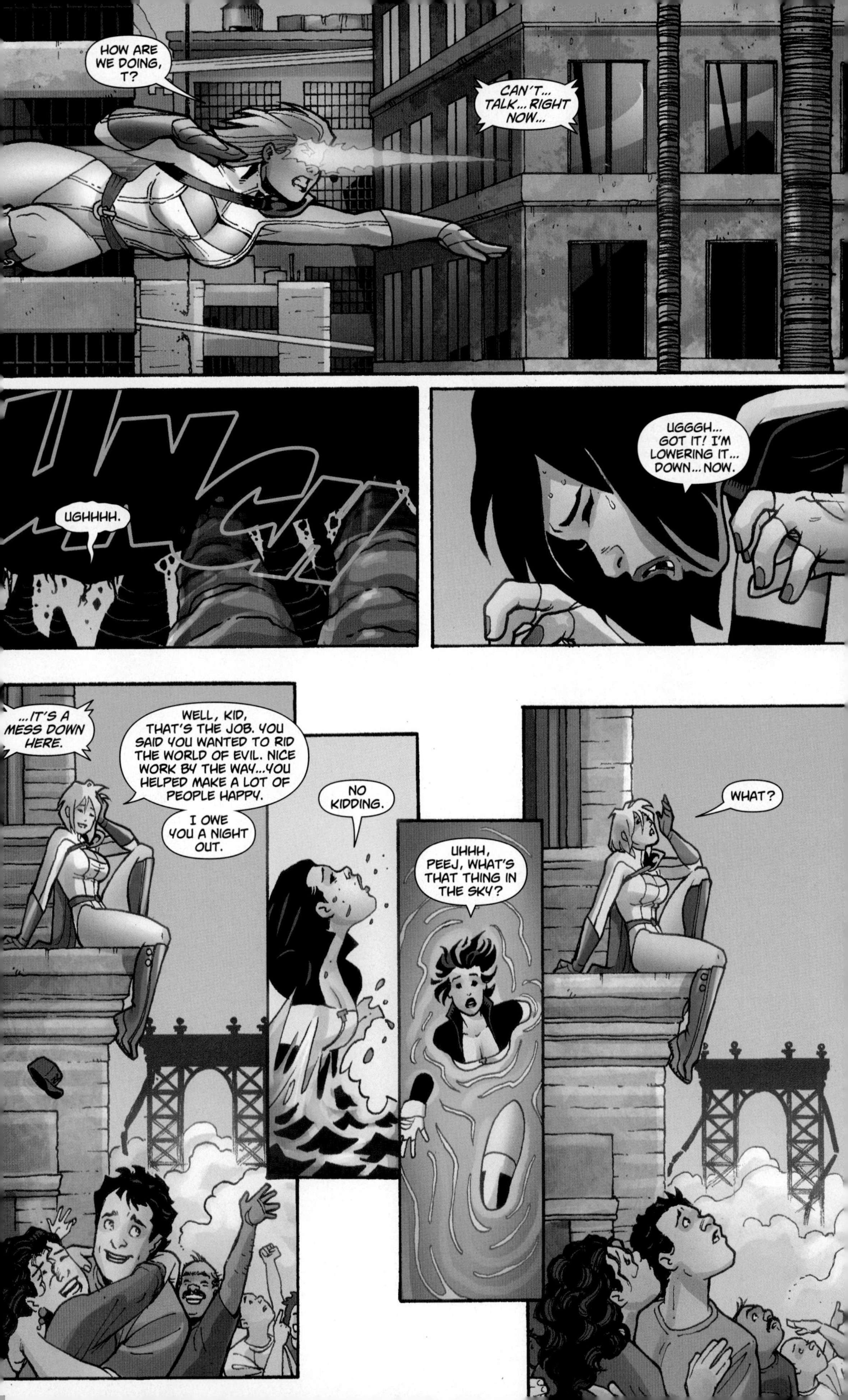
HOW ARE WE DOING, T?
CAN'T... TALK... RIGHT NOW...
UGHHHH.
UGGGH... GOT IT! I'M LOWERING IT... DOWN... NOW.
...IT'S A MESS DOWN HERE.
WELL, KID, THAT'S THE JOB. YOU SAID YOU WANTED TO RID THE WORLD OF EVIL. NICE WORK BY THE WAY...YOU HELPED MAKE A LOT OF PEOPLE HAPPY.
I OWE YOU A NIGHT OUT.
NO KIDDING.
UHHH, PEEJ, WHAT'S THAT THING IN THE SKY?
WHAT?

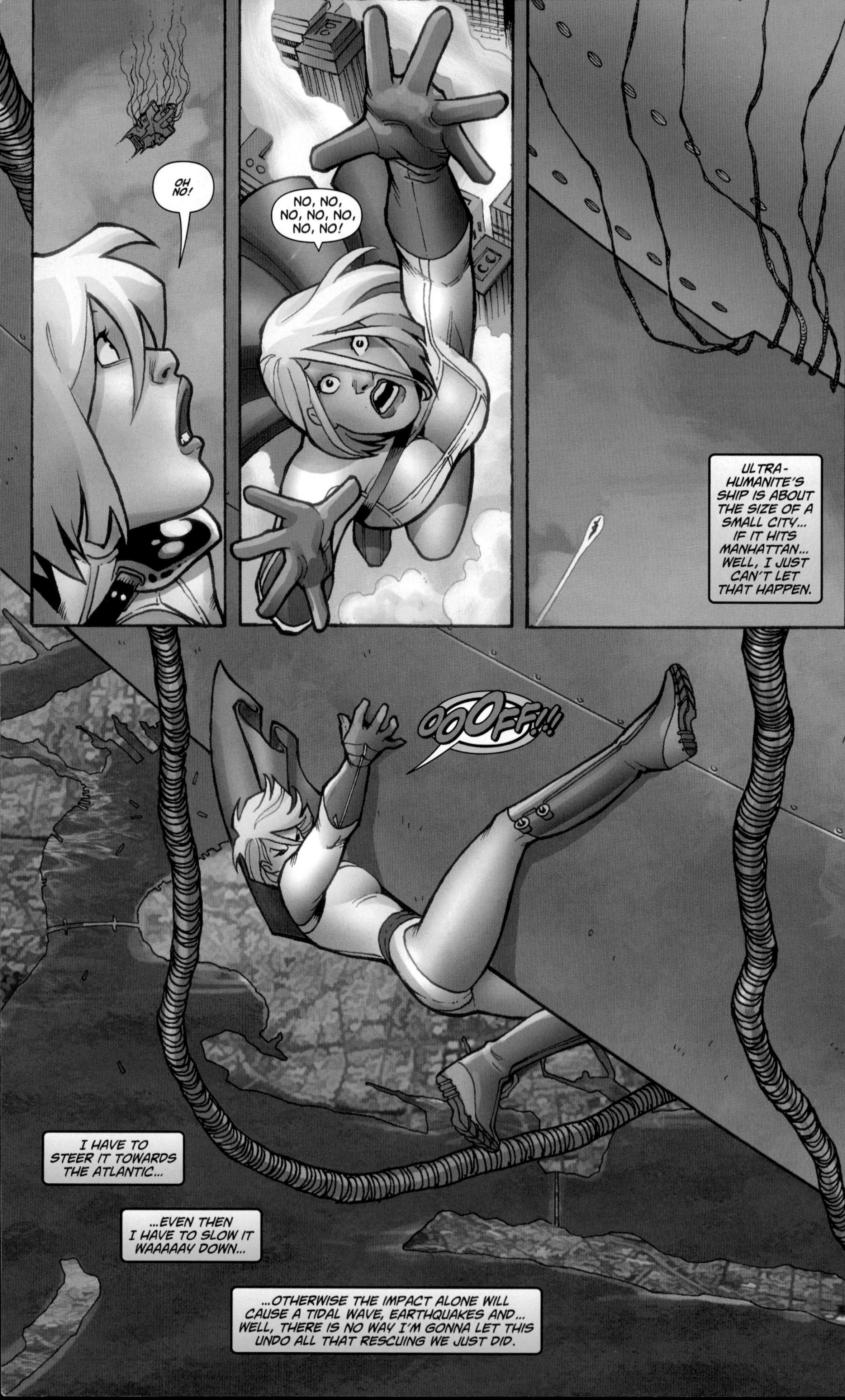
OH NO!
NO, NO, NO, NO, NO, NO, NO!
ULTRA-HUMANITE'S SHIP IS ABOUT THE SIZE OF A SMALL CITY... IF IT HITS MANHATTAN... WELL, I JUST CAN'T LET THAT HAPPEN.
OOOFF!!!
I HAVE TO STEER IT TOWARDS THE ATLANTIC...
...EVEN THEN I HAVE TO SLOW IT WAAAAAY DOWN...
...OTHERWISE THE IMPACT ALONE WILL CAUSE A TIDAL WAVE, EARTHQUAKES AND... WELL, THERE IS NO WAY I'M GONNA LET THIS UNDO ALL THAT RESCUING WE JUST DID.

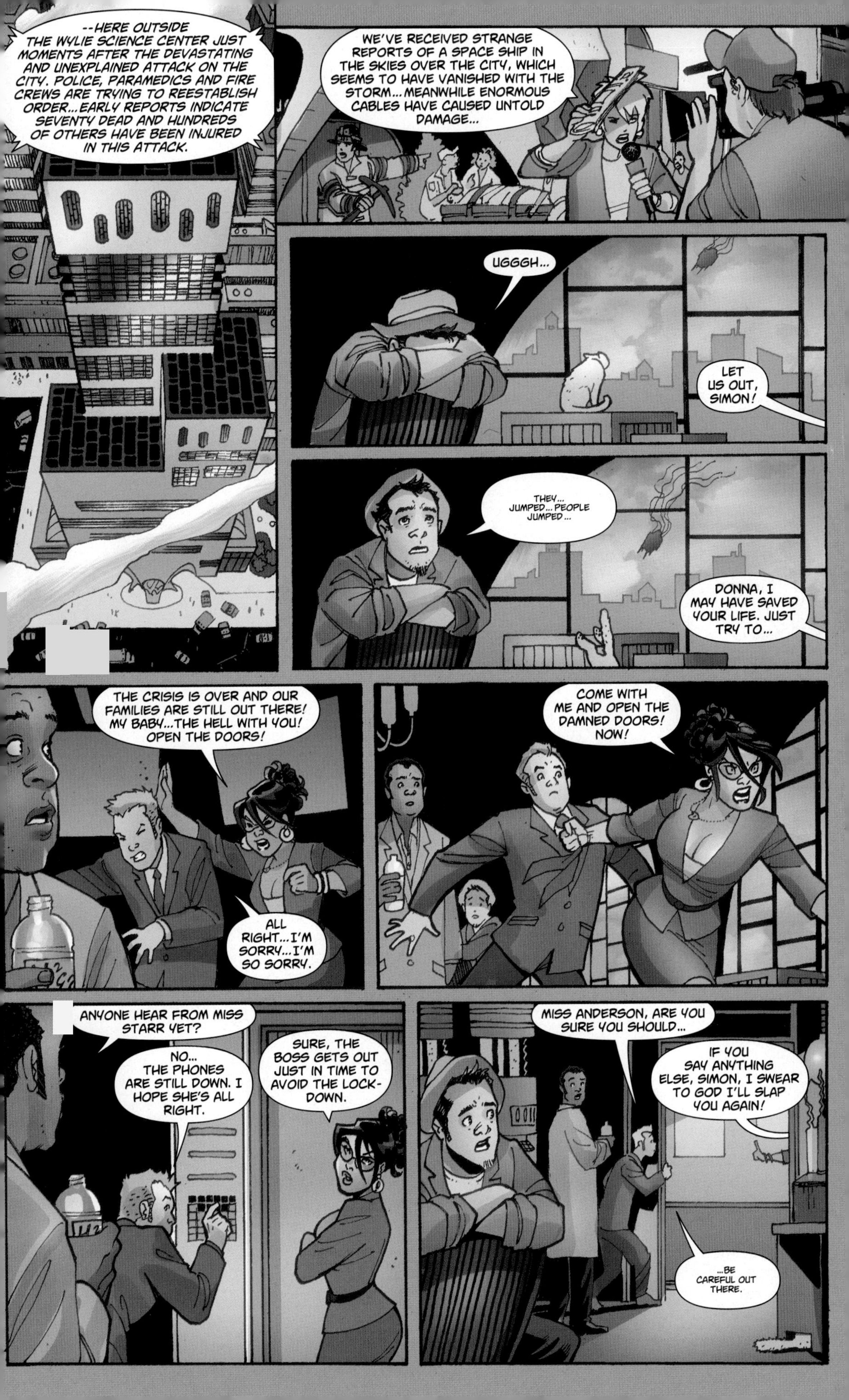
--HERE OUTSIDE THE WYLIE SCIENCE CENTER JUST MOMENTS AFTER THE DEVASTATING AND UNEXPLAINED ATTACK ON THE CITY. POLICE, PARAMEDICS AND FIRE CREWS ARE TRYING TO REESTABLISH ORDER...EARLY REPORTS INDICATE SEVENTY DEAD AND HUNDREDS OF OTHERS HAVE BEEN INJURED IN THIS ATTACK.
WE'VE RECEIVED STRANGE REPORTS OF A SPACE SHIP IN THE SKIES OVER THE CITY, WHICH SEEMS TO HAVE VANISHED WITH THE STORM...MEANWHILE ENORMOUS CABLES HAVE CAUSED UNTOLD DAMAGE...
UGGGH...
LET US OUT, SIMON!
THEY... JUMPED... PEOPLE JUMPED...
DONNA, I MAY HAVE SAVED YOUR LIFE. JUST TRY TO...
THE CRISIS IS OVER AND OUR FAMILIES ARE STILL OUT THERE! MY BABY...THE HELL WITH YOU! OPEN THE DOORS!
ALL RIGHT...I'M SORRY...I'M SO SORRY.
COME WITH ME AND OPEN THE DAMNED DOORS! NOW!
ANYONE HEAR FROM MISS STARR YET?
NO... THE PHONES ARE STILL DOWN. I HOPE SHE'S ALL RIGHT.
SURE, THE BOSS GETS OUT JUST IN TIME TO AVOID THE LOCK-DOWN.
MISS ANDERSON, ARE YOU SURE YOU SHOULD...
IF YOU SAY ANYTHING ELSE, SIMON, I SWEAR TO GOD I'LL SLAP YOU AGAIN!
...BE CAREFUL OUT THERE.

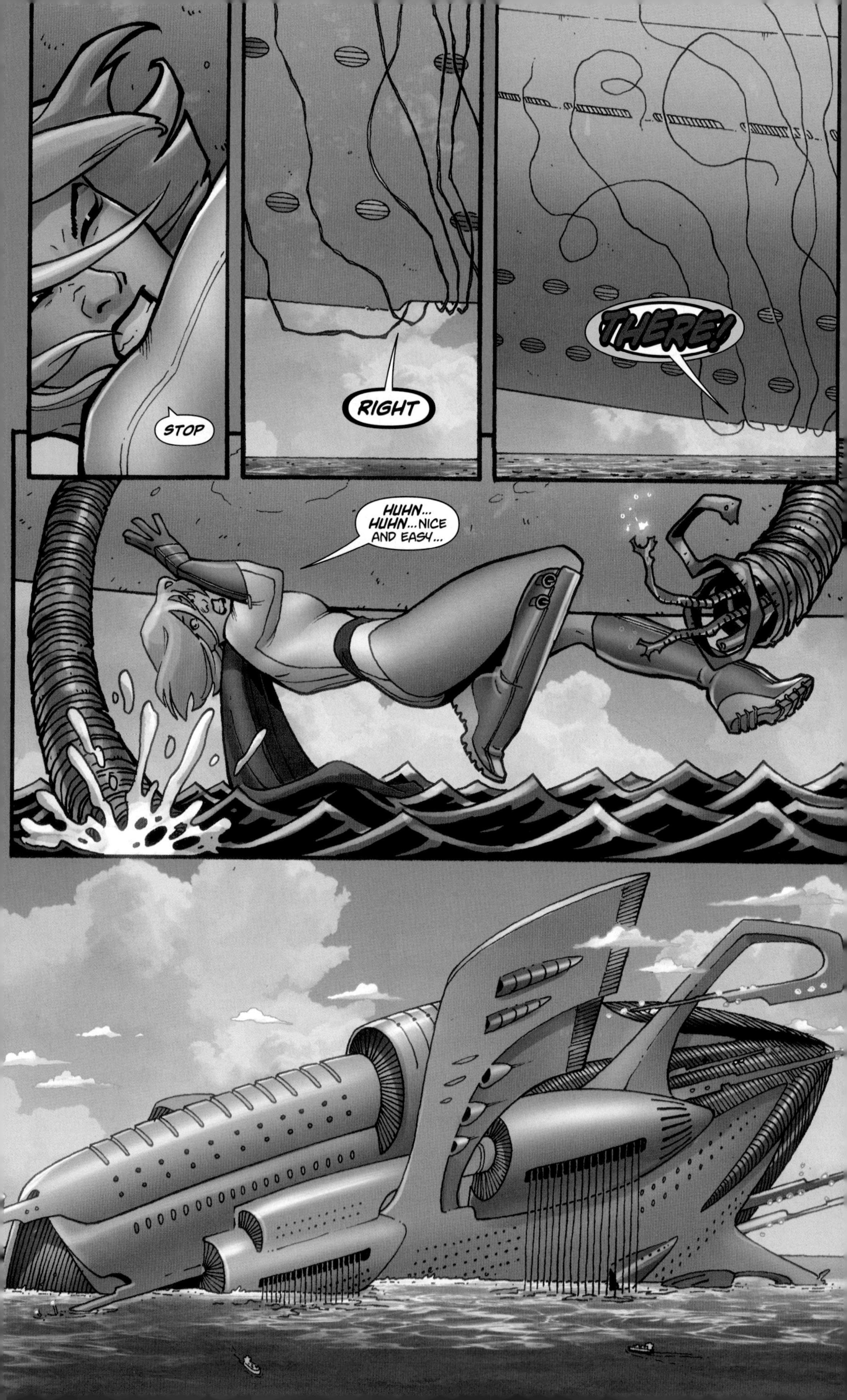
STOP
RIGHT
THERE!
HUHN... HUHN...NICE AND EASY...

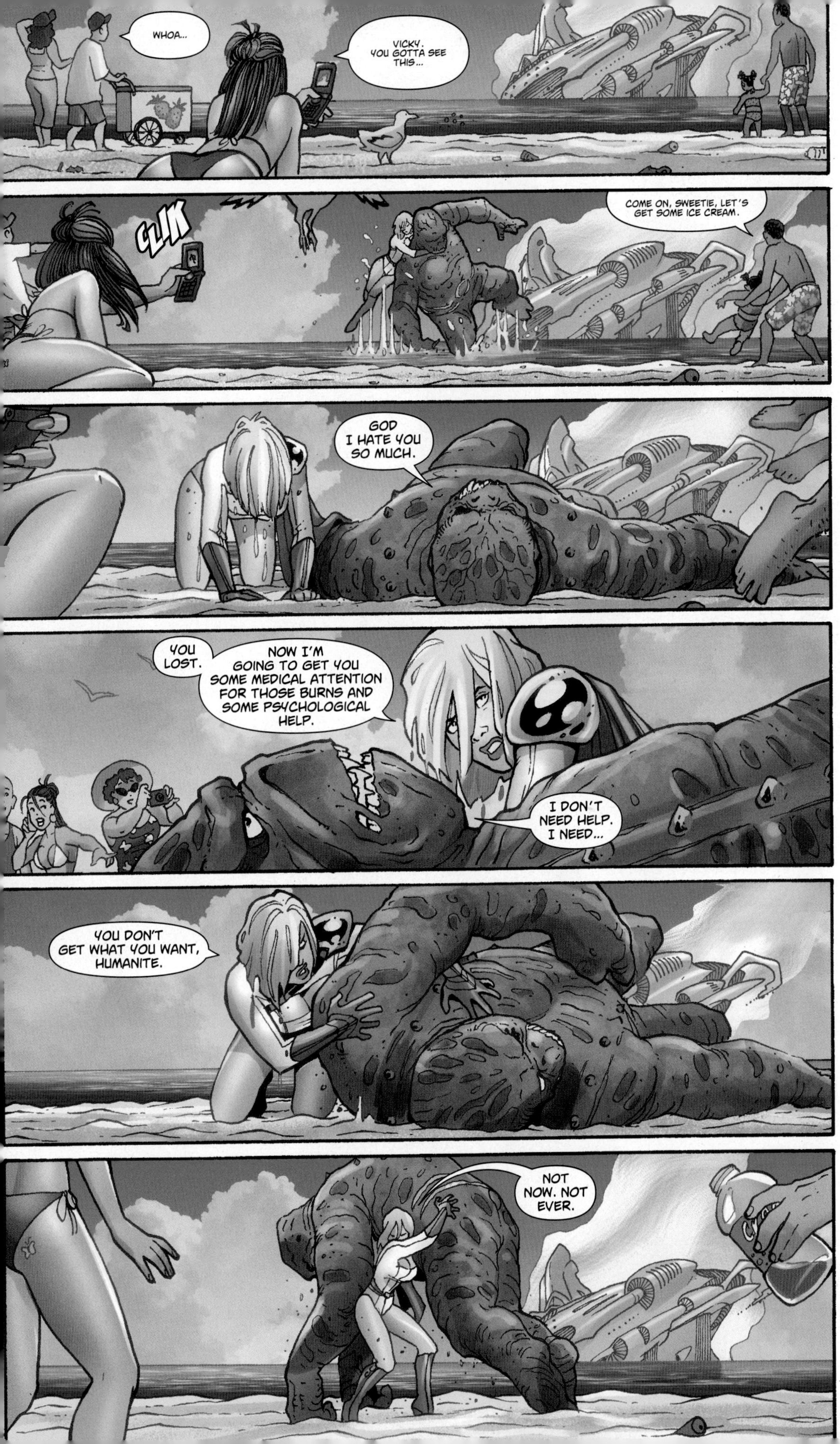
WHOA...
VICKY. YOU GOTTA SEE THIS...
CLIK
COME ON, SWEETIE, LET'S GET SOME ICE CREAM.
GOD I HATE YOU SO MUCH.
YOU LOST.
NOW I'M GOING TO GET YOU SOME MEDICAL ATTENTION FOR THOSE BURNS AND SOME PSYCHOLOGICAL HELP.
I DON'T NEED HELP. I NEED...
YOU DON'T GET WHAT YOU WANT, HUMANITE.
NOT NOW. NOT EVER.

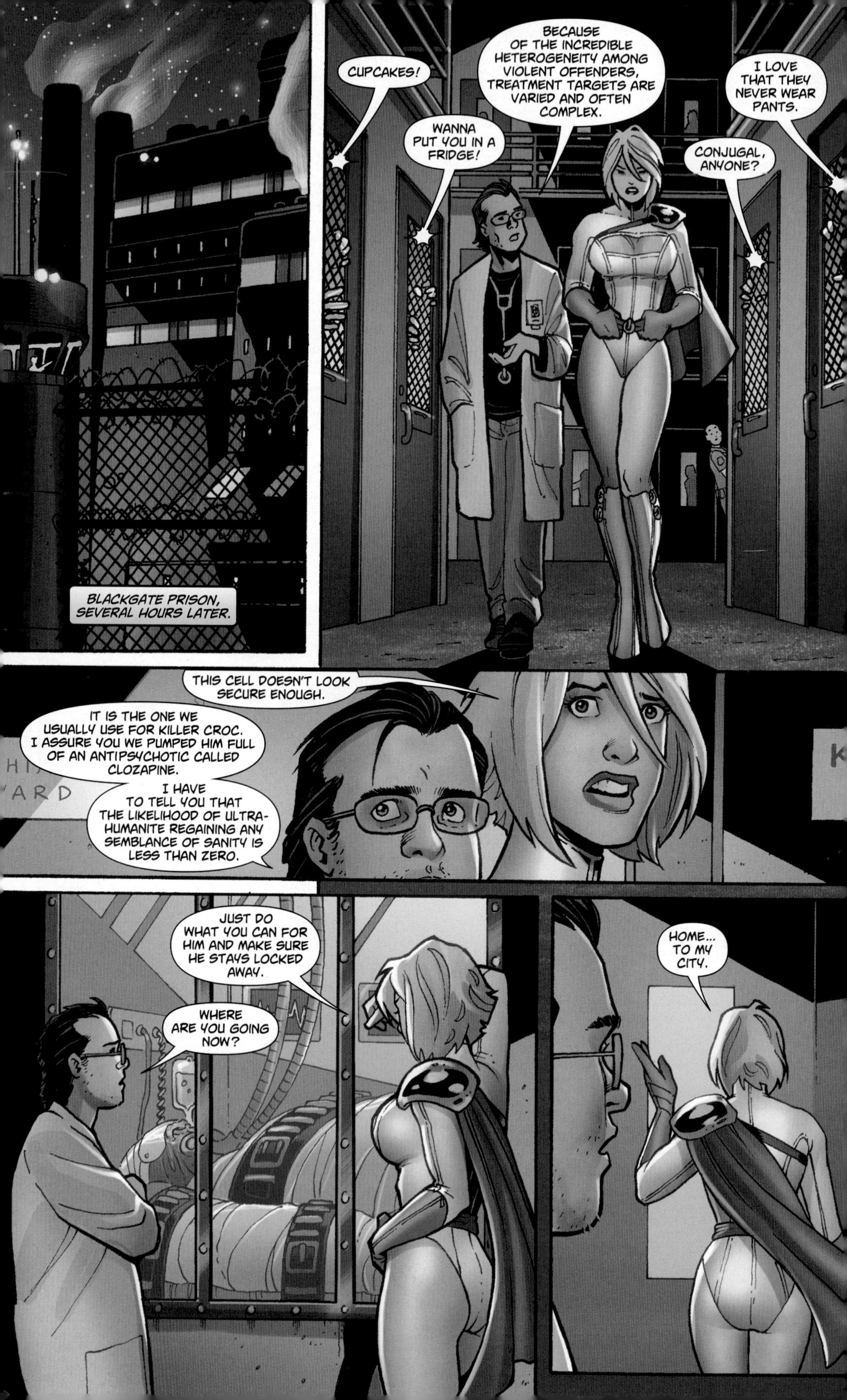
BLACKGATE PRISON, SEVERAL HOURS LATER.
CUPCAKES!
BECAUSE OF THE INCREDIBLE HETEROGENEITY AMONG VIOLENT OFFENDERS, TREATMENT TARGETS ARE VARIED AND OFTEN COMPLEX.
WANNA PUT YOU IN A FRIDGE!
I LOVE THAT THEY NEVER WEAR PANTS.
CONJUGAL, ANYONE?
THIS CELL DOESN'T LOOK SECURE ENOUGH.
IT IS THE ONE WE USUALLY USE FOR KILLER CROC. I ASSURE YOU WE PUMPED HIM FULL OF AN ANTIPSYCHOTIC CALLED CLOZAPINE.
I HAVE TO TELL YOU THAT THE LIKELIHOOD OF ULTRA-HUMANITE REGAINING ANY SEMBLANCE OF SANITY IS LESS THAN ZERO.
JUST DO WHAT YOU CAN FOR HIM AND MAKE SURE HE STAYS LOCKED AWAY.
WHERE ARE YOU GOING NOW?
HOME... TO MY CITY.

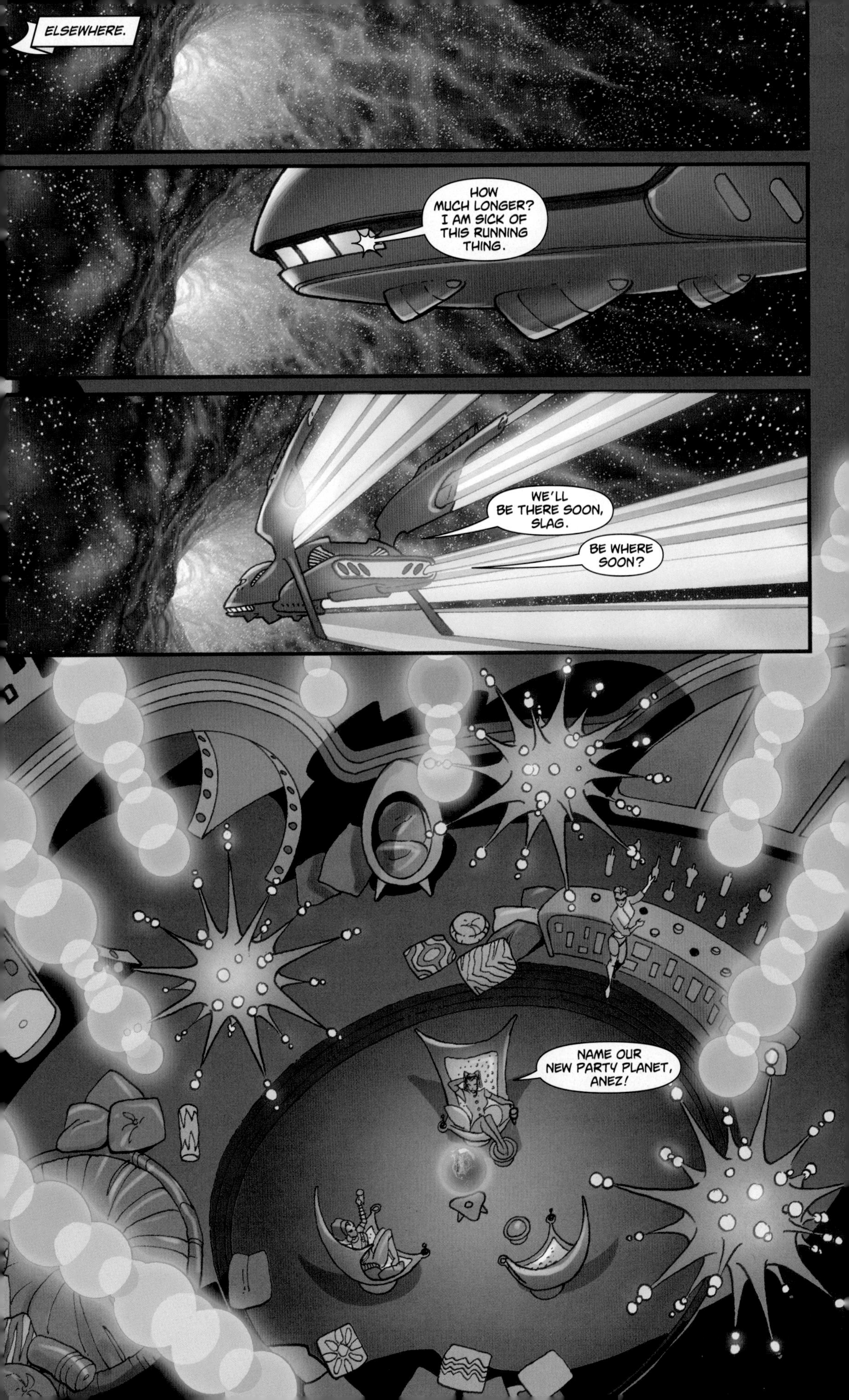
ELSEWHERE.
HOW MUCH LONGER? I AM SICK OF THIS RUNNING THING.
WE'LL BE THERE SOON, SLAG.
BE WHERE SOON?
NAME OUR NEW PARTY PLANET, ANEZ!

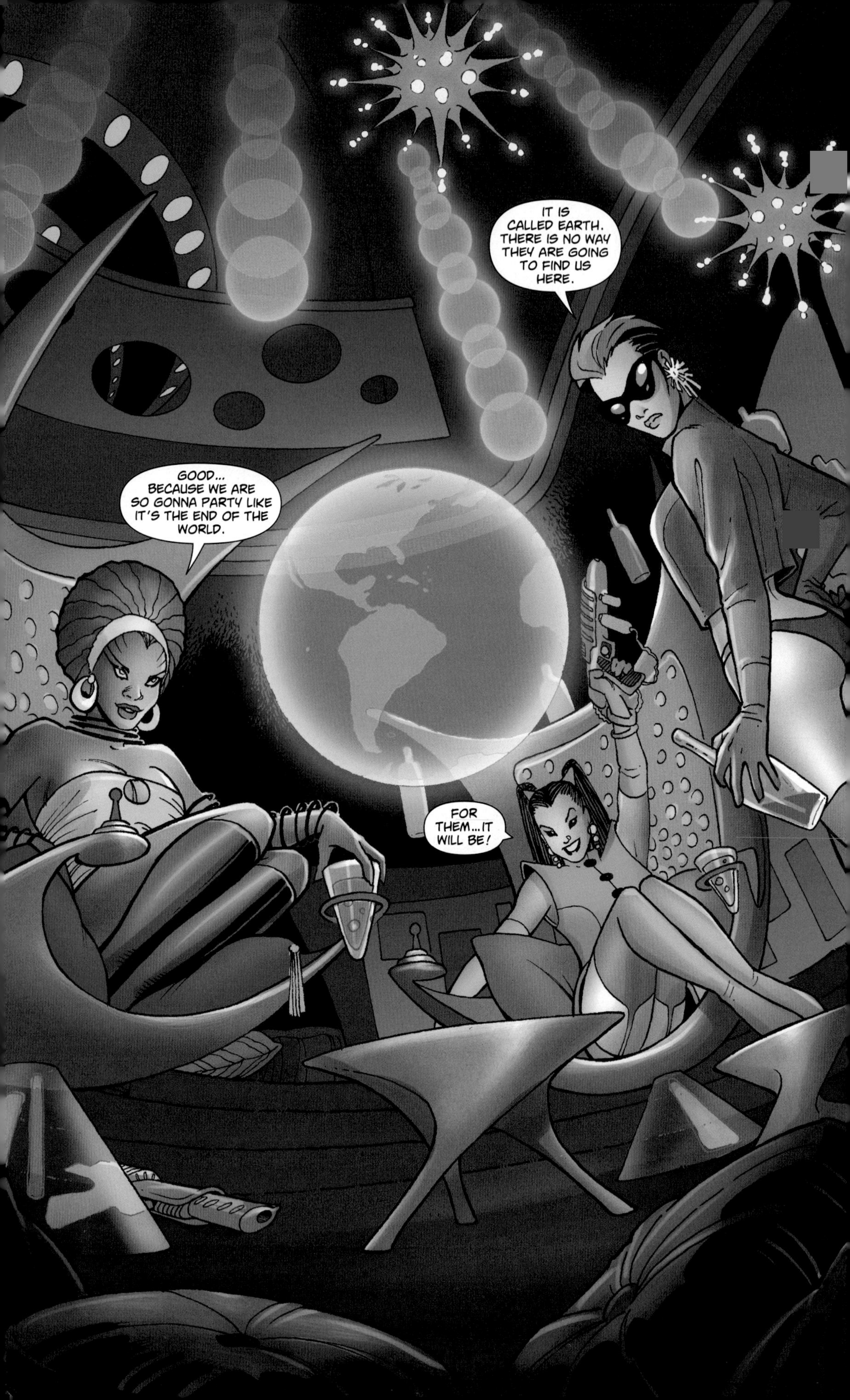
IT IS CALLED EARTH. THERE IS NO WAY THEY ARE GOING TO FIND US HERE.
GOOD... BECAUSE WE ARE SO GONNA PARTY LIKE IT'S THE END OF THE WORLD.
FOR THEM...IT WILL BE!

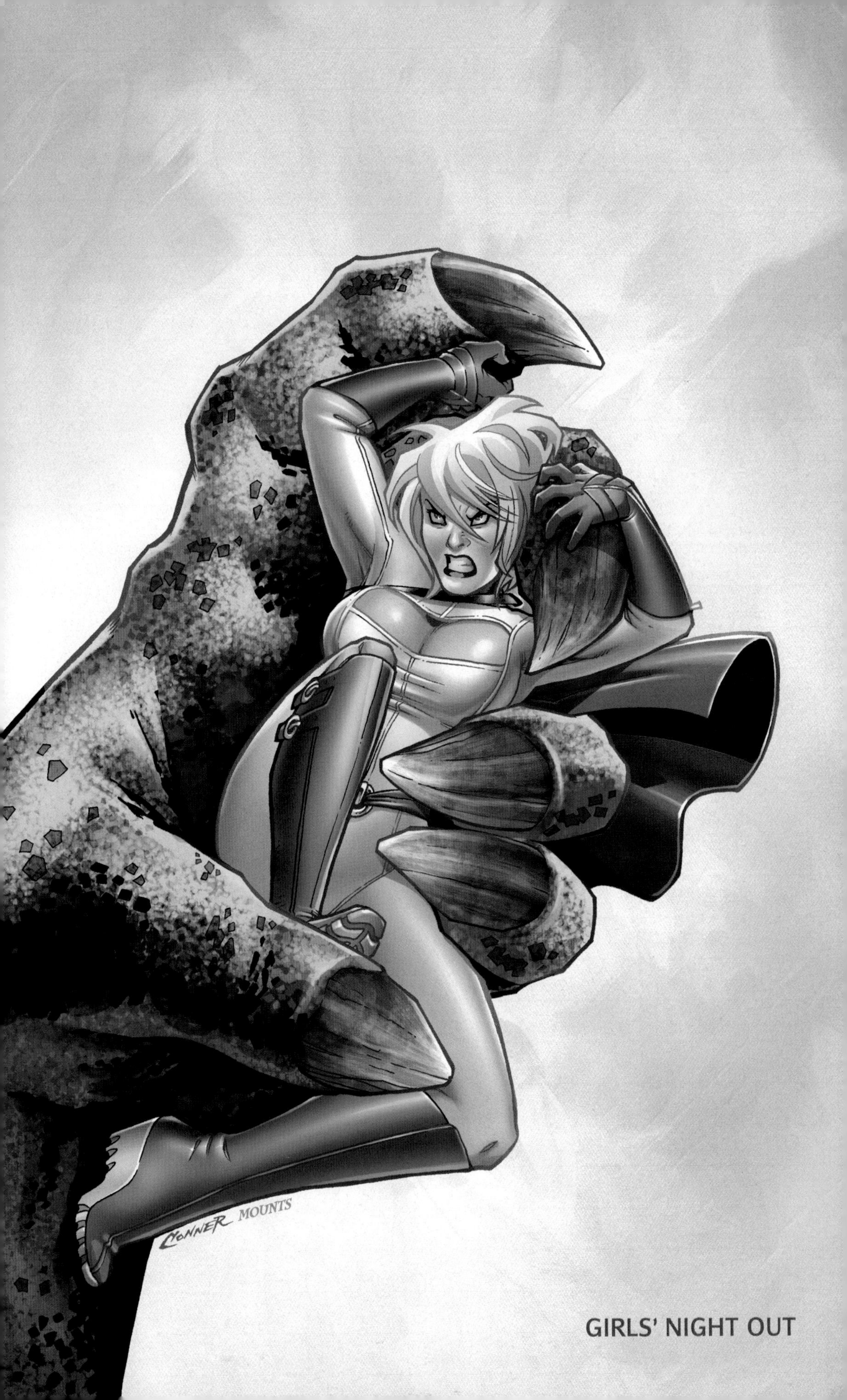
CONNER MOUNTS

GIRLS' NIGHT OUT

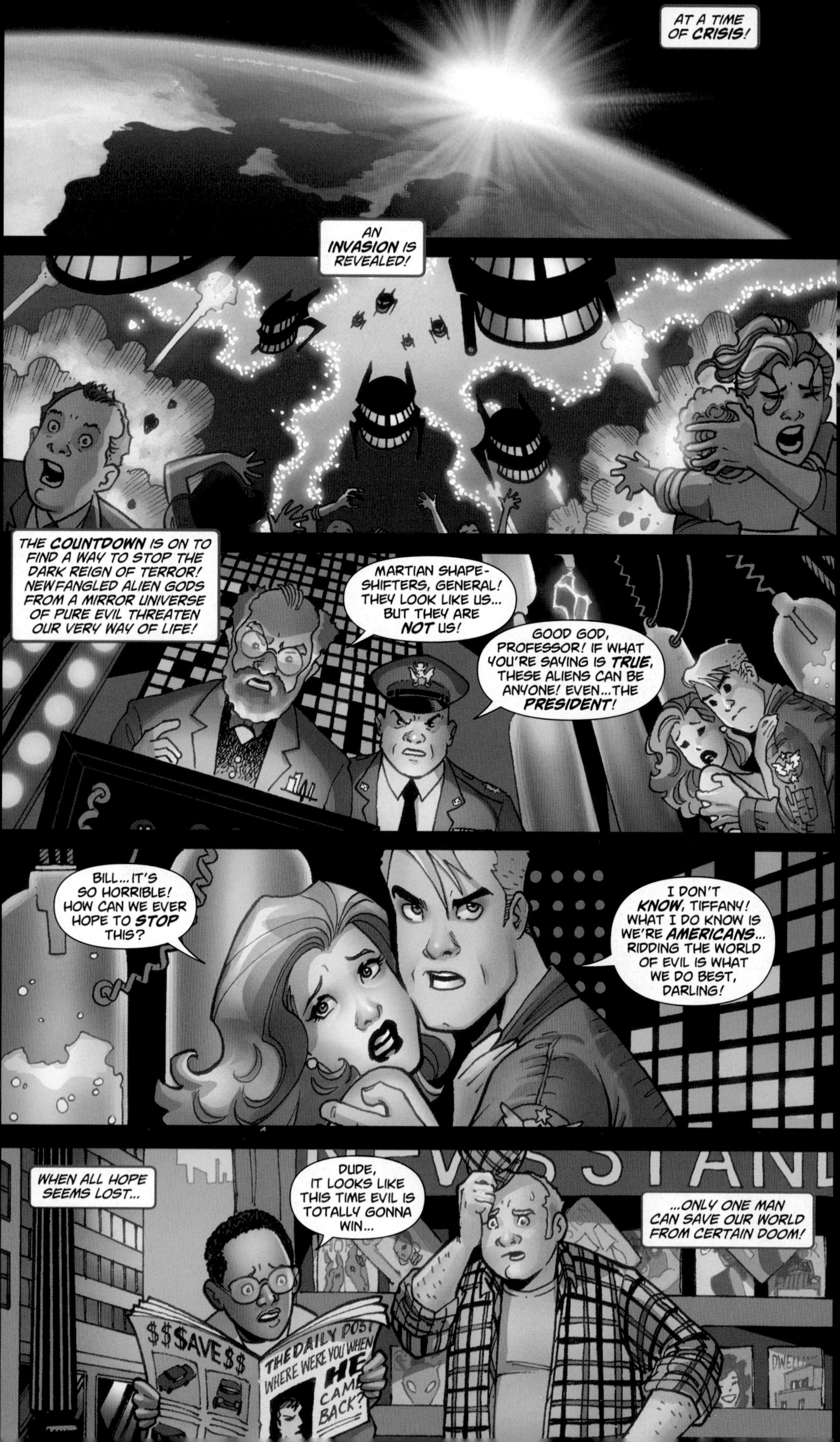

AT A TIME OF CRISIS!
AN INVASION IS REVEALED!
THE COUNTDOWN IS ON TO FIND A WAY TO STOP THE DARK REIGN OF TERROR! NEWFANGLED ALIEN GODS FROM A MIRROR UNIVERSE OF PURE EVIL THREATEN OUR VERY WAY OF LIFE!
MARTIAN SHAPE-SHIFTERS, GENERAL! THEY LOOK LIKE US... BUT THEY ARE NOT US!
GOOD GOD, PROFESSOR! IF WHAT YOU'RE SAYING IS TRUE, THESE ALIENS CAN BE ANYONE! EVEN...THE PRESIDENT!
BILL...IT'S SO HORRIBLE! HOW CAN WE EVER HOPE TO STOP THIS?
I DON'T KNOW, TIFFANY! WHAT I DO KNOW IS WE'RE AMERICANS... RIDDING THE WORLD OF EVIL IS WHAT WE DO BEST, DARLING!
WHEN ALL HOPE SEEMS LOST...
DUDE, IT LOOKS LIKE THIS TIME EVIL IS TOTALLY GONNA WIN...
...ONLY ONE MAN CAN SAVE OUR WORLD FROM CERTAIN DOOM!
$$$AVE$$
WHERE WERE YOU WHEN HE

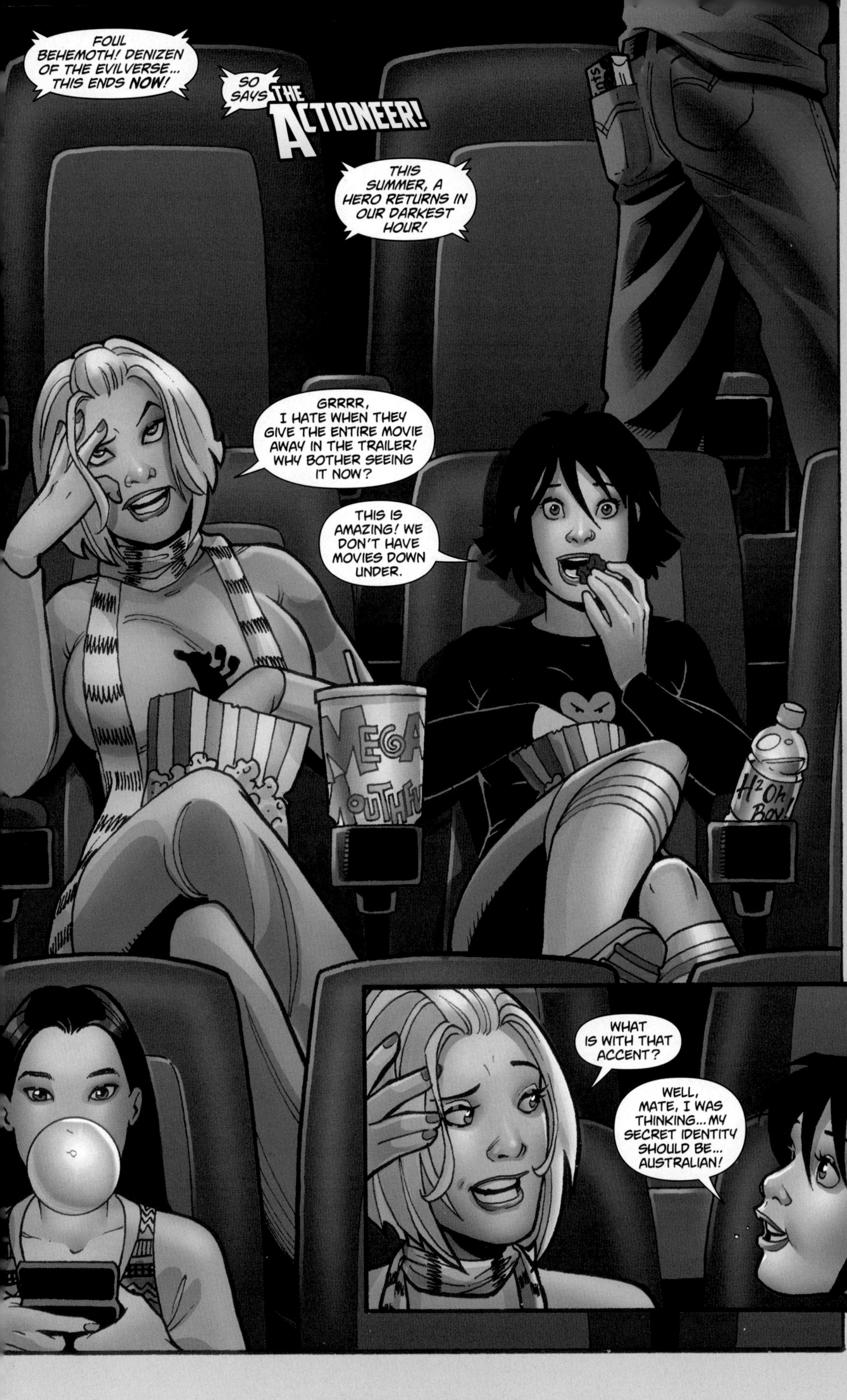
FOUL BEHEMOTH! DENIZEN OF THE EVILVERSE... THIS ENDS NOW!
SO SAYS THE ACTIONEER!
THIS SUMMER, A HERO RETURNS IN OUR DARKEST HOUR!
GRRRR, I HATE WHEN THEY GIVE THE ENTIRE MOVIE AWAY IN THE TRAILER! WHY BOTHER SEEING IT NOW?
THIS IS AMAZING! WE DON'T HAVE MOVIES DOWN UNDER.
MEGA MOUTHFU
H2 Oh Boy!
WHAT IS WITH THAT ACCENT?
WELL, MATE, I WAS THINKING... MY SECRET IDENTITY SHOULD BE... AUSTRALIAN!

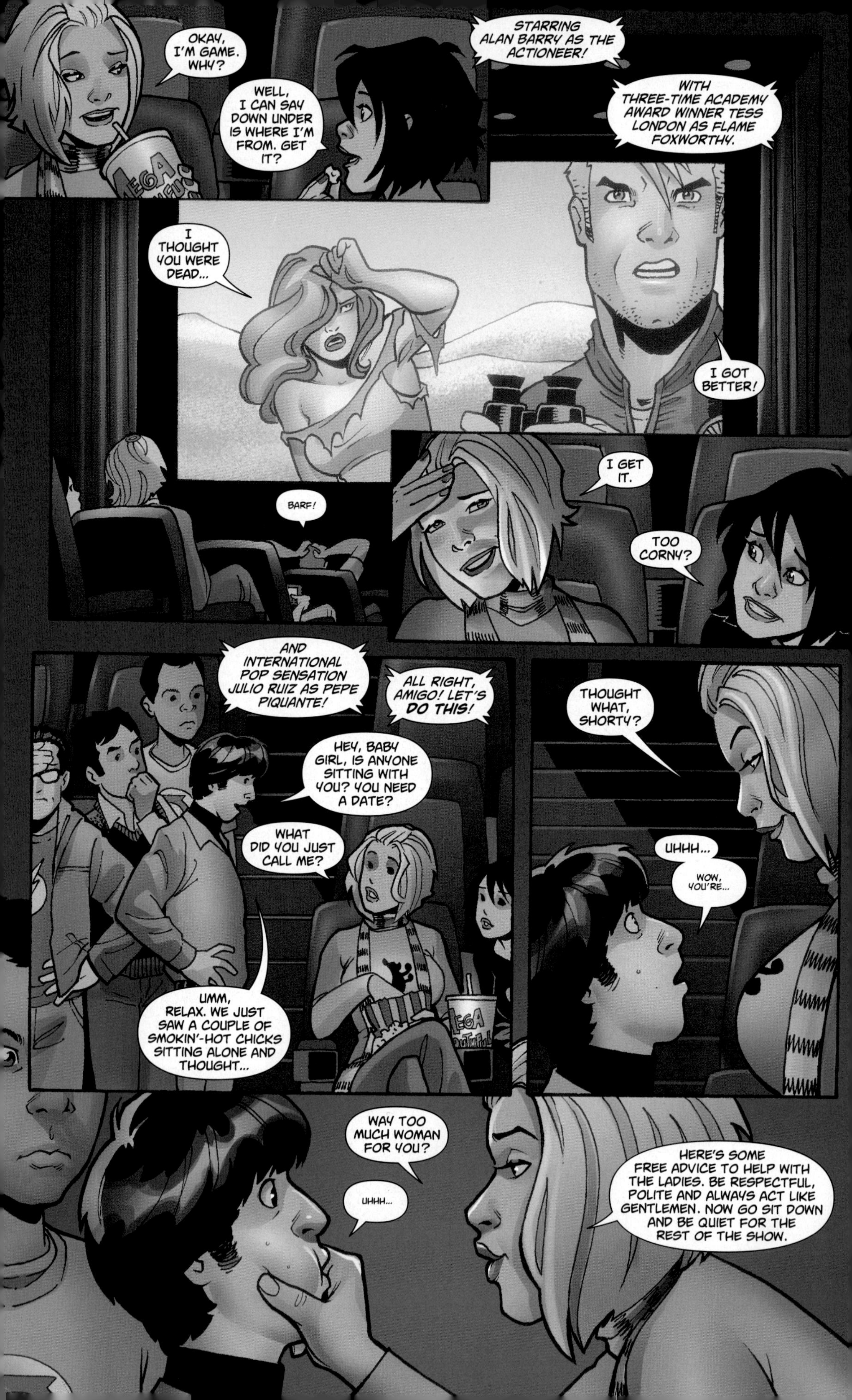

OKAY, I'M GAME. WHY?
WELL, I CAN SAY DOWN UNDER IS WHERE I'M FROM. GET IT?
STARRING ALAN BARRY AS THE ACTIONEER!
WITH THREE-TIME ACADEMY AWARD WINNER TESS LONDON AS FLAME FOXWORTHY.
I THOUGHT YOU WERE DEAD...
I GOT BETTER!
BARF!
I GET IT.
TOO CORNY?
AND INTERNATIONAL POP SENSATION JULIO RUIZ AS PEPE PIQUANTE!
ALL RIGHT, AMIGO! LET'S DO THIS!
HEY, BABY GIRL, IS ANYONE SITTING WITH YOU? YOU NEED A DATE?
WHAT DID YOU JUST CALL ME?
UMM, RELAX. WE JUST SAW A COUPLE OF SMOKIN'-HOT CHICKS SITTING ALONE AND THOUGHT...
THOUGHT WHAT, SHORTY?
UHHH...
WOW, YOU'RE...
WAY TOO MUCH WOMAN FOR YOU?
UHHH...
HERE'S SOME FREE ADVICE TO HELP WITH THE LADIES. BE RESPECTFUL, POLITE AND ALWAYS ACT LIKE GENTLEMEN. NOW GO SIT DOWN AND BE QUIET FOR THE REST OF THE SHOW.

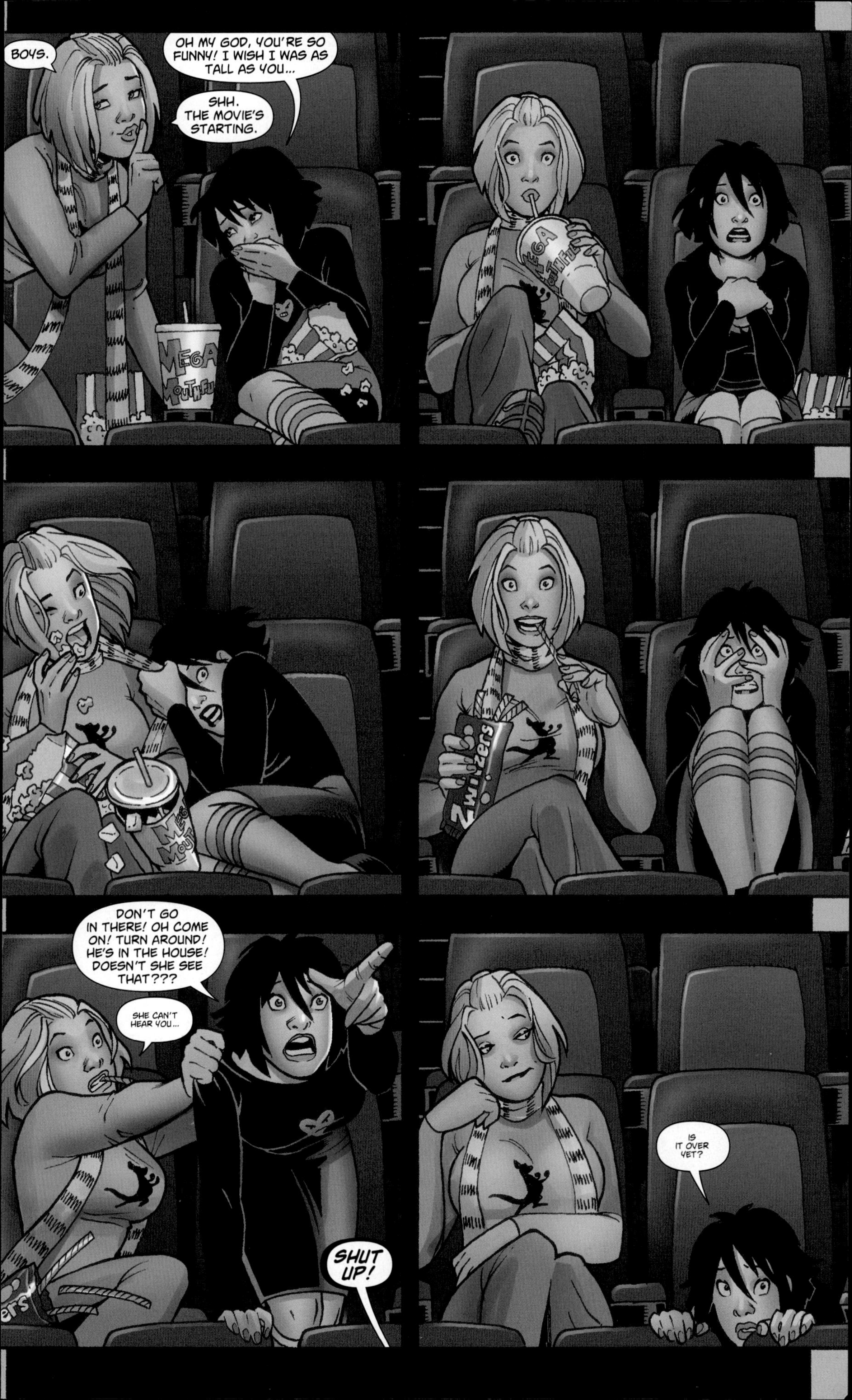
BOYS.
OH MY GOD, YOU'RE SO FUNNY! I WISH I WAS AS TALL AS YOU...
SHH. THE MOVIE'S STARTING.
DON'T GO IN THERE! OH COME ON! TURN AROUND! HE'S IN THE HOUSE! DOESN'T SHE SEE THAT???
SHE CAN'T HEAR YOU...
SHUT UP!
IS IT OVER YET?

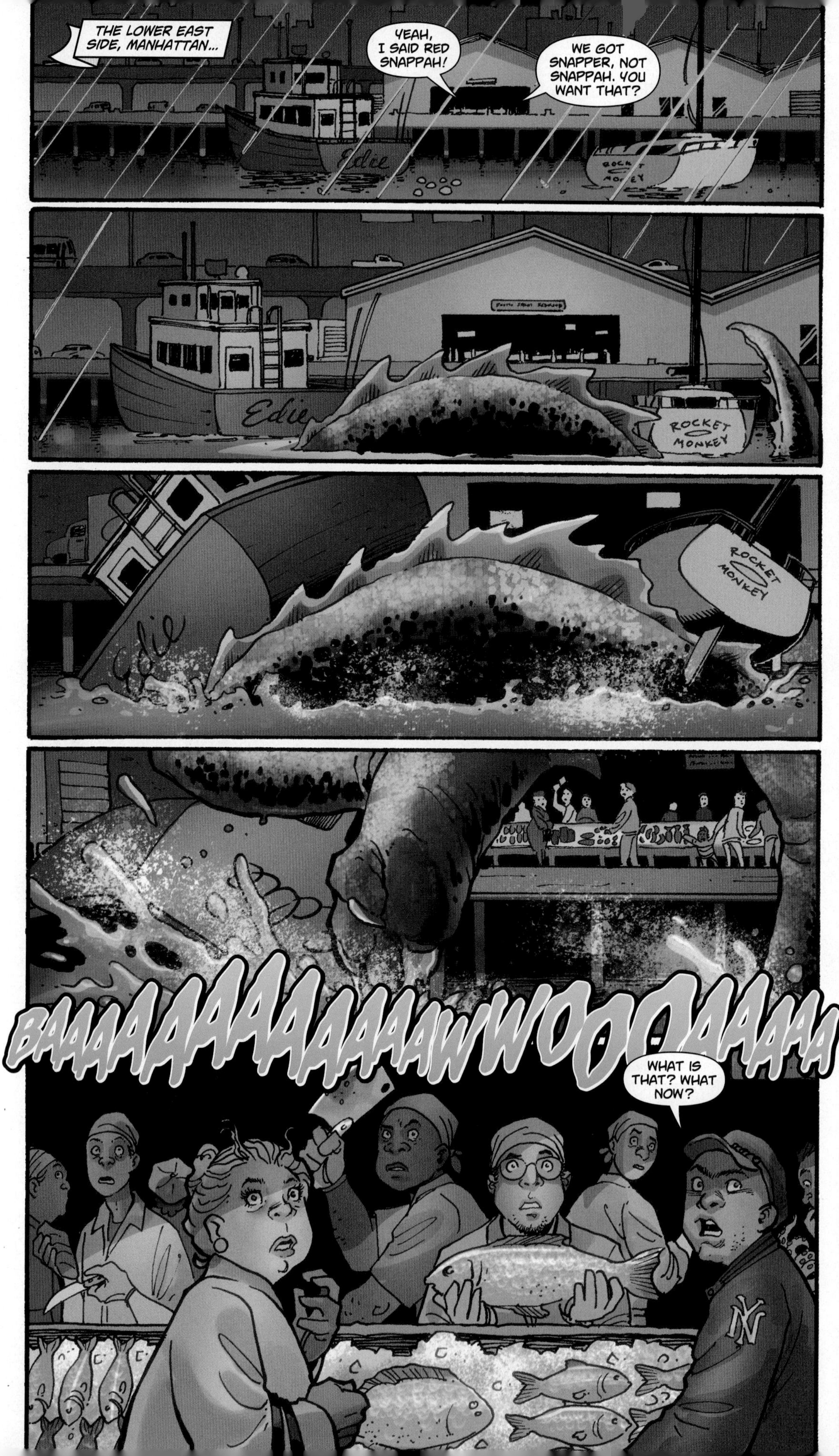
THE LOWER EAST SIDE, MANHATTAN...
YEAH, I SAID RED SNAPPAH!
WE GOT SNAPPER, NOT SNAPPAH. YOU WANT THAT?
Edie
ROCKET MONKEY
BAAAAAAAAAAAAAAWOOOAAAAA
WHAT IS THAT? WHAT NOW?

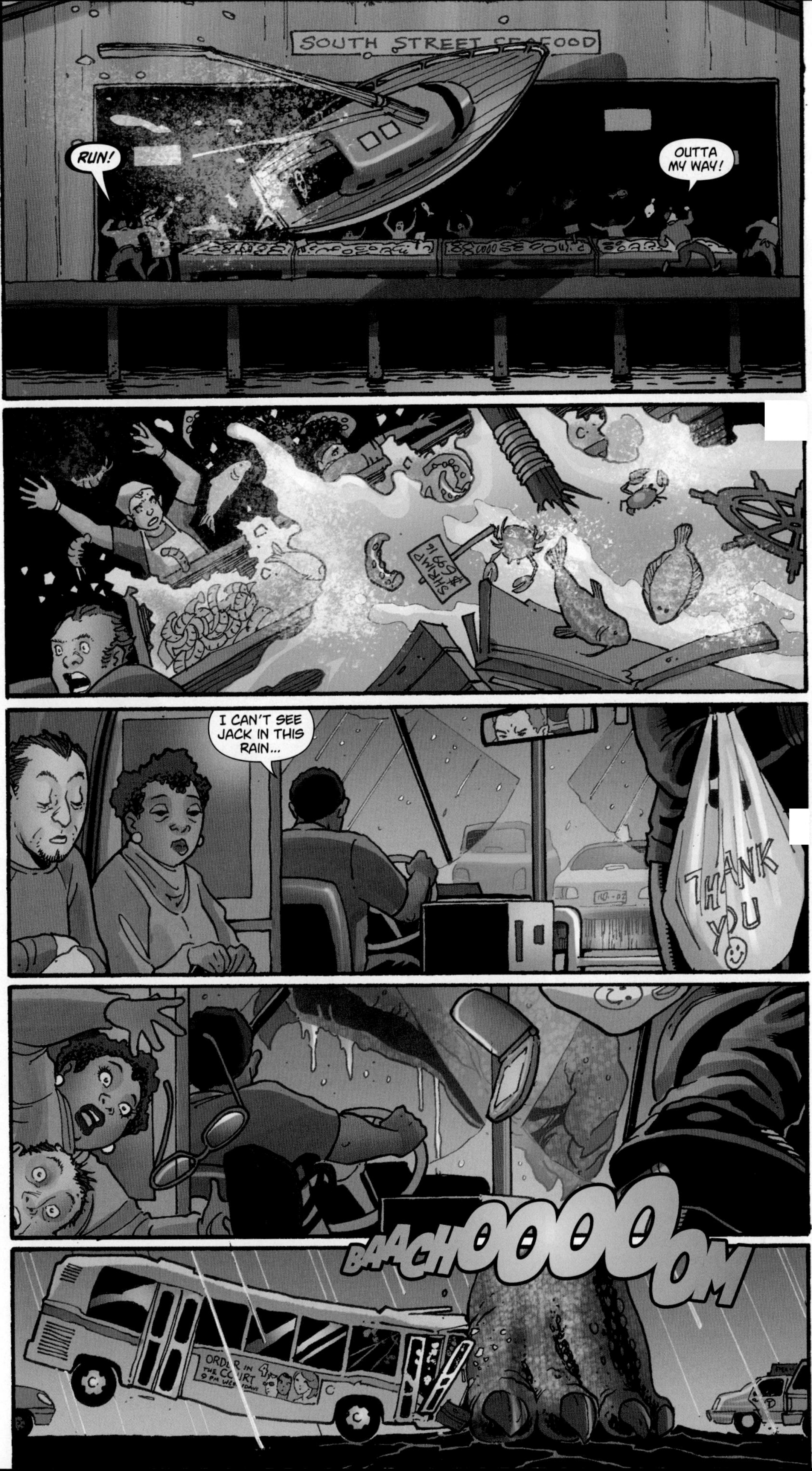
SOUTH STREET SEAFOOD
RUN!
OUTTA MY WAY!
I CAN'T SEE JACK IN THIS RAIN...
THANK YOU
ORDER IN THE COURT
BAACHOOOOOM

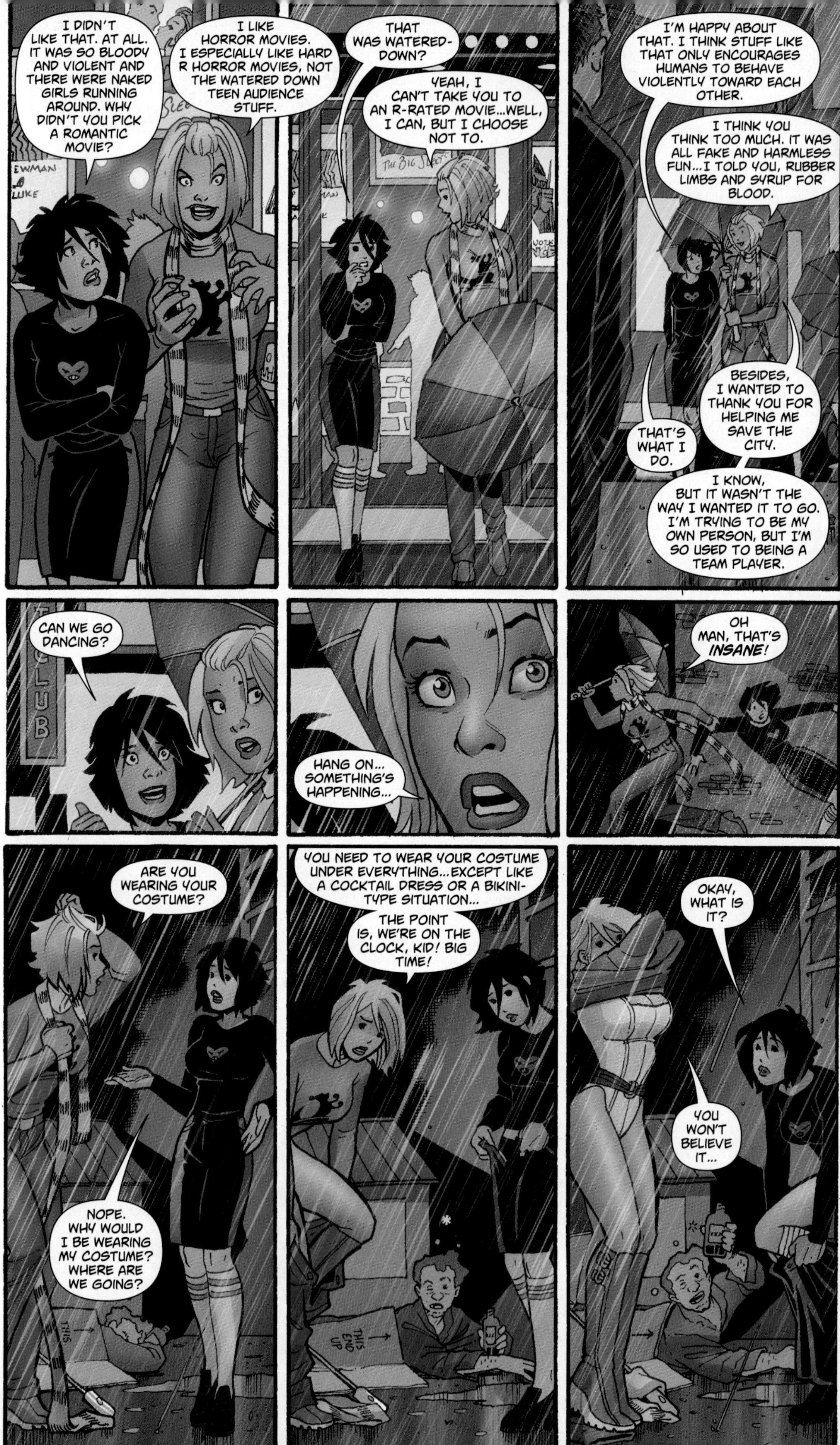
I DIDN'T LIKE THAT. AT ALL. IT WAS SO BLOODY AND VIOLENT AND THERE WERE NAKED GIRLS RUNNING AROUND. WHY DIDN'T YOU PICK A ROMANTIC MOVIE?
I LIKE HORROR MOVIES. I ESPECIALLY LIKE HARD R HORROR MOVIES, NOT THE WATERED DOWN TEEN AUDIENCE STUFF.
THAT WAS WATERED-DOWN?
YEAH, I CAN'T TAKE YOU TO AN R-RATED MOVIE...WELL, I CAN, BUT I CHOOSE NOT TO.
I'M HAPPY ABOUT THAT. I THINK STUFF LIKE THAT ONLY ENCOURAGES HUMANS TO BEHAVE VIOLENTLY TOWARD EACH OTHER.
I THINK YOU THINK TOO MUCH. IT WAS ALL FAKE AND HARMLESS FUN...I TOLD YOU, RUBBER LIMBS AND SYRUP FOR BLOOD.
BESIDES, I WANTED TO THANK YOU FOR HELPING ME SAVE THE CITY.
THAT'S WHAT I DO.
I KNOW, BUT IT WASN'T THE WAY I WANTED IT TO GO. I'M TRYING TO BE MY OWN PERSON, BUT I'M SO USED TO BEING A TEAM PLAYER.
CLUB
CAN WE GO DANCING?
HANG ON... SOMETHING'S HAPPENING...
OH MAN, THAT'S *INSANE*!
ARE YOU WEARING YOUR COSTUME?
NOPE. WHY WOULD I BE WEARING MY COSTUME? WHERE ARE WE GOING?
YOU NEED TO WEAR YOUR COSTUME UNDER EVERYTHING...EXCEPT LIKE A COCKTAIL DRESS OR A BIKINI-TYPE SITUATION...
THE POINT IS, WE'RE ON THE CLOCK, KID! BIG TIME!
THIS END UP
OKAY, WHAT IS IT?
YOU WON'T BELIEVE IT...

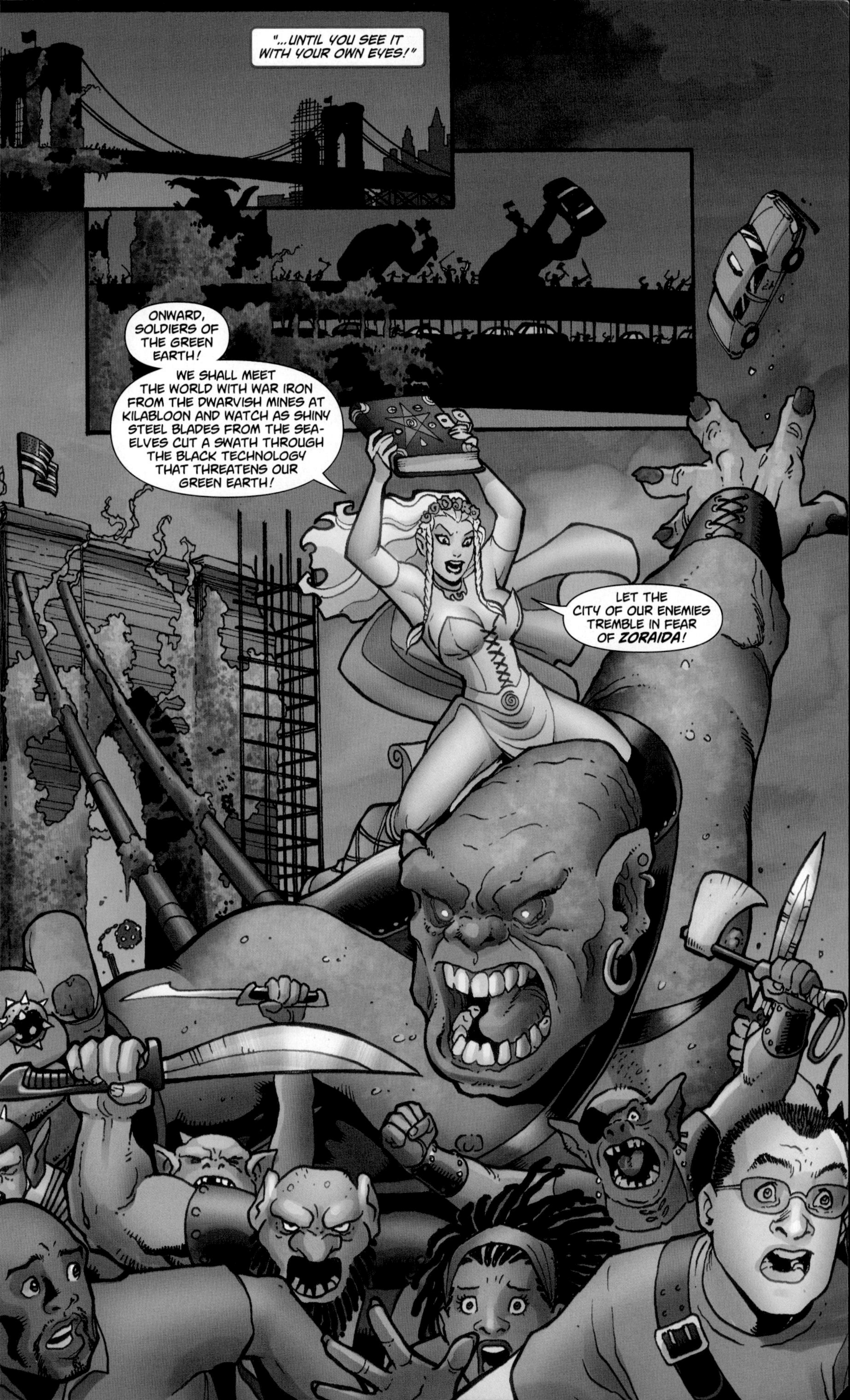
"...UNTIL YOU SEE IT WITH YOUR OWN EYES!"
ONWARD, SOLDIERS OF THE GREEN EARTH!
WE SHALL MEET THE WORLD WITH WAR IRON FROM THE DWARVISH MINES AT KILABLOON AND WATCH AS SHINY STEEL BLADES FROM THE SEA-ELVES CUT A SWATH THROUGH THE BLACK TECHNOLOGY THAT THREATENS OUR GREEN EARTH!
LET THE CITY OF OUR ENEMIES TREMBLE IN FEAR OF ZORAIDA!

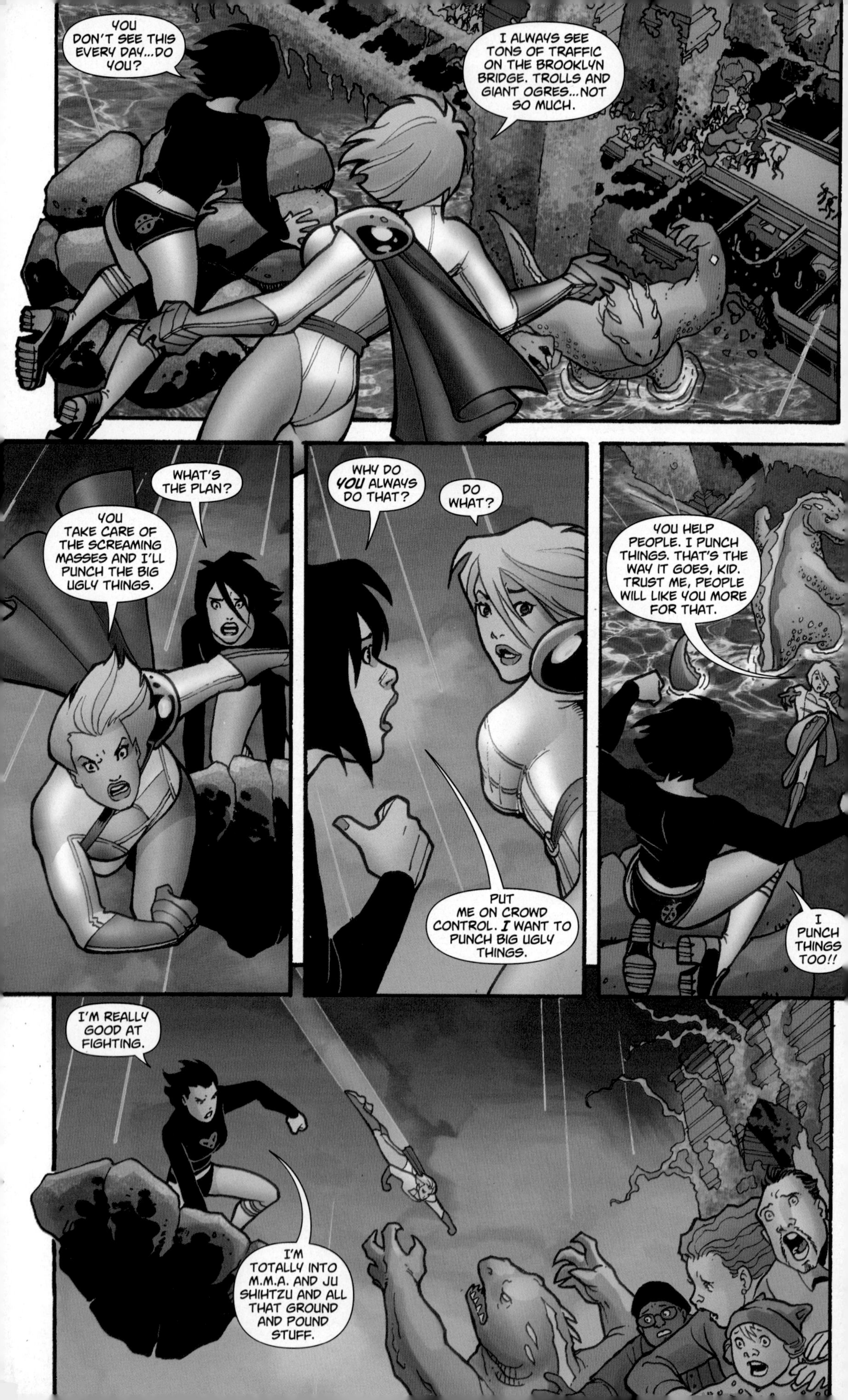
YOU DON'T SEE THIS EVERY DAY...DO YOU?
I ALWAYS SEE TONS OF TRAFFIC ON THE BROOKLYN BRIDGE. TROLLS AND GIANT OGRES...NOT SO MUCH.
WHAT'S THE PLAN?
YOU TAKE CARE OF THE SCREAMING MASSES AND I'LL PUNCH THE BIG UGLY THINGS.
WHY DO *YOU* ALWAYS DO THAT?
DO WHAT?
PUT ME ON CROWD CONTROL. *I* WANT TO PUNCH BIG UGLY THINGS.
YOU HELP PEOPLE. I PUNCH THINGS. THAT'S THE WAY IT GOES, KID. TRUST ME, PEOPLE WILL LIKE YOU MORE FOR THAT.
I PUNCH THINGS TOO!!
I'M REALLY GOOD AT FIGHTING.
I'M TOTALLY INTO M.M.A. AND JU SHIHTZU AND ALL THAT GROUND AND POUND STUFF.

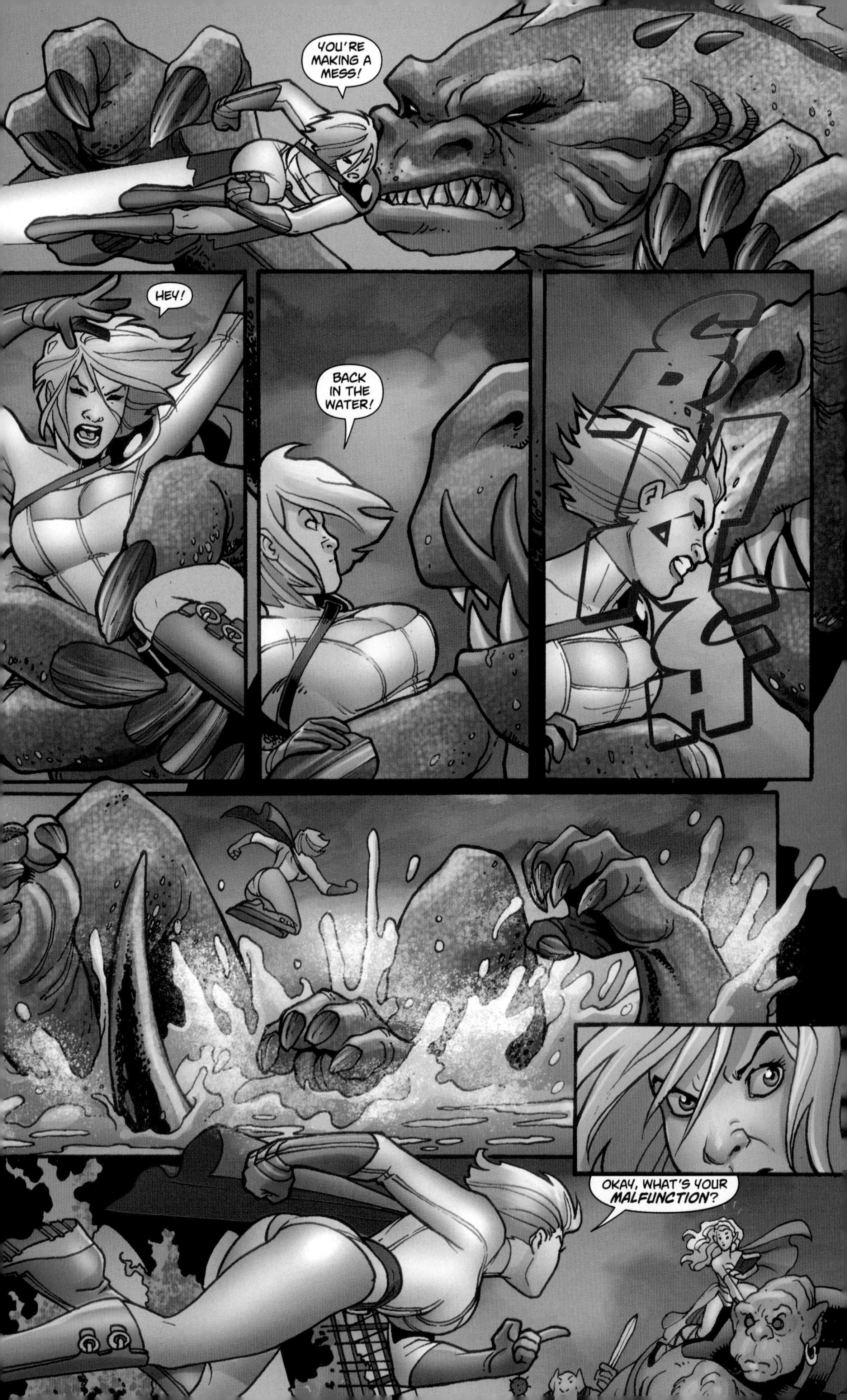
YOU'RE MAKING A MESS!
HEY!
BACK IN THE WATER!
OKAY, WHAT'S YOUR *MALFUNCTION*?

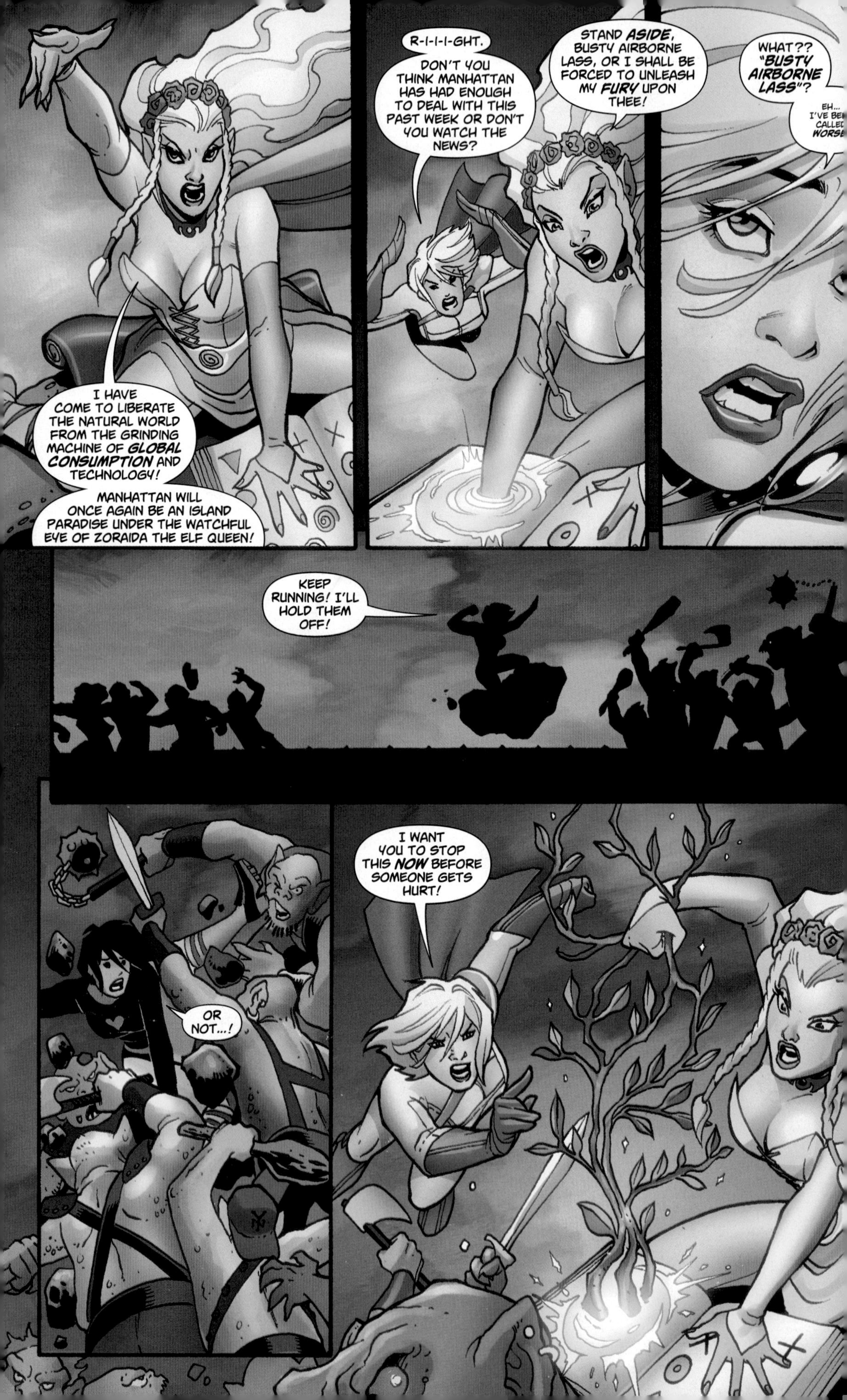
I HAVE COME TO LIBERATE THE NATURAL WORLD FROM THE GRINDING MACHINE OF GLOBAL CONSUMPTION AND TECHNOLOGY!
MANHATTAN WILL ONCE AGAIN BE AN ISLAND PARADISE UNDER THE WATCHFUL EYE OF ZORAIDA THE ELF QUEEN!
R-I-I-I-GHT.
DON'T YOU THINK MANHATTAN HAS HAD ENOUGH TO DEAL WITH THIS PAST WEEK OR DON'T YOU WATCH THE NEWS?
STAND ASIDE, BUSTY AIRBORNE LASS, OR I SHALL BE FORCED TO UNLEASH MY FURY UPON THEE!
WHAT?? "BUSTY AIRBORNE LASS"?
EH... I'VE BE CALLED WORSE
KEEP RUNNING! I'LL HOLD THEM OFF!
OR NOT...!
I WANT YOU TO STOP THIS NOW BEFORE SOMEONE GETS HURT!

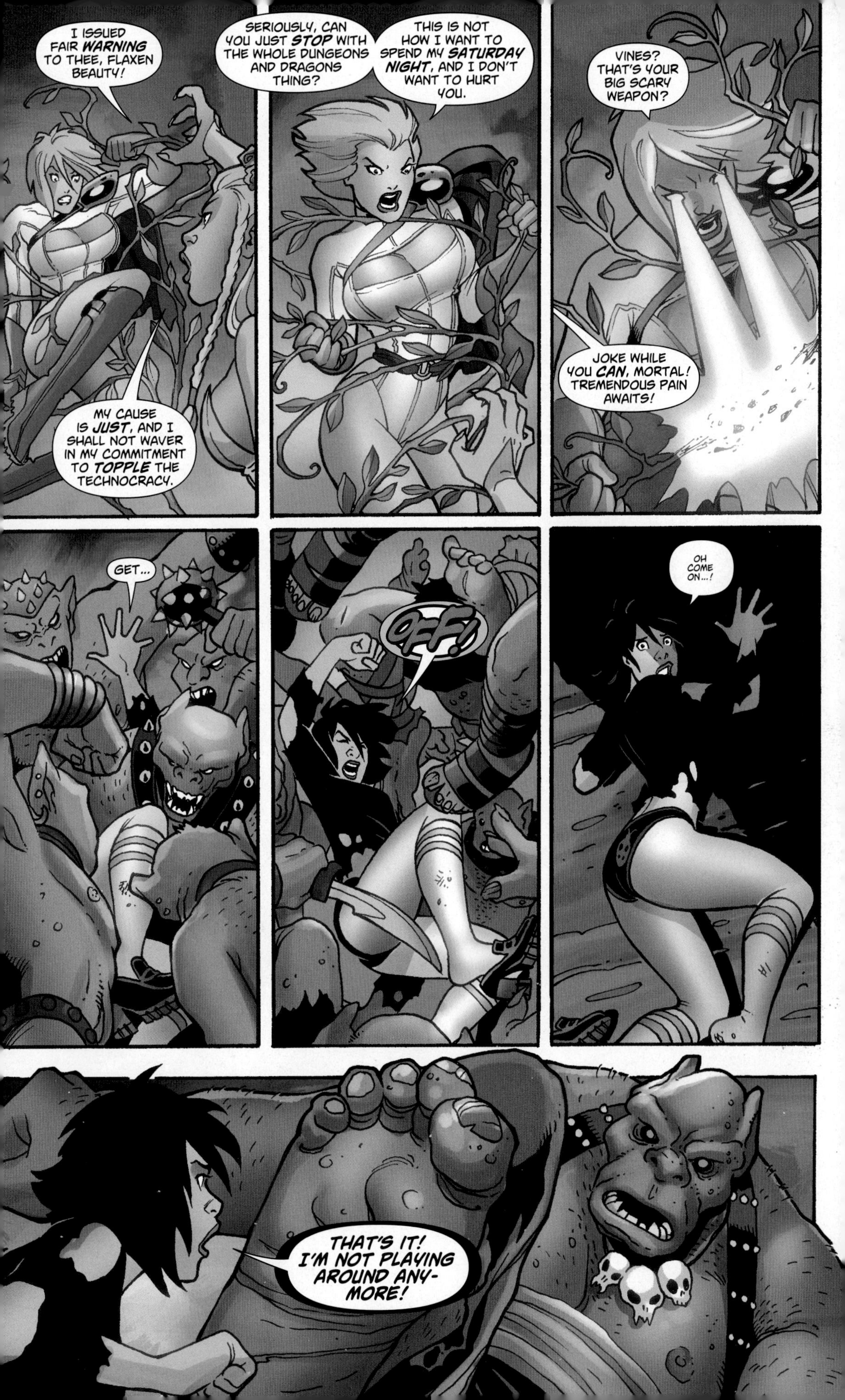
I ISSUED FAIR WARNING TO THEE, FLAXEN BEAUTY!
MY CAUSE IS JUST, AND I SHALL NOT WAVER IN MY COMMITMENT TO TOPPLE THE TECHNOCRACY.
SERIOUSLY, CAN YOU JUST STOP WITH THE WHOLE DUNGEONS AND DRAGONS THING?
THIS IS NOT HOW I WANT TO SPEND MY SATURDAY NIGHT, AND I DON'T WANT TO HURT YOU.
VINES? THAT'S YOUR BIG SCARY WEAPON?
JOKE WHILE YOU CAN, MORTAL! TREMENDOUS PAIN AWAITS!
GET...
OFF!
OH COME ON...!
THAT'S IT! I'M NOT PLAYING AROUND ANY-MORE!

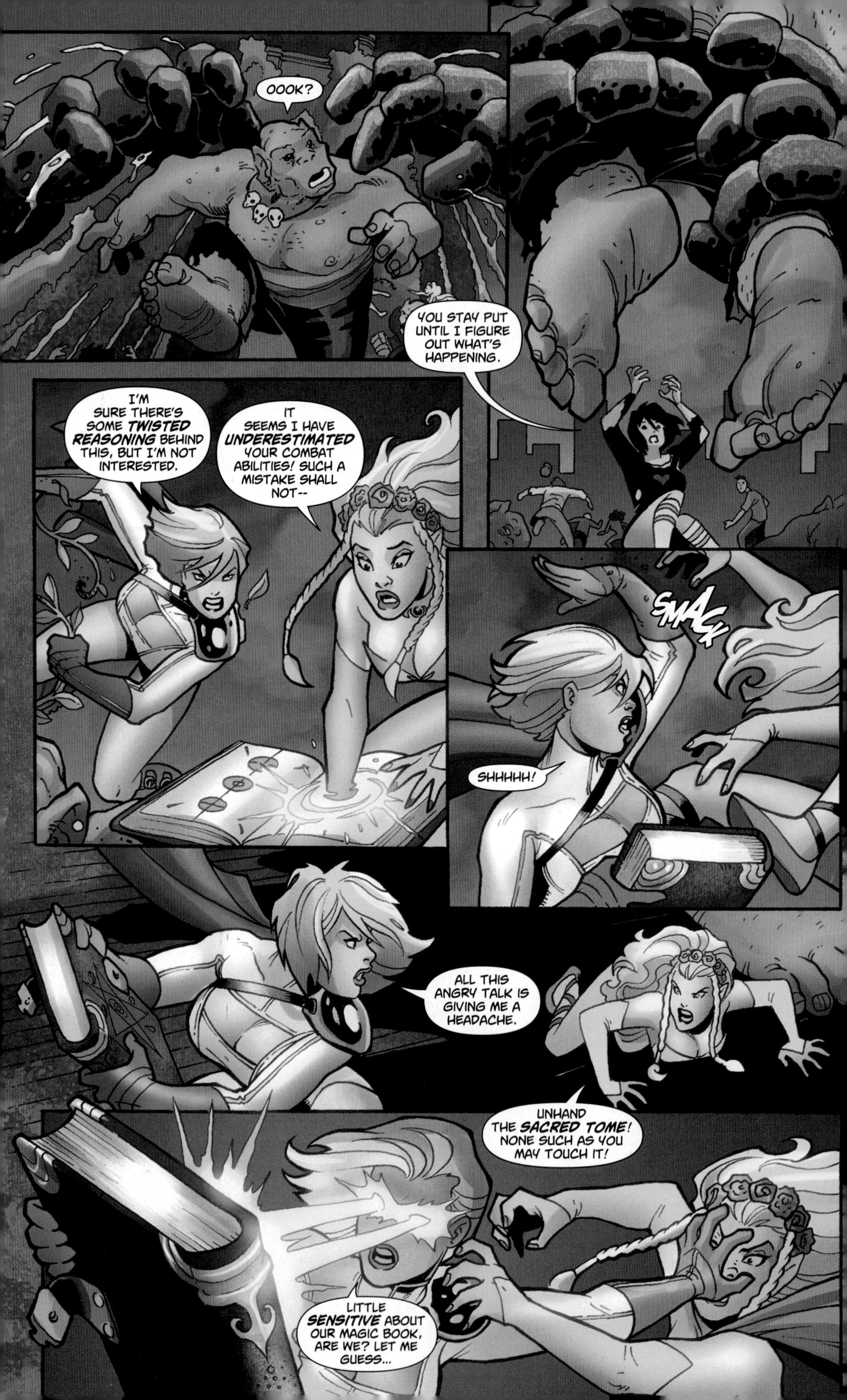
OOOK?
YOU STAY PUT UNTIL I FIGURE OUT WHAT'S HAPPENING.
I'M SURE THERE'S SOME **TWISTED REASONING** BEHIND THIS, BUT I'M NOT INTERESTED.
IT SEEMS I HAVE **UNDERESTIMATED** YOUR COMBAT ABILITIES! SUCH A MISTAKE SHALL NOT--
SMACK
SHHHHH!
ALL THIS ANGRY TALK IS GIVING ME A HEADACHE.
UNHAND THE **SACRED TOME**! NONE SUCH AS YOU MAY TOUCH IT!
LITTLE **SENSITIVE** ABOUT OUR MAGIC BOOK, ARE WE? LET ME GUESS...

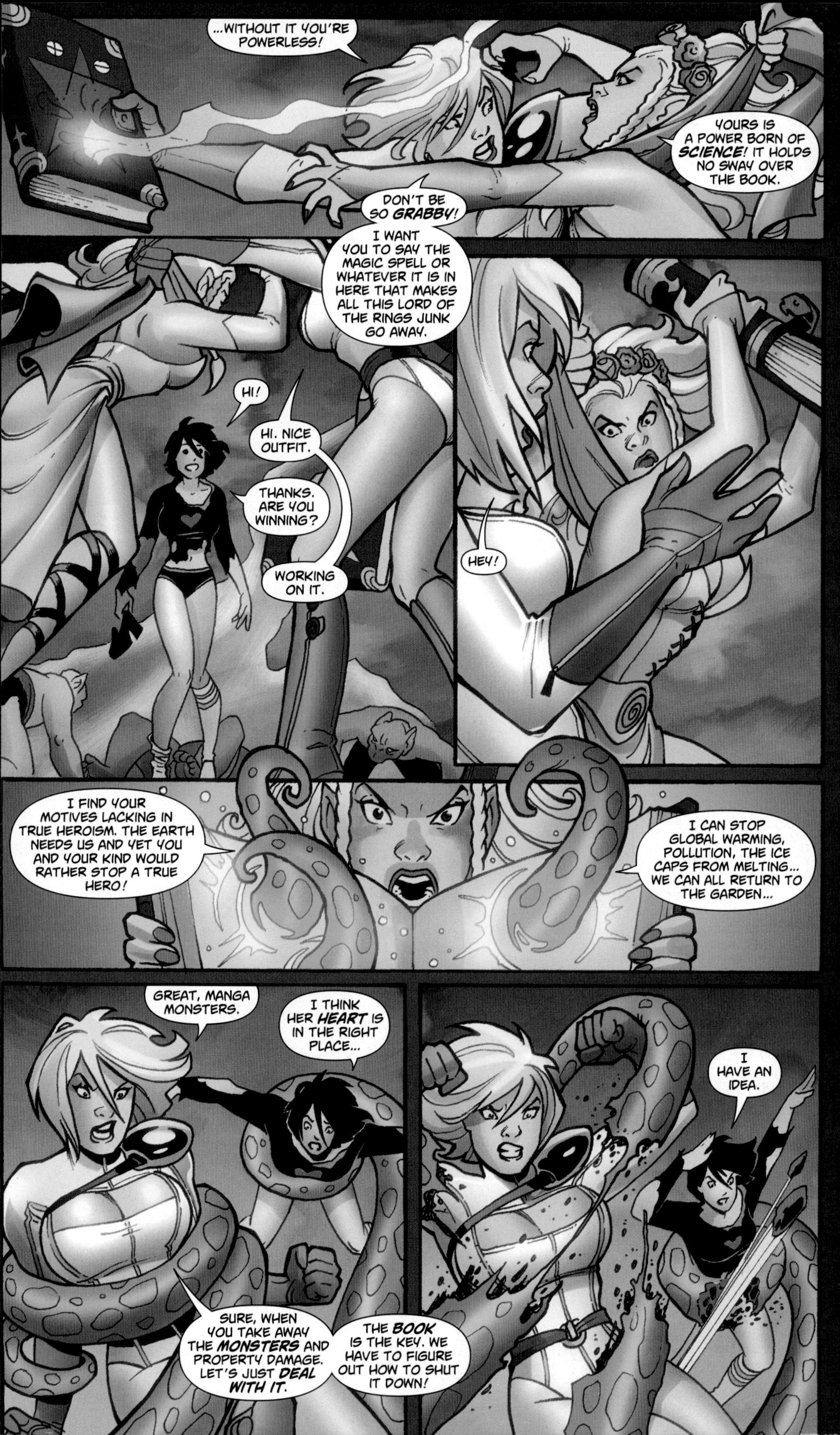
...WITHOUT IT YOU'RE POWERLESS!
YOURS IS A POWER BORN OF SCIENCE! IT HOLDS NO SWAY OVER THE BOOK.
DON'T BE SO GRABBY!
I WANT YOU TO SAY THE MAGIC SPELL OR WHATEVER IT IS IN HERE THAT MAKES ALL THIS LORD OF THE RINGS JUNK GO AWAY.
HI!
HI. NICE OUTFIT.
THANKS. ARE YOU WINNING?
WORKING ON IT.
HEY!
I FIND YOUR MOTIVES LACKING IN TRUE HEROISM. THE EARTH NEEDS US AND YET YOU AND YOUR KIND WOULD RATHER STOP A TRUE HERO!
I CAN STOP GLOBAL WARMING, POLLUTION, THE ICE CAPS FROM MELTING... WE CAN ALL RETURN TO THE GARDEN...
GREAT, MANGA MONSTERS.
I THINK HER HEART IS IN THE RIGHT PLACE...
SURE, WHEN YOU TAKE AWAY THE MONSTERS AND PROPERTY DAMAGE. LET'S JUST DEAL WITH IT.
THE BOOK IS THE KEY. WE HAVE TO FIGURE OUT HOW TO SHUT IT DOWN!
I HAVE AN IDEA.

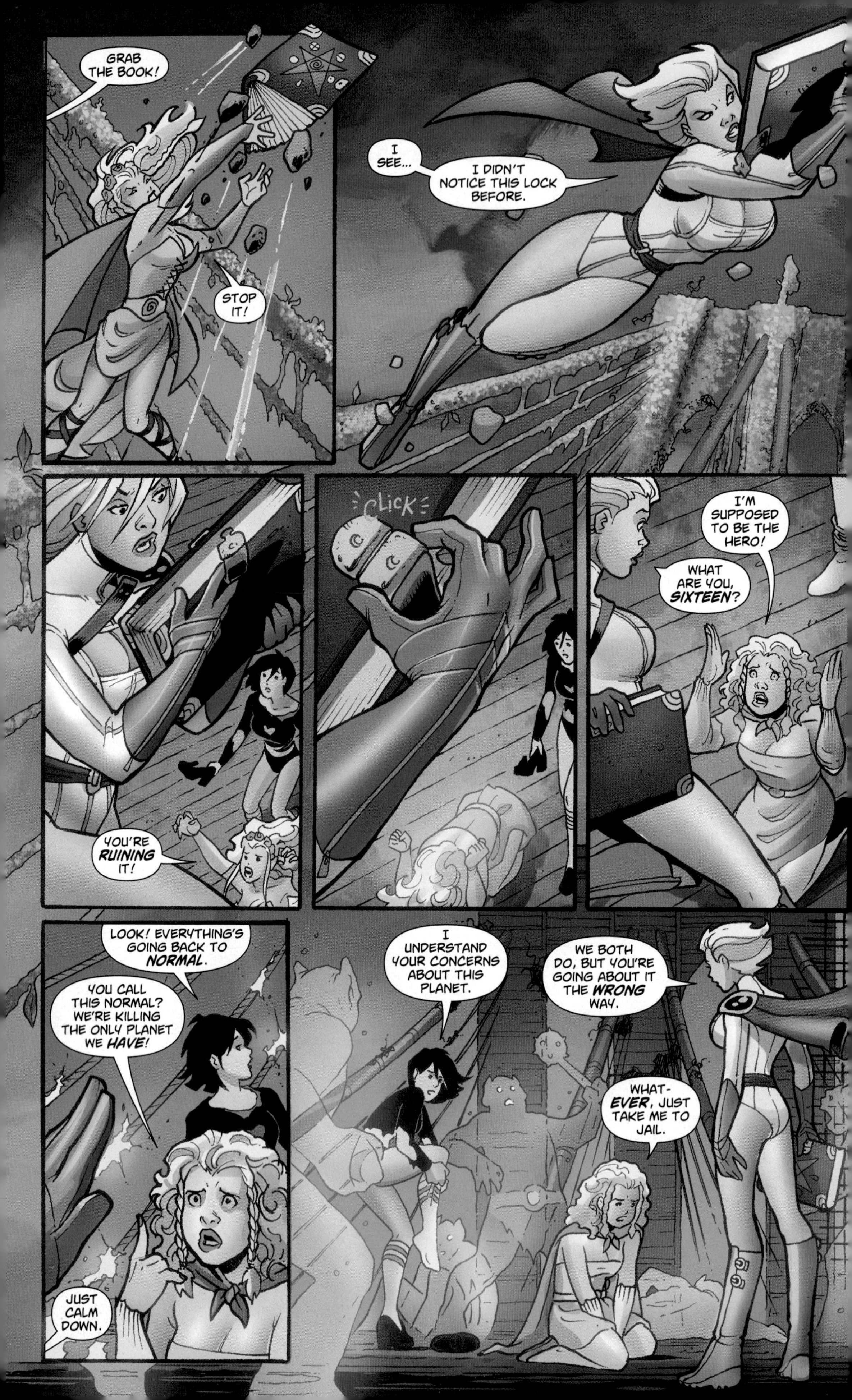
GRAB THE BOOK!
STOP IT!
I SEE...
I DIDN'T NOTICE THIS LOCK BEFORE.
YOU'RE **RUINING** IT!
CLICK
I'M SUPPOSED TO BE THE HERO!
WHAT ARE YOU, **SIXTEEN**?
LOOK! EVERYTHING'S GOING BACK TO **NORMAL**.
YOU CALL THIS NORMAL? WE'RE KILLING THE ONLY PLANET WE **HAVE**!
JUST CALM DOWN.
I UNDERSTAND YOUR CONCERNS ABOUT THIS PLANET.
WE BOTH DO, BUT YOU'RE GOING ABOUT IT THE **WRONG** WAY.
WHAT-**EVER**, JUST TAKE ME TO JAIL.

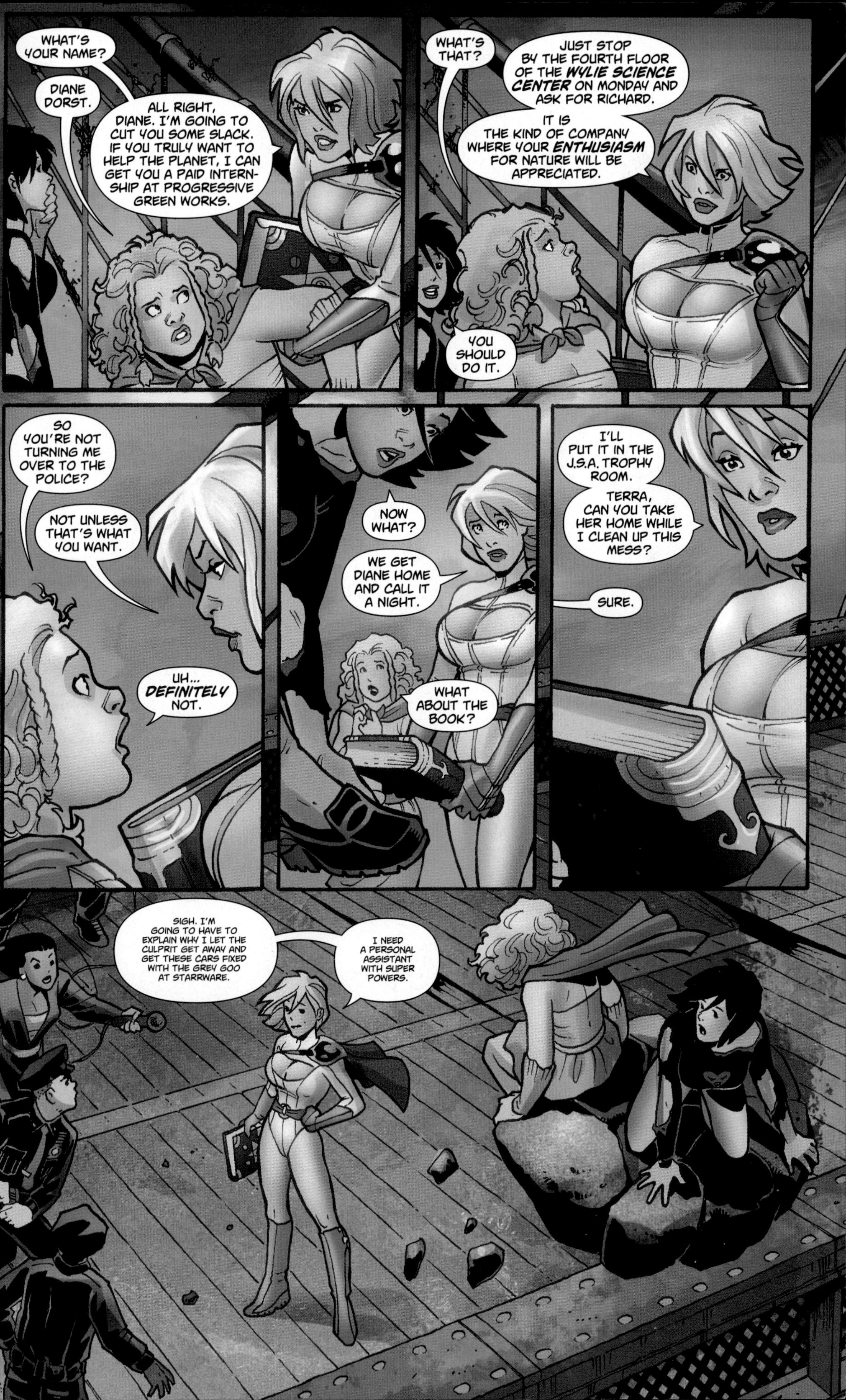

WHAT'S YOUR NAME?
DIANE DORST.
ALL RIGHT, DIANE. I'M GOING TO CUT YOU SOME SLACK. IF YOU TRULY WANT TO HELP THE PLANET, I CAN GET YOU A PAID INTERN-SHIP AT PROGRESSIVE GREEN WORKS.
WHAT'S THAT?
JUST STOP BY THE FOURTH FLOOR OF THE WYLIE SCIENCE CENTER ON MONDAY AND ASK FOR RICHARD.
IT IS THE KIND OF COMPANY WHERE YOUR ENTHUSIASM FOR NATURE WILL BE APPRECIATED.
YOU SHOULD DO IT.
SO YOU'RE NOT TURNING ME OVER TO THE POLICE?
NOT UNLESS THAT'S WHAT YOU WANT.
UH... DEFINITELY NOT.
NOW WHAT?
WE GET DIANE HOME AND CALL IT A NIGHT.
WHAT ABOUT THE BOOK?
I'LL PUT IT IN THE J.S.A. TROPHY ROOM.
TERRA, CAN YOU TAKE HER HOME WHILE I CLEAN UP THIS MESS?
SURE.
SIGH. I'M GOING TO HAVE TO EXPLAIN WHY I LET THE CULPRIT GET AWAY AND GET THESE CARS FIXED WITH THE GREY GOO AT STARRWARE.
I NEED A PERSONAL ASSISTANT WITH SUPER POWERS.

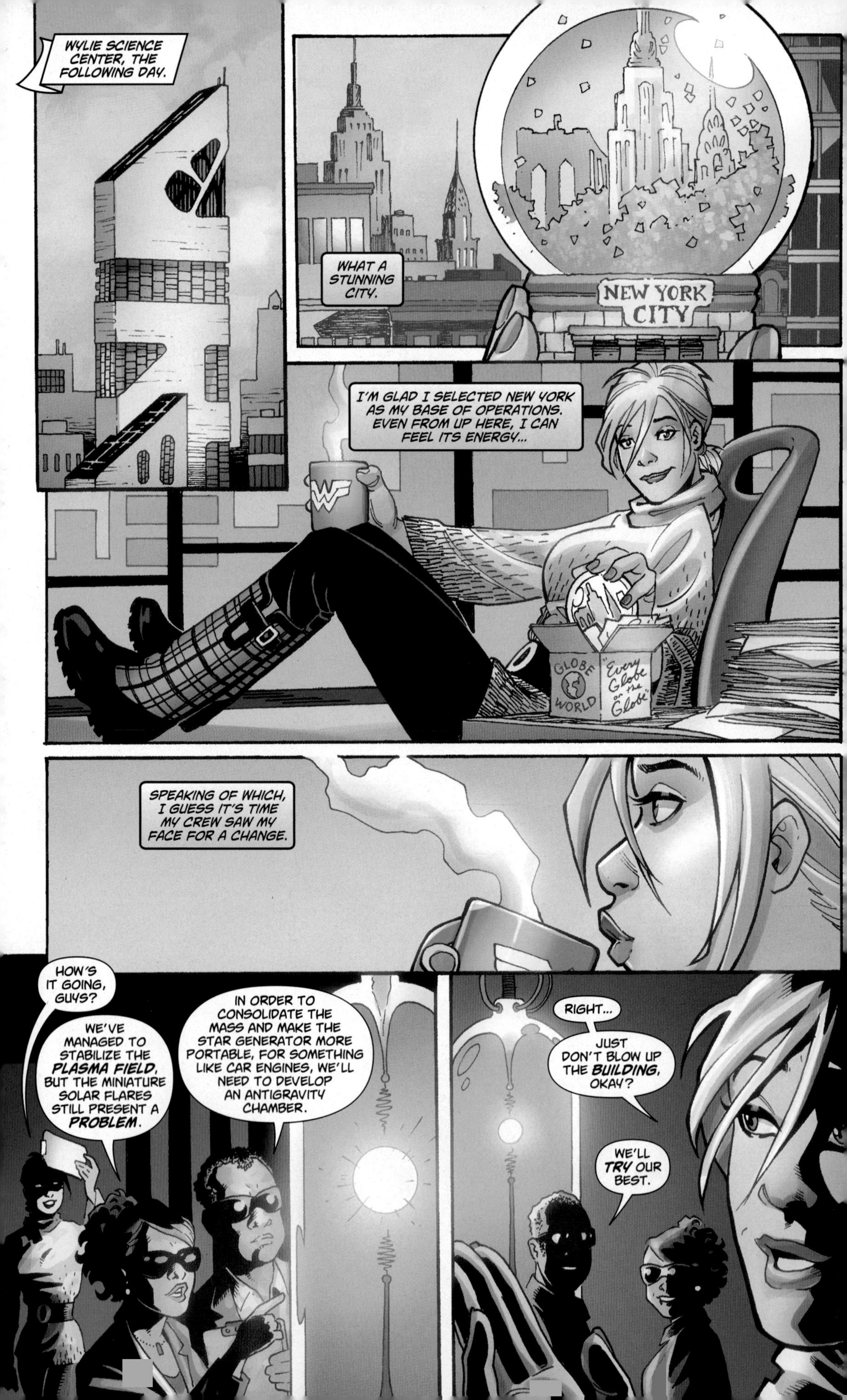
WYLIE SCIENCE CENTER, THE FOLLOWING DAY.
WHAT A STUNNING CITY.
NEW YORK CITY
I'M GLAD I SELECTED NEW YORK AS MY BASE OF OPERATIONS. EVEN FROM UP HERE, I CAN FEEL ITS ENERGY...
GLOBE WORLD
"Every Globe on the Globe"
SPEAKING OF WHICH, I GUESS IT'S TIME MY CREW SAW MY FACE FOR A CHANGE.
HOW'S IT GOING, GUYS?
WE'VE MANAGED TO STABILIZE THE PLASMA FIELD, BUT THE MINIATURE SOLAR FLARES STILL PRESENT A PROBLEM.
IN ORDER TO CONSOLIDATE THE MASS AND MAKE THE STAR GENERATOR MORE PORTABLE, FOR SOMETHING LIKE CAR ENGINES, WE'LL NEED TO DEVELOP AN ANTIGRAVITY CHAMBER.
RIGHT...
JUST DON'T BLOW UP THE BUILDING, OKAY?
WE'LL TRY OUR BEST.

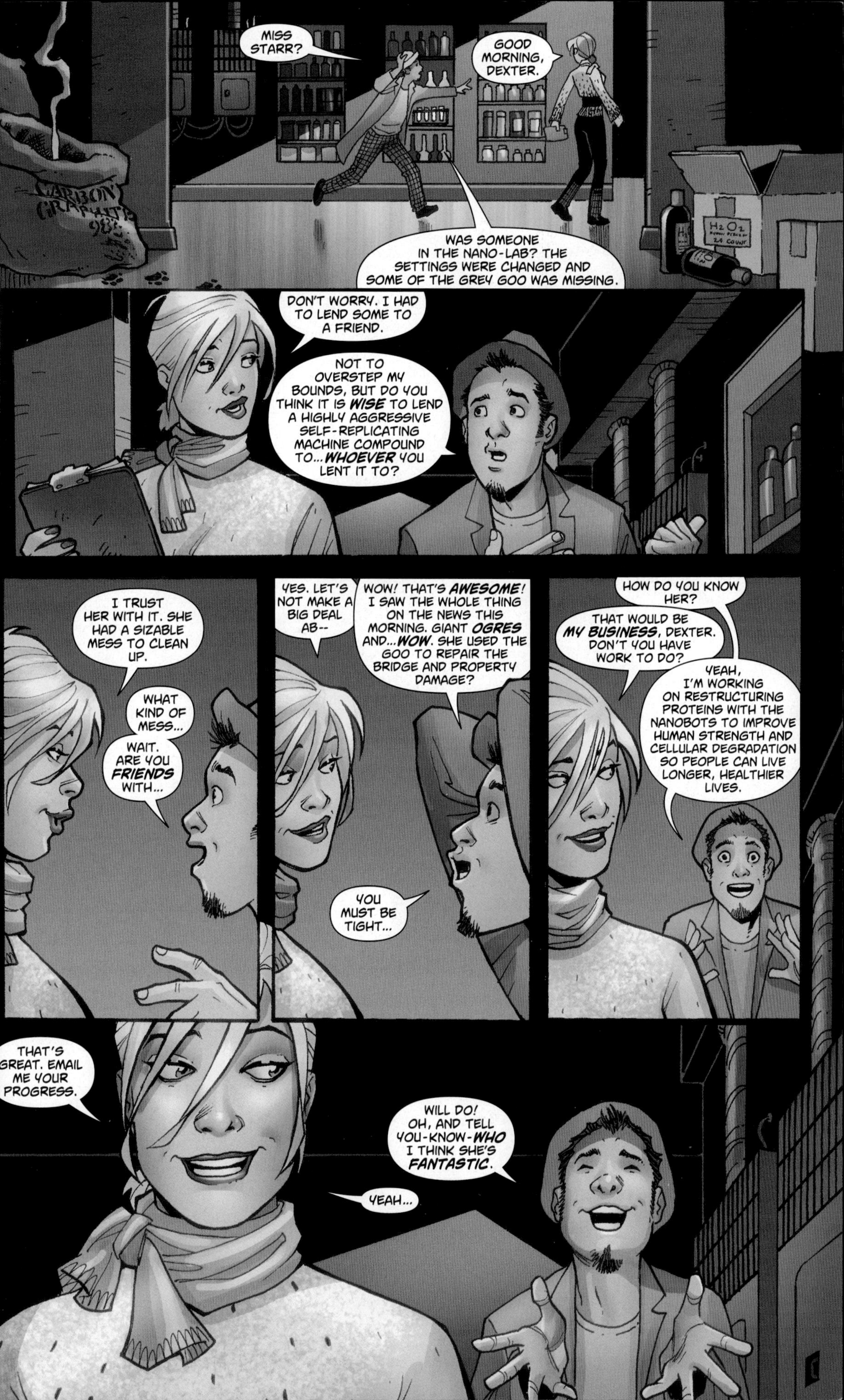
MISS STARR?
GOOD MORNING, DEXTER.
WAS SOMEONE IN THE NANO-LAB? THE SETTINGS WERE CHANGED AND SOME OF THE GREY GOO WAS MISSING.
DON'T WORRY. I HAD TO LEND SOME TO A FRIEND.
NOT TO OVERSTEP MY BOUNDS, BUT DO YOU THINK IT IS *WISE* TO LEND A HIGHLY AGGRESSIVE SELF-REPLICATING MACHINE COMPOUND TO...*WHOEVER* YOU LENT IT TO?
I TRUST HER WITH IT. SHE HAD A SIZABLE MESS TO CLEAN UP.
WHAT KIND OF MESS...
WAIT. ARE YOU *FRIENDS* WITH...
YES. LET'S NOT MAKE A BIG DEAL AB--
WOW! THAT'S *AWESOME*! I SAW THE WHOLE THING ON THE NEWS THIS MORNING. GIANT *OGRES* AND...*WOW*. SHE USED THE GOO TO REPAIR THE BRIDGE AND PROPERTY DAMAGE?
YOU MUST BE TIGHT...
HOW DO YOU KNOW HER?
THAT WOULD BE *MY BUSINESS*, DEXTER. DON'T YOU HAVE WORK TO DO?
YEAH, I'M WORKING ON RESTRUCTURING PROTEINS WITH THE NANOBOTS TO IMPROVE HUMAN STRENGTH AND CELLULAR DEGRADATION SO PEOPLE CAN LIVE LONGER, HEALTHIER LIVES.
THAT'S GREAT. EMAIL ME YOUR PROGRESS.
WILL DO! OH, AND TELL YOU-KNOW-*WHO* I THINK SHE'S *FANTASTIC*.
YEAH...

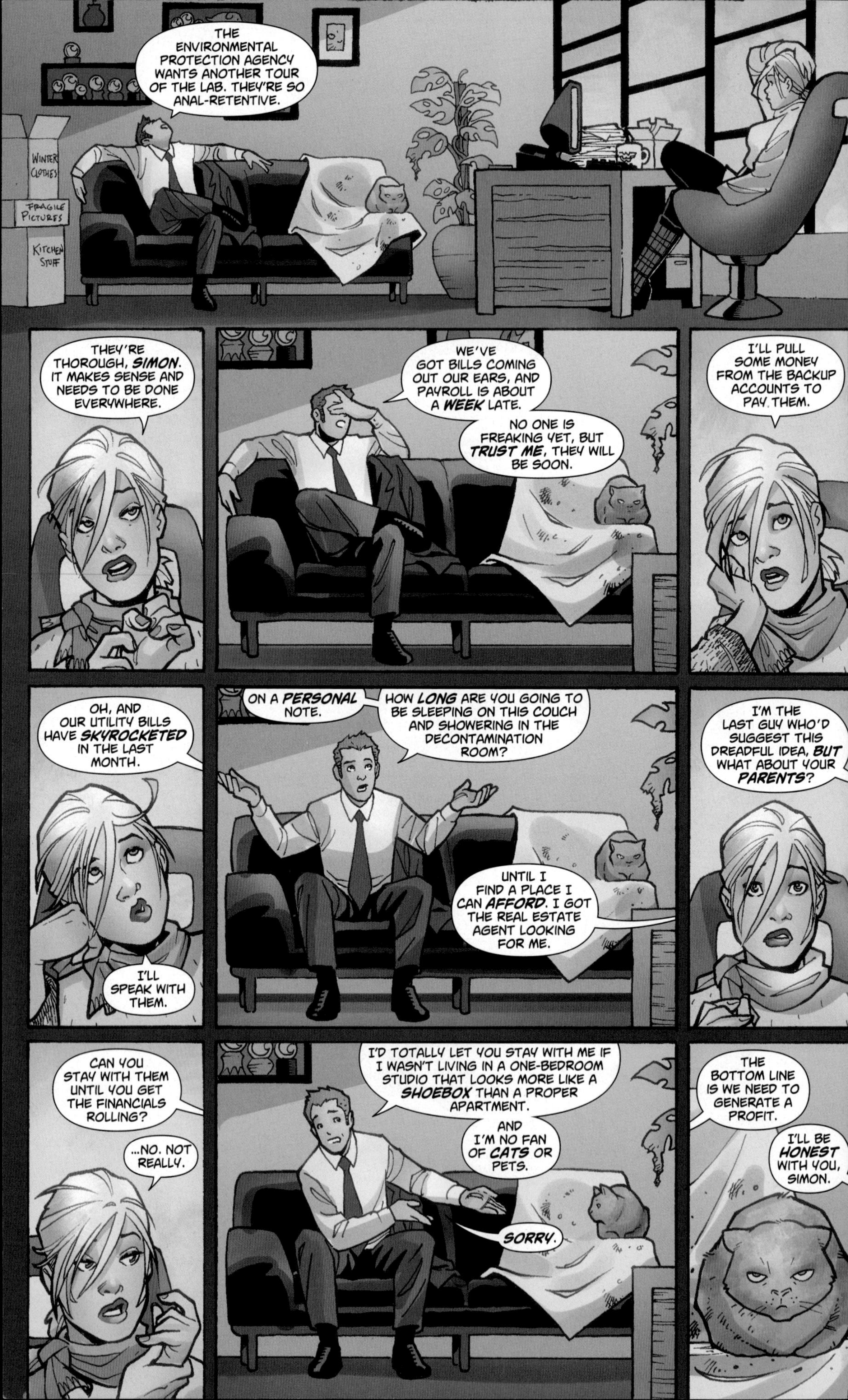
THE ENVIRONMENTAL PROTECTION AGENCY WANTS ANOTHER TOUR OF THE LAB. THEY'RE SO ANAL-RETENTIVE.
WINTER CLOTHES
FRAGILE PICTURES
KITCHEN STUFF
THEY'RE THOROUGH, SIMON. IT MAKES SENSE AND NEEDS TO BE DONE EVERYWHERE.
WE'VE GOT BILLS COMING OUT OUR EARS, AND PAYROLL IS ABOUT A WEEK LATE.
NO ONE IS FREAKING YET, BUT TRUST ME, THEY WILL BE SOON.
I'LL PULL SOME MONEY FROM THE BACKUP ACCOUNTS TO PAY THEM.
OH, AND OUR UTILITY BILLS HAVE SKYROCKETED IN THE LAST MONTH.
I'LL SPEAK WITH THEM.
ON A PERSONAL NOTE.
HOW LONG ARE YOU GOING TO BE SLEEPING ON THIS COUCH AND SHOWERING IN THE DECONTAMINATION ROOM?
UNTIL I FIND A PLACE I CAN AFFORD. I GOT THE REAL ESTATE AGENT LOOKING FOR ME.
I'M THE LAST GUY WHO'D SUGGEST THIS DREADFUL IDEA, BUT WHAT ABOUT YOUR PARENTS?
CAN YOU STAY WITH THEM UNTIL YOU GET THE FINANCIALS ROLLING?
...NO. NOT REALLY.
I'D TOTALLY LET YOU STAY WITH ME IF I WASN'T LIVING IN A ONE-BEDROOM STUDIO THAT LOOKS MORE LIKE A SHOEBOX THAN A PROPER APARTMENT.
AND I'M NO FAN OF CATS OR PETS.
SORRY.
THE BOTTOM LINE IS WE NEED TO GENERATE A PROFIT.
I'LL BE HONEST WITH YOU, SIMON.

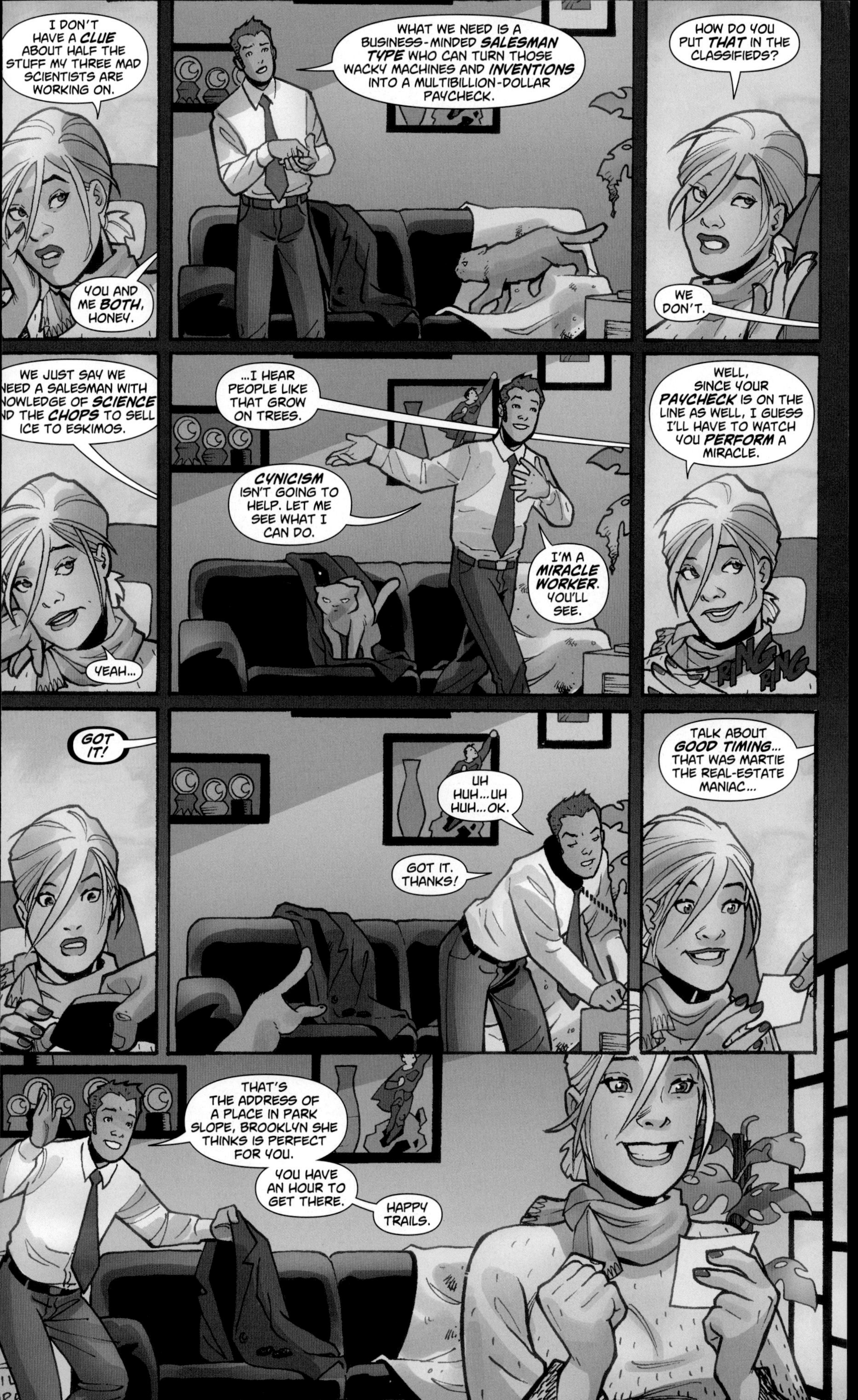
I DON'T HAVE A CLUE ABOUT HALF THE STUFF MY THREE MAD SCIENTISTS ARE WORKING ON.
YOU AND ME BOTH, HONEY.
WHAT WE NEED IS A BUSINESS-MINDED SALESMAN TYPE WHO CAN TURN THOSE WACKY MACHINES AND INVENTIONS INTO A MULTIBILLION-DOLLAR PAYCHECK.
HOW DO YOU PUT THAT IN THE CLASSIFIEDS?
WE DON'T.
WE JUST SAY WE NEED A SALESMAN WITH NOWLEDGE OF SCIENCE ND THE CHOPS TO SELL ICE TO ESKIMOS.
YEAH...
...I HEAR PEOPLE LIKE THAT GROW ON TREES.
CYNICISM ISN'T GOING TO HELP. LET ME SEE WHAT I CAN DO.
I'M A MIRACLE WORKER. YOU'LL SEE.
WELL, SINCE YOUR PAYCHECK IS ON THE LINE AS WELL, I GUESS I'LL HAVE TO WATCH YOU PERFORM A MIRACLE.
RING RING
GOT IT!
UH HUH...UH HUH...OK.
GOT IT. THANKS!
TALK ABOUT GOOD TIMING... THAT WAS MARTIE THE REAL-ESTATE MANIAC...
THAT'S THE ADDRESS OF A PLACE IN PARK SLOPE, BROOKLYN SHE THINKS IS PERFECT FOR YOU.
YOU HAVE AN HOUR TO GET THERE.
HAPPY TRAILS.

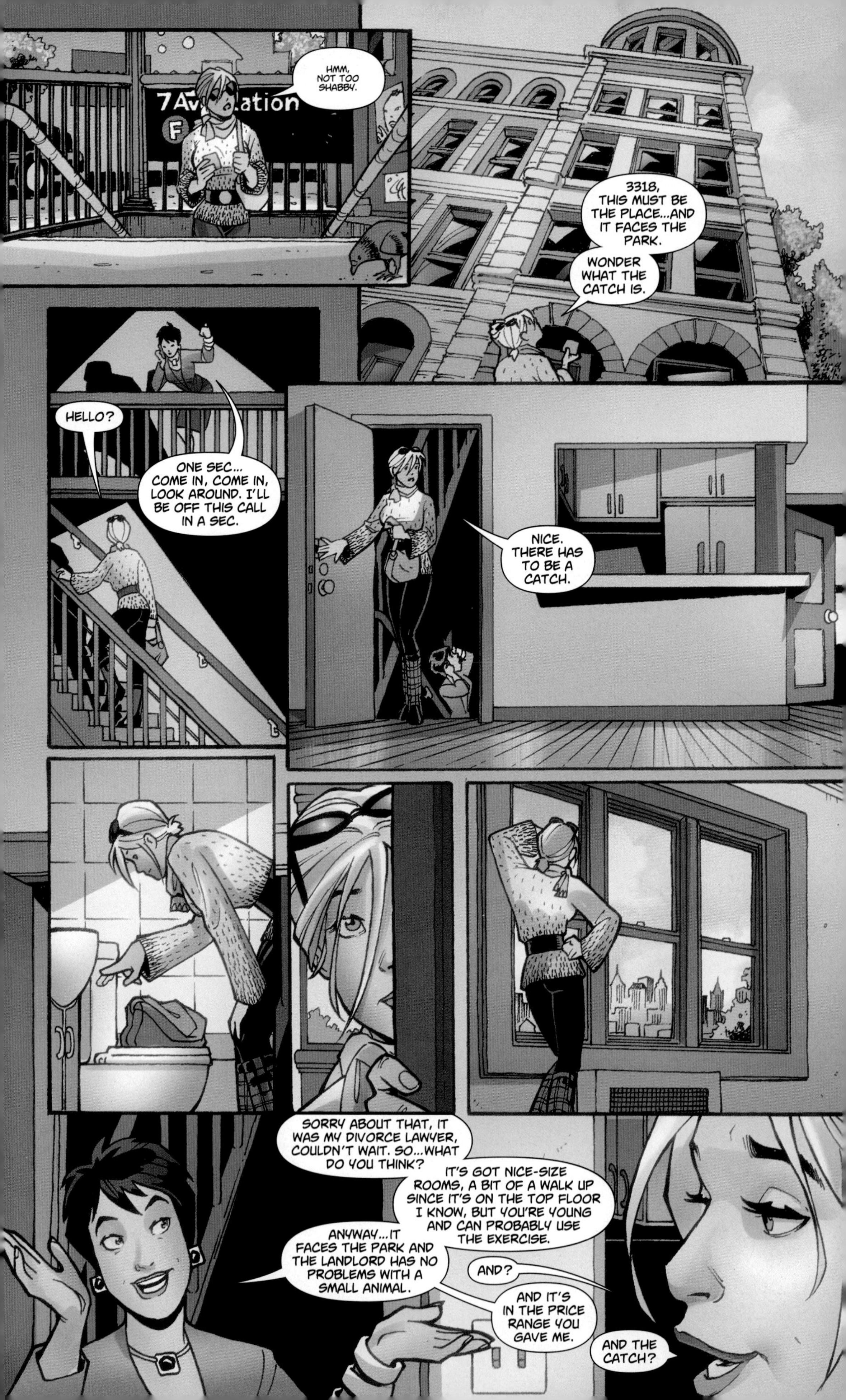

7Av. Station
F
HMM, NOT TOO SHABBY.
3318, THIS MUST BE THE PLACE...AND IT FACES THE PARK.
WONDER WHAT THE CATCH IS.
HELLO?
ONE SEC... COME IN, COME IN, LOOK AROUND. I'LL BE OFF THIS CALL IN A SEC.
NICE. THERE HAS TO BE A CATCH.
SORRY ABOUT THAT, IT WAS MY DIVORCE LAWYER, COULDN'T WAIT. SO...WHAT DO YOU THINK?
IT'S GOT NICE-SIZE ROOMS, A BIT OF A WALK UP SINCE IT'S ON THE TOP FLOOR I KNOW, BUT YOU'RE YOUNG AND CAN PROBABLY USE THE EXERCISE.
ANYWAY...IT FACES THE PARK AND THE LANDLORD HAS NO PROBLEMS WITH A SMALL ANIMAL.
AND?
AND IT'S IN THE PRICE RANGE YOU GAVE ME.
AND THE CATCH?

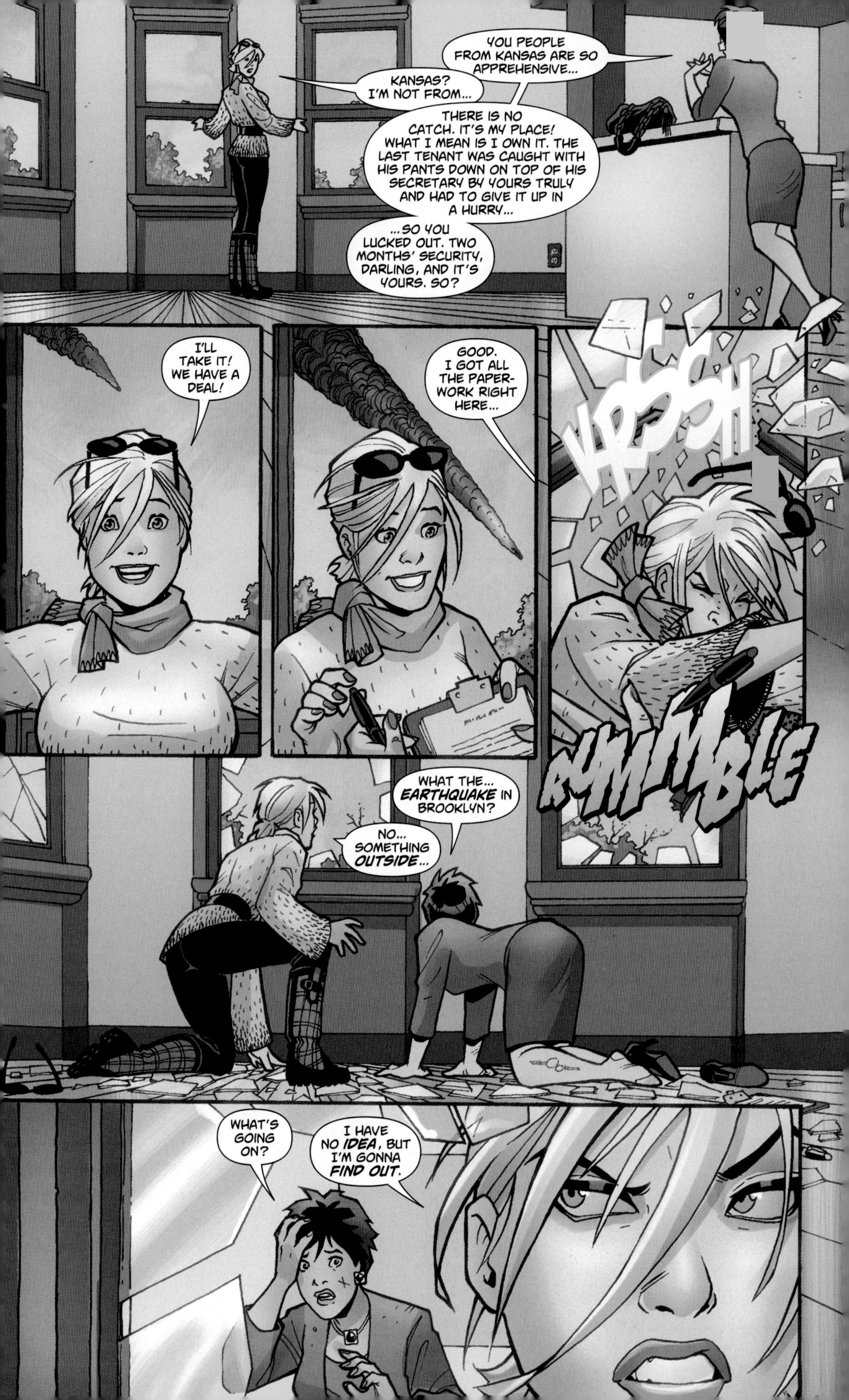

YOU PEOPLE FROM KANSAS ARE SO APPREHENSIVE...
KANSAS? I'M NOT FROM...
THERE IS NO CATCH. IT'S MY PLACE! WHAT I MEAN IS I OWN IT. THE LAST TENANT WAS CAUGHT WITH HIS PANTS DOWN ON TOP OF HIS SECRETARY BY YOURS TRULY AND HAD TO GIVE IT UP IN A HURRY...
...SO YOU LUCKED OUT. TWO MONTHS' SECURITY, DARLING, AND IT'S YOURS. SO?
I'LL TAKE IT! WE HAVE A DEAL!
GOOD. I GOT ALL THE PAPER-WORK RIGHT HERE...
KRSSH
RUMMMBLE
WHAT THE... EARTHQUAKE IN BROOKLYN?
NO... SOMETHING OUTSIDE...
WHAT'S GOING ON?
I HAVE NO IDEA, BUT I'M GONNA FIND OUT.

SPACE GIRLS GONE WILD part one

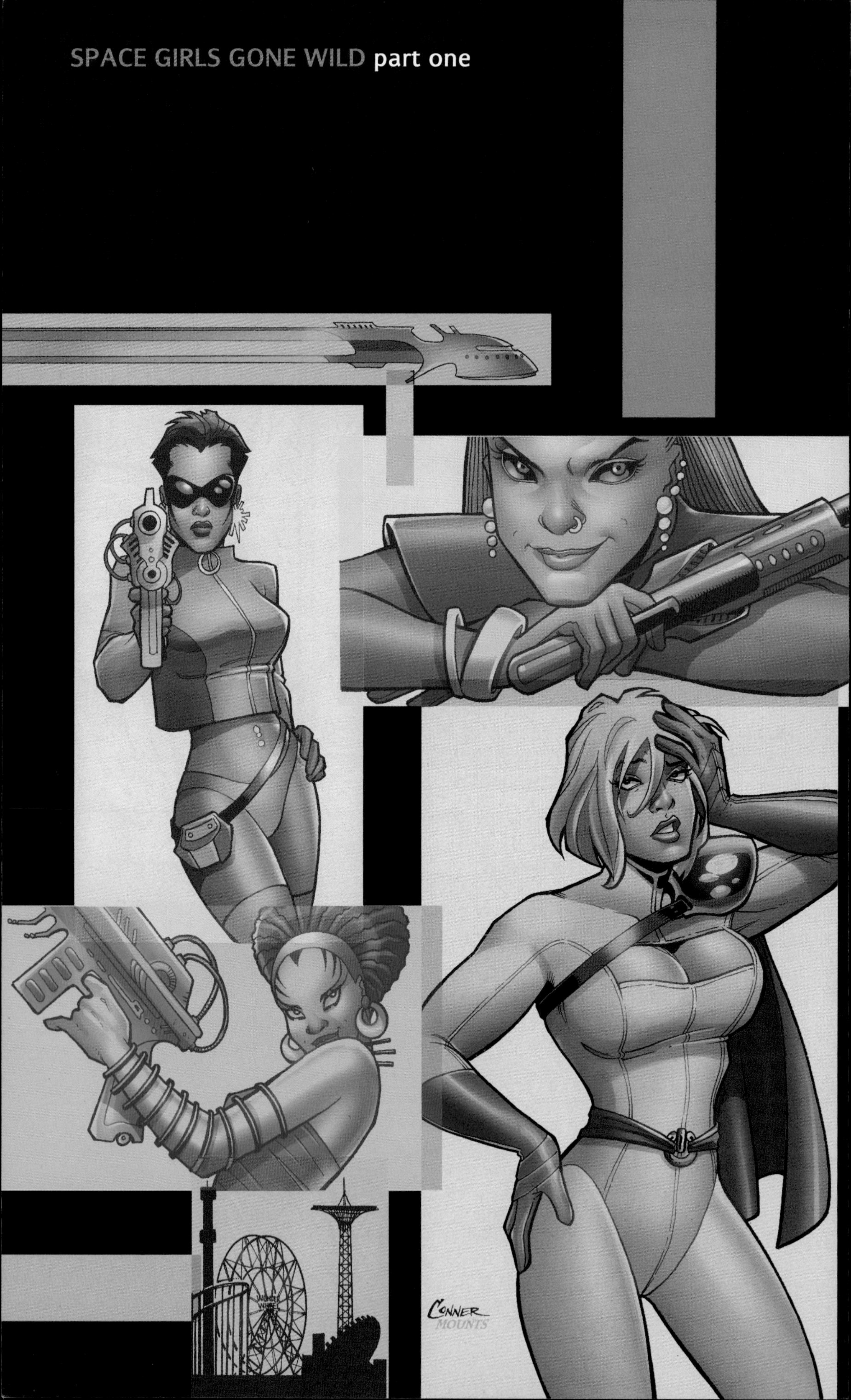
CONNER
MOUNTS

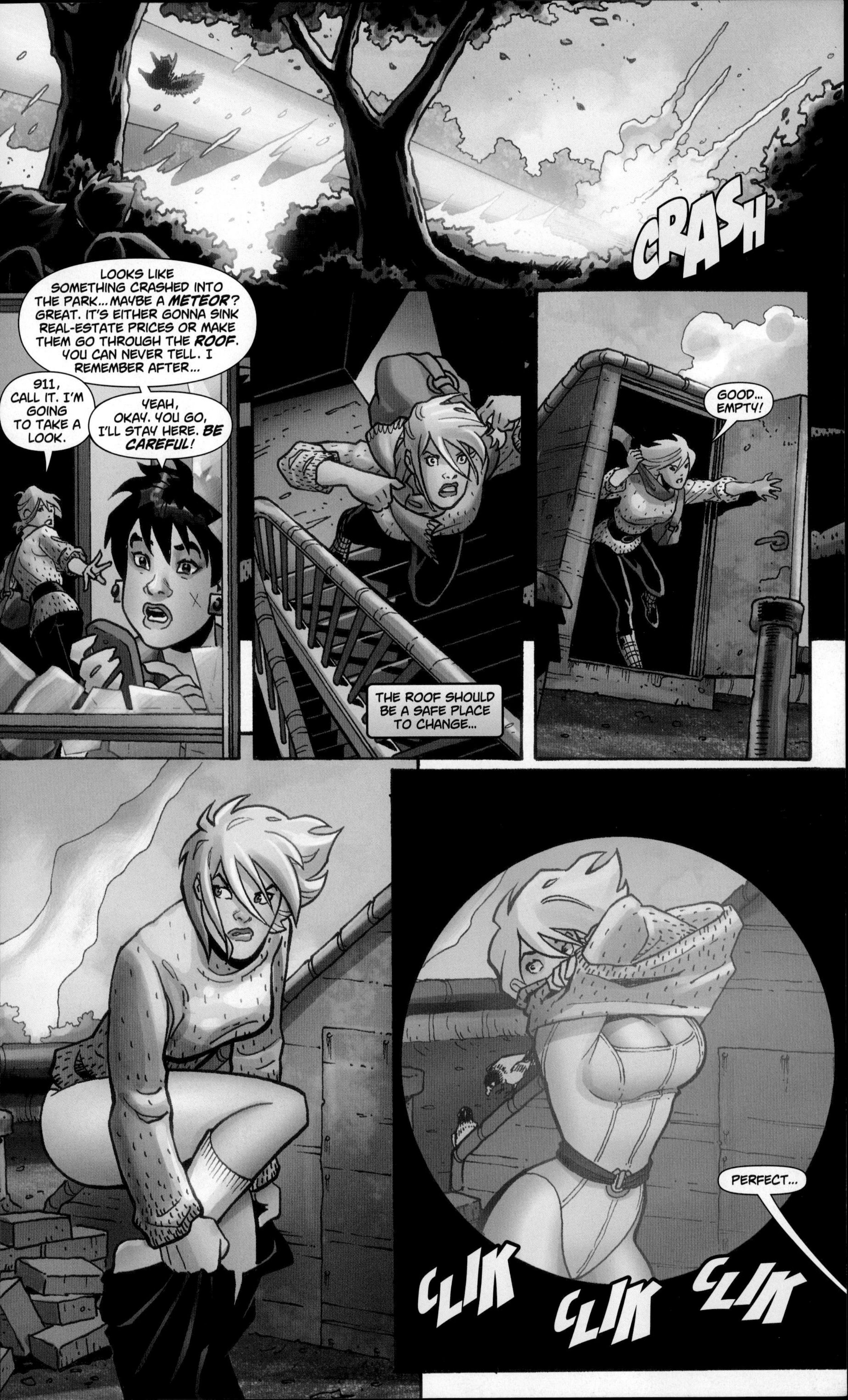
CRASH
LOOKS LIKE SOMETHING CRASHED INTO THE PARK... MAYBE A *METEOR*? GREAT. IT'S EITHER GONNA SINK REAL-ESTATE PRICES OR MAKE THEM GO THROUGH THE *ROOF*. YOU CAN NEVER TELL. I REMEMBER AFTER...
911, CALL IT. I'M GOING TO TAKE A LOOK.
YEAH, OKAY. YOU GO, I'LL STAY HERE. *BE CAREFUL*!
THE ROOF SHOULD BE A SAFE PLACE TO CHANGE...
GOOD... EMPTY!
PERFECT...
CLIK
CLIK
CLIK

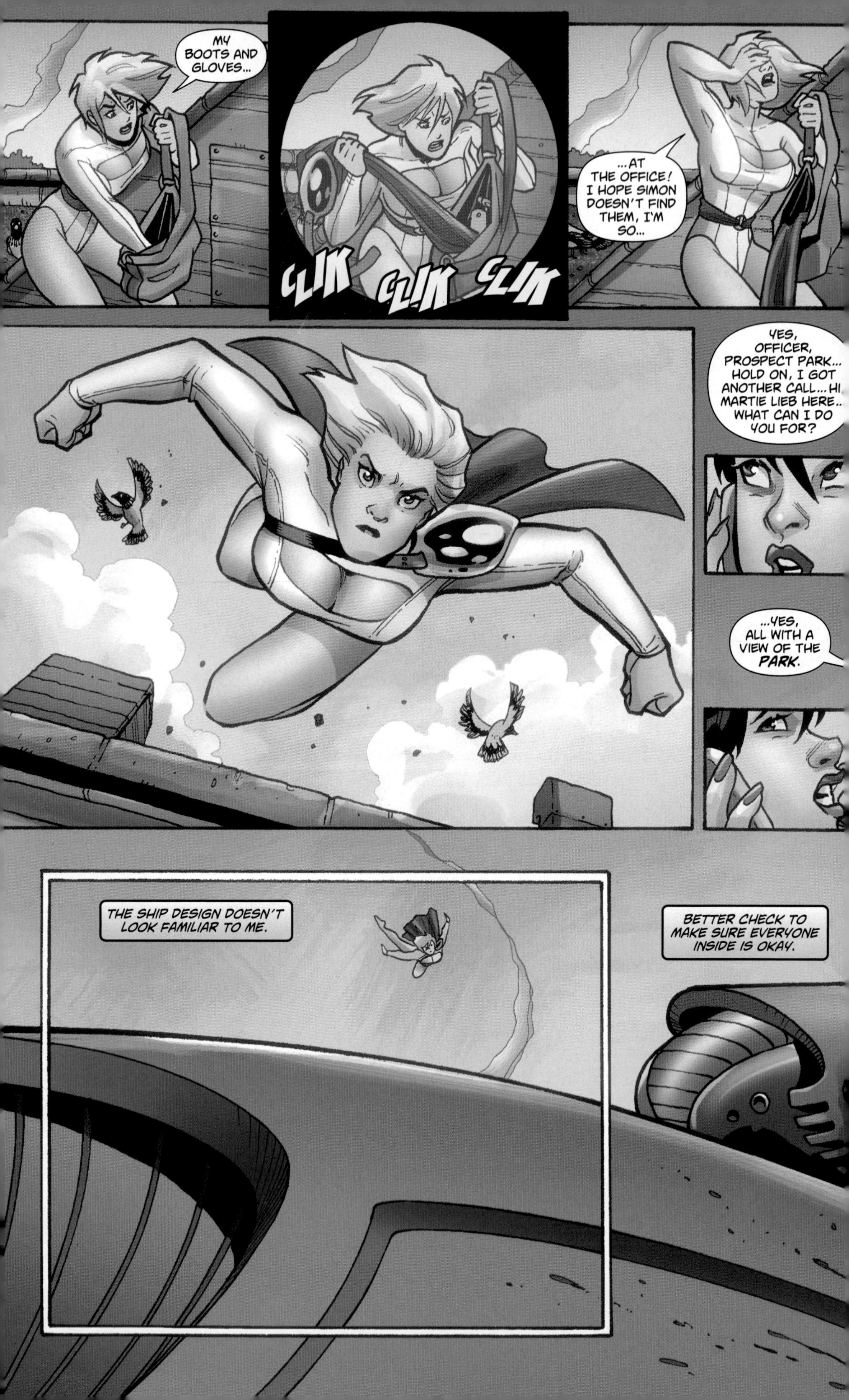
MY BOOTS AND GLOVES...
CLIK CLIK CLIK
...AT THE OFFICE! I HOPE SIMON DOESN'T FIND THEM, I'M SO...
YES, OFFICER, PROSPECT PARK... HOLD ON, I GOT ANOTHER CALL... HI, MARTIE LIEB HERE... WHAT CAN I DO YOU FOR?
...YES, ALL WITH A VIEW OF THE PARK.
THE SHIP DESIGN DOESN'T LOOK FAMILIAR TO ME.
BETTER CHECK TO MAKE SURE EVERYONE INSIDE IS OKAY.

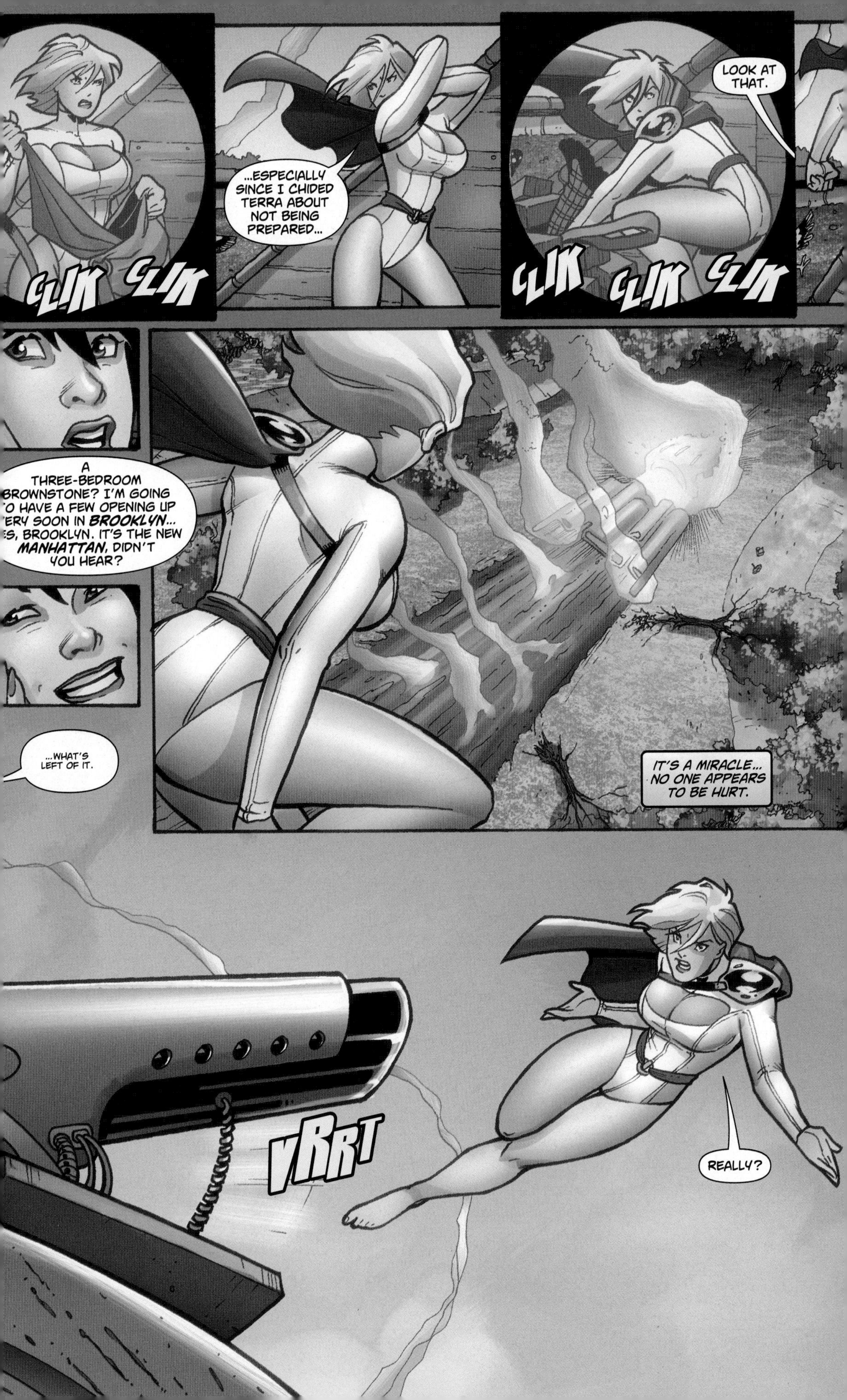

CLIK CLIK
...ESPECIALLY SINCE I CHIDED TERRA ABOUT NOT BEING PREPARED...
LOOK AT THAT.
CLIK CLIK CLIK
A THREE-BEDROOM BROWNSTONE? I'M GOING TO HAVE A FEW OPENING UP VERY SOON IN BROOKLYN... YES, BROOKLYN. IT'S THE NEW MANHATTAN, DIDN'T YOU HEAR?
...WHAT'S LEFT OF IT.
IT'S A MIRACLE... NO ONE APPEARS TO BE HURT.
VRRT
REALLY?

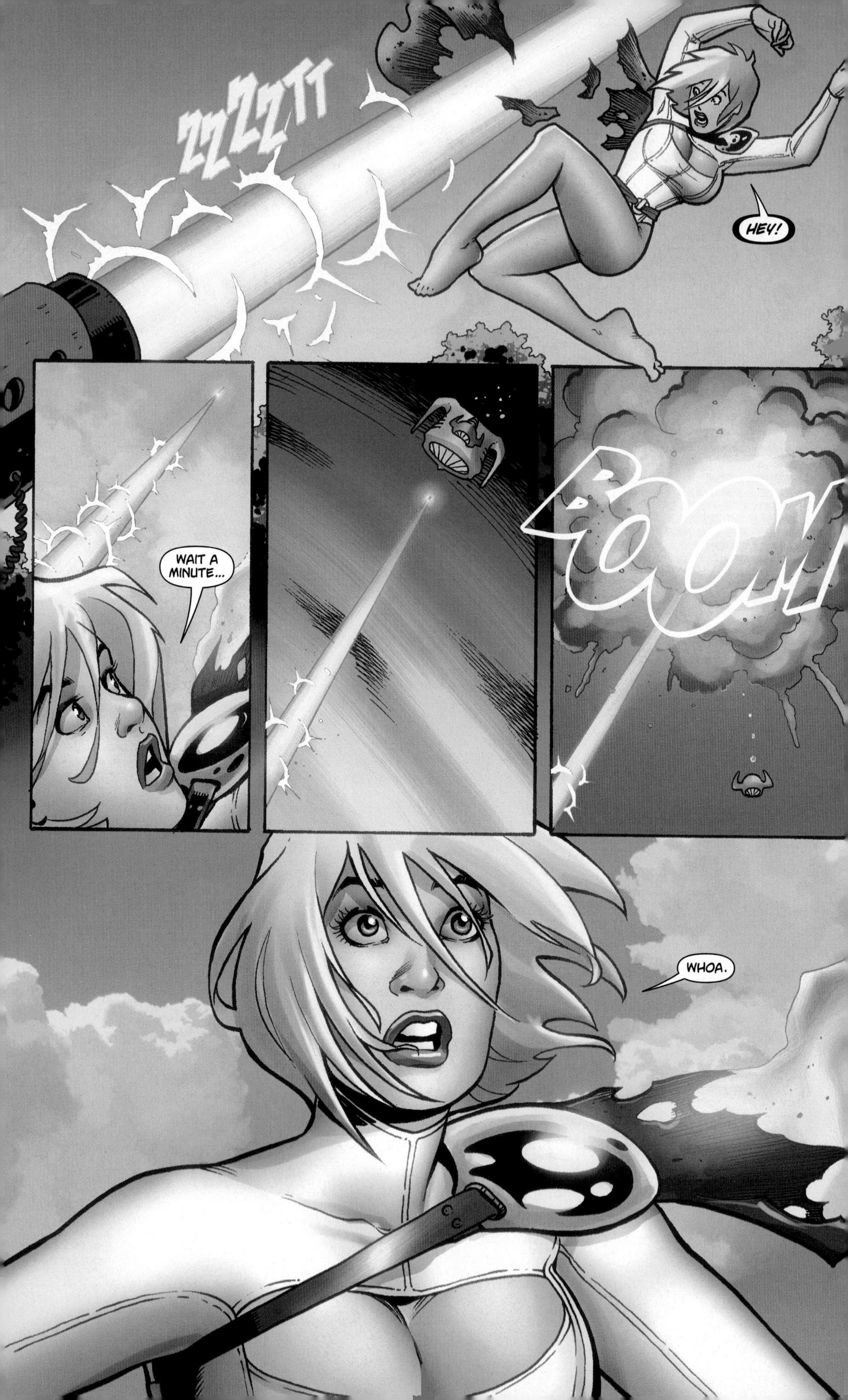
ZZZZTT
HEY!
WAIT A MINUTE...
BOOM
WHOA.

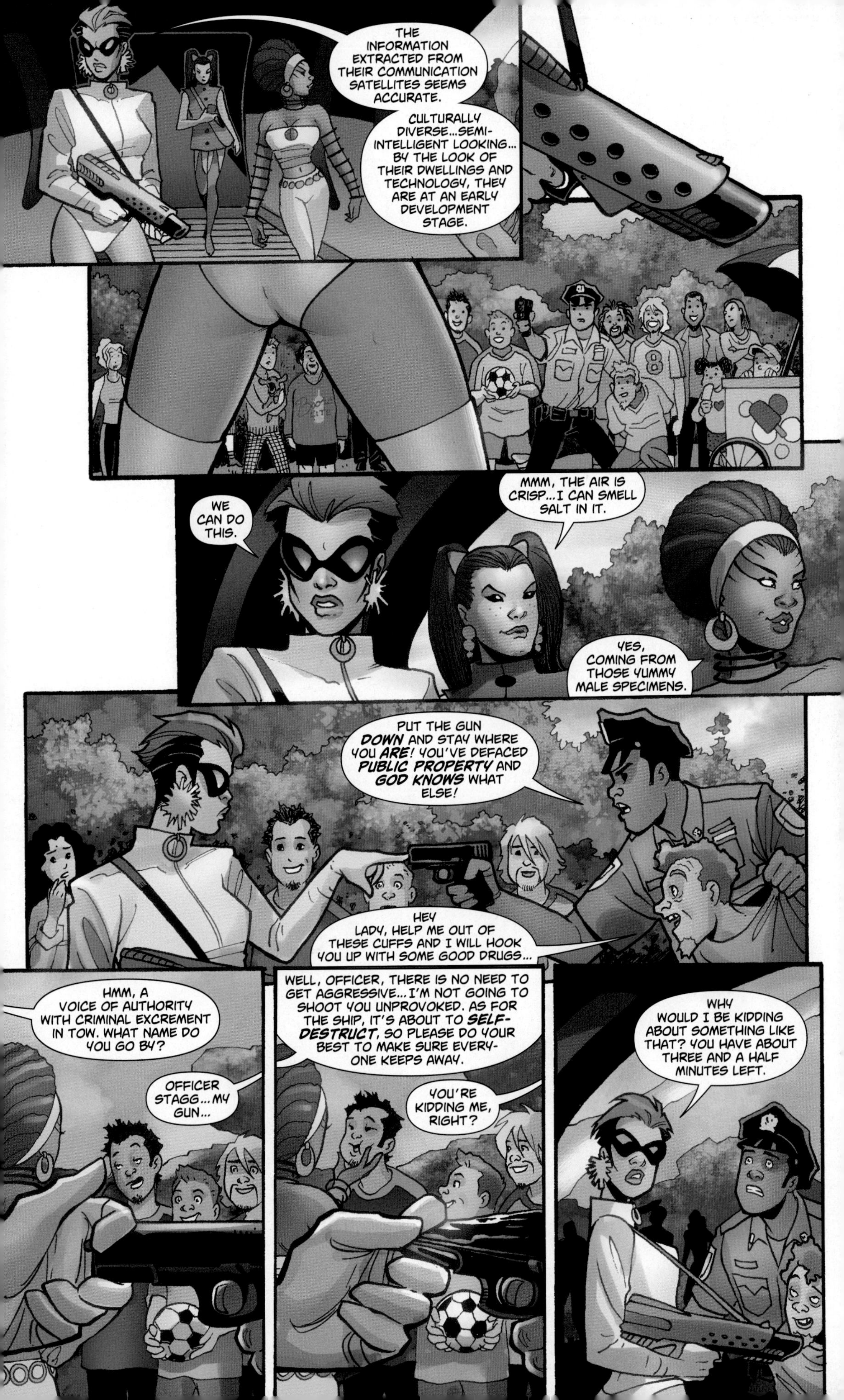
THE INFORMATION EXTRACTED FROM THEIR COMMUNICATION SATELLITES SEEMS ACCURATE.
CULTURALLY DIVERSE...SEMI-INTELLIGENT LOOKING... BY THE LOOK OF THEIR DWELLINGS AND TECHNOLOGY, THEY ARE AT AN EARLY DEVELOPMENT STAGE.
WE CAN DO THIS.
MMM, THE AIR IS CRISP...I CAN SMELL SALT IN IT.
YES, COMING FROM THOSE YUMMY MALE SPECIMENS.
PUT THE GUN DOWN AND STAY WHERE YOU ARE! YOU'VE DEFACED PUBLIC PROPERTY AND GOD KNOWS WHAT ELSE!
HEY LADY, HELP ME OUT OF THESE CUFFS AND I WILL HOOK YOU UP WITH SOME GOOD DRUGS...
HMM, A VOICE OF AUTHORITY WITH CRIMINAL EXCREMENT IN TOW. WHAT NAME DO YOU GO BY?
OFFICER STAGG...MY GUN...
WELL, OFFICER, THERE IS NO NEED TO GET AGGRESSIVE...I'M NOT GOING TO SHOOT YOU UNPROVOKED. AS FOR THE SHIP, IT'S ABOUT TO SELF-DESTRUCT, SO PLEASE DO YOUR BEST TO MAKE SURE EVERYONE KEEPS AWAY.
YOU'RE KIDDING ME, RIGHT?
WHY WOULD I BE KIDDING ABOUT SOMETHING LIKE THAT? YOU HAVE ABOUT THREE AND A HALF MINUTES LEFT.

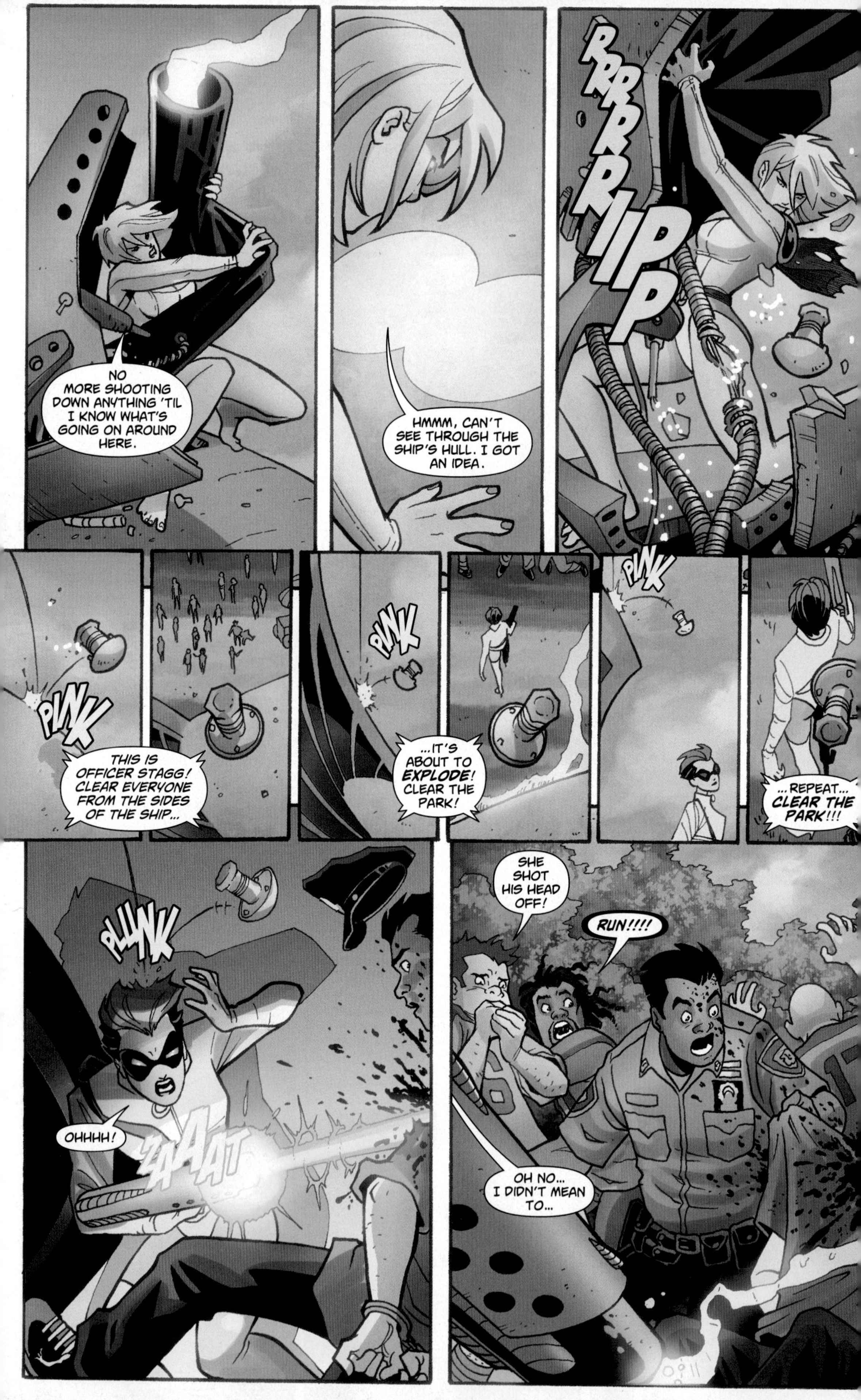
NO MORE SHOOTING DOWN ANYTHING 'TIL I KNOW WHAT'S GOING ON AROUND HERE.
HMMM, CAN'T SEE THROUGH THE SHIP'S HULL. I GOT AN IDEA.
RRRRRIIIPP
PINK
THIS IS OFFICER STAGG! CLEAR EVERYONE FROM THE SIDES OF THE SHIP...
PINK
...IT'S ABOUT TO EXPLODE! CLEAR THE PARK!
PINK
...REPEAT... CLEAR THE PARK!!!
PLUNK
OHHHH!
ZAAAT
SHE SHOT HIS HEAD OFF!
RUN!!!!
OH NO... I DIDN'T MEAN TO...

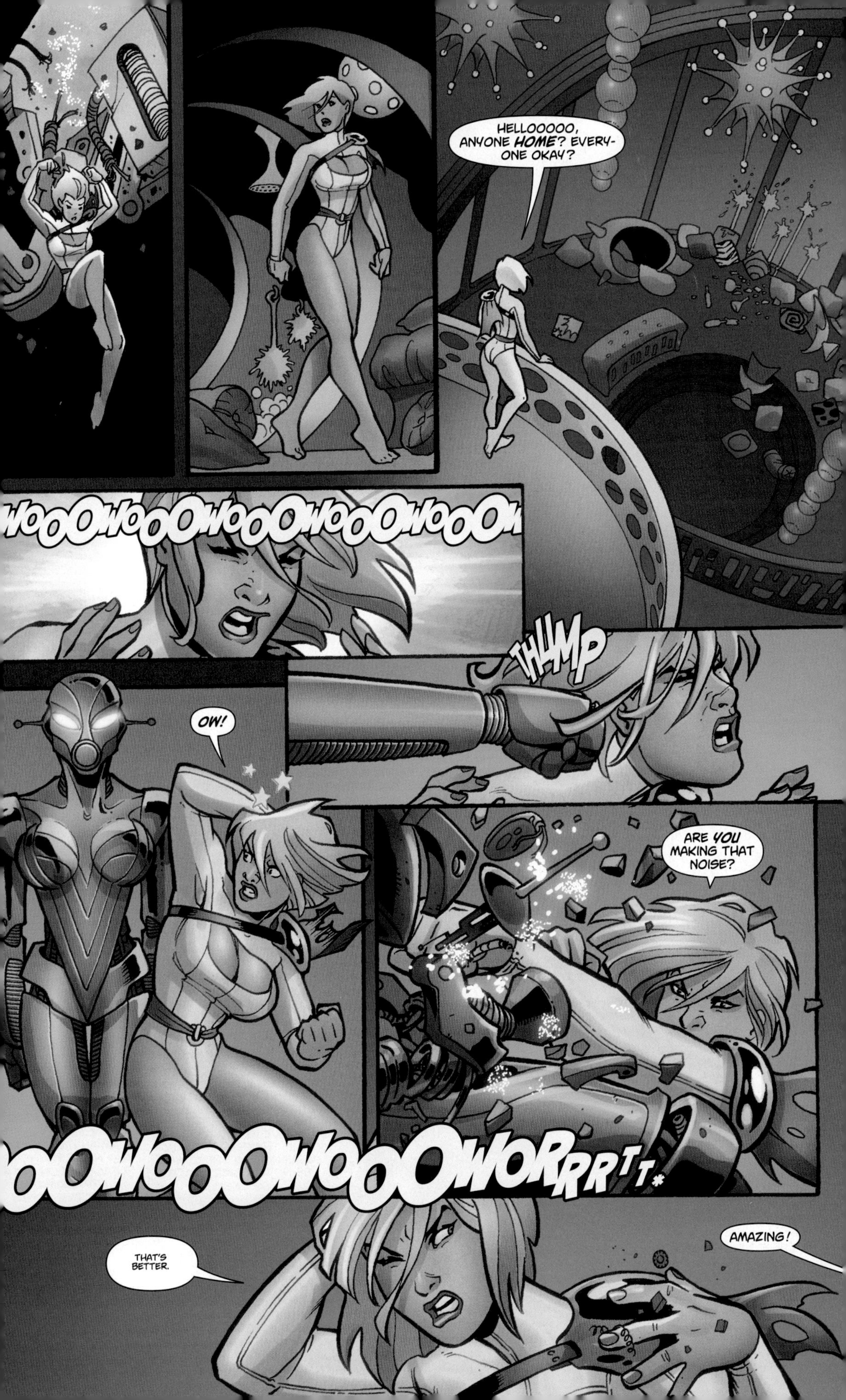
HELLOOOOO, ANYONE HOME? EVERY-ONE OKAY?
WOOOWOOOWOOOWOOOWOOOW
THUMP
OW!
ARE YOU MAKING THAT NOISE?
OOOWOOOWOOOWORRRTT*
THAT'S BETTER.
AMAZING!

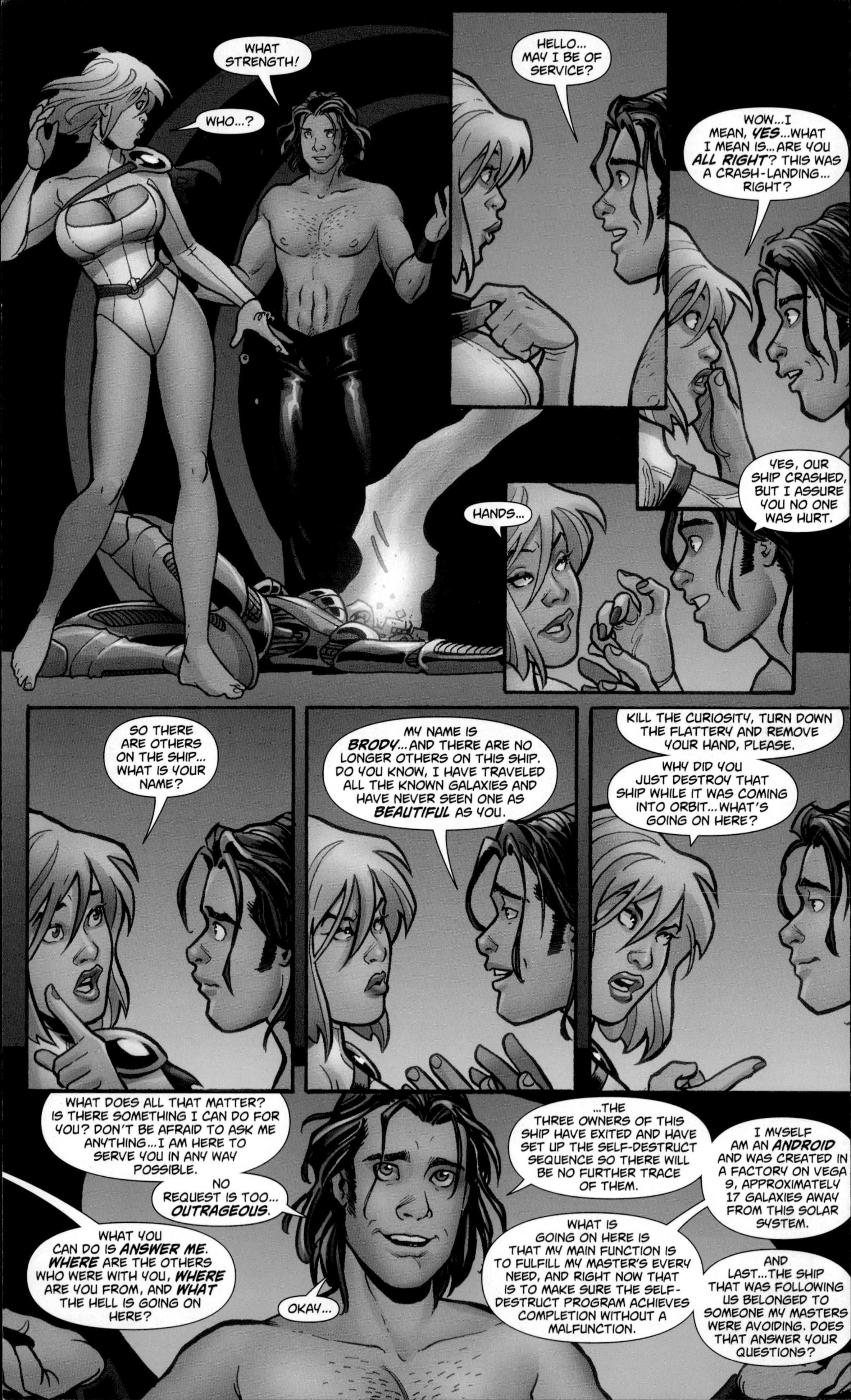
WHAT STRENGTH!
WHO...?
HELLO... MAY I BE OF SERVICE?
WOW...I MEAN, YES...WHAT I MEAN IS...ARE YOU ALL RIGHT? THIS WAS A CRASH-LANDING... RIGHT?
YES, OUR SHIP CRASHED, BUT I ASSURE YOU NO ONE WAS HURT.
HANDS...
SO THERE ARE OTHERS ON THE SHIP... WHAT IS YOUR NAME?
MY NAME IS BRODY...AND THERE ARE NO LONGER OTHERS ON THIS SHIP. DO YOU KNOW, I HAVE TRAVELED ALL THE KNOWN GALAXIES AND HAVE NEVER SEEN ONE AS BEAUTIFUL AS YOU.
KILL THE CURIOSITY, TURN DOWN THE FLATTERY AND REMOVE YOUR HAND, PLEASE.
WHY DID YOU JUST DESTROY THAT SHIP WHILE IT WAS COMING INTO ORBIT...WHAT'S GOING ON HERE?
WHAT DOES ALL THAT MATTER? IS THERE SOMETHING I CAN DO FOR YOU? DON'T BE AFRAID TO ASK ME ANYTHING...I AM HERE TO SERVE YOU IN ANY WAY POSSIBLE.
NO REQUEST IS TOO... OUTRAGEOUS.
WHAT YOU CAN DO IS ANSWER ME. WHERE ARE THE OTHERS WHO WERE WITH YOU, WHERE ARE YOU FROM, AND WHAT THE HELL IS GOING ON HERE?
OKAY...
...THE THREE OWNERS OF THIS SHIP HAVE EXITED AND HAVE SET UP THE SELF-DESTRUCT SEQUENCE SO THERE WILL BE NO FURTHER TRACE OF THEM.
I MYSELF AM AN ANDROID AND WAS CREATED IN A FACTORY ON VEGA 9, APPROXIMATELY 17 GALAXIES AWAY FROM THIS SOLAR SYSTEM.
WHAT IS GOING ON HERE IS THAT MY MAIN FUNCTION IS TO FULFILL MY MASTER'S EVERY NEED, AND RIGHT NOW THAT IS TO MAKE SURE THE SELF-DESTRUCT PROGRAM ACHIEVES COMPLETION WITHOUT A MALFUNCTION.
AND LAST...THE SHIP THAT WAS FOLLOWING US BELONGED TO SOMEONE MY MASTERS WERE AVOIDING. DOES THAT ANSWER YOUR QUESTIONS?

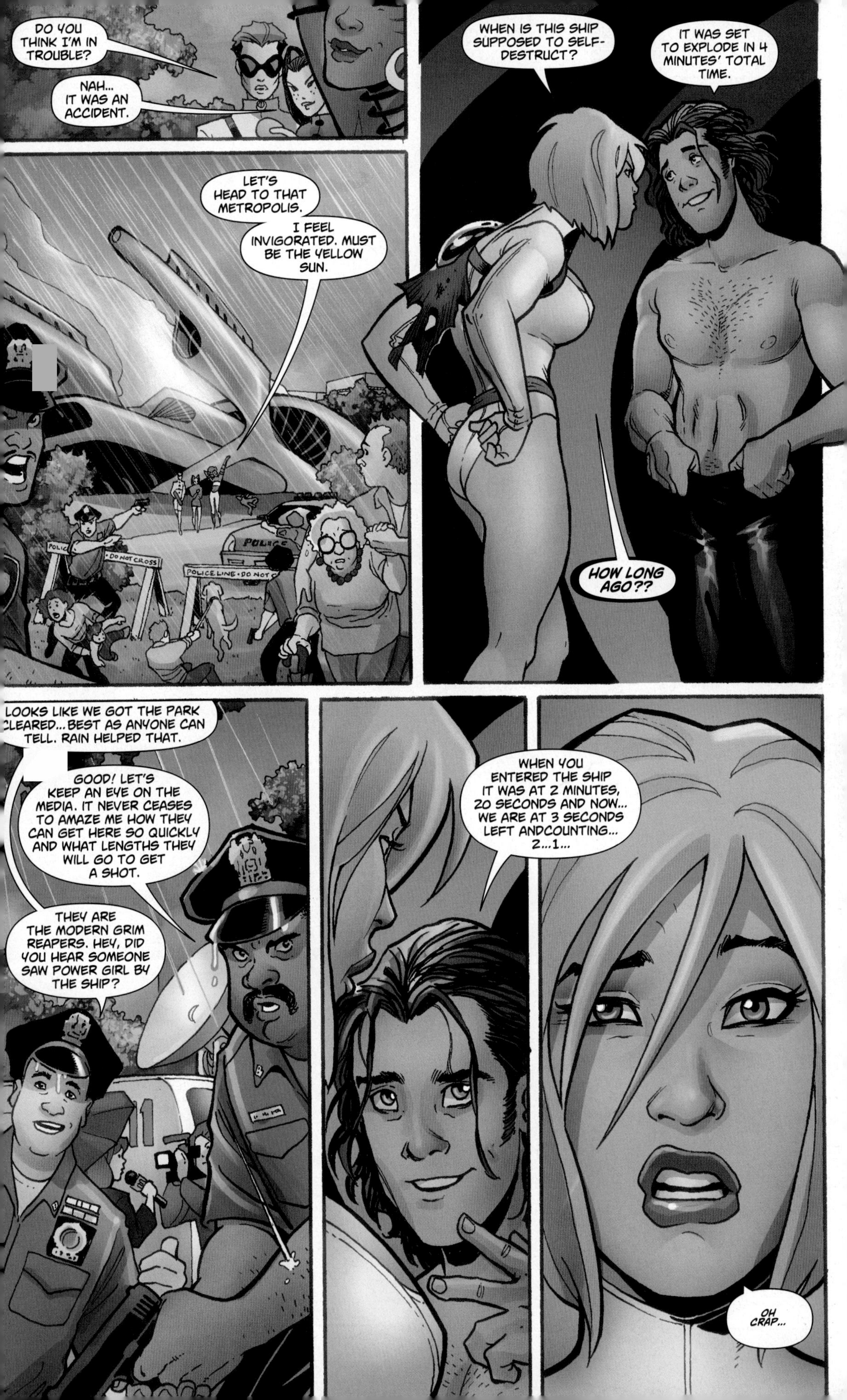
DO YOU THINK I'M IN TROUBLE?
NAH... IT WAS AN ACCIDENT.
LET'S HEAD TO THAT METROPOLIS.
I FEEL INVIGORATED. MUST BE THE YELLOW SUN.
POLICE LINE • DO NOT CROSS
POLICE LINE • DO NOT
POLICE
WHEN IS THIS SHIP SUPPOSED TO SELF-DESTRUCT?
IT WAS SET TO EXPLODE IN 4 MINUTES' TOTAL TIME.
HOW LONG AGO??
LOOKS LIKE WE GOT THE PARK CLEARED...BEST AS ANYONE CAN TELL. RAIN HELPED THAT.
GOOD! LET'S KEEP AN EYE ON THE MEDIA. IT NEVER CEASES TO AMAZE ME HOW THEY CAN GET HERE SO QUICKLY AND WHAT LENGTHS THEY WILL GO TO GET A SHOT.
THEY ARE THE MODERN GRIM REAPERS. HEY, DID YOU HEAR SOMEONE SAW POWER GIRL BY THE SHIP?
WHEN YOU ENTERED THE SHIP IT WAS AT 2 MINUTES, 20 SECONDS AND NOW... WE ARE AT 3 SECONDS LEFT ANDCOUNTING... 2...1...
OH CRAP...

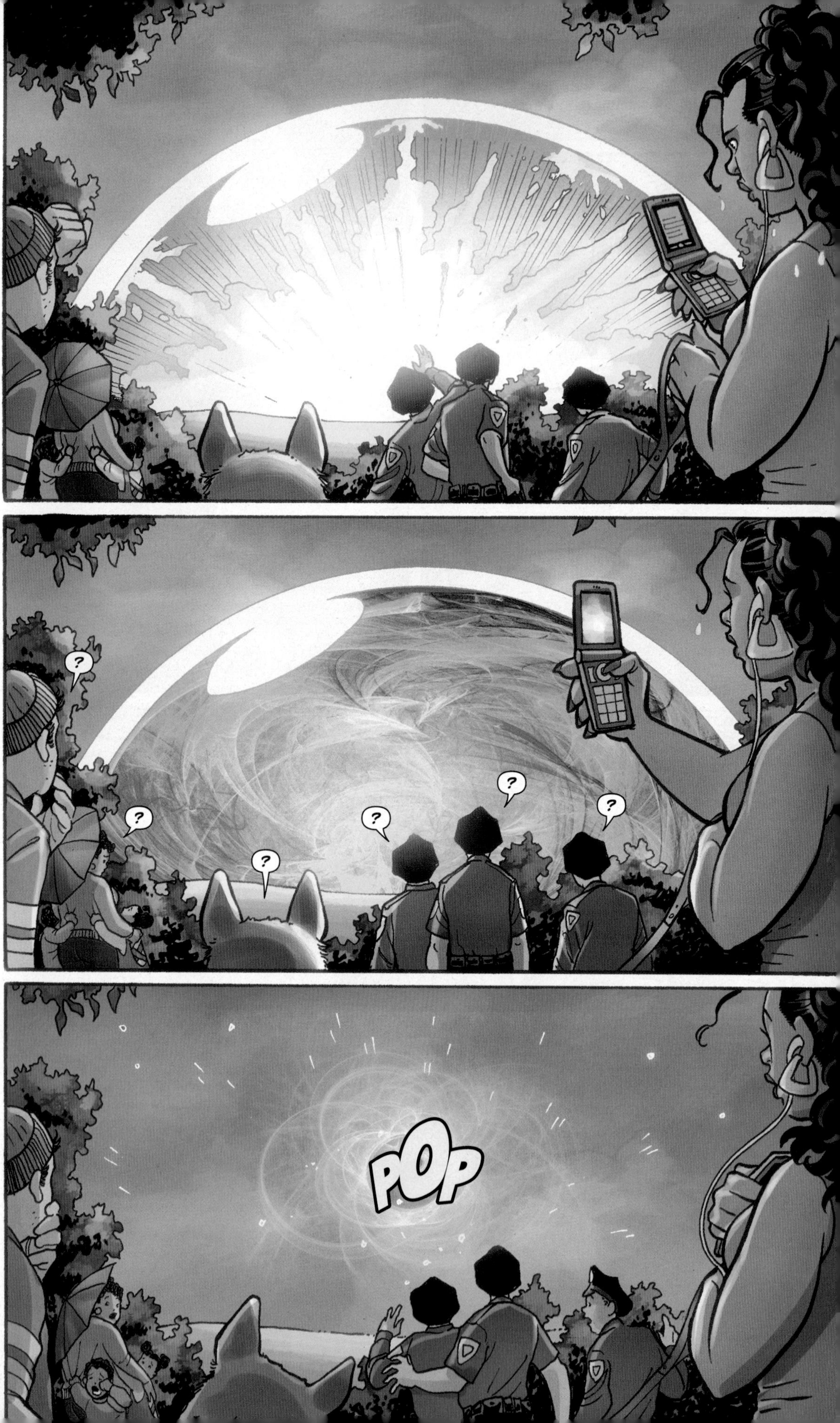
?
?
?
?
?
?
POP

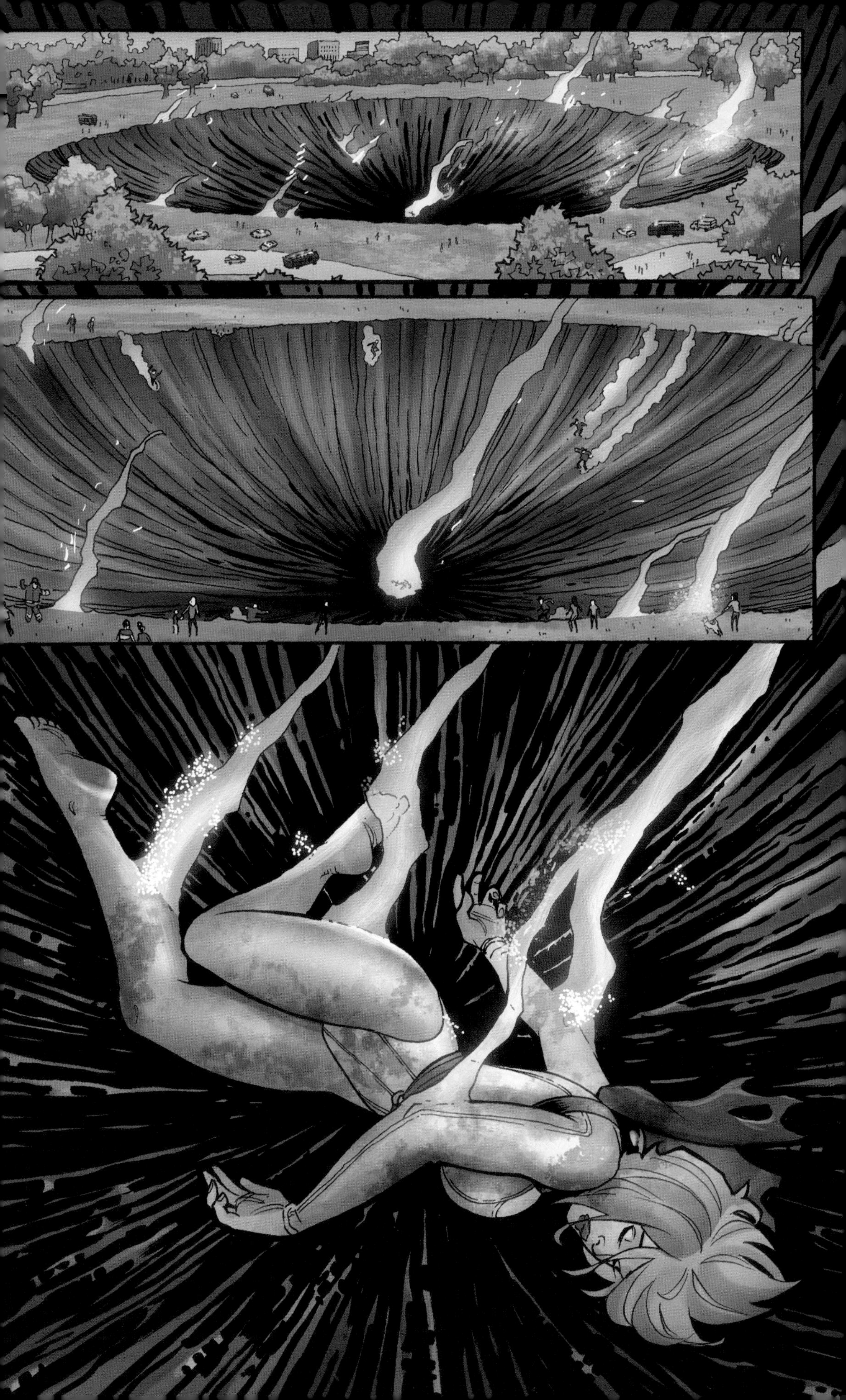

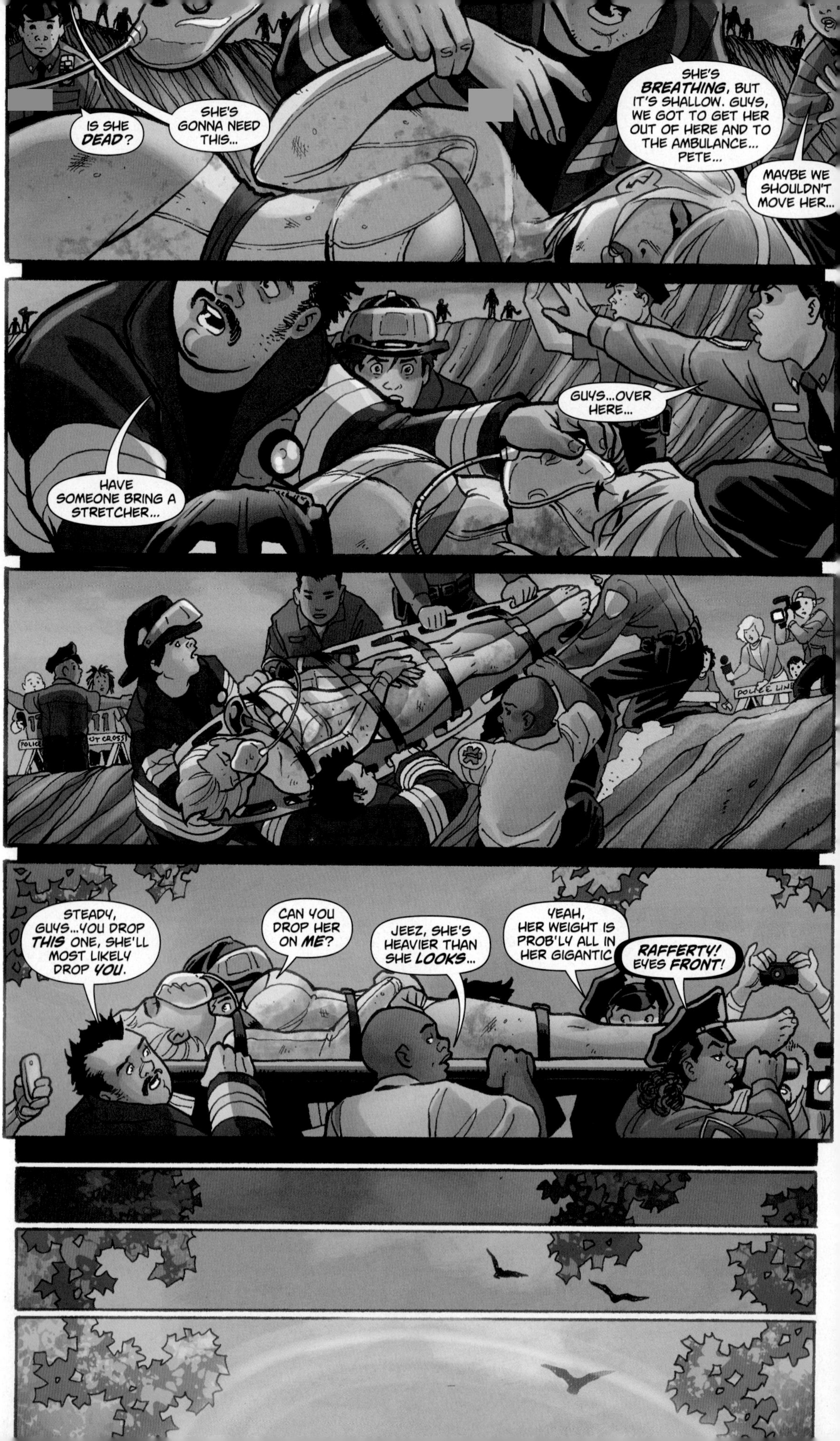

IS SHE DEAD?
SHE'S GONNA NEED THIS...
SHE'S BREATHING, BUT IT'S SHALLOW. GUYS, WE GOT TO GET HER OUT OF HERE AND TO THE AMBULANCE... PETE...
MAYBE WE SHOULDN'T MOVE HER...
GUYS...OVER HERE...
HAVE SOMEONE BRING A STRETCHER...
STEADY, GUYS...YOU DROP THIS ONE, SHE'LL MOST LIKELY DROP YOU.
CAN YOU DROP HER ON ME?
JEEZ, SHE'S HEAVIER THAN SHE LOOKS...
YEAH, HER WEIGHT IS PROB'LY ALL IN HER GIGANTIC
RAFFERTY! EYES FRONT!

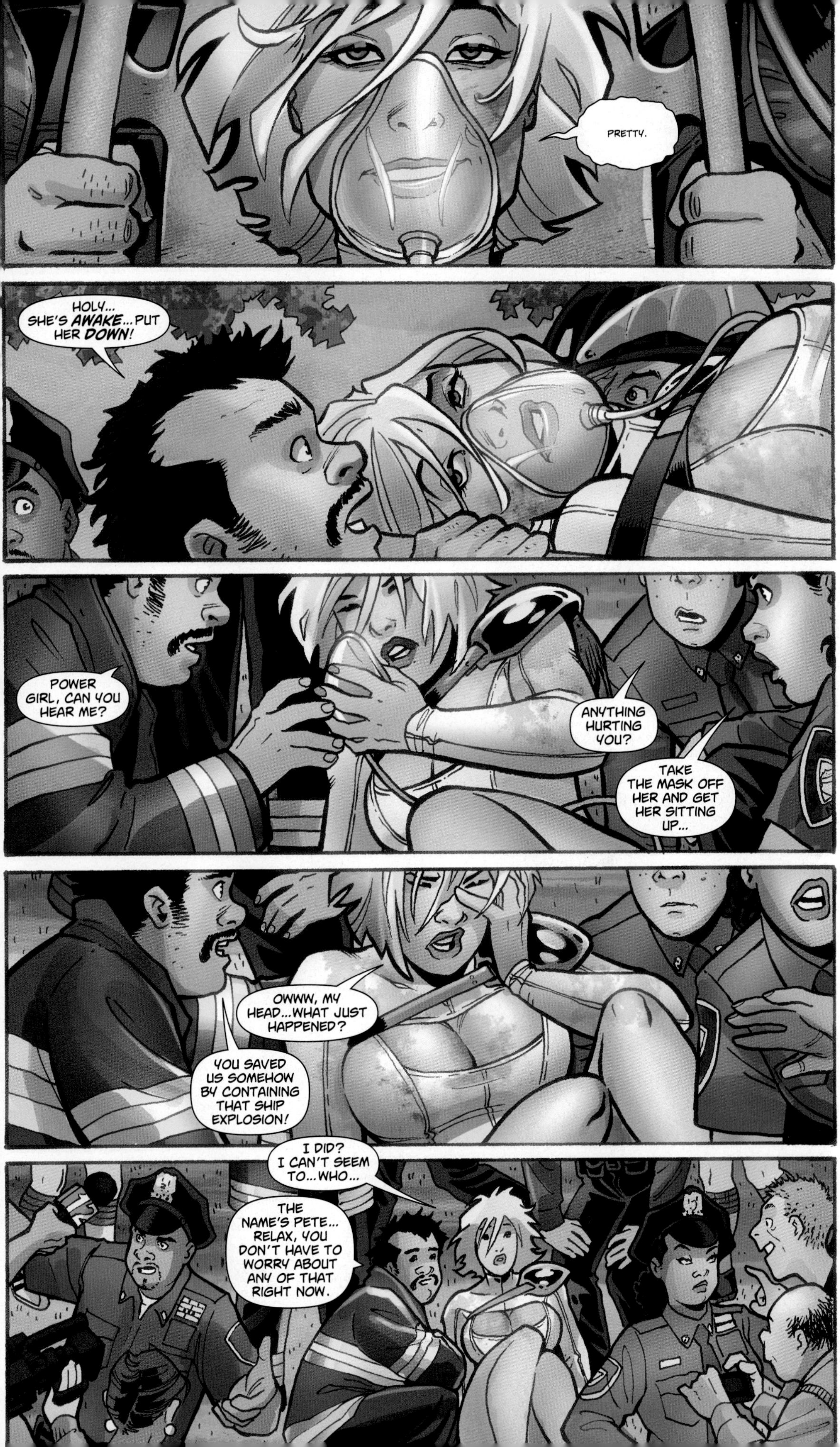
PRETTY.
HOLY... SHE'S AWAKE...PUT HER DOWN!
POWER GIRL, CAN YOU HEAR ME?
ANYTHING HURTING YOU?
TAKE THE MASK OFF HER AND GET HER SITTING UP...
OWWW, MY HEAD...WHAT JUST HAPPENED?
YOU SAVED US SOMEHOW BY CONTAINING THAT SHIP EXPLOSION!
I DID? I CAN'T SEEM TO...WHO...
THE NAME'S PETE... RELAX, YOU DON'T HAVE TO WORRY ABOUT ANY OF THAT RIGHT NOW.

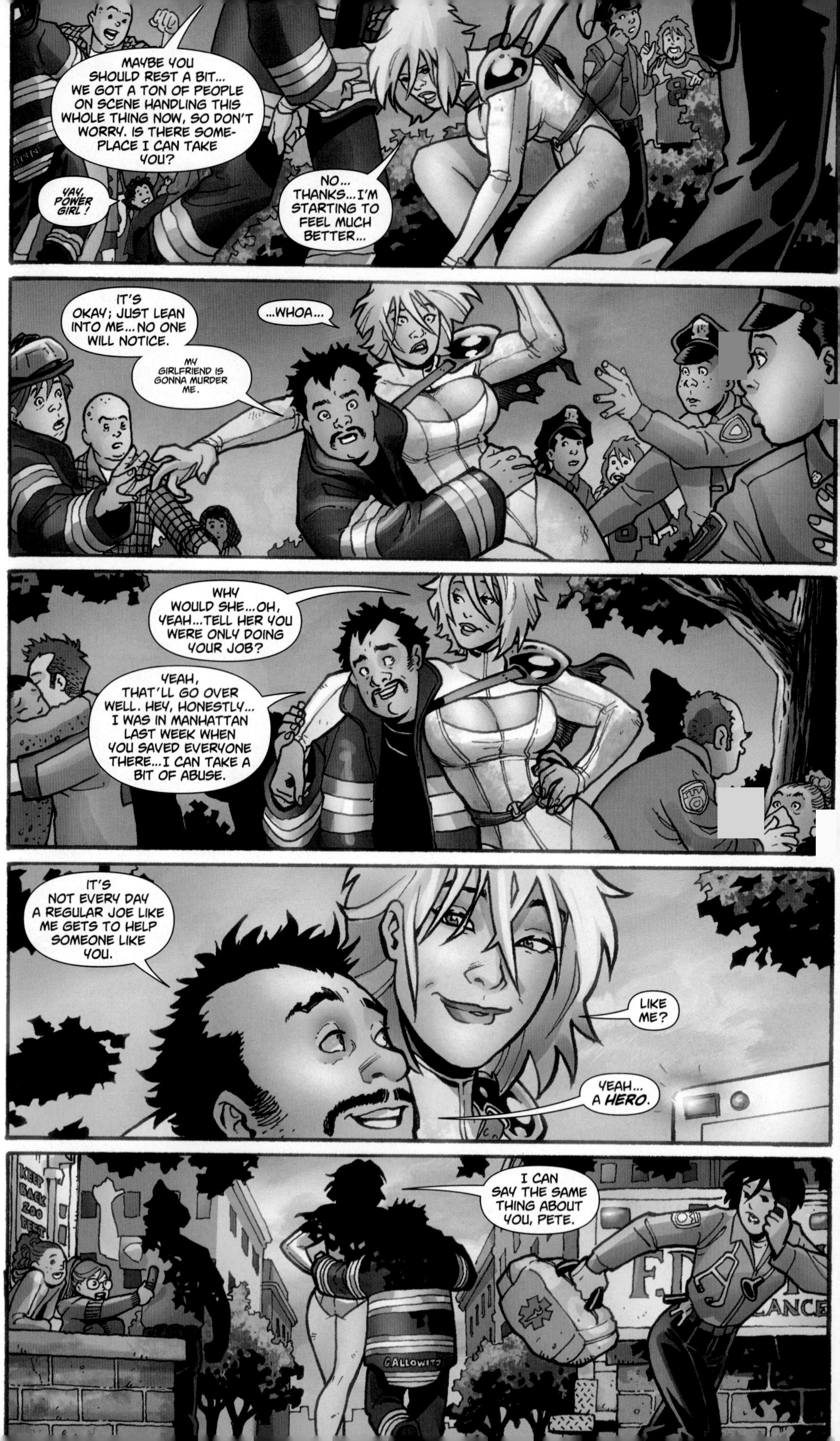
MAYBE YOU SHOULD REST A BIT... WE GOT A TON OF PEOPLE ON SCENE HANDLING THIS WHOLE THING NOW, SO DON'T WORRY. IS THERE SOME-PLACE I CAN TAKE YOU?
YAY, POWER GIRL!
NO... THANKS...I'M STARTING TO FEEL MUCH BETTER...
IT'S OKAY; JUST LEAN INTO ME...NO ONE WILL NOTICE.
...WHOA...
MY GIRLFRIEND IS GONNA MURDER ME.
WHY WOULD SHE...OH, YEAH...TELL HER YOU WERE ONLY DOING YOUR JOB?
YEAH, THAT'LL GO OVER WELL. HEY, HONESTLY... I WAS IN MANHATTAN LAST WEEK WHEN YOU SAVED EVERYONE THERE...I CAN TAKE A BIT OF ABUSE.
IT'S NOT EVERY DAY A REGULAR JOE LIKE ME GETS TO HELP SOMEONE LIKE YOU.
LIKE ME?
YEAH... A **HERO**.
KEEP BACK 200 FEET
I CAN SAY THE SAME THING ABOUT YOU, PETE.
GALLOWITZ

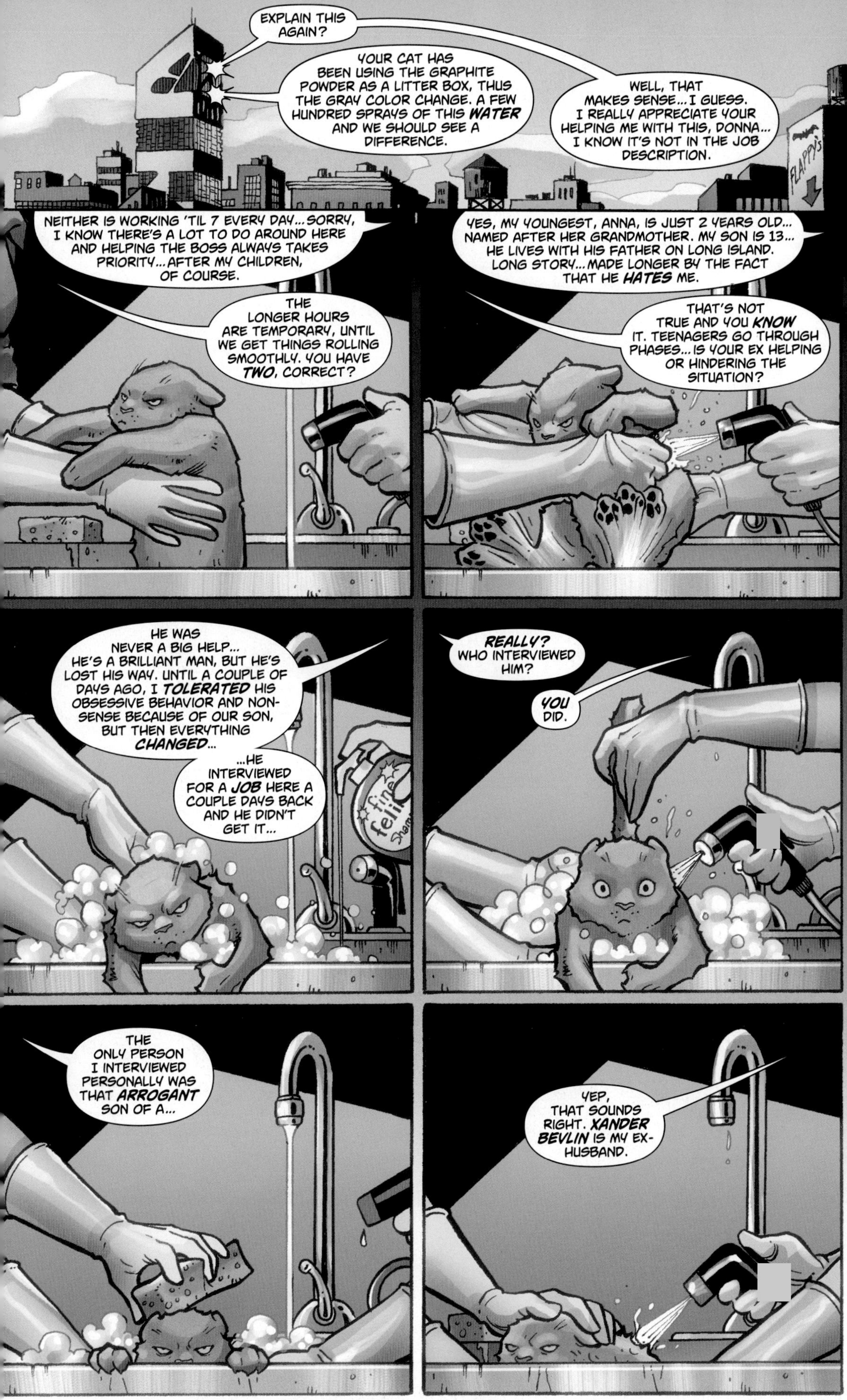
EXPLAIN THIS AGAIN?
YOUR CAT HAS BEEN USING THE GRAPHITE POWDER AS A LITTER BOX, THUS THE GRAY COLOR CHANGE. A FEW HUNDRED SPRAYS OF THIS WATER AND WE SHOULD SEE A DIFFERENCE.
WELL, THAT MAKES SENSE... I GUESS. I REALLY APPRECIATE YOUR HELPING ME WITH THIS, DONNA... I KNOW IT'S NOT IN THE JOB DESCRIPTION.
FLAPPY'S
NEITHER IS WORKING 'TIL 7 EVERY DAY... SORRY, I KNOW THERE'S A LOT TO DO AROUND HERE AND HELPING THE BOSS ALWAYS TAKES PRIORITY... AFTER MY CHILDREN, OF COURSE.
THE LONGER HOURS ARE TEMPORARY, UNTIL WE GET THINGS ROLLING SMOOTHLY. YOU HAVE TWO, CORRECT?
YES, MY YOUNGEST, ANNA, IS JUST 2 YEARS OLD... NAMED AFTER HER GRANDMOTHER. MY SON IS 13... HE LIVES WITH HIS FATHER ON LONG ISLAND. LONG STORY... MADE LONGER BY THE FACT THAT HE HATES ME.
THAT'S NOT TRUE AND YOU KNOW IT. TEENAGERS GO THROUGH PHASES... IS YOUR EX HELPING OR HINDERING THE SITUATION?
HE WAS NEVER A BIG HELP... HE'S A BRILLIANT MAN, BUT HE'S LOST HIS WAY. UNTIL A COUPLE OF DAYS AGO, I TOLERATED HIS OBSESSIVE BEHAVIOR AND NON-SENSE BECAUSE OF OUR SON, BUT THEN EVERYTHING CHANGED...
...HE INTERVIEWED FOR A JOB HERE A COUPLE DAYS BACK AND HE DIDN'T GET IT...
REALLY? WHO INTERVIEWED HIM?
YOU DID.
THE ONLY PERSON I INTERVIEWED PERSONALLY WAS THAT ARROGANT SON OF A...
YEP, THAT SOUNDS RIGHT. XANDER BEVLIN IS MY EX-HUSBAND.

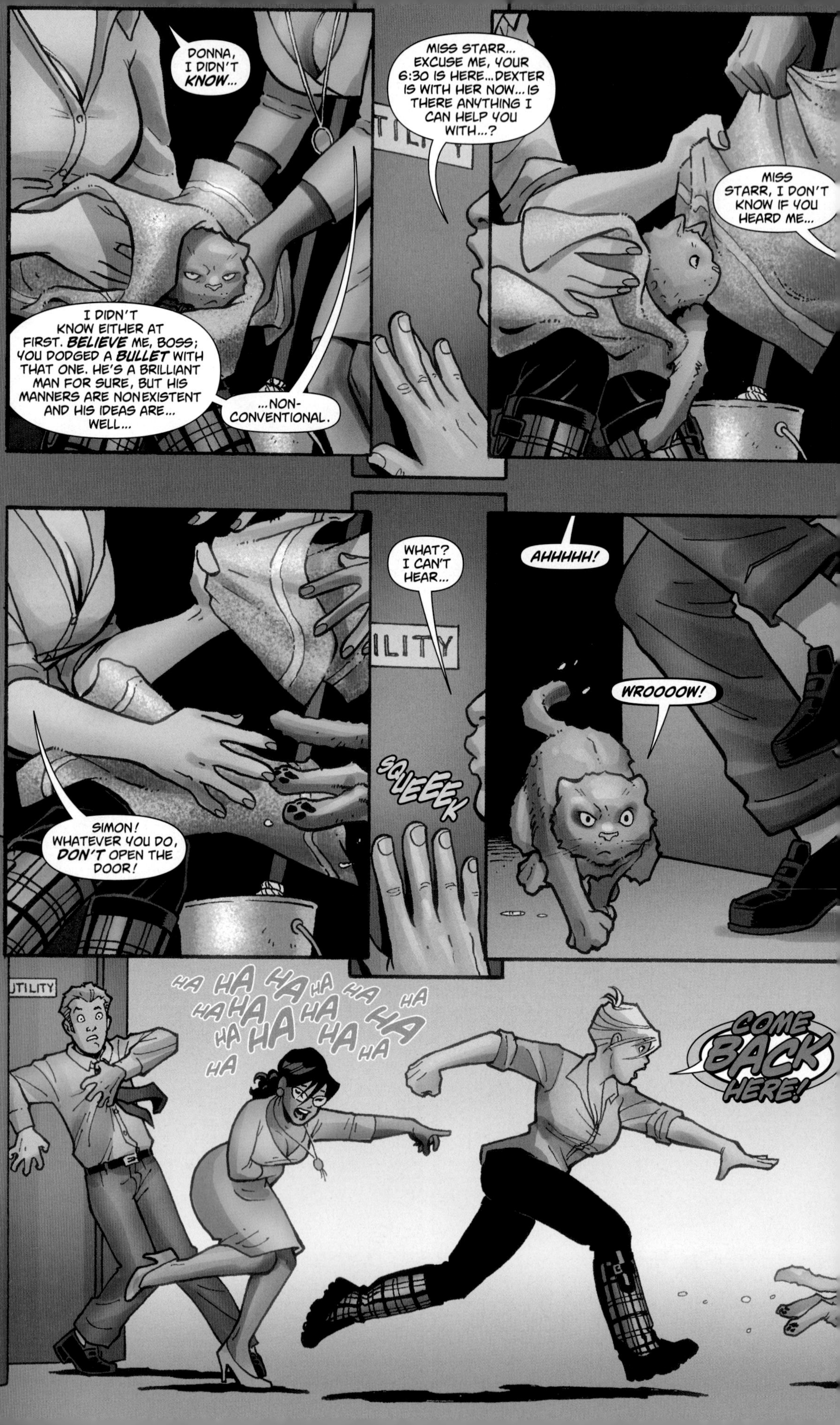
DONNA, I DIDN'T KNOW...
I DIDN'T KNOW EITHER AT FIRST. BELIEVE ME, BOSS; YOU DODGED A BULLET WITH THAT ONE. HE'S A BRILLIANT MAN FOR SURE, BUT HIS MANNERS ARE NONEXISTENT AND HIS IDEAS ARE... WELL...
...NON-CONVENTIONAL.
MISS STARR... EXCUSE ME, YOUR 6:30 IS HERE... DEXTER IS WITH HER NOW... IS THERE ANYTHING I CAN HELP YOU WITH...?
UTILITY
MISS STARR, I DON'T KNOW IF YOU HEARD ME...
SIMON! WHATEVER YOU DO, DON'T OPEN THE DOOR!
WHAT? I CAN'T HEAR...
ILITY
SQUEEEK
AHHHHH!
WROOOOW!
UTILITY
HA HA HA HA HA HA HA HA HA HA HA HA HA HA HA HA HA
COME BACK HERE!

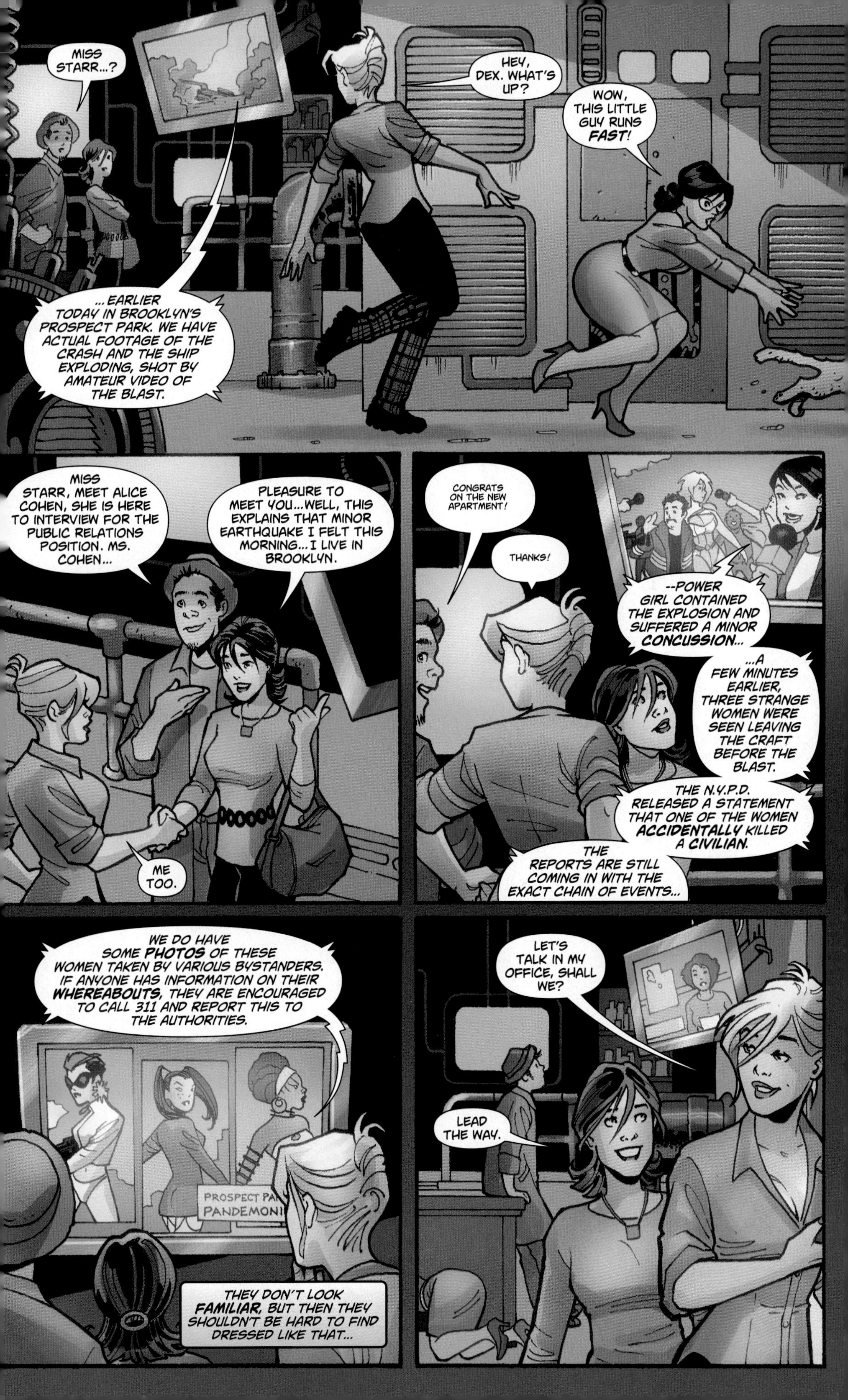
MISS STARR...?
HEY, DEX. WHAT'S UP?
WOW, THIS LITTLE GUY RUNS FAST!
...EARLIER TODAY IN BROOKLYN'S PROSPECT PARK. WE HAVE ACTUAL FOOTAGE OF THE CRASH AND THE SHIP EXPLODING, SHOT BY AMATEUR VIDEO OF THE BLAST.
MISS STARR, MEET ALICE COHEN, SHE IS HERE TO INTERVIEW FOR THE PUBLIC RELATIONS POSITION. MS. COHEN...
PLEASURE TO MEET YOU...WELL, THIS EXPLAINS THAT MINOR EARTHQUAKE I FELT THIS MORNING...I LIVE IN BROOKLYN.
ME TOO.
CONGRATS ON THE NEW APARTMENT!
THANKS!
--POWER GIRL CONTAINED THE EXPLOSION AND SUFFERED A MINOR CONCUSSION...
...A FEW MINUTES EARLIER, THREE STRANGE WOMEN WERE SEEN LEAVING THE CRAFT BEFORE THE BLAST.
THE N.Y.P.D. RELEASED A STATEMENT THAT ONE OF THE WOMEN ACCIDENTALLY KILLED A CIVILIAN.
THE REPORTS ARE STILL COMING IN WITH THE EXACT CHAIN OF EVENTS...
WE DO HAVE SOME PHOTOS OF THESE WOMEN TAKEN BY VARIOUS BYSTANDERS. IF ANYONE HAS INFORMATION ON THEIR WHEREABOUTS, THEY ARE ENCOURAGED TO CALL 311 AND REPORT THIS TO THE AUTHORITIES.
PROSPECT PA
PANDEMONI
THEY DON'T LOOK FAMILIAR, BUT THEN THEY SHOULDN'T BE HARD TO FIND DRESSED LIKE THAT...
LET'S TALK IN MY OFFICE, SHALL WE?
LEAD THE WAY.

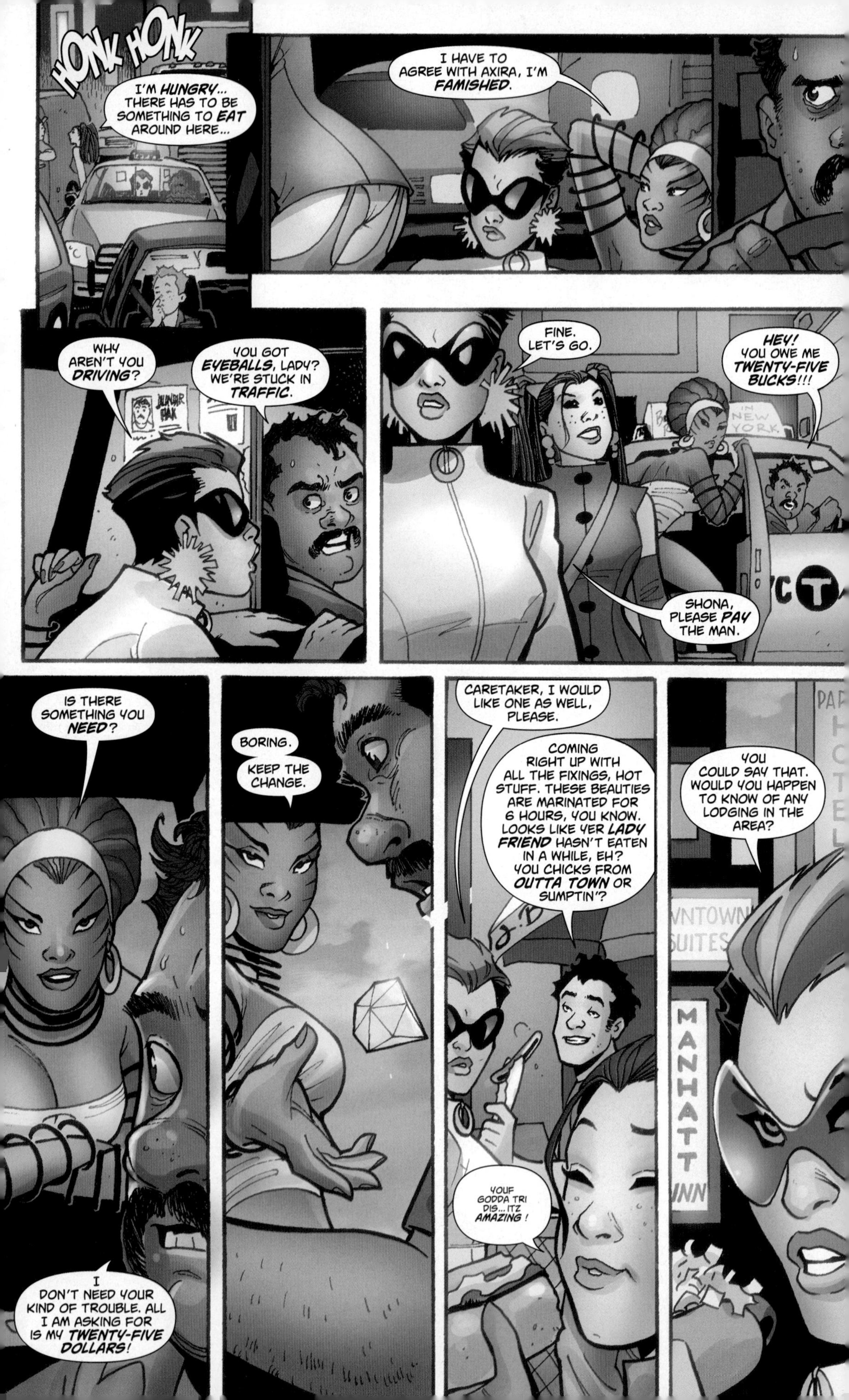
HONK HONK
I'M HUNGRY... THERE HAS TO BE SOMETHING TO EAT AROUND HERE...
I HAVE TO AGREE WITH AXIRA, I'M FAMISHED.
WHY AREN'T YOU DRIVING?
YOU GOT EYEBALLS, LADY? WE'RE STUCK IN TRAFFIC.
FINE. LET'S GO.
HEY! YOU OWE ME TWENTY-FIVE BUCKS!!!
SHONA, PLEASE PAY THE MAN.
IN NEW YORK
IS THERE SOMETHING YOU NEED?
I DON'T NEED YOUR KIND OF TROUBLE. ALL I AM ASKING FOR IS MY TWENTY-FIVE DOLLARS!
BORING.
KEEP THE CHANGE.
CARETAKER, I WOULD LIKE ONE AS WELL, PLEASE.
COMING RIGHT UP WITH ALL THE FIXINGS, HOT STUFF. THESE BEAUTIES ARE MARINATED FOR 6 HOURS, YOU KNOW. LOOKS LIKE YER LADY FRIEND HASN'T EATEN IN A WHILE, EH? YOU CHICKS FROM OUTTA TOWN OR SUMPTIN'?
YOUF GODDA TRI DIS... ITZ AMAZING!
YOU COULD SAY THAT. WOULD YOU HAPPEN TO KNOW OF ANY LODGING IN THE AREA?
HOTEL
SUITES
MANHATT INN

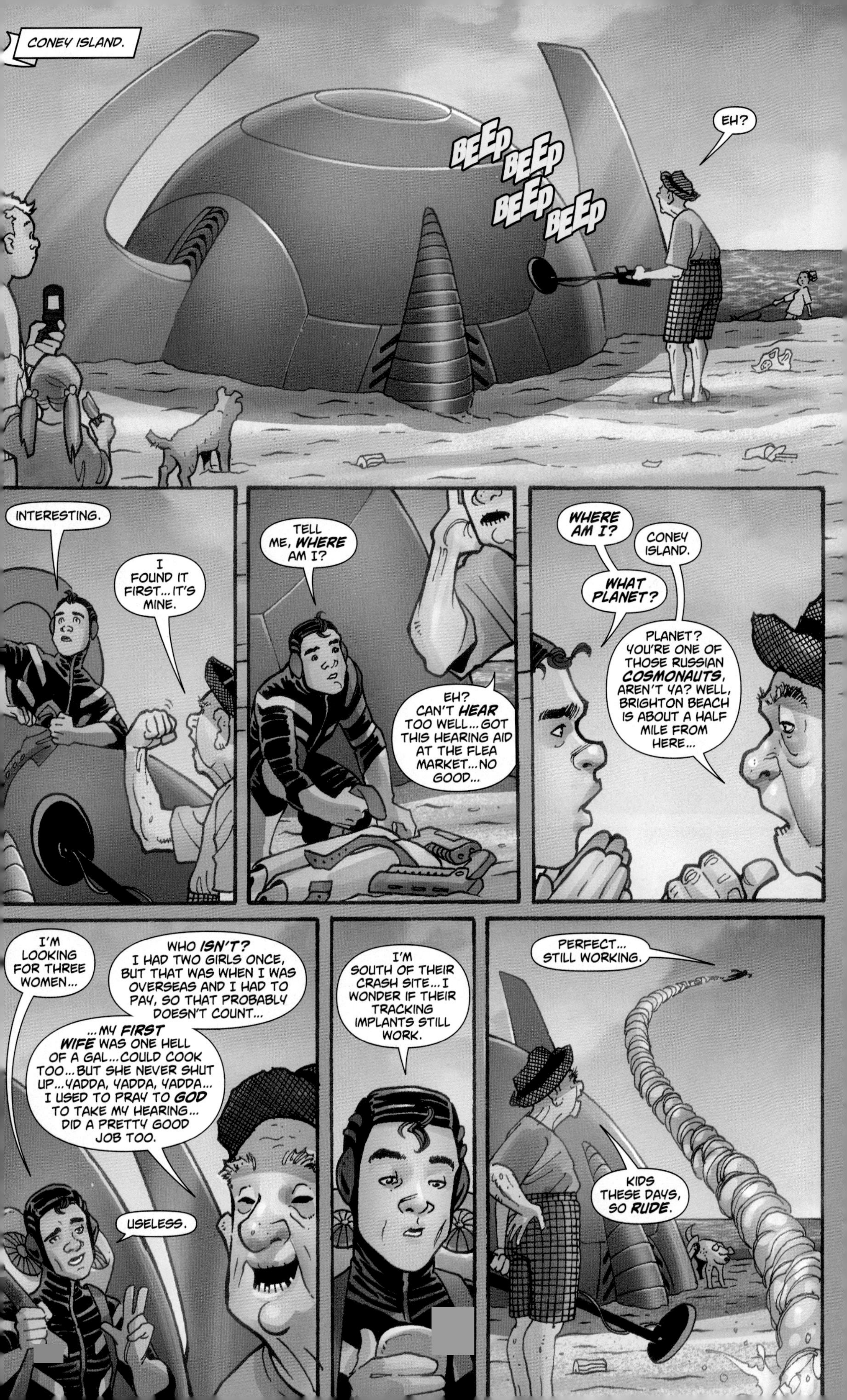
CONEY ISLAND.
BEEP BEEP BEEP BEEP
EH?
INTERESTING.
I FOUND IT FIRST... IT'S MINE.
TELL ME, WHERE AM I?
EH? CAN'T HEAR TOO WELL... GOT THIS HEARING AID AT THE FLEA MARKET... NO GOOD...
WHERE AM I?
CONEY ISLAND.
WHAT PLANET?
PLANET? YOU'RE ONE OF THOSE RUSSIAN COSMONAUTS, AREN'T YA? WELL, BRIGHTON BEACH IS ABOUT A HALF MILE FROM HERE...
I'M LOOKING FOR THREE WOMEN...
WHO ISN'T? I HAD TWO GIRLS ONCE, BUT THAT WAS WHEN I WAS OVERSEAS AND I HAD TO PAY, SO THAT PROBABLY DOESN'T COUNT...
...MY FIRST WIFE WAS ONE HELL OF A GAL... COULD COOK TOO... BUT SHE NEVER SHUT UP... YADDA, YADDA, YADDA... I USED TO PRAY TO GOD TO TAKE MY HEARING... DID A PRETTY GOOD JOB TOO.
USELESS.
I'M SOUTH OF THEIR CRASH SITE... I WONDER IF THEIR TRACKING IMPLANTS STILL WORK.
PERFECT... STILL WORKING.
KIDS THESE DAYS, SO RUDE.

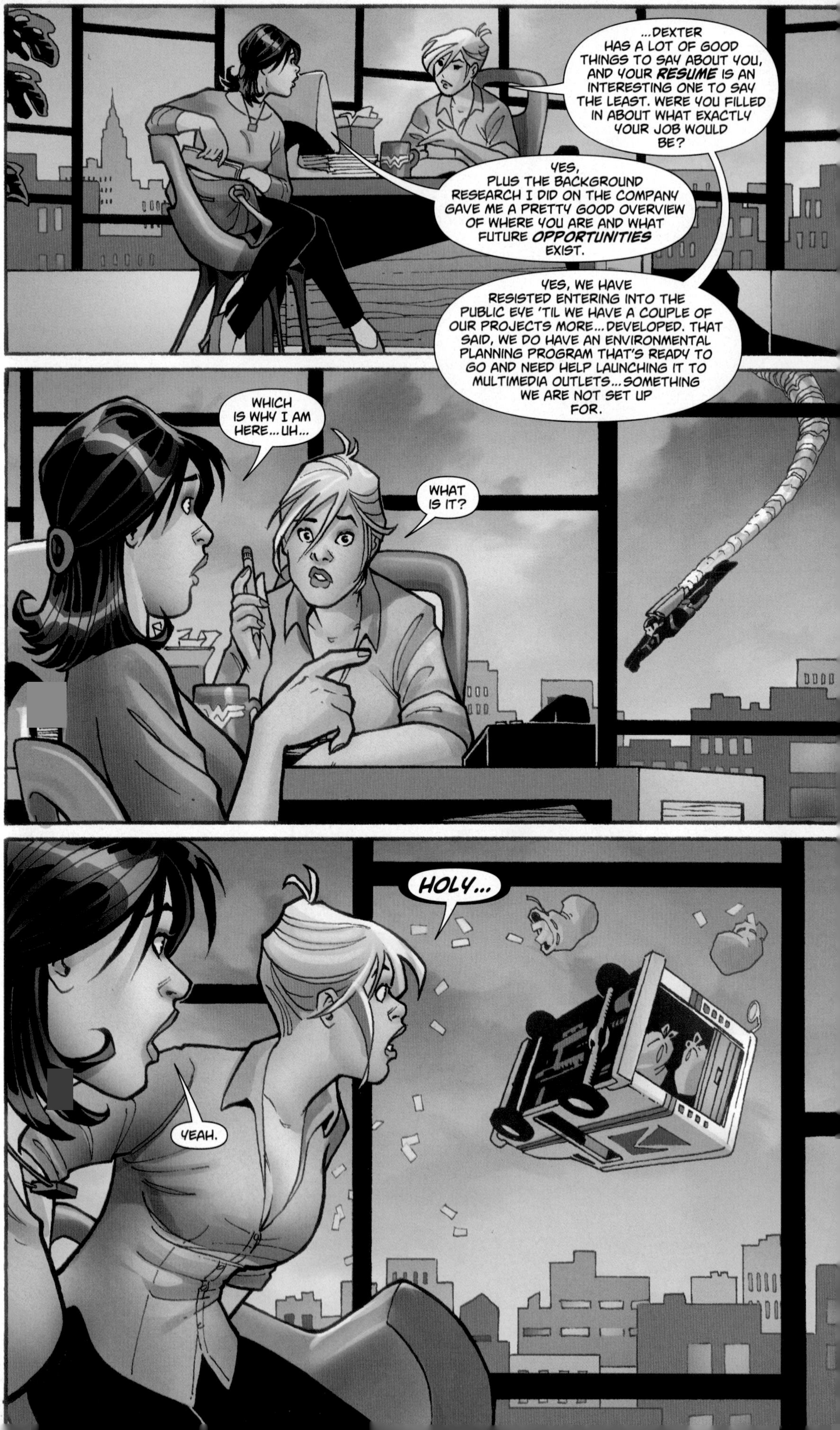
...DEXTER HAS A LOT OF GOOD THINGS TO SAY ABOUT YOU, AND YOUR **RESUME** IS AN INTERESTING ONE TO SAY THE LEAST. WERE YOU FILLED IN ABOUT WHAT EXACTLY YOUR JOB WOULD BE?
YES, PLUS THE BACKGROUND RESEARCH I DID ON THE COMPANY GAVE ME A PRETTY GOOD OVERVIEW OF WHERE YOU ARE AND WHAT FUTURE **OPPORTUNITIES** EXIST.
YES, WE HAVE RESISTED ENTERING INTO THE PUBLIC EYE 'TIL WE HAVE A COUPLE OF OUR PROJECTS MORE...DEVELOPED. THAT SAID, WE DO HAVE AN ENVIRONMENTAL PLANNING PROGRAM THAT'S READY TO GO AND NEED HELP LAUNCHING IT TO MULTIMEDIA OUTLETS...SOMETHING WE ARE NOT SET UP FOR.
WHICH IS WHY I AM HERE...UH...
WHAT IS IT?
HOLY...
YEAH.

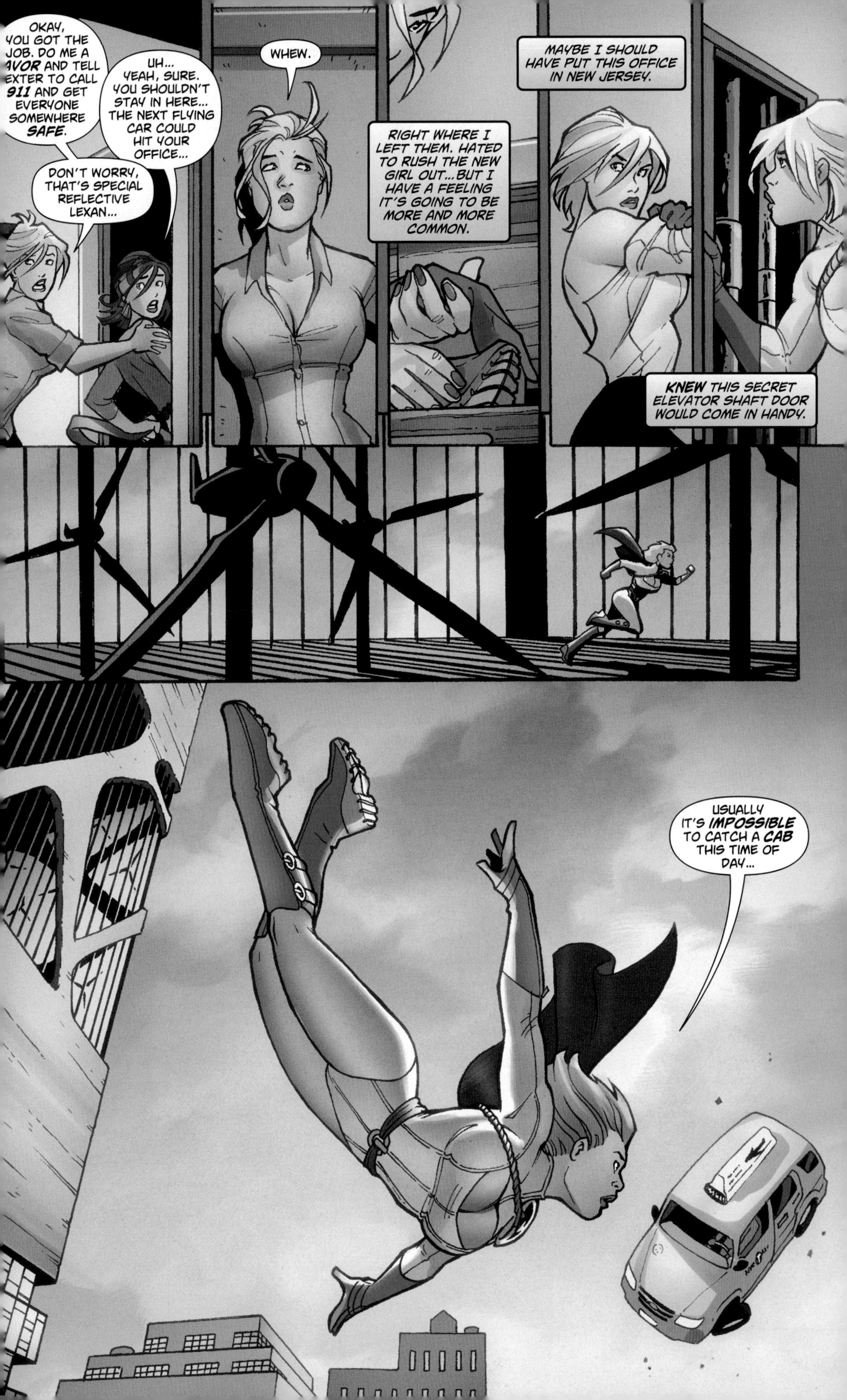
OKAY, YOU GOT THE JOB. DO ME A AVOR AND TELL EXTER TO CALL 911 AND GET EVERYONE SOMEWHERE SAFE.
UH... YEAH, SURE. YOU SHOULDN'T STAY IN HERE... THE NEXT FLYING CAR COULD HIT YOUR OFFICE...
DON'T WORRY, THAT'S SPECIAL REFLECTIVE LEXAN...
WHEW.
RIGHT WHERE I LEFT THEM. HATED TO RUSH THE NEW GIRL OUT...BUT I HAVE A FEELING IT'S GOING TO BE MORE AND MORE COMMON.
MAYBE I SHOULD HAVE PUT THIS OFFICE IN NEW JERSEY.
KNEW THIS SECRET ELEVATOR SHAFT DOOR WOULD COME IN HANDY.
USUALLY IT'S IMPOSSIBLE TO CATCH A CAB THIS TIME OF DAY...

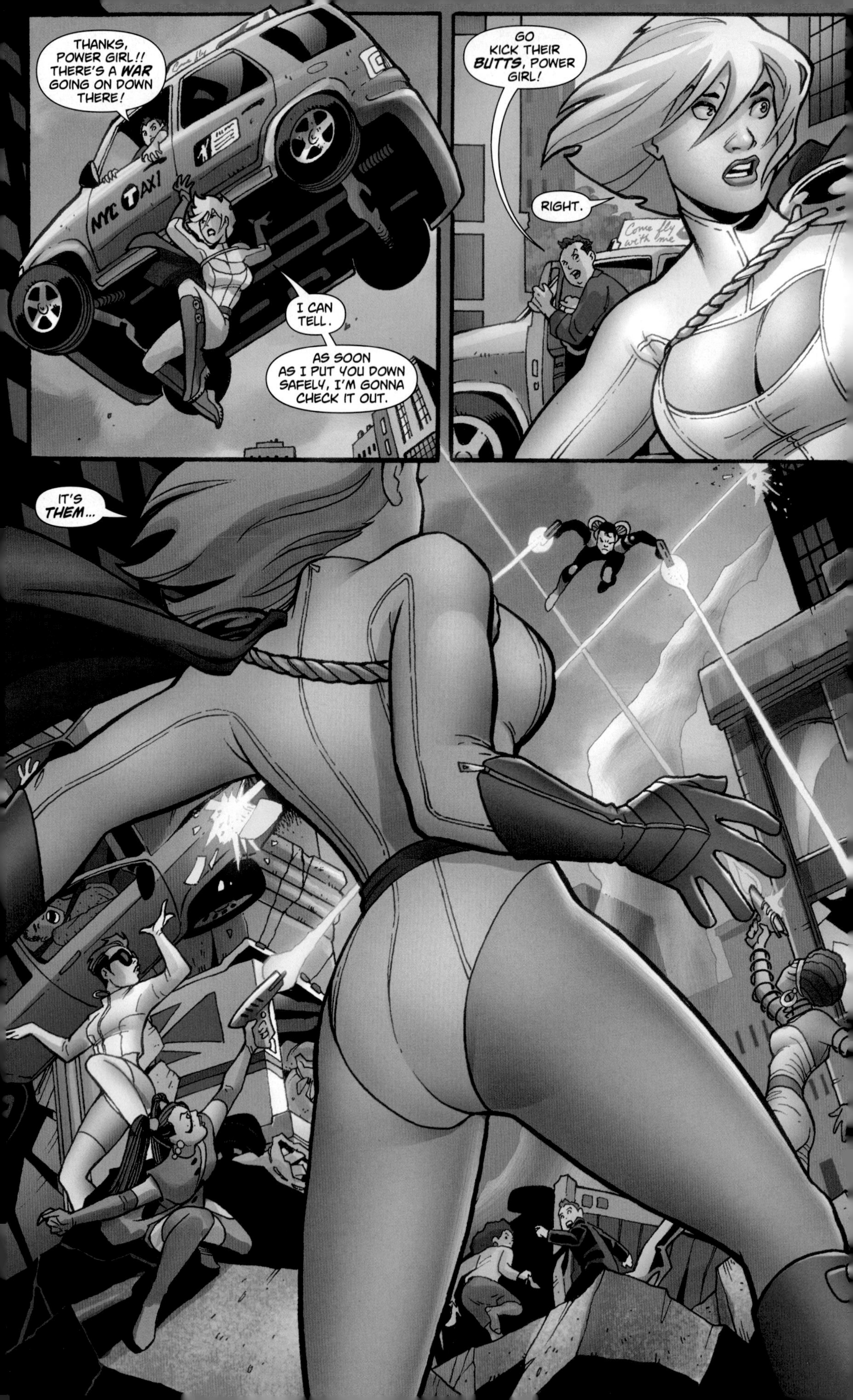
THANKS, POWER GIRL!! THERE'S A **WAR** GOING ON DOWN THERE!
I CAN TELL.
AS SOON AS I PUT YOU DOWN SAFELY, I'M GONNA CHECK IT OUT.
GO KICK THEIR **BUTTS**, POWER GIRL!
RIGHT.
IT'S **THEM**...

SPACE GIRLS GONE WILD part two

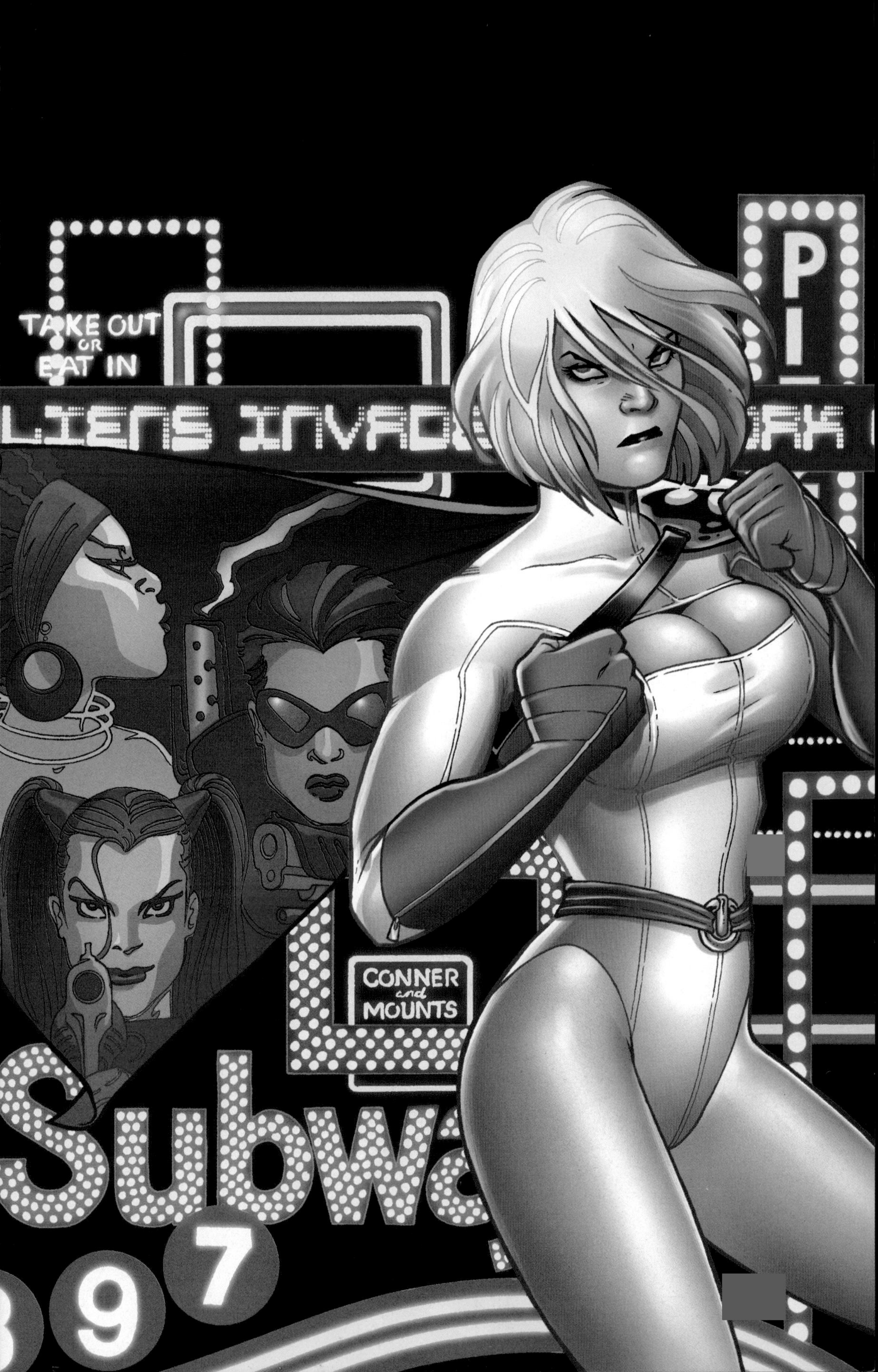
TAKE OUT OR EAT IN
CONNER and MOUNTS

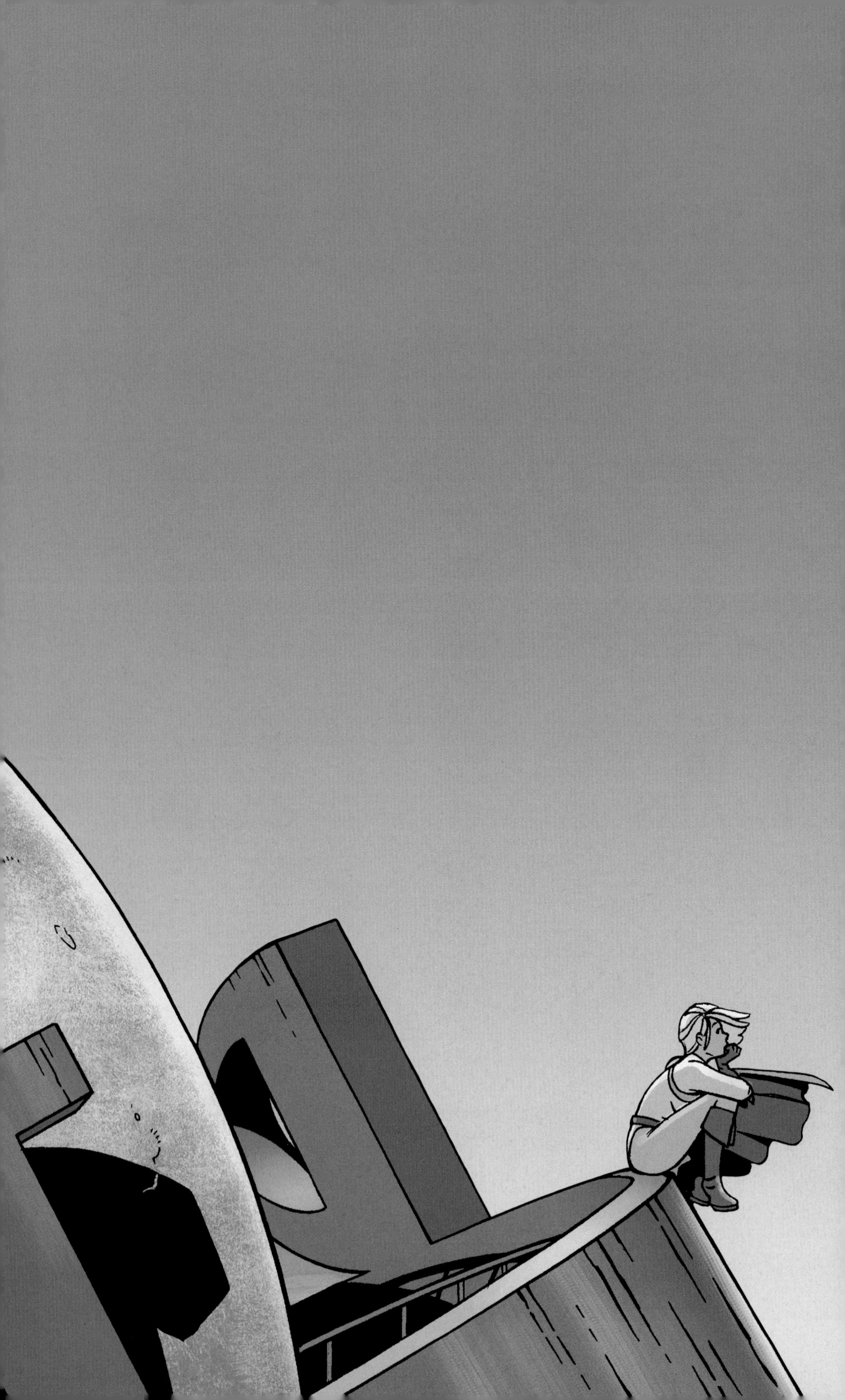

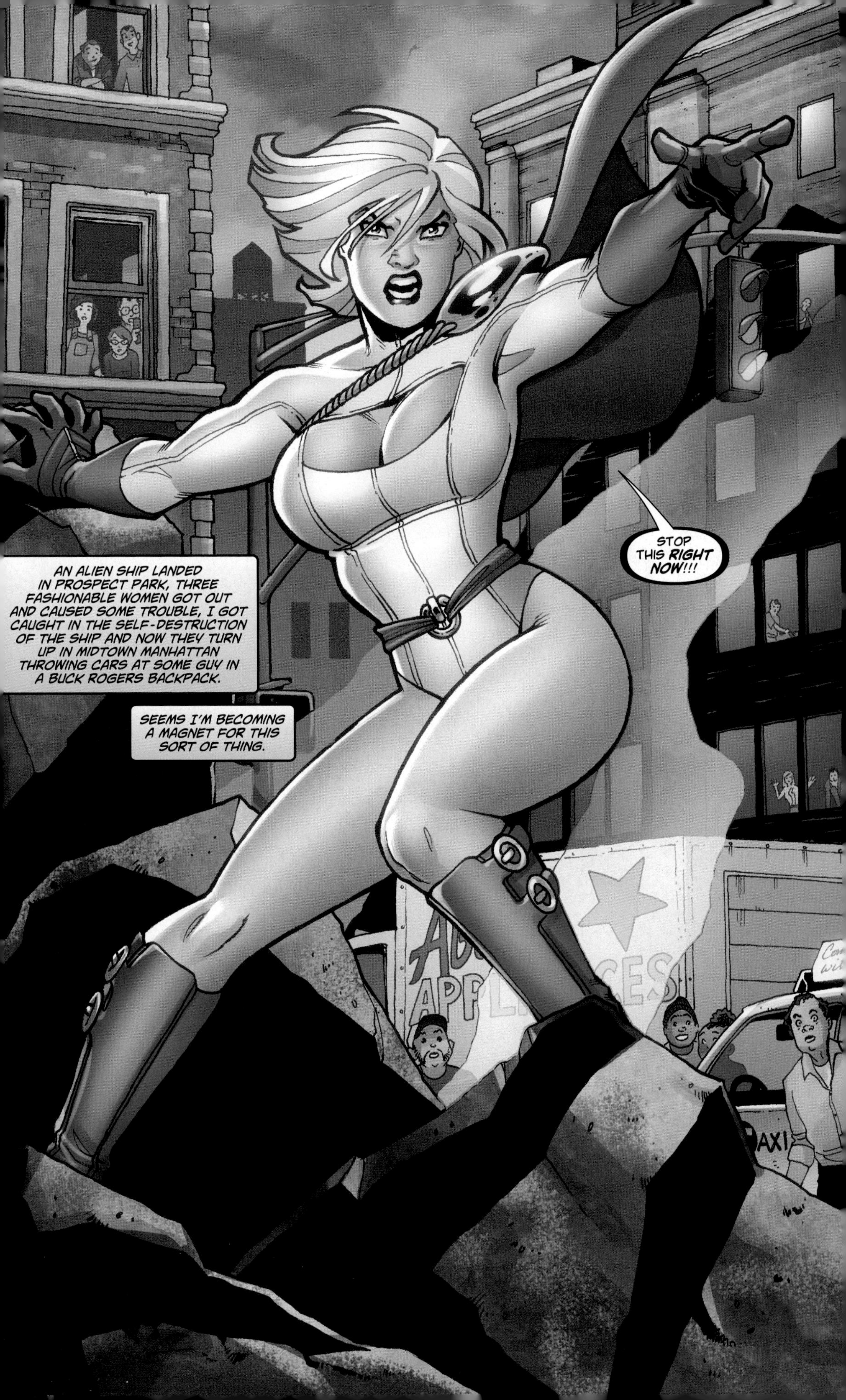

AN ALIEN SHIP LANDED IN PROSPECT PARK, THREE FASHIONABLE WOMEN GOT OUT AND CAUSED SOME TROUBLE, I GOT CAUGHT IN THE SELF-DESTRUCTION OF THE SHIP AND NOW THEY TURN UP IN MIDTOWN MANHATTAN THROWING CARS AT SOME GUY IN A BUCK ROGERS BACKPACK.
SEEMS I'M BECOMING A MAGNET FOR THIS SORT OF THING.
STOP THIS RIGHT NOW!!!

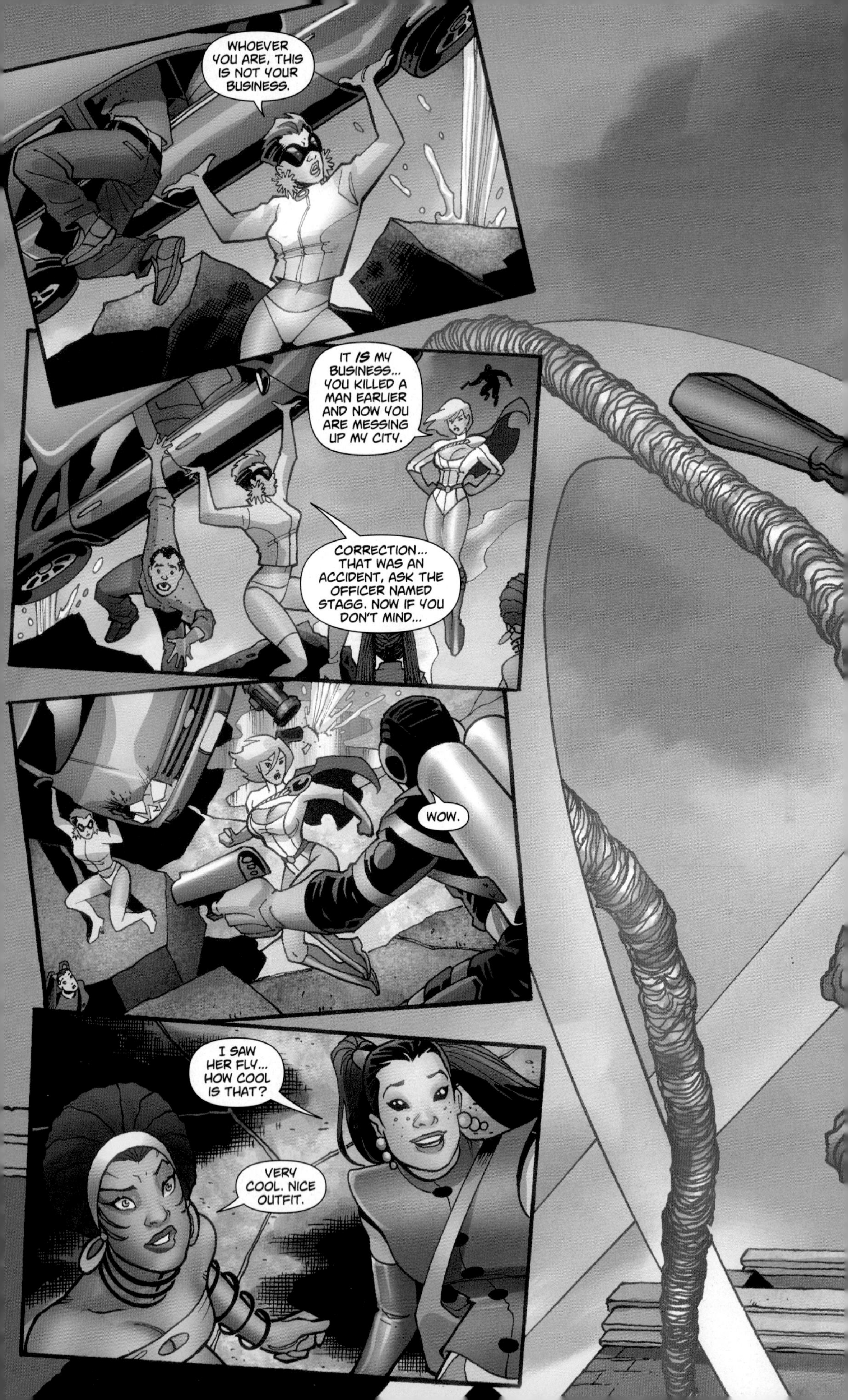
WHOEVER YOU ARE, THIS IS NOT YOUR BUSINESS.
IT IS MY BUSINESS... YOU KILLED A MAN EARLIER AND NOW YOU ARE MESSING UP MY CITY.
CORRECTION... THAT WAS AN ACCIDENT, ASK THE OFFICER NAMED STAGG. NOW IF YOU DON'T MIND...
WOW.
I SAW HER FLY... HOW COOL IS THAT?
VERY COOL. NICE OUTFIT.

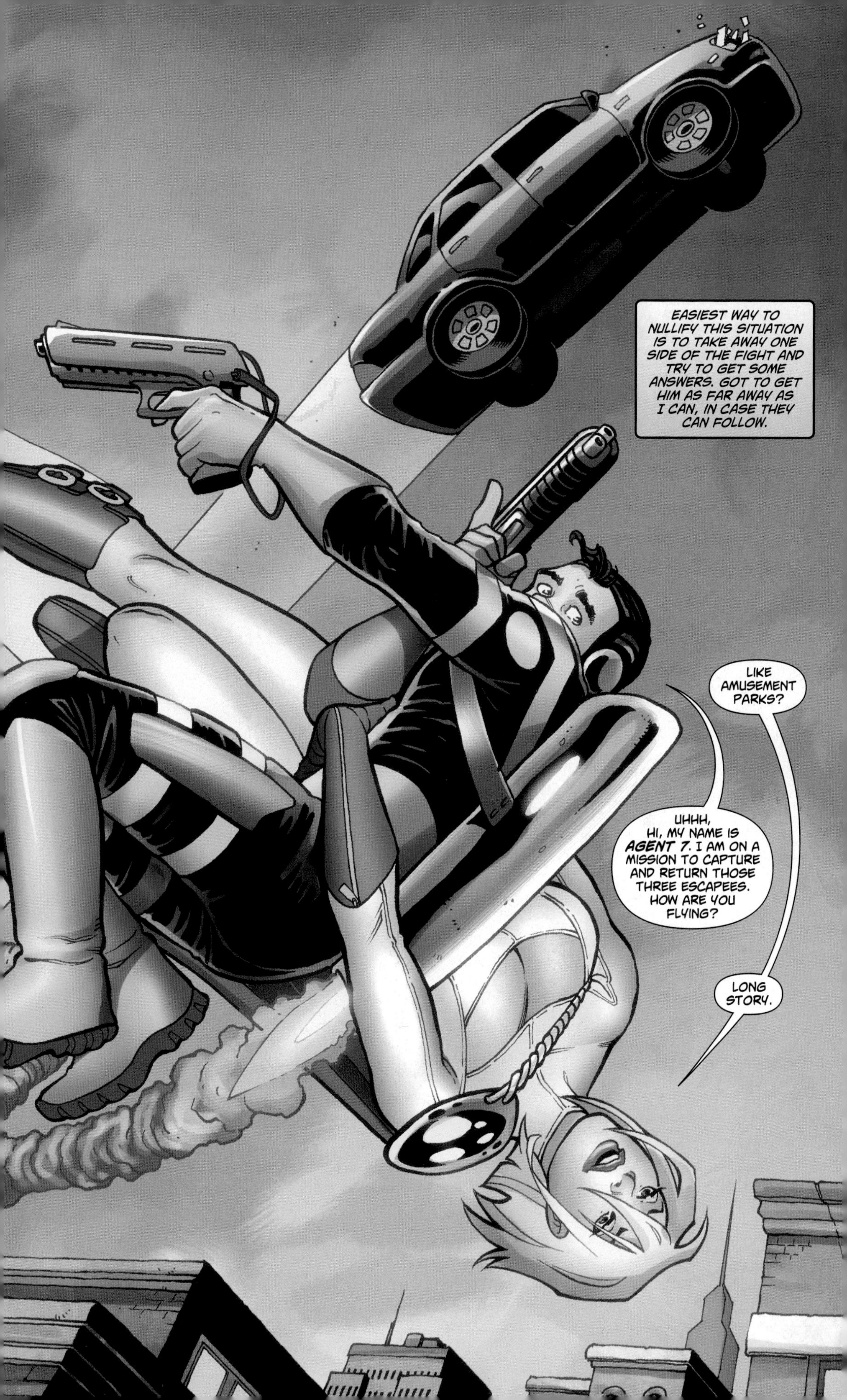
EASIEST WAY TO NULLIFY THIS SITUATION IS TO TAKE AWAY ONE SIDE OF THE FIGHT AND TRY TO GET SOME ANSWERS. GOT TO GET HIM AS FAR AWAY AS I CAN, IN CASE THEY CAN FOLLOW.
LIKE AMUSEMENT PARKS?
UHHH, HI, MY NAME IS **AGENT 7**. I AM ON A MISSION TO CAPTURE AND RETURN THOSE THREE ESCAPEES. HOW ARE YOU FLYING?
LONG STORY.

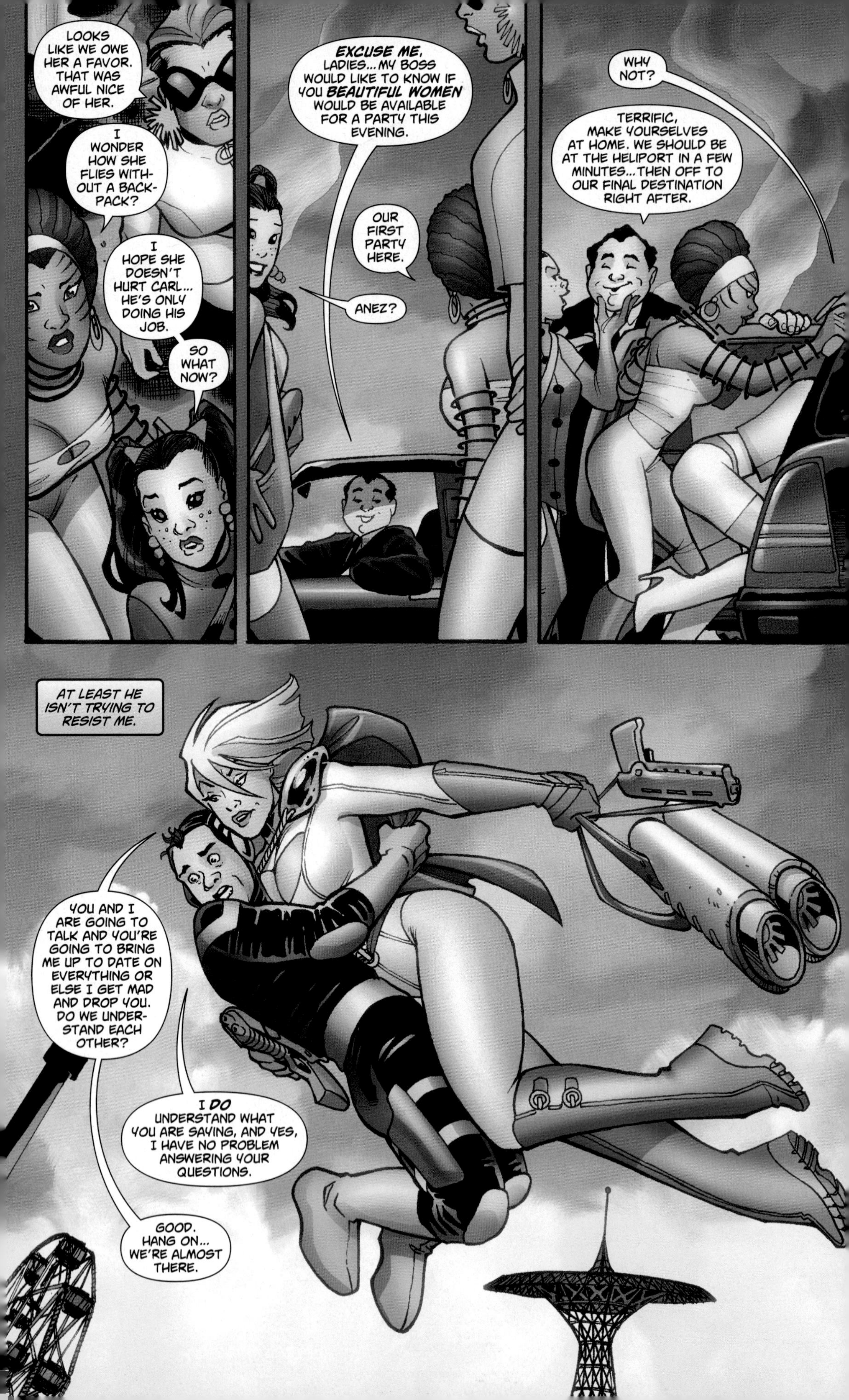
LOOKS LIKE WE OWE HER A FAVOR. THAT WAS AWFUL NICE OF HER.
I WONDER HOW SHE FLIES WITH-OUT A BACK-PACK?
I HOPE SHE DOESN'T HURT CARL... HE'S ONLY DOING HIS JOB.
SO WHAT NOW?
EXCUSE ME, LADIES... MY BOSS WOULD LIKE TO KNOW IF YOU BEAUTIFUL WOMEN WOULD BE AVAILABLE FOR A PARTY THIS EVENING.
OUR FIRST PARTY HERE.
ANEZ?
WHY NOT?
TERRIFIC, MAKE YOURSELVES AT HOME. WE SHOULD BE AT THE HELIPORT IN A FEW MINUTES...THEN OFF TO OUR FINAL DESTINATION RIGHT AFTER.
AT LEAST HE ISN'T TRYING TO RESIST ME.
YOU AND I ARE GOING TO TALK AND YOU'RE GOING TO BRING ME UP TO DATE ON EVERYTHING OR ELSE I GET MAD AND DROP YOU. DO WE UNDER-STAND EACH OTHER?
I DO UNDERSTAND WHAT YOU ARE SAYING, AND YES, I HAVE NO PROBLEM ANSWERING YOUR QUESTIONS.
GOOD. HANG ON... WE'RE ALMOST THERE.

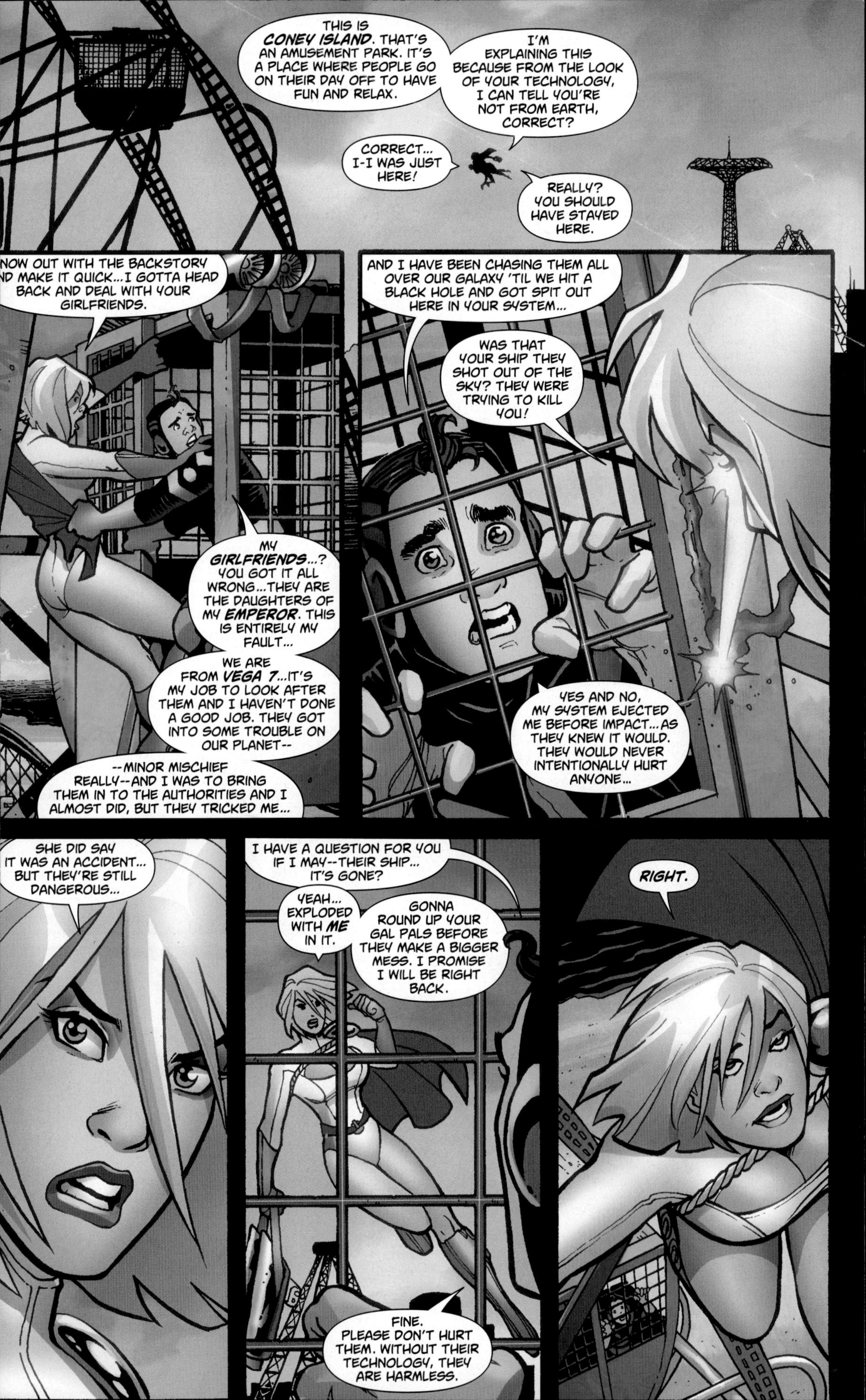
THIS IS CONEY ISLAND. THAT'S AN AMUSEMENT PARK. IT'S A PLACE WHERE PEOPLE GO ON THEIR DAY OFF TO HAVE FUN AND RELAX.
I'M EXPLAINING THIS BECAUSE FROM THE LOOK OF YOUR TECHNOLOGY, I CAN TELL YOU'RE NOT FROM EARTH, CORRECT?
CORRECT... I-I WAS JUST HERE!
REALLY? YOU SHOULD HAVE STAYED HERE.
NOW OUT WITH THE BACKSTORY AND MAKE IT QUICK... I GOTTA HEAD BACK AND DEAL WITH YOUR GIRLFRIENDS.
MY GIRLFRIENDS...? YOU GOT IT ALL WRONG... THEY ARE THE DAUGHTERS OF MY EMPEROR. THIS IS ENTIRELY MY FAULT...
WE ARE FROM VEGA 7... IT'S MY JOB TO LOOK AFTER THEM AND I HAVEN'T DONE A GOOD JOB. THEY GOT INTO SOME TROUBLE ON OUR PLANET--
--MINOR MISCHIEF REALLY--AND I WAS TO BRING THEM IN TO THE AUTHORITIES AND I ALMOST DID, BUT THEY TRICKED ME...
AND I HAVE BEEN CHASING THEM ALL OVER OUR GALAXY 'TIL WE HIT A BLACK HOLE AND GOT SPIT OUT HERE IN YOUR SYSTEM...
WAS THAT YOUR SHIP THEY SHOT OUT OF THE SKY? THEY WERE TRYING TO KILL YOU!
YES AND NO, MY SYSTEM EJECTED ME BEFORE IMPACT... AS THEY KNEW IT WOULD. THEY WOULD NEVER INTENTIONALLY HURT ANYONE...
SHE DID SAY IT WAS AN ACCIDENT... BUT THEY'RE STILL DANGEROUS...
I HAVE A QUESTION FOR YOU IF I MAY--THEIR SHIP... IT'S GONE?
YEAH... EXPLODED WITH ME IN IT.
GONNA ROUND UP YOUR GAL PALS BEFORE THEY MAKE A BIGGER MESS. I PROMISE I WILL BE RIGHT BACK.
FINE. PLEASE DON'T HURT THEM. WITHOUT THEIR TECHNOLOGY, THEY ARE HARMLESS.
RIGHT.

DO YOU EVEN KNOW WHAT DIRECTION THEY *WENT*?

MIXED REPORTS ACTUALLY...SOME SAID A LIMO PICKED THEM UP, OTHERS SAY THEY TOOK THE TRAIN TO CATCH A YANKEES GAME. HONEST, WHEN YOU LEFT, THEY SPLIT.

WE HAD AN ALL-POINTS BULLETIN OUT ON ONE OF THE GALS BUT NOT ANYMORE...

...THEY ARE NOW SAYING THE DEATH SHE CAUSED WAS ACCIDENTAL. SORRY I CAN'T BE OF MORE HELP.

ACTUALLY THAT *IS* HELPFUL, OFFICER. THANKS.

HMMM, HUNDREDS OF LIMOS...AND NOTHING. IF THEY WENT INTO THE BOROUGHS...

WELL...MAYBE A QUICK RUN THROUGH THE SUBWAY.

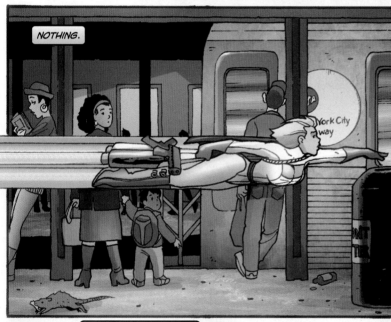

NOTHING.

BACK TO MY FRIEND IN CONEY FOR SOME HELP, I GUESS.

FIGURES.

WELL, THAT'S THAT 'TIL THEY SHOW UP ON THE RADAR...OR THE AUTHORITIES FIND THEM. AT LEAST IT'S NOT A COMPLETE LOSS...

...THIS FIREARM AND BACKPACK HAVE FASCINATING TECHNOLOGY THAT MY LAB BOYS CAN ANALYZE.

TIME TO GET BACK TO WORK.

HALF DAY, DEXTER?

SIX O'CLOCK, I'M THE LAST OF THE STAFF HERE...NEED ME TO STAY?

NO...IT'S ALL RIGHT. I GOT SOME PAPERWORK TO CATCH UP ON. I'LL CLOSE UP.

COOL... 'NIGHT.

THIS DAY IS ONE FOR THE BOOKS. LAST THING I WANT TO DO IS WORK.

HEY KITTY...INTERESTED IN CHECKING OUT YOUR NEW DIGS?

PRRRRRRRT?

I'LL TAKE THAT AS A YES... I KNOW YOU DON'T LIKE TO FLY, SO...

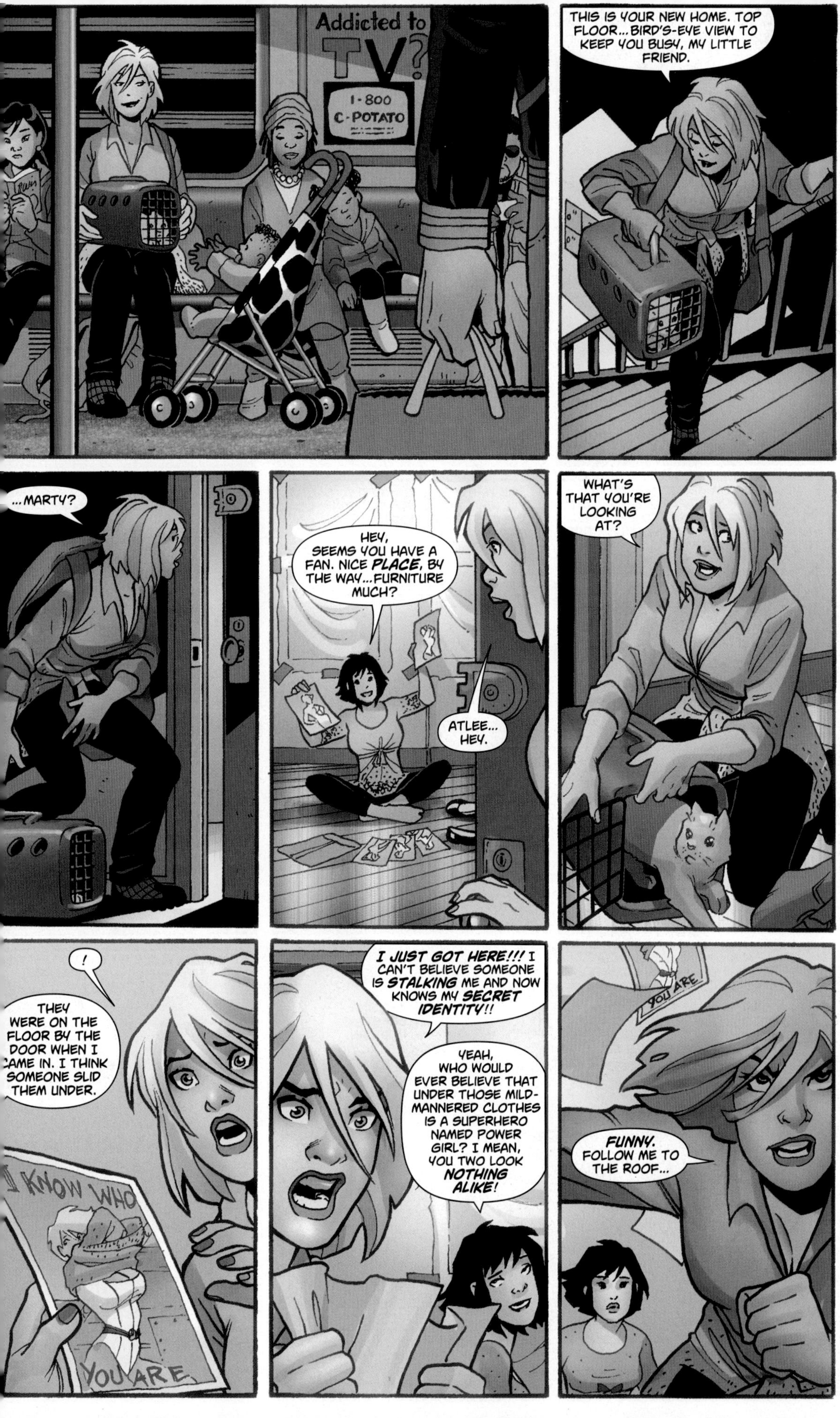

Addicted to TV?
1-800 C-POTATO
THIS IS YOUR NEW HOME. TOP FLOOR... BIRD'S-EYE VIEW TO KEEP YOU BUSY, MY LITTLE FRIEND.
...MARTY?
HEY, SEEMS YOU HAVE A FAN. NICE PLACE, BY THE WAY... FURNITURE MUCH?
ATLEE... HEY.
WHAT'S THAT YOU'RE LOOKING AT?
!
THEY WERE ON THE FLOOR BY THE DOOR WHEN I CAME IN. I THINK SOMEONE SLID THEM UNDER.
I KNOW WHO YOU ARE
I JUST GOT HERE!!! I CAN'T BELIEVE SOMEONE IS STALKING ME AND NOW KNOWS MY SECRET IDENTITY!!
YEAH, WHO WOULD EVER BELIEVE THAT UNDER THOSE MILD-MANNERED CLOTHES IS A SUPERHERO NAMED POWER GIRL? I MEAN, YOU TWO LOOK NOTHING ALIKE!
YOU ARE
FUNNY. FOLLOW ME TO THE ROOF...

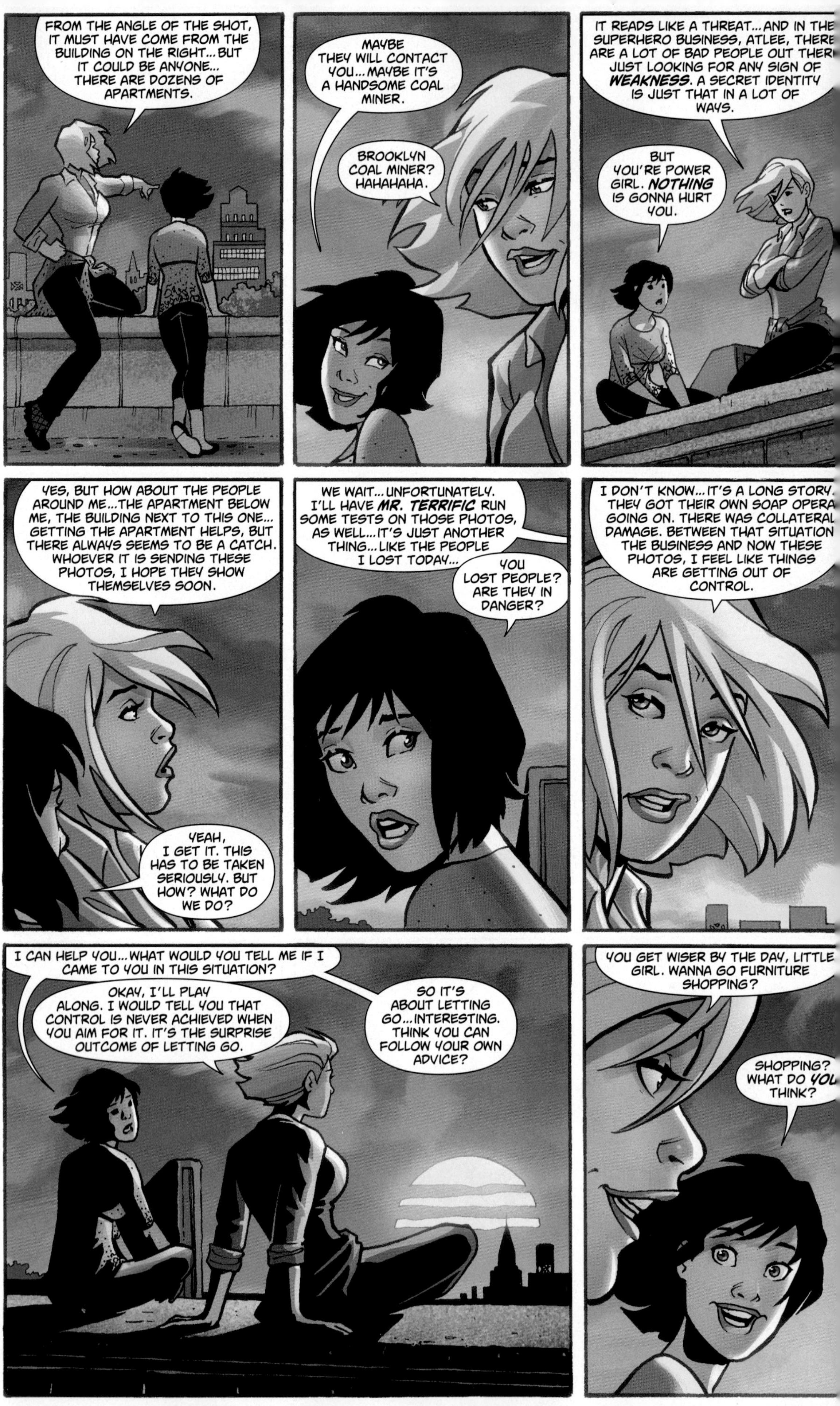
FROM THE ANGLE OF THE SHOT, IT MUST HAVE COME FROM THE BUILDING ON THE RIGHT... BUT IT COULD BE ANYONE... THERE ARE DOZENS OF APARTMENTS.
MAYBE THEY WILL CONTACT YOU... MAYBE IT'S A HANDSOME COAL MINER.
BROOKLYN COAL MINER? HAHAHAHA.
IT READS LIKE A THREAT... AND IN THE SUPERHERO BUSINESS, ATLEE, THERE ARE A LOT OF BAD PEOPLE OUT THERE JUST LOOKING FOR ANY SIGN OF WEAKNESS. A SECRET IDENTITY IS JUST THAT IN A LOT OF WAYS.
BUT YOU'RE POWER GIRL. NOTHING IS GONNA HURT YOU.
YES, BUT HOW ABOUT THE PEOPLE AROUND ME... THE APARTMENT BELOW ME, THE BUILDING NEXT TO THIS ONE... GETTING THE APARTMENT HELPS, BUT THERE ALWAYS SEEMS TO BE A CATCH. WHOEVER IT IS SENDING THESE PHOTOS, I HOPE THEY SHOW THEMSELVES SOON.
YEAH, I GET IT. THIS HAS TO BE TAKEN SERIOUSLY. BUT HOW? WHAT DO WE DO?
WE WAIT... UNFORTUNATELY. I'LL HAVE MR. TERRIFIC RUN SOME TESTS ON THOSE PHOTOS, AS WELL... IT'S JUST ANOTHER THING... LIKE THE PEOPLE I LOST TODAY...
YOU LOST PEOPLE? ARE THEY IN DANGER?
I DON'T KNOW... IT'S A LONG STORY. THEY GOT THEIR OWN SOAP OPERA GOING ON. THERE WAS COLLATERAL DAMAGE. BETWEEN THAT SITUATION THE BUSINESS AND NOW THESE PHOTOS, I FEEL LIKE THINGS ARE GETTING OUT OF CONTROL.
I CAN HELP YOU... WHAT WOULD YOU TELL ME IF I CAME TO YOU IN THIS SITUATION?
OKAY, I'LL PLAY ALONG. I WOULD TELL YOU THAT CONTROL IS NEVER ACHIEVED WHEN YOU AIM FOR IT. IT'S THE SURPRISE OUTCOME OF LETTING GO.
SO IT'S ABOUT LETTING GO... INTERESTING. THINK YOU CAN FOLLOW YOUR OWN ADVICE?
YOU GET WISER BY THE DAY, LITTLE GIRL. WANNA GO FURNITURE SHOPPING?
SHOPPING? WHAT DO YOU THINK?

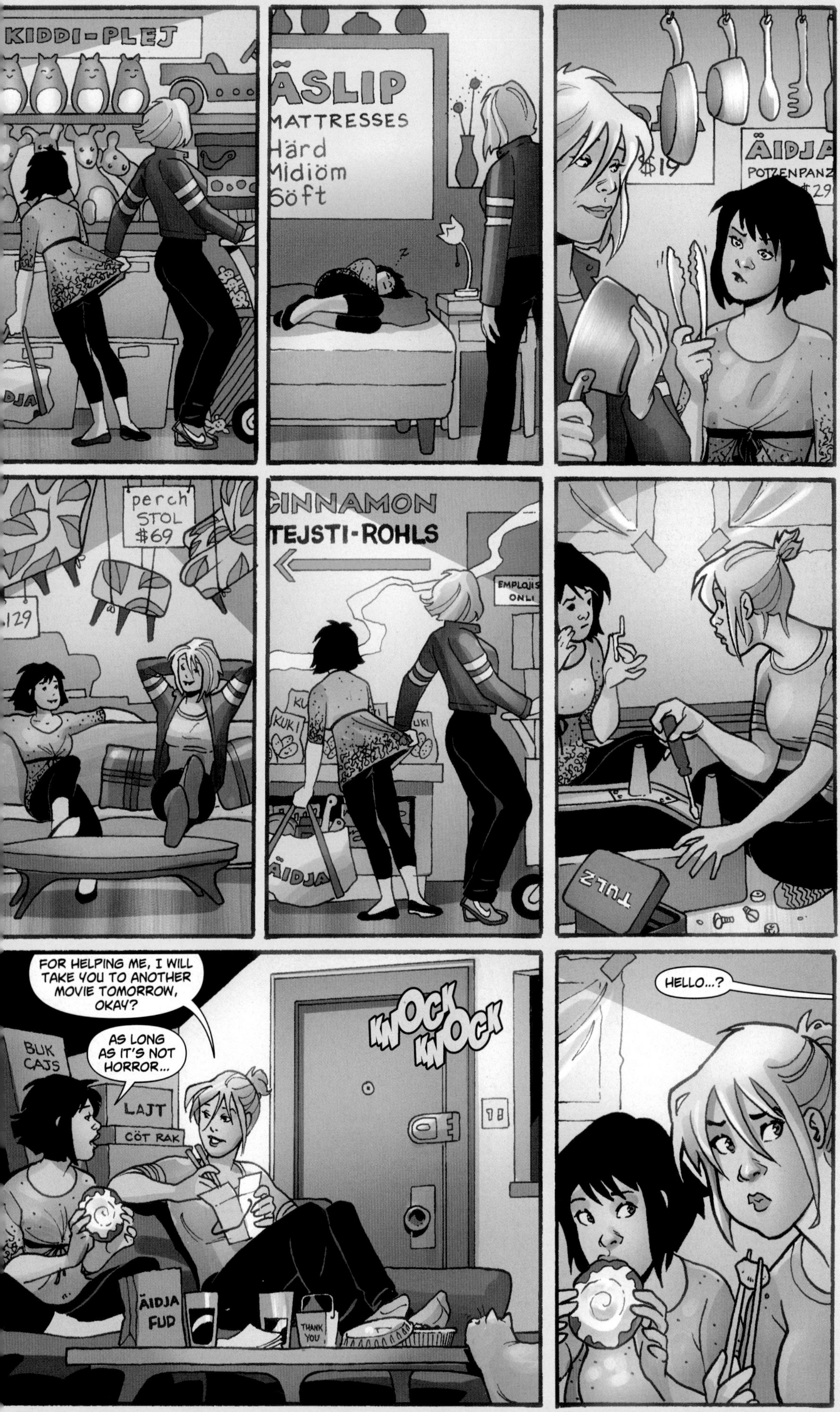
KIDDI-PLEJ
ÄIDJA
ÄSLIP
MATTRESSES
Härd
Midiöm
Söft
$19
ÄIDJA
POTZENPANZ
perch
STOL
$69
CINNAMON
TEJSTI-ROHLS
EMPLOJIS ONLI
KUKI
ÄIDJA
TULZ
FOR HELPING ME, I WILL TAKE YOU TO ANOTHER MOVIE TOMORROW, OKAY?
AS LONG AS IT'S NOT HORROR...
BUK CAJS
LAJT
CÖT RAK
ÄIDJA FUD
THANK YOU
KNOCK KNOCK
HELLO...?

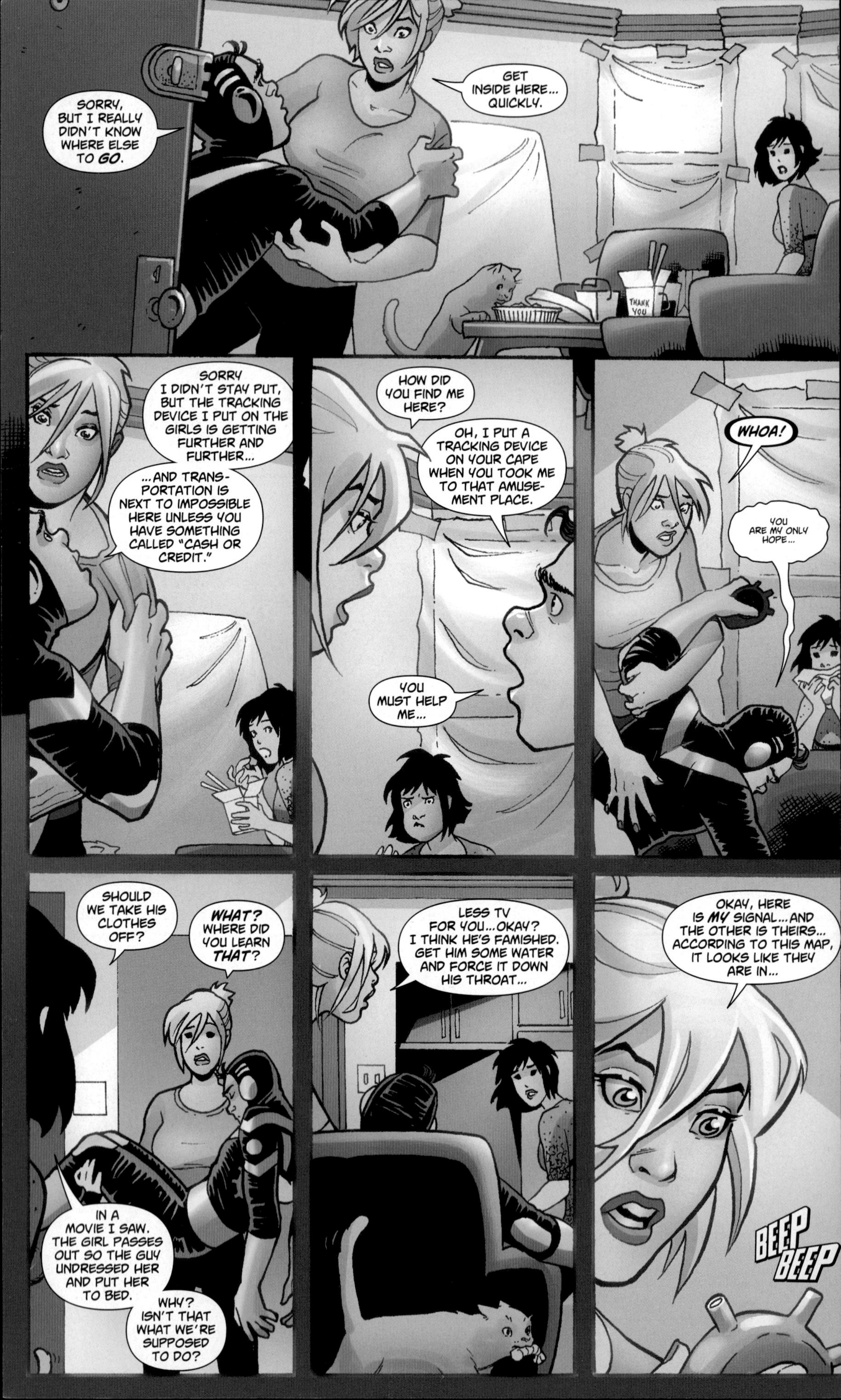
SORRY, BUT I REALLY DIDN'T KNOW WHERE ELSE TO GO.
GET INSIDE HERE... QUICKLY.
THANK YOU
SORRY I DIDN'T STAY PUT, BUT THE TRACKING DEVICE I PUT ON THE GIRLS IS GETTING FURTHER AND FURTHER...
...AND TRANSPORTATION IS NEXT TO IMPOSSIBLE HERE UNLESS YOU HAVE SOMETHING CALLED "CASH OR CREDIT."
HOW DID YOU FIND ME HERE?
OH, I PUT A TRACKING DEVICE ON YOUR CAPE WHEN YOU TOOK ME TO THAT AMUSEMENT PLACE.
YOU MUST HELP ME...
WHOA!
YOU ARE MY ONLY HOPE...
SHOULD WE TAKE HIS CLOTHES OFF?
WHAT? WHERE DID YOU LEARN THAT?
IN A MOVIE I SAW. THE GIRL PASSES OUT SO THE GUY UNDRESSED HER AND PUT HER TO BED.
WHY? ISN'T THAT WHAT WE'RE SUPPOSED TO DO?
LESS TV FOR YOU...OKAY? I THINK HE'S FAMISHED. GET HIM SOME WATER AND FORCE IT DOWN HIS THROAT...
OKAY, HERE IS MY SIGNAL...AND THE OTHER IS THEIRS... ACCORDING TO THIS MAP, IT LOOKS LIKE THEY ARE IN...
BEEP BEEP

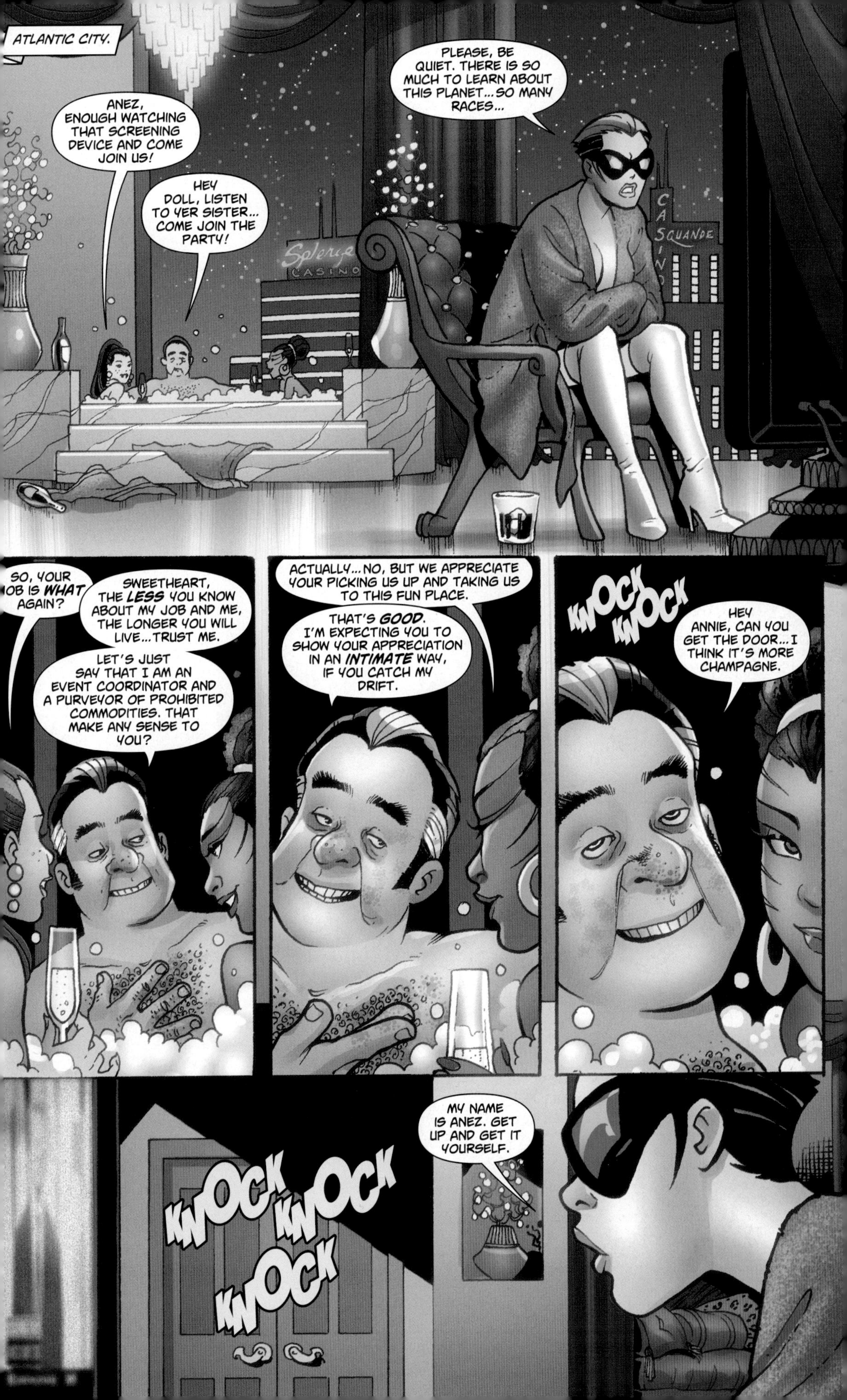

ATLANTIC CITY.
ANEZ, ENOUGH WATCHING THAT SCREENING DEVICE AND COME JOIN US!
HEY DOLL, LISTEN TO YER SISTER... COME JOIN THE PARTY!
PLEASE, BE QUIET. THERE IS SO MUCH TO LEARN ABOUT THIS PLANET... SO MANY RACES...
SPLERGE CASINO
CASINO
SQUANDE
SO, YOUR JOB IS WHAT AGAIN?
SWEETHEART, THE LESS YOU KNOW ABOUT MY JOB AND ME, THE LONGER YOU WILL LIVE... TRUST ME.
LET'S JUST SAY THAT I AM AN EVENT COORDINATOR AND A PURVEYOR OF PROHIBITED COMMODITIES. THAT MAKE ANY SENSE TO YOU?
ACTUALLY... NO, BUT WE APPRECIATE YOUR PICKING US UP AND TAKING US TO THIS FUN PLACE.
THAT'S GOOD. I'M EXPECTING YOU TO SHOW YOUR APPRECIATION IN AN INTIMATE WAY, IF YOU CATCH MY DRIFT.
KNOCK KNOCK
HEY ANNIE, CAN YOU GET THE DOOR... I THINK IT'S MORE CHAMPAGNE.
KNOCK KNOCK KNOCK
MY NAME IS ANEZ. GET UP AND GET IT YOURSELF.

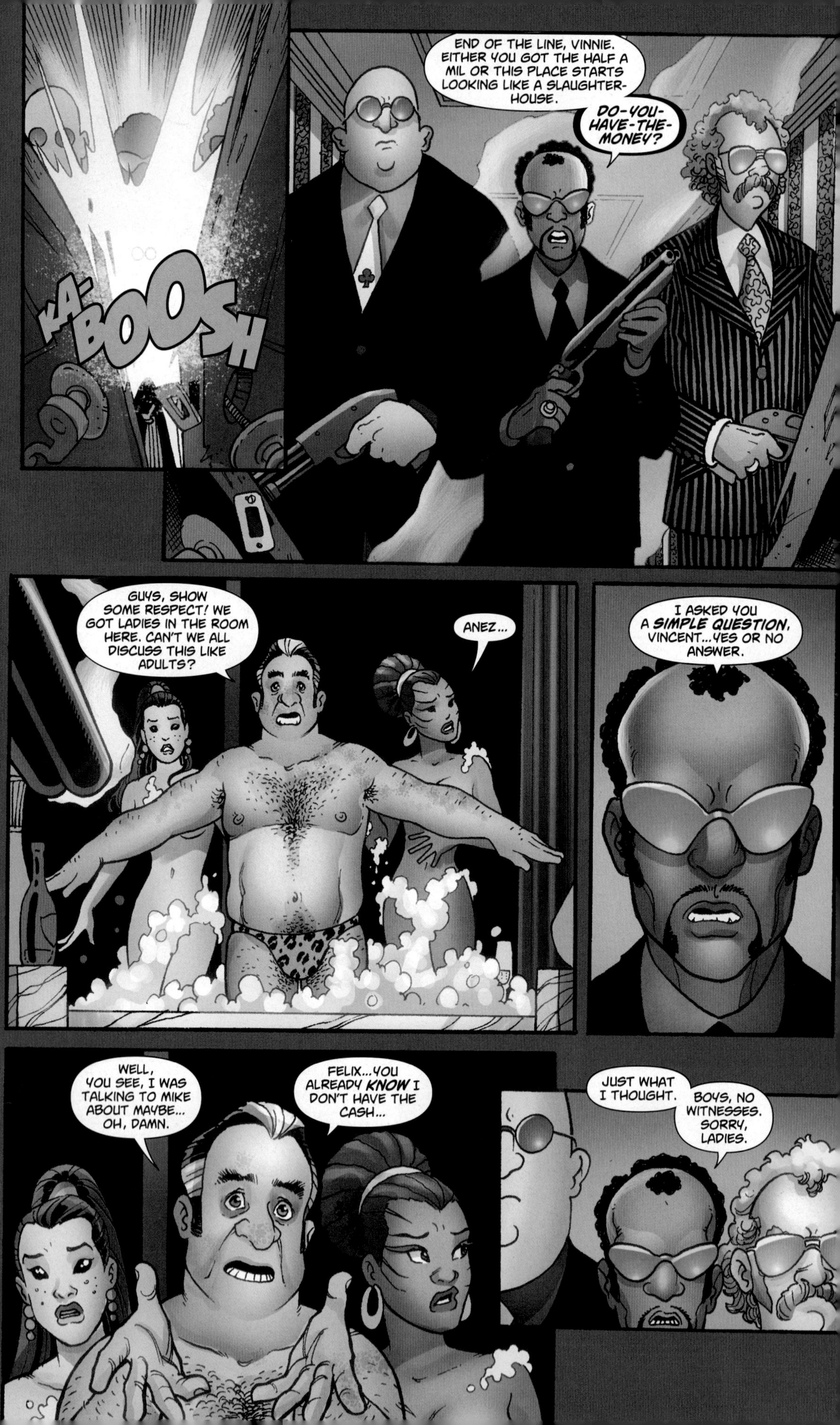
KA-BOOOSH
END OF THE LINE, VINNIE. EITHER YOU GOT THE HALF A MIL OR THIS PLACE STARTS LOOKING LIKE A SLAUGHTER-HOUSE.
DO-YOU-HAVE-THE-MONEY?
GUYS, SHOW SOME RESPECT! WE GOT LADIES IN THE ROOM HERE. CAN'T WE ALL DISCUSS THIS LIKE ADULTS?
ANEZ...
I ASKED YOU A SIMPLE QUESTION, VINCENT...YES OR NO ANSWER.
WELL, YOU SEE, I WAS TALKING TO MIKE ABOUT MAYBE... OH, DAMN.
FELIX...YOU ALREADY KNOW I DON'T HAVE THE CASH...
JUST WHAT I THOUGHT.
BOYS, NO WITNESSES. SORRY, LADIES.

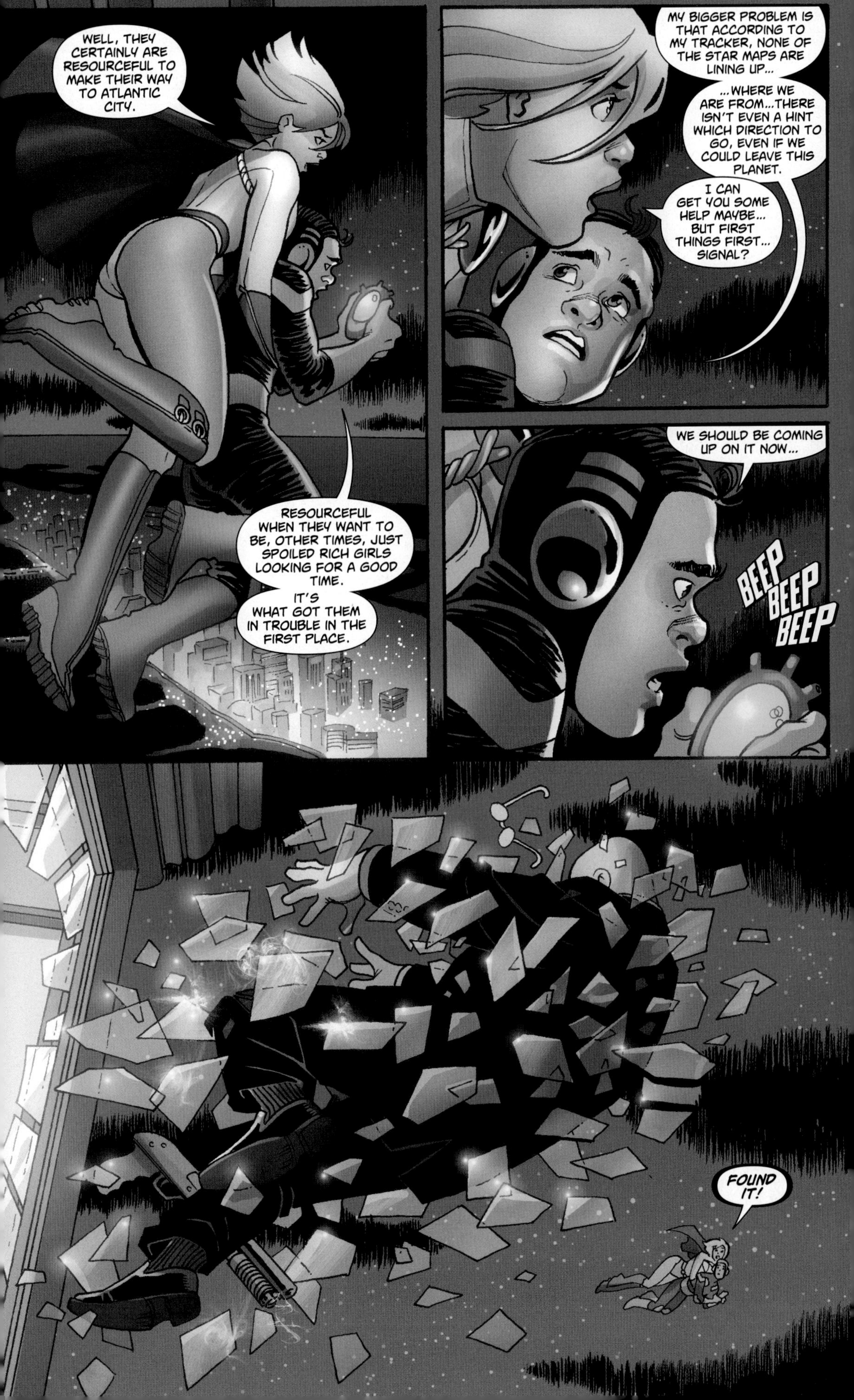
WELL, THEY CERTAINLY ARE RESOURCEFUL TO MAKE THEIR WAY TO ATLANTIC CITY.
RESOURCEFUL WHEN THEY WANT TO BE, OTHER TIMES, JUST SPOILED RICH GIRLS LOOKING FOR A GOOD TIME.
IT'S WHAT GOT THEM IN TROUBLE IN THE FIRST PLACE.
MY BIGGER PROBLEM IS THAT ACCORDING TO MY TRACKER, NONE OF THE STAR MAPS ARE LINING UP...
...WHERE WE ARE FROM...THERE ISN'T EVEN A HINT WHICH DIRECTION TO GO, EVEN IF WE COULD LEAVE THIS PLANET.
I CAN GET YOU SOME HELP MAYBE... BUT FIRST THINGS FIRST... SIGNAL?
WE SHOULD BE COMING UP ON IT NOW...
BEEP BEEP BEEP
FOUND IT!

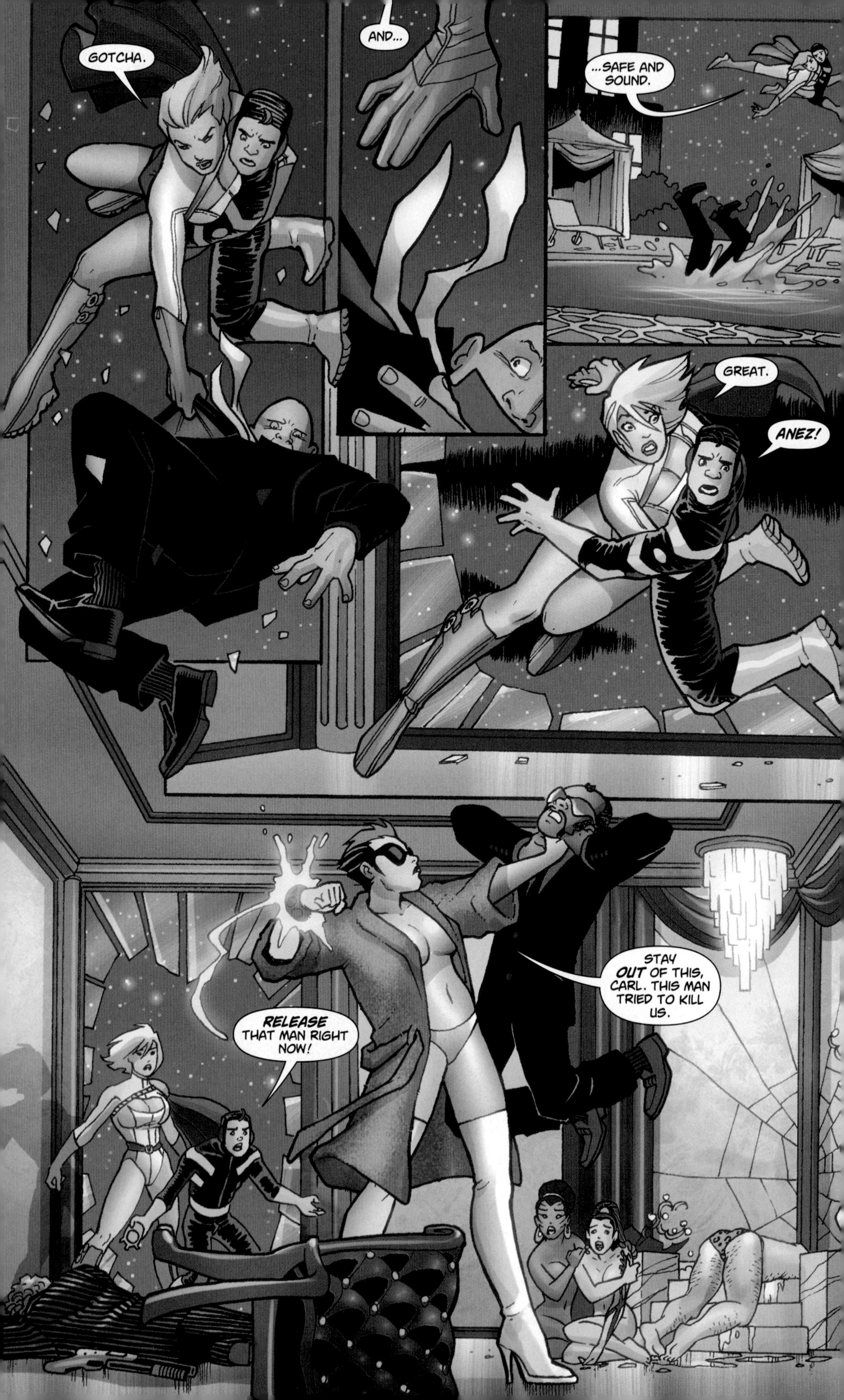
GOTCHA.
AND...
...SAFE AND SOUND.
GREAT.
ANEZ!
STAY OUT OF THIS, CARL. THIS MAN TRIED TO KILL US.
RELEASE THAT MAN RIGHT NOW!

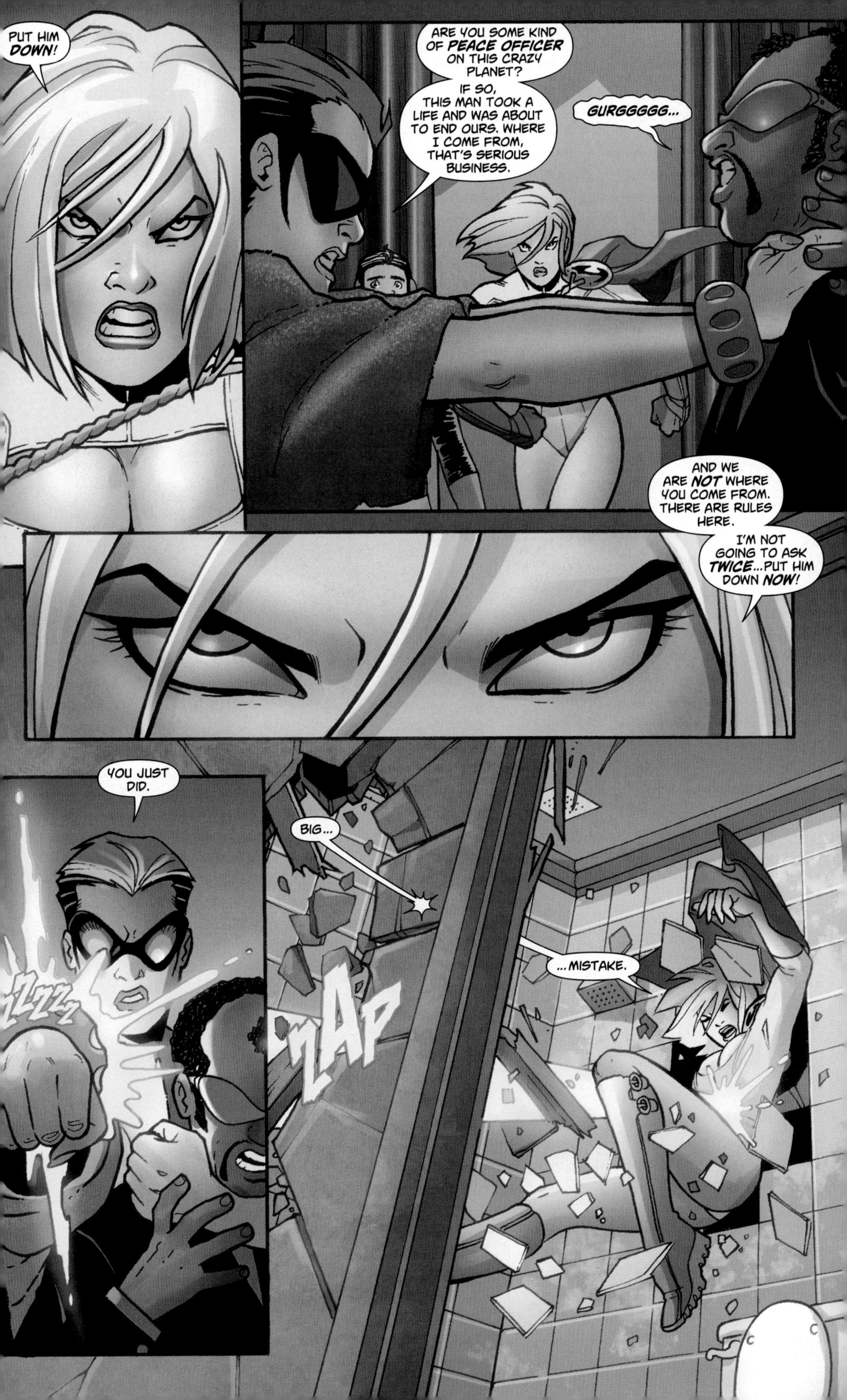
PUT HIM DOWN!
ARE YOU SOME KIND OF PEACE OFFICER ON THIS CRAZY PLANET?
IF SO, THIS MAN TOOK A LIFE AND WAS ABOUT TO END OURS. WHERE I COME FROM, THAT'S SERIOUS BUSINESS.
GURGGGGG...
AND WE ARE NOT WHERE YOU COME FROM. THERE ARE RULES HERE.
I'M NOT GOING TO ASK TWICE...PUT HIM DOWN NOW!
YOU JUST DID.
ZZZZ
BIG...
...MISTAKE.
ZAP

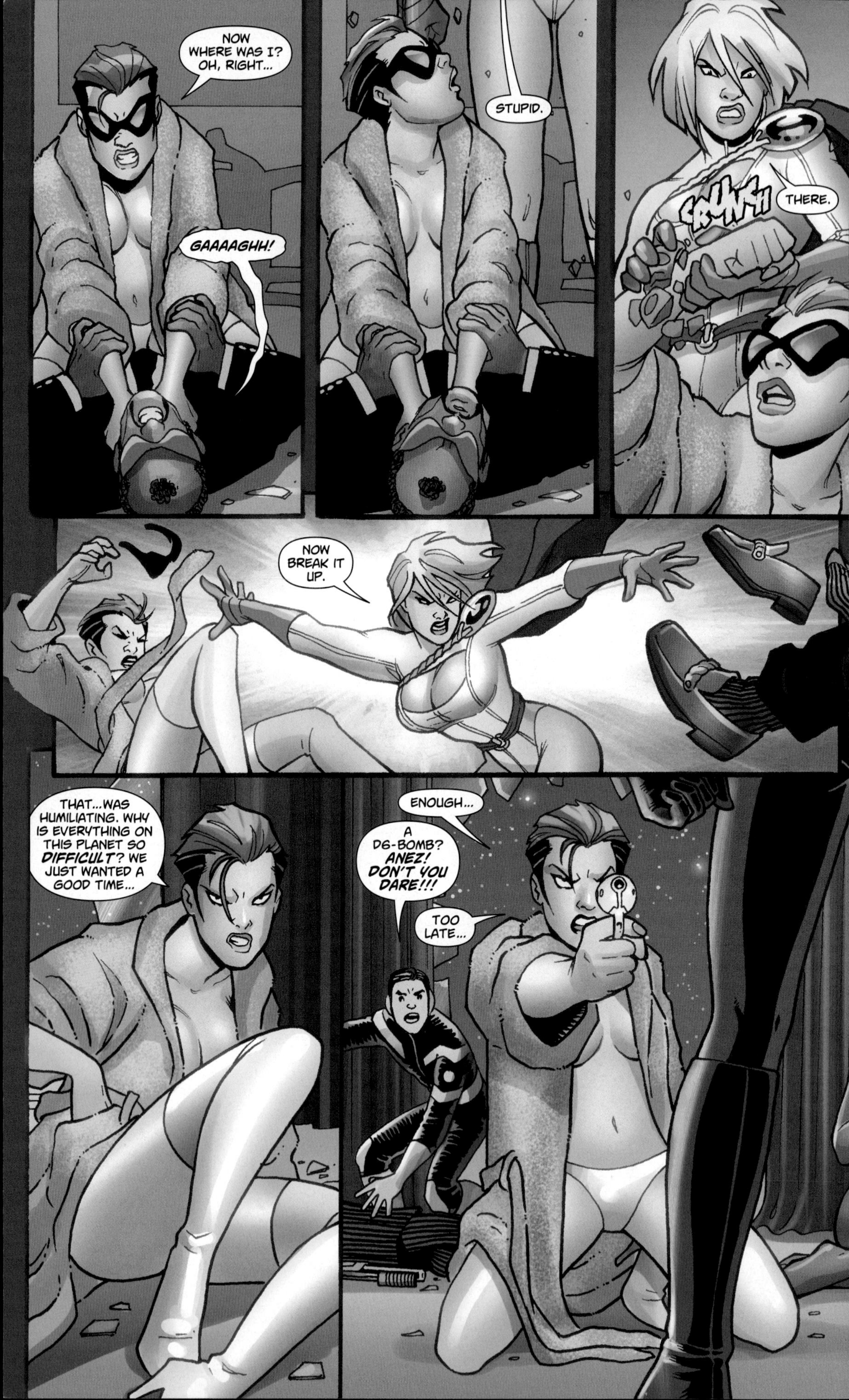
NOW WHERE WAS I? OH, RIGHT...
GAAAAGHH!
STUPID.
CRUNCH
THERE.
NOW BREAK IT UP.
THAT...WAS HUMILIATING. WHY IS EVERYTHING ON THIS PLANET SO *DIFFICULT*? WE JUST WANTED A GOOD TIME...
ENOUGH...
A D6-BOMB? ***ANEZ! DON'T YOU DARE!!!***
TOO LATE...

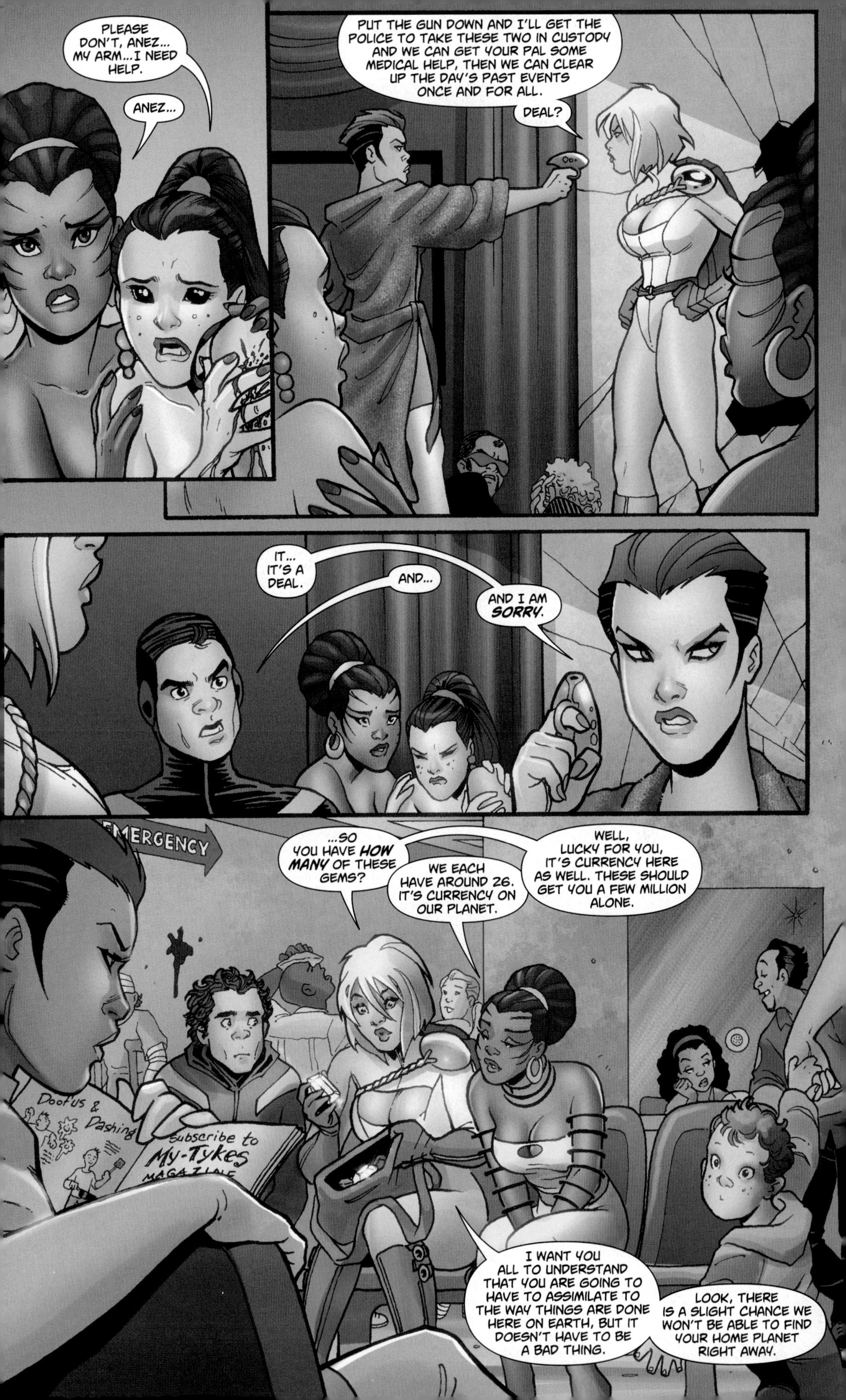
PLEASE DON'T, ANEZ... MY ARM...I NEED HELP.
ANEZ...
PUT THE GUN DOWN AND I'LL GET THE POLICE TO TAKE THESE TWO IN CUSTODY AND WE CAN GET YOUR PAL SOME MEDICAL HELP, THEN WE CAN CLEAR UP THE DAY'S PAST EVENTS ONCE AND FOR ALL.
DEAL?
IT... IT'S A DEAL.
AND...
AND I AM SORRY.
EMERGENCY
...SO YOU HAVE HOW MANY OF THESE GEMS?
WE EACH HAVE AROUND 26. IT'S CURRENCY ON OUR PLANET.
WELL, LUCKY FOR YOU, IT'S CURRENCY HERE AS WELL. THESE SHOULD GET YOU A FEW MILLION ALONE.
Doofus & Dashing
Subscribe to My-Tykes MAGAZINE
I WANT YOU ALL TO UNDERSTAND THAT YOU ARE GOING TO HAVE TO ASSIMILATE TO THE WAY THINGS ARE DONE HERE ON EARTH, BUT IT DOESN'T HAVE TO BE A BAD THING.
LOOK, THERE IS A SLIGHT CHANCE WE WON'T BE ABLE TO FIND YOUR HOME PLANET RIGHT AWAY.

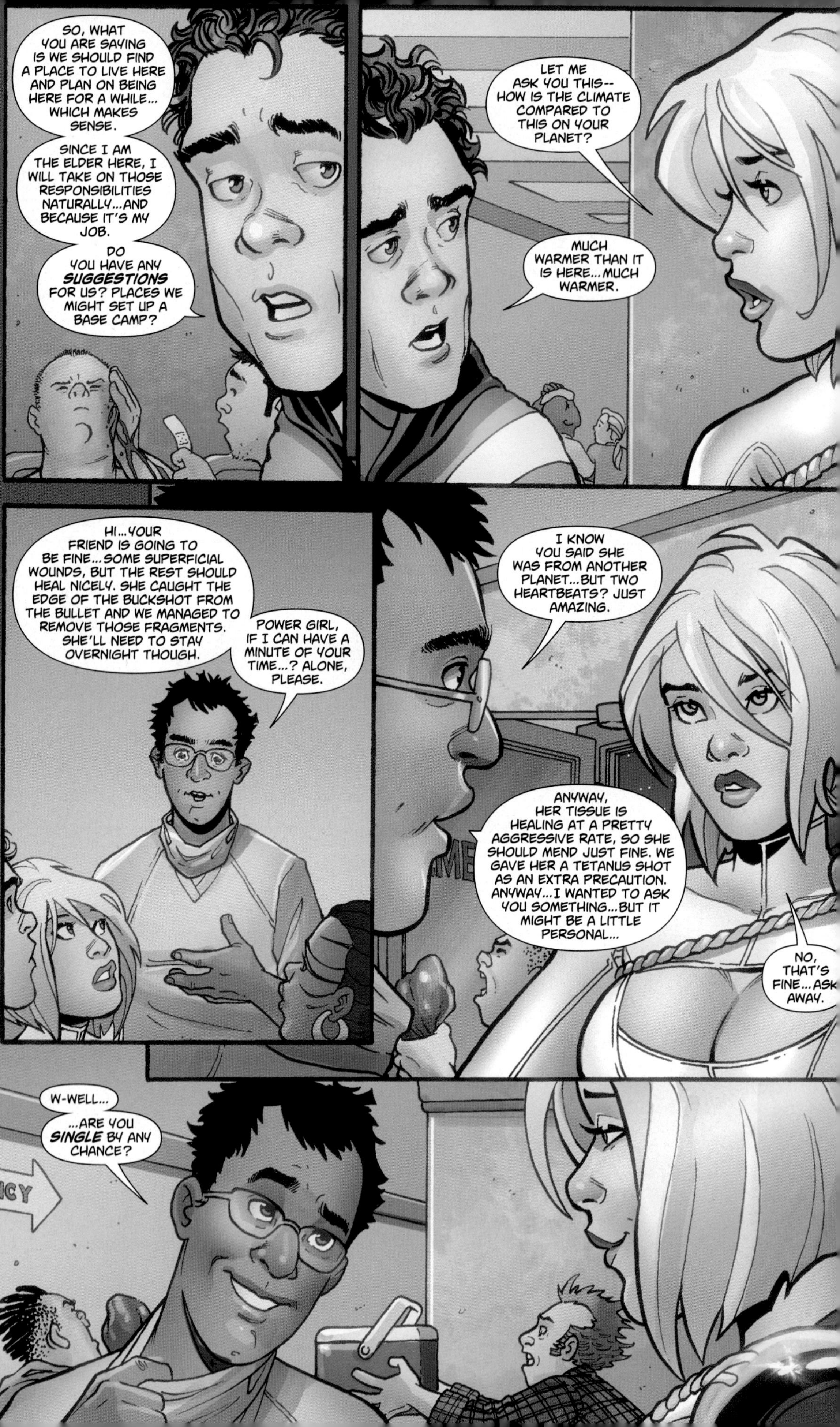
SO, WHAT YOU ARE SAYING IS WE SHOULD FIND A PLACE TO LIVE HERE AND PLAN ON BEING HERE FOR A WHILE... WHICH MAKES SENSE.
SINCE I AM THE ELDER HERE, I WILL TAKE ON THOSE RESPONSIBILITIES NATURALLY...AND BECAUSE IT'S MY JOB.
DO YOU HAVE ANY SUGGESTIONS FOR US? PLACES WE MIGHT SET UP A BASE CAMP?
LET ME ASK YOU THIS-- HOW IS THE CLIMATE COMPARED TO THIS ON YOUR PLANET?
MUCH WARMER THAN IT IS HERE...MUCH WARMER.
HI...YOUR FRIEND IS GOING TO BE FINE...SOME SUPERFICIAL WOUNDS, BUT THE REST SHOULD HEAL NICELY. SHE CAUGHT THE EDGE OF THE BUCKSHOT FROM THE BULLET AND WE MANAGED TO REMOVE THOSE FRAGMENTS. SHE'LL NEED TO STAY OVERNIGHT THOUGH.
POWER GIRL, IF I CAN HAVE A MINUTE OF YOUR TIME...? ALONE, PLEASE.
I KNOW YOU SAID SHE WAS FROM ANOTHER PLANET...BUT TWO HEARTBEATS? JUST AMAZING.
ANYWAY, HER TISSUE IS HEALING AT A PRETTY AGGRESSIVE RATE, SO SHE SHOULD MEND JUST FINE. WE GAVE HER A TETANUS SHOT AS AN EXTRA PRECAUTION. ANYWAY...I WANTED TO ASK YOU SOMETHING...BUT IT MIGHT BE A LITTLE PERSONAL...
NO, THAT'S FINE...ASK AWAY.
W-WELL...
...ARE YOU SINGLE BY ANY CHANCE?
ENCY

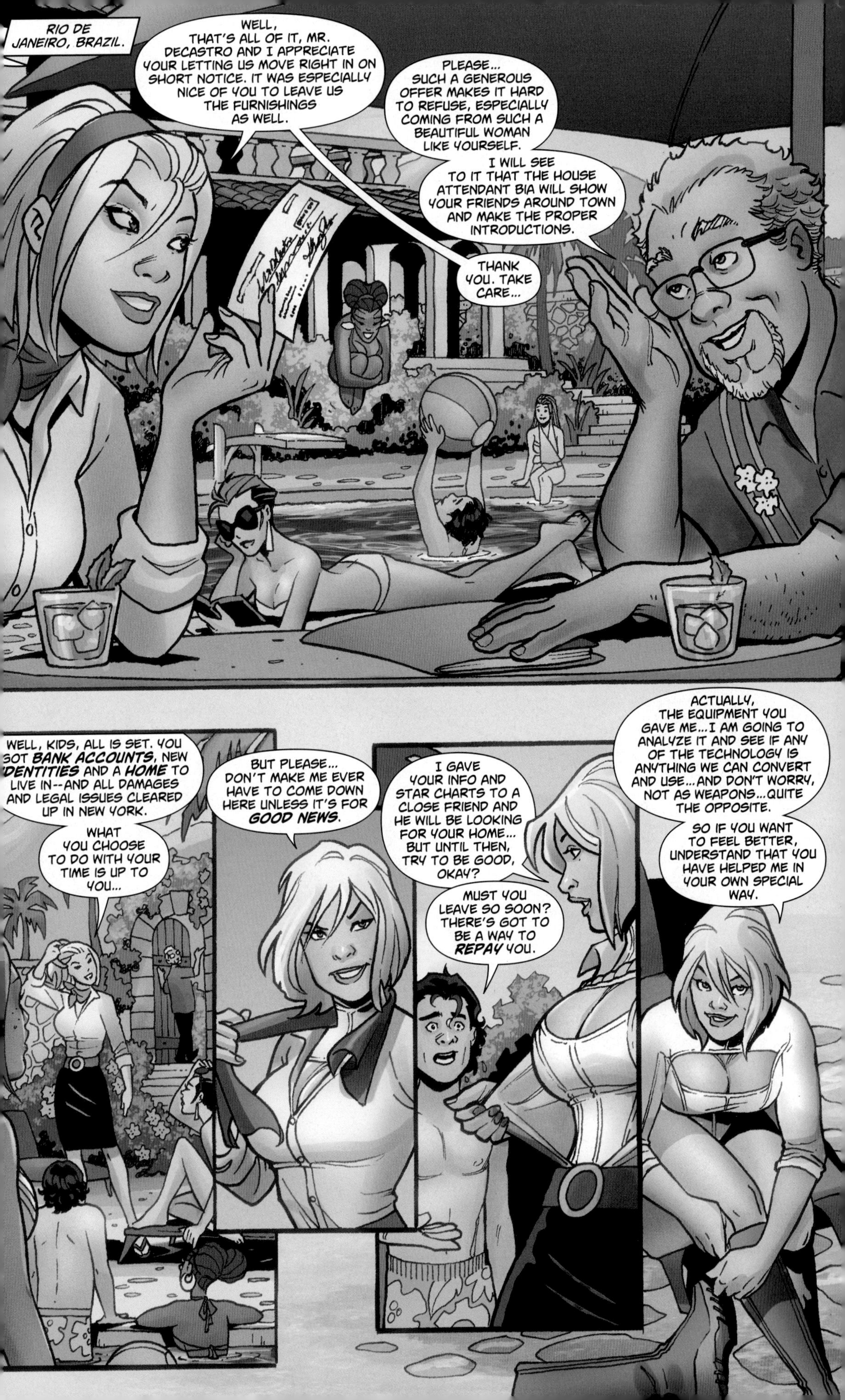

RIO DE JANEIRO, BRAZIL.
WELL, THAT'S ALL OF IT, MR. DECASTRO AND I APPRECIATE YOUR LETTING US MOVE RIGHT IN ON SHORT NOTICE. IT WAS ESPECIALLY NICE OF YOU TO LEAVE US THE FURNISHINGS AS WELL.
PLEASE... SUCH A GENEROUS OFFER MAKES IT HARD TO REFUSE, ESPECIALLY COMING FROM SUCH A BEAUTIFUL WOMAN LIKE YOURSELF.
I WILL SEE TO IT THAT THE HOUSE ATTENDANT BIA WILL SHOW YOUR FRIENDS AROUND TOWN AND MAKE THE PROPER INTRODUCTIONS.
THANK YOU. TAKE CARE...
WELL, KIDS, ALL IS SET. YOU GOT **BANK ACCOUNTS**, NEW IDENTITIES AND A **HOME** TO LIVE IN--AND ALL DAMAGES AND LEGAL ISSUES CLEARED UP IN NEW YORK.
WHAT YOU CHOOSE TO DO WITH YOUR TIME IS UP TO YOU...
BUT PLEASE... DON'T MAKE ME EVER HAVE TO COME DOWN HERE UNLESS IT'S FOR **GOOD NEWS**.
I GAVE YOUR INFO AND STAR CHARTS TO A CLOSE FRIEND AND HE WILL BE LOOKING FOR YOUR HOME... BUT UNTIL THEN, TRY TO BE GOOD, OKAY?
MUST YOU LEAVE SO SOON? THERE'S GOT TO BE A WAY TO **REPAY** YOU.
ACTUALLY, THE EQUIPMENT YOU GAVE ME... I AM GOING TO ANALYZE IT AND SEE IF ANY OF THE TECHNOLOGY IS ANYTHING WE CAN CONVERT AND USE... AND DON'T WORRY, NOT AS WEAPONS... QUITE THE OPPOSITE.
SO IF YOU WANT TO FEEL BETTER, UNDERSTAND THAT YOU HAVE HELPED ME IN YOUR OWN SPECIAL WAY.

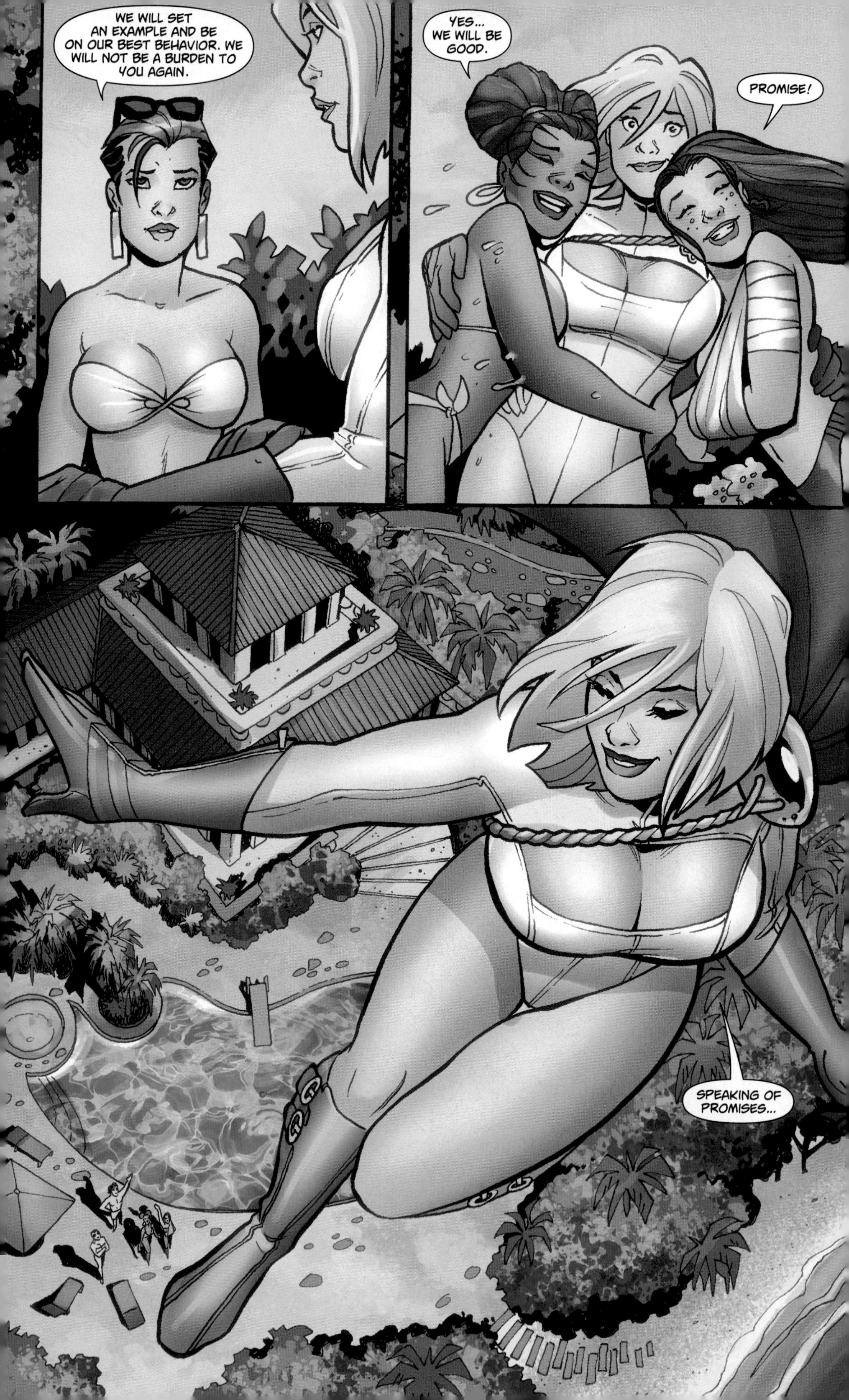
WE WILL SET AN EXAMPLE AND BE ON OUR BEST BEHAVIOR. WE WILL NOT BE A BURDEN TO YOU AGAIN.
YES... WE WILL BE GOOD.
PROMISE!
SPEAKING OF PROMISES...

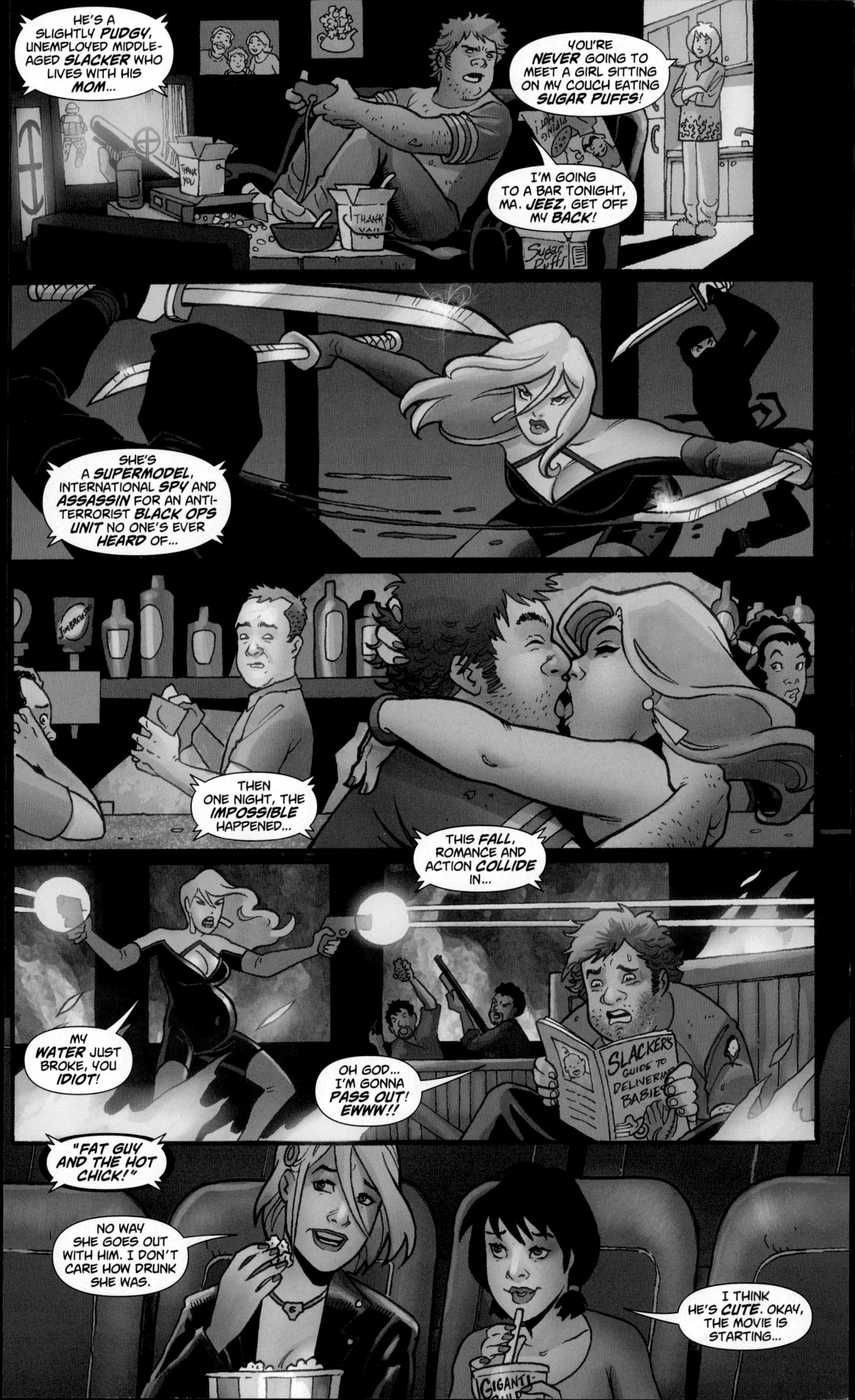
HE'S A SLIGHTLY PUDGY, UNEMPLOYED MIDDLE-AGED SLACKER WHO LIVES WITH HIS MOM...
YOU'RE NEVER GOING TO MEET A GIRL SITTING ON MY COUCH EATING SUGAR PUFFS!
I'M GOING TO A BAR TONIGHT, MA. JEEZ, GET OFF MY BACK!
THANK YOU
THANK YOU
Sugar Puffs
SHE'S A SUPERMODEL, INTERNATIONAL SPY AND ASSASSIN FOR AN ANTI-TERRORIST BLACK OPS UNIT NO ONE'S EVER HEARD OF...
THEN ONE NIGHT, THE IMPOSSIBLE HAPPENED...
THIS FALL, ROMANCE AND ACTION COLLIDE IN...
MY WATER JUST BROKE, YOU IDIOT!
OH GOD... I'M GONNA PASS OUT! EWWW!!
SLACKER'S GUIDE TO DELIVERING BABIES
"FAT GUY AND THE HOT CHICK!"
NO WAY SHE GOES OUT WITH HIM. I DON'T CARE HOW DRUNK SHE WAS.
I THINK HE'S CUTE. OKAY, THE MOVIE IS STARTING...

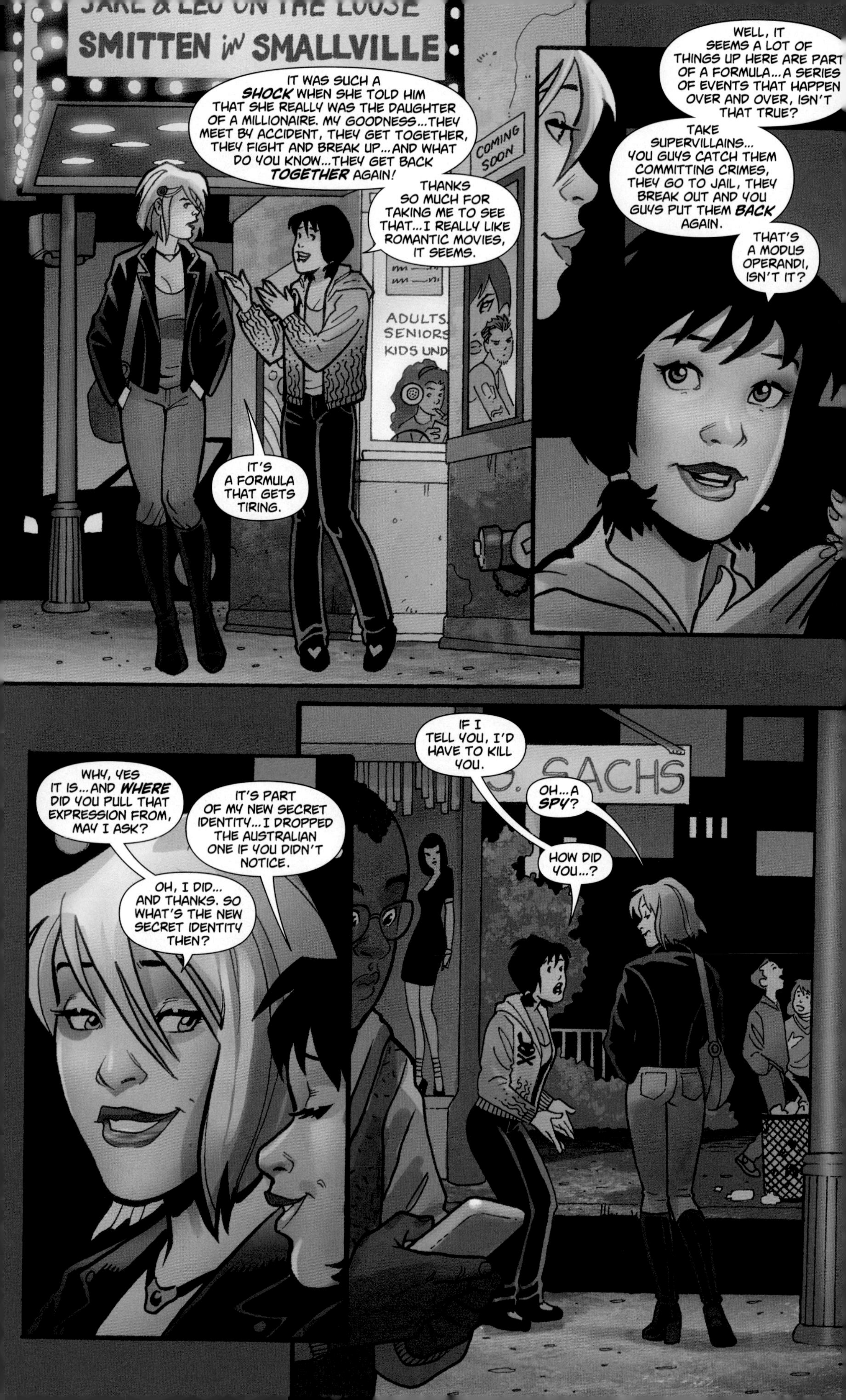
JAKE & LEO ON THE LOOSE
SMITTEN IN SMALLVILLE
IT WAS SUCH A SHOCK WHEN SHE TOLD HIM THAT SHE REALLY WAS THE DAUGHTER OF A MILLIONAIRE. MY GOODNESS...THEY MEET BY ACCIDENT, THEY GET TOGETHER, THEY FIGHT AND BREAK UP...AND WHAT DO YOU KNOW...THEY GET BACK TOGETHER AGAIN!
COMING SOON
THANKS SO MUCH FOR TAKING ME TO SEE THAT...I REALLY LIKE ROMANTIC MOVIES, IT SEEMS.
ADULTS SENIORS KIDS UND
IT'S A FORMULA THAT GETS TIRING.
WELL, IT SEEMS A LOT OF THINGS UP HERE ARE PART OF A FORMULA...A SERIES OF EVENTS THAT HAPPEN OVER AND OVER, ISN'T THAT TRUE?
TAKE SUPERVILLAINS... YOU GUYS CATCH THEM COMMITTING CRIMES, THEY GO TO JAIL, THEY BREAK OUT AND YOU GUYS PUT THEM BACK AGAIN.
THAT'S A MODUS OPERANDI, ISN'T IT?
WHY, YES IT IS...AND WHERE DID YOU PULL THAT EXPRESSION FROM, MAY I ASK?
IT'S PART OF MY NEW SECRET IDENTITY...I DROPPED THE AUSTRALIAN ONE IF YOU DIDN'T NOTICE.
OH, I DID... AND THANKS. SO WHAT'S THE NEW SECRET IDENTITY THEN?
IF I TELL YOU, I'D HAVE TO KILL YOU.
SACHS
OH...A SPY?
HOW DID YOU...?

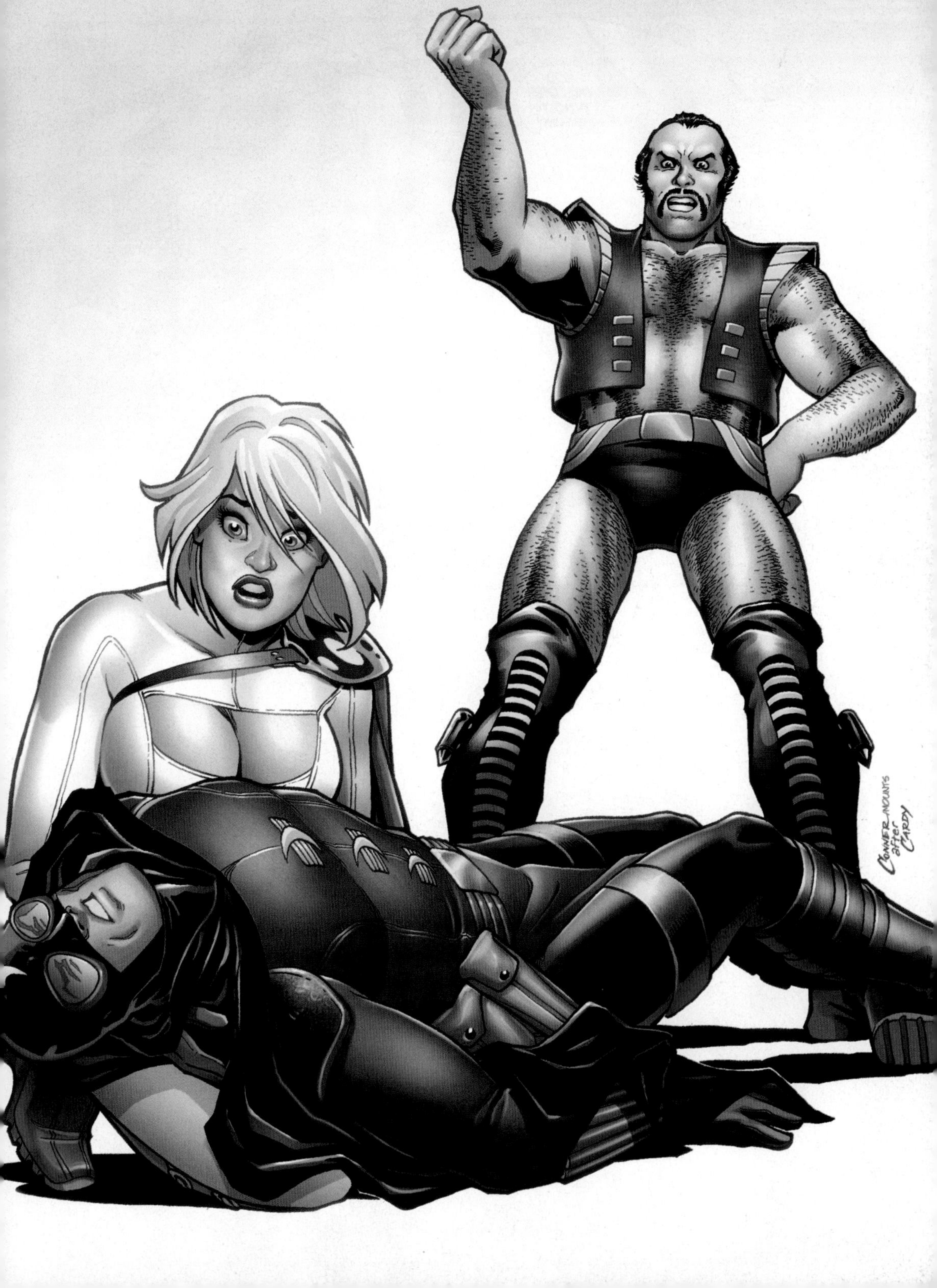

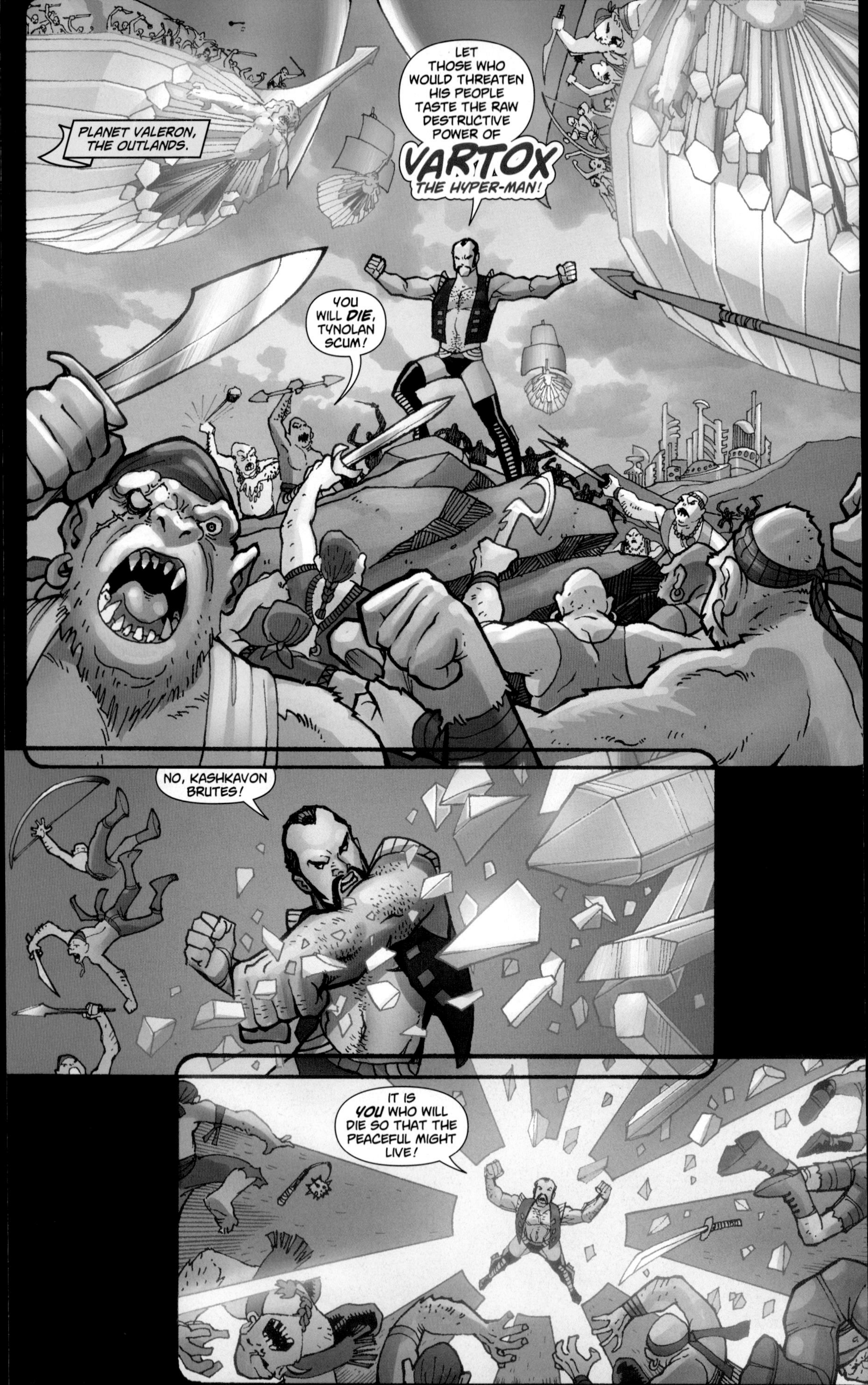
PLANET VALERON, THE OUTLANDS.
LET THOSE WHO WOULD THREATEN HIS PEOPLE TASTE THE RAW DESTRUCTIVE POWER OF VARTOX THE HYPER-MAN!
YOU WILL DIE, TYNOLAN SCUM!
NO, KASHKAVON BRUTES!
IT IS YOU WHO WILL DIE SO THAT THE PEACEFUL MIGHT LIVE!

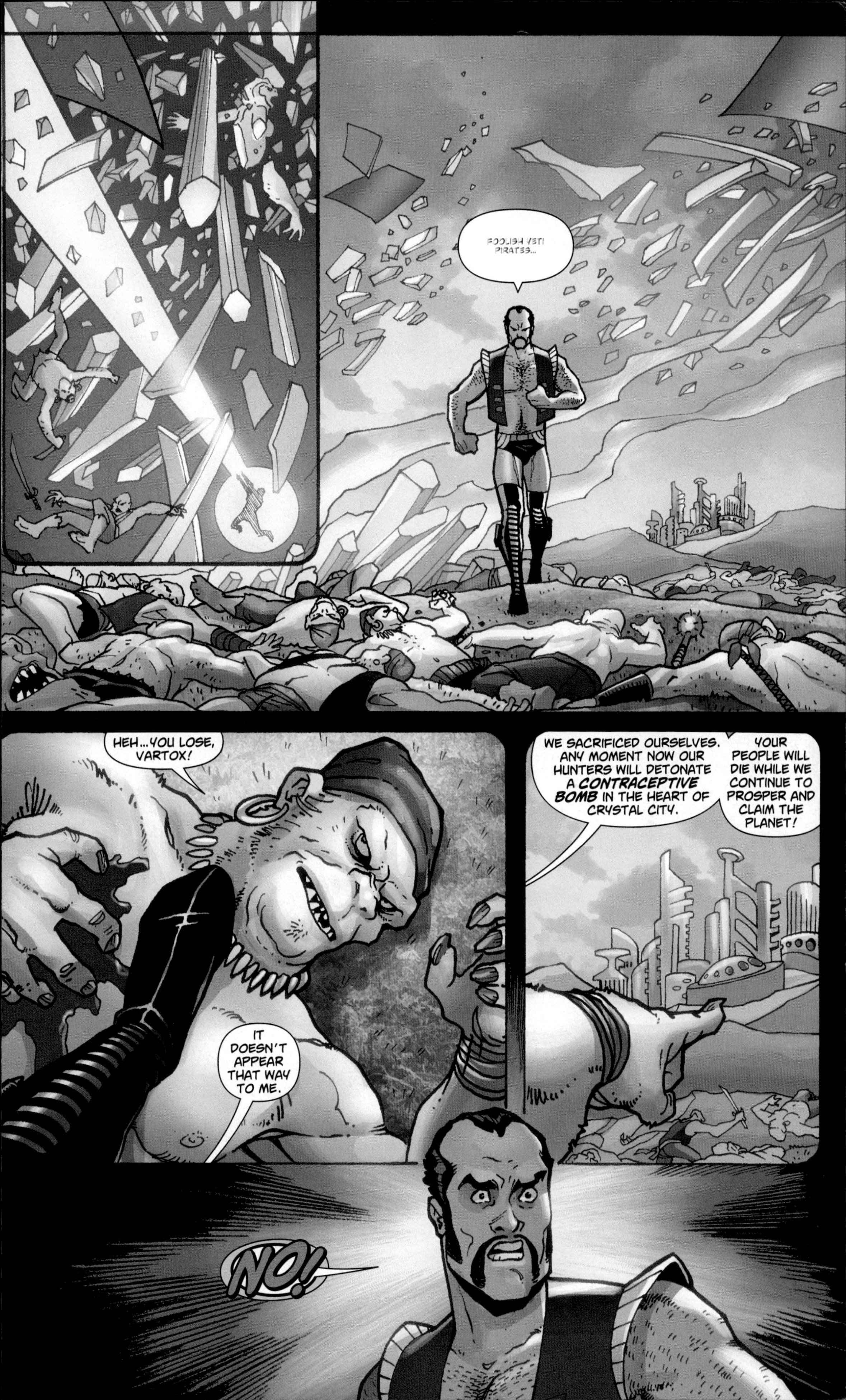
FOOLISH YETI PIRATES...
HEH...YOU LOSE, VARTOX!
IT DOESN'T APPEAR THAT WAY TO ME.
WE SACRIFICED OURSELVES. ANY MOMENT NOW OUR HUNTERS WILL DETONATE A CONTRACEPTIVE BOMB IN THE HEART OF CRYSTAL CITY.
YOUR PEOPLE WILL DIE WHILE WE CONTINUE TO PROSPER AND CLAIM THE PLANET!
NO!

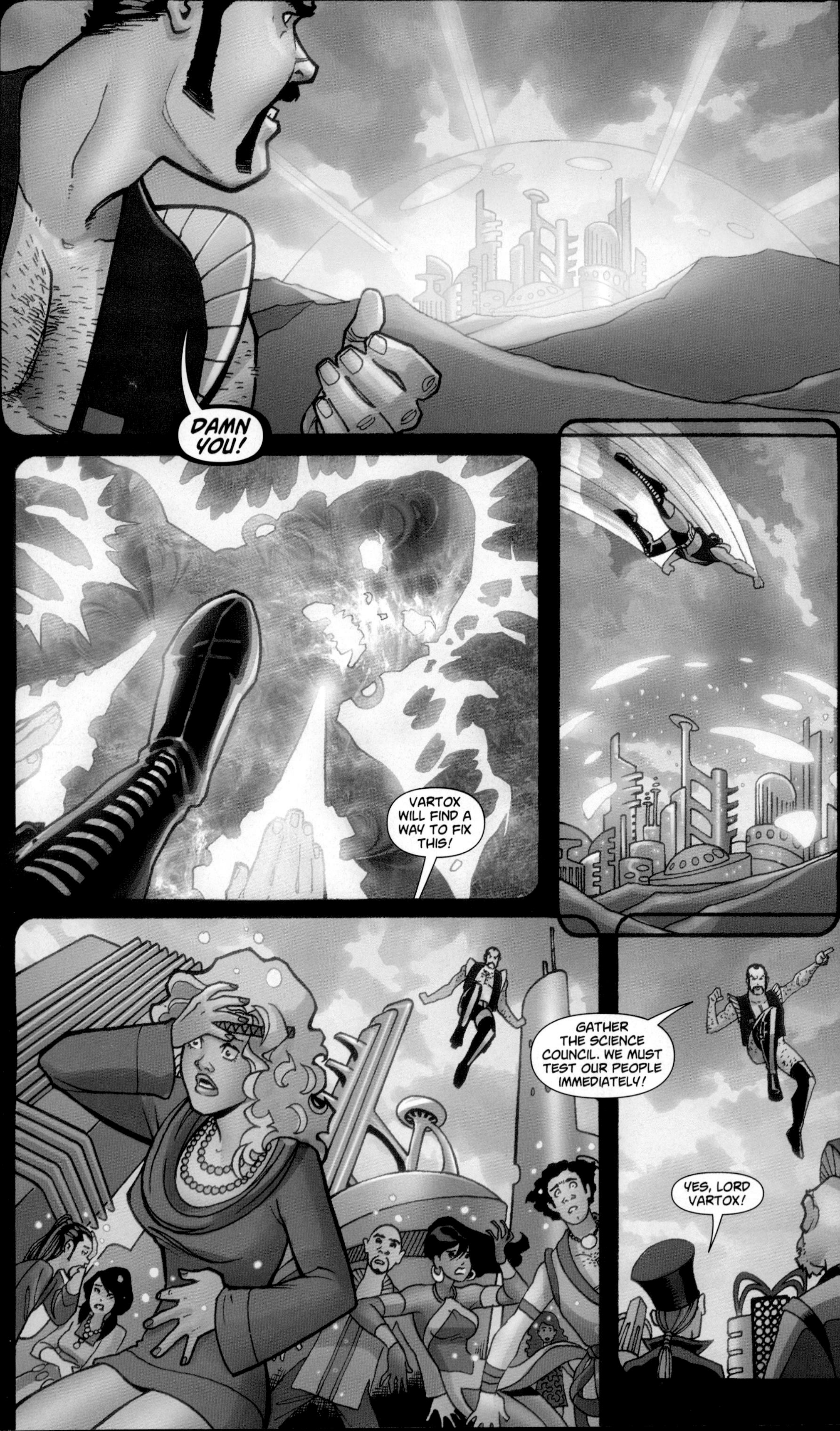
DAMN YOU!
VARTOX WILL FIND A WAY TO FIX THIS!
GATHER THE SCIENCE COUNCIL. WE MUST TEST OUR PEOPLE IMMEDIATELY!
YES, LORD VARTOX!

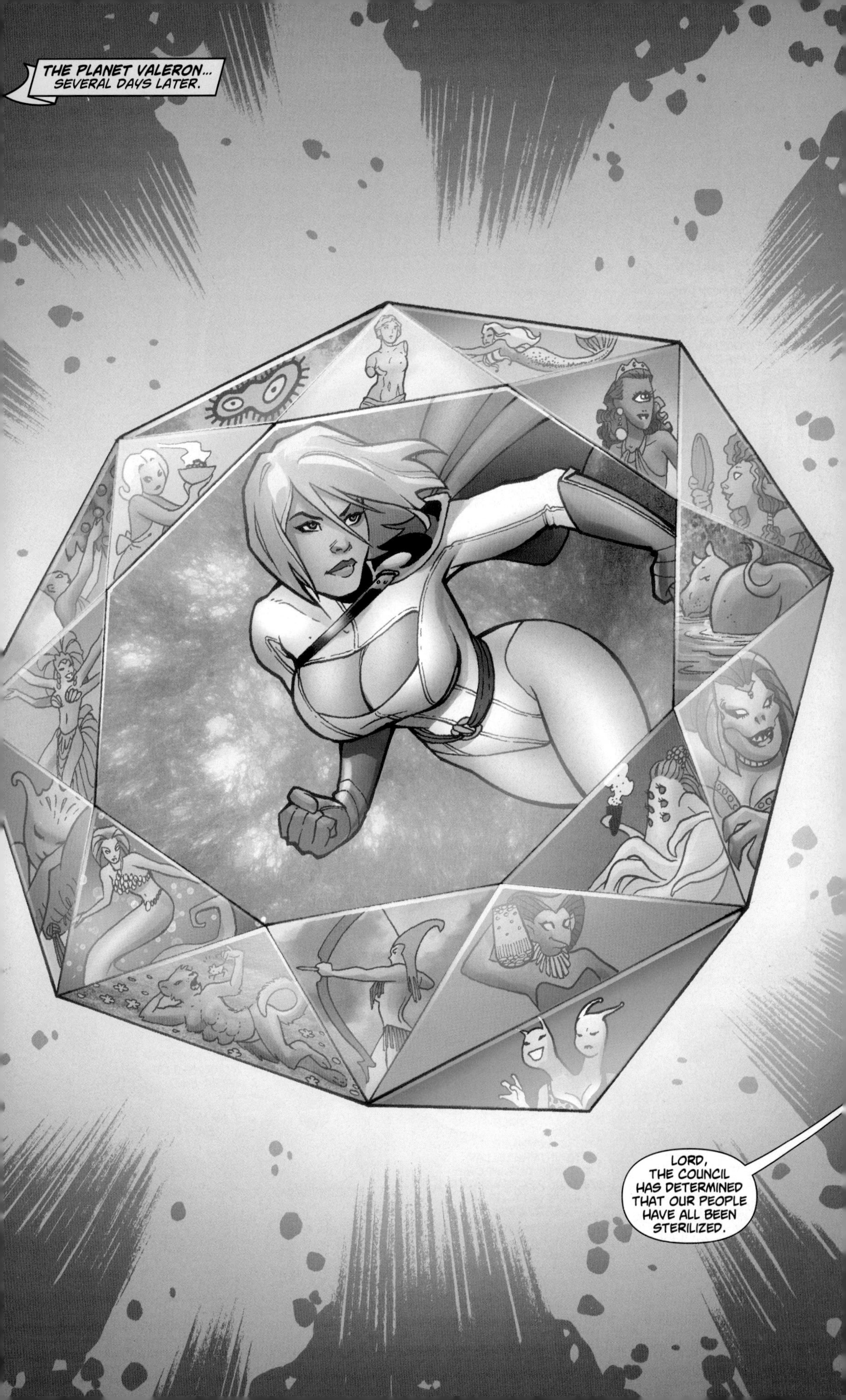
THE PLANET VALERON... SEVERAL DAYS LATER.
LORD, THE COUNCIL HAS DETERMINED THAT OUR PEOPLE HAVE ALL BEEN STERILIZED.

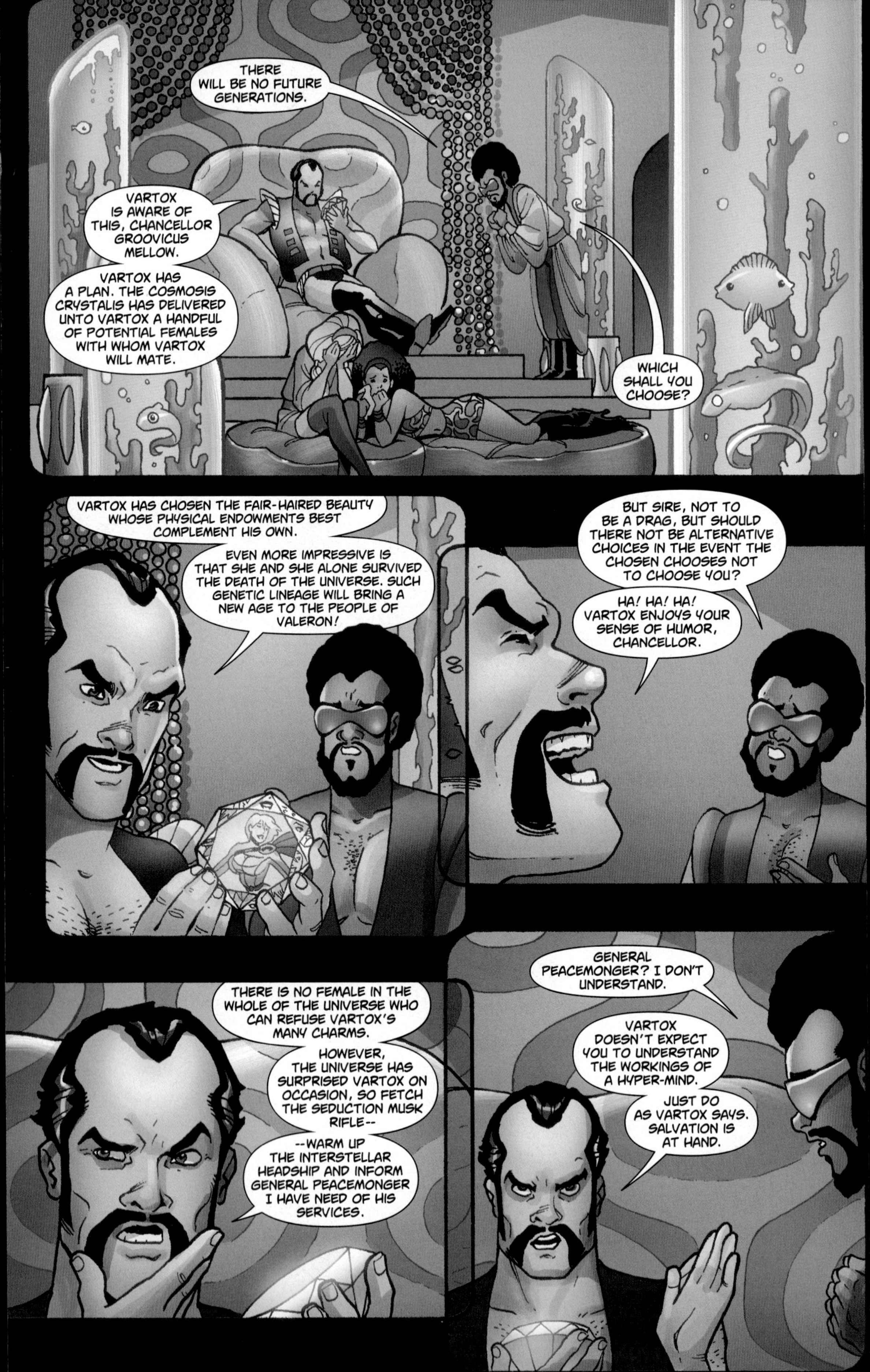
THERE WILL BE NO FUTURE GENERATIONS.
VARTOX IS AWARE OF THIS, CHANCELLOR GROOVICUS MELLOW.
VARTOX HAS A PLAN. THE COSMOSIS CRYSTALIS HAS DELIVERED UNTO VARTOX A HANDFUL OF POTENTIAL FEMALES WITH WHOM VARTOX WILL MATE.
WHICH SHALL YOU CHOOSE?
VARTOX HAS CHOSEN THE FAIR-HAIRED BEAUTY WHOSE PHYSICAL ENDOWMENTS BEST COMPLEMENT HIS OWN.
EVEN MORE IMPRESSIVE IS THAT SHE AND SHE ALONE SURVIVED THE DEATH OF THE UNIVERSE. SUCH GENETIC LINEAGE WILL BRING A NEW AGE TO THE PEOPLE OF VALERON!
BUT SIRE, NOT TO BE A DRAG, BUT SHOULD THERE NOT BE ALTERNATIVE CHOICES IN THE EVENT THE CHOSEN CHOOSES NOT TO CHOOSE YOU?
HA! HA! HA! VARTOX ENJOYS YOUR SENSE OF HUMOR, CHANCELLOR.
THERE IS NO FEMALE IN THE WHOLE OF THE UNIVERSE WHO CAN REFUSE VARTOX'S MANY CHARMS.
HOWEVER, THE UNIVERSE HAS SURPRISED VARTOX ON OCCASION, SO FETCH THE SEDUCTION MUSK RIFLE--
--WARM UP THE INTERSTELLAR HEADSHIP AND INFORM GENERAL PEACEMONGER I HAVE NEED OF HIS SERVICES.
GENERAL PEACEMONGER? I DON'T UNDERSTAND.
VARTOX DOESN'T EXPECT YOU TO UNDERSTAND THE WORKINGS OF A HYPER-MIND.
JUST DO AS VARTOX SAYS. SALVATION IS AT HAND.

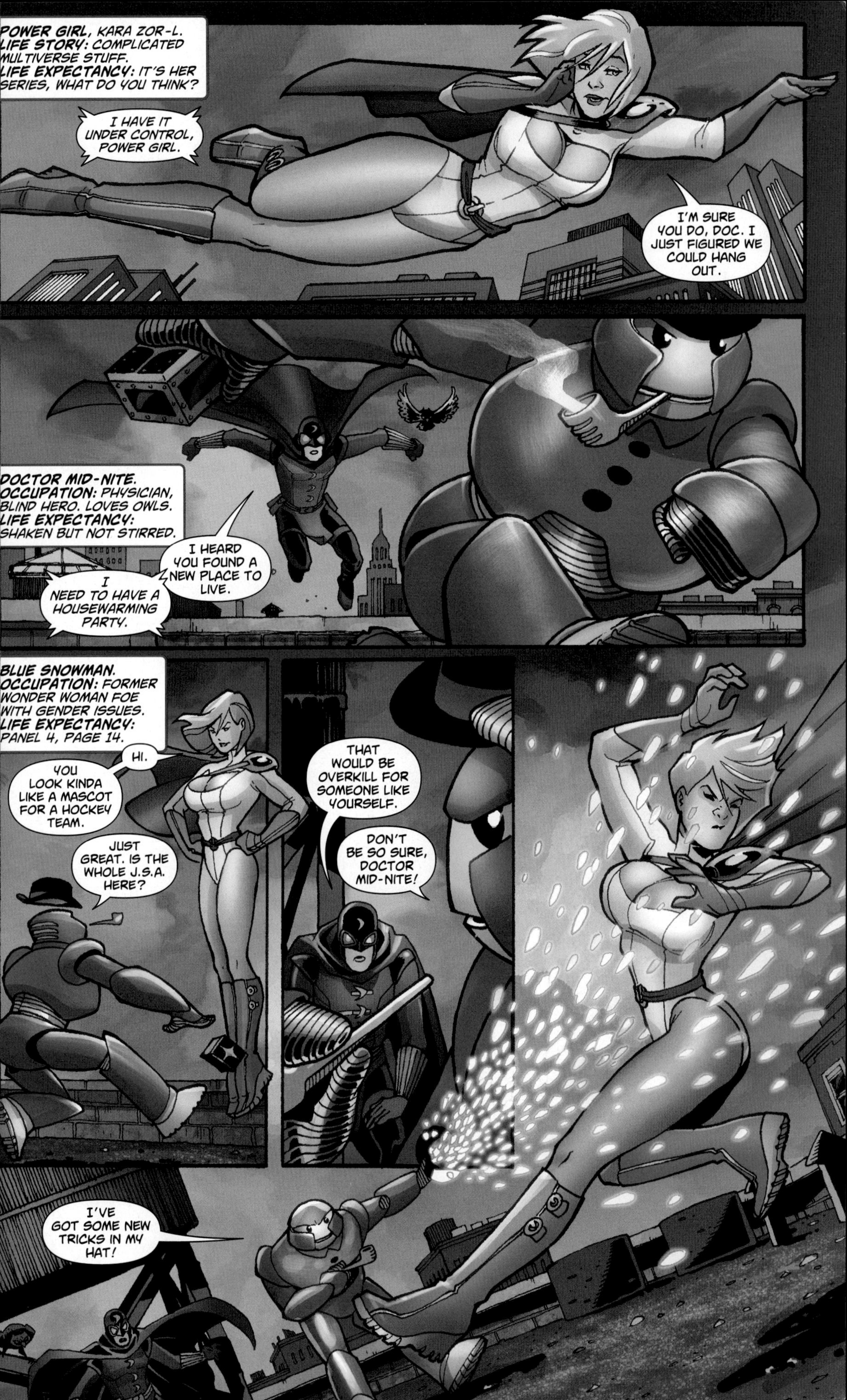
POWER GIRL, KARA ZOR-L.
LIFE STORY: COMPLICATED MULTIVERSE STUFF.
LIFE EXPECTANCY: IT'S HER SERIES, WHAT DO YOU THINK?
I HAVE IT UNDER CONTROL, POWER GIRL.
I'M SURE YOU DO, DOC. I JUST FIGURED WE COULD HANG OUT.
DOCTOR MID-NITE.
OCCUPATION: PHYSICIAN, BLIND HERO. LOVES OWLS.
LIFE EXPECTANCY: SHAKEN BUT NOT STIRRED.
I HEARD YOU FOUND A NEW PLACE TO LIVE.
I NEED TO HAVE A HOUSEWARMING PARTY.
BLUE SNOWMAN.
OCCUPATION: FORMER WONDER WOMAN FOE WITH GENDER ISSUES.
LIFE EXPECTANCY: PANEL 4, PAGE 14.
HI.
YOU LOOK KINDA LIKE A MASCOT FOR A HOCKEY TEAM.
JUST GREAT. IS THE WHOLE J.S.A. HERE?
THAT WOULD BE OVERKILL FOR SOMEONE LIKE YOURSELF.
DON'T BE SO SURE, DOCTOR MID-NITE!
I'VE GOT SOME NEW TRICKS IN MY HAT!

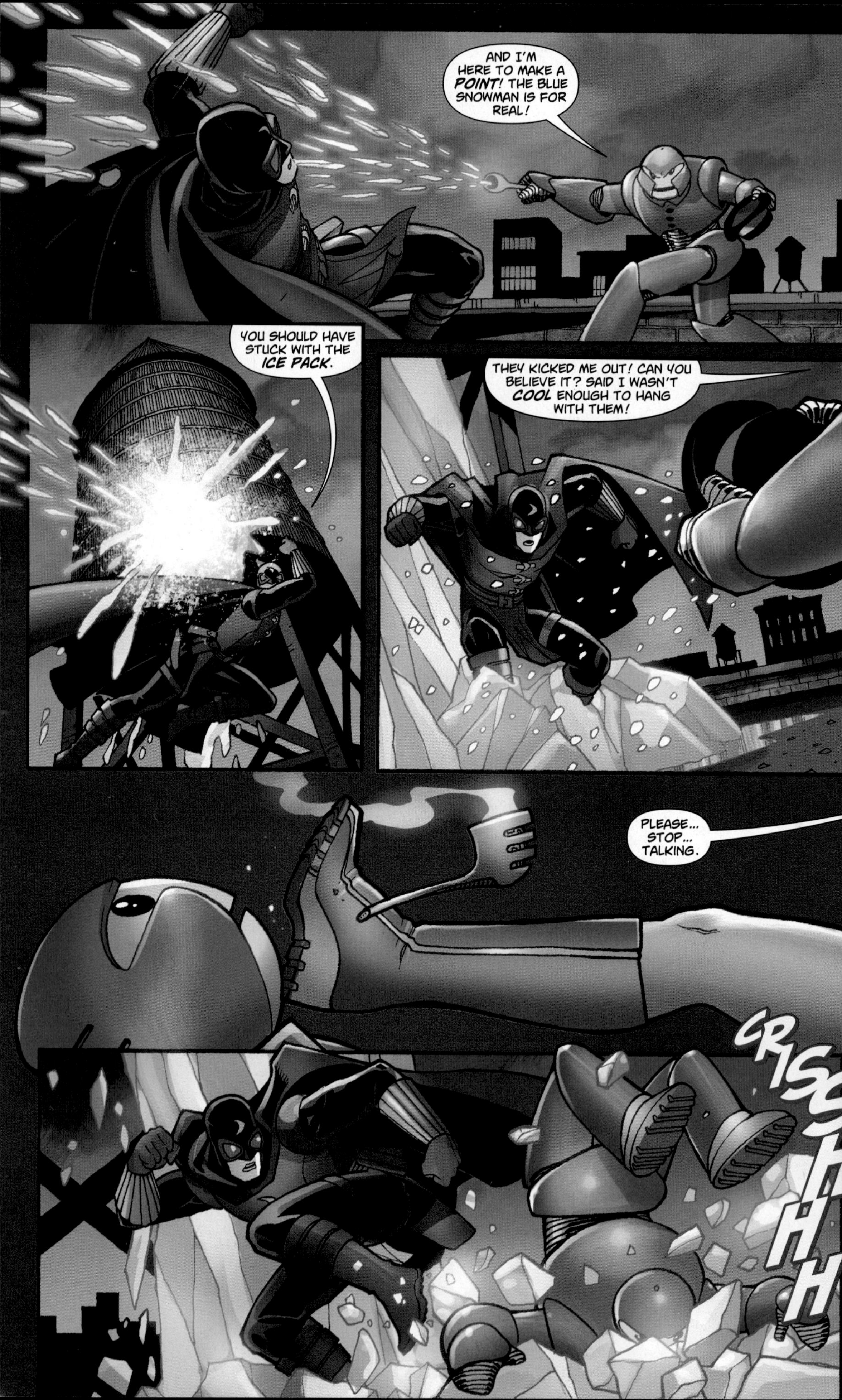
AND I'M HERE TO MAKE A POINT! THE BLUE SNOWMAN IS FOR REAL!
YOU SHOULD HAVE STUCK WITH THE ICE PACK.
THEY KICKED ME OUT! CAN YOU BELIEVE IT? SAID I WASN'T COOL ENOUGH TO HANG WITH THEM!
PLEASE... STOP... TALKING.
CRISSSHHHH

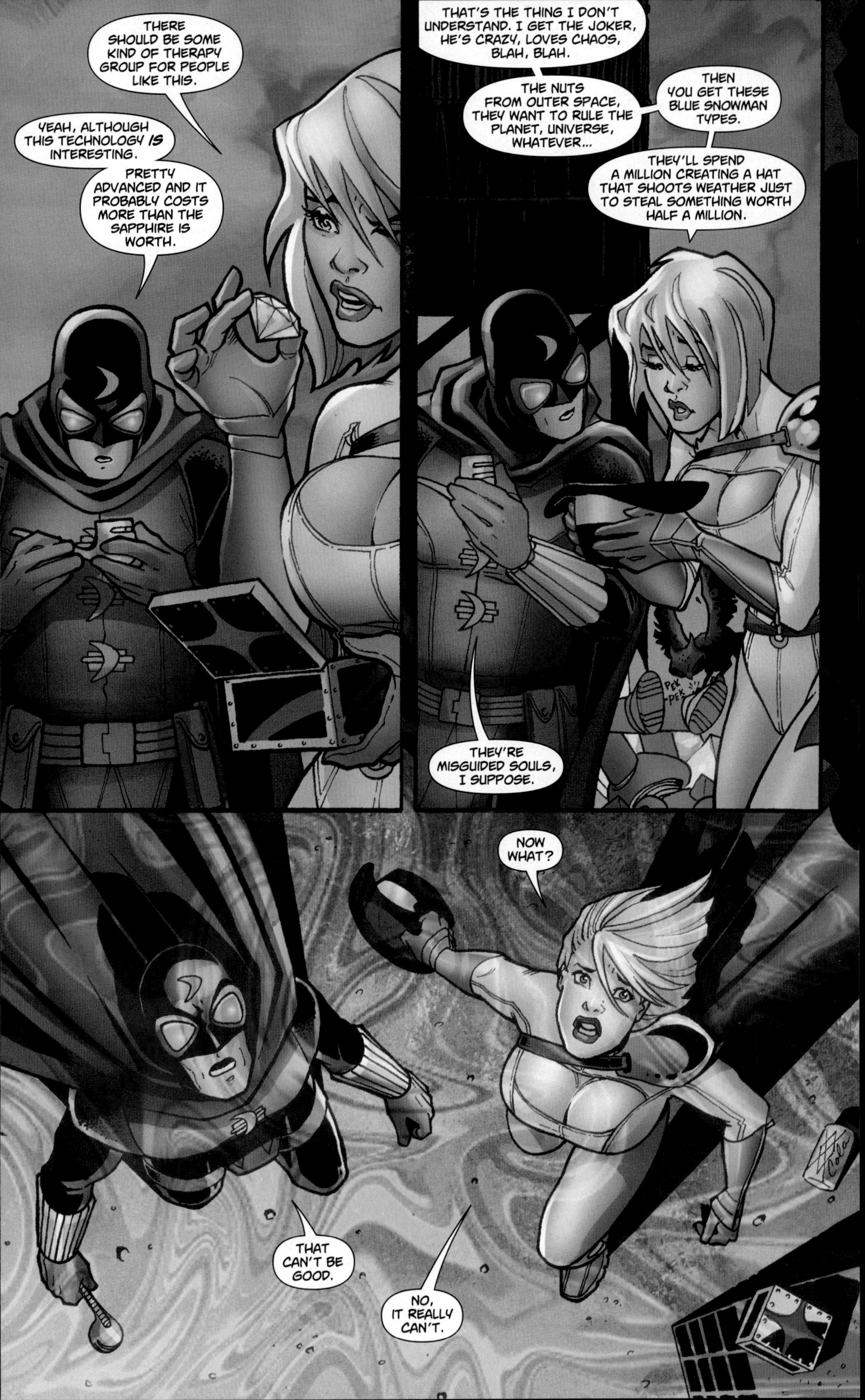
THERE SHOULD BE SOME KIND OF THERAPY GROUP FOR PEOPLE LIKE THIS.
YEAH, ALTHOUGH THIS TECHNOLOGY *IS* INTERESTING.
PRETTY ADVANCED AND IT PROBABLY COSTS MORE THAN THE SAPPHIRE IS WORTH.
THAT'S THE THING I DON'T UNDERSTAND. I GET THE JOKER, HE'S CRAZY, LOVES CHAOS, BLAH, BLAH.
THE NUTS FROM OUTER SPACE, THEY WANT TO RULE THE PLANET, UNIVERSE, WHATEVER...
THEN YOU GET THESE BLUE SNOWMAN TYPES.
THEY'LL SPEND A MILLION CREATING A HAT THAT SHOOTS WEATHER JUST TO STEAL SOMETHING WORTH HALF A MILLION.
PEK PEK
THEY'RE MISGUIDED SOULS, I SUPPOSE.
NOW WHAT?
THAT CAN'T BE GOOD.
NO, IT REALLY CAN'T.

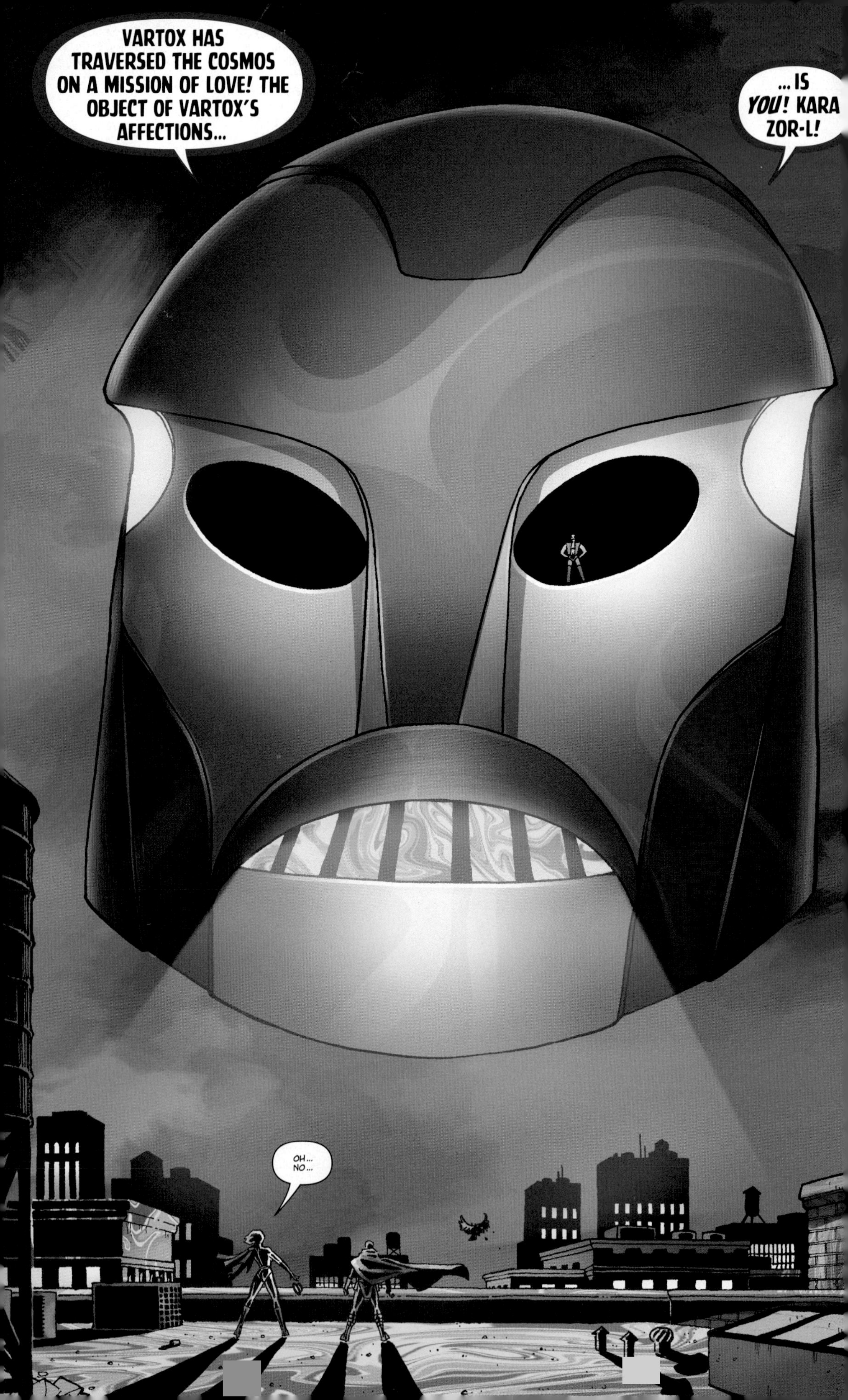
VARTOX HAS TRAVERSED THE COSMOS ON A MISSION OF LOVE! THE OBJECT OF VARTOX'S AFFECTIONS...
...IS YOU! KARA ZOR-L!
OH... NO...

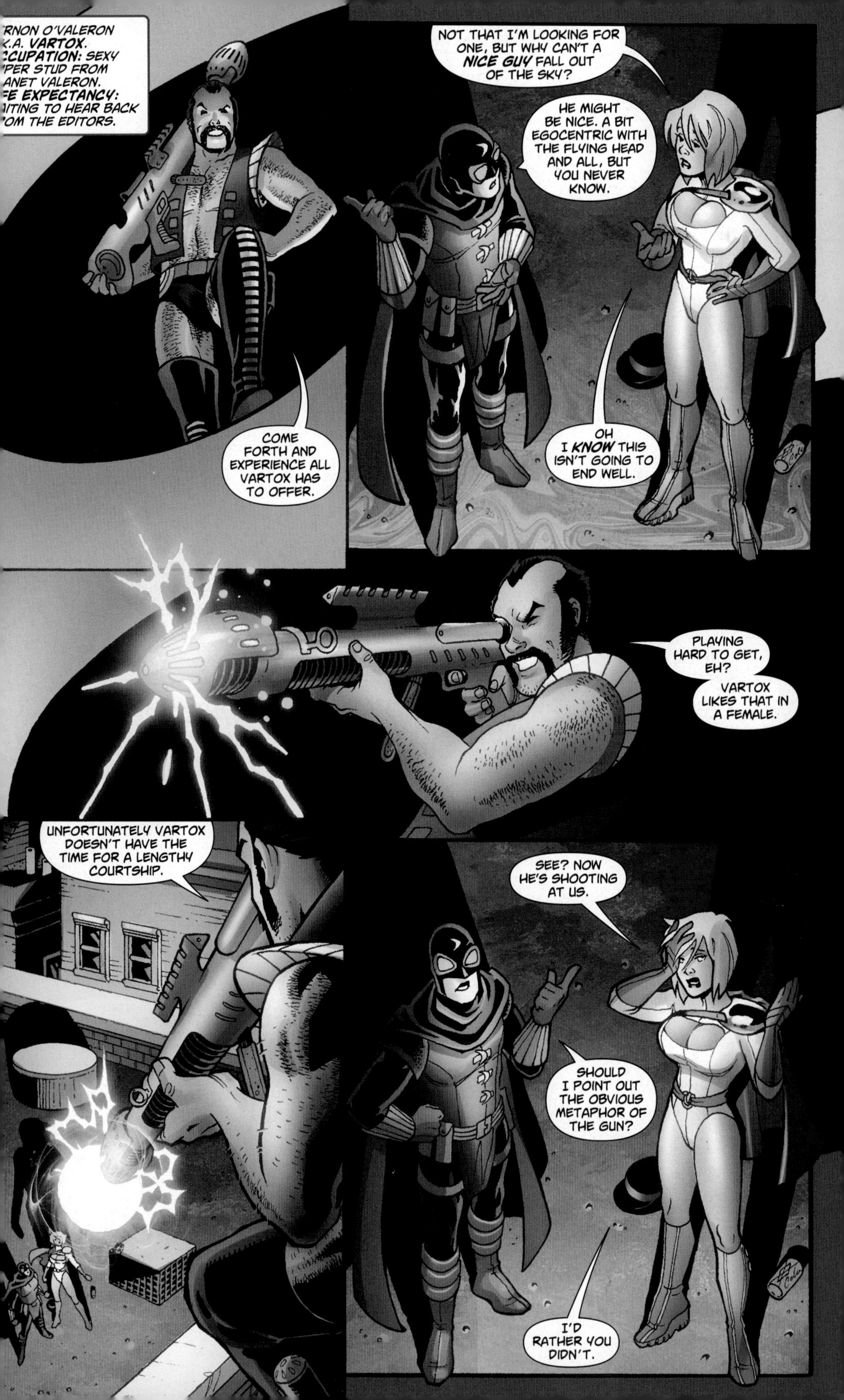

RNON O'VALERON
.A. VARTOX.
CUPATION: SEXY
PER STUD FROM
ANET VALERON.
FE EXPECTANCY:
ITING TO HEAR BACK
OM THE EDITORS.
COME FORTH AND EXPERIENCE ALL VARTOX HAS TO OFFER.
NOT THAT I'M LOOKING FOR ONE, BUT WHY CAN'T A NICE GUY FALL OUT OF THE SKY?
HE MIGHT BE NICE. A BIT EGOCENTRIC WITH THE FLYING HEAD AND ALL, BUT YOU NEVER KNOW.
OH I KNOW THIS ISN'T GOING TO END WELL.
PLAYING HARD TO GET, EH?
VARTOX LIKES THAT IN A FEMALE.
UNFORTUNATELY VARTOX DOESN'T HAVE THE TIME FOR A LENGTHY COURTSHIP.
SEE? NOW HE'S SHOOTING AT US.
SHOULD I POINT OUT THE OBVIOUS METAPHOR OF THE GUN?
I'D RATHER YOU DIDN'T.

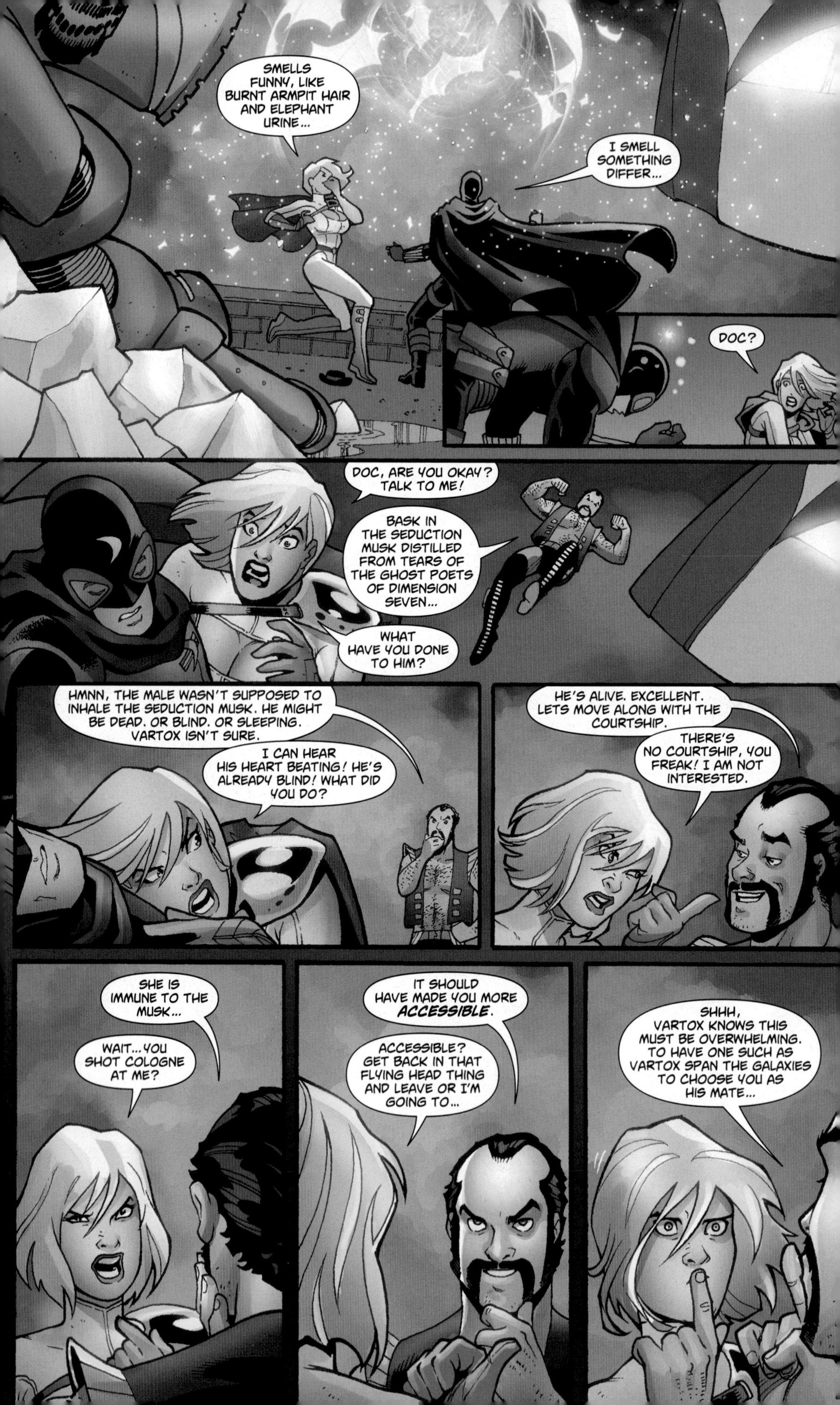
SMELLS FUNNY, LIKE BURNT ARMPIT HAIR AND ELEPHANT URINE...
I SMELL SOMETHING DIFFER...
DOC?
DOC, ARE YOU OKAY? TALK TO ME!
BASK IN THE SEDUCTION MUSK DISTILLED FROM TEARS OF THE GHOST POETS OF DIMENSION SEVEN...
WHAT HAVE YOU DONE TO HIM?
HMNN, THE MALE WASN'T SUPPOSED TO INHALE THE SEDUCTION MUSK. HE MIGHT BE DEAD. OR BLIND. OR SLEEPING. VARTOX ISN'T SURE.
I CAN HEAR HIS HEART BEATING! HE'S ALREADY BLIND! WHAT DID YOU DO?
HE'S ALIVE. EXCELLENT. LETS MOVE ALONG WITH THE COURTSHIP.
THERE'S NO COURTSHIP, YOU FREAK! I AM NOT INTERESTED.
SHE IS IMMUNE TO THE MUSK...
WAIT...YOU SHOT COLOGNE AT ME?
IT SHOULD HAVE MADE YOU MORE ***ACCESSIBLE***.
ACCESSIBLE? GET BACK IN THAT FLYING HEAD THING AND LEAVE OR I'M GOING TO...
SHHH, VARTOX KNOWS THIS MUST BE OVERWHELMING. TO HAVE ONE SUCH AS VARTOX SPAN THE GALAXIES TO CHOOSE YOU AS HIS MATE...

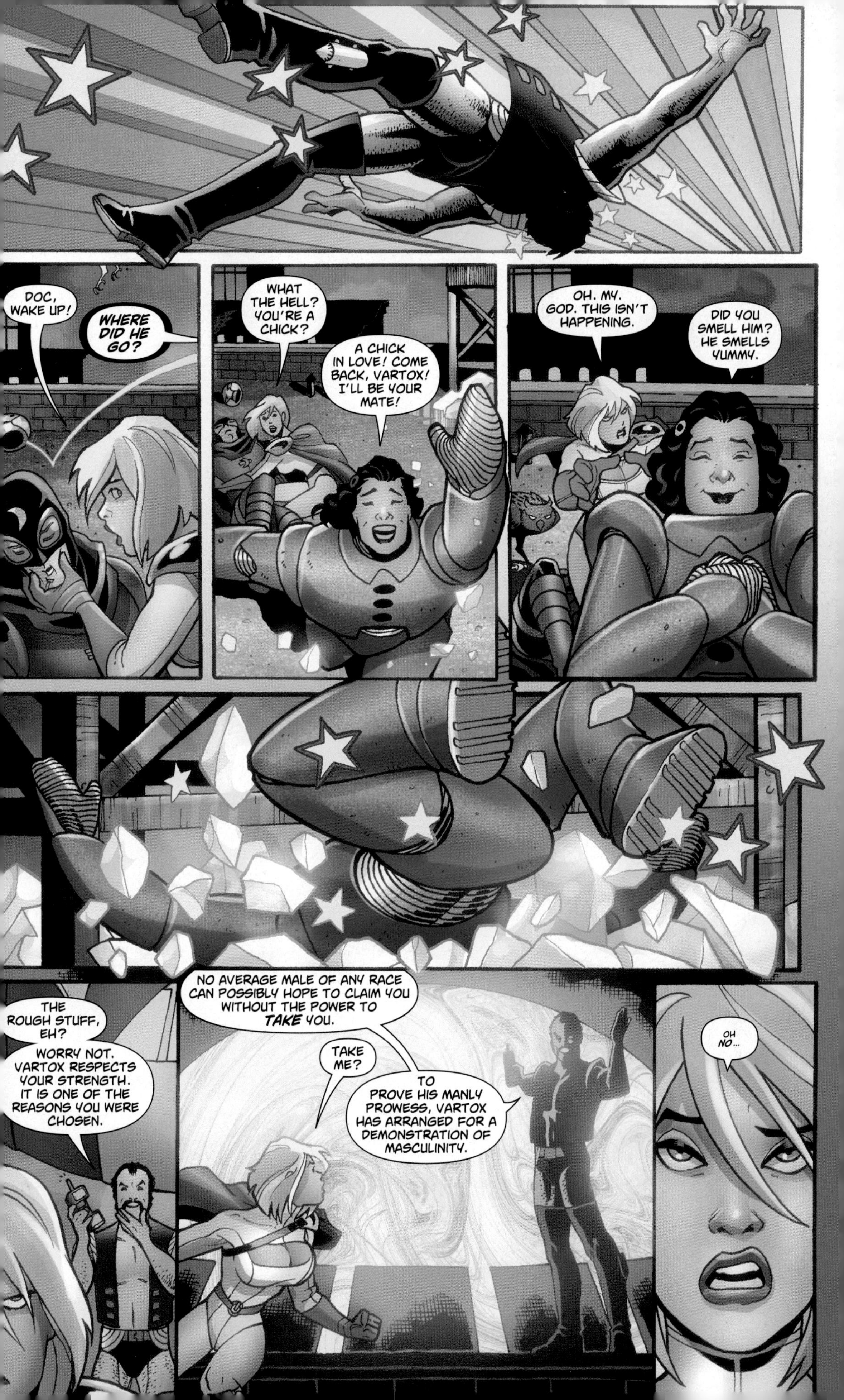
DOC, WAKE UP!
WHERE DID HE GO?
WHAT THE HELL? YOU'RE A CHICK?
A CHICK IN LOVE! COME BACK, VARTOX! I'LL BE YOUR MATE!
OH. MY. GOD. THIS ISN'T HAPPENING.
DID YOU SMELL HIM? HE SMELLS YUMMY.
THE ROUGH STUFF, EH?
WORRY NOT. VARTOX RESPECTS YOUR STRENGTH. IT IS ONE OF THE REASONS YOU WERE CHOSEN.
NO AVERAGE MALE OF ANY RACE CAN POSSIBLY HOPE TO CLAIM YOU WITHOUT THE POWER TO TAKE YOU.
TAKE ME?
TO PROVE HIS MANLY PROWESS, VARTOX HAS ARRANGED FOR A DEMONSTRATION OF MASCULINITY.
OH NO...

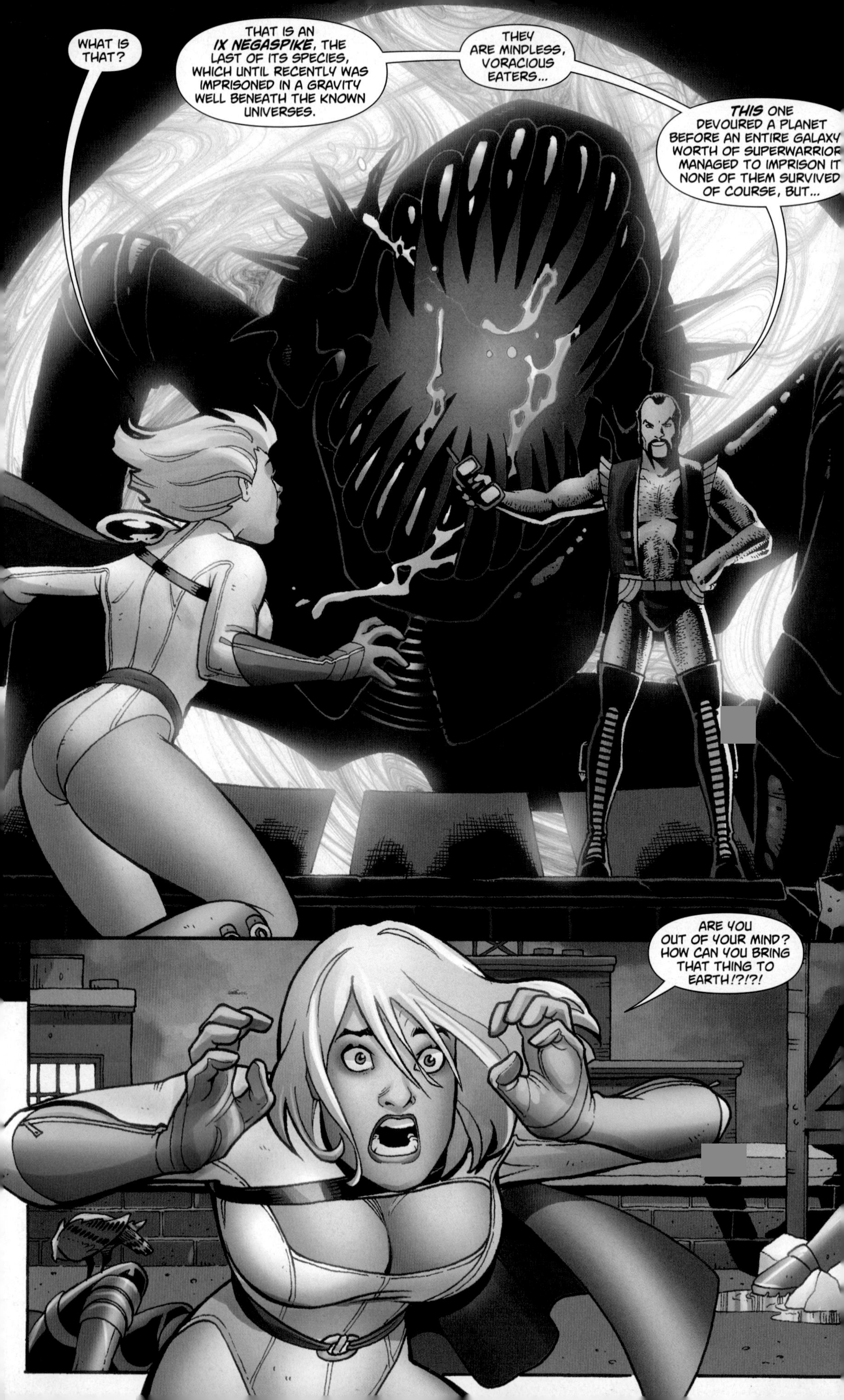
WHAT IS THAT?
THAT IS AN IX NEGASPIKE, THE LAST OF ITS SPECIES, WHICH UNTIL RECENTLY WAS IMPRISONED IN A GRAVITY WELL BENEATH THE KNOWN UNIVERSES.
THEY ARE MINDLESS, VORACIOUS EATERS...
THIS ONE DEVOURED A PLANET BEFORE AN ENTIRE GALAXY WORTH OF SUPERWARRIOR MANAGED TO IMPRISON IT NONE OF THEM SURVIVED OF COURSE, BUT...
ARE YOU OUT OF YOUR MIND? HOW CAN YOU BRING THAT THING TO EARTH!?!?!

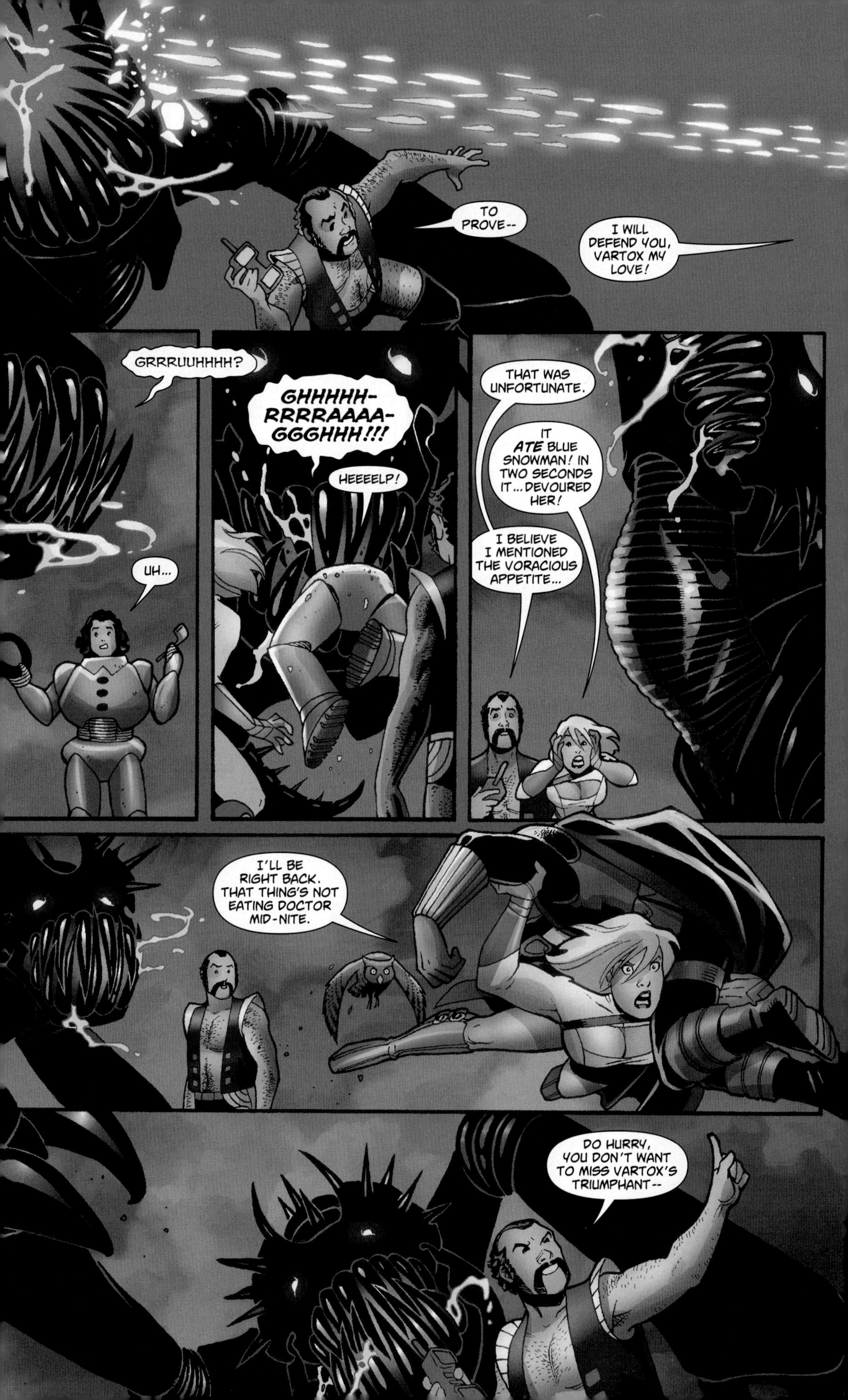
TO PROVE--
I WILL DEFEND YOU, VARTOX MY LOVE!
GRRRUUHHHH?
UH...
GHHHHH-RRRRAAAA-GGGHHH!!!
HEEEELP!
THAT WAS UNFORTUNATE.
IT ATE BLUE SNOWMAN! IN TWO SECONDS IT... DEVOURED HER!
I BELIEVE I MENTIONED THE VORACIOUS APPETITE...
I'LL BE RIGHT BACK. THAT THING'S NOT EATING DOCTOR MID-NITE.
DO HURRY, YOU DON'T WANT TO MISS VARTOX'S TRIUMPHANT--

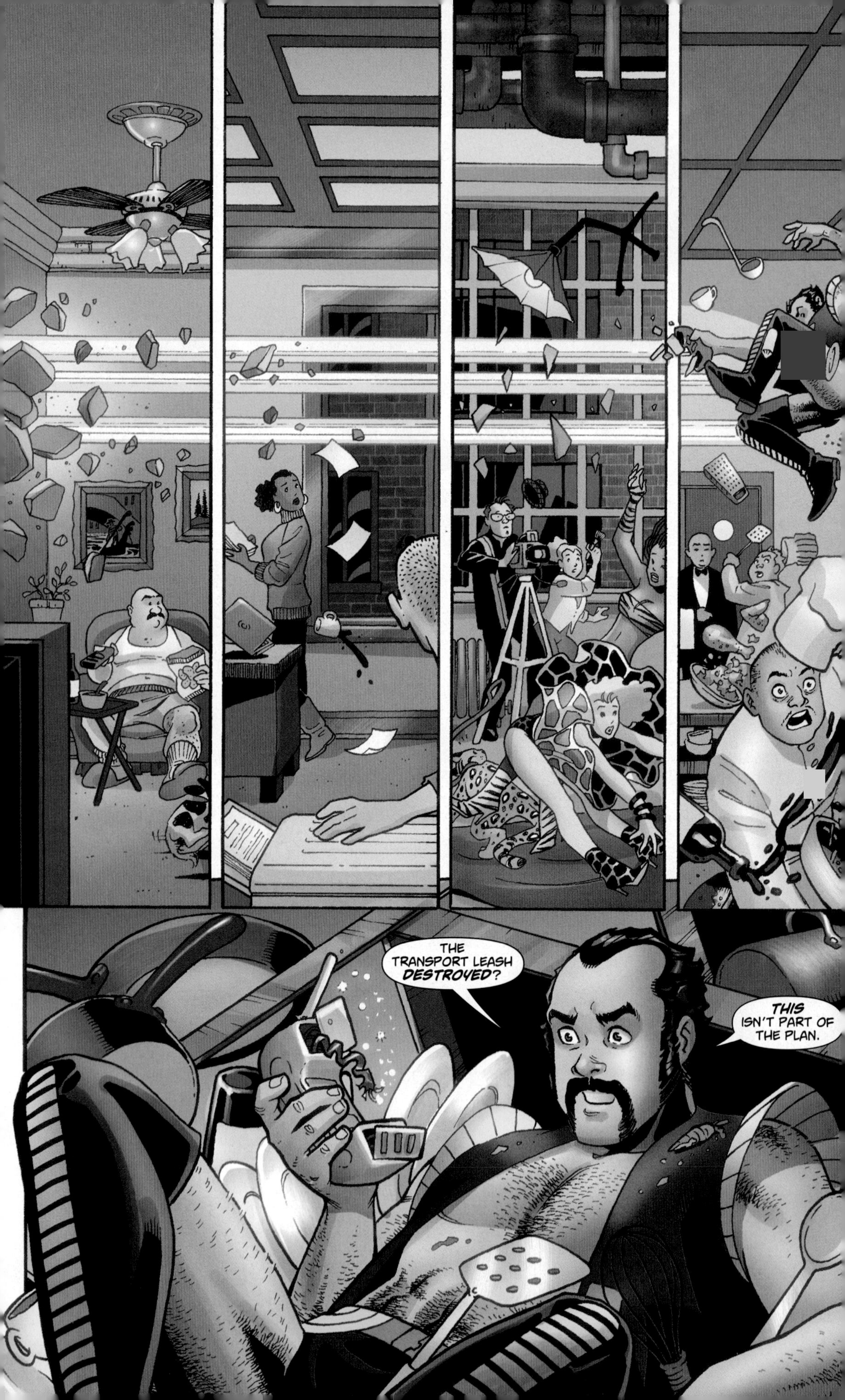
THE TRANSPORT LEASH DESTROYED?
THIS ISN'T PART OF THE PLAN.

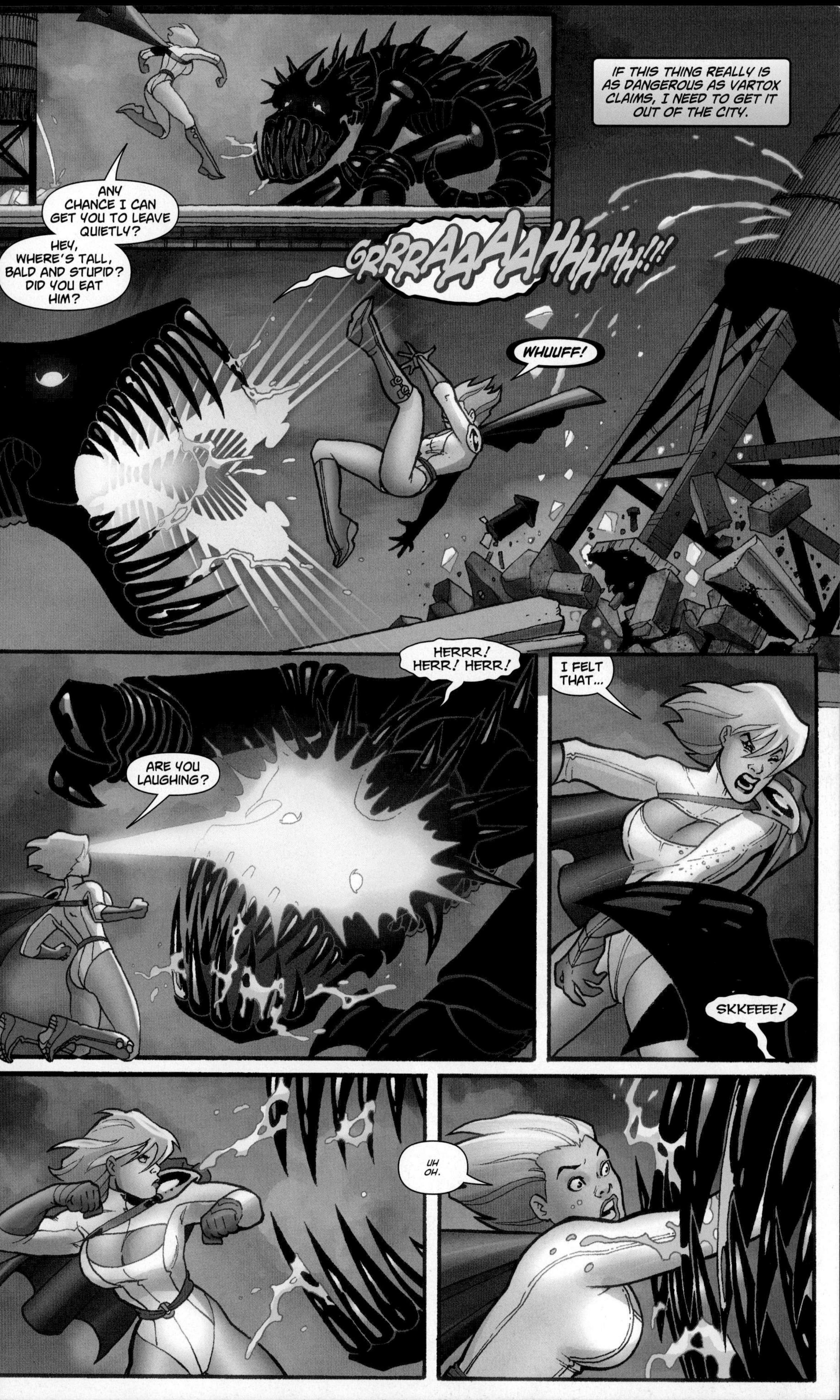
IF THIS THING REALLY IS AS DANGEROUS AS VARTOX CLAIMS, I NEED TO GET IT OUT OF THE CITY.
ANY CHANCE I CAN GET YOU TO LEAVE QUIETLY?
HEY, WHERE'S TALL, BALD AND STUPID? DID YOU EAT HIM?
GRRRAAAAAHHHHH!!!
WHUUFF!
HERRR! HERR! HERR!
ARE YOU LAUGHING?
I FELT THAT...
SKKEEEE!
UH OH.

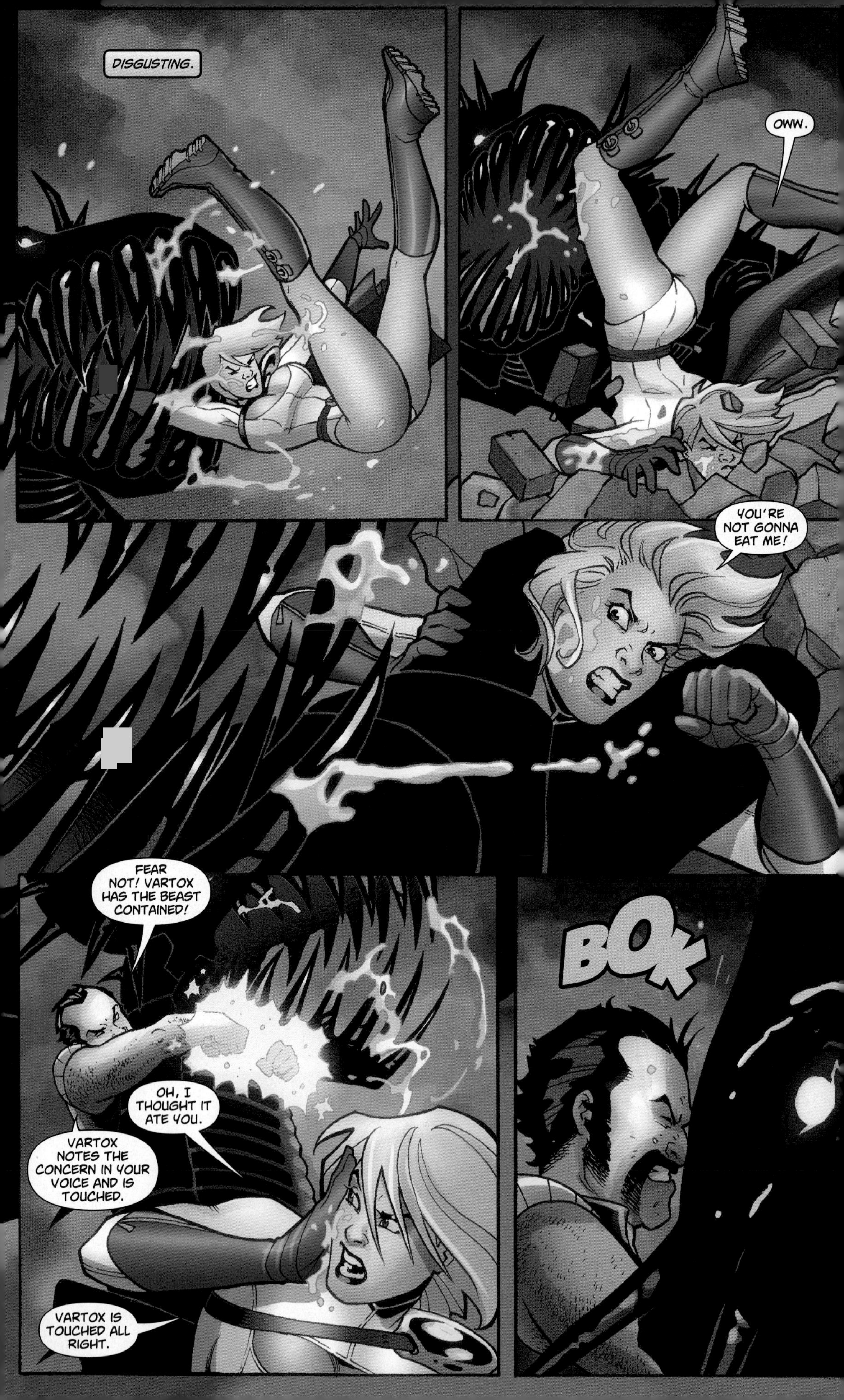
DISGUSTING.
OWW.
YOU'RE NOT GONNA EAT ME!
FEAR NOT! VARTOX HAS THE BEAST CONTAINED!
OH, I THOUGHT IT ATE YOU.
VARTOX NOTES THE CONCERN IN YOUR VOICE AND IS TOUCHED.
VARTOX IS TOUCHED ALL RIGHT.
BOK

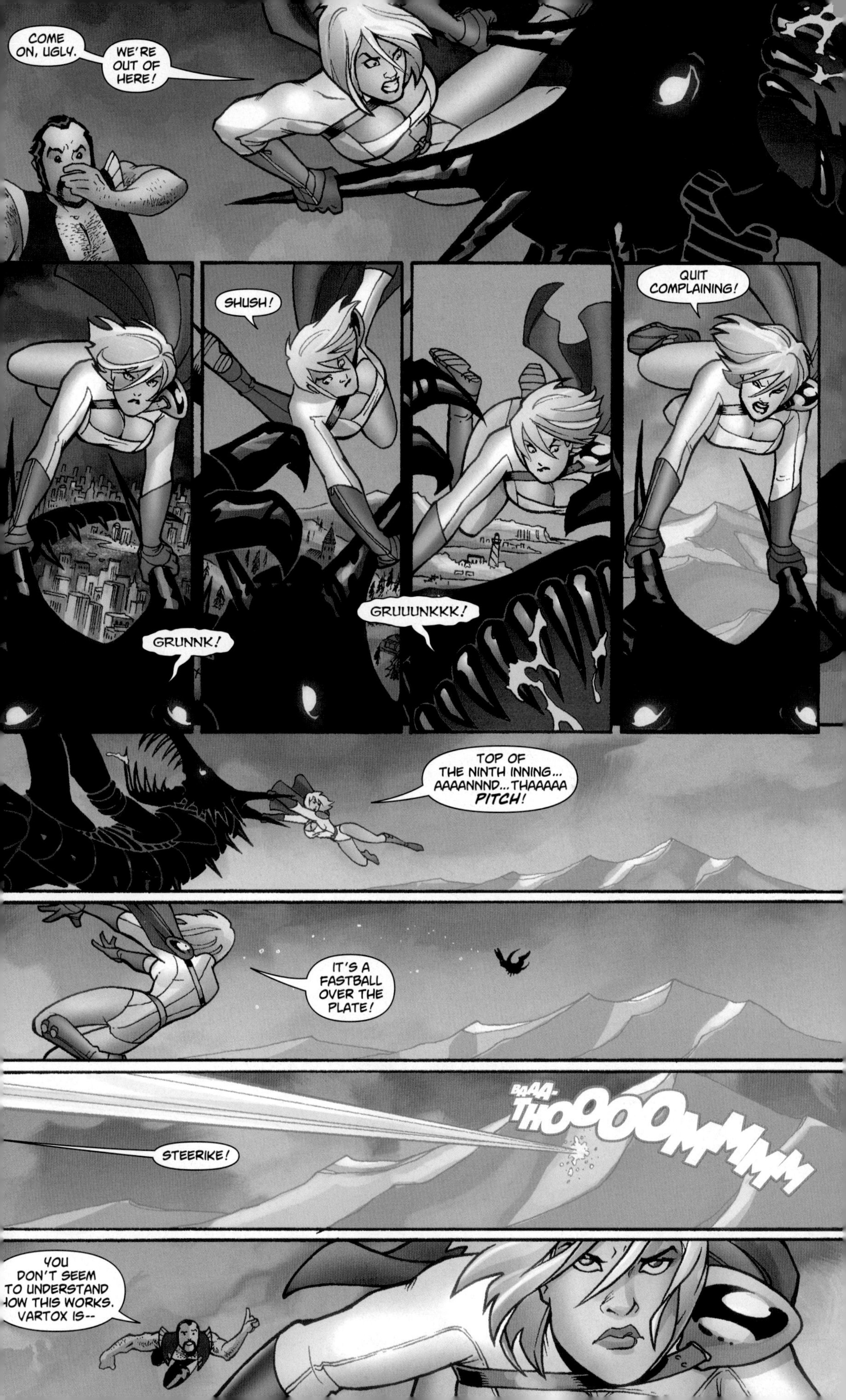
COME ON, UGLY.
WE'RE OUT OF HERE!
SHUSH!
GRUNNK!
GRUUUNKKK!
QUIT COMPLAINING!
TOP OF THE NINTH INNING... AAAANNND...THAAAAA PITCH!
IT'S A FASTBALL OVER THE PLATE!
BAAA-THOOOOOMMMMM
STEERIKE!
YOU DON'T SEEM TO UNDERSTAND HOW THIS WORKS. VARTOX IS--

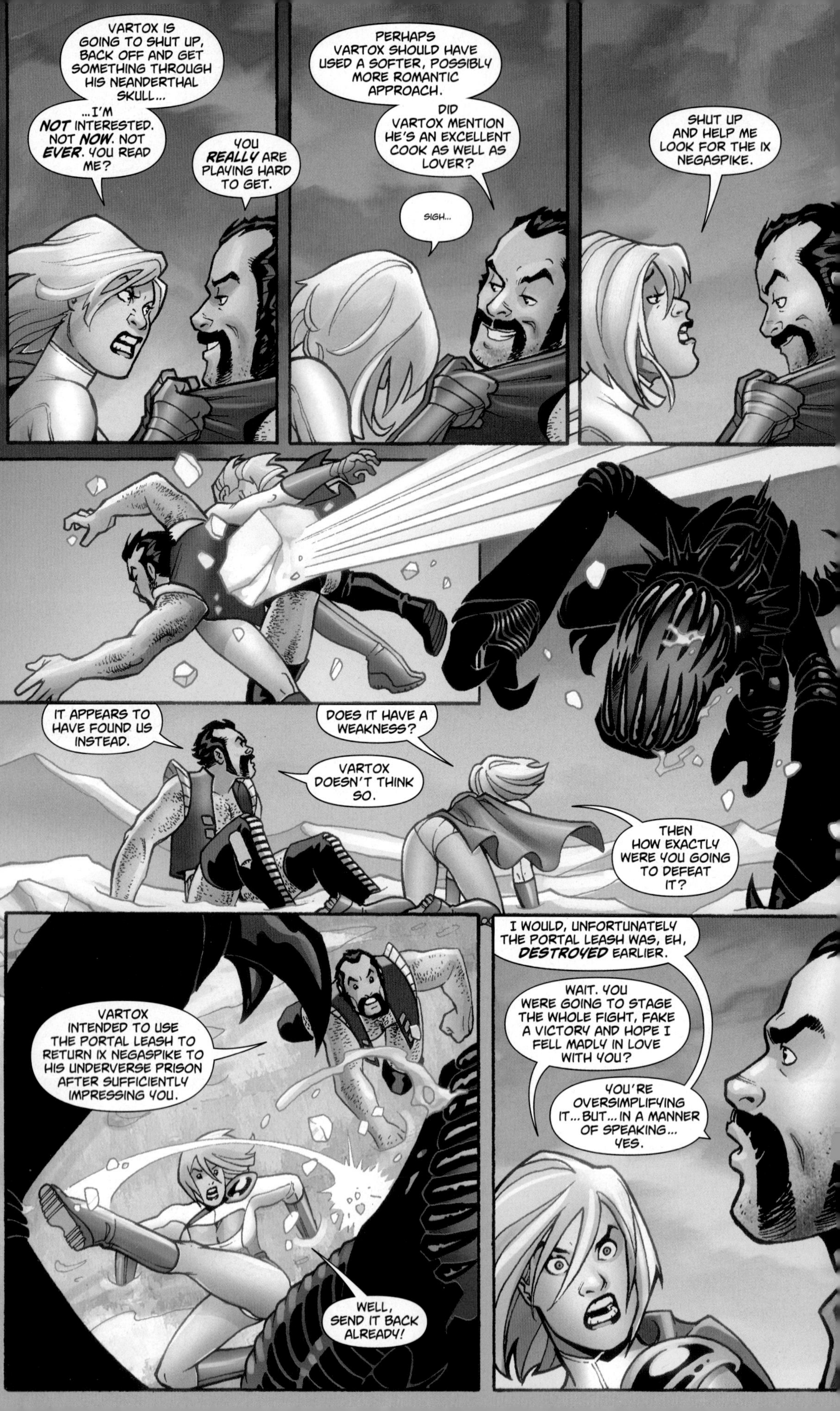
VARTOX IS GOING TO SHUT UP, BACK OFF AND GET SOMETHING THROUGH HIS NEANDERTHAL SKULL...
...I'M NOT INTERESTED. NOT NOW. NOT EVER. YOU READ ME?
YOU REALLY ARE PLAYING HARD TO GET.
PERHAPS VARTOX SHOULD HAVE USED A SOFTER, POSSIBLY MORE ROMANTIC APPROACH.
DID VARTOX MENTION HE'S AN EXCELLENT COOK AS WELL AS LOVER?
SIGH...
SHUT UP AND HELP ME LOOK FOR THE IX NEGASPIKE.
IT APPEARS TO HAVE FOUND US INSTEAD.
DOES IT HAVE A WEAKNESS?
VARTOX DOESN'T THINK SO.
THEN HOW EXACTLY WERE YOU GOING TO DEFEAT IT?
VARTOX INTENDED TO USE THE PORTAL LEASH TO RETURN IX NEGASPIKE TO HIS UNDERVERSE PRISON AFTER SUFFICIENTLY IMPRESSING YOU.
WELL, SEND IT BACK ALREADY!
I WOULD, UNFORTUNATELY THE PORTAL LEASH WAS, EH, DESTROYED EARLIER.
WAIT. YOU WERE GOING TO STAGE THE WHOLE FIGHT, FAKE A VICTORY AND HOPE I FELL MADLY IN LOVE WITH YOU?
YOU'RE OVERSIMPLIFYING IT...BUT...IN A MANNER OF SPEAKING... YES.

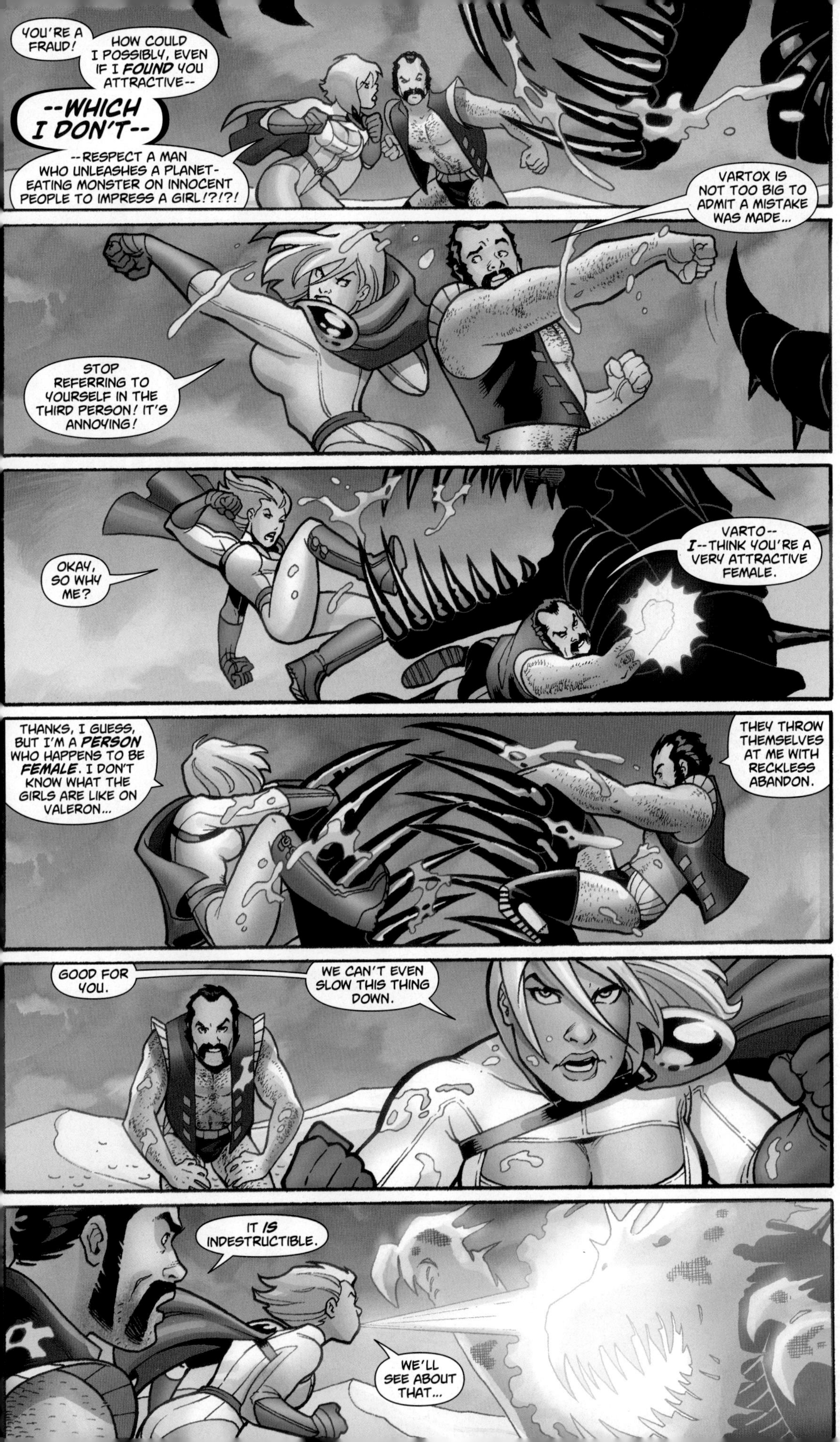
YOU'RE A FRAUD!
HOW COULD I POSSIBLY, EVEN IF I FOUND YOU ATTRACTIVE--
--WHICH I DON'T--
--RESPECT A MAN WHO UNLEASHES A PLANET-EATING MONSTER ON INNOCENT PEOPLE TO IMPRESS A GIRL!?!?!
VARTOX IS NOT TOO BIG TO ADMIT A MISTAKE WAS MADE...
STOP REFERRING TO YOURSELF IN THE THIRD PERSON! IT'S ANNOYING!
OKAY, SO WHY ME?
VARTO-- I--THINK YOU'RE A VERY ATTRACTIVE FEMALE.
THANKS, I GUESS, BUT I'M A PERSON WHO HAPPENS TO BE FEMALE. I DON'T KNOW WHAT THE GIRLS ARE LIKE ON VALERON...
THEY THROW THEMSELVES AT ME WITH RECKLESS ABANDON.
GOOD FOR YOU.
WE CAN'T EVEN SLOW THIS THING DOWN.
IT IS INDESTRUCTIBLE.
WE'LL SEE ABOUT THAT...

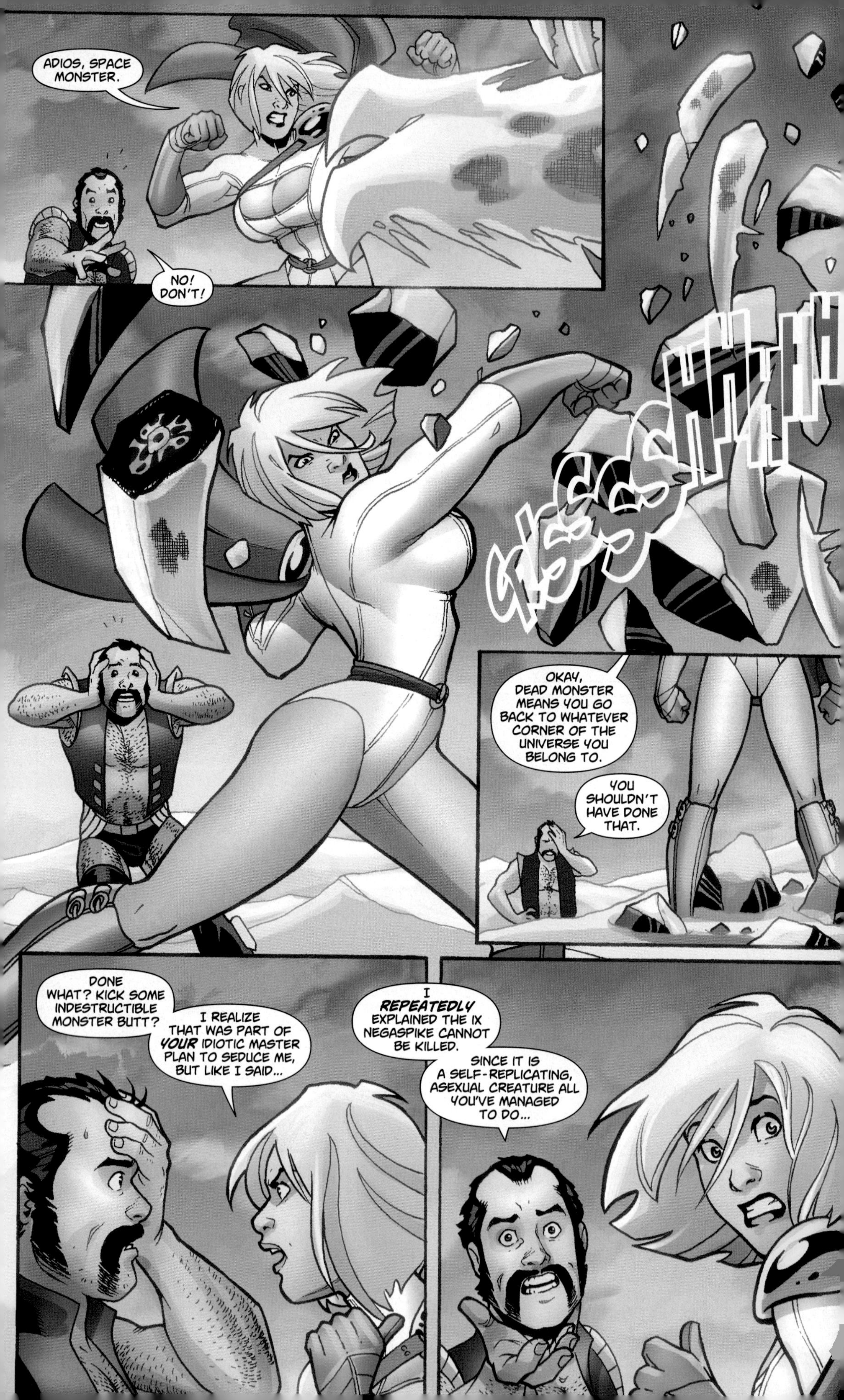
ADIOS, SPACE MONSTER.
NO! DON'T!
OKAY, DEAD MONSTER MEANS YOU GO BACK TO WHATEVER CORNER OF THE UNIVERSE YOU BELONG TO.
YOU SHOULDN'T HAVE DONE THAT.
DONE WHAT? KICK SOME INDESTRUCTIBLE MONSTER BUTT?
I REALIZE THAT WAS PART OF YOUR IDIOTIC MASTER PLAN TO SEDUCE ME, BUT LIKE I SAID...
I REPEATEDLY EXPLAINED THE IX NEGASPIKE CANNOT BE KILLED.
SINCE IT IS A SELF-REPLICATING, ASEXUAL CREATURE ALL YOU'VE MANAGED TO DO...

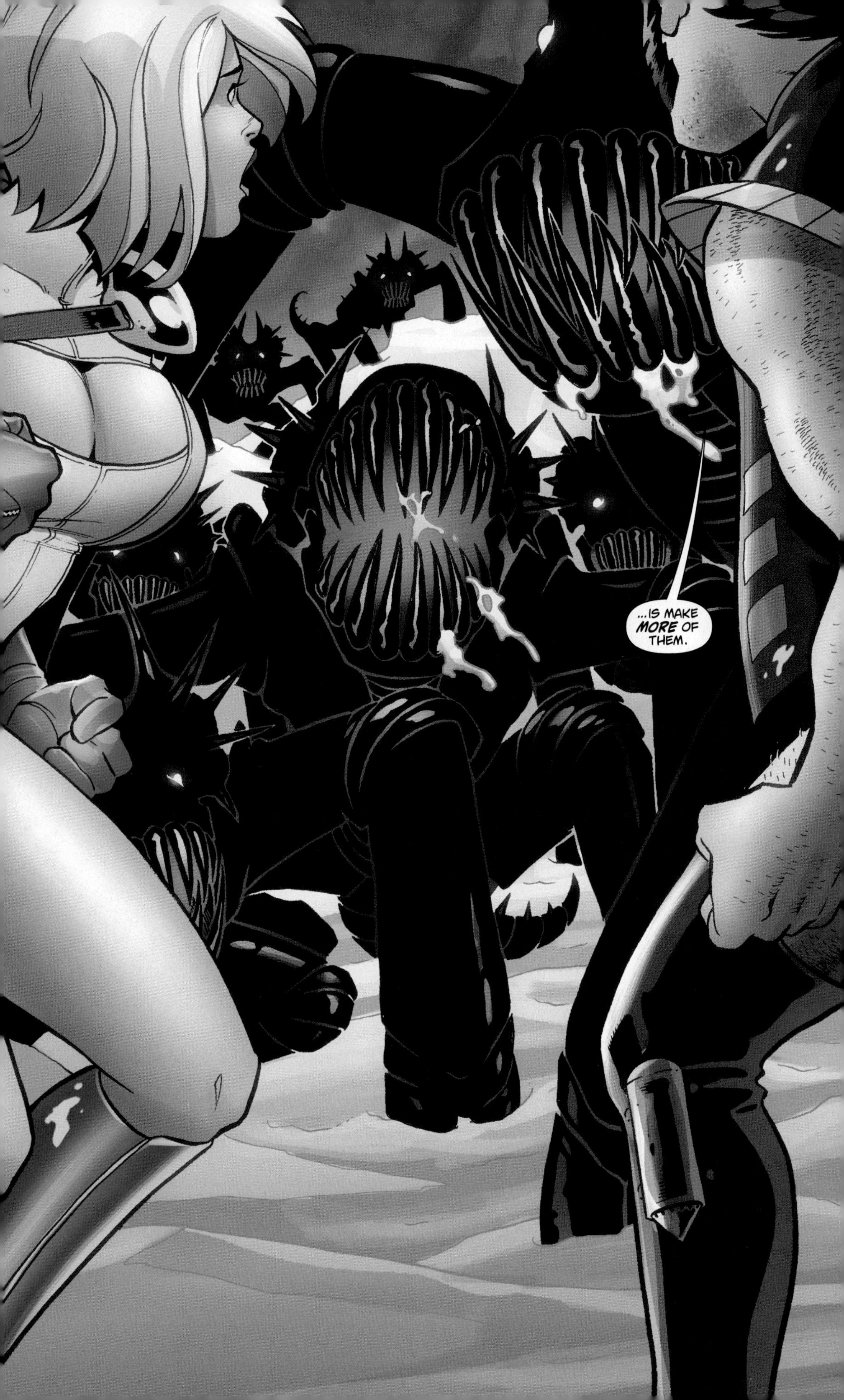
...IS MAKE MORE OF THEM.

A GROOVY KIND OF LOVE

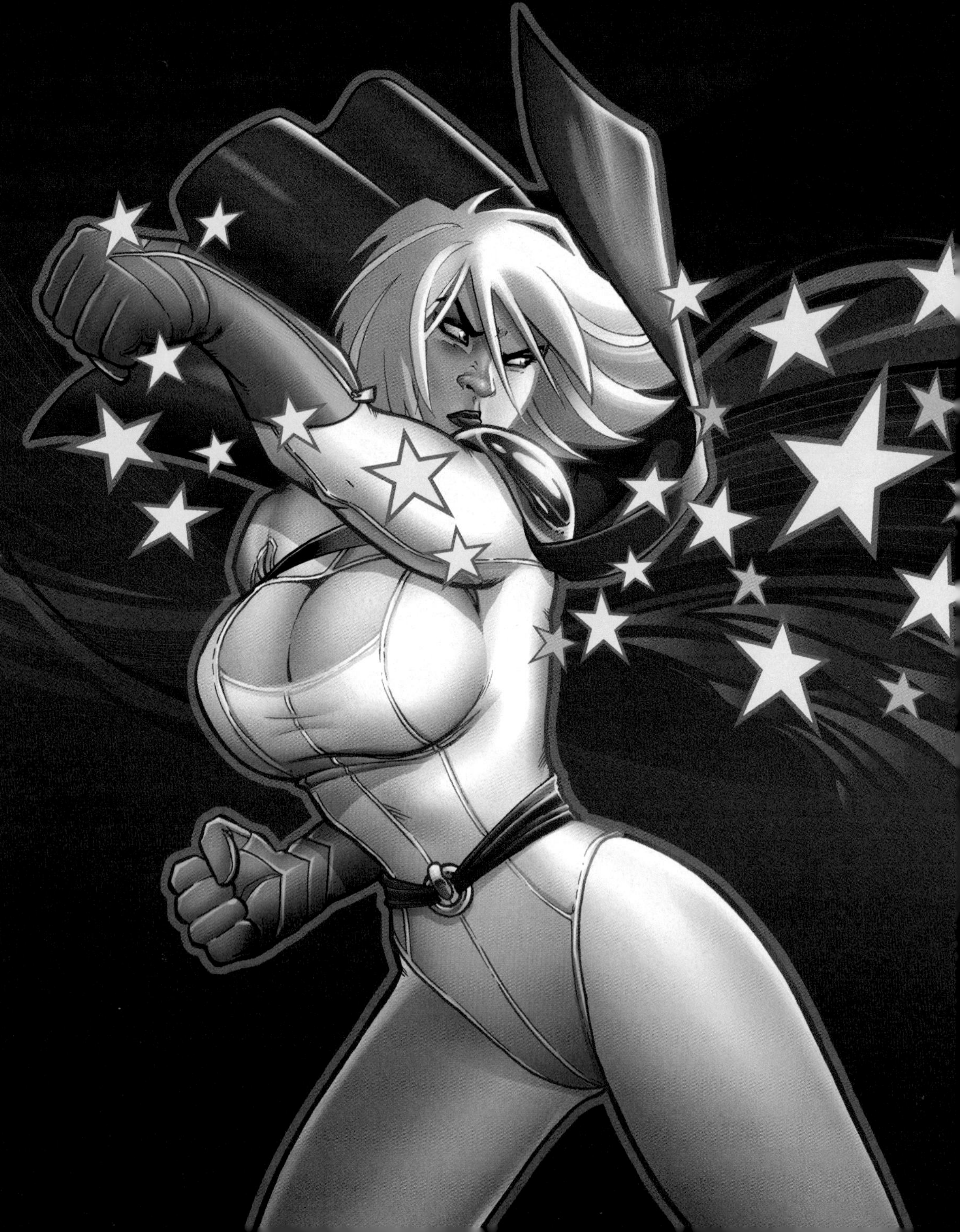

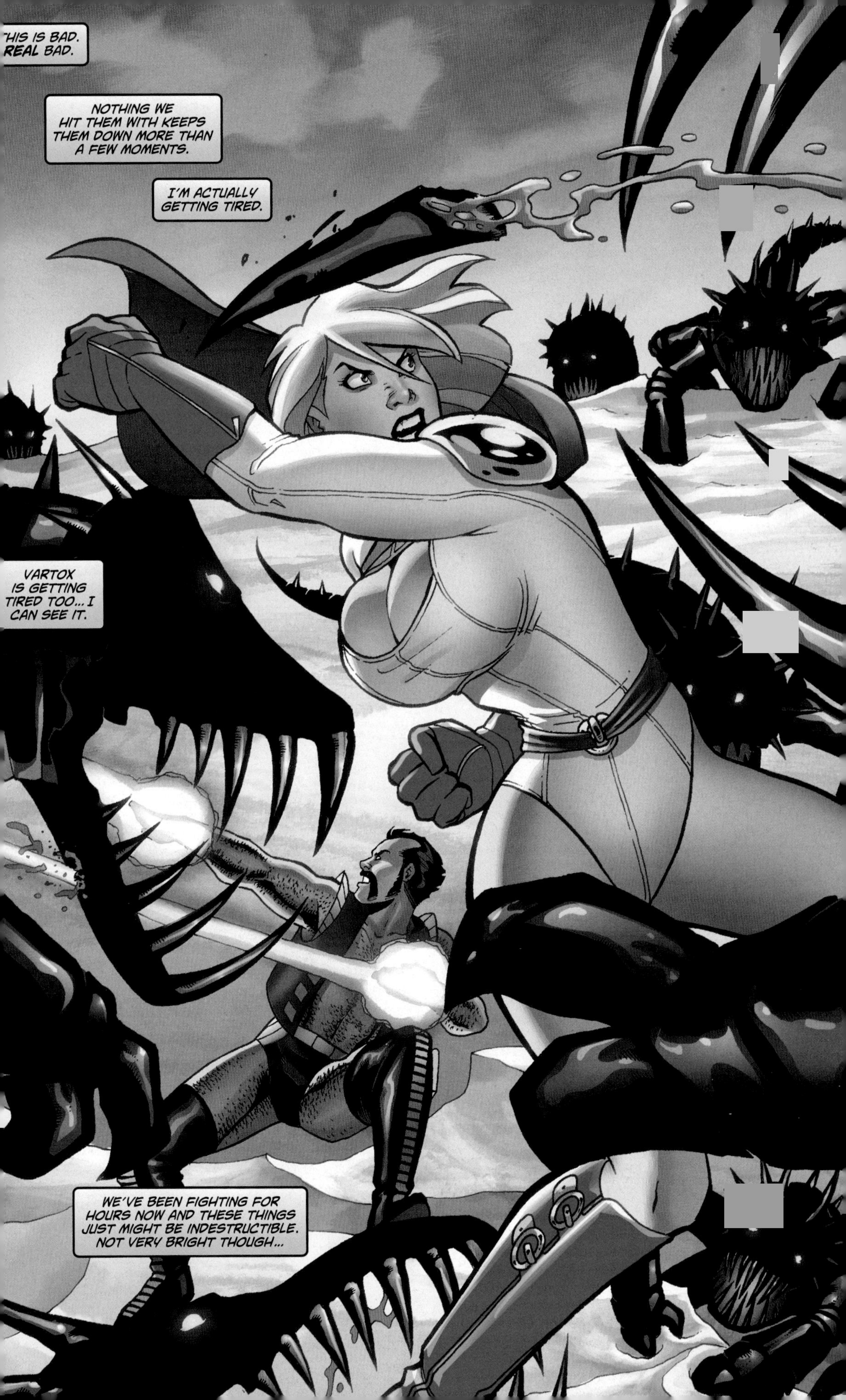
THIS IS BAD. REAL BAD.
NOTHING WE HIT THEM WITH KEEPS THEM DOWN MORE THAN A FEW MOMENTS.
I'M ACTUALLY GETTING TIRED.
VARTOX IS GETTING TIRED TOO... I CAN SEE IT.
WE'VE BEEN FIGHTING FOR HOURS NOW AND THESE THINGS JUST MIGHT BE INDESTRUCTIBLE. NOT VERY BRIGHT THOUGH...

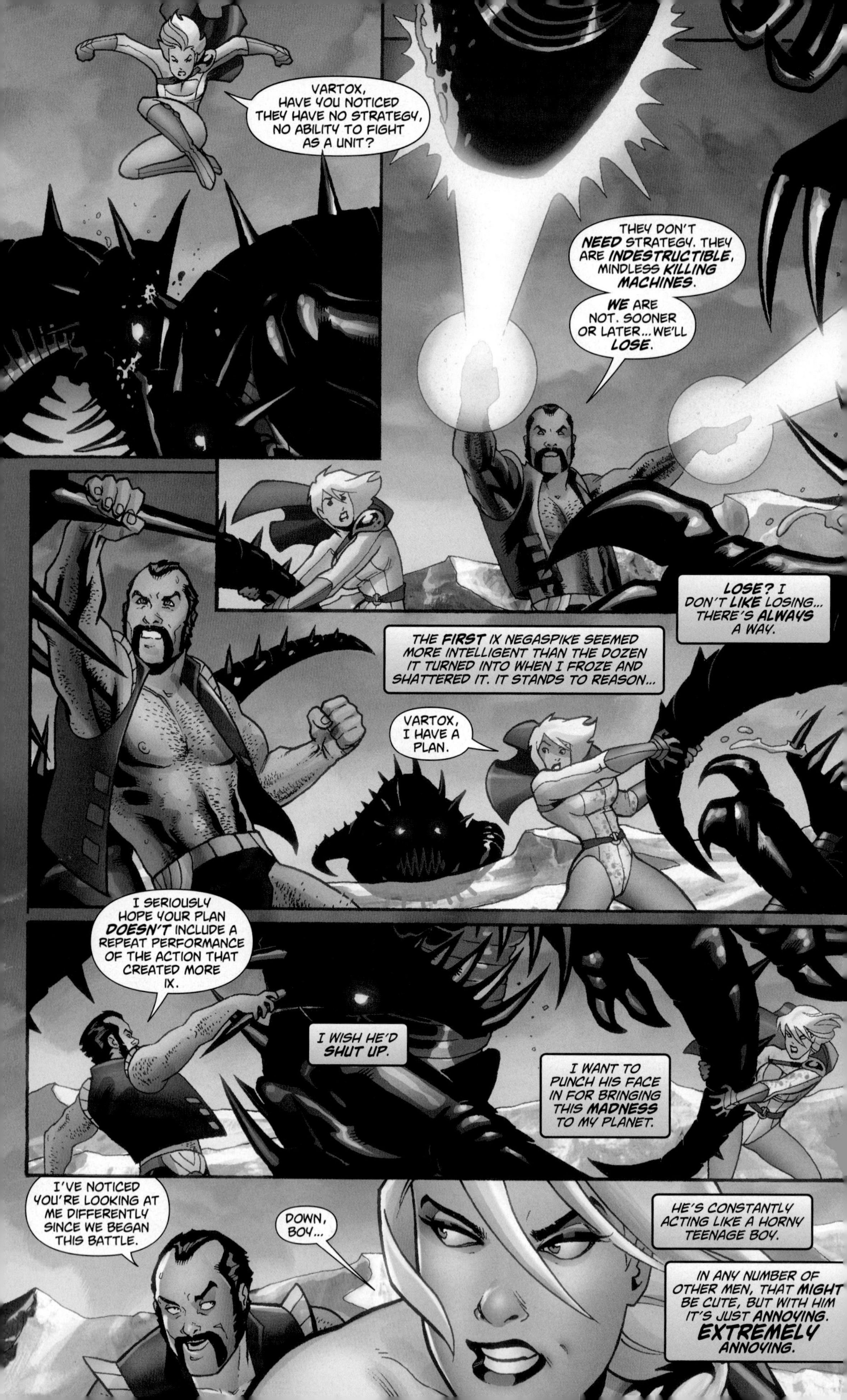

VARTOX, HAVE YOU NOTICED THEY HAVE NO STRATEGY, NO ABILITY TO FIGHT AS A UNIT?
THEY DON'T NEED STRATEGY. THEY ARE INDESTRUCTIBLE, MINDLESS KILLING MACHINES.
WE ARE NOT. SOONER OR LATER... WE'LL LOSE.
LOSE? I DON'T LIKE LOSING... THERE'S ALWAYS A WAY.
THE FIRST IX NEGASPIKE SEEMED MORE INTELLIGENT THAN THE DOZEN IT TURNED INTO WHEN I FROZE AND SHATTERED IT. IT STANDS TO REASON...
VARTOX, I HAVE A PLAN.
I SERIOUSLY HOPE YOUR PLAN DOESN'T INCLUDE A REPEAT PERFORMANCE OF THE ACTION THAT CREATED MORE IX.
I WISH HE'D SHUT UP.
I WANT TO PUNCH HIS FACE IN FOR BRINGING THIS MADNESS TO MY PLANET.
I'VE NOTICED YOU'RE LOOKING AT ME DIFFERENTLY SINCE WE BEGAN THIS BATTLE.
DOWN, BOY...
HE'S CONSTANTLY ACTING LIKE A HORNY TEENAGE BOY.
IN ANY NUMBER OF OTHER MEN, THAT MIGHT BE CUTE, BUT WITH HIM IT'S JUST ANNOYING. EXTREMELY ANNOYING.

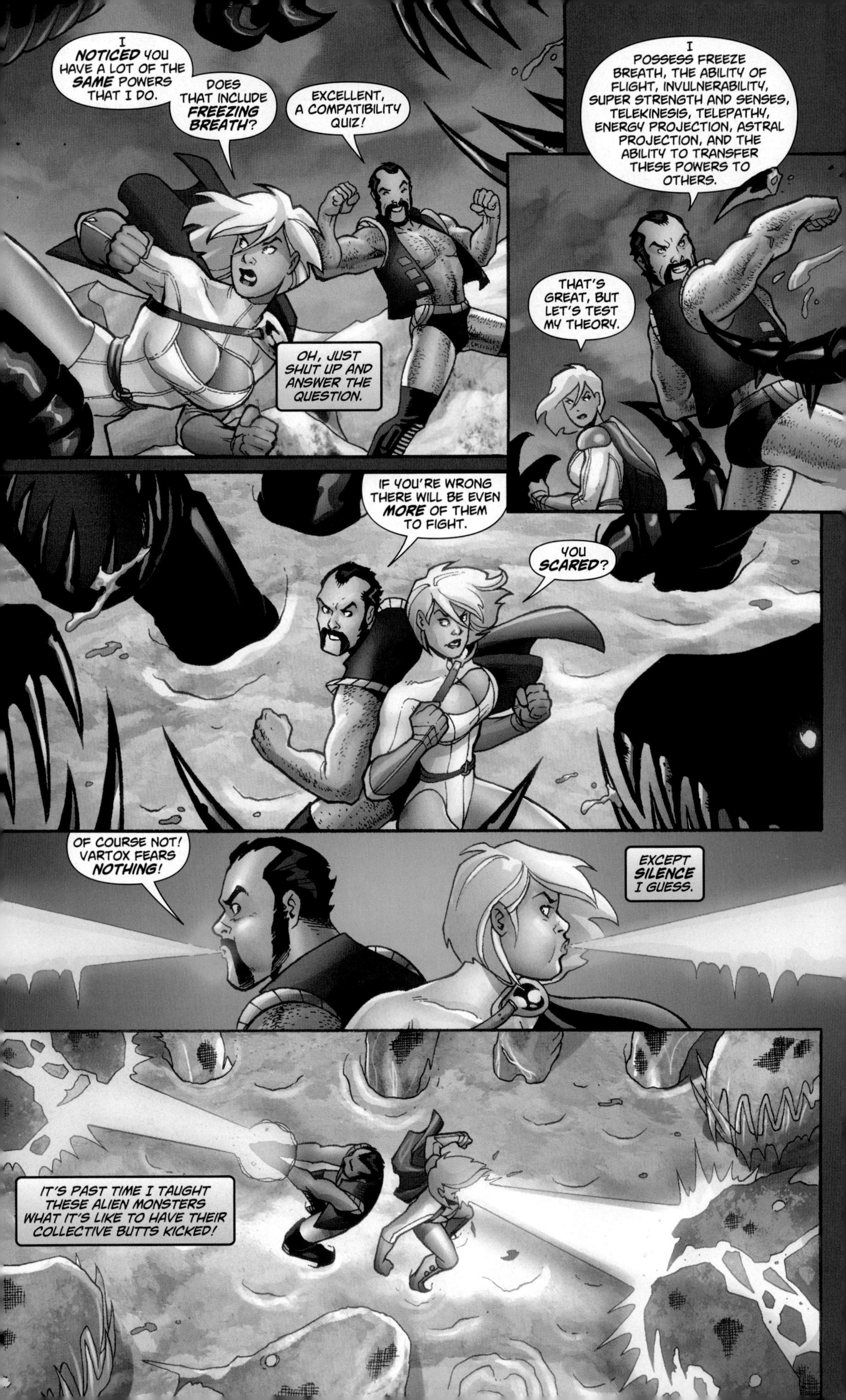

I NOTICED YOU HAVE A LOT OF THE SAME POWERS THAT I DO.
DOES THAT INCLUDE FREEZING BREATH?
EXCELLENT, A COMPATIBILITY QUIZ!
OH, JUST SHUT UP AND ANSWER THE QUESTION.
I POSSESS FREEZE BREATH, THE ABILITY OF FLIGHT, INVULNERABILITY, SUPER STRENGTH AND SENSES, TELEKINESIS, TELEPATHY, ENERGY PROJECTION, ASTRAL PROJECTION, AND THE ABILITY TO TRANSFER THESE POWERS TO OTHERS.
THAT'S GREAT, BUT LET'S TEST MY THEORY.
IF YOU'RE WRONG THERE WILL BE EVEN MORE OF THEM TO FIGHT.
YOU SCARED?
OF COURSE NOT! VARTOX FEARS NOTHING!
EXCEPT SILENCE I GUESS.
IT'S PAST TIME I TAUGHT THESE ALIEN MONSTERS WHAT IT'S LIKE TO HAVE THEIR COLLECTIVE BUTTS KICKED!

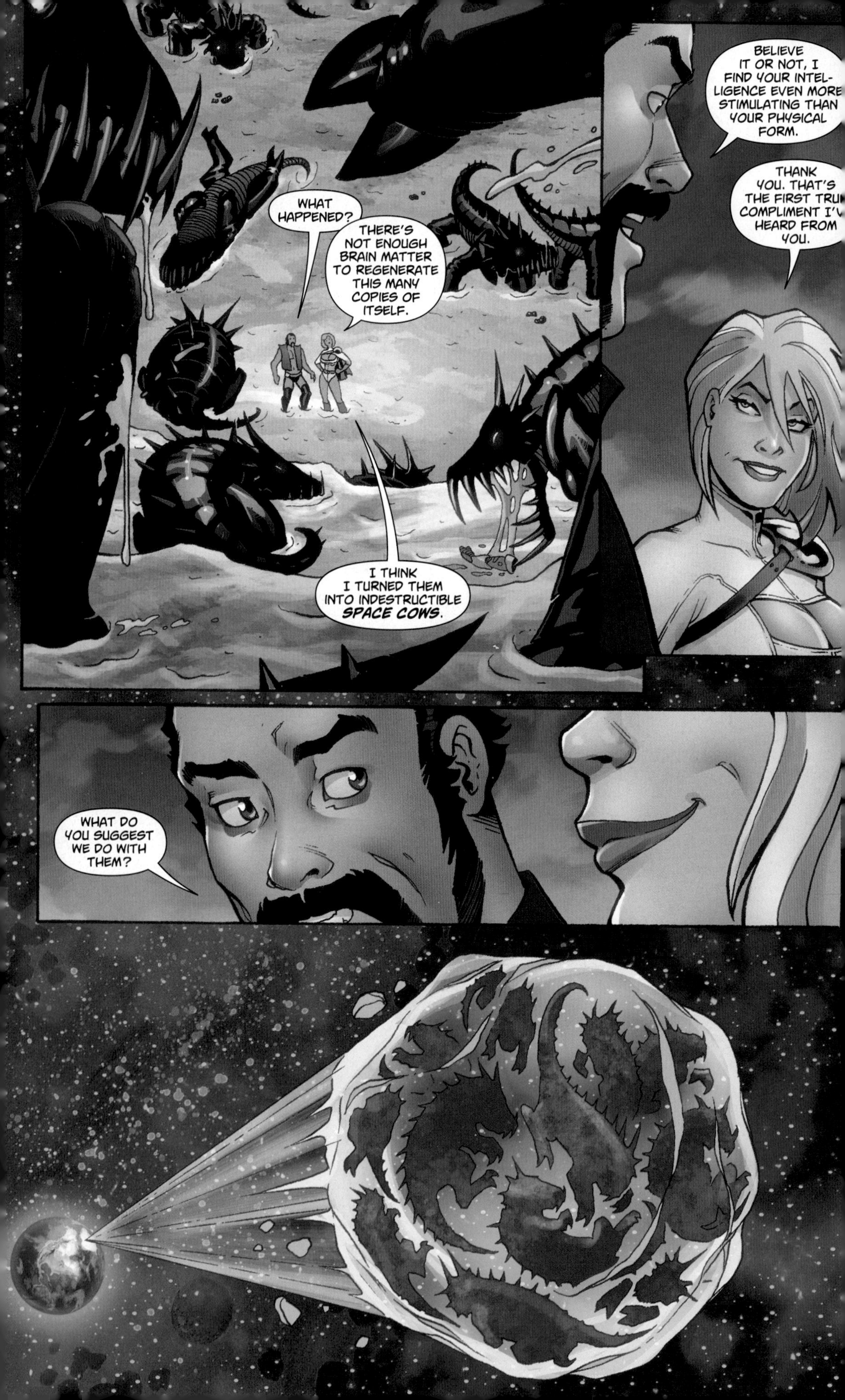
WHAT HAPPENED?
THERE'S NOT ENOUGH BRAIN MATTER TO REGENERATE THIS MANY COPIES OF ITSELF.
I THINK I TURNED THEM INTO INDESTRUCTIBLE ***SPACE COWS***.
BELIEVE IT OR NOT, I FIND YOUR INTEL-LIGENCE EVEN MORE STIMULATING THAN YOUR PHYSICAL FORM.
THANK YOU. THAT'S THE FIRST TRU COMPLIMENT I'V HEARD FROM YOU.
WHAT DO YOU SUGGEST WE DO WITH THEM?

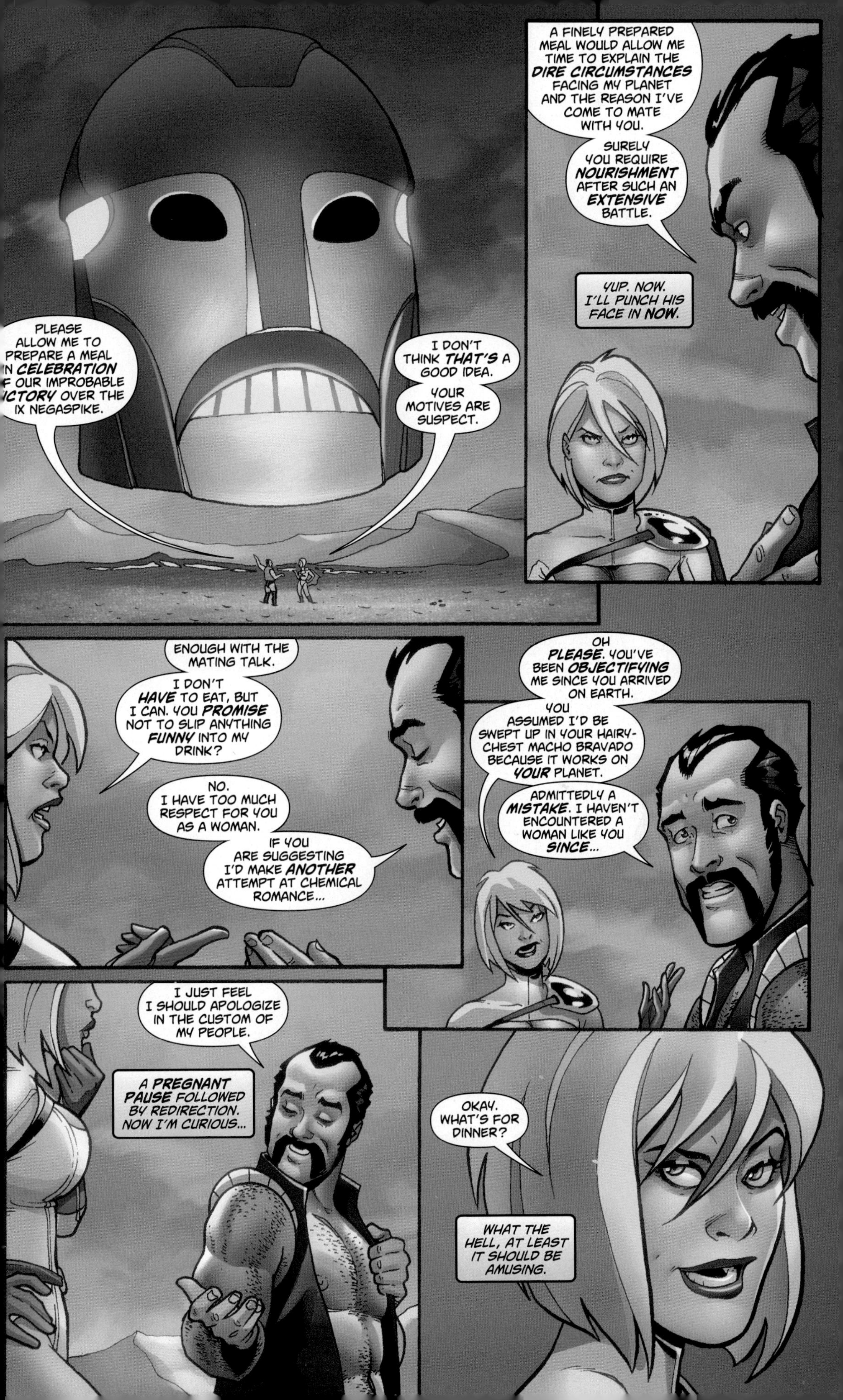

PLEASE ALLOW ME TO PREPARE A MEAL IN CELEBRATION OF OUR IMPROBABLE VICTORY OVER THE IX NEGASPIKE.
I DON'T THINK THAT'S A GOOD IDEA.
YOUR MOTIVES ARE SUSPECT.
A FINELY PREPARED MEAL WOULD ALLOW ME TIME TO EXPLAIN THE DIRE CIRCUMSTANCES FACING MY PLANET AND THE REASON I'VE COME TO MATE WITH YOU.
SURELY YOU REQUIRE NOURISHMENT AFTER SUCH AN EXTENSIVE BATTLE.
YUP. NOW. I'LL PUNCH HIS FACE IN NOW.
ENOUGH WITH THE MATING TALK.
I DON'T HAVE TO EAT, BUT I CAN. YOU PROMISE NOT TO SLIP ANYTHING FUNNY INTO MY DRINK?
NO. I HAVE TOO MUCH RESPECT FOR YOU AS A WOMAN.
IF YOU ARE SUGGESTING I'D MAKE ANOTHER ATTEMPT AT CHEMICAL ROMANCE...
OH PLEASE. YOU'VE BEEN OBJECTIFYING ME SINCE YOU ARRIVED ON EARTH.
YOU ASSUMED I'D BE SWEPT UP IN YOUR HAIRY-CHEST MACHO BRAVADO BECAUSE IT WORKS ON YOUR PLANET.
ADMITTEDLY A MISTAKE. I HAVEN'T ENCOUNTERED A WOMAN LIKE YOU SINCE...
I JUST FEEL I SHOULD APOLOGIZE IN THE CUSTOM OF MY PEOPLE.
A PREGNANT PAUSE FOLLOWED BY REDIRECTION. NOW I'M CURIOUS...
OKAY. WHAT'S FOR DINNER?
WHAT THE HELL, AT LEAST IT SHOULD BE AMUSING.

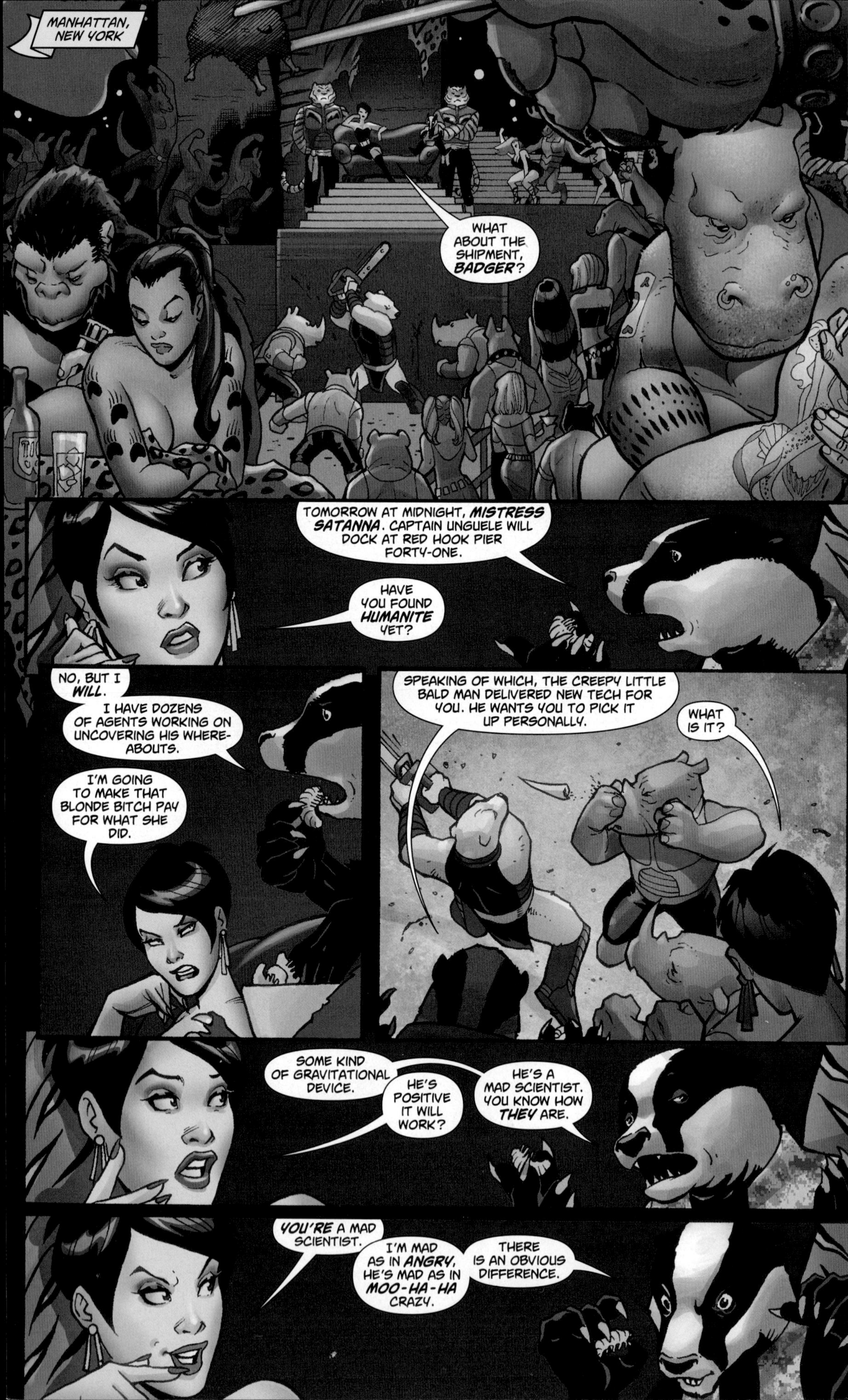
MANHATTAN, NEW YORK
WHAT ABOUT THE SHIPMENT, BADGER?
TOMORROW AT MIDNIGHT, MISTRESS SATANNA. CAPTAIN UNGUELE WILL DOCK AT RED HOOK PIER FORTY-ONE.
HAVE YOU FOUND HUMANITE YET?
NO, BUT I WILL.
I HAVE DOZENS OF AGENTS WORKING ON UNCOVERING HIS WHERE-ABOUTS.
I'M GOING TO MAKE THAT BLONDE BITCH PAY FOR WHAT SHE DID.
SPEAKING OF WHICH, THE CREEPY LITTLE BALD MAN DELIVERED NEW TECH FOR YOU. HE WANTS YOU TO PICK IT UP PERSONALLY.
WHAT IS IT?
SOME KIND OF GRAVITATIONAL DEVICE.
HE'S POSITIVE IT WILL WORK?
HE'S A MAD SCIENTIST. YOU KNOW HOW THEY ARE.
YOU'RE A MAD SCIENTIST.
I'M MAD AS IN ANGRY, HE'S MAD AS IN MOO-HA-HA CRAZY.
THERE IS AN OBVIOUS DIFFERENCE.

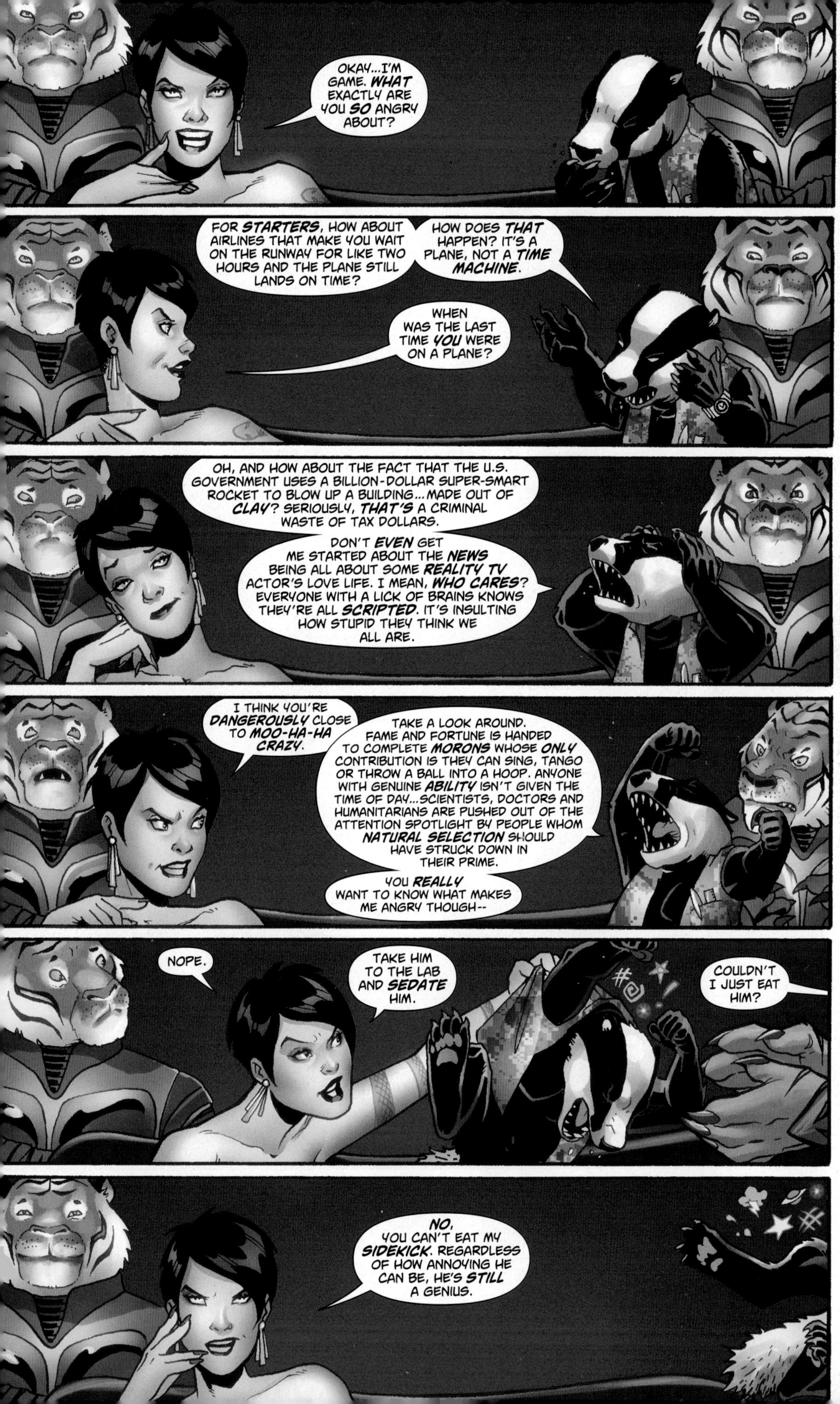
OKAY...I'M GAME. WHAT EXACTLY ARE YOU SO ANGRY ABOUT?
FOR STARTERS, HOW ABOUT AIRLINES THAT MAKE YOU WAIT ON THE RUNWAY FOR LIKE TWO HOURS AND THE PLANE STILL LANDS ON TIME?
HOW DOES THAT HAPPEN? IT'S A PLANE, NOT A TIME MACHINE.
WHEN WAS THE LAST TIME YOU WERE ON A PLANE?
OH, AND HOW ABOUT THE FACT THAT THE U.S. GOVERNMENT USES A BILLION-DOLLAR SUPER-SMART ROCKET TO BLOW UP A BUILDING... MADE OUT OF CLAY? SERIOUSLY, THAT'S A CRIMINAL WASTE OF TAX DOLLARS.
DON'T EVEN GET ME STARTED ABOUT THE NEWS BEING ALL ABOUT SOME REALITY TV ACTOR'S LOVE LIFE. I MEAN, WHO CARES? EVERYONE WITH A LICK OF BRAINS KNOWS THEY'RE ALL SCRIPTED. IT'S INSULTING HOW STUPID THEY THINK WE ALL ARE.
I THINK YOU'RE DANGEROUSLY CLOSE TO MOO-HA-HA CRAZY.
TAKE A LOOK AROUND. FAME AND FORTUNE IS HANDED TO COMPLETE MORONS WHOSE ONLY CONTRIBUTION IS THEY CAN SING, TANGO OR THROW A BALL INTO A HOOP. ANYONE WITH GENUINE ABILITY ISN'T GIVEN THE TIME OF DAY...SCIENTISTS, DOCTORS AND HUMANITARIANS ARE PUSHED OUT OF THE ATTENTION SPOTLIGHT BY PEOPLE WHOM NATURAL SELECTION SHOULD HAVE STRUCK DOWN IN THEIR PRIME.
YOU REALLY WANT TO KNOW WHAT MAKES ME ANGRY THOUGH--
NOPE.
TAKE HIM TO THE LAB AND SEDATE HIM.
COULDN'T I JUST EAT HIM?
NO, YOU CAN'T EAT MY SIDEKICK. REGARDLESS OF HOW ANNOYING HE CAN BE, HE'S STILL A GENIUS.

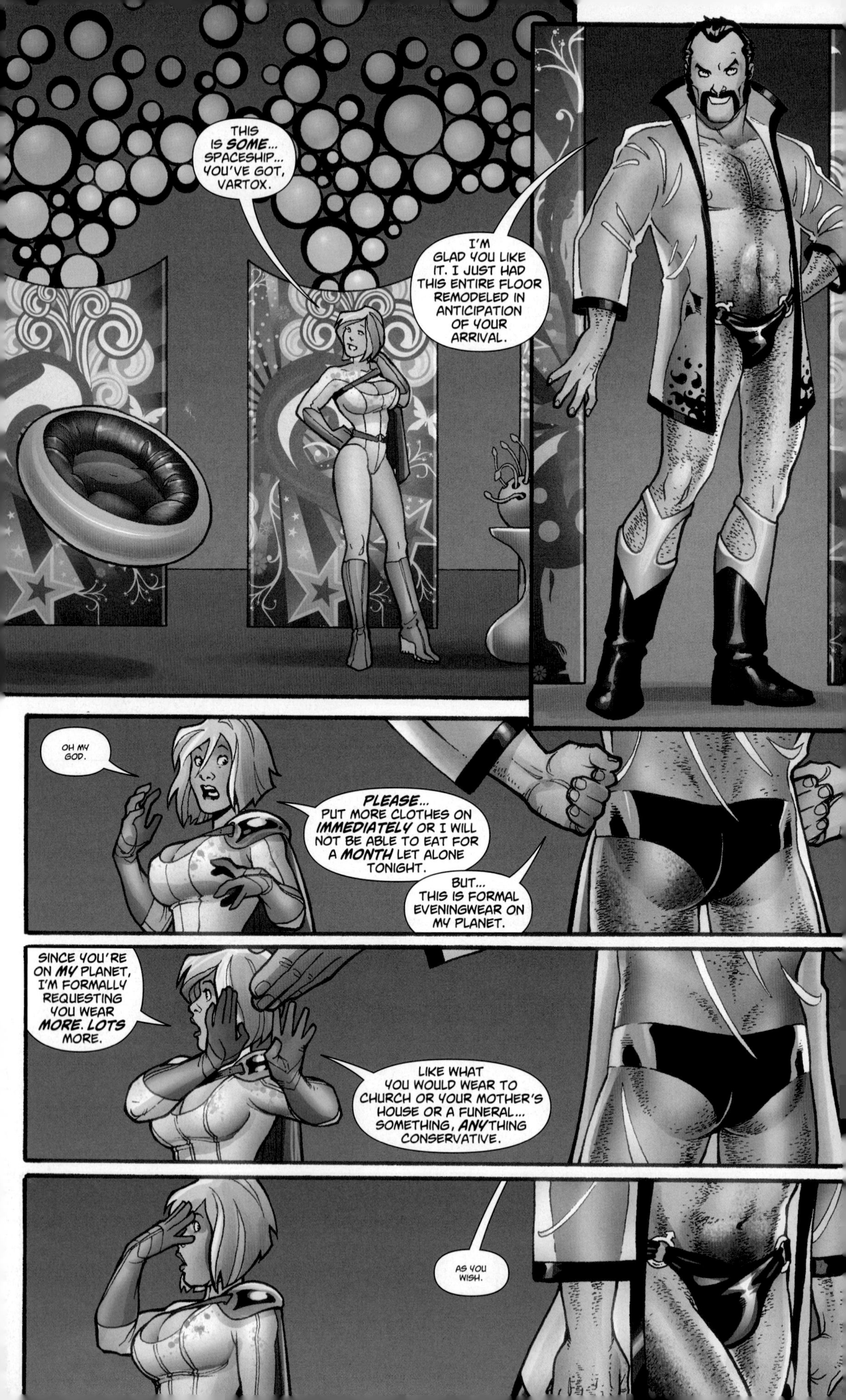
THIS IS SOME... SPACESHIP... YOU'VE GOT, VARTOX.
I'M GLAD YOU LIKE IT. I JUST HAD THIS ENTIRE FLOOR REMODELED IN ANTICIPATION OF YOUR ARRIVAL.
OH MY GOD.
PLEASE... PUT MORE CLOTHES ON IMMEDIATELY OR I WILL NOT BE ABLE TO EAT FOR A MONTH LET ALONE TONIGHT.
BUT... THIS IS FORMAL EVENINGWEAR ON MY PLANET.
SINCE YOU'RE ON MY PLANET, I'M FORMALLY REQUESTING YOU WEAR MORE. LOTS MORE.
LIKE WHAT YOU WOULD WEAR TO CHURCH OR YOUR MOTHER'S HOUSE OR A FUNERAL... SOMETHING, ANYTHING CONSERVATIVE.
AS YOU WISH.

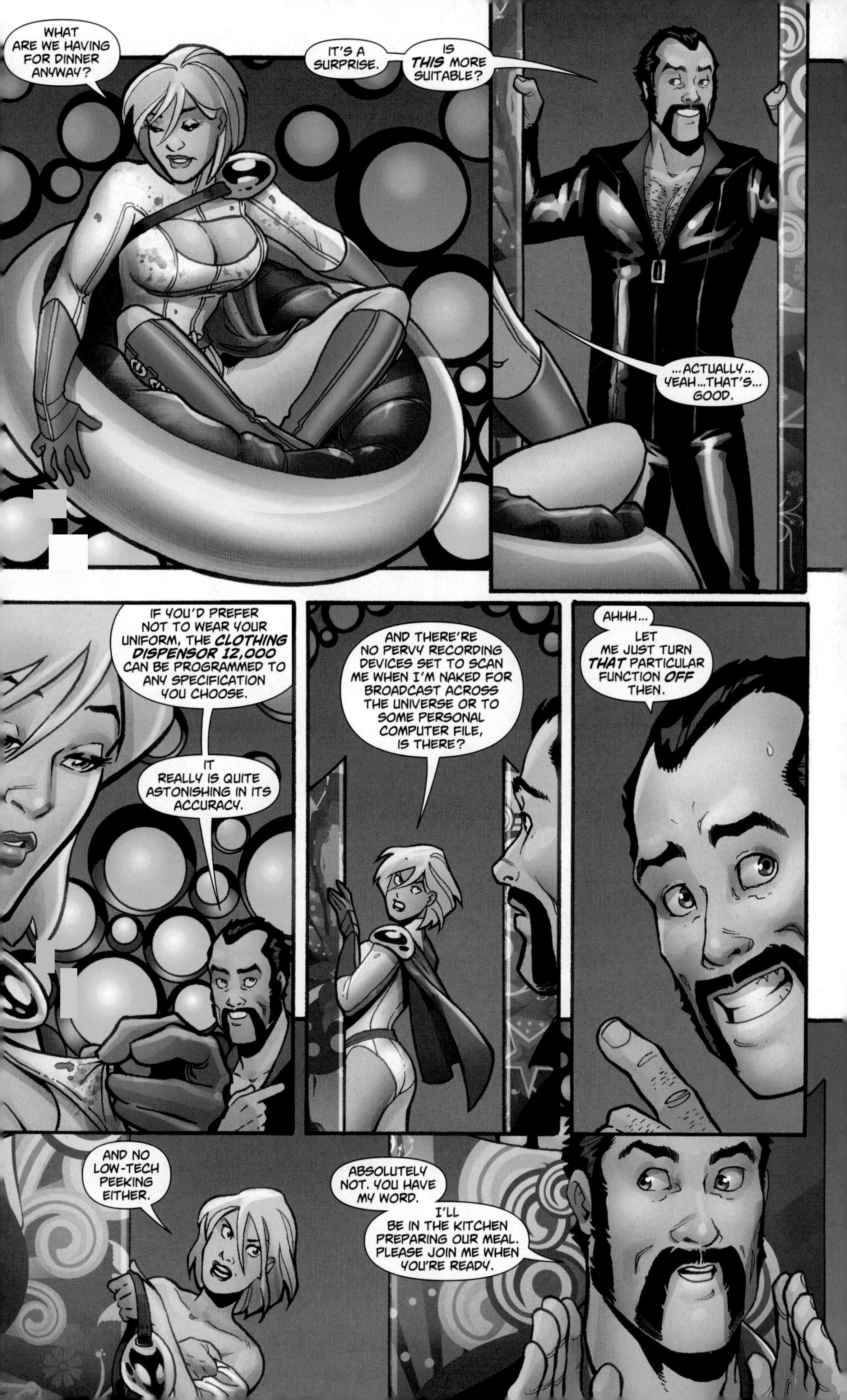
WHAT ARE WE HAVING FOR DINNER ANYWAY?
IT'S A SURPRISE.
IS THIS MORE SUITABLE?
...ACTUALLY... YEAH...THAT'S... GOOD.
IF YOU'D PREFER NOT TO WEAR YOUR UNIFORM, THE CLOTHING DISPENSOR 12,000 CAN BE PROGRAMMED TO ANY SPECIFICATION YOU CHOOSE.
IT REALLY IS QUITE ASTONISHING IN ITS ACCURACY.
AND THERE'RE NO PERVY RECORDING DEVICES SET TO SCAN ME WHEN I'M NAKED FOR BROADCAST ACROSS THE UNIVERSE OR TO SOME PERSONAL COMPUTER FILE, IS THERE?
AHHH...
LET ME JUST TURN THAT PARTICULAR FUNCTION OFF THEN.
AND NO LOW-TECH PEEKING EITHER.
ABSOLUTELY NOT. YOU HAVE MY WORD.
I'LL BE IN THE KITCHEN PREPARING OUR MEAL. PLEASE JOIN ME WHEN YOU'RE READY.

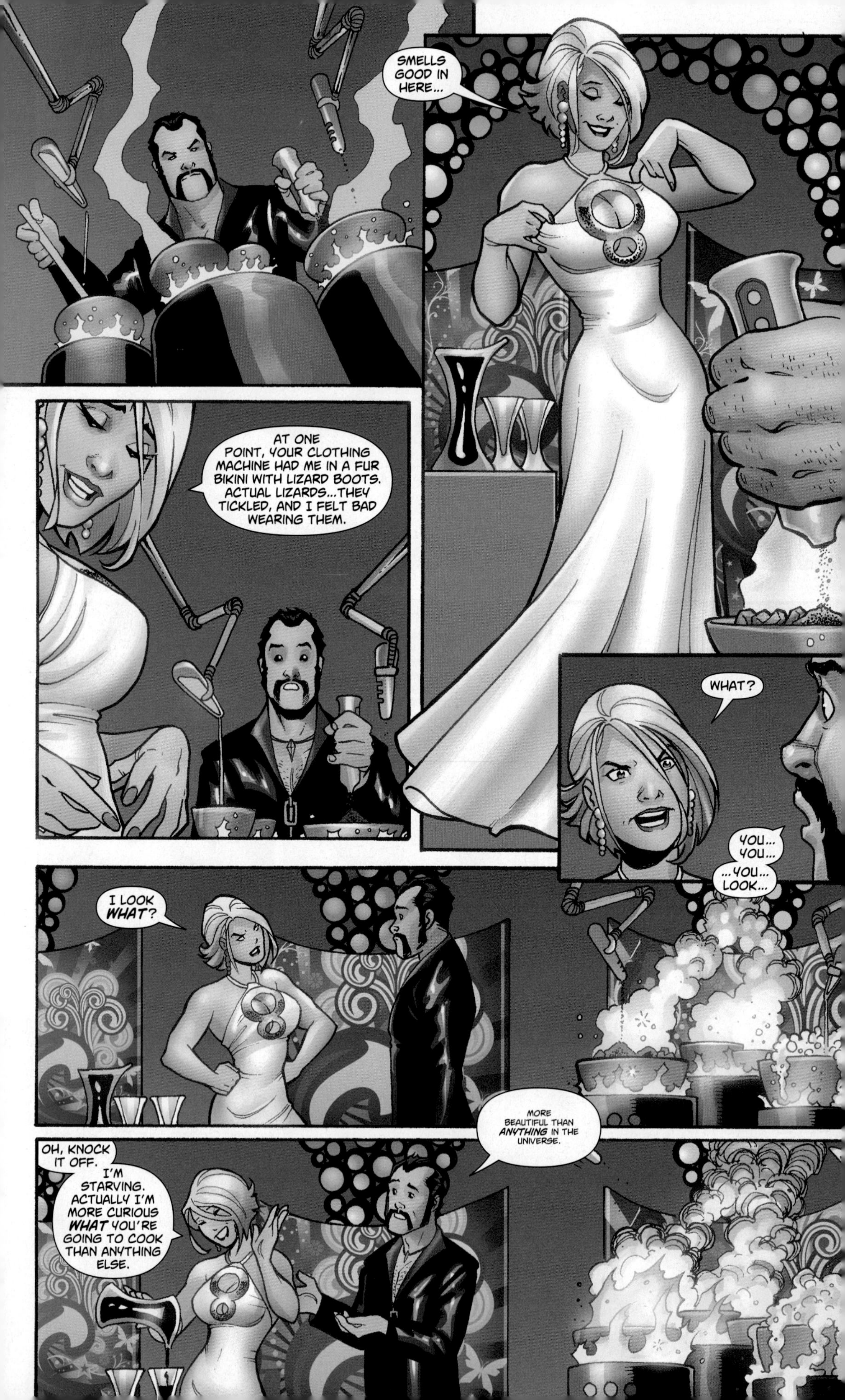
SMELLS GOOD IN HERE...
AT ONE POINT, YOUR CLOTHING MACHINE HAD ME IN A FUR BIKINI WITH LIZARD BOOTS. ACTUAL LIZARDS...THEY TICKLED, AND I FELT BAD WEARING THEM.
WHAT?
YOU... YOU... ...YOU... LOOK...
I LOOK WHAT?
MORE BEAUTIFUL THAN ANYTHING IN THE UNIVERSE.
OH, KNOCK IT OFF.
I'M STARVING. ACTUALLY I'M MORE CURIOUS WHAT YOU'RE GOING TO COOK THAN ANYTHING ELSE.

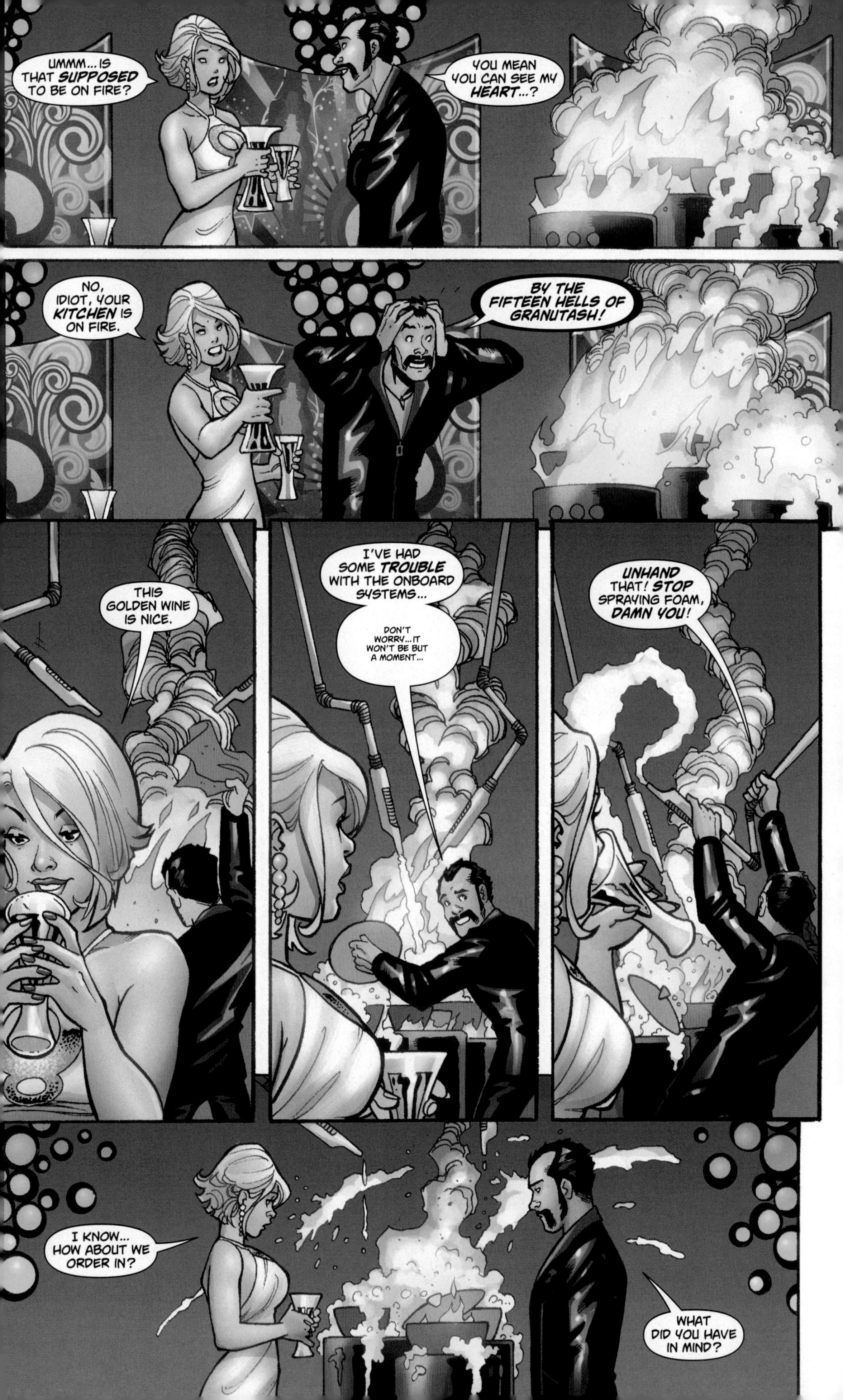

UMMM... IS THAT SUPPOSED TO BE ON FIRE?
YOU MEAN YOU CAN SEE MY HEART...?
NO, IDIOT, YOUR KITCHEN IS ON FIRE.
BY THE FIFTEEN HELLS OF GRANUTASH!
THIS GOLDEN WINE IS NICE.
I'VE HAD SOME TROUBLE WITH THE ONBOARD SYSTEMS...
DON'T WORRY... IT WON'T BE BUT A MOMENT...
UNHAND THAT! STOP SPRAYING FOAM, DAMN YOU!
I KNOW... HOW ABOUT WE ORDER IN?
WHAT DID YOU HAVE IN MIND?

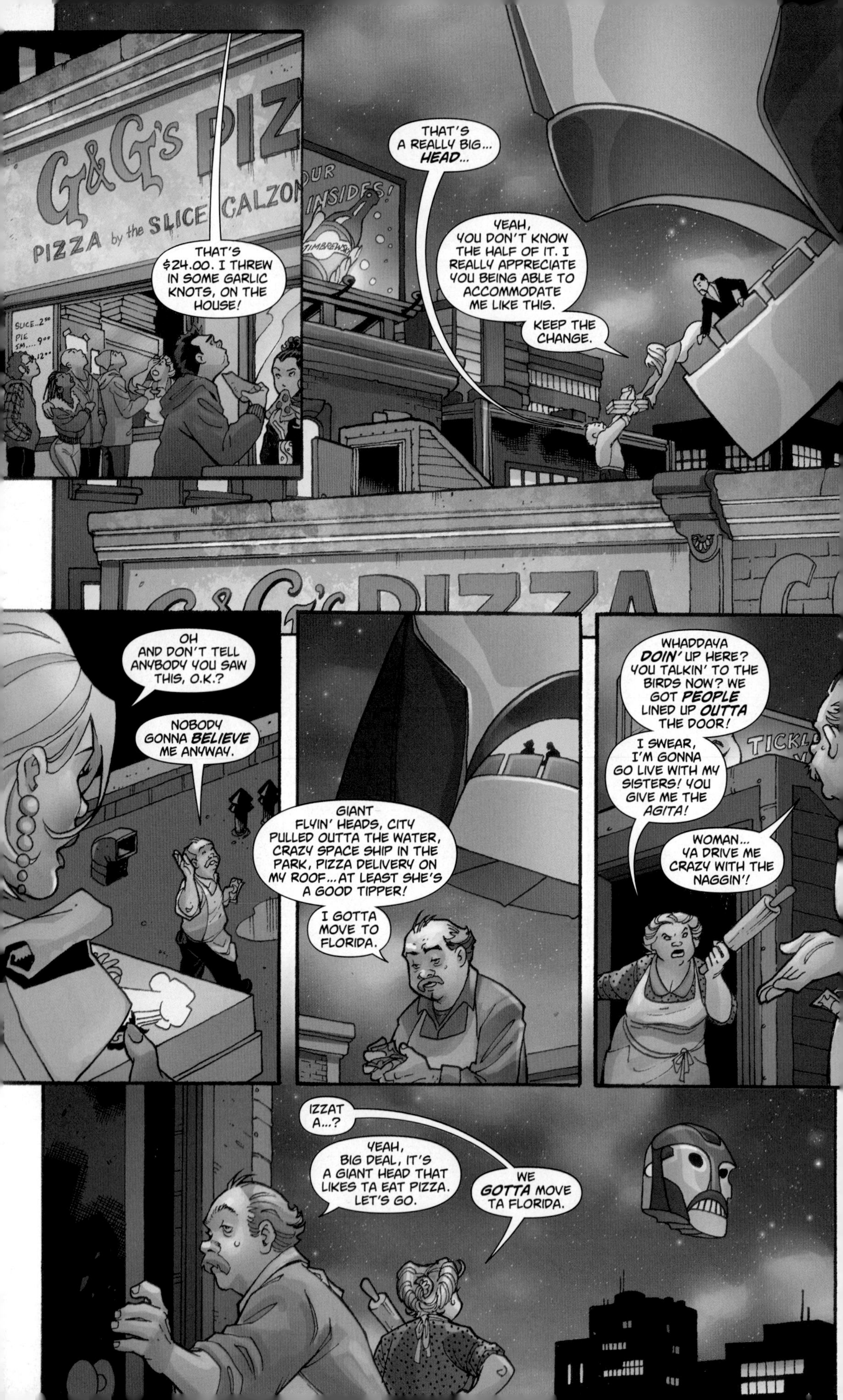

G&G's PIZ
PIZZA by the SLICE CALZON
SLICE..2.00 PIE SM.... 9.00
THAT'S $24.00. I THREW IN SOME GARLIC KNOTS, ON THE HOUSE!
THAT'S A REALLY BIG... HEAD...
YEAH, YOU DON'T KNOW THE HALF OF IT. I REALLY APPRECIATE YOU BEING ABLE TO ACCOMMODATE ME LIKE THIS.
KEEP THE CHANGE.
G&G's PIZZA
OH AND DON'T TELL ANYBODY YOU SAW THIS, O.K.?
NOBODY GONNA BELIEVE ME ANYWAY.
GIANT FLYIN' HEADS, CITY PULLED OUTTA THE WATER, CRAZY SPACE SHIP IN THE PARK, PIZZA DELIVERY ON MY ROOF...AT LEAST SHE'S A GOOD TIPPER!
I GOTTA MOVE TO FLORIDA.
WHADDAYA DOIN' UP HERE? YOU TALKIN' TO THE BIRDS NOW? WE GOT PEOPLE LINED UP OUTTA THE DOOR!
I SWEAR, I'M GONNA GO LIVE WITH MY SISTERS! YOU GIVE ME THE AGITA!
WOMAN... YA DRIVE ME CRAZY WITH THE NAGGIN'!
IZZAT A...?
YEAH, BIG DEAL, IT'S A GIANT HEAD THAT LIKES TA EAT PIZZA. LET'S GO.
WE GOTTA MOVE TA FLORIDA.

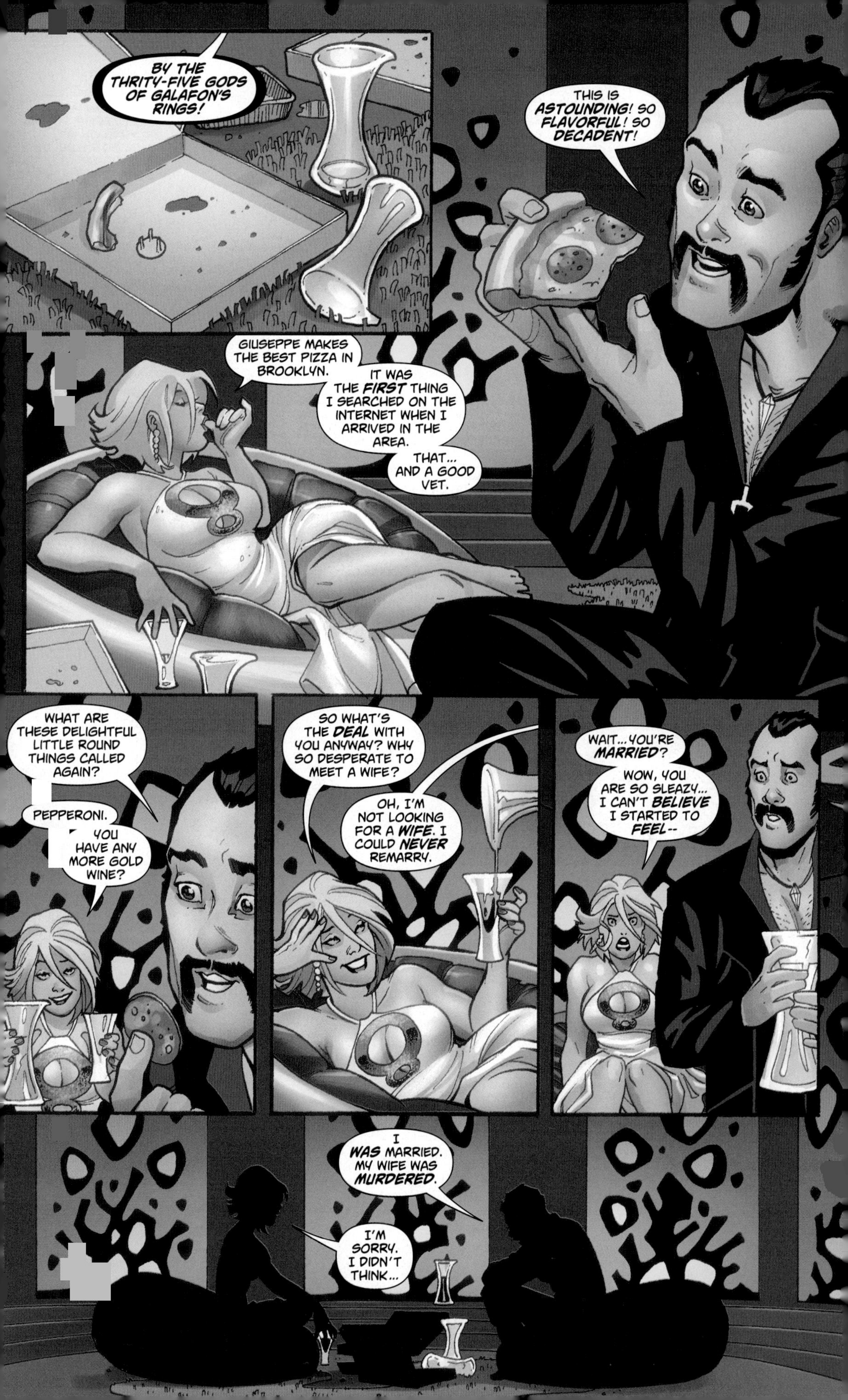
BY THE THRITY-FIVE GODS OF GALAFON'S RINGS!
THIS IS ASTOUNDING! SO FLAVORFUL! SO DECADENT!
GIUSEPPE MAKES THE BEST PIZZA IN BROOKLYN.
IT WAS THE FIRST THING I SEARCHED ON THE INTERNET WHEN I ARRIVED IN THE AREA.
THAT... AND A GOOD VET.
WHAT ARE THESE DELIGHTFUL LITTLE ROUND THINGS CALLED AGAIN?
PEPPERONI.
YOU HAVE ANY MORE GOLD WINE?
SO WHAT'S THE DEAL WITH YOU ANYWAY? WHY SO DESPERATE TO MEET A WIFE?
OH, I'M NOT LOOKING FOR A WIFE. I COULD NEVER REMARRY.
WAIT... YOU'RE MARRIED?
WOW, YOU ARE SO SLEAZY... I CAN'T BELIEVE I STARTED TO FEEL--
I WAS MARRIED. MY WIFE WAS MURDERED.
I'M SORRY. I DIDN'T THINK...

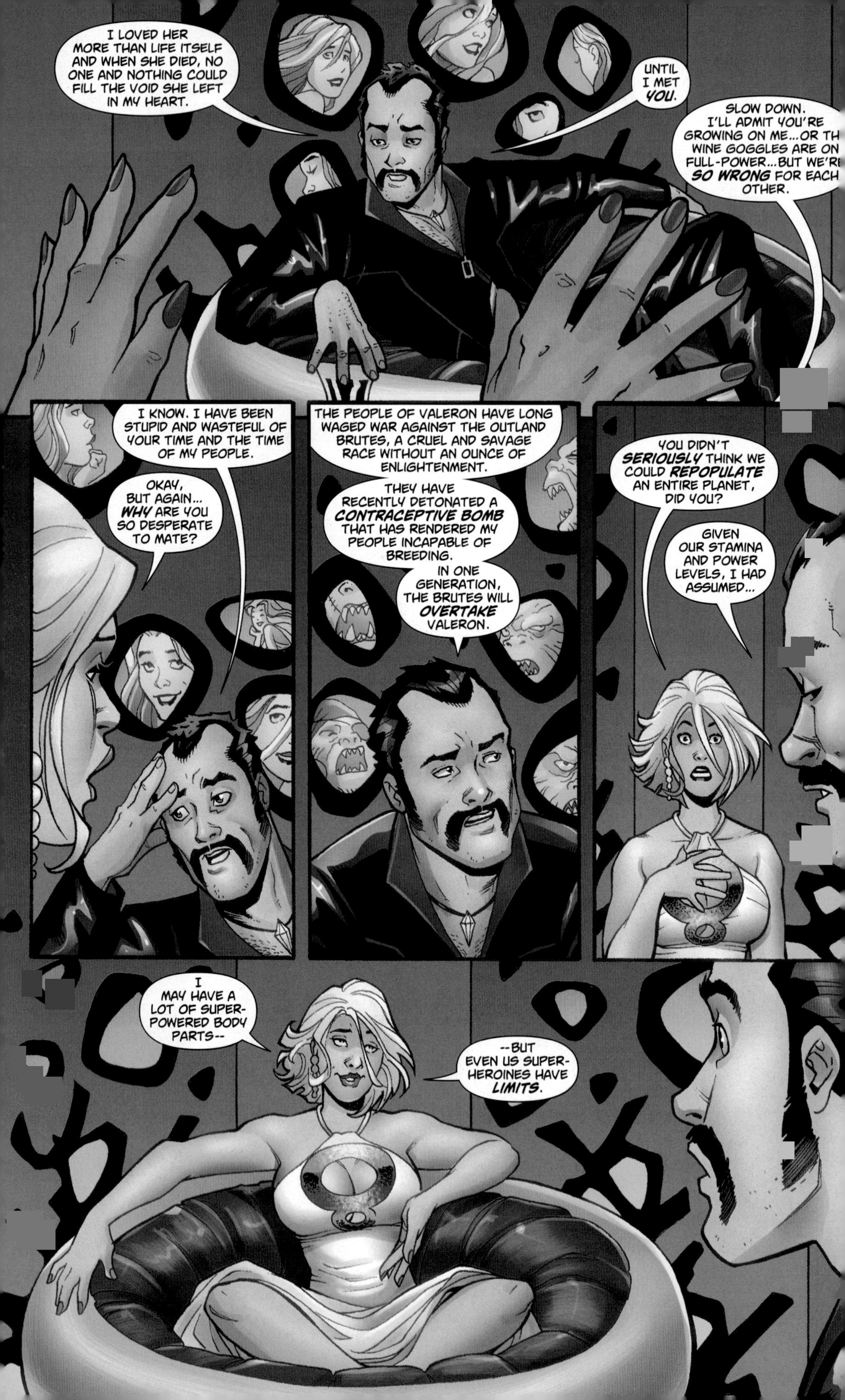
I LOVED HER MORE THAN LIFE ITSELF AND WHEN SHE DIED, NO ONE AND NOTHING COULD FILL THE VOID SHE LEFT IN MY HEART.
UNTIL I MET YOU.
SLOW DOWN. I'LL ADMIT YOU'RE GROWING ON ME...OR TH WINE GOGGLES ARE ON FULL-POWER...BUT WE'R SO WRONG FOR EACH OTHER.
I KNOW. I HAVE BEEN STUPID AND WASTEFUL OF YOUR TIME AND THE TIME OF MY PEOPLE.
OKAY, BUT AGAIN... WHY ARE YOU SO DESPERATE TO MATE?
THE PEOPLE OF VALERON HAVE LONG WAGED WAR AGAINST THE OUTLAND BRUTES, A CRUEL AND SAVAGE RACE WITHOUT AN OUNCE OF ENLIGHTENMENT.
THEY HAVE RECENTLY DETONATED A CONTRACEPTIVE BOMB THAT HAS RENDERED MY PEOPLE INCAPABLE OF BREEDING.
IN ONE GENERATION, THE BRUTES WILL OVERTAKE VALERON.
YOU DIDN'T SERIOUSLY THINK WE COULD REPOPULATE AN ENTIRE PLANET, DID YOU?
GIVEN OUR STAMINA AND POWER LEVELS, I HAD ASSUMED...
I MAY HAVE A LOT OF SUPER-POWERED BODY PARTS--
--BUT EVEN US SUPER-HEROINES HAVE LIMITS.

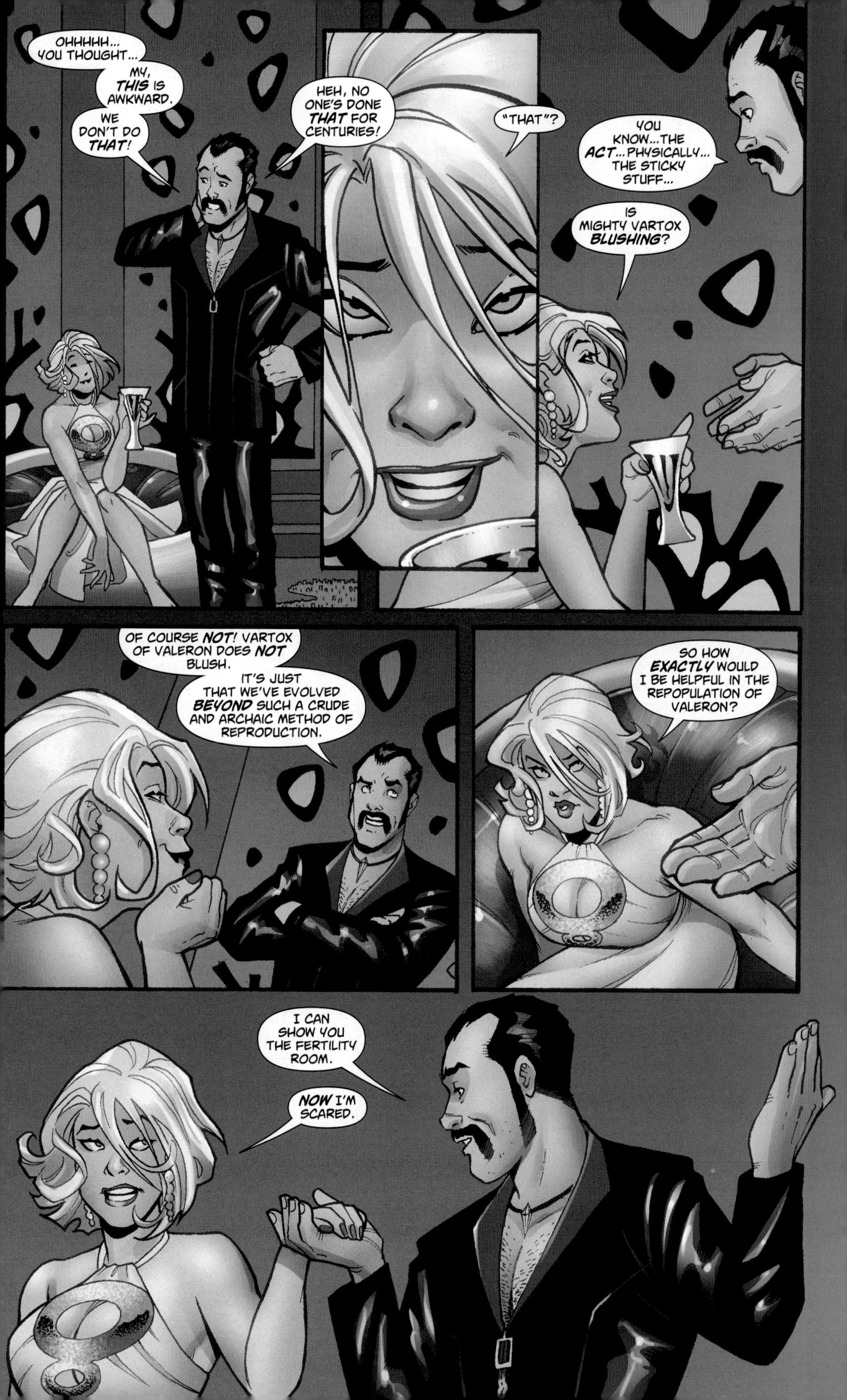

OHHHHH... YOU THOUGHT...
MY, THIS IS AWKWARD.
WE DON'T DO THAT!
HEH, NO ONE'S DONE THAT FOR CENTURIES!
"THAT"?
YOU KNOW...THE ACT...PHYSICALLY... THE STICKY STUFF...
IS MIGHTY VARTOX BLUSHING?
OF COURSE NOT! VARTOX OF VALERON DOES NOT BLUSH.
IT'S JUST THAT WE'VE EVOLVED BEYOND SUCH A CRUDE AND ARCHAIC METHOD OF REPRODUCTION.
SO HOW EXACTLY WOULD I BE HELPFUL IN THE REPOPULATION OF VALERON?
I CAN SHOW YOU THE FERTILITY ROOM.
NOW I'M SCARED.

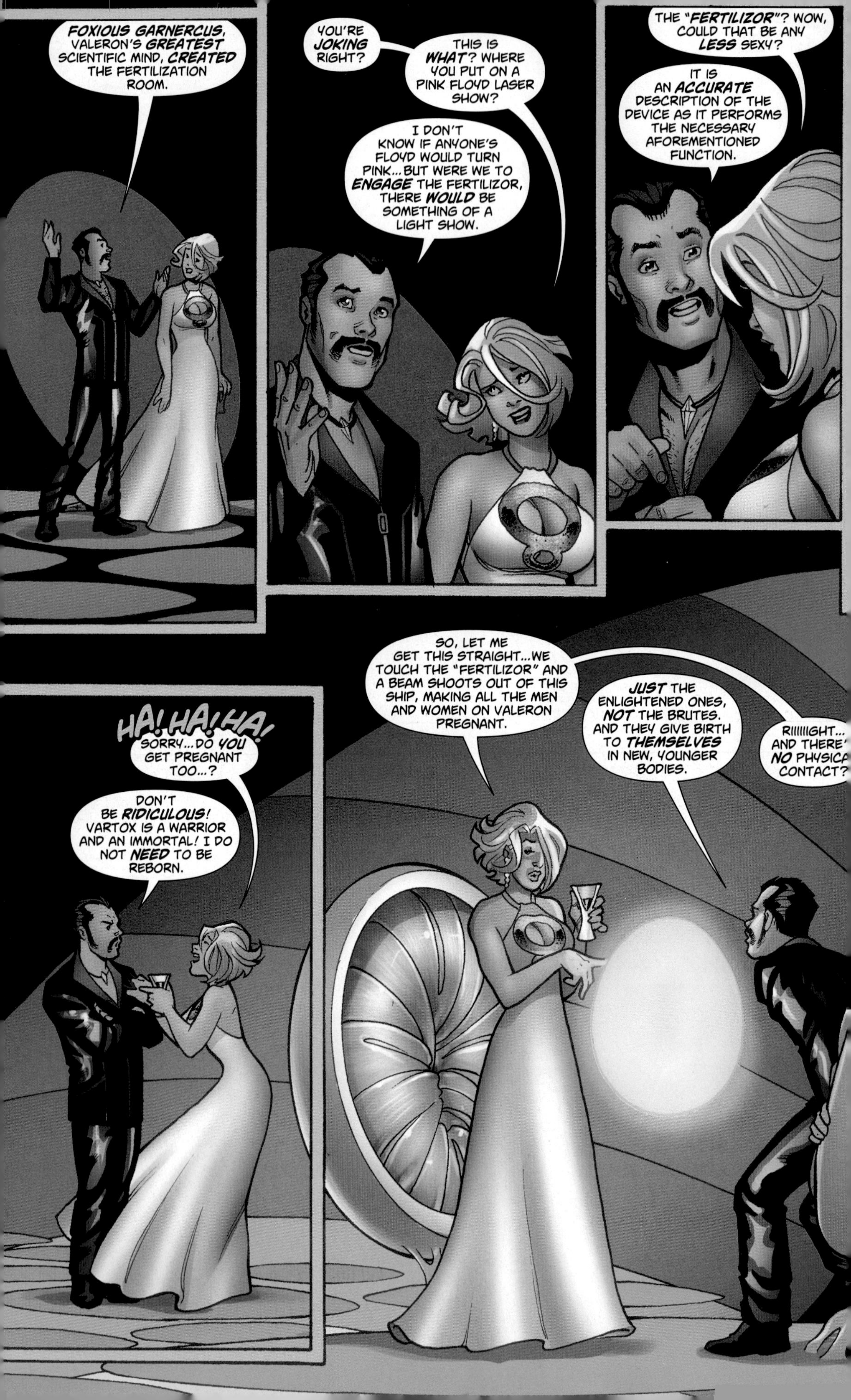
FOXIOUS GARNERCUS, VALERON'S GREATEST SCIENTIFIC MIND, CREATED THE FERTILIZATION ROOM.
YOU'RE JOKING RIGHT?
THIS IS WHAT? WHERE YOU PUT ON A PINK FLOYD LASER SHOW?
I DON'T KNOW IF ANYONE'S FLOYD WOULD TURN PINK... BUT WERE WE TO ENGAGE THE FERTILIZOR, THERE WOULD BE SOMETHING OF A LIGHT SHOW.
THE "FERTILIZOR"? WOW, COULD THAT BE ANY LESS SEXY?
IT IS AN ACCURATE DESCRIPTION OF THE DEVICE AS IT PERFORMS THE NECESSARY AFOREMENTIONED FUNCTION.
SO, LET ME GET THIS STRAIGHT...WE TOUCH THE "FERTILIZOR" AND A BEAM SHOOTS OUT OF THIS SHIP, MAKING ALL THE MEN AND WOMEN ON VALERON PREGNANT.
JUST THE ENLIGHTENED ONES, NOT THE BRUTES. AND THEY GIVE BIRTH TO THEMSELVES IN NEW, YOUNGER BODIES.
RIIIIIGHT... AND THERE' NO PHYSICA CONTACT?
HA! HA! HA!
SORRY... DO YOU GET PREGNANT TOO...?
DON'T BE RIDICULOUS! VARTOX IS A WARRIOR AND AN IMMORTAL! I DO NOT NEED TO BE REBORN.

YOU SEE, ONCE PROPERLY *STIMULATED*, THE *FERTILIZOR* FIRES A *PREGNO-RAY*--

"*PREGNO-RAY*"? *SERIOUSLY*? YOU JUST SAID PREGNO-RAY *OUT LOUD*?

MAY I *FINISH*?

≥ SNICKER ≥... GO AHEAD.

THE *PREGNO-RAY*--

--STOP *GIGGLING*--

--FIRES FROM HERE TO *VALERON*, EFFECTIVELY REVERSING THE EFFECTS OF THE *BRUTES'* CONTRACEPTIVE BOMB, WHILE *SIMULTANEOUSLY* IMPREGNATING ALL OF THE *MALES* AND *FEMALES*.

THE *MALES*!

DID YOU JUST SAY "*MALES*"?

YES, THE MALES OF VALERON *ALSO* CARRY THEIR CHILDREN TO TERM.

I *FAIL* TO SEE THE *HUMOR* IN WHAT IS ONE OF THE MORE *ELEGANT* AND *IMPERSONAL* MATING RITUALS IN THE ENTIRE UNIVERSE.

BETWEEN *US* I MEAN. I DON'T HAVE TO TAKE MY CLOTHES OFF OR *ANYTHING*?

NOT UNLESS YOU *WANTED* TO.

OKAY, SUPPOSE I DO IT--

--*NOT* THE CLOTHES THING, THEY'RE STAYING *ON*--

--AM I GOING TO HAVE A BUNCH OF *KIDS* SHOWING UP HERE ON EARTH CALLING ME "*MOMMY*"?

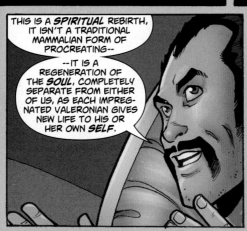

THIS IS A *SPIRITUAL* REBIRTH, IT ISN'T A TRADITIONAL *MAMMALIAN* FORM OF PROCREATING--

--IT IS A REGENERATION OF THE *SOUL*, COMPLETELY SEPARATE FROM EITHER OF US, AS EACH IMPREGNATED VALERONIAN GIVES NEW LIFE TO HIS OR HER OWN *SELF*.

I'M GONNA NEED MORE WINE TO DECIPHER WHAT THE HELL YOU'RE SAYING AND TAKE IT ALL IN... BUT I'LL HELP.

I *THINK*.

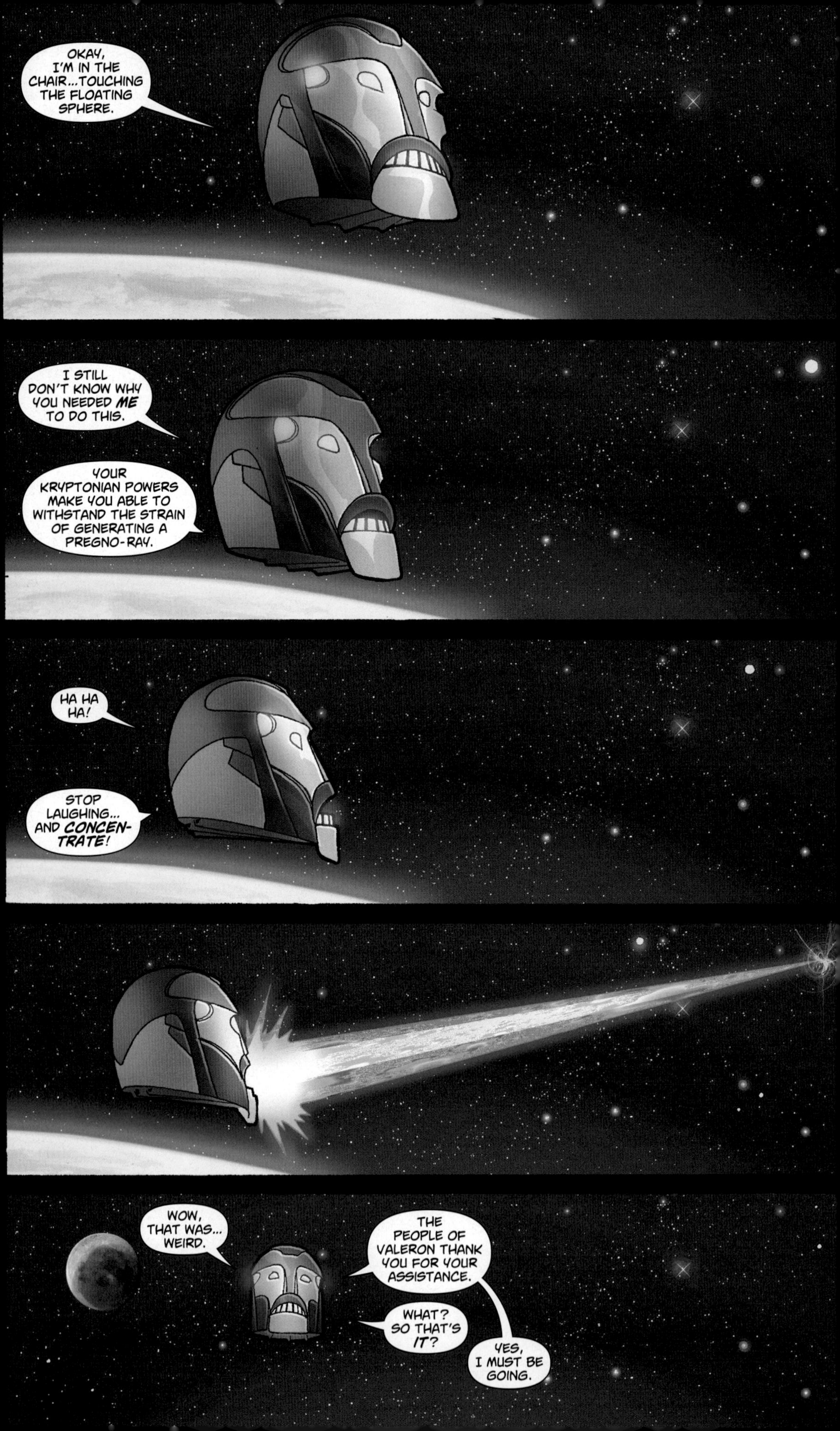
OKAY, I'M IN THE CHAIR...TOUCHING THE FLOATING SPHERE.
I STILL DON'T KNOW WHY YOU NEEDED ME TO DO THIS.
YOUR KRYPTONIAN POWERS MAKE YOU ABLE TO WITHSTAND THE STRAIN OF GENERATING A PREGNO-RAY.
HA HA HA!
STOP LAUGHING... AND CONCEN-TRATE!
WOW, THAT WAS... WEIRD.
THE PEOPLE OF VALERON THANK YOU FOR YOUR ASSISTANCE.
WHAT? SO THAT'S IT?
YES, I MUST BE GOING.

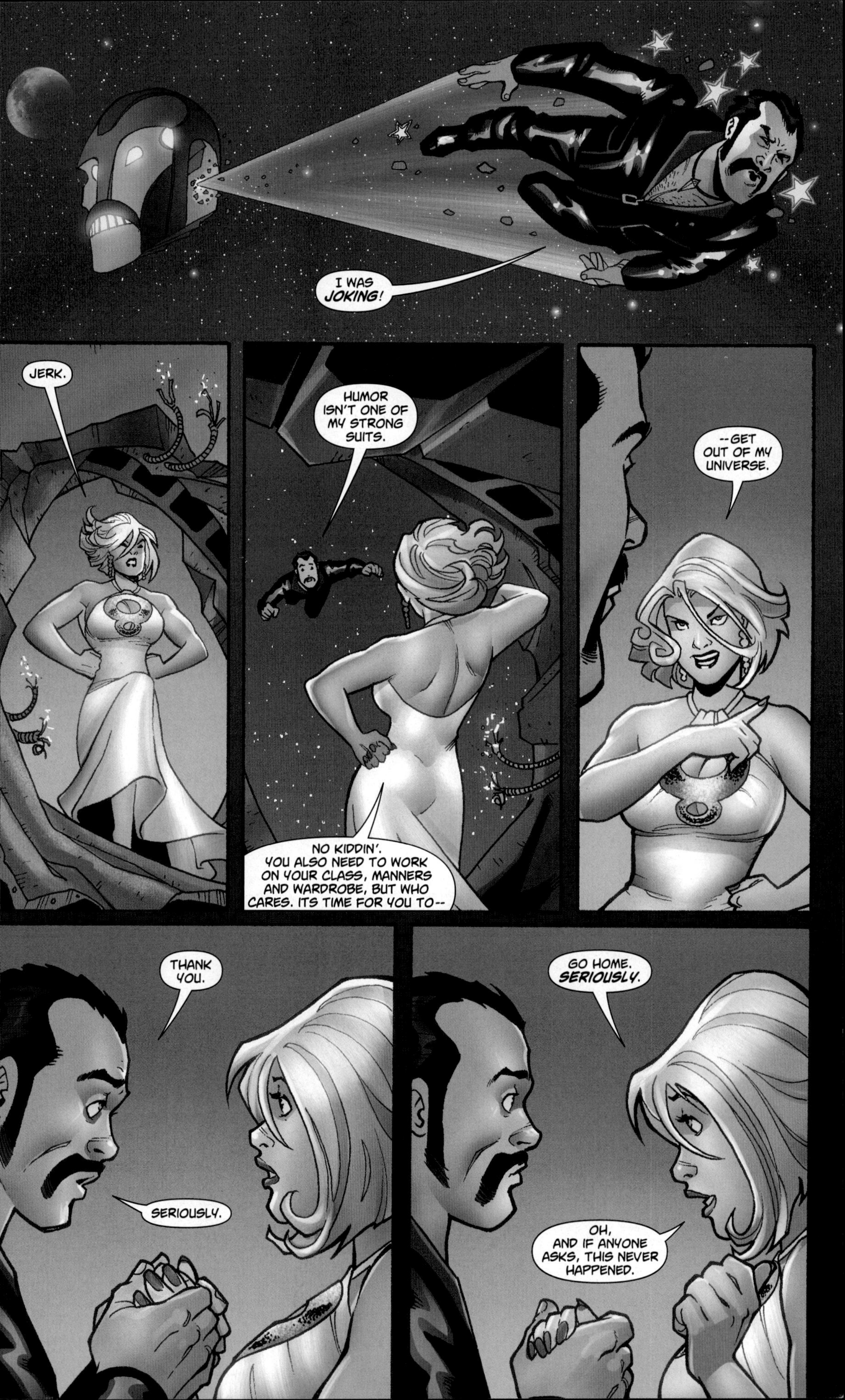
I WAS JOKING!
JERK.
HUMOR ISN'T ONE OF MY STRONG SUITS.
NO KIDDIN'. YOU ALSO NEED TO WORK ON YOUR CLASS, MANNERS AND WARDROBE, BUT WHO CARES. ITS TIME FOR YOU TO--
--GET OUT OF MY UNIVERSE.
THANK YOU.
SERIOUSLY.
GO HOME. SERIOUSLY.
OH, AND IF ANYONE ASKS, THIS NEVER HAPPENED.

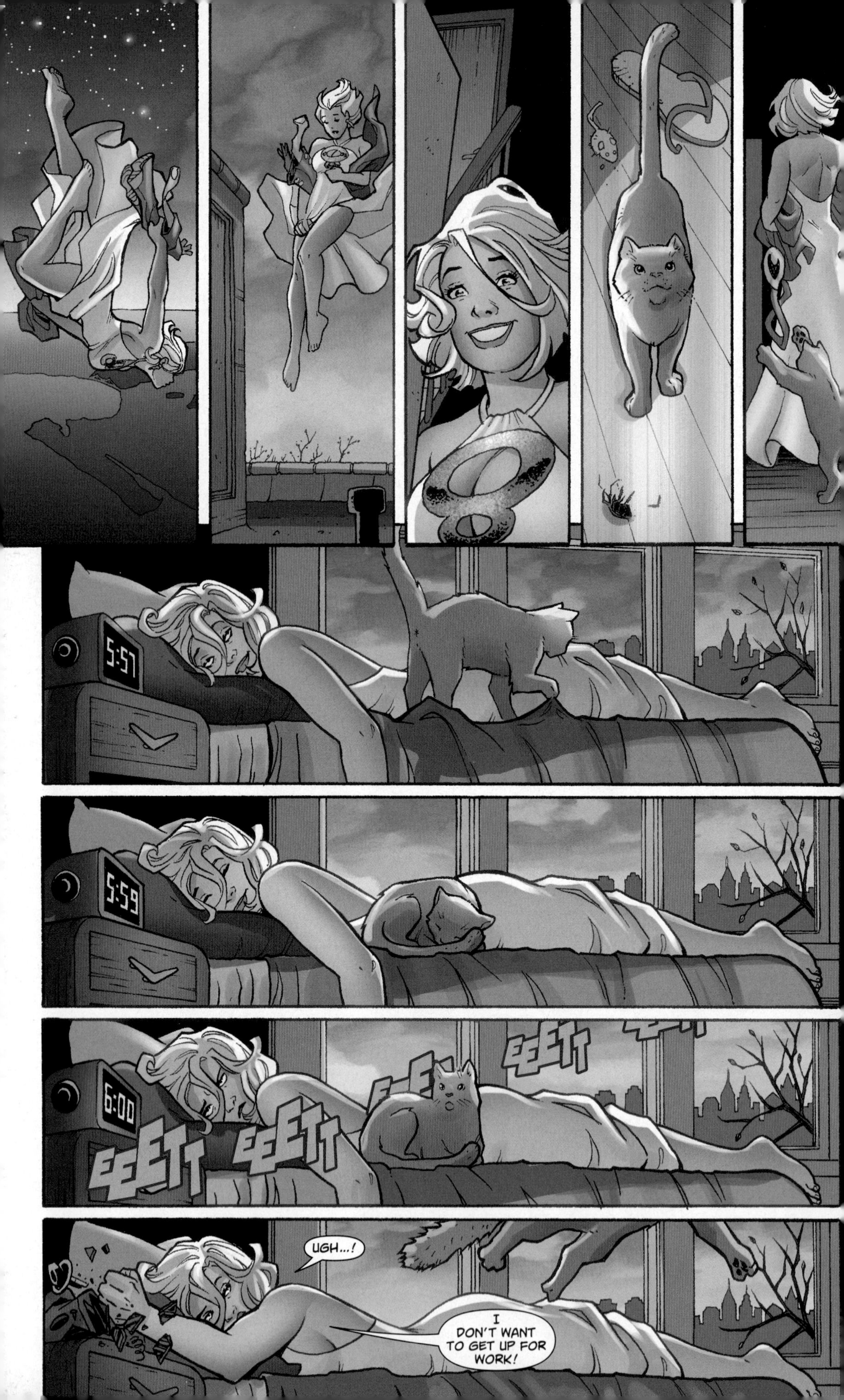
5:57
5:59
6:00
EEEETT
EEEETT
E-E
EEETT
UGH...!
I DON'T WANT TO GET UP FOR WORK!

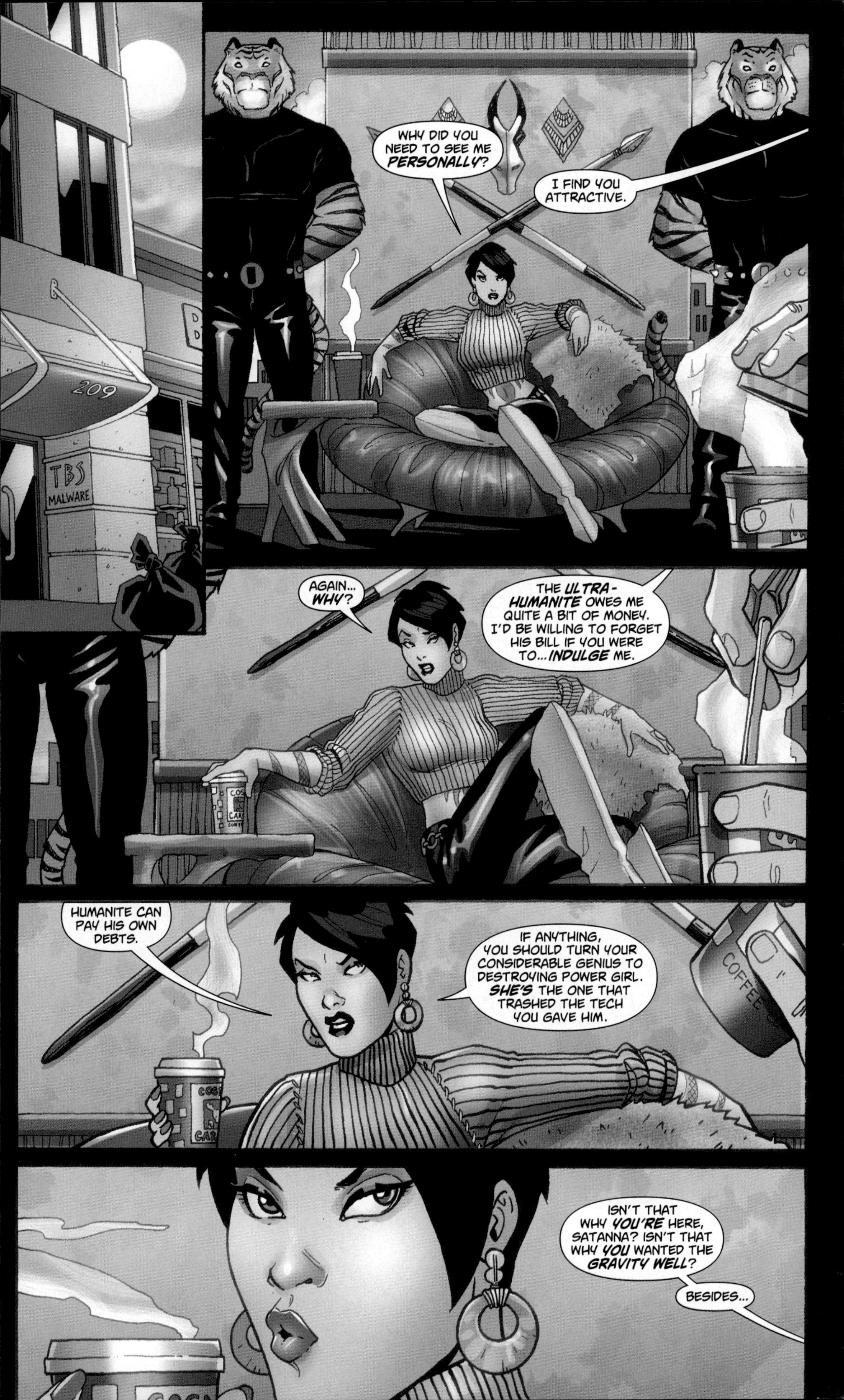

209
TBS
MALWARE
WHY DID YOU NEED TO SEE ME PERSONALLY?
I FIND YOU ATTRACTIVE.
AGAIN... WHY?
THE ULTRA-HUMANITE OWES ME QUITE A BIT OF MONEY. I'D BE WILLING TO FORGET HIS BILL IF YOU WERE TO...INDULGE ME.
HUMANITE CAN PAY HIS OWN DEBTS.
IF ANYTHING, YOU SHOULD TURN YOUR CONSIDERABLE GENIUS TO DESTROYING POWER GIRL. SHE'S THE ONE THAT TRASHED THE TECH YOU GAVE HIM.
ISN'T THAT WHY YOU'RE HERE, SATANNA? ISN'T THAT WHY YOU WANTED THE GRAVITY WELL?
BESIDES...

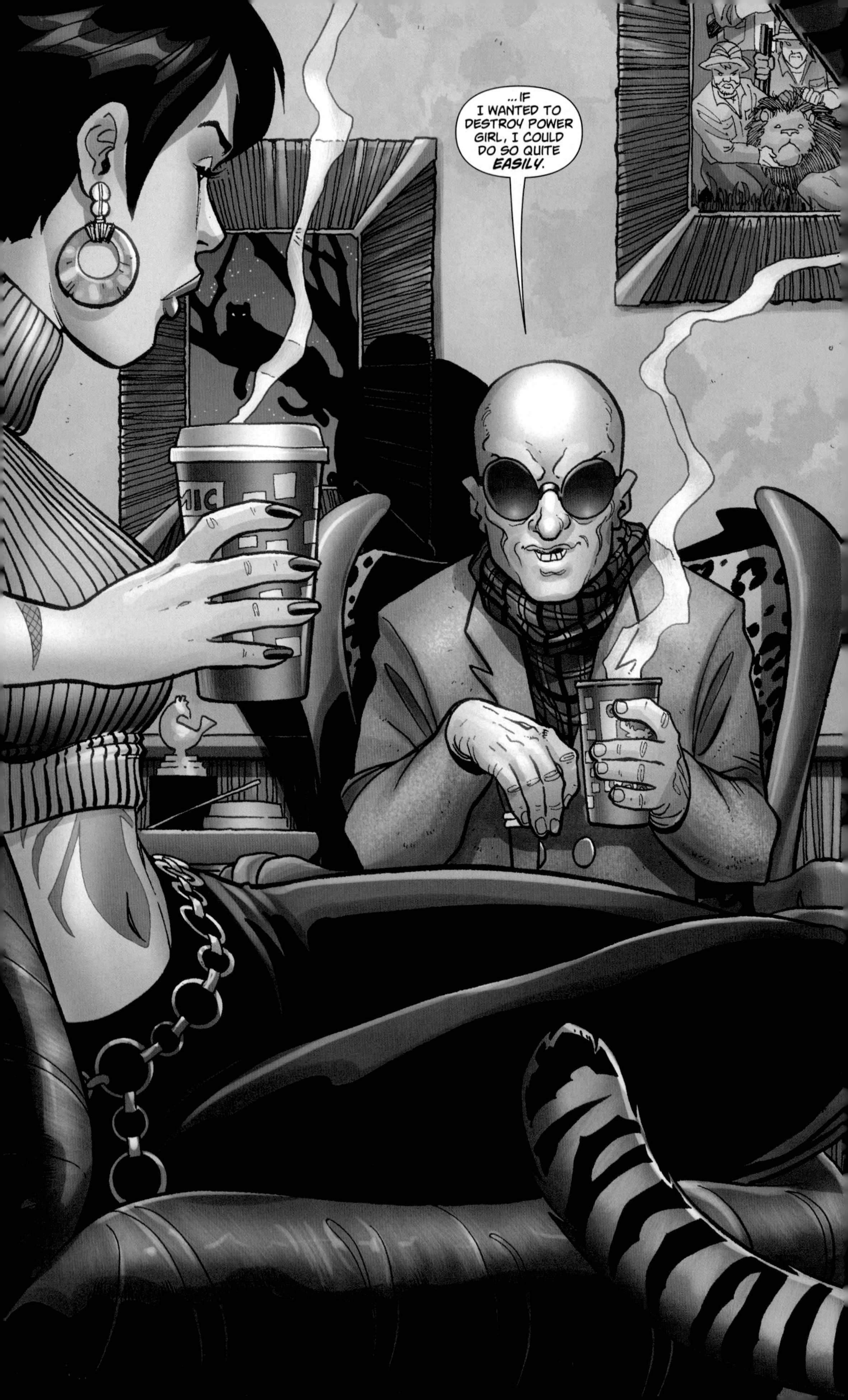
...IF I WANTED TO DESTROY POWER GIRL, I COULD DO SO QUITE EASILY.

THIS CITY IS A ZOO

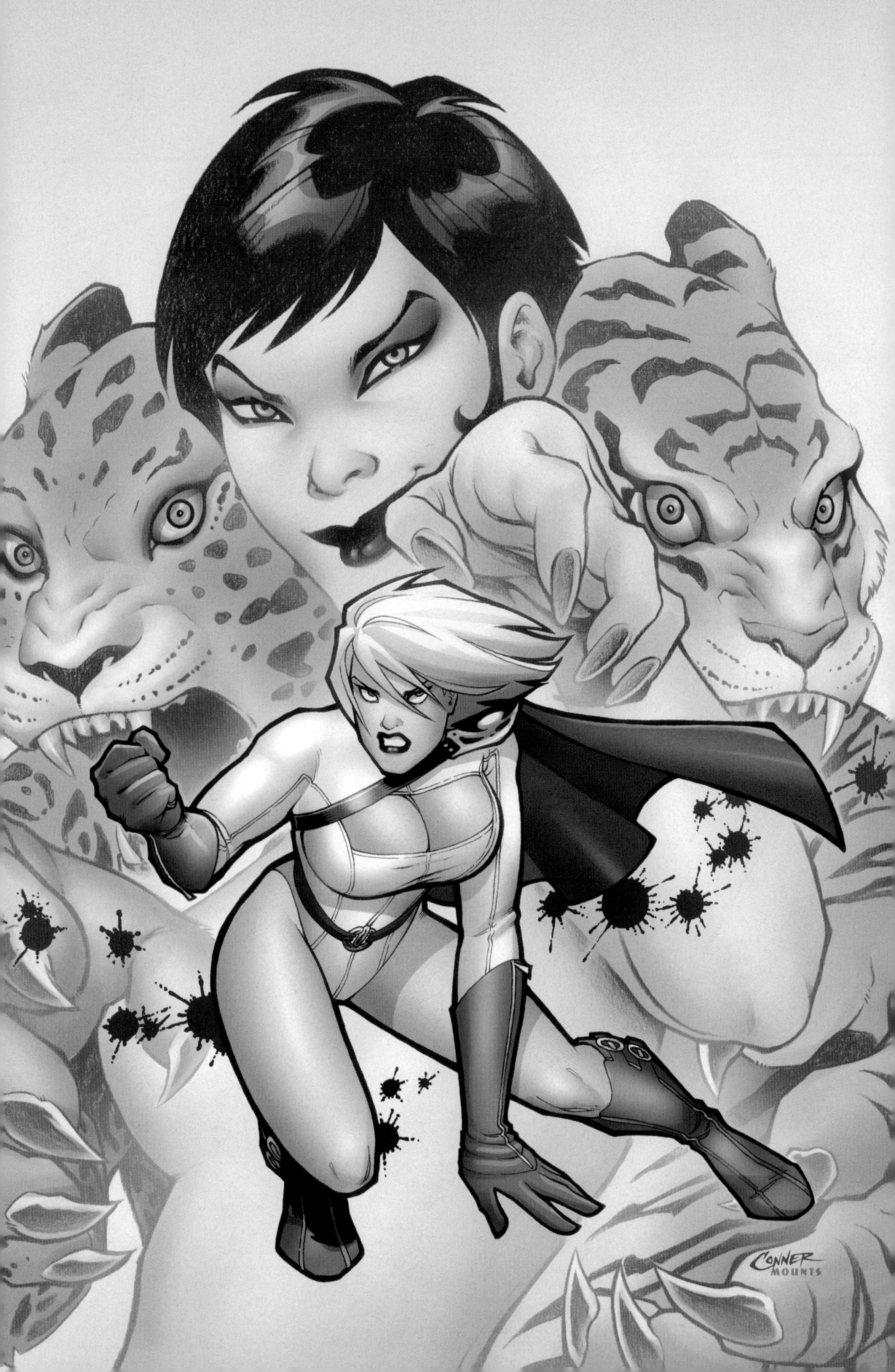
CONNER
MOUNTS

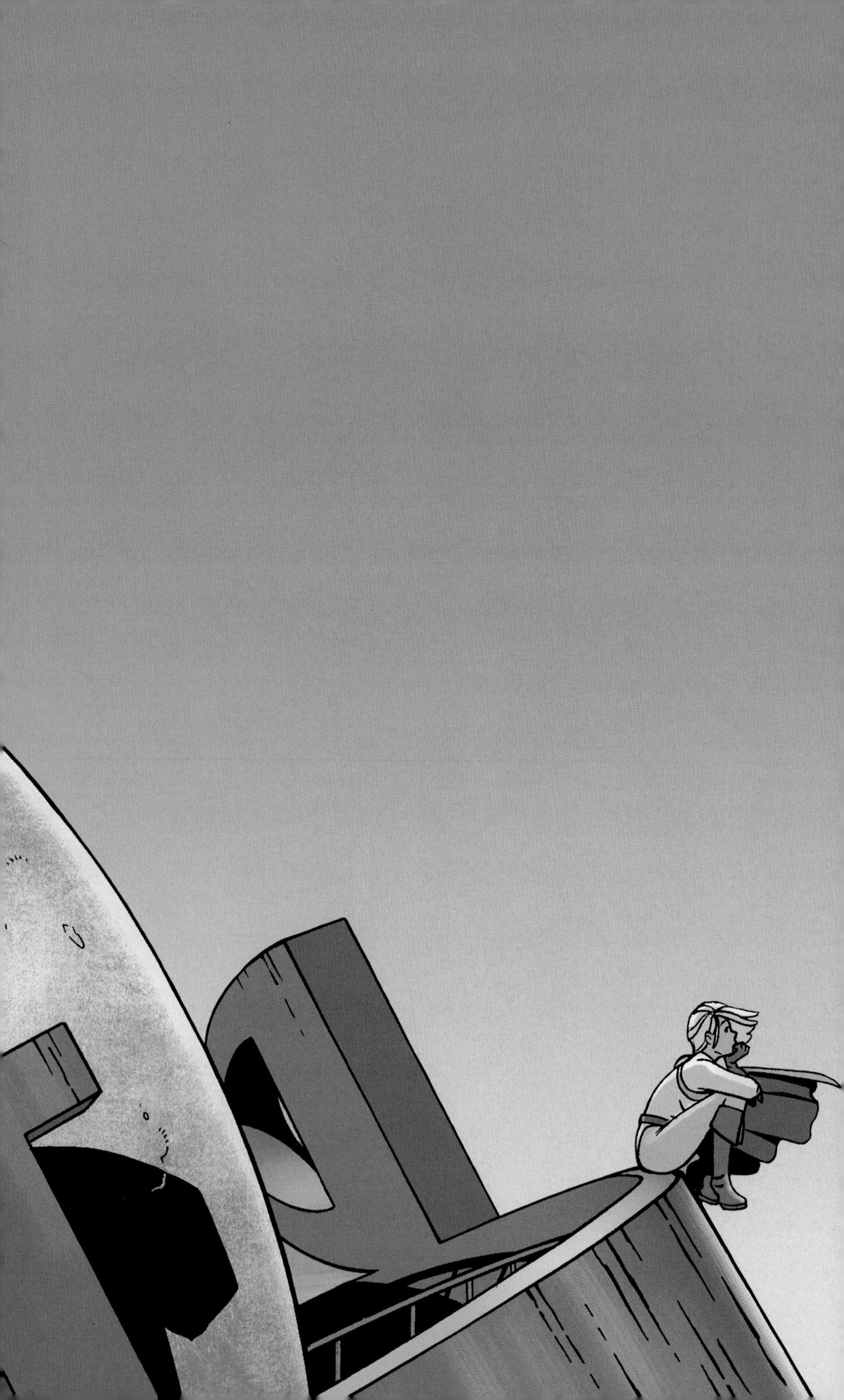

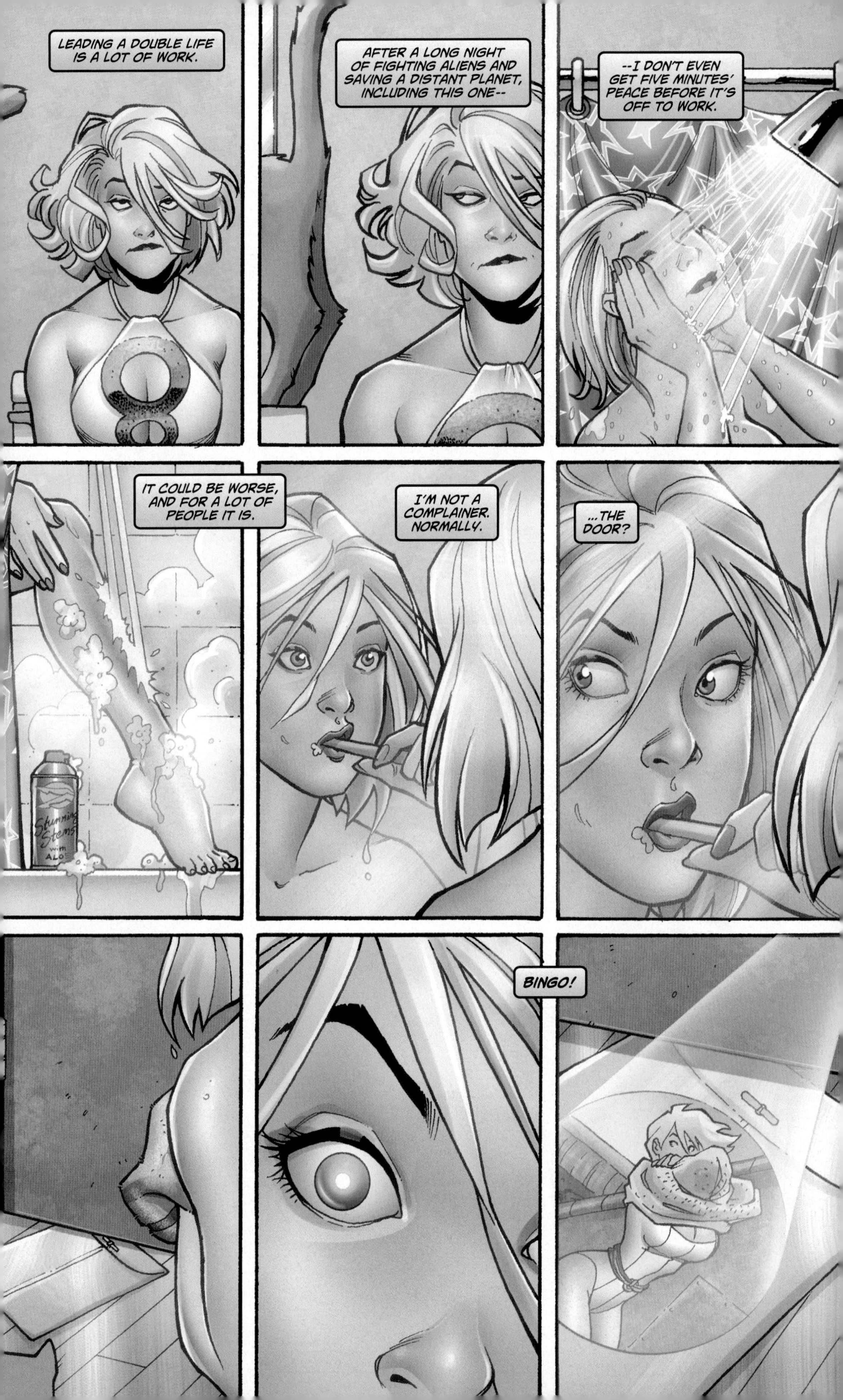
LEADING A DOUBLE LIFE IS A LOT OF WORK.
AFTER A LONG NIGHT OF FIGHTING ALIENS AND SAVING A DISTANT PLANET, INCLUDING THIS ONE--
--I DON'T EVEN GET FIVE MINUTES' PEACE BEFORE IT'S OFF TO WORK.
IT COULD BE WORSE, AND FOR A LOT OF PEOPLE IT IS.
I'M NOT A COMPLAINER. NORMALLY.
...THE DOOR?
BINGO!

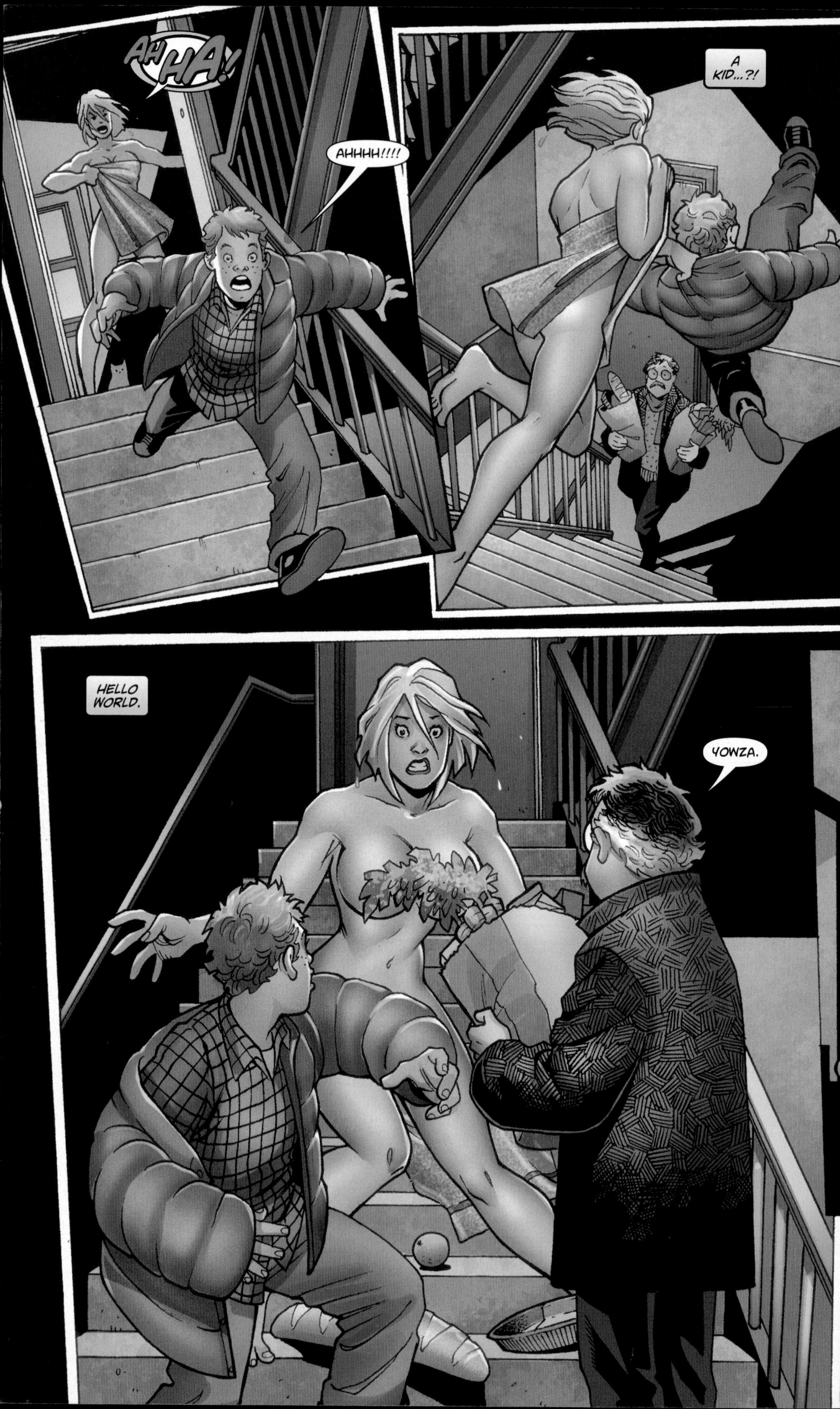
AH HA!
AHHHH!!!!
A KID...?!
HELLO WORLD.
YOWZA.

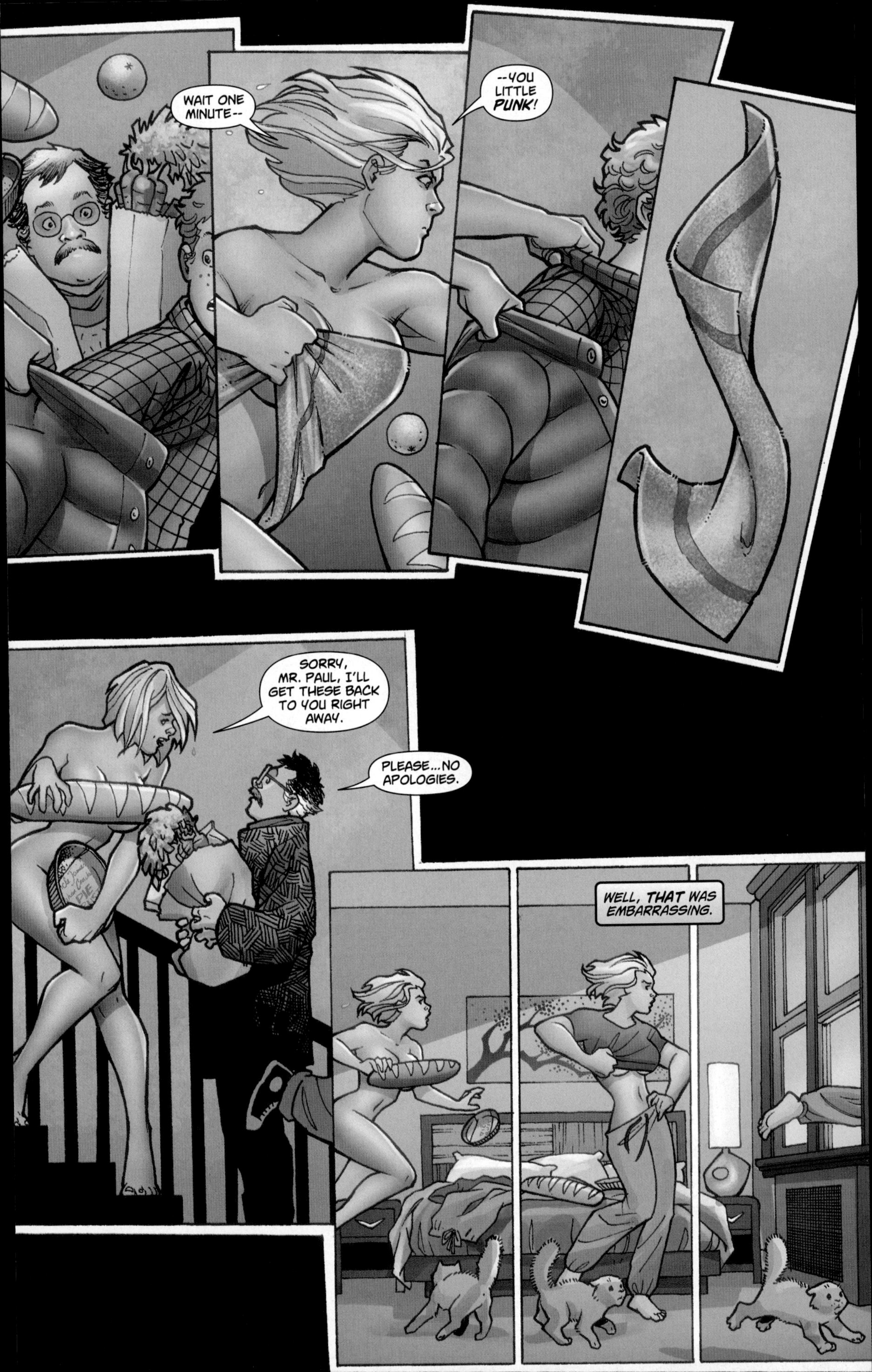
WAIT ONE MINUTE--
--YOU LITTLE PUNK!
SORRY, MR. PAUL, I'LL GET THESE BACK TO YOU RIGHT AWAY.
PLEASE...NO APOLOGIES.
WELL, THAT WAS EMBARRASSING.

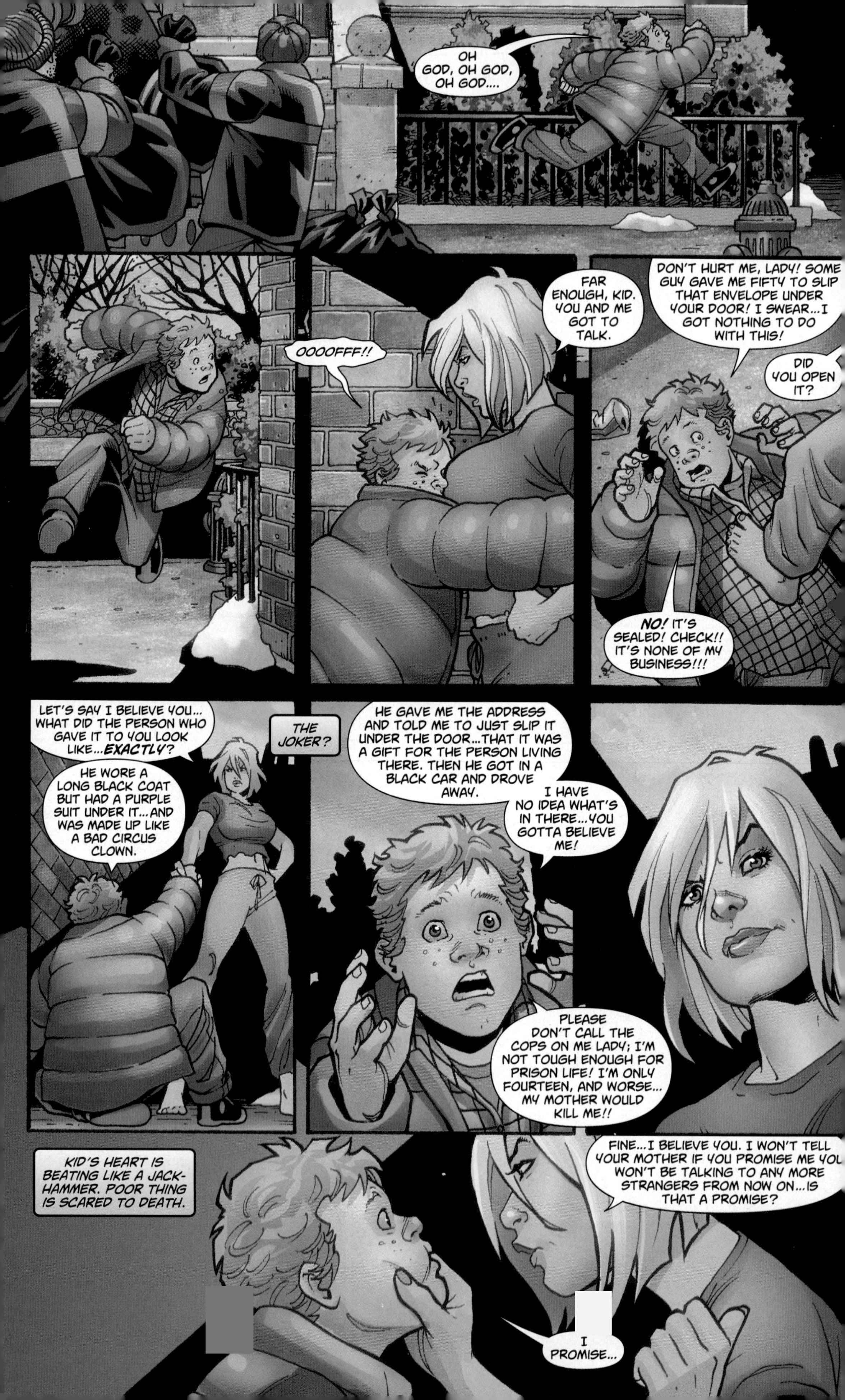
OH GOD, OH GOD, OH GOD....
OOOOFFF!!
FAR ENOUGH, KID. YOU AND ME GOT TO TALK.
DON'T HURT ME, LADY! SOME GUY GAVE ME FIFTY TO SLIP THAT ENVELOPE UNDER YOUR DOOR! I SWEAR...I GOT NOTHING TO DO WITH THIS!
DID YOU OPEN IT?
NO! IT'S SEALED! CHECK!! IT'S NONE OF MY BUSINESS!!!
LET'S SAY I BELIEVE YOU... WHAT DID THE PERSON WHO GAVE IT TO YOU LOOK LIKE...EXACTLY?
HE WORE A LONG BLACK COAT BUT HAD A PURPLE SUIT UNDER IT...AND WAS MADE UP LIKE A BAD CIRCUS CLOWN.
THE JOKER?
HE GAVE ME THE ADDRESS AND TOLD ME TO JUST SLIP IT UNDER THE DOOR...THAT IT WAS A GIFT FOR THE PERSON LIVING THERE. THEN HE GOT IN A BLACK CAR AND DROVE AWAY.
I HAVE NO IDEA WHAT'S IN THERE...YOU GOTTA BELIEVE ME!
PLEASE DON'T CALL THE COPS ON ME LADY; I'M NOT TOUGH ENOUGH FOR PRISON LIFE! I'M ONLY FOURTEEN, AND WORSE... MY MOTHER WOULD KILL ME!!
KID'S HEART IS BEATING LIKE A JACK-HAMMER. POOR THING IS SCARED TO DEATH.
FINE...I BELIEVE YOU. I WON'T TELL YOUR MOTHER IF YOU PROMISE ME YOU WON'T BE TALKING TO ANY MORE STRANGERS FROM NOW ON...IS THAT A PROMISE?
I PROMISE...

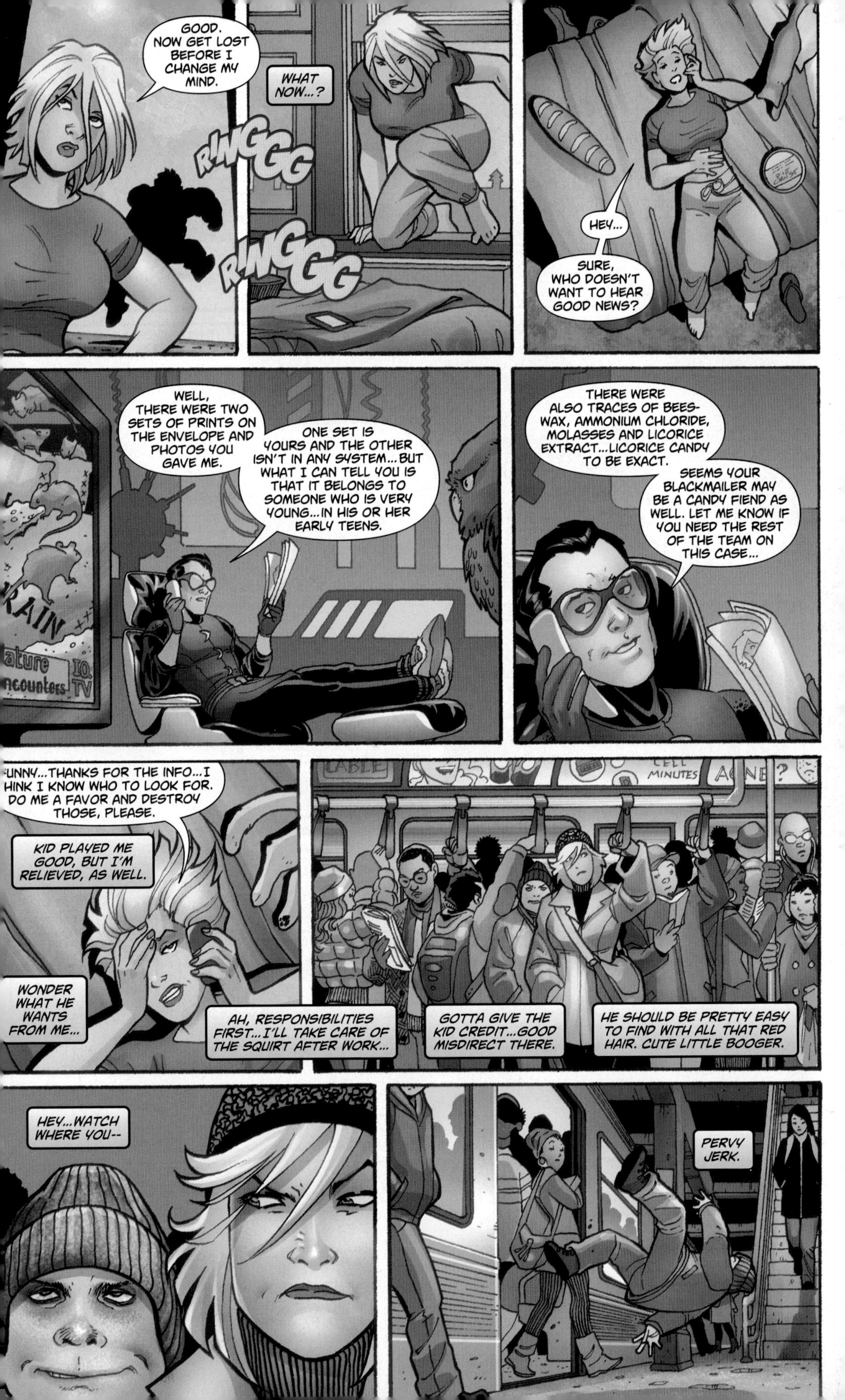
GOOD. NOW GET LOST BEFORE I CHANGE MY MIND.
RINGGG
WHAT NOW...?
RINGGG
HEY...
SURE, WHO DOESN'T WANT TO HEAR GOOD NEWS?
WELL, THERE WERE TWO SETS OF PRINTS ON THE ENVELOPE AND PHOTOS YOU GAVE ME.
ONE SET IS YOURS AND THE OTHER ISN'T IN ANY SYSTEM...BUT WHAT I CAN TELL YOU IS THAT IT BELONGS TO SOMEONE WHO IS VERY YOUNG...IN HIS OR HER EARLY TEENS.
THERE WERE ALSO TRACES OF BEES-WAX, AMMONIUM CHLORIDE, MOLASSES AND LICORICE EXTRACT...LICORICE CANDY TO BE EXACT.
SEEMS YOUR BLACKMAILER MAY BE A CANDY FIEND AS WELL. LET ME KNOW IF YOU NEED THE REST OF THE TEAM ON THIS CASE...
FUNNY...THANKS FOR THE INFO...I THINK I KNOW WHO TO LOOK FOR. DO ME A FAVOR AND DESTROY THOSE, PLEASE.
KID PLAYED ME GOOD, BUT I'M RELIEVED, AS WELL.
WONDER WHAT HE WANTS FROM ME...
AH, RESPONSIBILITIES FIRST...I'LL TAKE CARE OF THE SQUIRT AFTER WORK...
GOTTA GIVE THE KID CREDIT...GOOD MISDIRECT THERE.
HE SHOULD BE PRETTY EASY TO FIND WITH ALL THAT RED HAIR. CUTE LITTLE BOOGER.
HEY...WATCH WHERE YOU--
PERVY JERK.

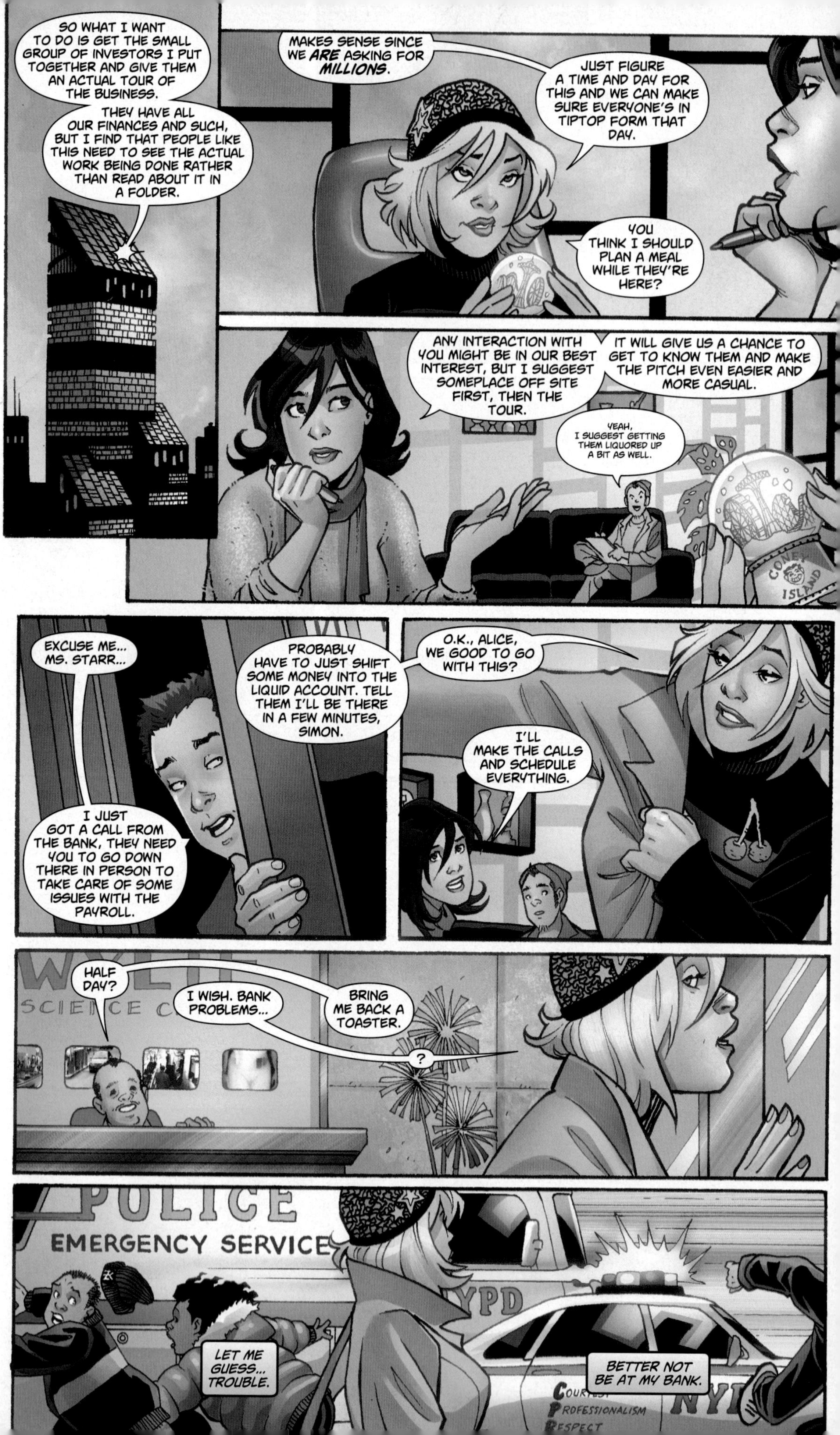
SO WHAT I WANT TO DO IS GET THE SMALL GROUP OF INVESTORS I PUT TOGETHER AND GIVE THEM AN ACTUAL TOUR OF THE BUSINESS.
THEY HAVE ALL OUR FINANCES AND SUCH, BUT I FIND THAT PEOPLE LIKE THIS NEED TO SEE THE ACTUAL WORK BEING DONE RATHER THAN READ ABOUT IT IN A FOLDER.
MAKES SENSE SINCE WE ARE ASKING FOR MILLIONS.
JUST FIGURE A TIME AND DAY FOR THIS AND WE CAN MAKE SURE EVERYONE'S IN TIPTOP FORM THAT DAY.
YOU THINK I SHOULD PLAN A MEAL WHILE THEY'RE HERE?
ANY INTERACTION WITH YOU MIGHT BE IN OUR BEST INTEREST, BUT I SUGGEST SOMEPLACE OFF SITE FIRST, THEN THE TOUR.
IT WILL GIVE US A CHANCE TO GET TO KNOW THEM AND MAKE THE PITCH EVEN EASIER AND MORE CASUAL.
YEAH, I SUGGEST GETTING THEM LIQUORED UP A BIT AS WELL.
CONEY ISLAND
EXCUSE ME... MS. STARR...
I JUST GOT A CALL FROM THE BANK, THEY NEED YOU TO GO DOWN THERE IN PERSON TO TAKE CARE OF SOME ISSUES WITH THE PAYROLL.
PROBABLY HAVE TO JUST SHIFT SOME MONEY INTO THE LIQUID ACCOUNT. TELL THEM I'LL BE THERE IN A FEW MINUTES, SIMON.
O.K., ALICE, WE GOOD TO GO WITH THIS?
I'LL MAKE THE CALLS AND SCHEDULE EVERYTHING.
SCIENCE C
HALF DAY?
I WISH. BANK PROBLEMS...
BRING ME BACK A TOASTER.
?
POLICE
EMERGENCY SERVICE
NYPD
LET ME GUESS... TROUBLE.
BETTER NOT BE AT MY BANK.
COURTESY
PROFESSIONALISM
RESPECT

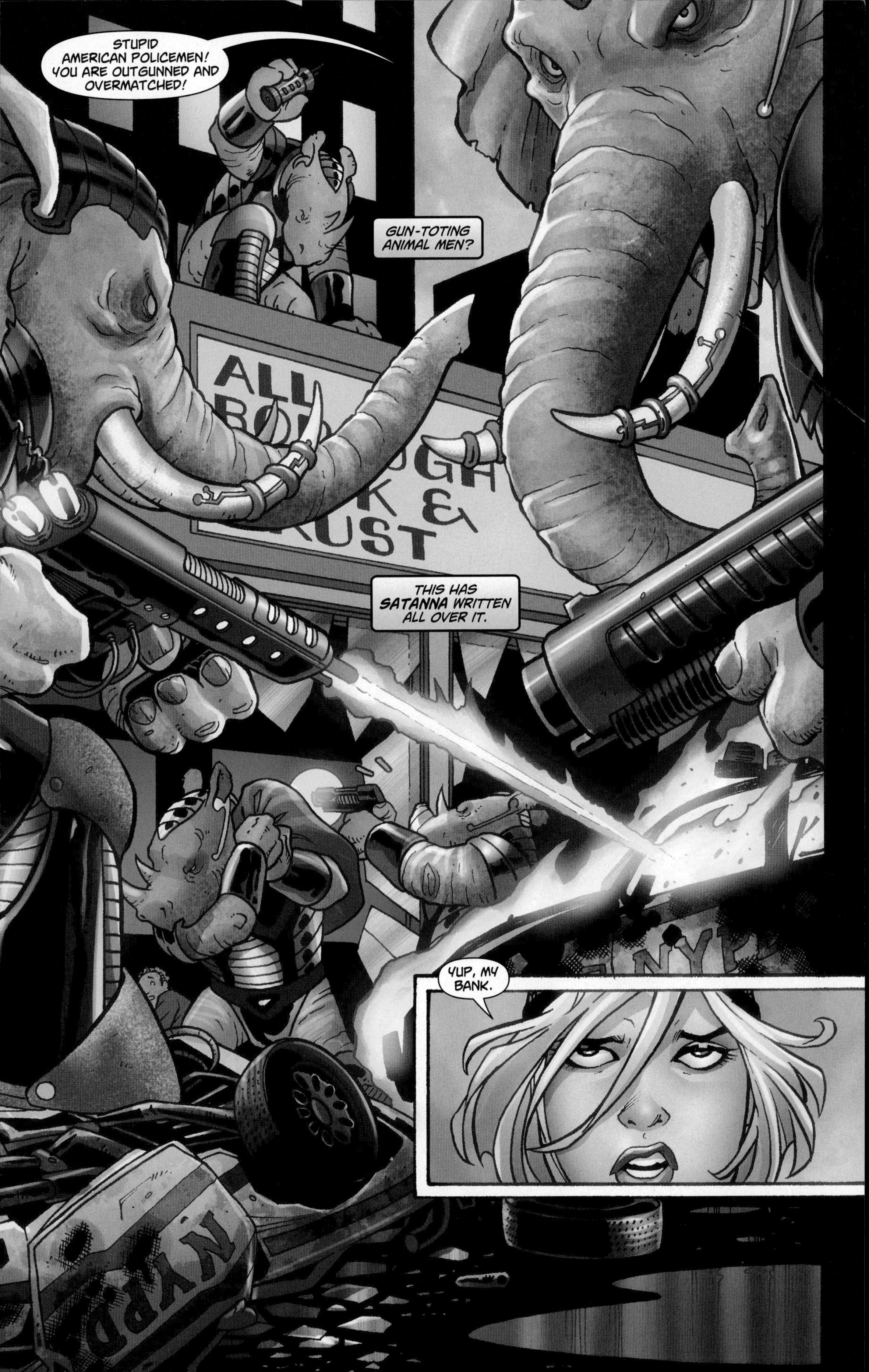
STUPID AMERICAN POLICEMEN! YOU ARE OUTGUNNED AND OVERMATCHED!
GUN-TOTING ANIMAL MEN?
ALL
UGH
K &
RUST
THIS HAS SATANNA WRITTEN ALL OVER IT.
YUP, MY BANK.
NYPD

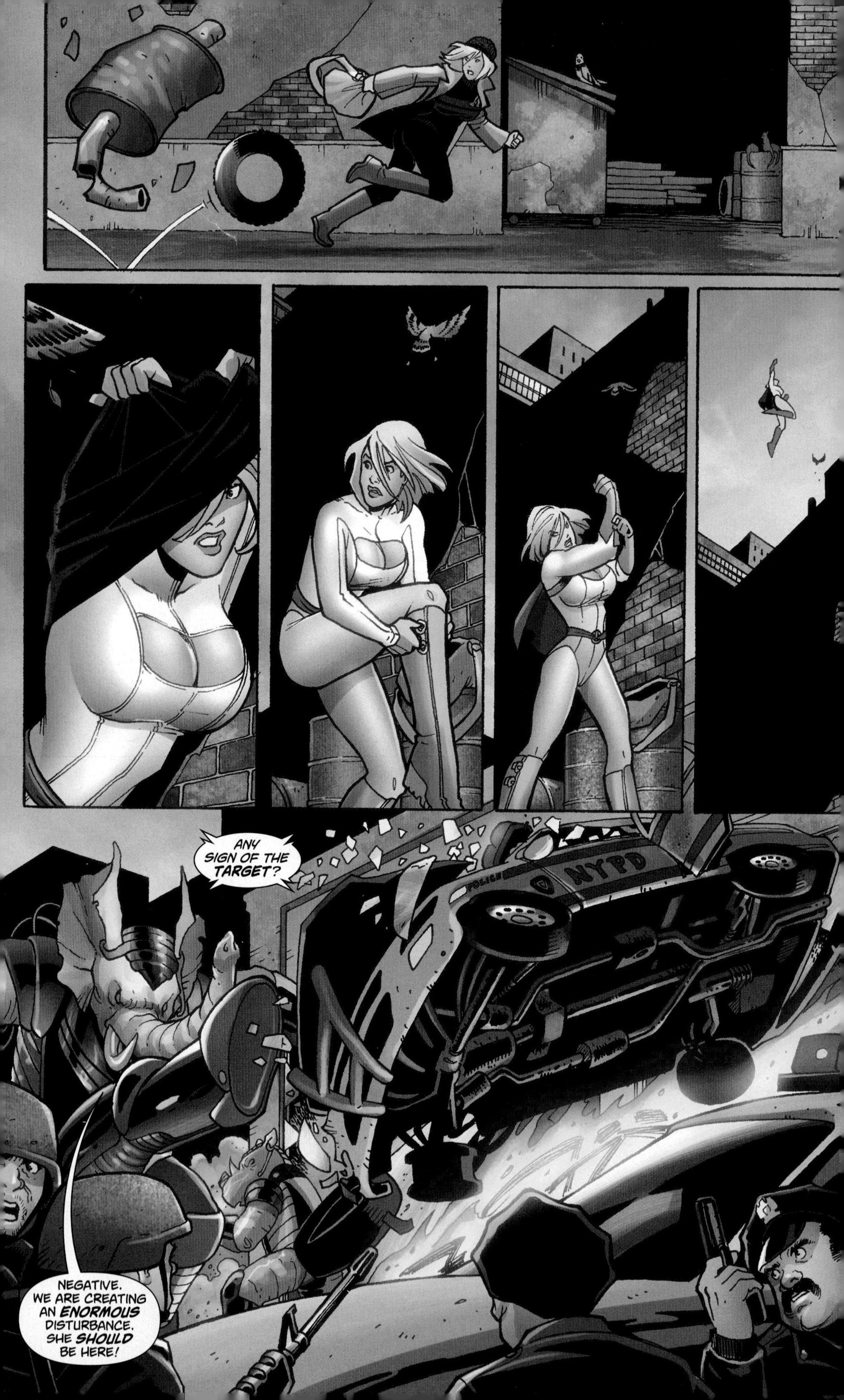
ANY SIGN OF THE TARGET?
NEGATIVE. WE ARE CREATING AN ENORMOUS DISTURBANCE. SHE SHOULD BE HERE!
NYPD
POLICE

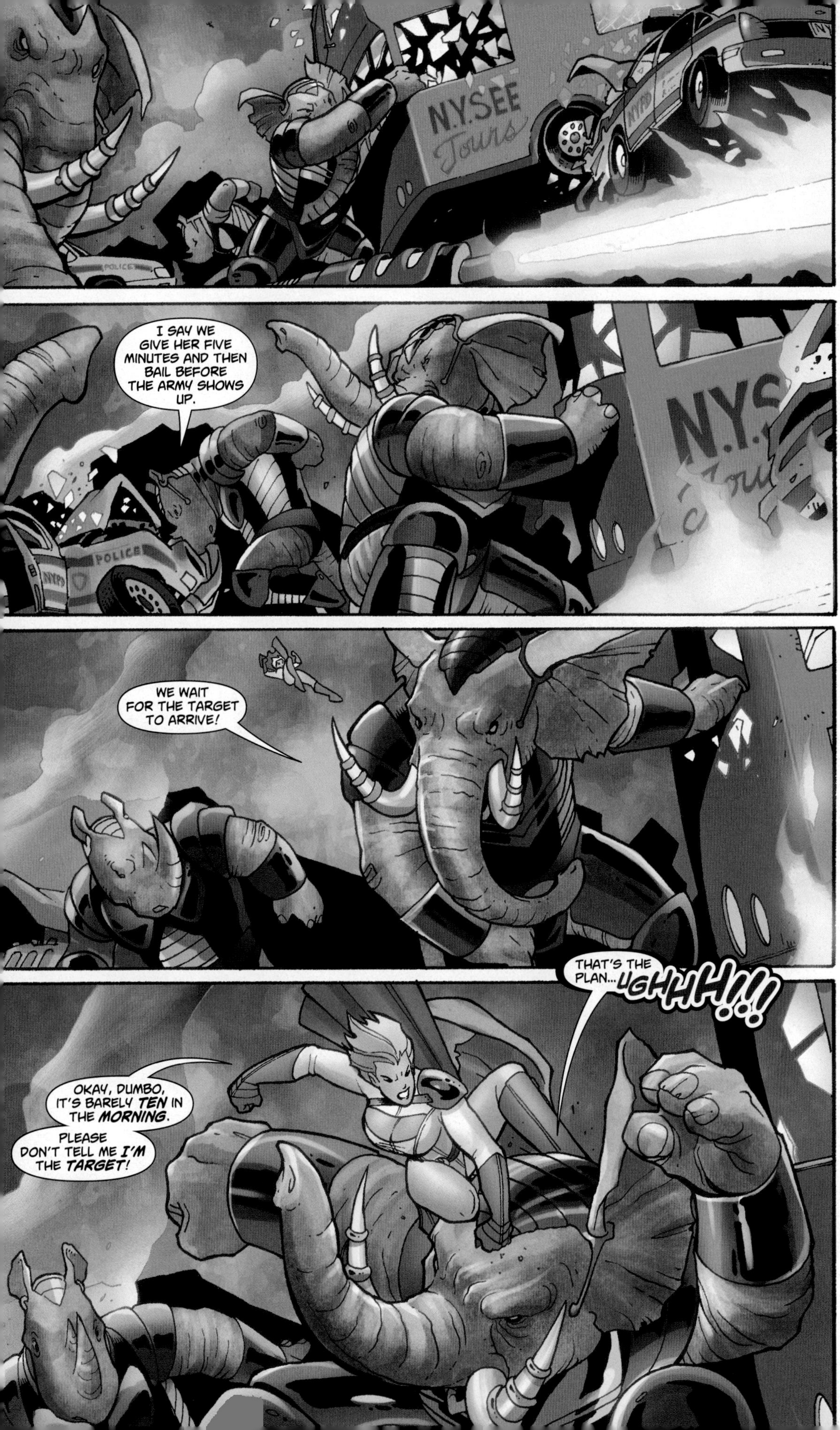
N.Y.SEE Tours
POLICE
NYPD
I SAY WE GIVE HER FIVE MINUTES AND THEN BAIL BEFORE THE ARMY SHOWS UP.
WE WAIT FOR THE TARGET TO ARRIVE!
THAT'S THE PLAN... UGHHH!!!
OKAY, DUMBO, IT'S BARELY TEN IN THE MORNING.
PLEASE DON'T TELL ME I'M THE TARGET!

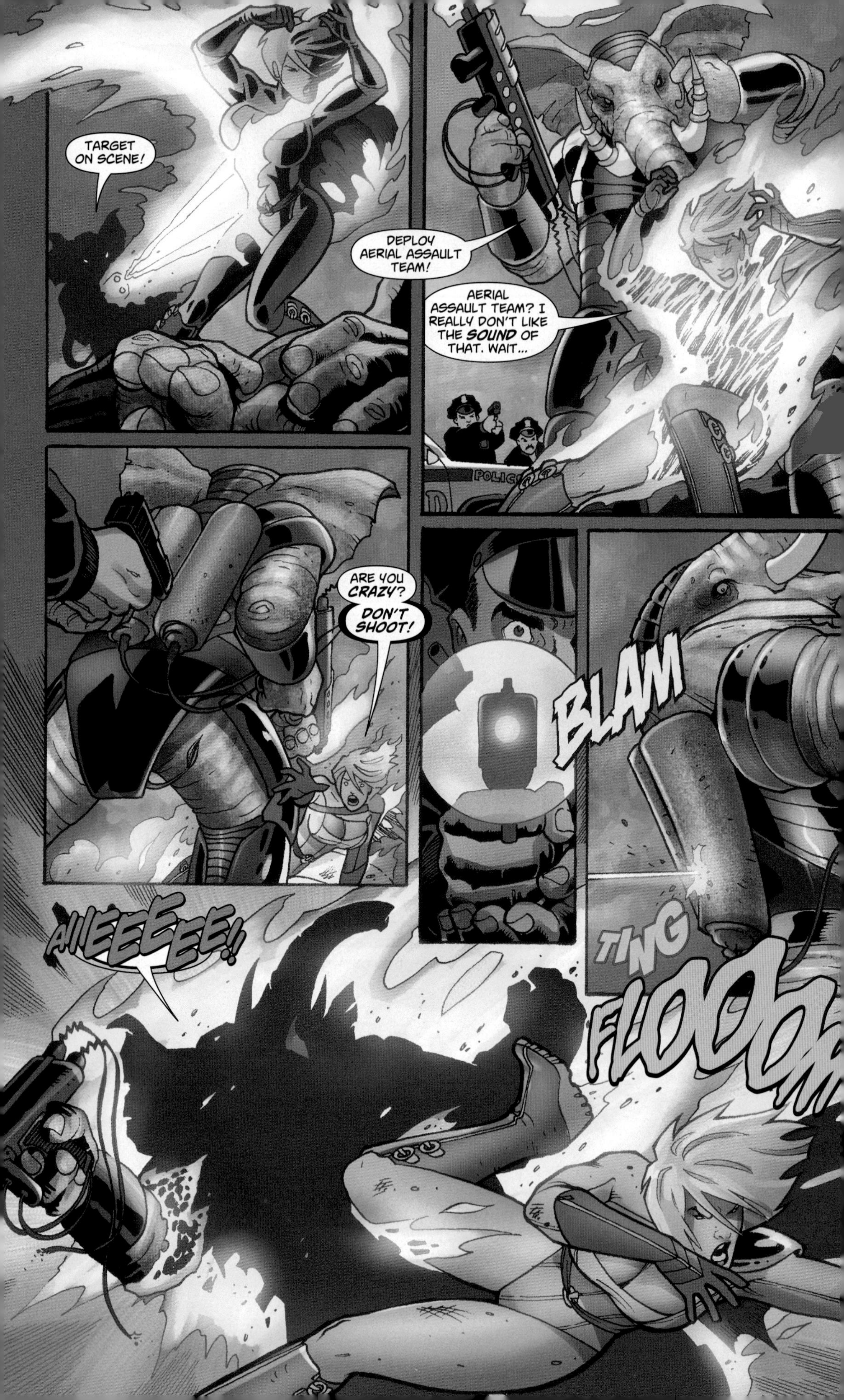
TARGET ON SCENE!
DEPLOY AERIAL ASSAULT TEAM!
AERIAL ASSAULT TEAM? I REALLY DON'T LIKE THE SOUND OF THAT. WAIT...
POLICE
ARE YOU CRAZY? DON'T SHOOT!
BLAM
TING
AIIEEEEEE!!
FLOOO

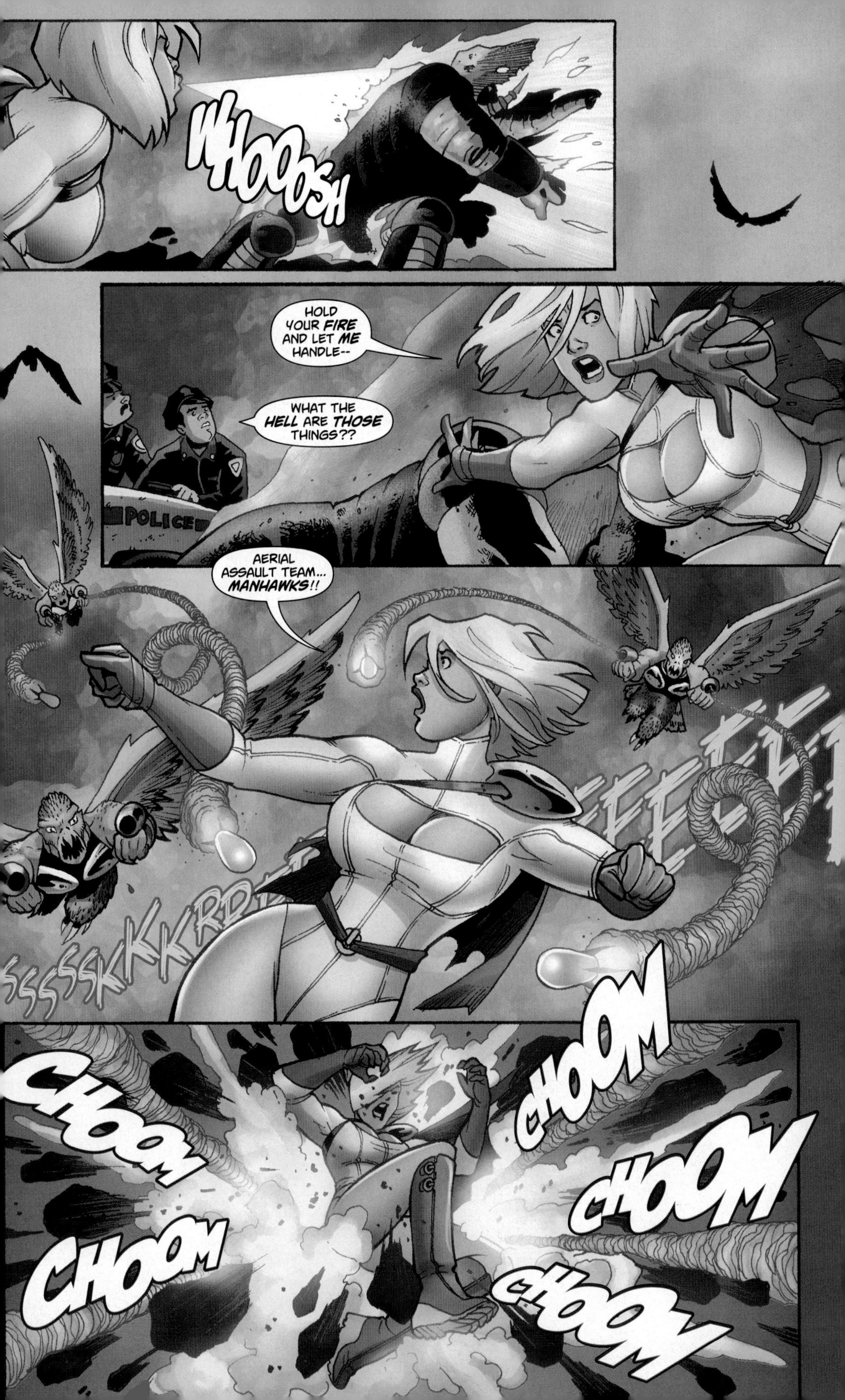
WHOOOSH
HOLD YOUR FIRE AND LET ME HANDLE--
WHAT THE HELL ARE THOSE THINGS??
POLICE
AERIAL ASSAULT TEAM... MANHAWKS!!
SSSSSSKKKRD
CHOOM
CHOOM
CHOOM
CHOOM
CHOOM

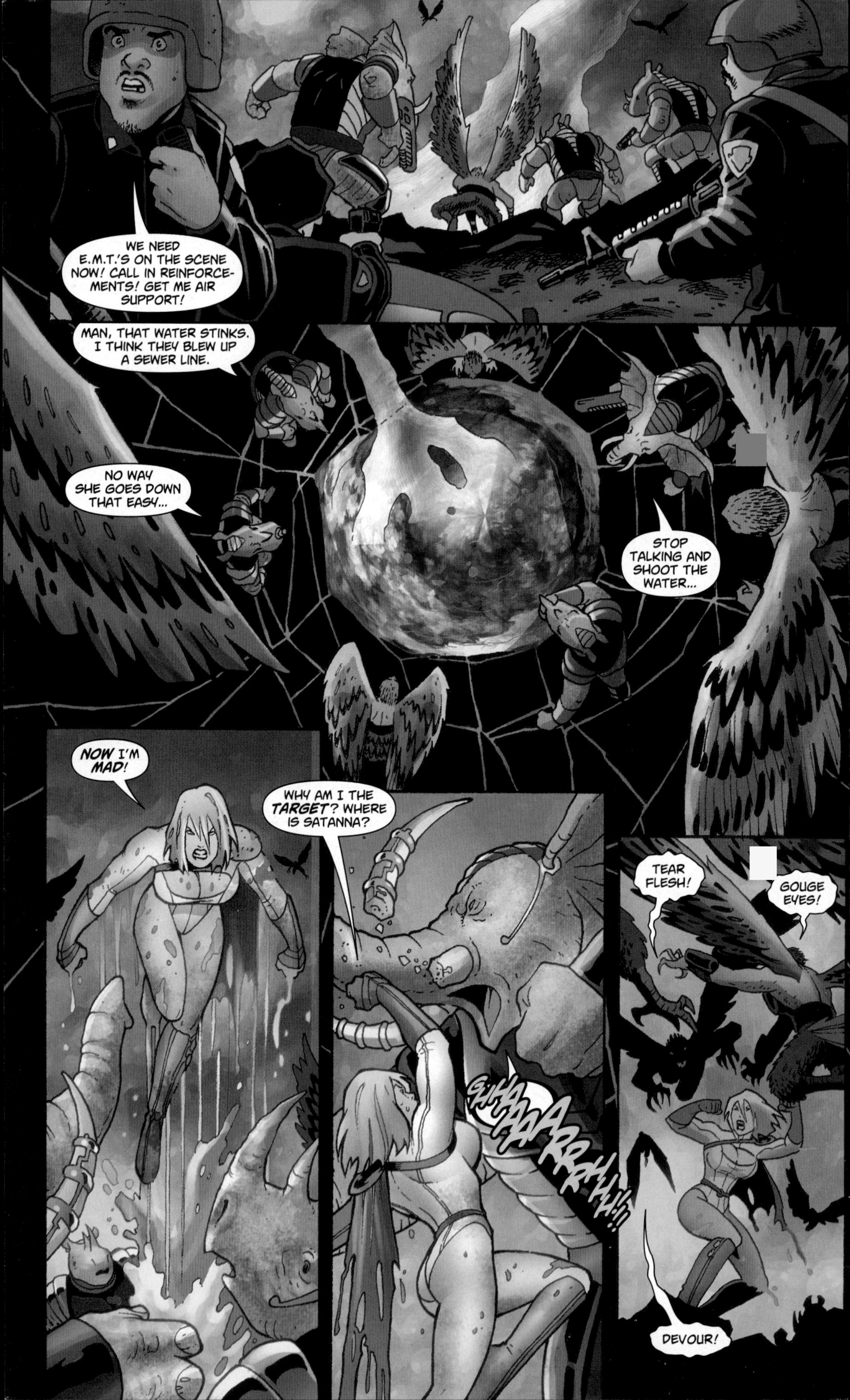
WE NEED E.M.T.'S ON THE SCENE NOW! CALL IN REINFORCEMENTS! GET ME AIR SUPPORT!
MAN, THAT WATER STINKS. I THINK THEY BLEW UP A SEWER LINE.
NO WAY SHE GOES DOWN THAT EASY...
STOP TALKING AND SHOOT THE WATER...
NOW I'M MAD!
WHY AM I THE TARGET? WHERE IS SATANNA?
GUHAAARRRHH!!
TEAR FLESH!
GOUGE EYES!
DEVOUR!

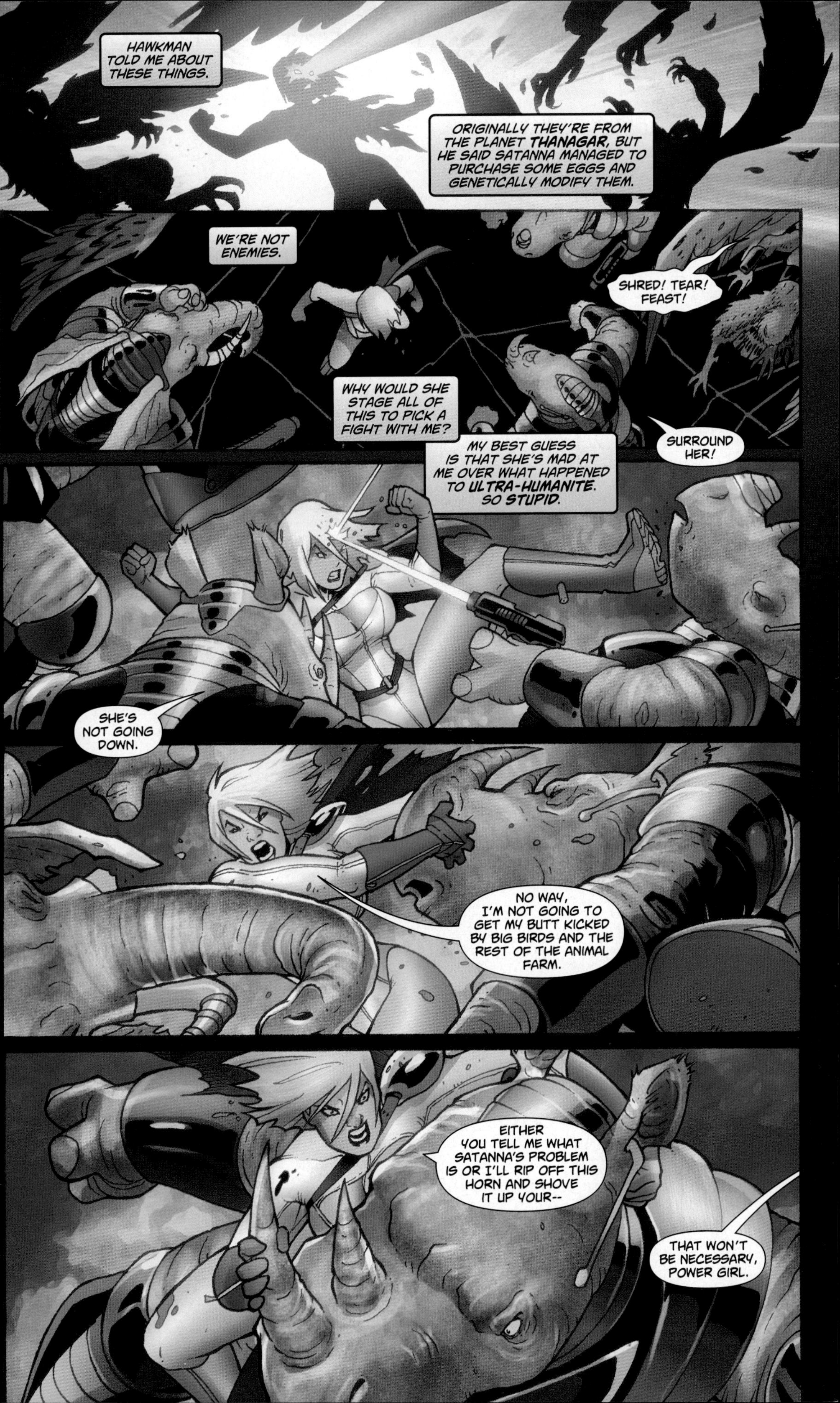
HAWKMAN TOLD ME ABOUT THESE THINGS.
ORIGINALLY THEY'RE FROM THE PLANET THANAGAR, BUT HE SAID SATANNA MANAGED TO PURCHASE SOME EGGS AND GENETICALLY MODIFY THEM.
WE'RE NOT ENEMIES.
SHRED! TEAR! FEAST!
WHY WOULD SHE STAGE ALL OF THIS TO PICK A FIGHT WITH ME?
SURROUND HER!
MY BEST GUESS IS THAT SHE'S MAD AT ME OVER WHAT HAPPENED TO ULTRA-HUMANITE. SO STUPID.
SHE'S NOT GOING DOWN.
NO WAY, I'M NOT GOING TO GET MY BUTT KICKED BY BIG BIRDS AND THE REST OF THE ANIMAL FARM.
EITHER YOU TELL ME WHAT SATANNA'S PROBLEM IS OR I'LL RIP OFF THIS HORN AND SHOVE IT UP YOUR--
THAT WON'T BE NECESSARY, POWER GIRL.

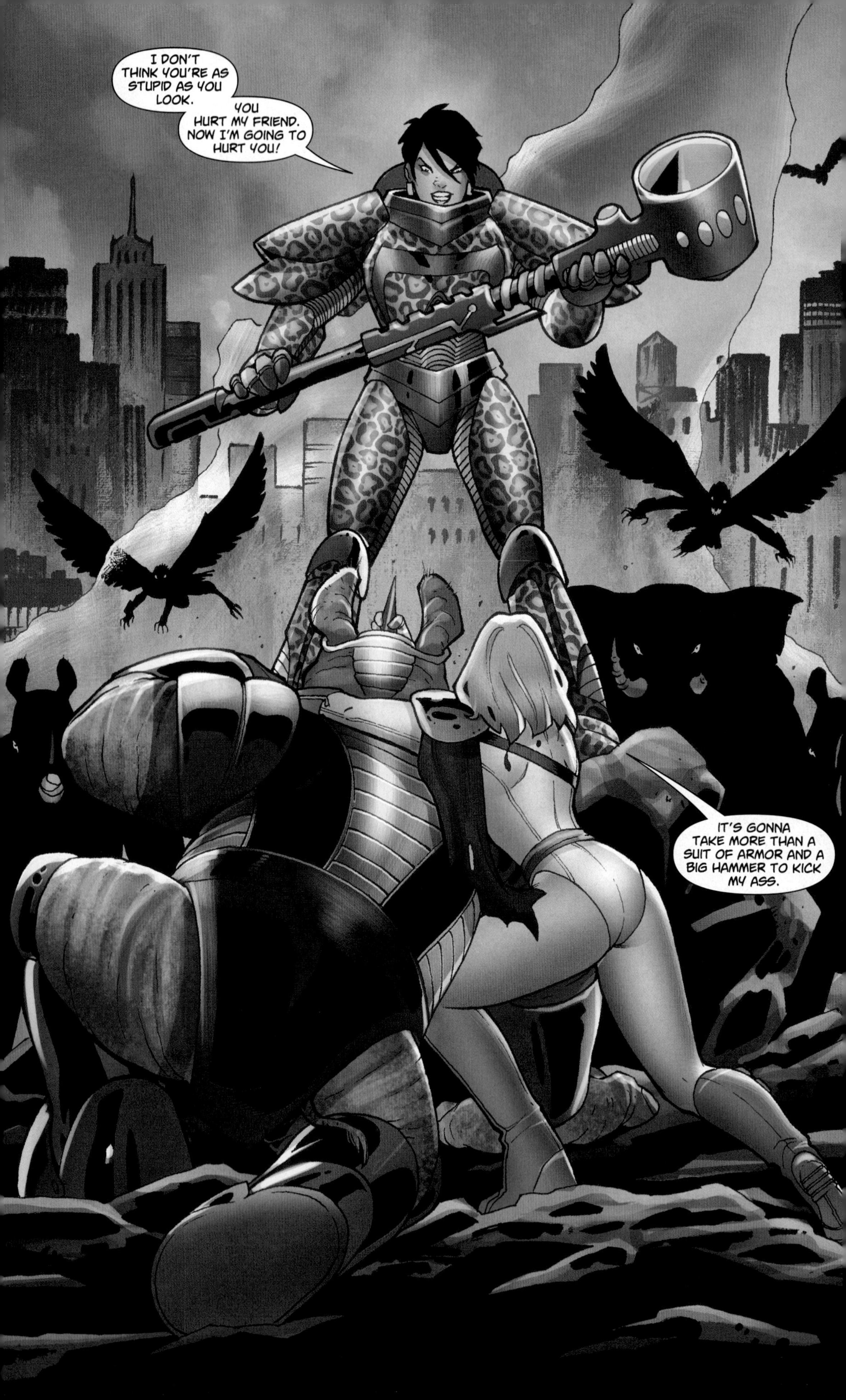
I DON'T THINK YOU'RE AS STUPID AS YOU LOOK.
YOU HURT MY FRIEND. NOW I'M GOING TO HURT YOU!
IT'S GONNA TAKE MORE THAN A SUIT OF ARMOR AND A BIG HAMMER TO KICK MY ASS.

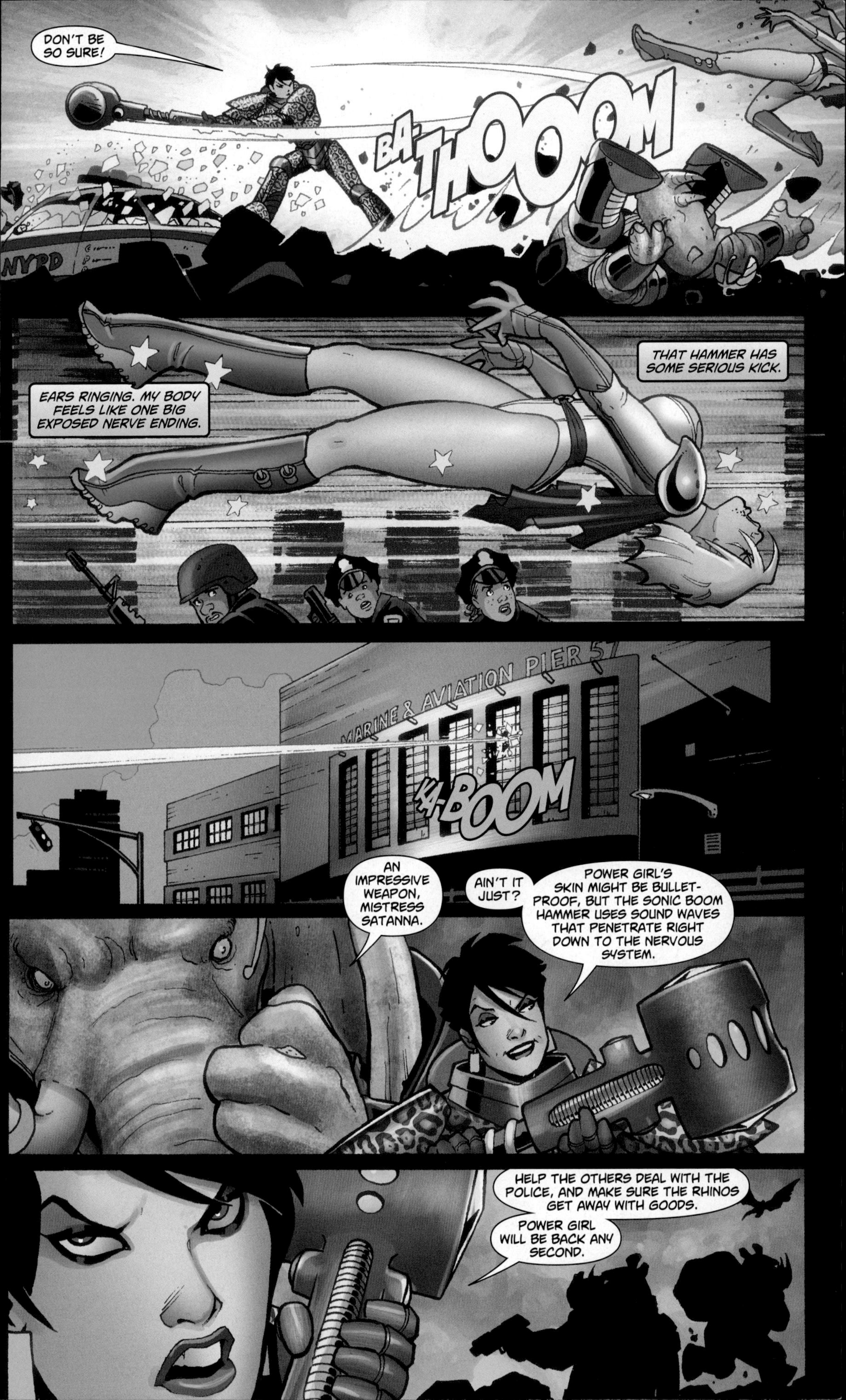
DON'T BE SO SURE!
BA-THOOOOM
NYPD
EARS RINGING. MY BODY FEELS LIKE ONE BIG EXPOSED NERVE ENDING.
THAT HAMMER HAS SOME SERIOUS KICK.
MARINE & AVIATION PIER 57
KA-BOOM
AN IMPRESSIVE WEAPON, MISTRESS SATANNA.
AIN'T IT JUST?
POWER GIRL'S SKIN MIGHT BE BULLET-PROOF, BUT THE SONIC BOOM HAMMER USES SOUND WAVES THAT PENETRATE RIGHT DOWN TO THE NERVOUS SYSTEM.
HELP THE OTHERS DEAL WITH THE POLICE, AND MAKE SURE THE RHINOS GET AWAY WITH GOODS.
POWER GIRL WILL BE BACK ANY SECOND.

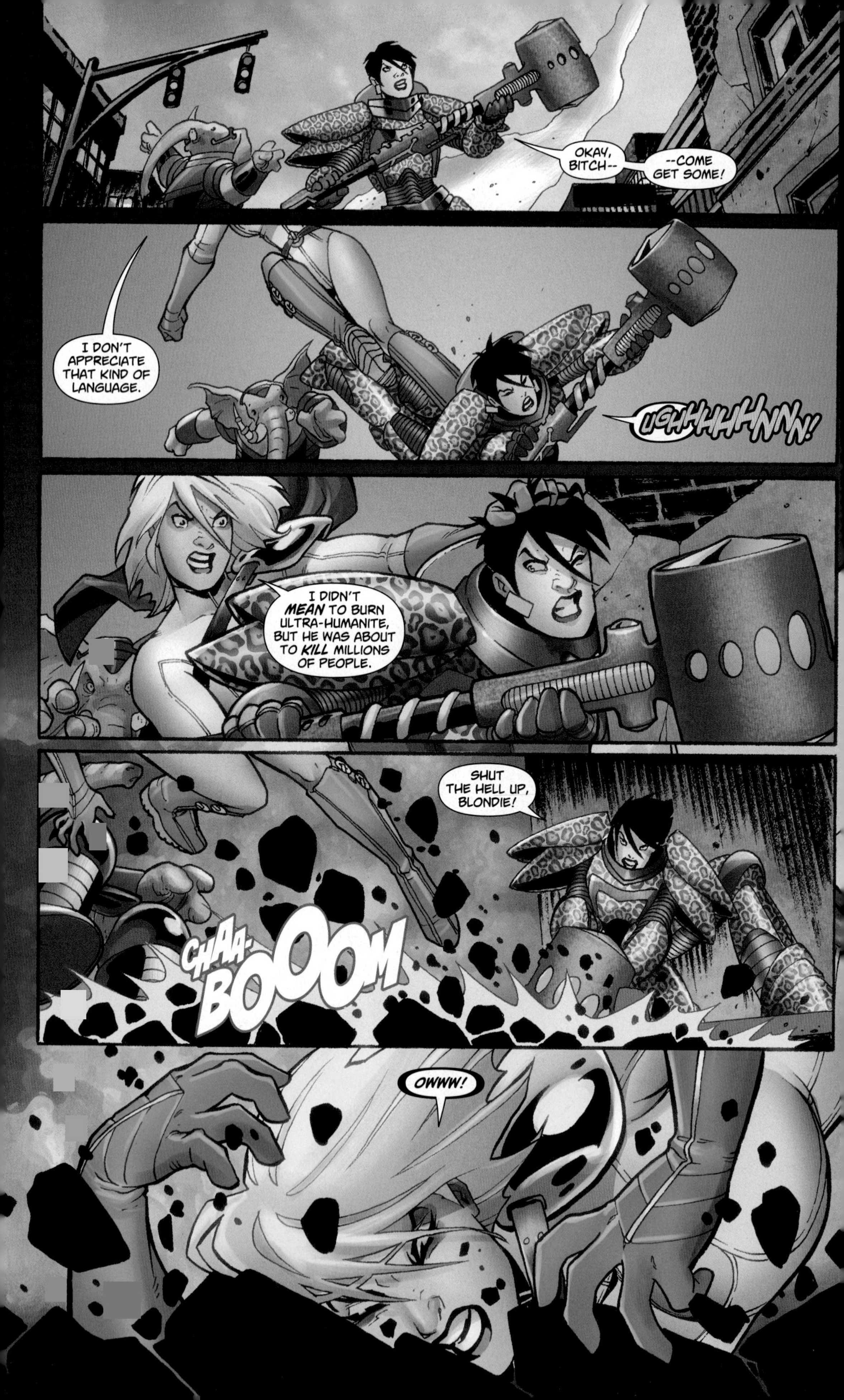
OKAY, BITCH--
--COME GET SOME!
I DON'T APPRECIATE THAT KIND OF LANGUAGE.
UGHHHHHNNN!
I DIDN'T MEAN TO BURN ULTRA-HUMANITE, BUT HE WAS ABOUT TO KILL MILLIONS OF PEOPLE.
SHUT THE HELL UP, BLONDIE!
CHAA-BOOOM
OWWW!

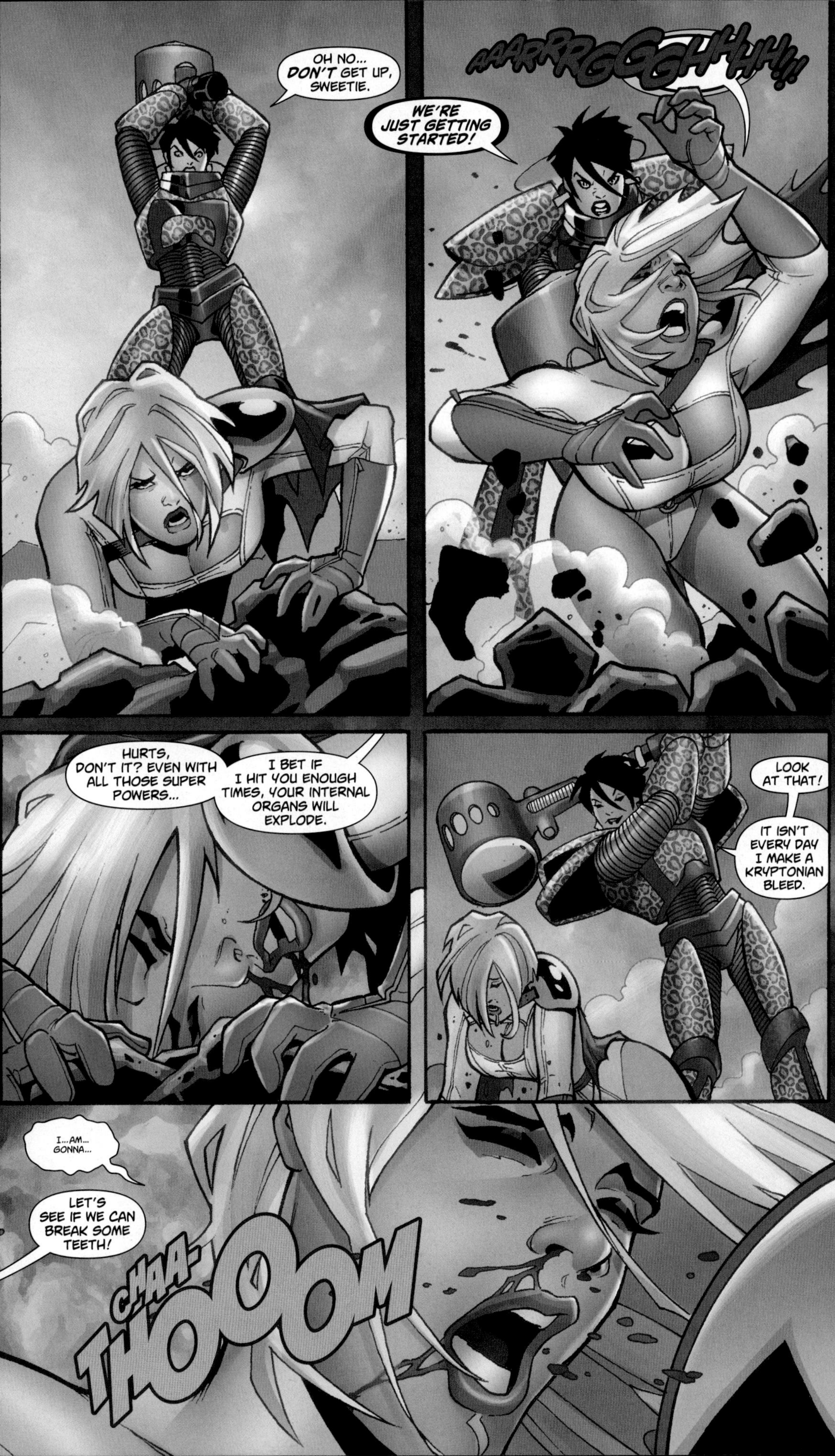

OH NO... DON'T GET UP, SWEETIE.
WE'RE JUST GETTING STARTED!
AAAARRRRGGGGHHHHH!!!
HURTS, DON'T IT? EVEN WITH ALL THOSE SUPER POWERS...
I BET IF I HIT YOU ENOUGH TIMES, YOUR INTERNAL ORGANS WILL EXPLODE.
LOOK AT THAT!
IT ISN'T EVERY DAY I MAKE A KRYPTONIAN BLEED.
I...AM... GONNA...
LET'S SEE IF WE CAN BREAK SOME TEETH!
CHAA-THOOOM

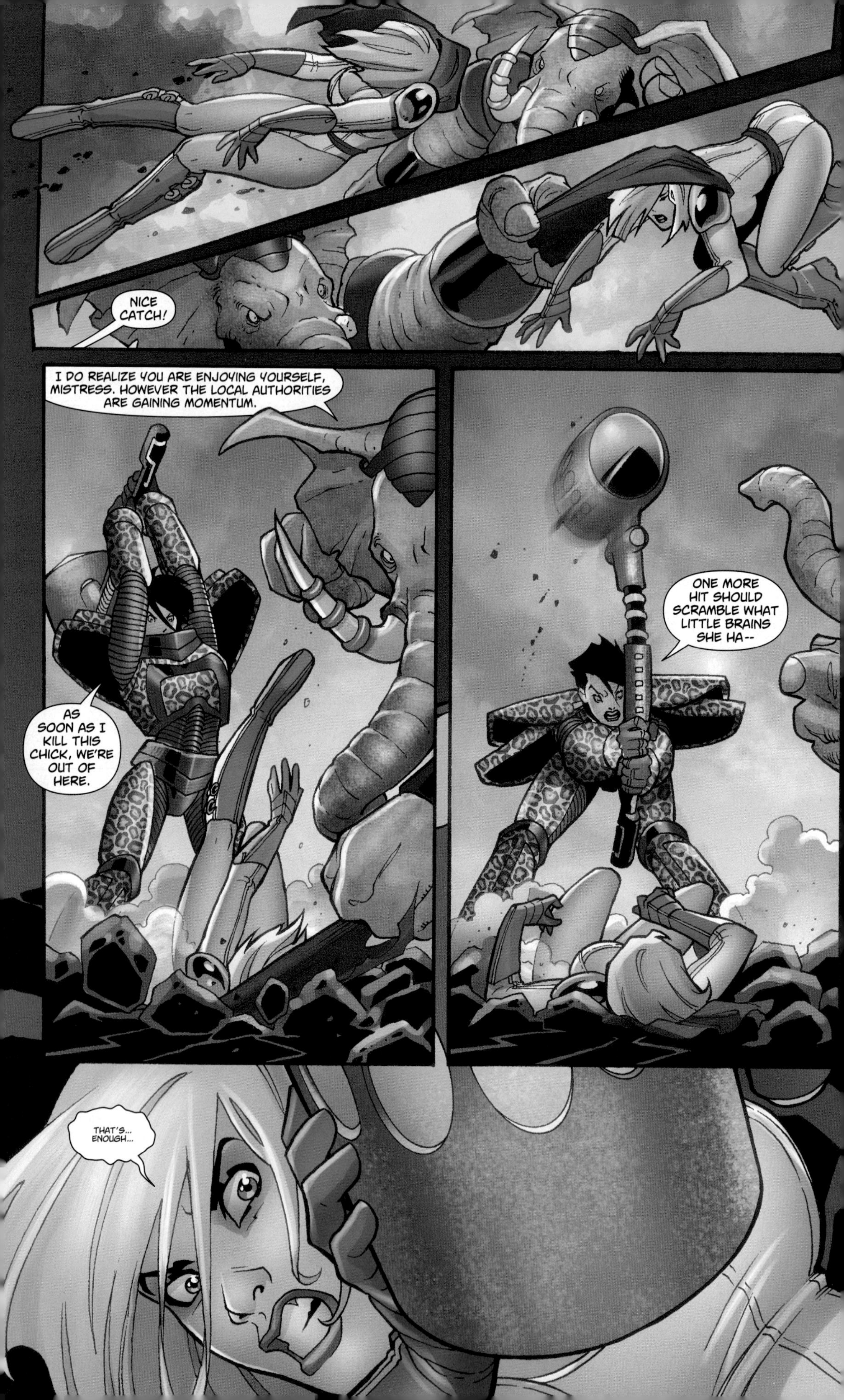
NICE CATCH!
I DO REALIZE YOU ARE ENJOYING YOURSELF, MISTRESS. HOWEVER THE LOCAL AUTHORITIES ARE GAINING MOMENTUM.
AS SOON AS I KILL THIS CHICK, WE'RE OUT OF HERE.
ONE MORE HIT SHOULD SCRAMBLE WHAT LITTLE BRAINS SHE HA--
THAT'S... ENOUGH...

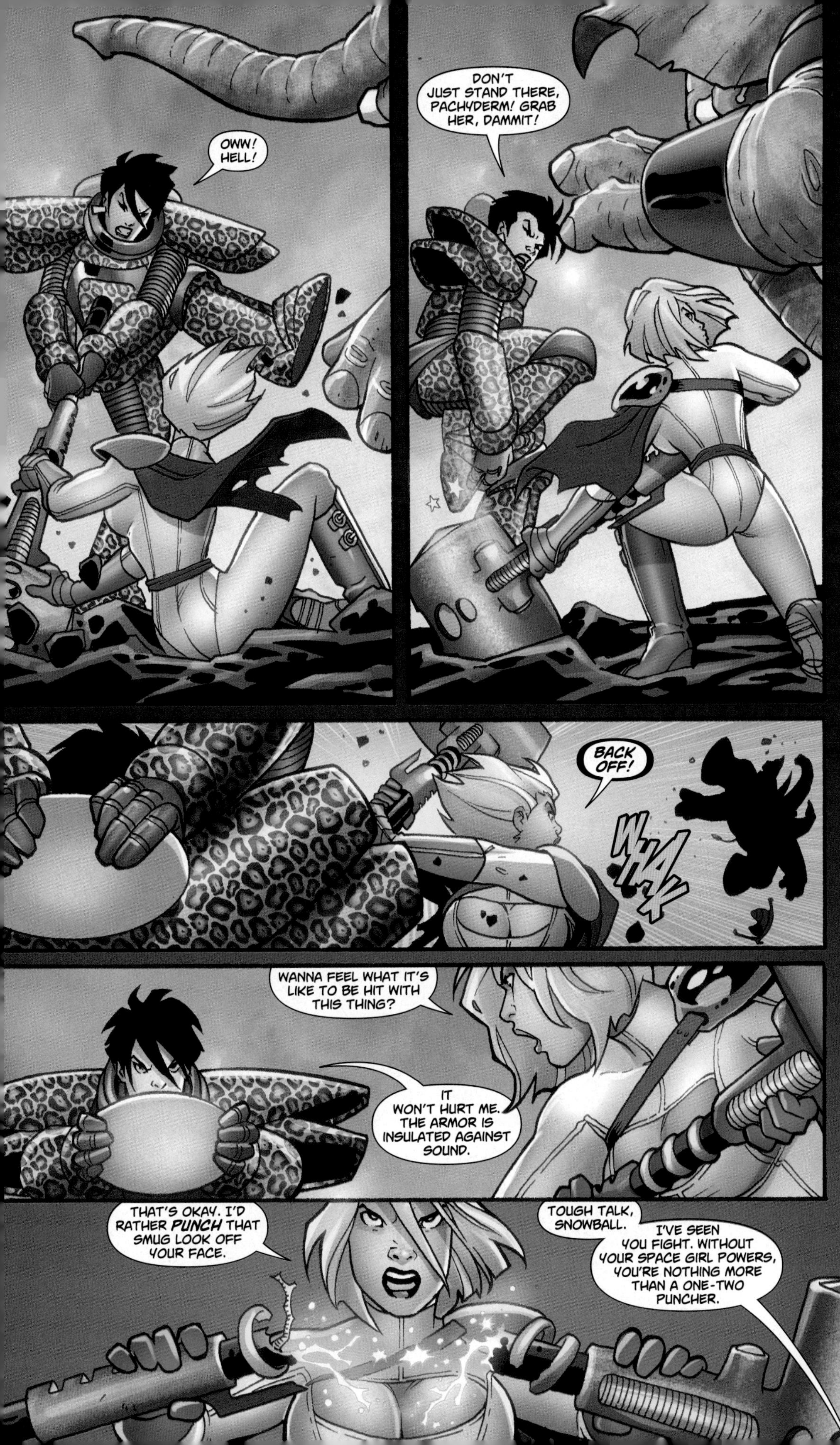
OWW! HELL!
DON'T JUST STAND THERE, PACHYDERM! GRAB HER, DAMMIT!
BACK OFF!
WHAK
WANNA FEEL WHAT IT'S LIKE TO BE HIT WITH THIS THING?
IT WON'T HURT ME. THE ARMOR IS INSULATED AGAINST SOUND.
THAT'S OKAY. I'D RATHER PUNCH THAT SMUG LOOK OFF YOUR FACE.
TOUGH TALK, SNOWBALL.
I'VE SEEN YOU FIGHT. WITHOUT YOUR SPACE GIRL POWERS, YOU'RE NOTHING MORE THAN A ONE-TWO PUNCHER.

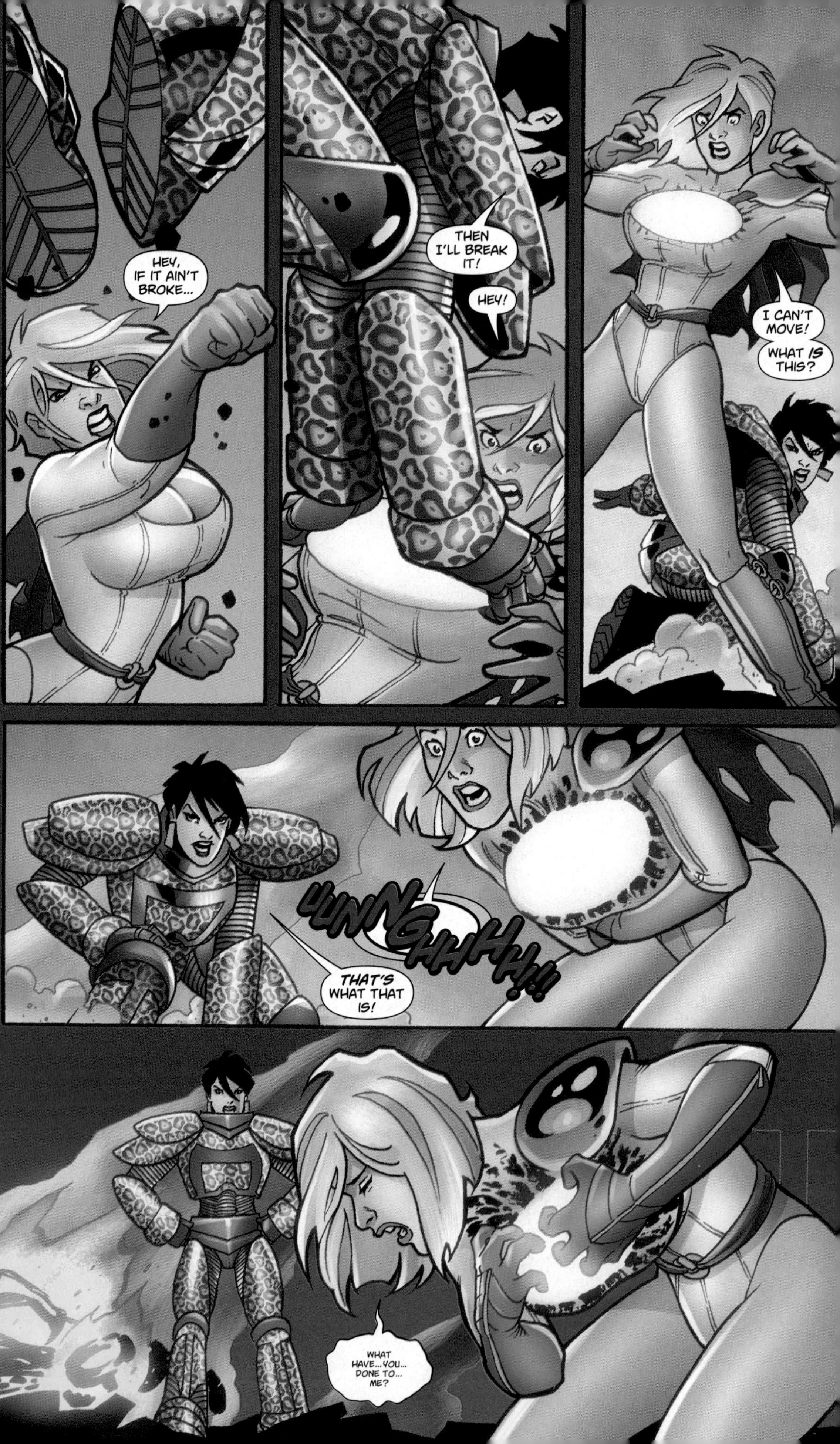
HEY, IF IT AIN'T BROKE...
THEN I'LL BREAK IT!
HEY!
I CAN'T MOVE! WHAT IS THIS?
UUNNGHHHHH!!!
THAT'S WHAT THAT IS!
WHAT HAVE...YOU... DONE TO... ME?

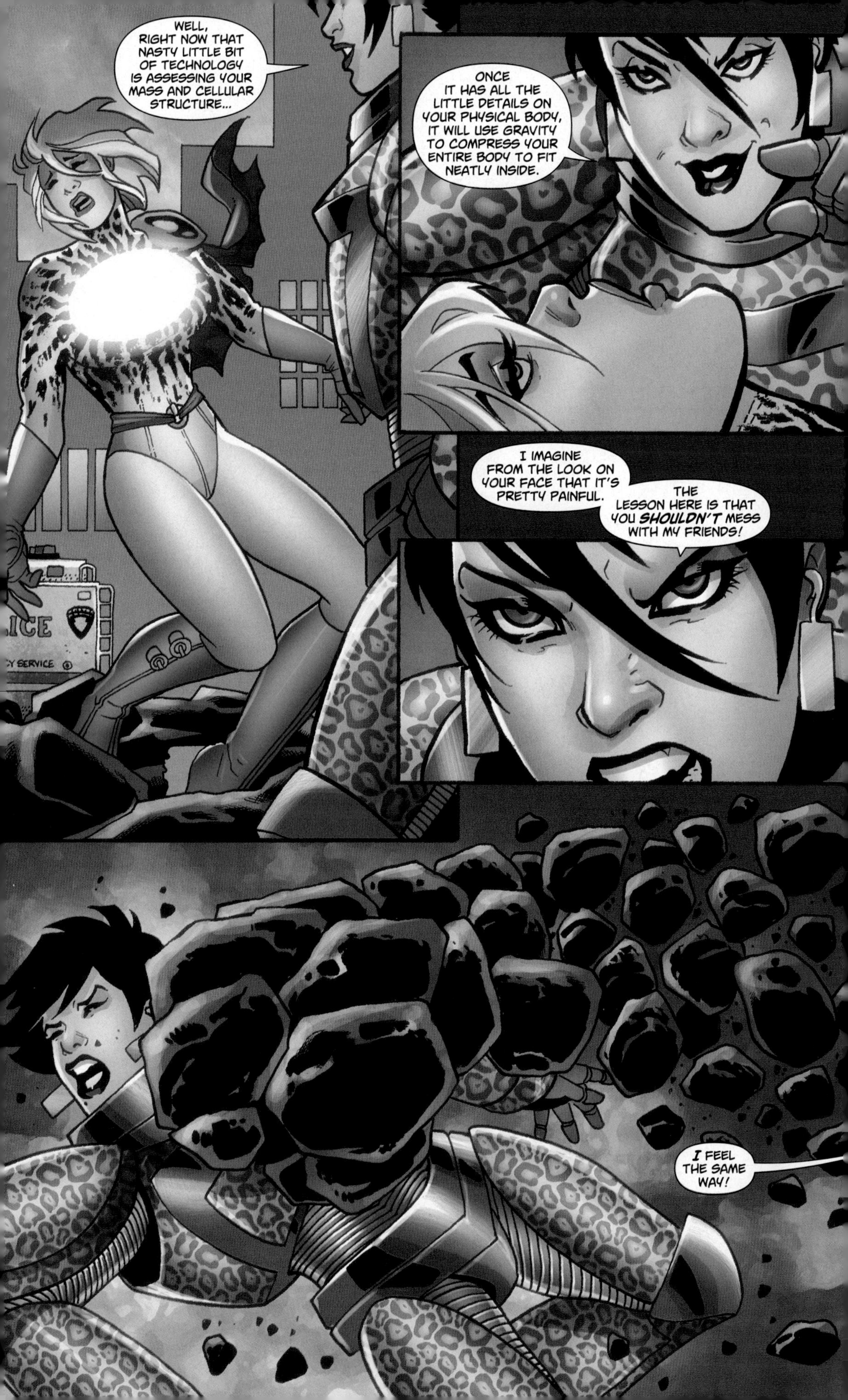
WELL, RIGHT NOW THAT NASTY LITTLE BIT OF TECHNOLOGY IS ASSESSING YOUR MASS AND CELLULAR STRUCTURE...
ONCE IT HAS ALL THE LITTLE DETAILS ON YOUR PHYSICAL BODY, IT WILL USE GRAVITY TO COMPRESS YOUR ENTIRE BODY TO FIT NEATLY INSIDE.
I IMAGINE FROM THE LOOK ON YOUR FACE THAT IT'S PRETTY PAINFUL.
THE LESSON HERE IS THAT YOU SHOULDN'T MESS WITH MY FRIENDS!
I FEEL THE SAME WAY!

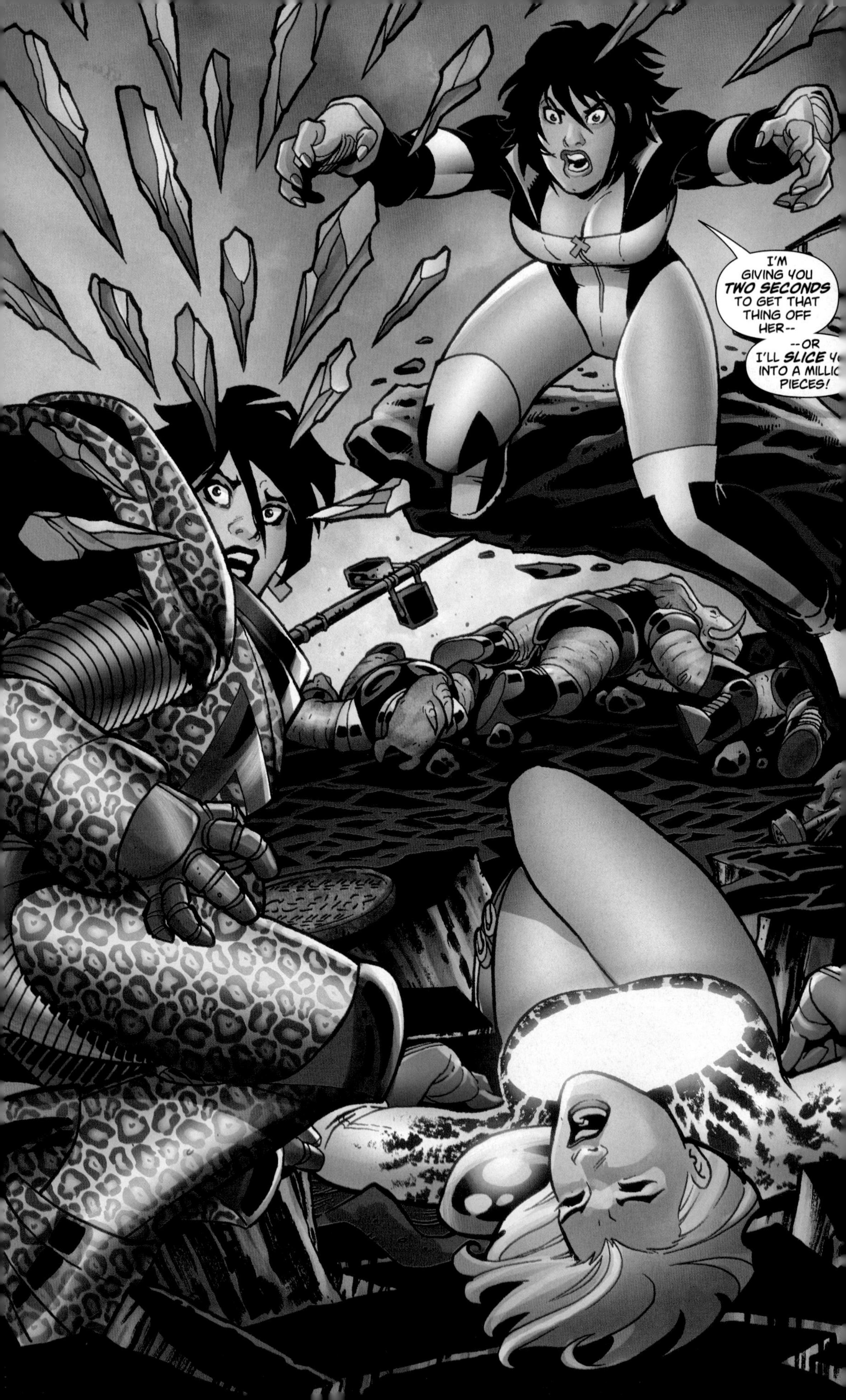
I'M GIVING YOU **TWO SECONDS** TO GET THAT THING OFF HER--
--OR I'LL **SLICE** YO INTO A MILLIO PIECES!

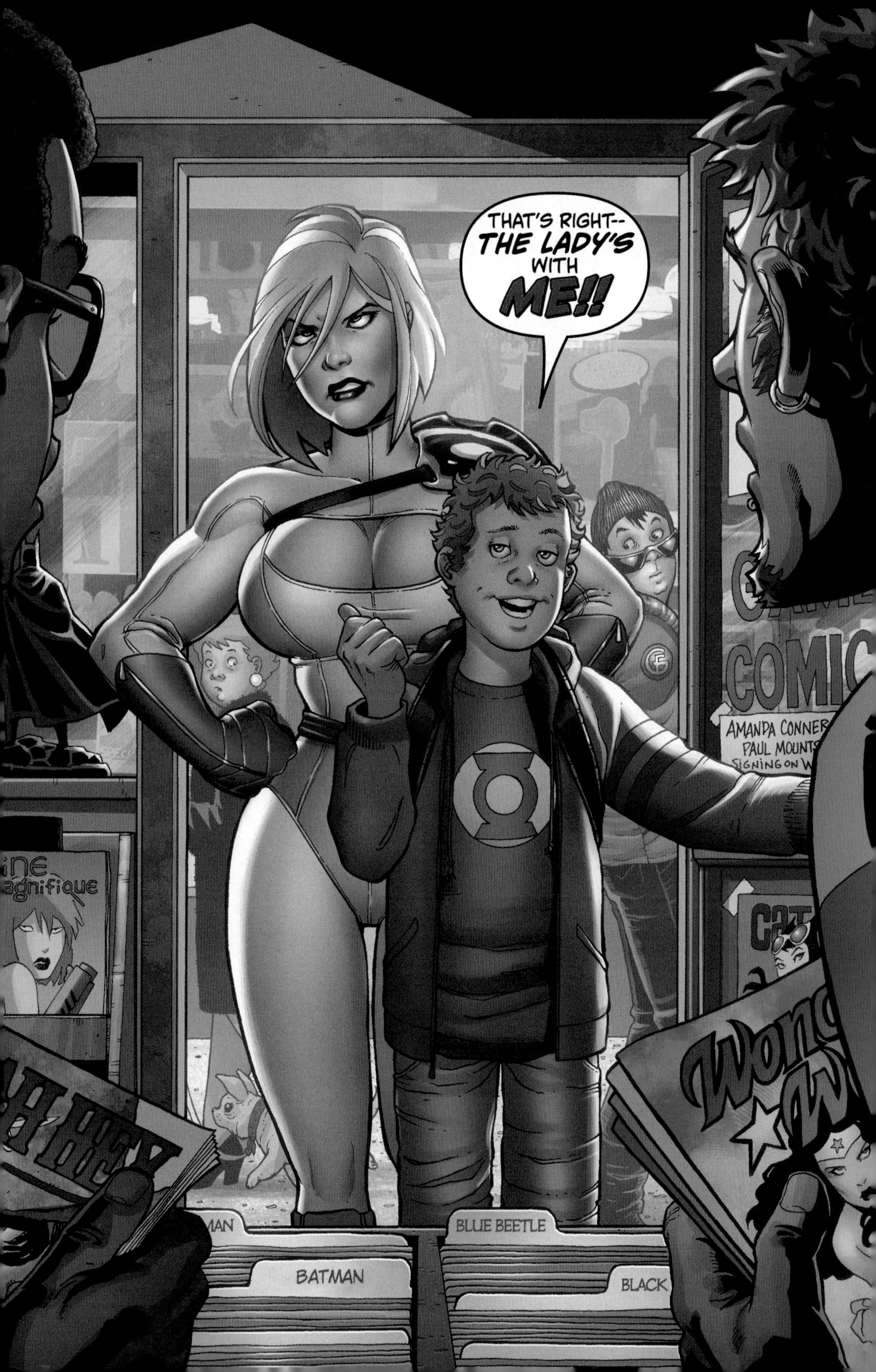
THAT'S RIGHT--
THE LADY'S
WITH
ME!!
AMANDA CONNER
PAUL MOUNTS
SIGNING ON W
COMIC
BLUE BEETLE
BATMAN
BLACK

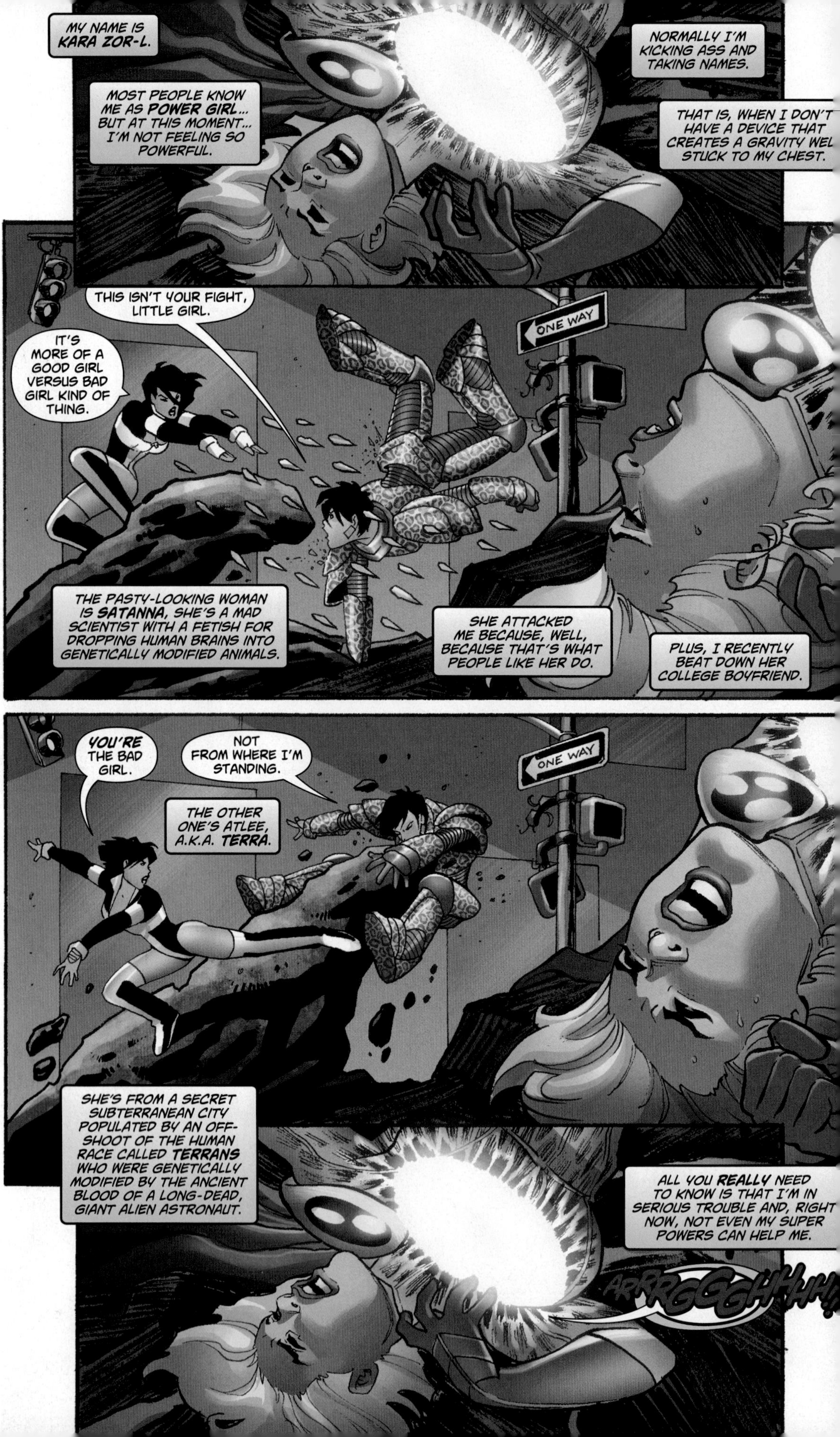

MY NAME IS KARA ZOR-L.
MOST PEOPLE KNOW ME AS POWER GIRL... BUT AT THIS MOMENT... I'M NOT FEELING SO POWERFUL.
NORMALLY I'M KICKING ASS AND TAKING NAMES.
THAT IS, WHEN I DON'T HAVE A DEVICE THAT CREATES A GRAVITY WEL STUCK TO MY CHEST.
THIS ISN'T YOUR FIGHT, LITTLE GIRL.
IT'S MORE OF A GOOD GIRL VERSUS BAD GIRL KIND OF THING.
ONE WAY
THE PASTY-LOOKING WOMAN IS SATANNA, SHE'S A MAD SCIENTIST WITH A FETISH FOR DROPPING HUMAN BRAINS INTO GENETICALLY MODIFIED ANIMALS.
SHE ATTACKED ME BECAUSE, WELL, BECAUSE THAT'S WHAT PEOPLE LIKE HER DO.
PLUS, I RECENTLY BEAT DOWN HER COLLEGE BOYFRIEND.
YOU'RE THE BAD GIRL.
NOT FROM WHERE I'M STANDING.
THE OTHER ONE'S ATLEE, A.K.A. TERRA.
ONE WAY
SHE'S FROM A SECRET SUBTERRANEAN CITY POPULATED BY AN OFF-SHOOT OF THE HUMAN RACE CALLED TERRANS WHO WERE GENETICALLY MODIFIED BY THE ANCIENT BLOOD OF A LONG-DEAD, GIANT ALIEN ASTRONAUT.
ALL YOU REALLY NEED TO KNOW IS THAT I'M IN SERIOUS TROUBLE AND, RIGHT NOW, NOT EVEN MY SUPER POWERS CAN HELP ME.
ARRRGGGHHHH!

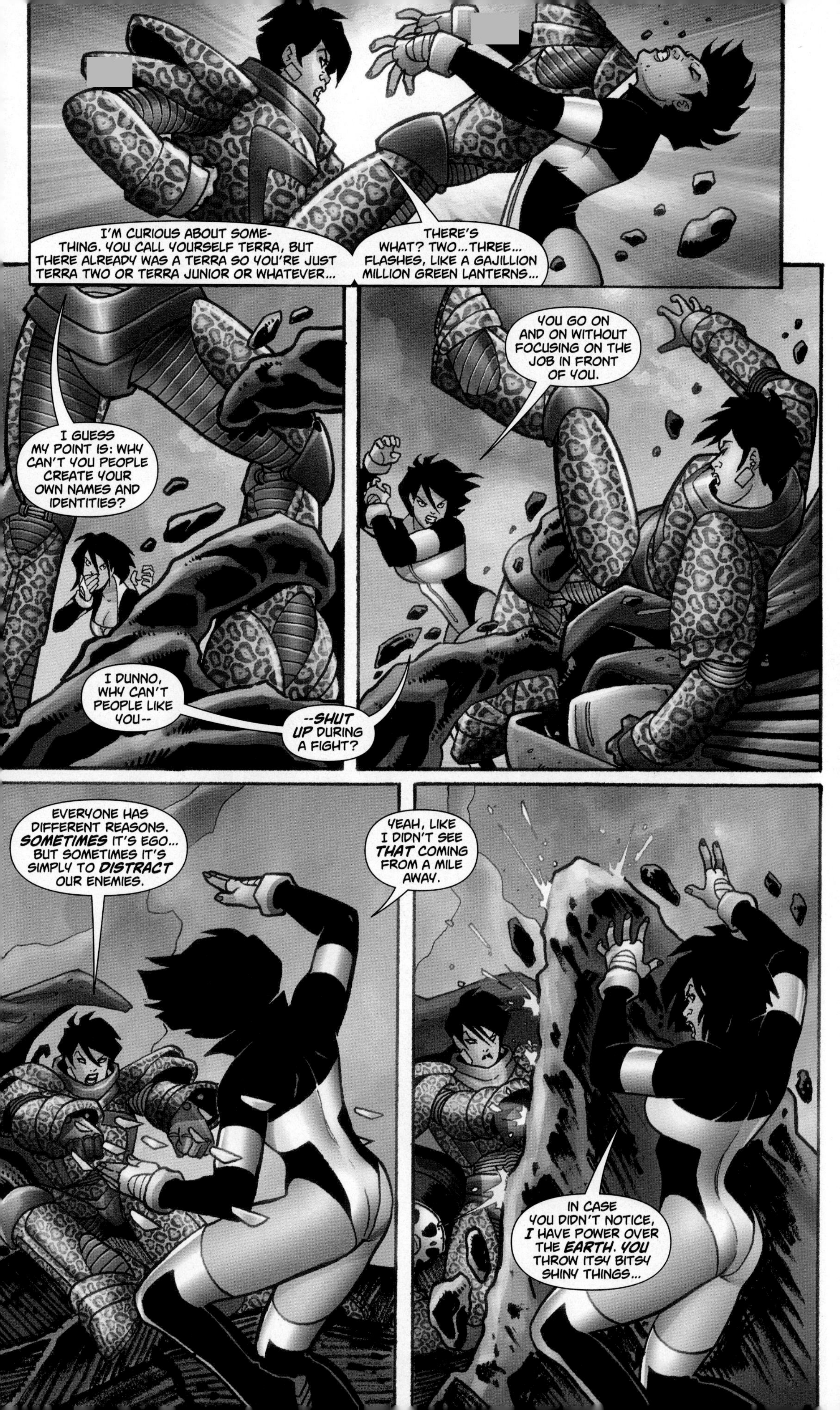
I'M CURIOUS ABOUT SOMETHING. YOU CALL YOURSELF TERRA, BUT THERE ALREADY WAS A TERRA SO YOU'RE JUST TERRA TWO OR TERRA JUNIOR OR WHATEVER...
THERE'S WHAT? TWO...THREE... FLASHES, LIKE A GAJILLION MILLION GREEN LANTERNS...
I GUESS MY POINT IS: WHY CAN'T YOU PEOPLE CREATE YOUR OWN NAMES AND IDENTITIES?
I DUNNO, WHY CAN'T PEOPLE LIKE YOU--
--**SHUT UP** DURING A FIGHT?
YOU GO ON AND ON WITHOUT FOCUSING ON THE JOB IN FRONT OF YOU.
EVERYONE HAS DIFFERENT REASONS. ***SOMETIMES*** IT'S EGO... BUT SOMETIMES IT'S SIMPLY TO ***DISTRACT*** OUR ENEMIES.
YEAH, LIKE I DIDN'T SEE ***THAT*** COMING FROM A MILE AWAY.
IN CASE YOU DIDN'T NOTICE, ***I*** HAVE POWER OVER THE ***EARTH***. ***YOU*** THROW ITSY BITSY SHINY THINGS...

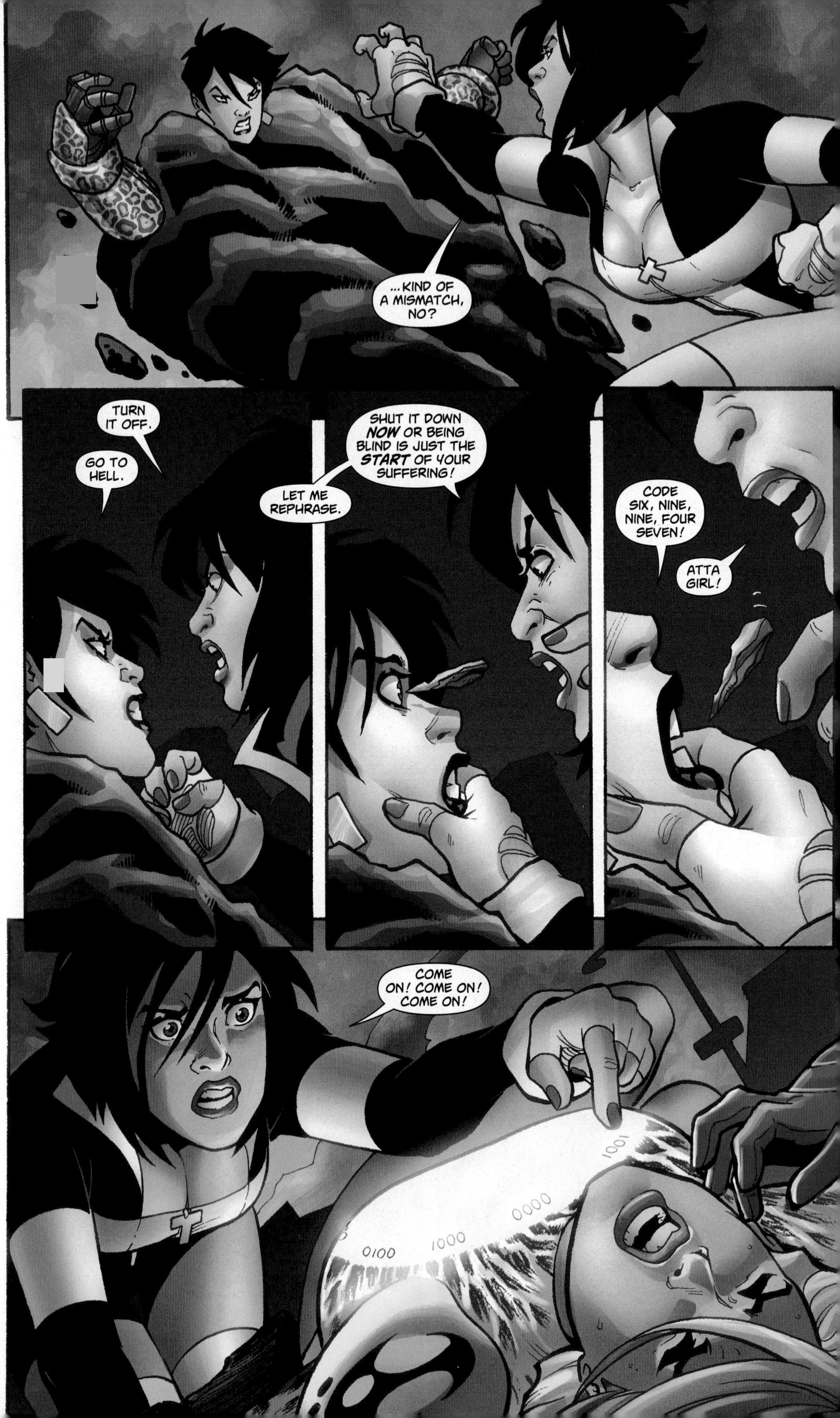
...KIND OF A MISMATCH, NO?
TURN IT OFF.
GO TO HELL.
LET ME REPHRASE.
SHUT IT DOWN NOW OR BEING BLIND IS JUST THE START OF YOUR SUFFERING!
CODE SIX, NINE, NINE, FOUR SEVEN!
ATTA GIRL!
COME ON! COME ON! COME ON!
1001
0000
1000
0100

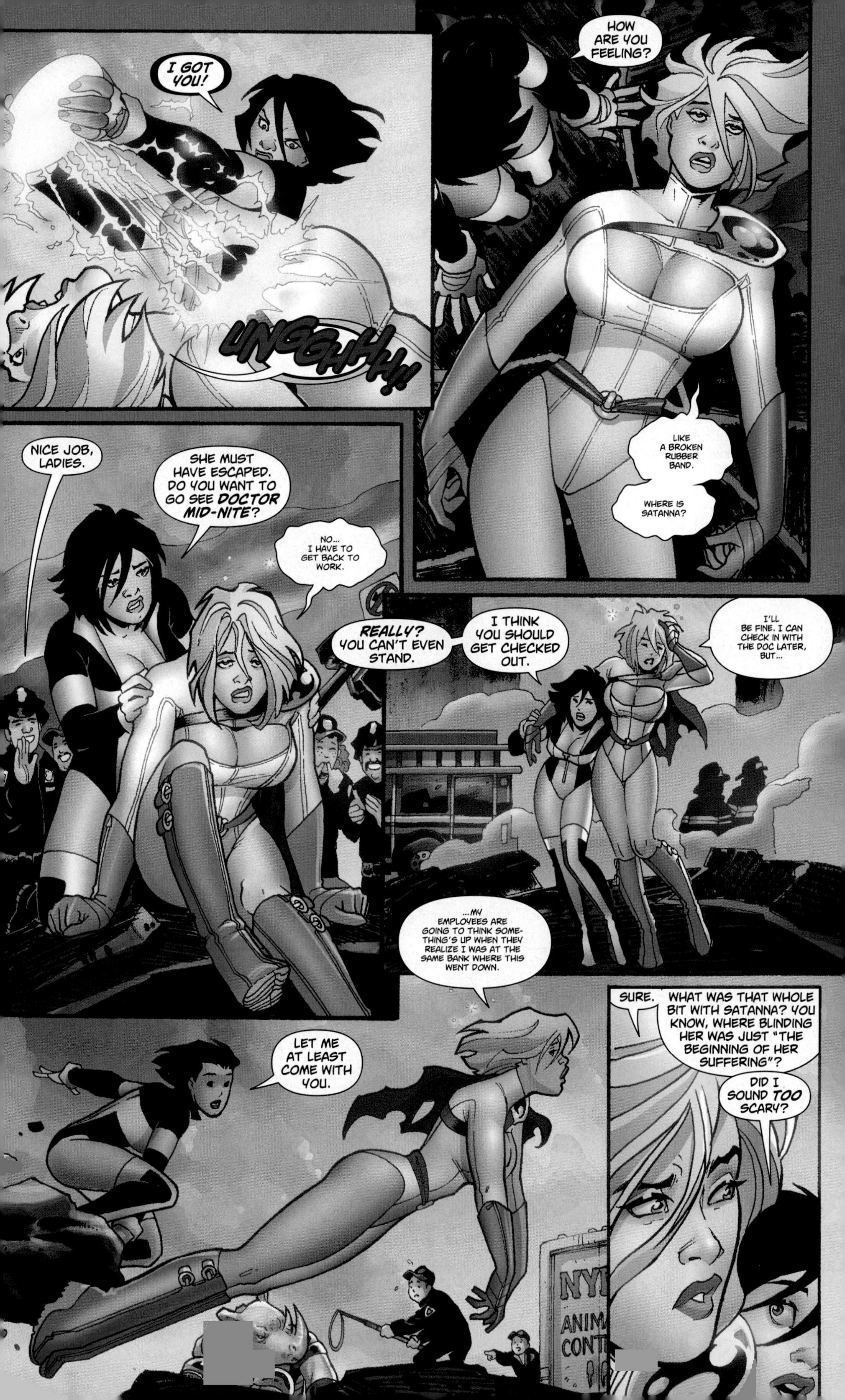
I GOT YOU!
UNGGHHH!!
HOW ARE YOU FEELING?
LIKE A BROKEN RUBBER BAND.
WHERE IS SATANNA?
NICE JOB, LADIES.
SHE MUST HAVE ESCAPED. DO YOU WANT TO GO SEE DOCTOR MID-NITE?
NO... I HAVE TO GET BACK TO WORK.
REALLY? YOU CAN'T EVEN STAND.
I THINK YOU SHOULD GET CHECKED OUT.
I'LL BE FINE. I CAN CHECK IN WITH THE DOC LATER, BUT...
...MY EMPLOYEES ARE GOING TO THINK SOME-THING'S UP WHEN THEY REALIZE I WAS AT THE SAME BANK WHERE THIS WENT DOWN.
LET ME AT LEAST COME WITH YOU.
SURE.
WHAT WAS THAT WHOLE BIT WITH SATANNA? YOU KNOW, WHERE BLINDING HER WAS JUST "THE BEGINNING OF HER SUFFERING"?
DID I SOUND TOO SCARY?

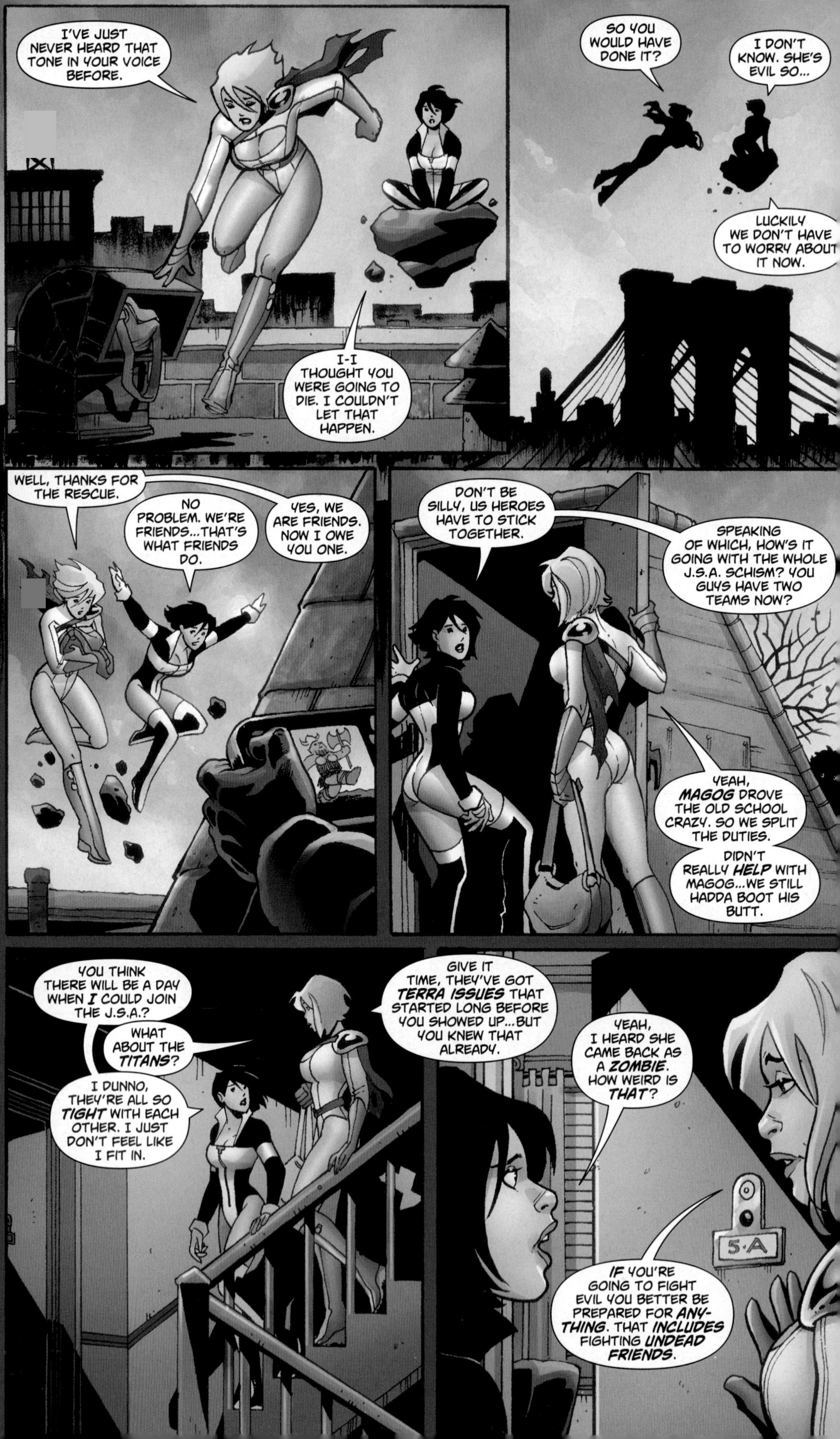
I'VE JUST NEVER HEARD THAT TONE IN YOUR VOICE BEFORE.
I-I THOUGHT YOU WERE GOING TO DIE. I COULDN'T LET THAT HAPPEN.
SO YOU WOULD HAVE DONE IT?
I DON'T KNOW. SHE'S EVIL SO...
LUCKILY WE DON'T HAVE TO WORRY ABOUT IT NOW.
WELL, THANKS FOR THE RESCUE.
NO PROBLEM. WE'RE FRIENDS...THAT'S WHAT FRIENDS DO.
YES, WE ARE FRIENDS. NOW I OWE YOU ONE.
DON'T BE SILLY, US HEROES HAVE TO STICK TOGETHER.
SPEAKING OF WHICH, HOW'S IT GOING WITH THE WHOLE J.S.A. SCHISM? YOU GUYS HAVE TWO TEAMS NOW?
YEAH, MAGOG DROVE THE OLD SCHOOL CRAZY. SO WE SPLIT THE DUTIES.
DIDN'T REALLY HELP WITH MAGOG...WE STILL HADDA BOOT HIS BUTT.
YOU THINK THERE WILL BE A DAY WHEN I COULD JOIN THE J.S.A.?
WHAT ABOUT THE TITANS?
I DUNNO, THEY'RE ALL SO TIGHT WITH EACH OTHER. I JUST DON'T FEEL LIKE I FIT IN.
GIVE IT TIME, THEY'VE GOT TERRA ISSUES THAT STARTED LONG BEFORE YOU SHOWED UP...BUT YOU KNEW THAT ALREADY.
YEAH, I HEARD SHE CAME BACK AS A ZOMBIE. HOW WEIRD IS THAT?
IF YOU'RE GOING TO FIGHT EVIL YOU BETTER BE PREPARED FOR ANYTHING. THAT INCLUDES FIGHTING UNDEAD FRIENDS.
5-A

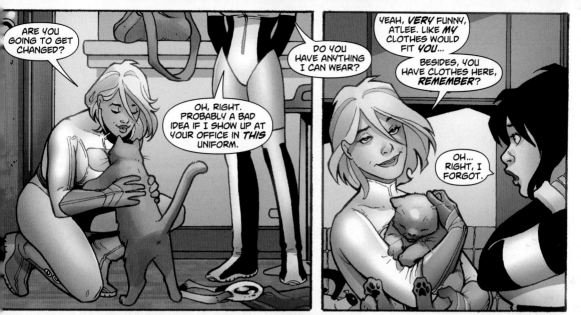

ARE YOU GOING TO GET CHANGED?

OH, RIGHT. PROBABLY A BAD IDEA IF I SHOW UP AT YOUR OFFICE IN *THIS* UNIFORM.

DO YOU HAVE ANYTHING I CAN WEAR?

YEAH, *VERY* FUNNY, ATLEE. LIKE *MY* CLOTHES WOULD FIT *YOU...* BESIDES, YOU HAVE CLOTHES HERE, *REMEMBER*?

OH... RIGHT, I FORGOT.

REMIND ME WHERE THEY ARE AGAIN?

CLOSET?

OF COURSE! THE CLOSET.

YOU OKAY, ATLEE? YOU'RE ACTING A LITTLE *WEIRD*.

NO, YEAH, TOTALLY COOL HERE, EVERYTHING'S FINE.

JUST *DISTRACTED* IS ALL. I THOUGHT YOU WERE GOING TO, LIKE, COLLAPSE INTO A BLACK HOLE OR SOMETHING.

THAT *WOULD* HAVE SUCKED.

OKAY, LET'S GET MOVING. THEY'RE PROBABLY FREAKING OUT AT *STARRWA--*.

OH NO, NOT *NOW*.

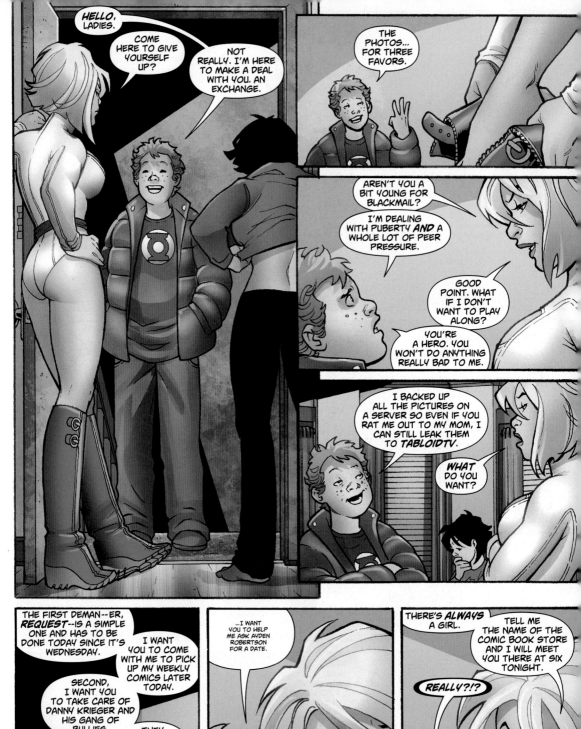

HELLO, LADIES.

COME HERE TO GIVE YOURSELF UP?

NOT REALLY. I'M HERE TO MAKE A DEAL WITH YOU. AN EXCHANGE.

THE PHOTOS... FOR THREE FAVORS.

AREN'T YOU A BIT YOUNG FOR BLACKMAIL?

I'M DEALING WITH PUBERTY *AND* A WHOLE LOT OF PEER PRESSURE.

GOOD POINT. WHAT IF I DON'T WANT TO PLAY ALONG?

YOU'RE A HERO. YOU WON'T DO ANYTHING REALLY BAD TO ME.

I BACKED UP ALL THE PICTURES ON A SERVER SO EVEN IF YOU RAT ME OUT TO MY MOM, I CAN STILL LEAK THEM TO *TABLOIDTV*.

WHAT DO YOU WANT?

THE FIRST DEMAN--ER, *REQUEST*--IS A SIMPLE ONE AND HAS TO BE DONE TODAY SINCE IT'S WEDNESDAY.

I WANT YOU TO COME WITH ME TO PICK UP MY WEEKLY COMICS LATER TODAY.

SECOND, I WANT YOU TO TAKE CARE OF DANNY KRIEGER AND HIS GANG OF BULLIES.

THEY BEAT ME UP EACH MORNING AND TAKE MY LUNCH MONEY... AND THIRD...

...I WANT YOU TO HELP ME ASK AYDEN ROBERTSON FOR A DATE.

THERE'S *ALWAYS* A GIRL.

TELL ME THE NAME OF THE COMIC BOOK STORE AND I WILL MEET YOU THERE AT SIX TONIGHT.

REALLY?!?

I MEAN, COOL...

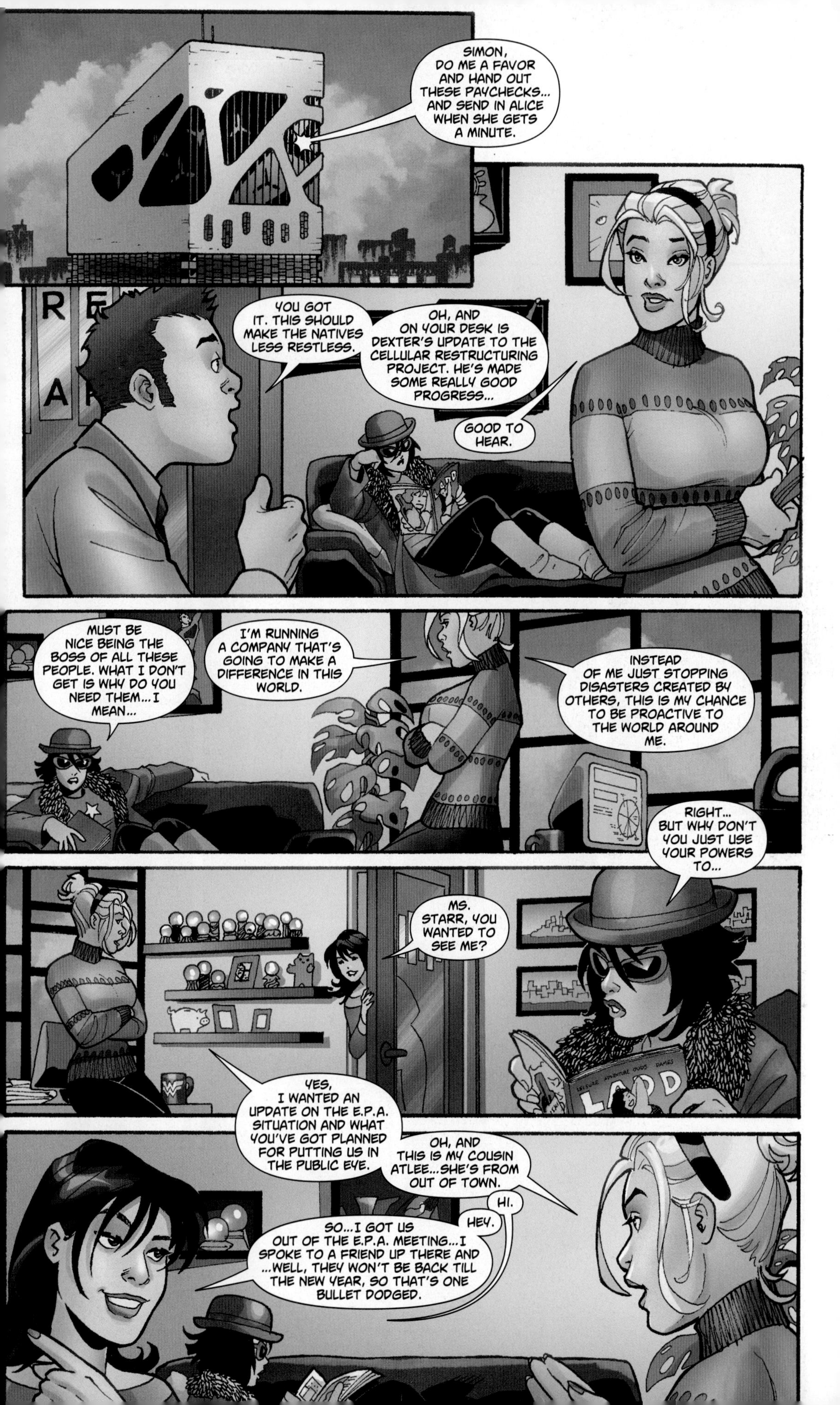

SIMON, DO ME A FAVOR AND HAND OUT THESE PAYCHECKS... AND SEND IN ALICE WHEN SHE GETS A MINUTE.
YOU GOT IT. THIS SHOULD MAKE THE NATIVES LESS RESTLESS.
OH, AND ON YOUR DESK IS DEXTER'S UPDATE TO THE CELLULAR RESTRUCTURING PROJECT. HE'S MADE SOME REALLY GOOD PROGRESS...
GOOD TO HEAR.
MUST BE NICE BEING THE BOSS OF ALL THESE PEOPLE. WHAT I DON'T GET IS WHY DO YOU NEED THEM... I MEAN...
I'M RUNNING A COMPANY THAT'S GOING TO MAKE A DIFFERENCE IN THIS WORLD.
INSTEAD OF ME JUST STOPPING DISASTERS CREATED BY OTHERS, THIS IS MY CHANCE TO BE PROACTIVE TO THE WORLD AROUND ME.
RIGHT... BUT WHY DON'T YOU JUST USE YOUR POWERS TO...
MS. STARR, YOU WANTED TO SEE ME?
YES, I WANTED AN UPDATE ON THE E.P.A. SITUATION AND WHAT YOU'VE GOT PLANNED FOR PUTTING US IN THE PUBLIC EYE.
LADD
OH, AND THIS IS MY COUSIN ATLEE... SHE'S FROM OUT OF TOWN.
HI.
HEY.
SO... I GOT US OUT OF THE E.P.A. MEETING... I SPOKE TO A FRIEND UP THERE AND ...WELL, THEY WON'T BE BACK TILL THE NEW YEAR, SO THAT'S ONE BULLET DODGED.

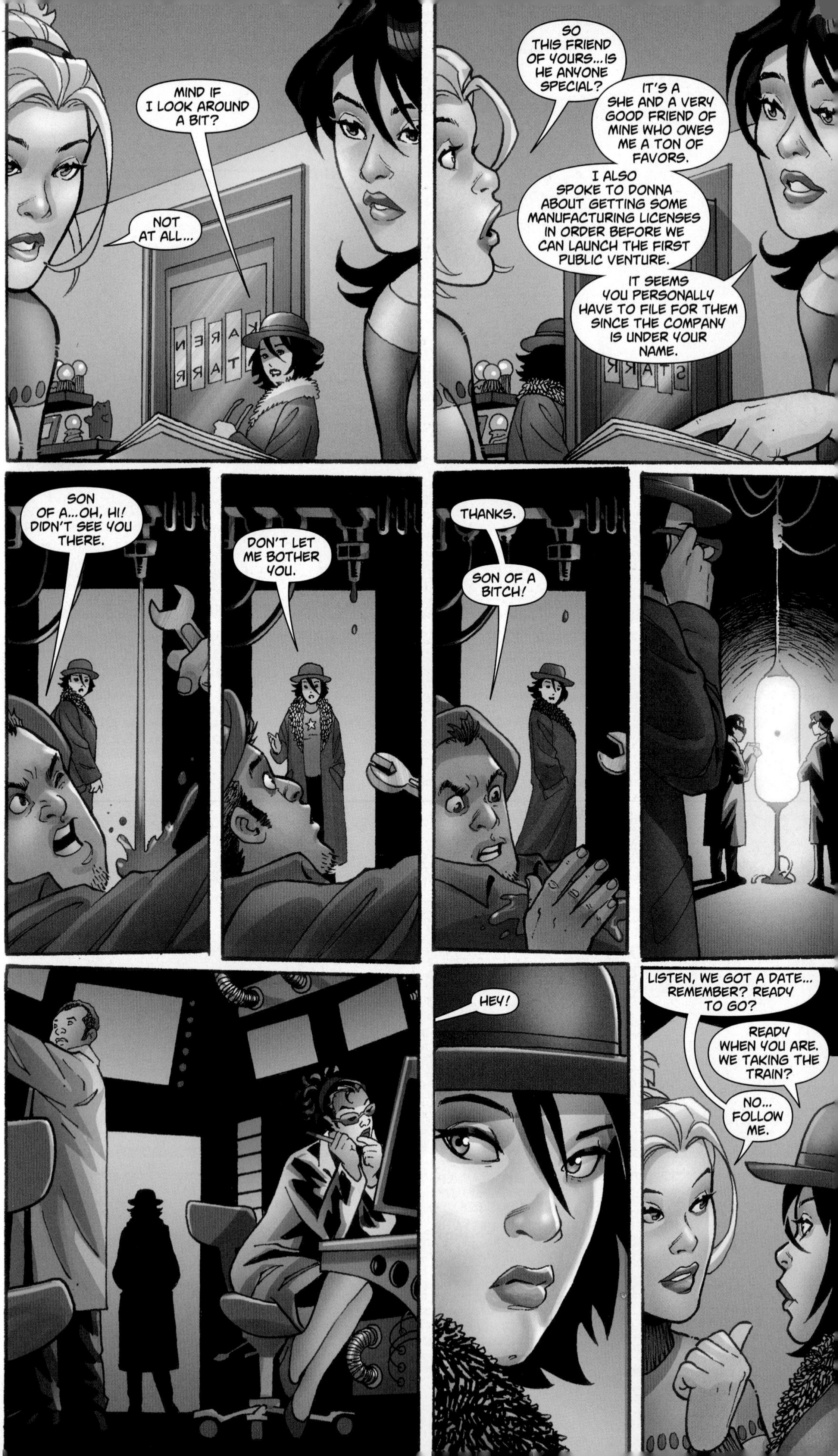
MIND IF I LOOK AROUND A BIT?
NOT AT ALL...
KAREN STARR
SO THIS FRIEND OF YOURS...IS HE ANYONE SPECIAL?
IT'S A SHE AND A VERY GOOD FRIEND OF MINE WHO OWES ME A TON OF FAVORS.
I ALSO SPOKE TO DONNA ABOUT GETTING SOME MANUFACTURING LICENSES IN ORDER BEFORE WE CAN LAUNCH THE FIRST PUBLIC VENTURE.
IT SEEMS YOU PERSONALLY HAVE TO FILE FOR THEM SINCE THE COMPANY IS UNDER YOUR NAME.
SON OF A...OH, HI! DIDN'T SEE YOU THERE.
DON'T LET ME BOTHER YOU.
THANKS.
SON OF A BITCH!
HEY!
LISTEN, WE GOT A DATE... REMEMBER? READY TO GO?
READY WHEN YOU ARE. WE TAKING THE TRAIN?
NO... FOLLOW ME.

...COMIC BOOKS... YOU KNOW, ILLUSTRATED MAGAZINES MADE UP OF NARRATIVE ARTWORK ACCOMPANIED BY DIALOGUE AND DESCRIPTIVE PROSE.

I STILL DON'T SEE WHY YOU JUST DON'T GO BACK TO HIS HOUSE, TAKE THE PHOTOS, MELT HIS CAMERA AND COMPUTER AND BE DONE WITH HIM.

BECAUSE AT THE END OF THE DAY, HE'S STILL A CHILD AND AN IMPRESSIONABLE ONE.

THIS IS A DELICATE SITUATION THAT I'M GOING TO DEAL WITH MY WAY.

STAY OUTSIDE; THIS SHOULD TAKE A MINUTE OR TWO TOPS.

C'MON, PEE-GEE. LET'S GO...

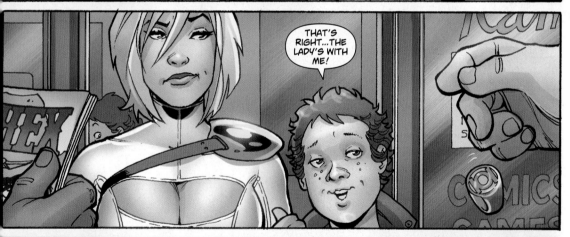

THAT'S RIGHT...THE LADY'S WITH ME!

OH MY GOD, IS THAT REALLY...?

IT'S GOT TO BE HER... NO ONE ELSE COULD...

THIS IS THE BEST COMIC BOOK STORE IN THE UNIVERSE...

WHAT IN HELL IS SHE DOING WITH FISHER?

HEY, FISHER... HOW ABOUT YOU INTRODUCE US TO YOUR...FRIEND?

OH, STEVE, ERIN, MEET POWER GIRL...SUPERHERO AND ALL THAT. HEY, IS THE NEW *CAPTAIN STEELGRIP* IN YET?

NO, THE ARTIST FELL BEHIND AND IT'S SKIPPING A MONTH.

WHAT A *RIP*!

SO, YOU LOSE A BET OR ARE YOU BABY-SITTING?

NEITHER. HE'S MY *HUSBAND*.

WE GOT *MARRIED* ON *JUPITER* LAST NIGHT AND WE INTERRUPTED OUR *HONEYMOON* TO COME BACK TO EARTH TO PICK UP HIS COMICS.

WELL... UM...THAT'S SWEET OF YOU.

DUDE, FISHER *MARRIED* HER.

NO *WAY*!

I HEARD IT TOO.

HE DOES HAVE NICE HAIR.

WELL, HE'S A GOOD KID, AND SMART... I HOPE YOU TWO HAVE A LONG AND HAPPY LIFE TOGETHER.

ANY CHANCE OF YOU STOPPING BY FOR FREE COMIC BOOK DAY?

SORRY... I HAVE A FULL-TIME JOB.

BUILD BODACIOUS BO AND MAGNIFIC MUSCL

COME ON, FISHER...TIME TO GO.

THE BOOKS ARE ON THE HOUSE THIS WEEK...AND THANKS FOR BRINGING YOUR FRIEND BY.

SHOPLIFTE WILL BE DEATH-RAY

COOL!

HEY...I'M GONNA HANG AROUND HERE. CATCH YOU LATER?

SURE, COME OUTSIDE A MINUTE.

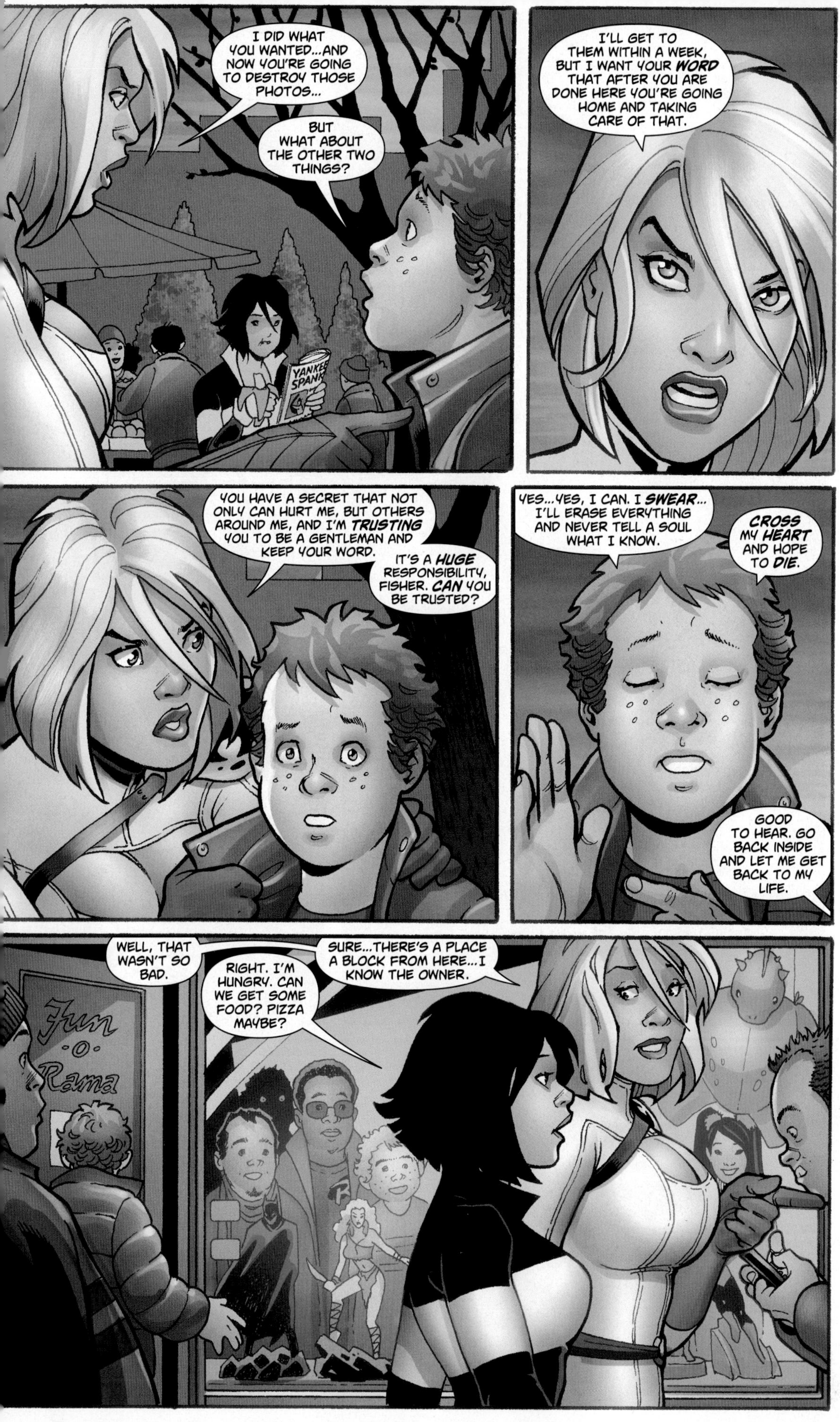
I DID WHAT YOU WANTED...AND NOW YOU'RE GOING TO DESTROY THOSE PHOTOS...
BUT WHAT ABOUT THE OTHER TWO THINGS?
YANKEE SPANK
I'LL GET TO THEM WITHIN A WEEK, BUT I WANT YOUR WORD THAT AFTER YOU ARE DONE HERE YOU'RE GOING HOME AND TAKING CARE OF THAT.
YOU HAVE A SECRET THAT NOT ONLY CAN HURT ME, BUT OTHERS AROUND ME, AND I'M TRUSTING YOU TO BE A GENTLEMAN AND KEEP YOUR WORD.
IT'S A HUGE RESPONSIBILITY, FISHER. CAN YOU BE TRUSTED?
YES...YES, I CAN. I SWEAR... I'LL ERASE EVERYTHING AND NEVER TELL A SOUL WHAT I KNOW.
CROSS MY HEART AND HOPE TO DIE.
GOOD TO HEAR. GO BACK INSIDE AND LET ME GET BACK TO MY LIFE.
WELL, THAT WASN'T SO BAD.
RIGHT. I'M HUNGRY. CAN WE GET SOME FOOD? PIZZA MAYBE?
SURE...THERE'S A PLACE A BLOCK FROM HERE...I KNOW THE OWNER.
Fun -o- Rama

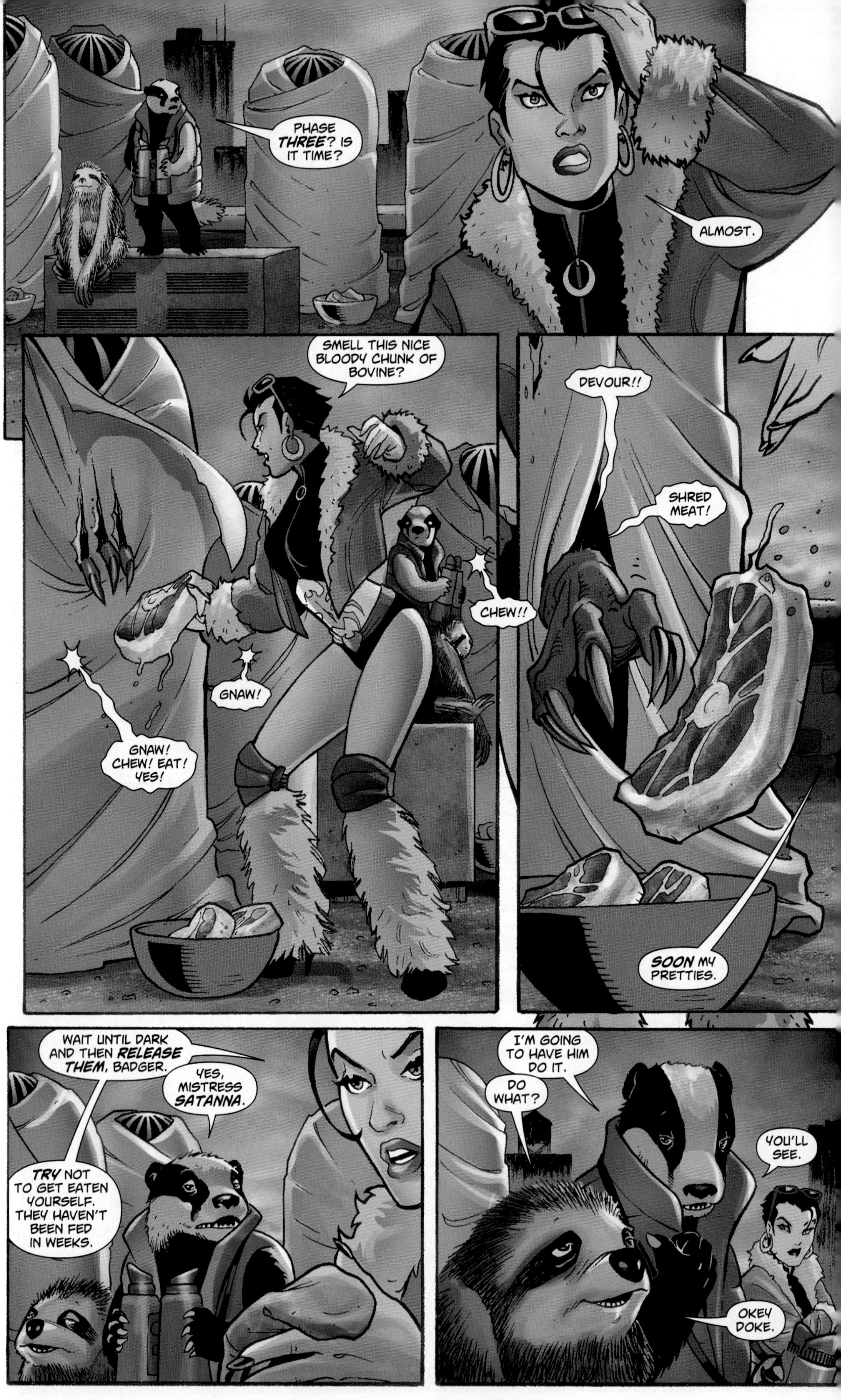
PHASE THREE? IS IT TIME?
ALMOST.
SMELL THIS NICE BLOODY CHUNK OF BOVINE?
CHEW!!
GNAW!
GNAW! CHEW! EAT! YES!
DEVOUR!!
SHRED MEAT!
SOON MY PRETTIES.
WAIT UNTIL DARK AND THEN RELEASE THEM, BADGER.
YES, MISTRESS SATANNA.
TRY NOT TO GET EATEN YOURSELF. THEY HAVEN'T BEEN FED IN WEEKS.
I'M GOING TO HAVE HIM DO IT.
DO WHAT?
YOU'LL SEE.
OKEY DOKE.

MM, THIS PIZZA IS **AMAZING**. I MEANT TO ASK...

WHAT'S THE **DEAL** WITH YOU AND SATANNA?

I GUESS IT HAS **SOMETHING** TO DO WITH THE **ULTRA-HUMANITE**.

POWER GIRL! CAN I GET AN **AUTOGRAPH**?

GROSS.

I KIND OF FEEL **BAD** FOR THE ULTRA.

WHY? HE'S AN **EVIL GORILLA**.

OH WOW! CAN I GET A **PICTURE** WITH YOU GUYS?

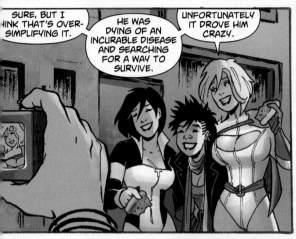

SURE, BUT I THINK THAT'S OVER-SIMPLIFYING IT.

HE WAS **DYING** OF AN **INCURABLE DISEASE** AND SEARCHING FOR A WAY TO SURVIVE.

UNFORTUNATELY IT DROVE HIM **CRAZY**.

THAT'S WHY I TRIED TO GET HIM PSYCHOLOGICAL **HELP** INSTEAD OF JUST TOSSING HIM IN JAIL.

SO YOU THINK YOU WERE DOING HIM A **FAVOR**?

WHY NOT? ISN'T THAT WHAT DEFINES US AS HEROES, OUR ABILITY TO FEEL **COMPASSION** FOR OUR ENEMIES?

OH, YOU HAVE **GOT** TO BE KIDDING.

IDIOT PERV.

CAN I GET A **COP** OVER HERE!?!

FWOOOSH

YOU DON'T HONESTLY **BELIEVE** THAT, DO YOU?

HELP!

IT IS **SO** CONDESCENDING.

OH, THESE **POOR** COSTUMED **LUNATICS** CAN'T HELP THEMSELVES SO WE HAVE TO STOP THEM AND PUT THEM IN **THERAPY**?

AND WHAT WOULD **YOU** SUGGEST WE DO WITH THEM?

DERMATOLOGY

MOHS SURGERY

EMA · PSORIASIS

LASER

IS WEEK'S ECIAL

E WILL FREEZE FF YOUR

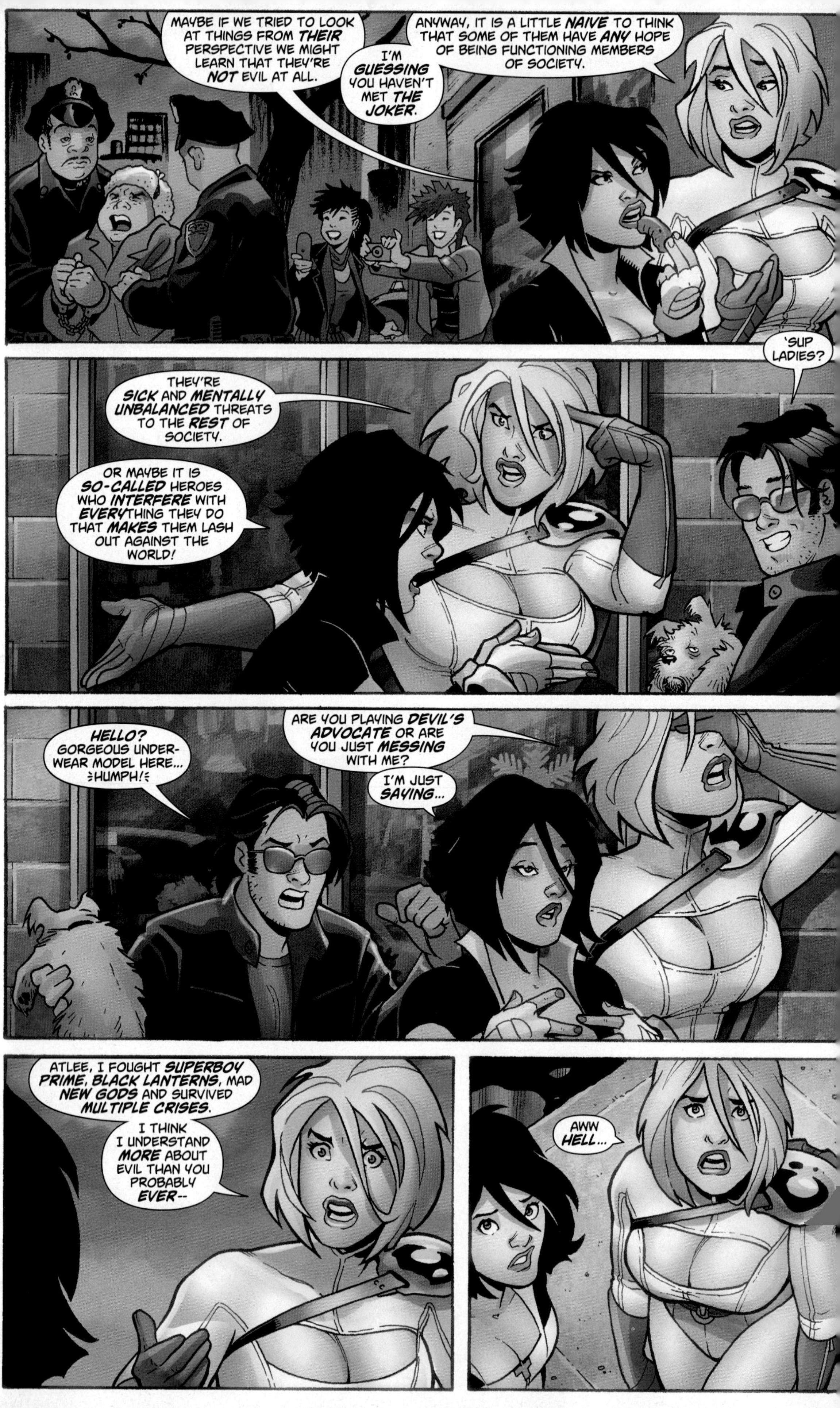

MAYBE IF WE TRIED TO LOOK AT THINGS FROM THEIR PERSPECTIVE WE MIGHT LEARN THAT THEY'RE NOT EVIL AT ALL.
I'M GUESSING YOU HAVEN'T MET THE JOKER.
ANYWAY, IT IS A LITTLE NAIVE TO THINK THAT SOME OF THEM HAVE ANY HOPE OF BEING FUNCTIONING MEMBERS OF SOCIETY.
THEY'RE SICK AND MENTALLY UNBALANCED THREATS TO THE REST OF SOCIETY.
OR MAYBE IT IS SO-CALLED HEROES WHO INTERFERE WITH EVERYTHING THEY DO THAT MAKES THEM LASH OUT AGAINST THE WORLD!
'SUP LADIES?
HELLO? GORGEOUS UNDER-WEAR MODEL HERE... HUMPH!
ARE YOU PLAYING DEVIL'S ADVOCATE OR ARE YOU JUST MESSING WITH ME?
I'M JUST SAYING...
ATLEE, I FOUGHT SUPERBOY PRIME, BLACK LANTERNS, MAD NEW GODS AND SURVIVED MULTIPLE CRISES.
I THINK I UNDERSTAND MORE ABOUT EVIL THAN YOU PROBABLY EVER--
AWW HELL...

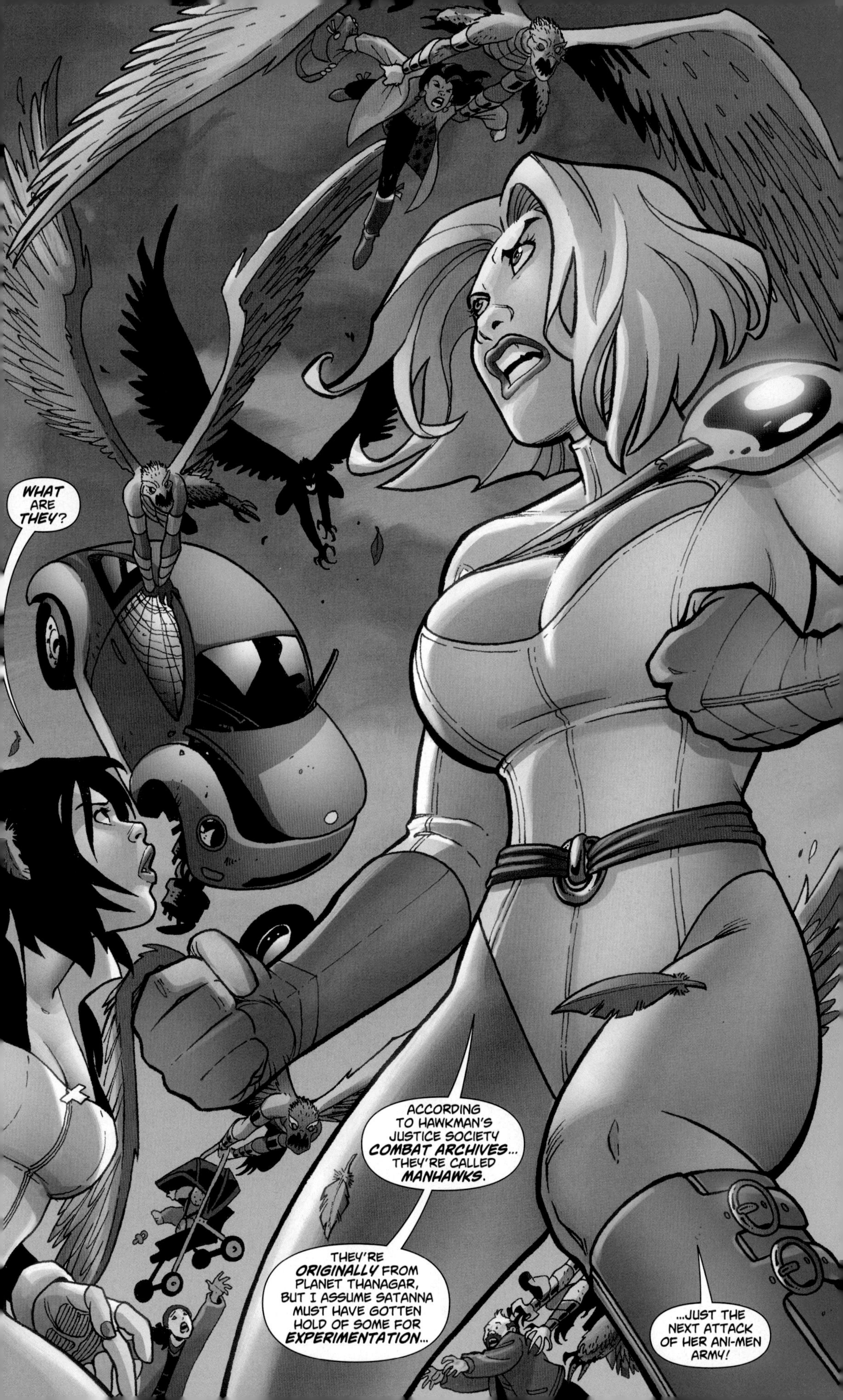
WHAT ARE THEY?
ACCORDING TO HAWKMAN'S JUSTICE SOCIETY COMBAT ARCHIVES... THEY'RE CALLED MANHAWKS.
THEY'RE ORIGINALLY FROM PLANET THANAGAR, BUT I ASSUME SATANNA MUST HAVE GOTTEN HOLD OF SOME FOR EXPERIMENTATION...
...JUST THE NEXT ATTACK OF HER ANI-MEN ARMY!

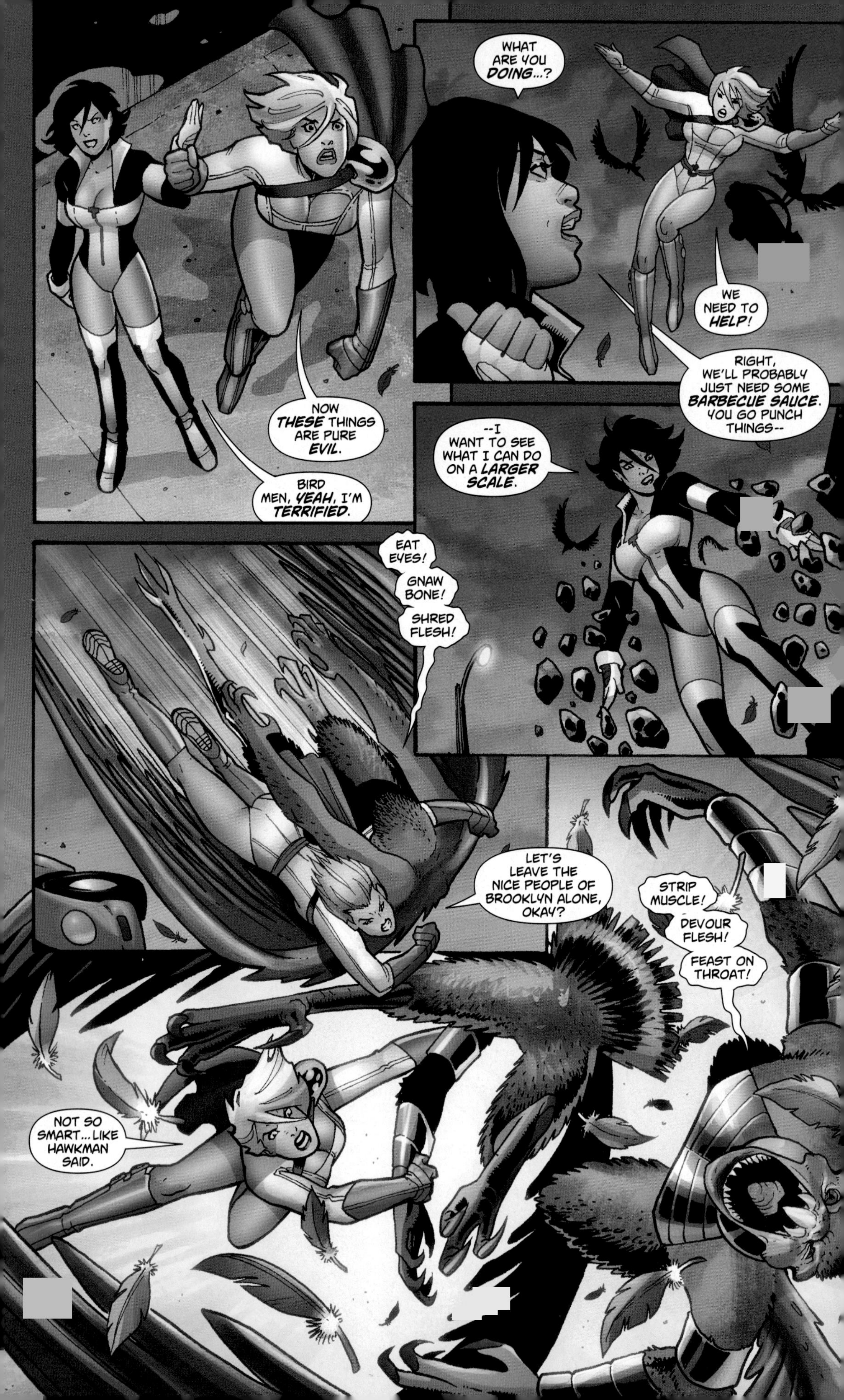
NOW THESE THINGS ARE PURE EVIL.
BIRD MEN, YEAH, I'M TERRIFIED.
WHAT ARE YOU DOING...?
WE NEED TO HELP!
RIGHT, WE'LL PROBABLY JUST NEED SOME BARBECUE SAUCE. YOU GO PUNCH THINGS--
--I WANT TO SEE WHAT I CAN DO ON A LARGER SCALE.
EAT EYES!
GNAW BONE!
SHRED FLESH!
LET'S LEAVE THE NICE PEOPLE OF BROOKLYN ALONE, OKAY?
STRIP MUSCLE!
DEVOUR FLESH!
FEAST ON THROAT!
NOT SO SMART... LIKE HAWKMAN SAID.

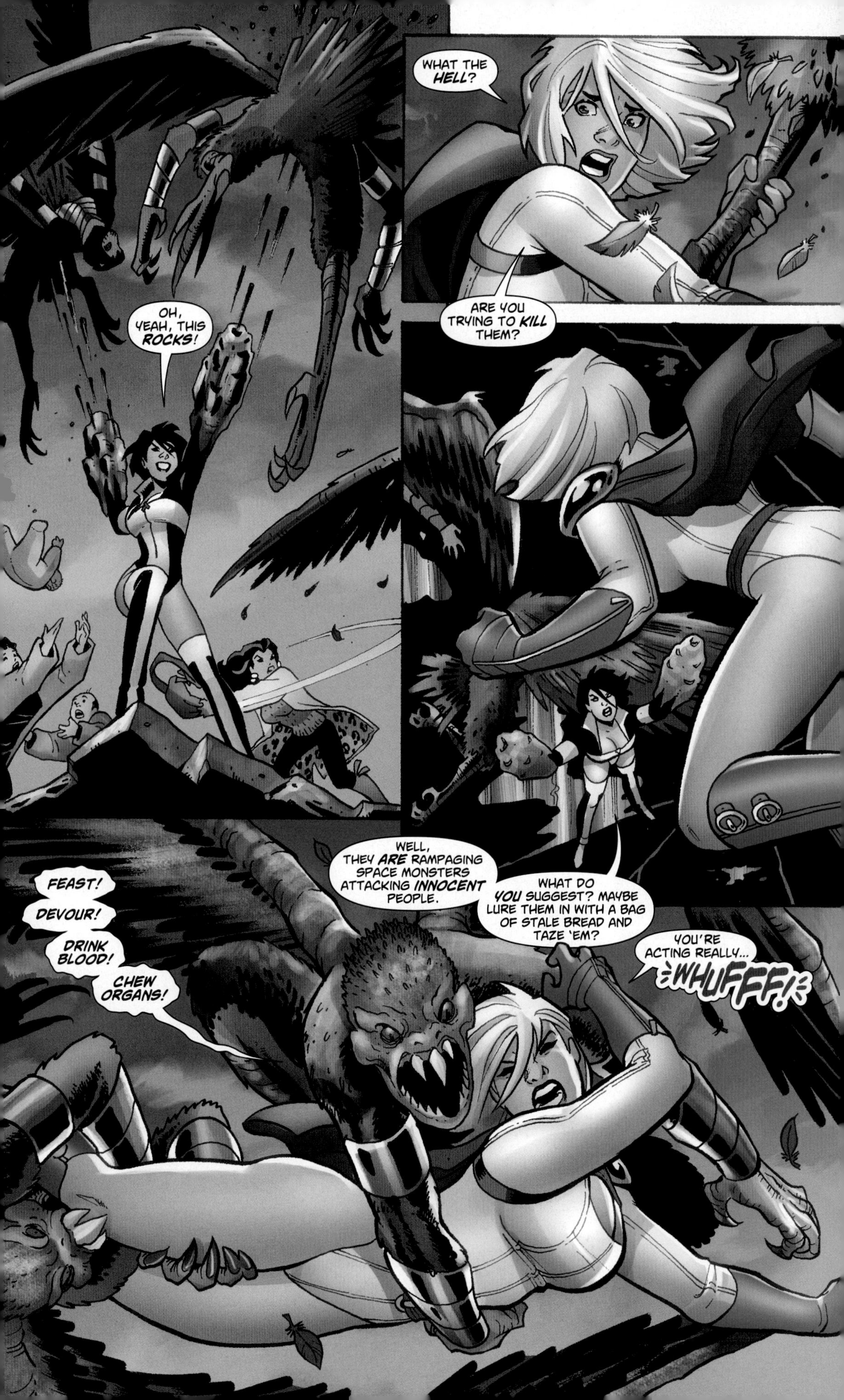
OH, YEAH, THIS ROCKS!
WHAT THE HELL?
ARE YOU TRYING TO KILL THEM?
WELL, THEY ARE RAMPAGING SPACE MONSTERS ATTACKING INNOCENT PEOPLE.
WHAT DO YOU SUGGEST? MAYBE LURE THEM IN WITH A BAG OF STALE BREAD AND TAZE 'EM?
FEAST!
DEVOUR!
DRINK BLOOD!
CHEW ORGANS!
YOU'RE ACTING REALLY...
WHUFFF!

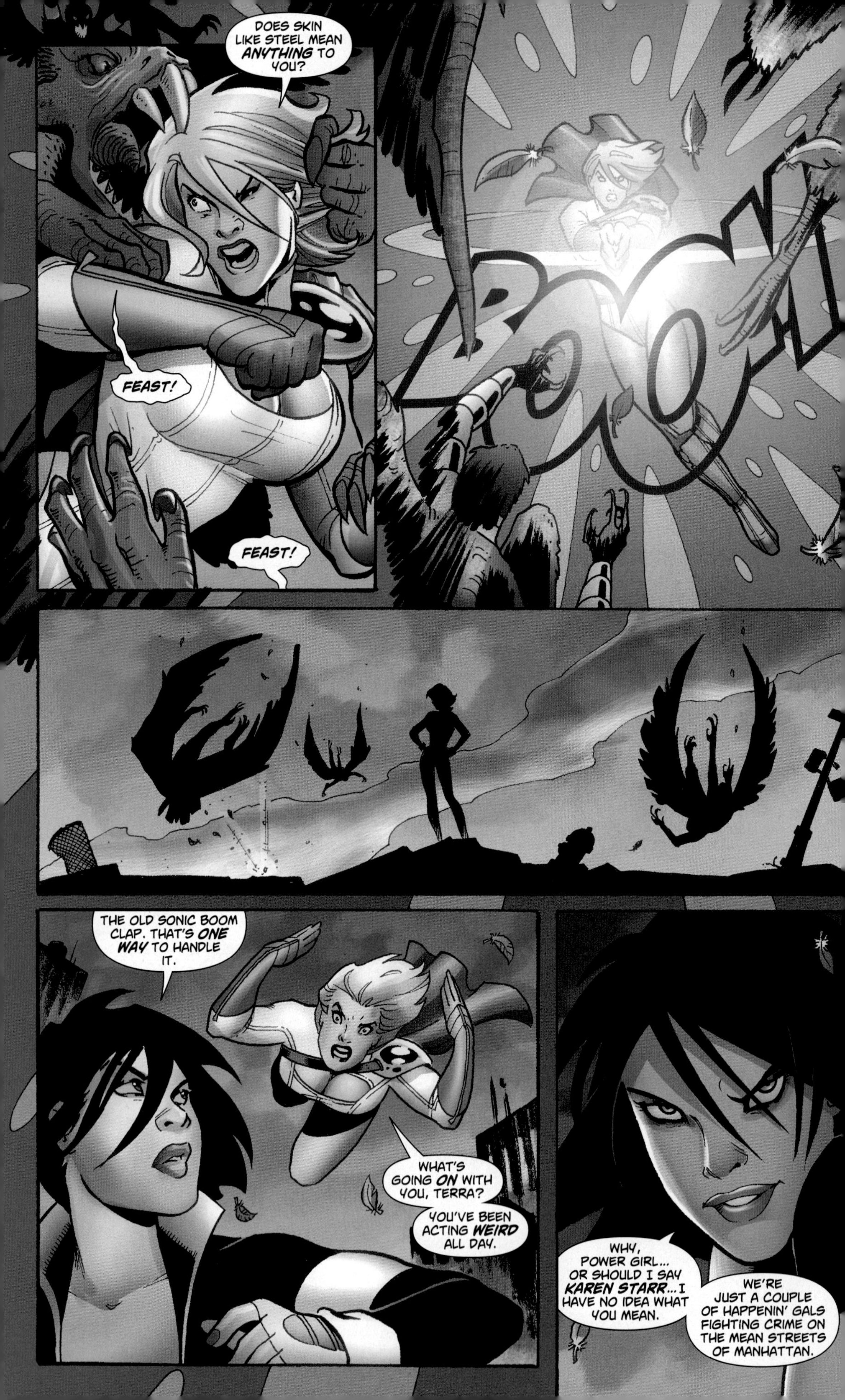
DOES SKIN LIKE STEEL MEAN *ANYTHING* TO YOU?
FEAST!
FEAST!
BOOM!
THE OLD SONIC BOOM CLAP. THAT'S *ONE WAY* TO HANDLE IT.
WHAT'S GOING *ON* WITH YOU, TERRA?
YOU'VE BEEN ACTING *WEIRD* ALL DAY.
WHY, POWER GIRL... OR SHOULD I SAY *KAREN STARR*... I HAVE NO IDEA WHAT YOU MEAN.
WE'RE JUST A COUPLE OF HAPPENIN' GALS FIGHTING CRIME ON THE MEAN STREETS OF MANHATTAN.

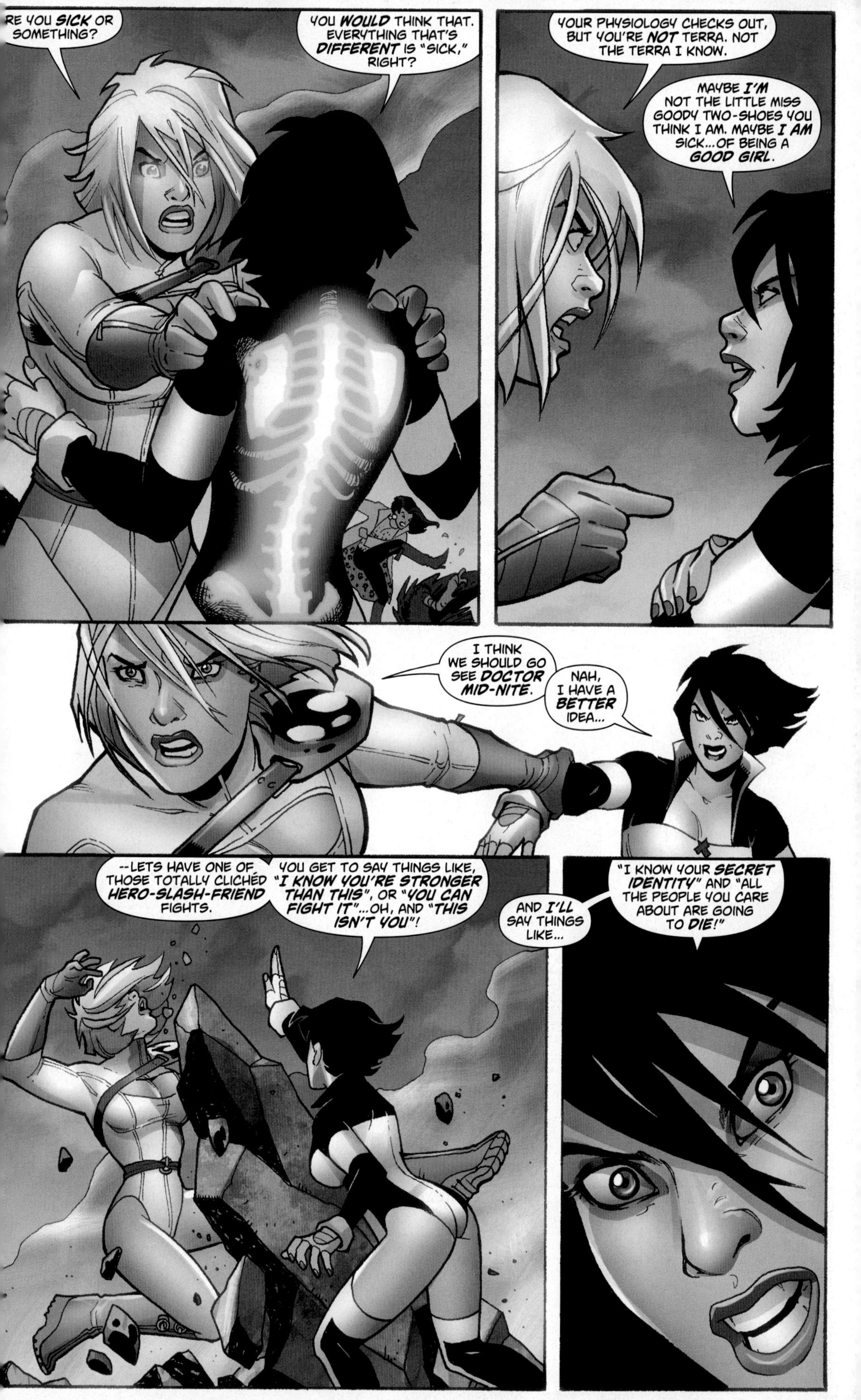

RE YOU SICK OR SOMETHING?
YOU WOULD THINK THAT. EVERYTHING THAT'S DIFFERENT IS "SICK," RIGHT?
YOUR PHYSIOLOGY CHECKS OUT, BUT YOU'RE NOT TERRA. NOT THE TERRA I KNOW.
MAYBE I'M NOT THE LITTLE MISS GOODY TWO-SHOES YOU THINK I AM. MAYBE I AM SICK...OF BEING A GOOD GIRL.
I THINK WE SHOULD GO SEE DOCTOR MID-NITE.
NAH, I HAVE A BETTER IDEA...
--LETS HAVE ONE OF THOSE TOTALLY CLICHÉD HERO-SLASH-FRIEND FIGHTS.
YOU GET TO SAY THINGS LIKE, "I KNOW YOU'RE STRONGER THAN THIS", OR "YOU CAN FIGHT IT"...OH, AND "THIS ISN'T YOU"!
AND I'LL SAY THINGS LIKE...
"I KNOW YOUR SECRET IDENTITY" AND "ALL THE PEOPLE YOU CARE ABOUT ARE GOING TO DIE!"

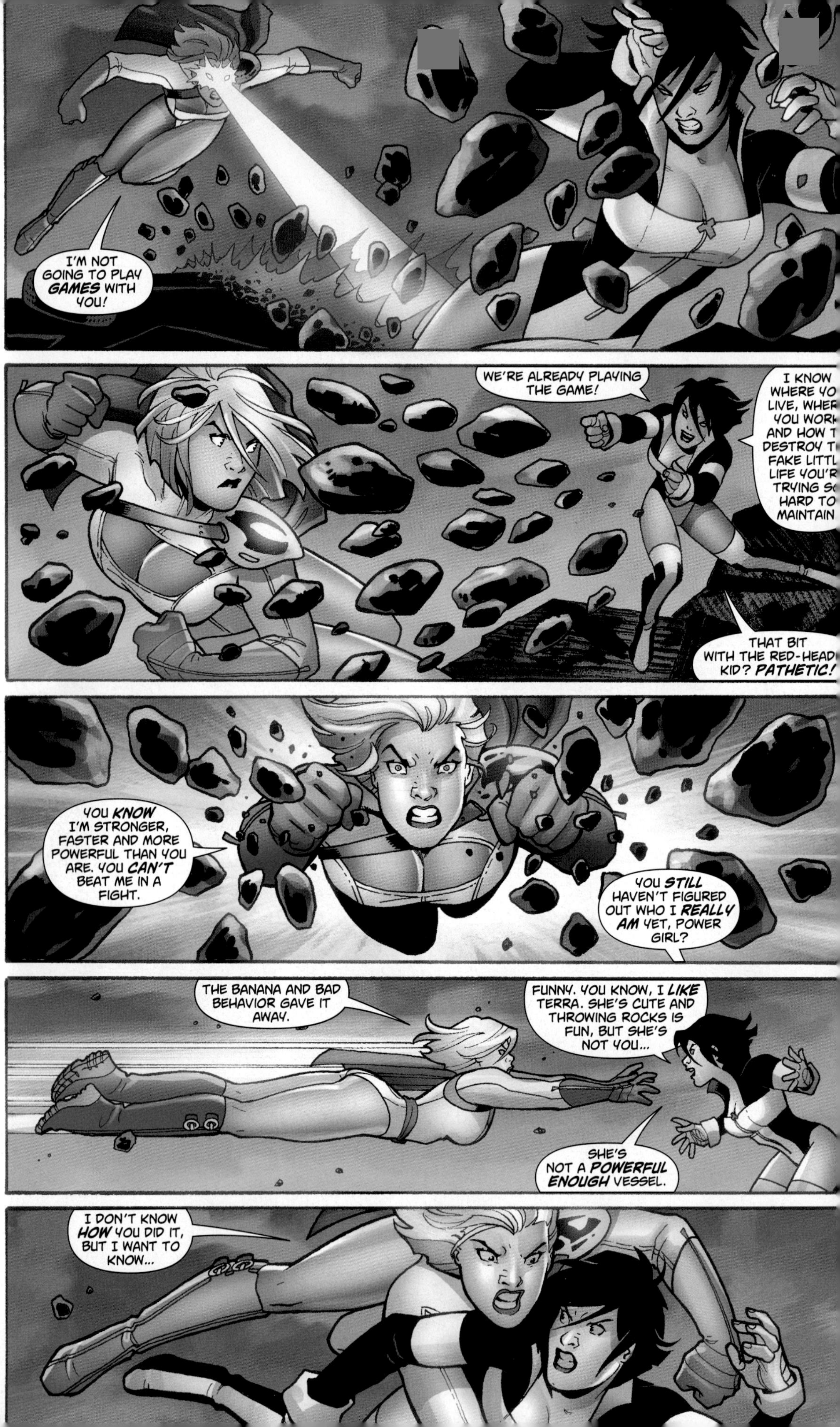
I'M NOT GOING TO PLAY GAMES WITH YOU!
WE'RE ALREADY PLAYING THE GAME!
I KNOW WHERE YO LIVE, WHER YOU WORK AND HOW T DESTROY T FAKE LITTL LIFE YOU'R TRYING S HARD TO MAINTAIN
THAT BIT WITH THE RED-HEAD KID? PATHETIC!
YOU KNOW I'M STRONGER, FASTER AND MORE POWERFUL THAN YOU ARE. YOU CAN'T BEAT ME IN A FIGHT.
YOU STILL HAVEN'T FIGURED OUT WHO I REALLY AM YET, POWER GIRL?
THE BANANA AND BAD BEHAVIOR GAVE IT AWAY.
FUNNY. YOU KNOW, I LIKE TERRA. SHE'S CUTE AND THROWING ROCKS IS FUN, BUT SHE'S NOT YOU...
SHE'S NOT A POWERFUL ENOUGH VESSEL.
I DON'T KNOW HOW YOU DID IT, BUT I WANT TO KNOW...

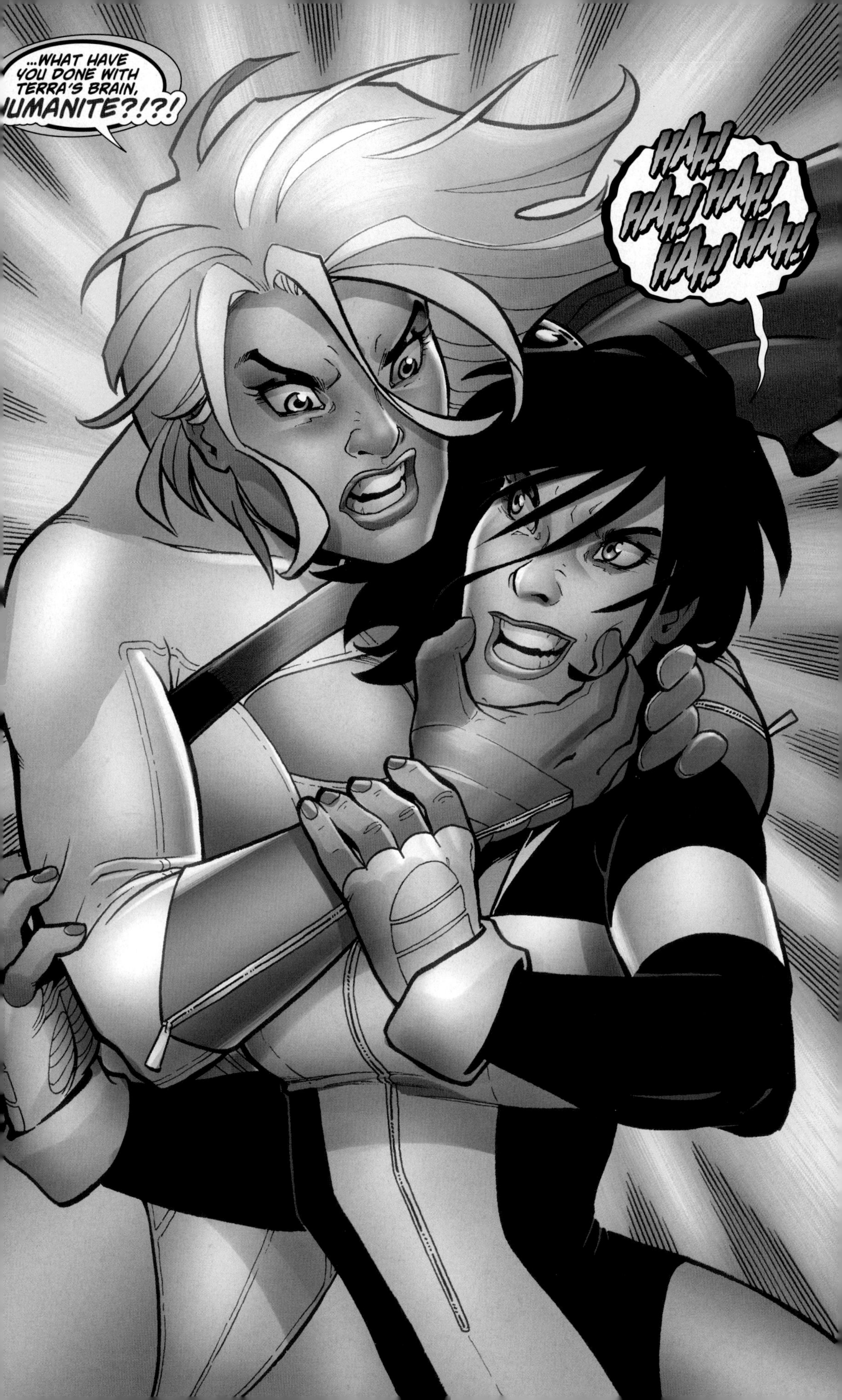
...WHAT HAVE YOU DONE WITH TERRA'S BRAIN, UMANITE?!?!
HAH! HAH! HAH! HAH! HAH! HAH!

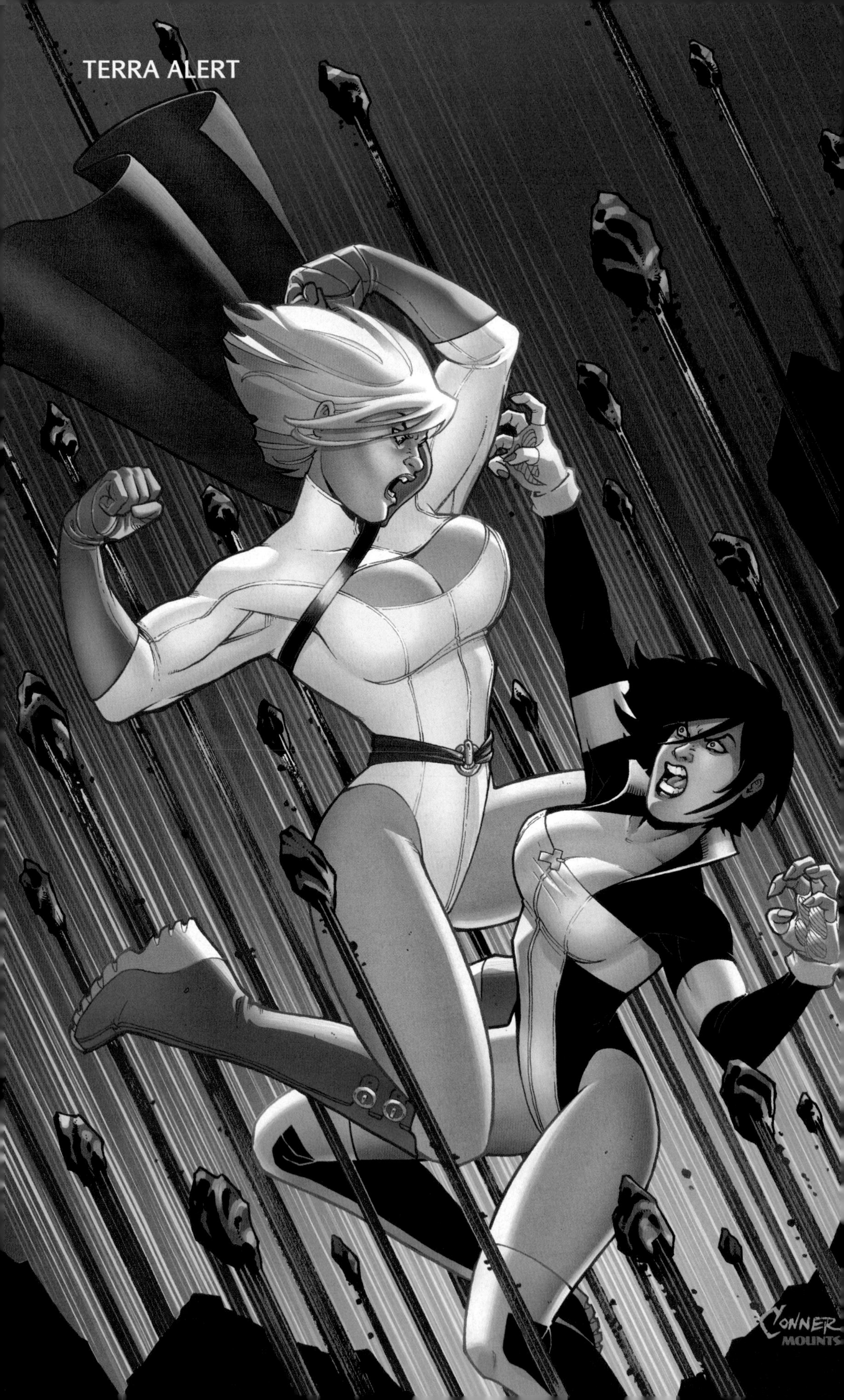
CONNER
MOUNTS
TERRA ALERT

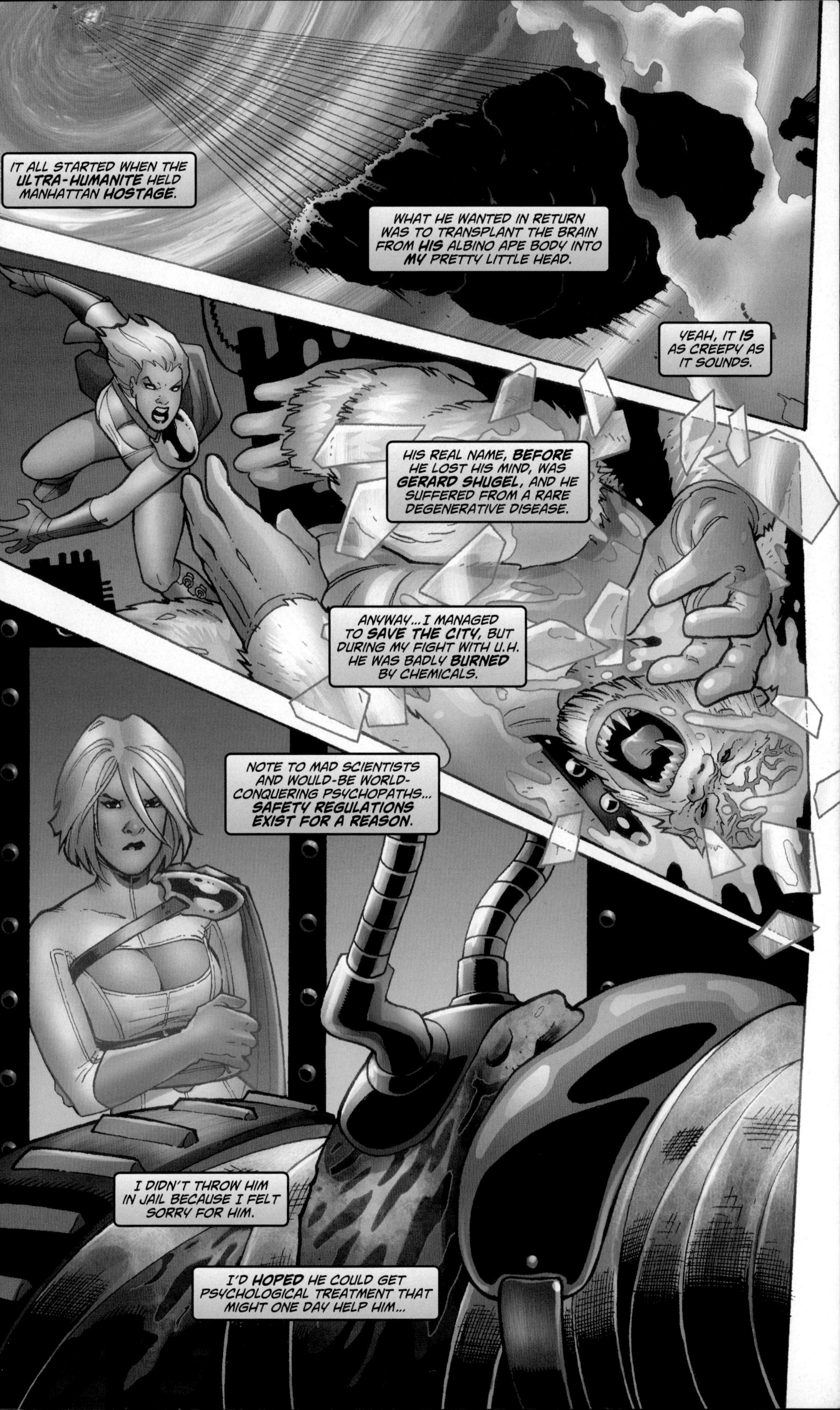

IT ALL STARTED WHEN THE ULTRA-HUMANITE HELD MANHATTAN HOSTAGE.
WHAT HE WANTED IN RETURN WAS TO TRANSPLANT THE BRAIN FROM HIS ALBINO APE BODY INTO MY PRETTY LITTLE HEAD.
YEAH, IT IS AS CREEPY AS IT SOUNDS.
HIS REAL NAME, BEFORE HE LOST HIS MIND, WAS GERARD SHUGEL, AND HE SUFFERED FROM A RARE DEGENERATIVE DISEASE.
ANYWAY... I MANAGED TO SAVE THE CITY, BUT DURING MY FIGHT WITH U.H. HE WAS BADLY BURNED BY CHEMICALS.
NOTE TO MAD SCIENTISTS AND WOULD-BE WORLD-CONQUERING PSYCHOPATHS... SAFETY REGULATIONS EXIST FOR A REASON.
I DIDN'T THROW HIM IN JAIL BECAUSE I FELT SORRY FOR HIM.
I'D HOPED HE COULD GET PSYCHOLOGICAL TREATMENT THAT MIGHT ONE DAY HELP HIM...

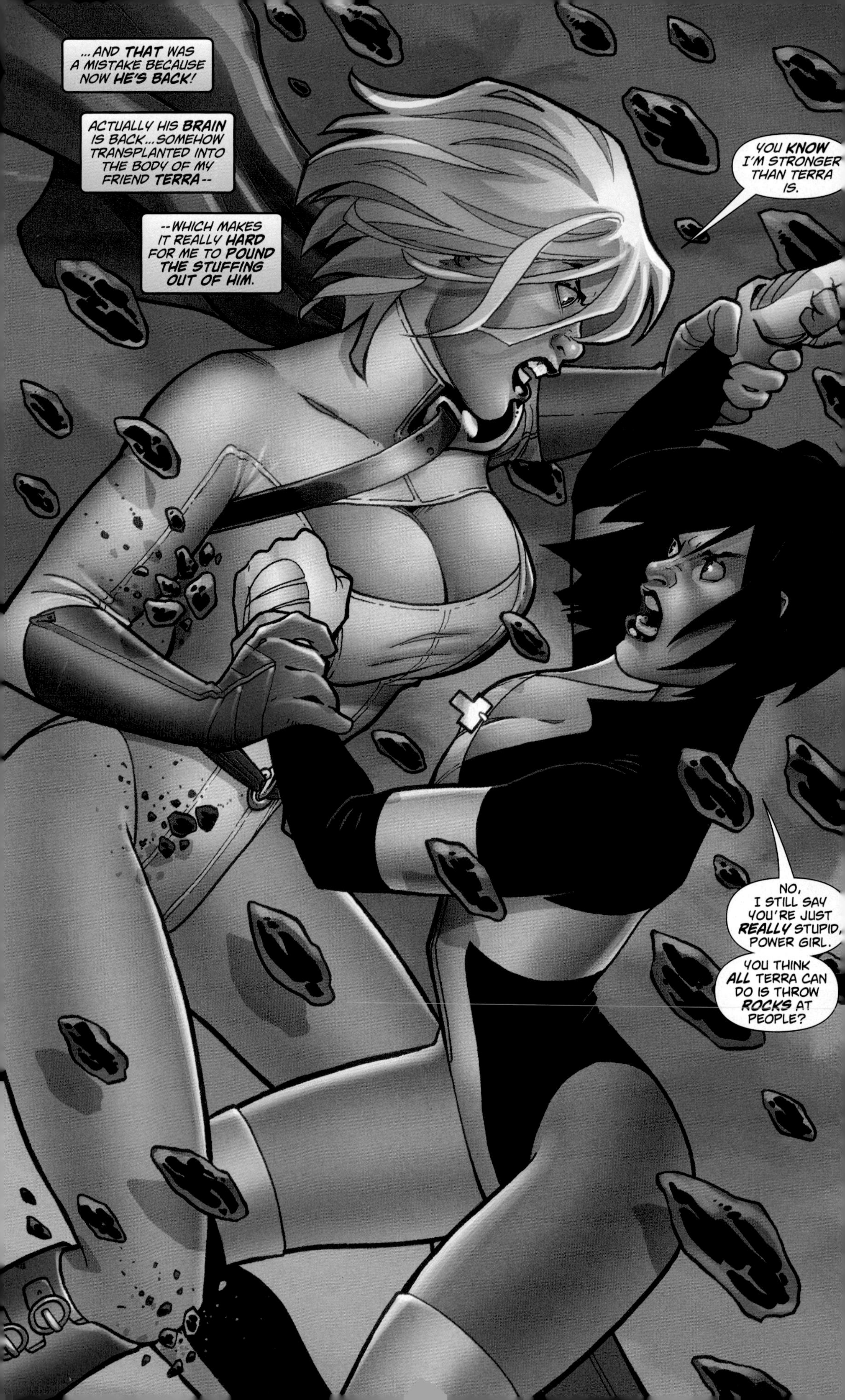
...AND THAT WAS A MISTAKE BECAUSE NOW HE'S BACK!
ACTUALLY HIS BRAIN IS BACK...SOMEHOW TRANSPLANTED INTO THE BODY OF MY FRIEND TERRA--
--WHICH MAKES IT REALLY HARD FOR ME TO POUND THE STUFFING OUT OF HIM.
YOU KNOW I'M STRONGER THAN TERRA IS.
NO, I STILL SAY YOU'RE JUST REALLY STUPID, POWER GIRL.
YOU THINK ALL TERRA CAN DO IS THROW ROCKS AT PEOPLE?

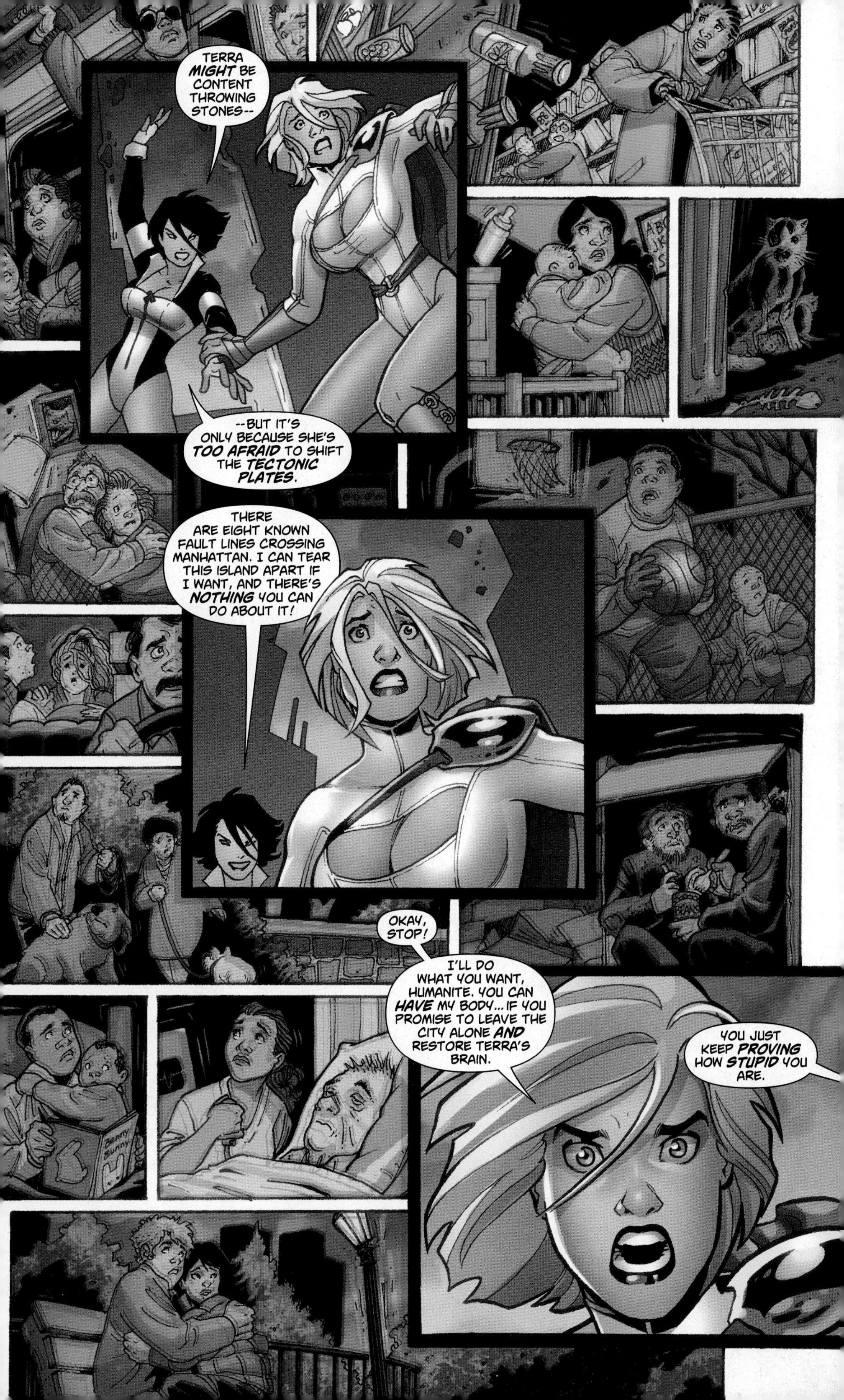
TERRA MIGHT BE CONTENT THROWING STONES--
--BUT IT'S ONLY BECAUSE SHE'S TOO AFRAID TO SHIFT THE TECTONIC PLATES.
THERE ARE EIGHT KNOWN FAULT LINES CROSSING MANHATTAN. I CAN TEAR THIS ISLAND APART IF I WANT, AND THERE'S NOTHING YOU CAN DO ABOUT IT!
OKAY, STOP!
I'LL DO WHAT YOU WANT, HUMANITE. YOU CAN HAVE MY BODY... IF YOU PROMISE TO LEAVE THE CITY ALONE AND RESTORE TERRA'S BRAIN.
YOU JUST KEEP PROVING HOW STUPID YOU ARE.

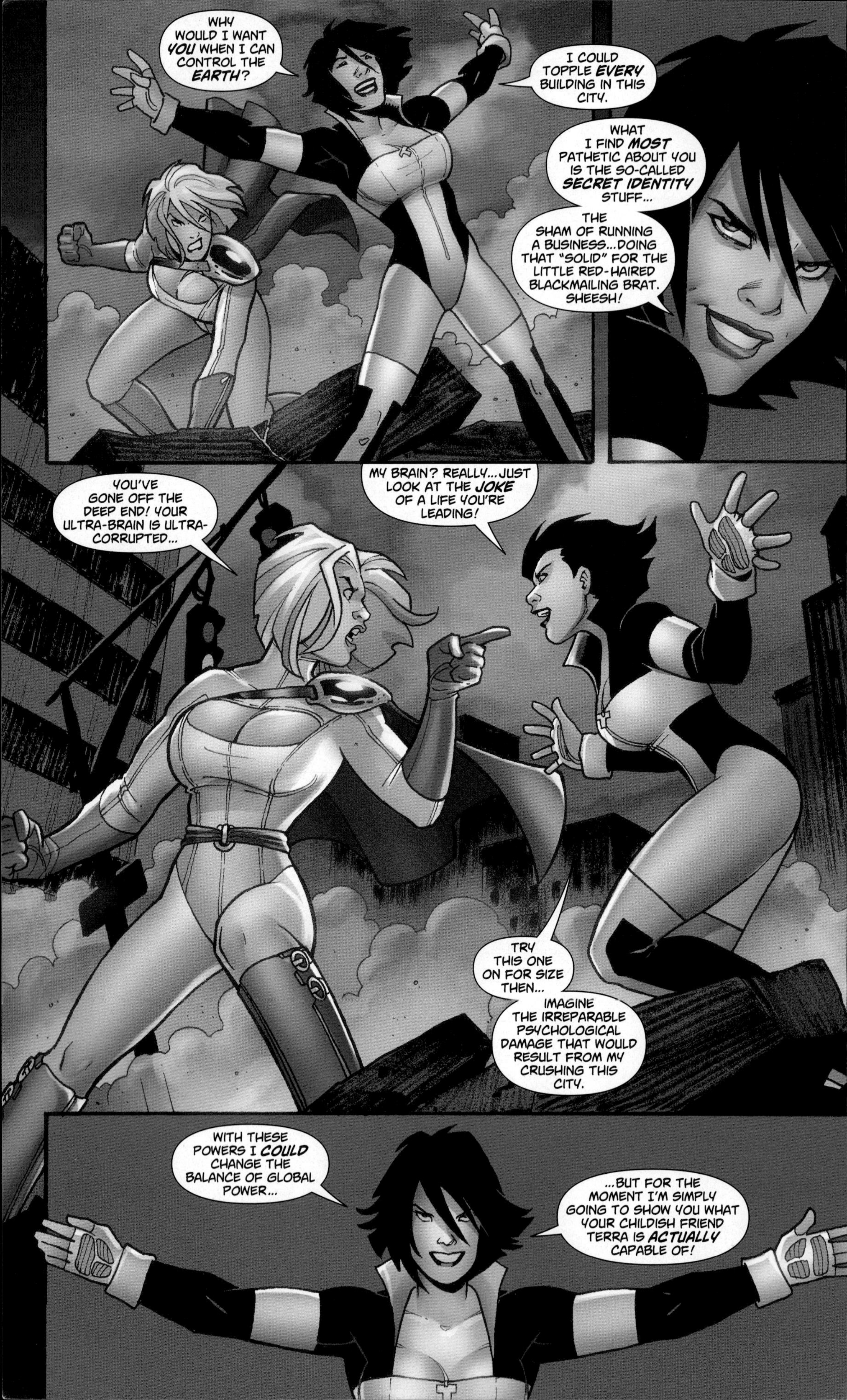
WHY WOULD I WANT YOU WHEN I CAN CONTROL THE EARTH?
I COULD TOPPLE EVERY BUILDING IN THIS CITY.
WHAT I FIND MOST PATHETIC ABOUT YOU IS THE SO-CALLED SECRET IDENTITY STUFF...
THE SHAM OF RUNNING A BUSINESS...DOING THAT "SOLID" FOR THE LITTLE RED-HAIRED BLACKMAILING BRAT. SHEESH!
YOU'VE GONE OFF THE DEEP END! YOUR ULTRA-BRAIN IS ULTRA-CORRUPTED...
MY BRAIN? REALLY...JUST LOOK AT THE JOKE OF A LIFE YOU'RE LEADING!
TRY THIS ONE ON FOR SIZE THEN...
IMAGINE THE IRREPARABLE PSYCHOLOGICAL DAMAGE THAT WOULD RESULT FROM MY CRUSHING THIS CITY.
WITH THESE POWERS I COULD CHANGE THE BALANCE OF GLOBAL POWER...
...BUT FOR THE MOMENT I'M SIMPLY GOING TO SHOW YOU WHAT YOUR CHILDISH FRIEND TERRA IS ACTUALLY CAPABLE OF!

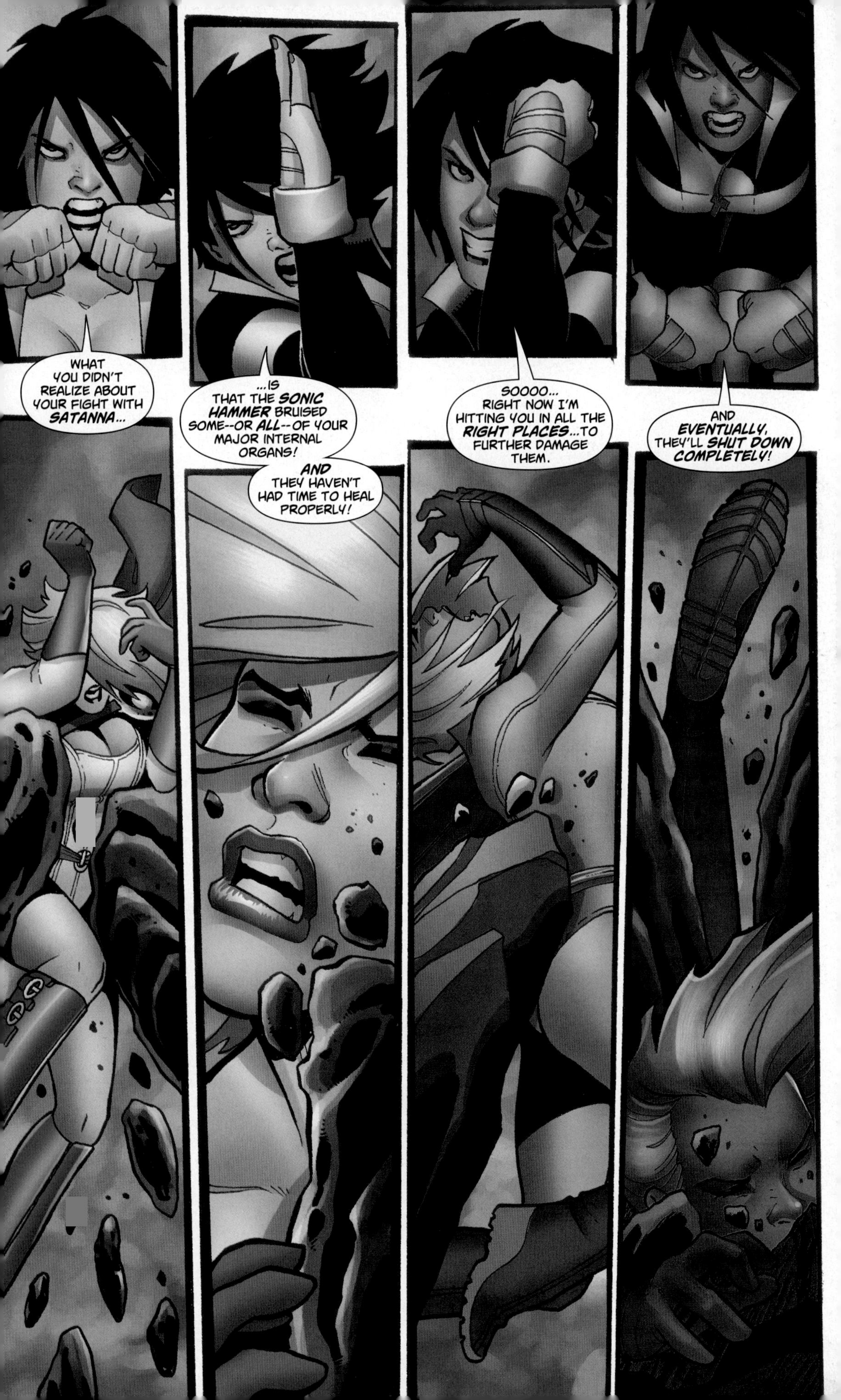

WHAT YOU DIDN'T REALIZE ABOUT YOUR FIGHT WITH SATANNA...
...IS THAT THE SONIC HAMMER BRUISED SOME--OR ALL--OF YOUR MAJOR INTERNAL ORGANS!
AND THEY HAVEN'T HAD TIME TO HEAL PROPERLY!
SOOOO... RIGHT NOW I'M HITTING YOU IN ALL THE RIGHT PLACES...TO FURTHER DAMAGE THEM.
AND EVENTUALLY, THEY'LL SHUT DOWN COMPLETELY!

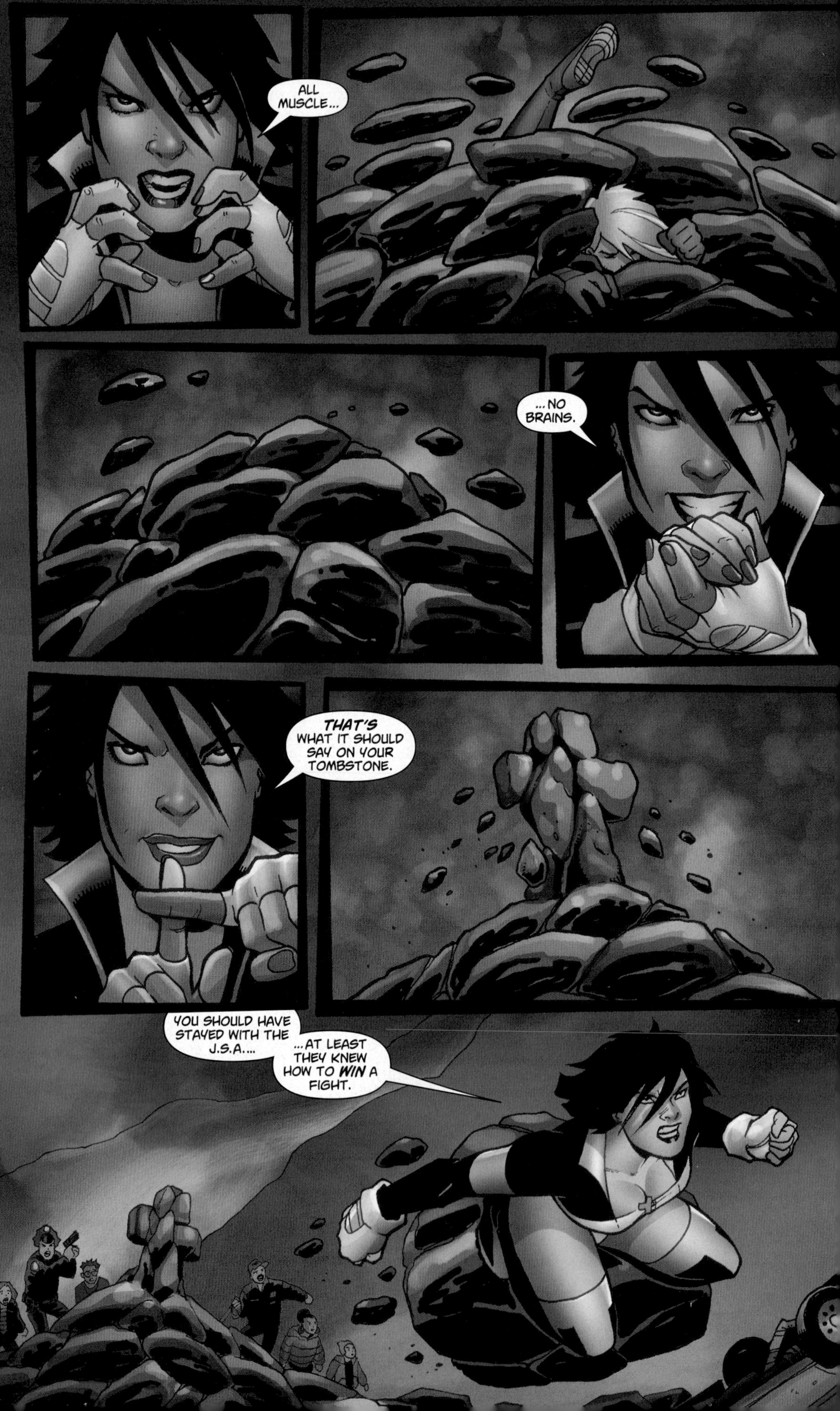
ALL MUSCLE...
...NO BRAINS.
THAT'S WHAT IT SHOULD SAY ON YOUR TOMBSTONE.
YOU SHOULD HAVE STAYED WITH THE J.S.A....
...AT LEAST THEY KNEW HOW TO WIN A FIGHT.

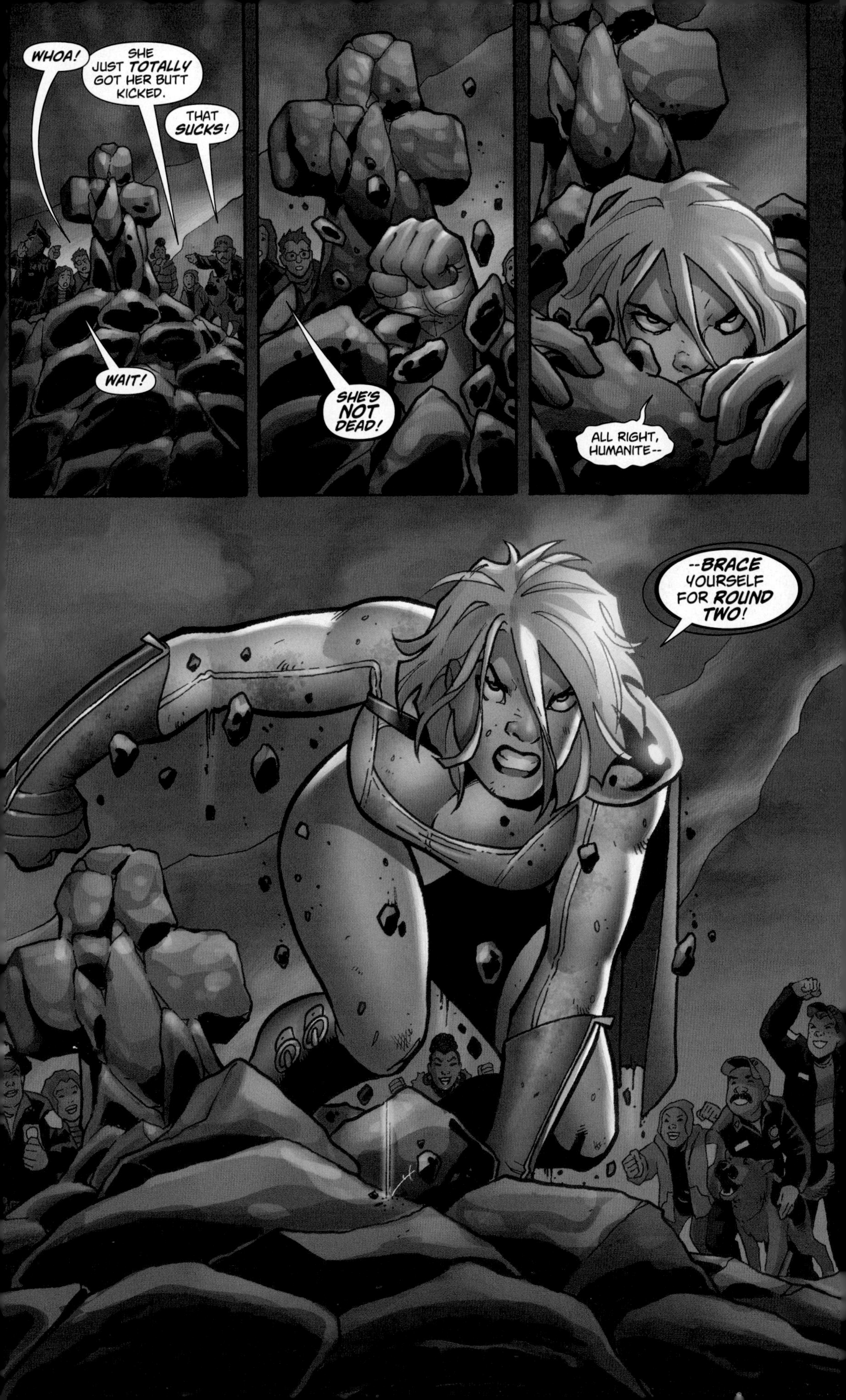
WHOA!
SHE JUST TOTALLY GOT HER BUTT KICKED.
THAT SUCKS!
WAIT!
SHE'S NOT DEAD!
ALL RIGHT, HUMANITE--
--BRACE YOURSELF FOR ROUND TWO!

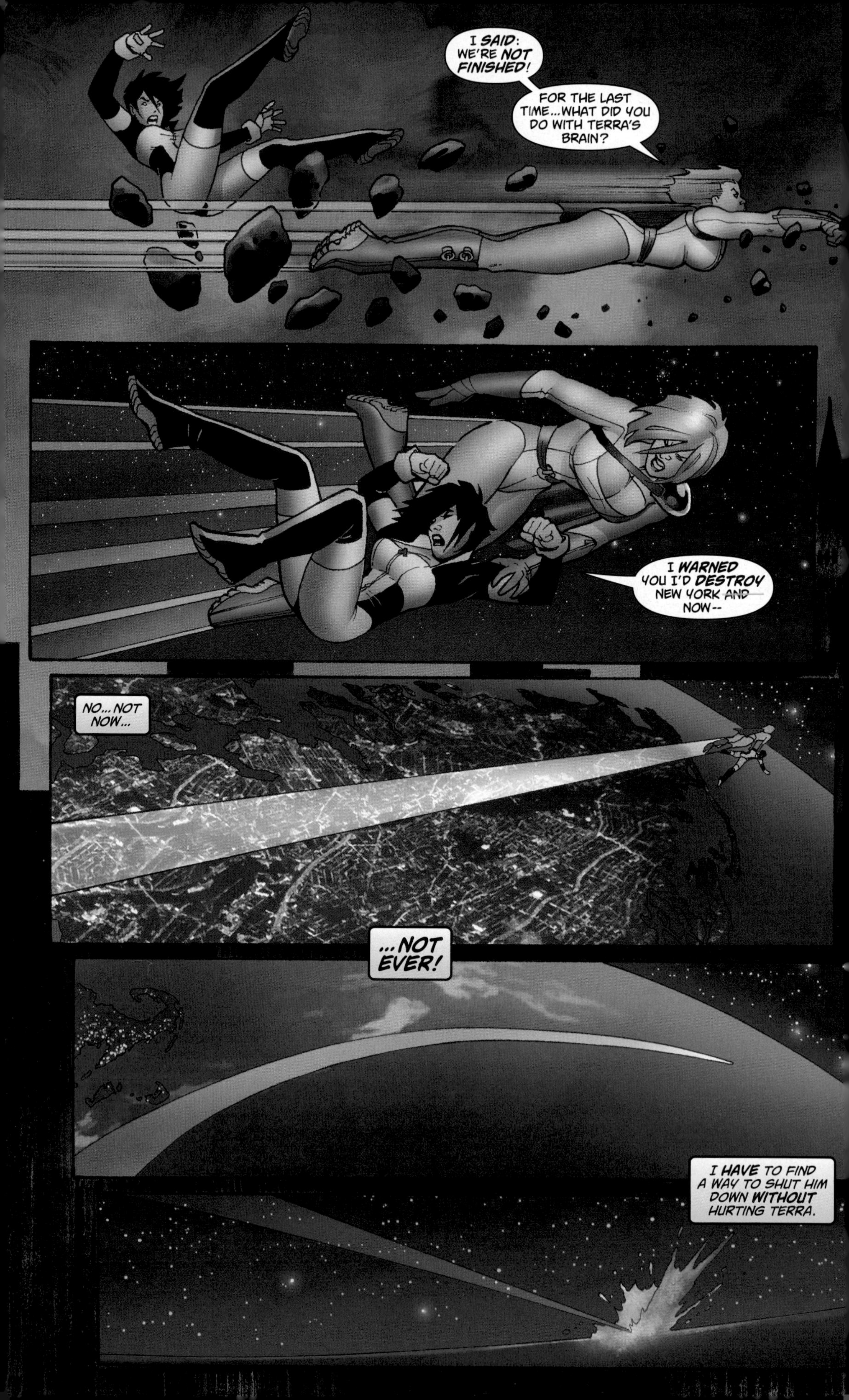
I SAID: WE'RE NOT FINISHED!
FOR THE LAST TIME...WHAT DID YOU DO WITH TERRA'S BRAIN?
I WARNED YOU I'D DESTROY NEW YORK AND NOW--
NO...NOT NOW...
...NOT EVER!
I HAVE TO FIND A WAY TO SHUT HIM DOWN WITHOUT HURTING TERRA.

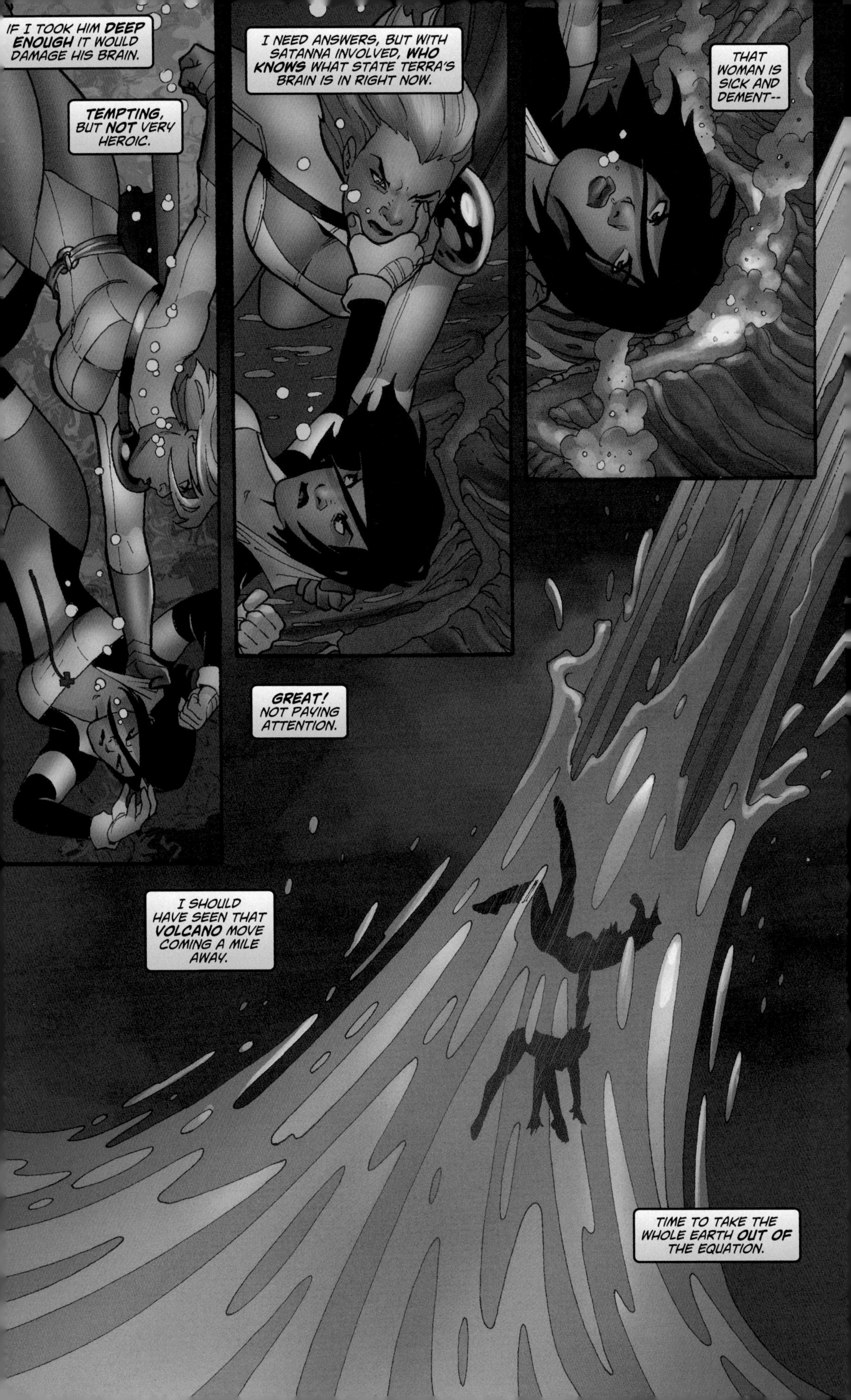

IF I TOOK HIM **DEEP ENOUGH** IT WOULD DAMAGE HIS BRAIN.
TEMPTING, BUT **NOT** VERY HEROIC.
I NEED ANSWERS, BUT WITH SATANNA INVOLVED, **WHO KNOWS** WHAT STATE TERRA'S BRAIN IS IN RIGHT NOW.
THAT WOMAN IS SICK AND DEMENT--
GREAT! NOT PAYING ATTENTION.
I SHOULD HAVE SEEN THAT **VOLCANO** MOVE COMING A MILE AWAY.
TIME TO TAKE THE WHOLE EARTH **OUT OF** THE EQUATION.

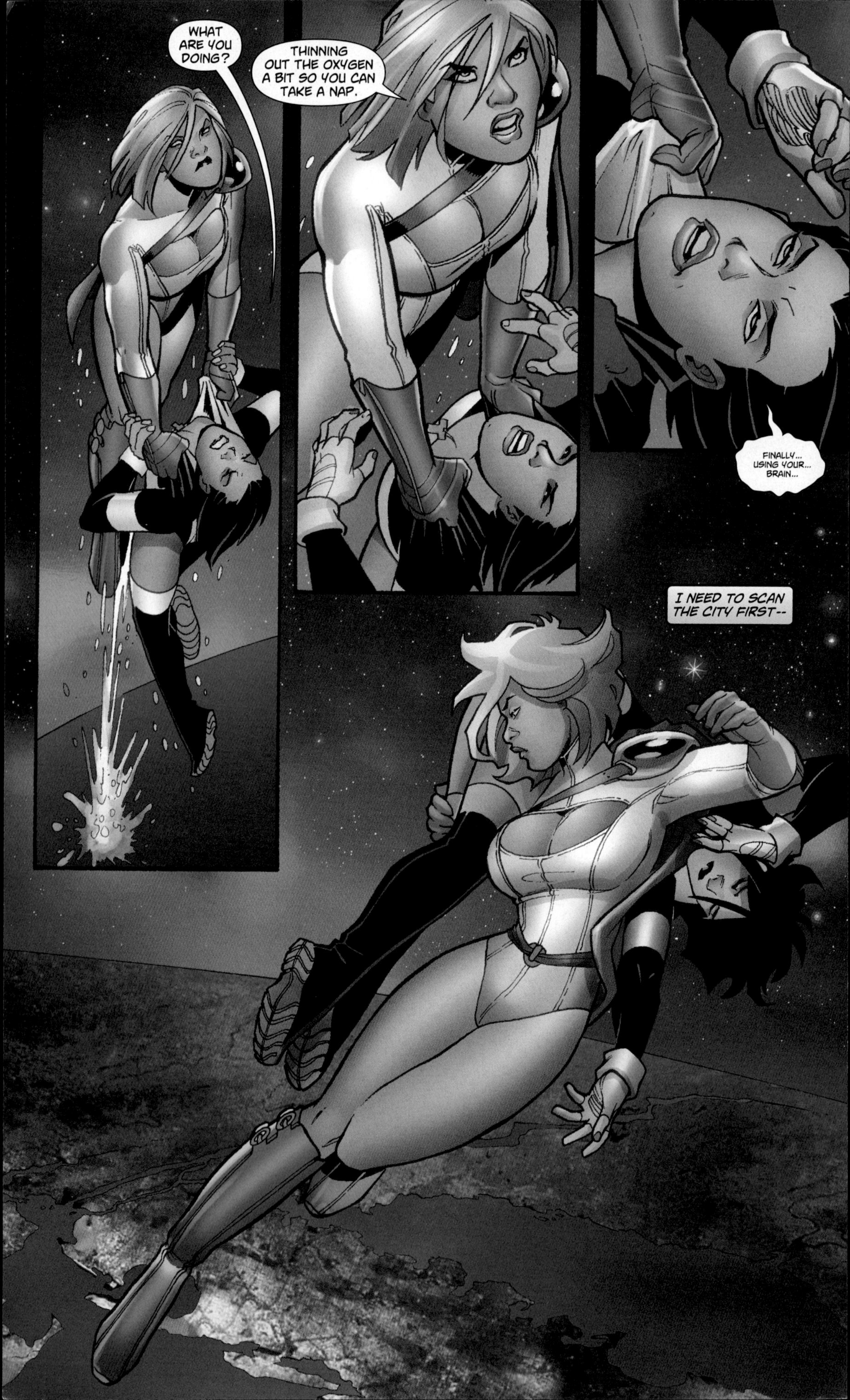
WHAT ARE YOU DOING?
THINNING OUT THE OXYGEN A BIT SO YOU CAN TAKE A NAP.
FINALLY... USING YOUR... BRAIN...
I NEED TO SCAN THE CITY FIRST--

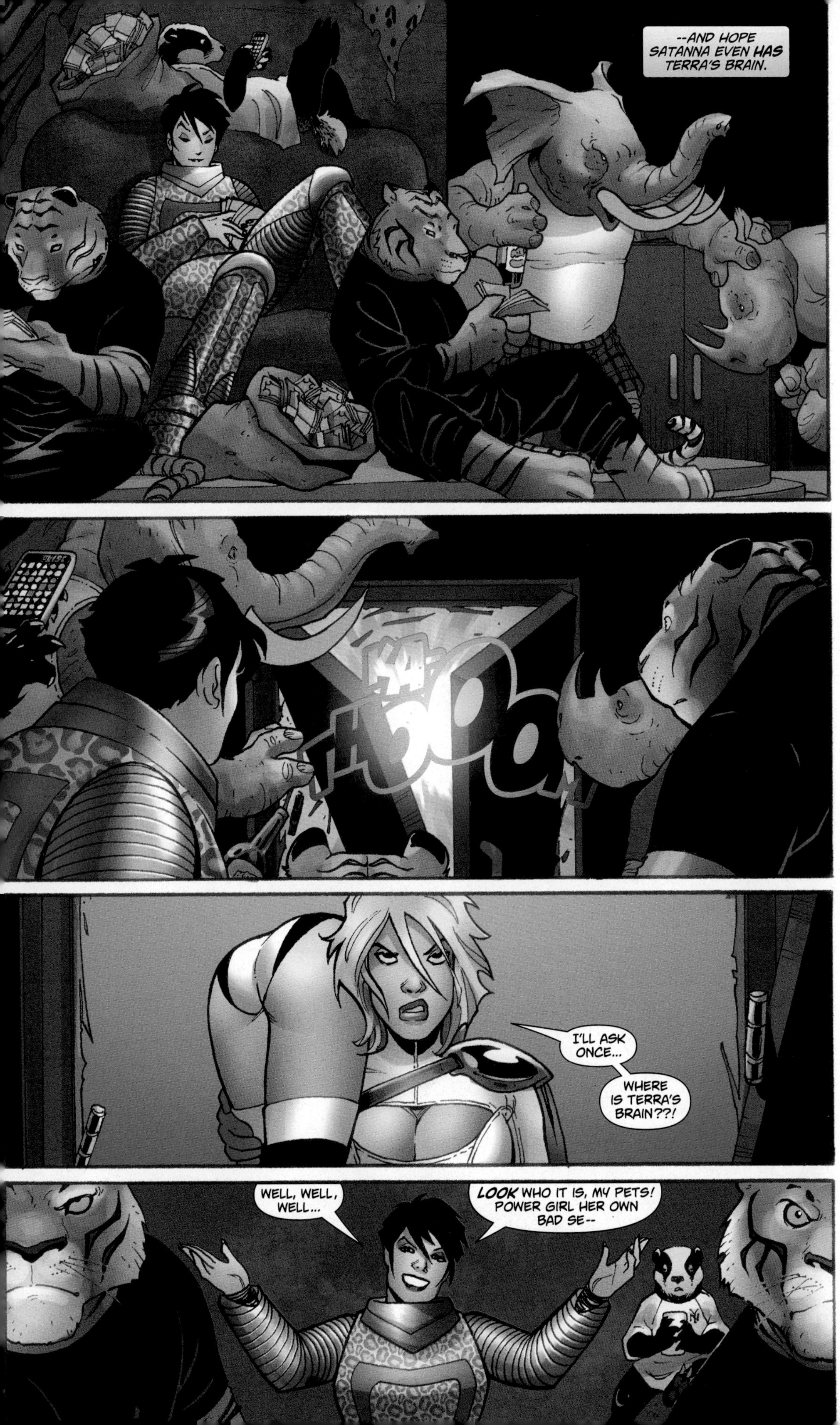
--AND HOPE SATANNA EVEN HAS TERRA'S BRAIN.
KA-THOOOM
I'LL ASK ONCE...
WHERE IS TERRA'S BRAIN??!
WELL, WELL, WELL...
LOOK WHO IT IS, MY PETS! POWER GIRL HER OWN BAD SE--

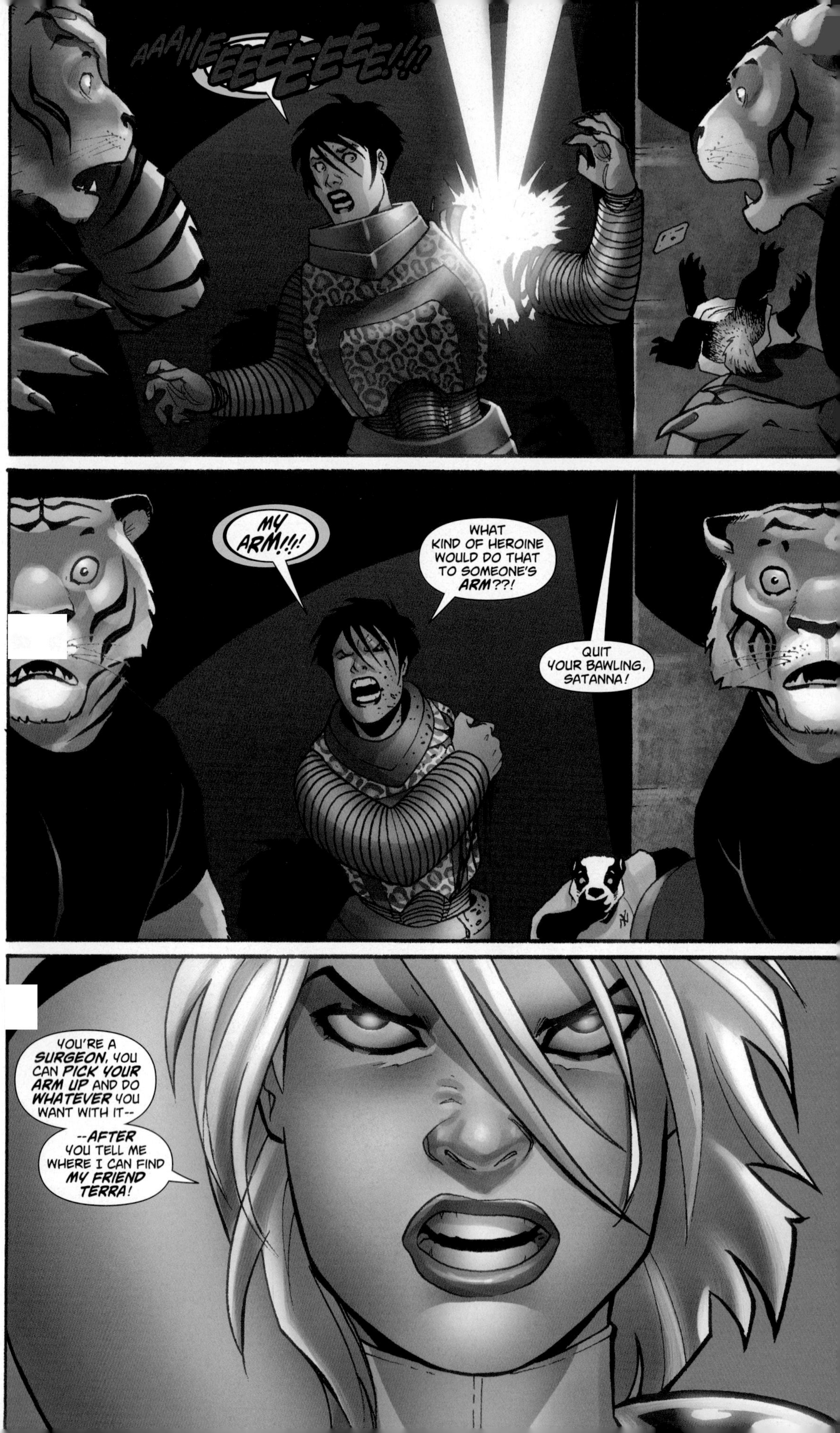
AAAIIIEEEEEEEEEEE!!!
MY ARM!!!!
WHAT KIND OF HEROINE WOULD DO THAT TO SOMEONE'S ARM??!
QUIT YOUR BAWLING, SATANNA!
YOU'RE A SURGEON, YOU CAN PICK YOUR ARM UP AND DO WHATEVER YOU WANT WITH IT--
--AFTER YOU TELL ME WHERE I CAN FIND MY FRIEND TERRA!

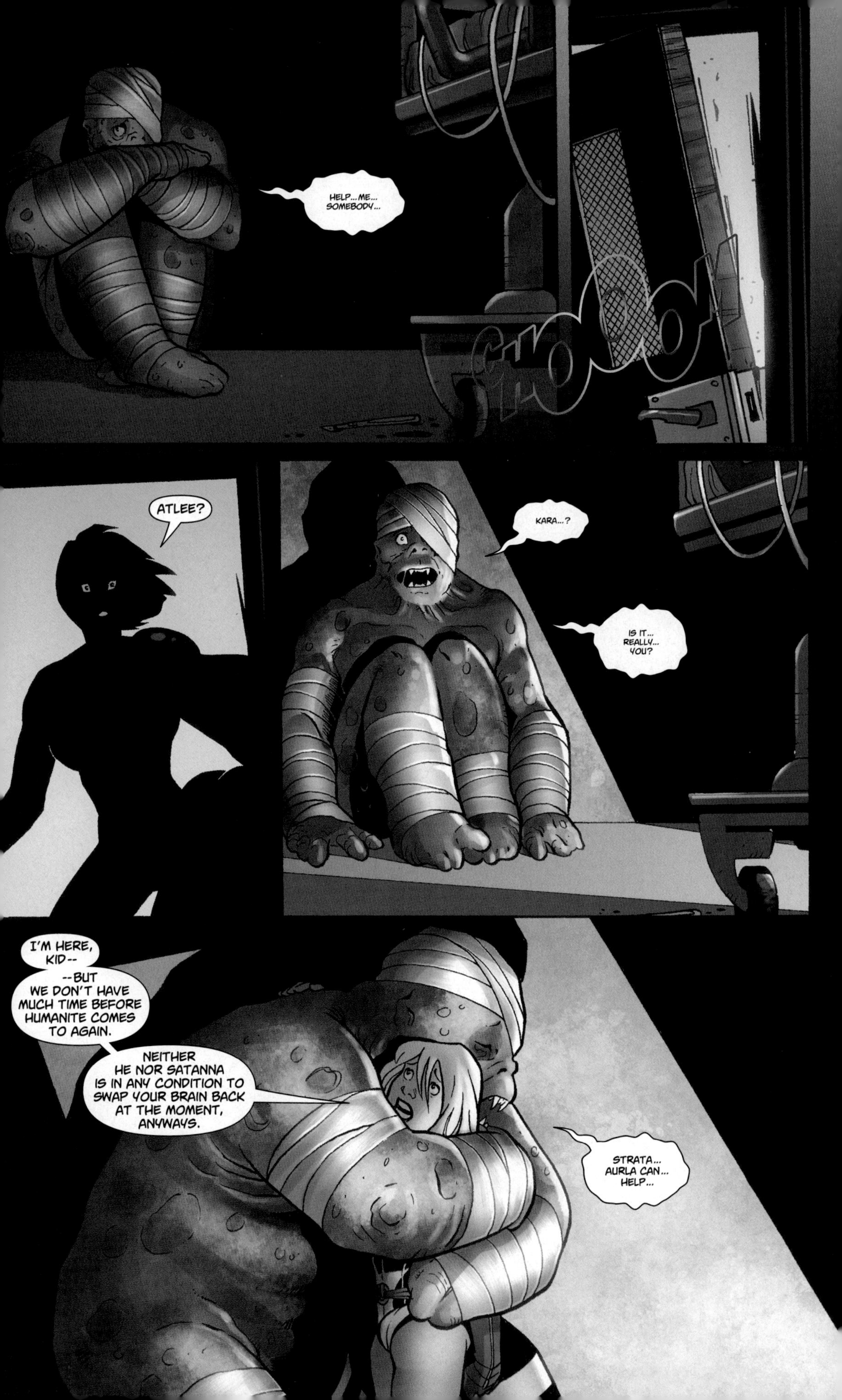
HELP... ME... SOMEBODY...
CHOOOOM
ATLEE?
KARA...?
IS IT... REALLY... YOU?
I'M HERE, KID--
--BUT WE DON'T HAVE MUCH TIME BEFORE HUMANITE COMES TO AGAIN.
NEITHER HE NOR SATANNA IS IN ANY CONDITION TO SWAP YOUR BRAIN BACK AT THE MOMENT, ANYWAYS.
STRATA... AURLA CAN... HELP...

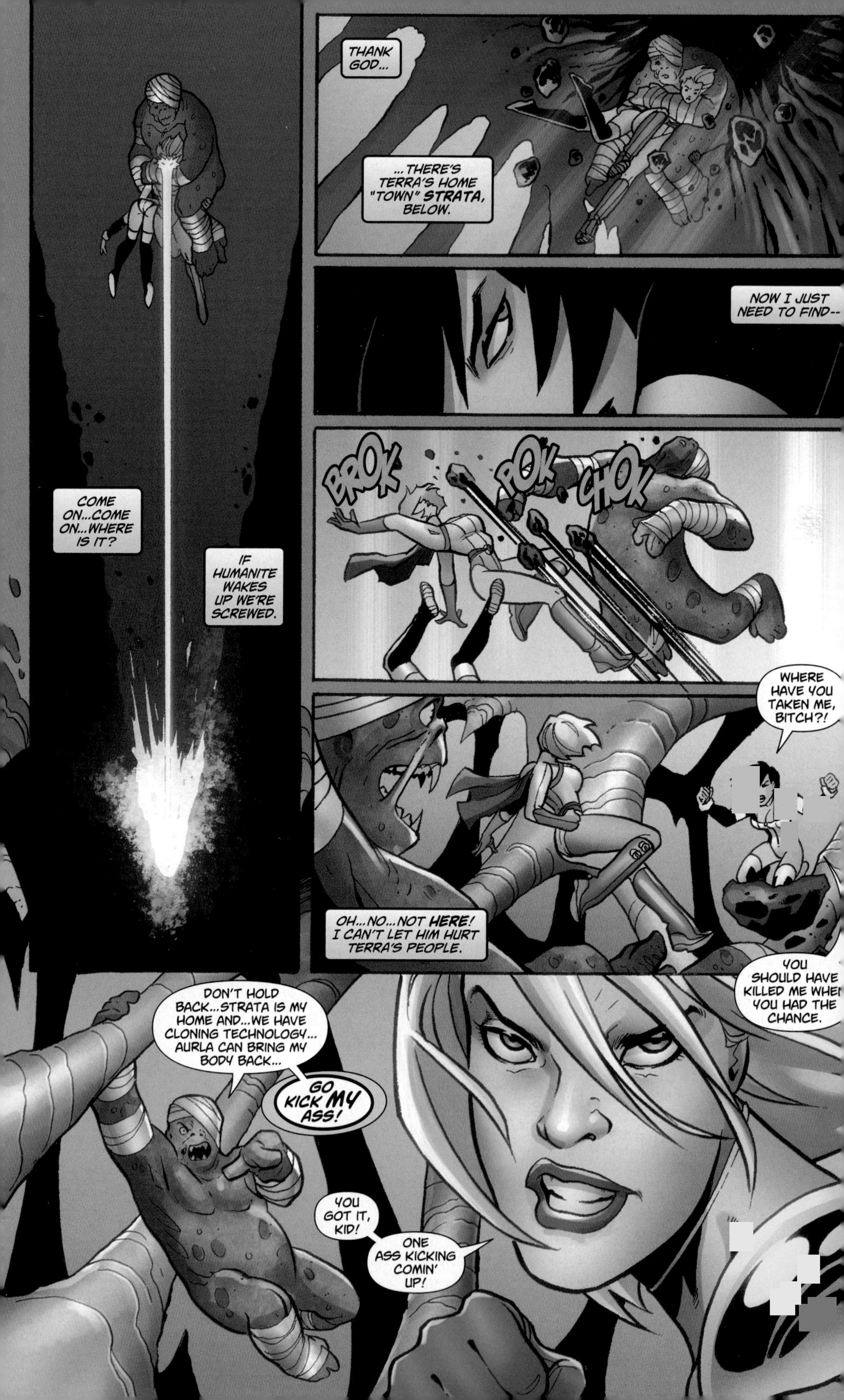

COME ON...COME ON...WHERE IS IT?
IF HUMANITE WAKES UP WE'RE SCREWED.
THANK GOD...
...THERE'S TERRA'S HOME "TOWN" STRATA, BELOW.
NOW I JUST NEED TO FIND--
BROK
POK
CHOK
WHERE HAVE YOU TAKEN ME, BITCH?!
OH...NO...NOT HERE! I CAN'T LET HIM HURT TERRA'S PEOPLE.
DON'T HOLD BACK...STRATA IS MY HOME AND...WE HAVE CLONING TECHNOLOGY... AURLA CAN BRING MY BODY BACK...
GO KICK MY ASS!
YOU SHOULD HAVE KILLED ME WHEN YOU HAD THE CHANCE.
YOU GOT IT, KID!
ONE ASS KICKING COMIN' UP!

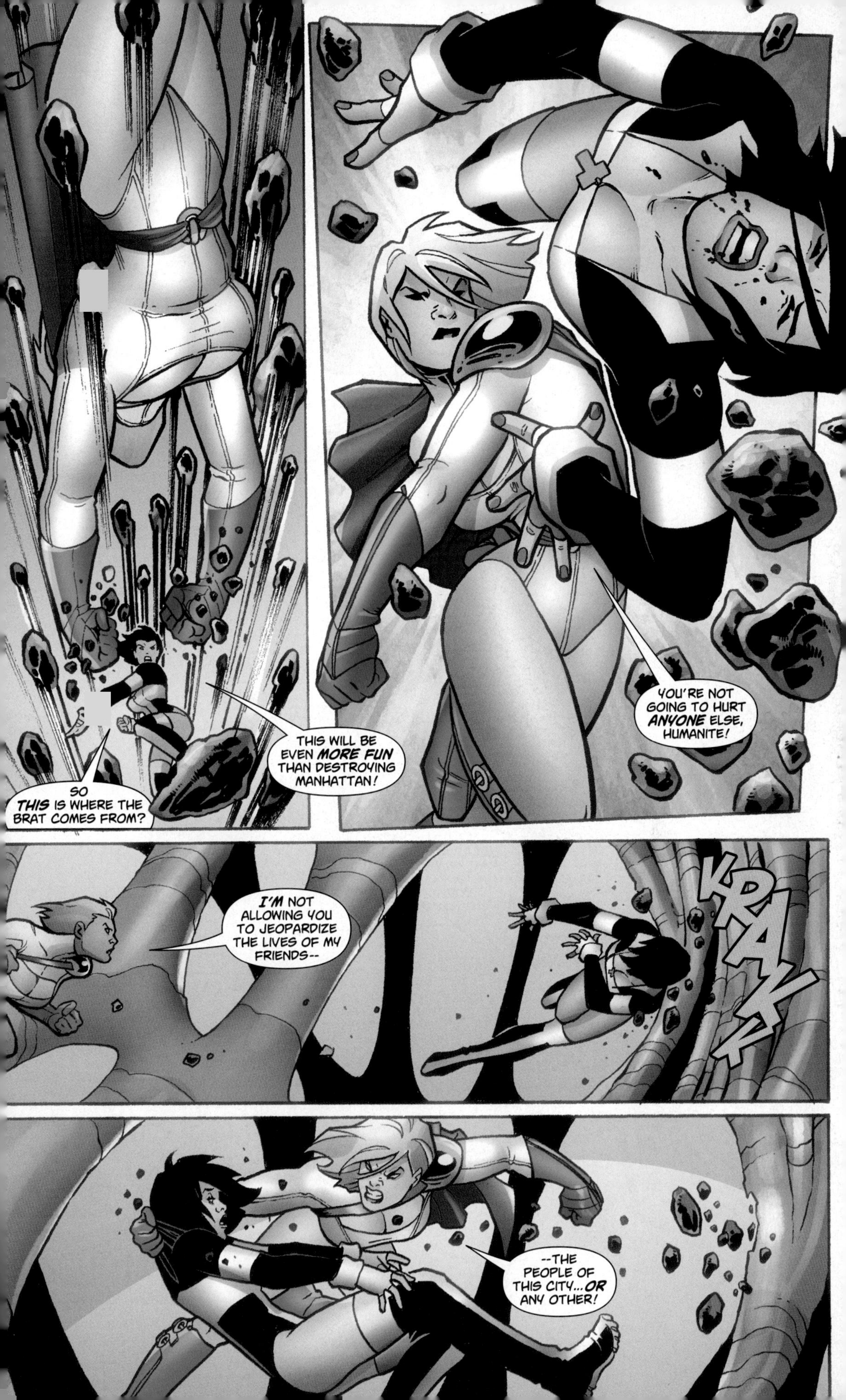
SO **THIS** IS WHERE THE BRAT COMES FROM?
THIS WILL BE EVEN **MORE FUN** THAN DESTROYING MANHATTAN!
YOU'RE NOT GOING TO HURT **ANYONE** ELSE, HUMANITE!
I'M NOT ALLOWING YOU TO JEOPARDIZE THE LIVES OF MY FRIENDS--
KRAKK
--THE PEOPLE OF THIS CITY... **OR** ANY OTHER!

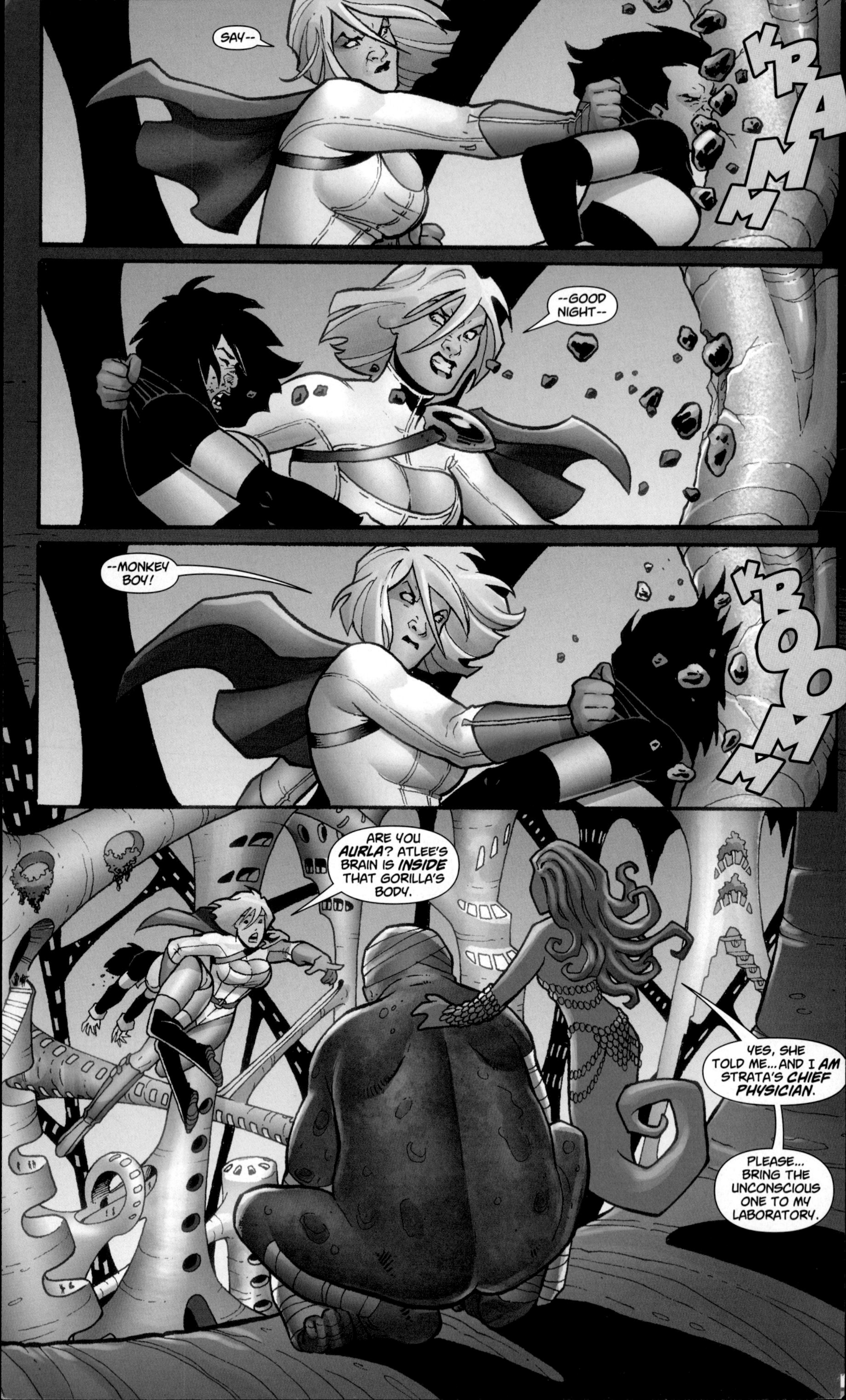
SAY--
KRAMMM
--GOOD NIGHT--
--MONKEY BOY!
KROOOMMM
ARE YOU AURLA? ATLEE'S BRAIN IS INSIDE THAT GORILLA'S BODY.
YES, SHE TOLD ME...AND I AM STRATA'S CHIEF PHYSICIAN.
PLEASE... BRING THE UNCONSCIOUS ONE TO MY LABORATORY.

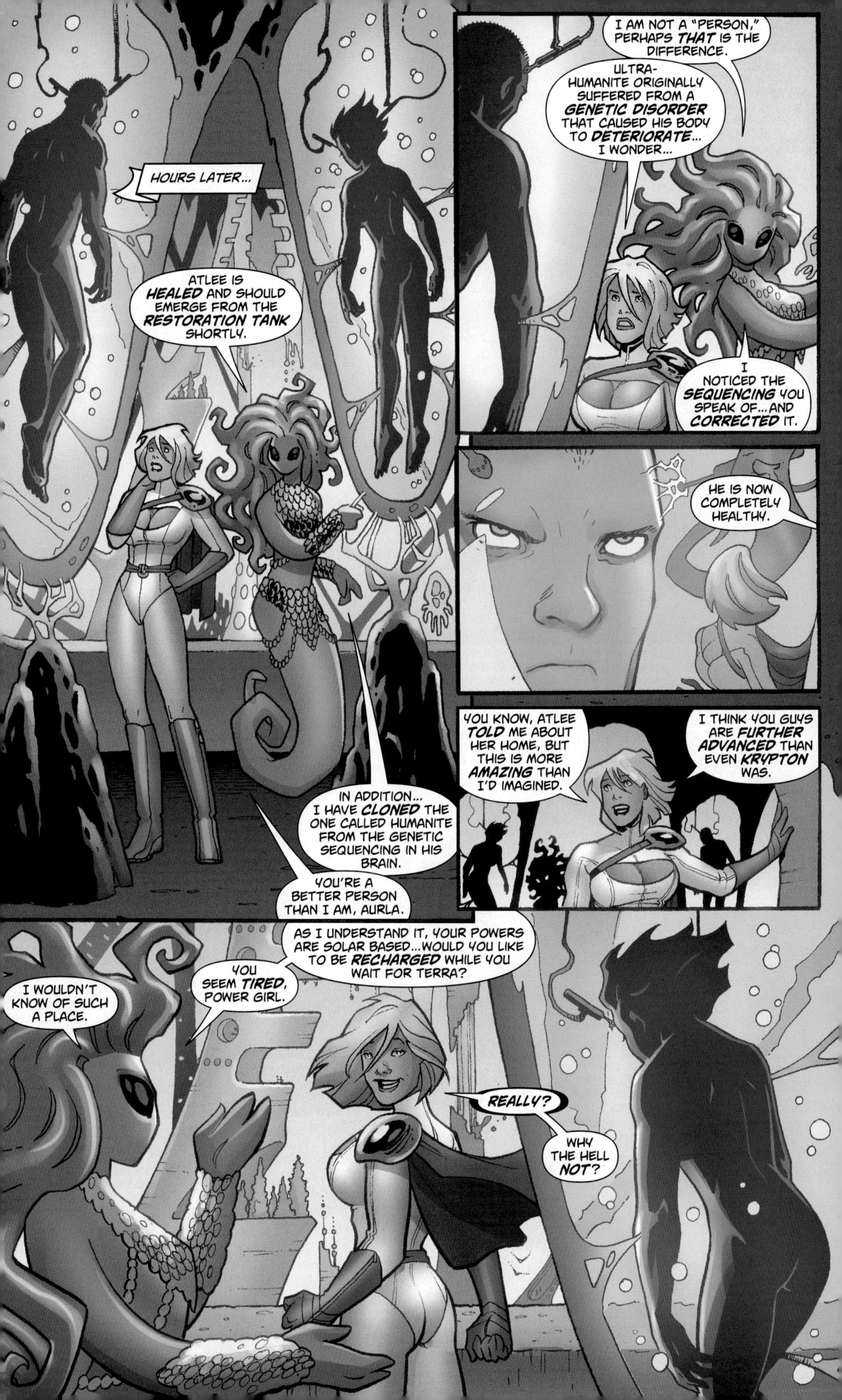
HOURS LATER...
ATLEE IS HEALED AND SHOULD EMERGE FROM THE RESTORATION TANK SHORTLY.
IN ADDITION... I HAVE CLONED THE ONE CALLED HUMANITE FROM THE GENETIC SEQUENCING IN HIS BRAIN.
YOU'RE A BETTER PERSON THAN I AM, AURLA.
I AM NOT A "PERSON," PERHAPS THAT IS THE DIFFERENCE.
ULTRA-HUMANITE ORIGINALLY SUFFERED FROM A GENETIC DISORDER THAT CAUSED HIS BODY TO DETERIORATE... I WONDER...
I NOTICED THE SEQUENCING YOU SPEAK OF... AND CORRECTED IT.
HE IS NOW COMPLETELY HEALTHY.
YOU KNOW, ATLEE TOLD ME ABOUT HER HOME, BUT THIS IS MORE AMAZING THAN I'D IMAGINED.
I THINK YOU GUYS ARE FURTHER ADVANCED THAN EVEN KRYPTON WAS.
I WOULDN'T KNOW OF SUCH A PLACE.
YOU SEEM TIRED, POWER GIRL.
AS I UNDERSTAND IT, YOUR POWERS ARE SOLAR BASED... WOULD YOU LIKE TO BE RECHARGED WHILE YOU WAIT FOR TERRA?
REALLY?
WHY THE HELL NOT?

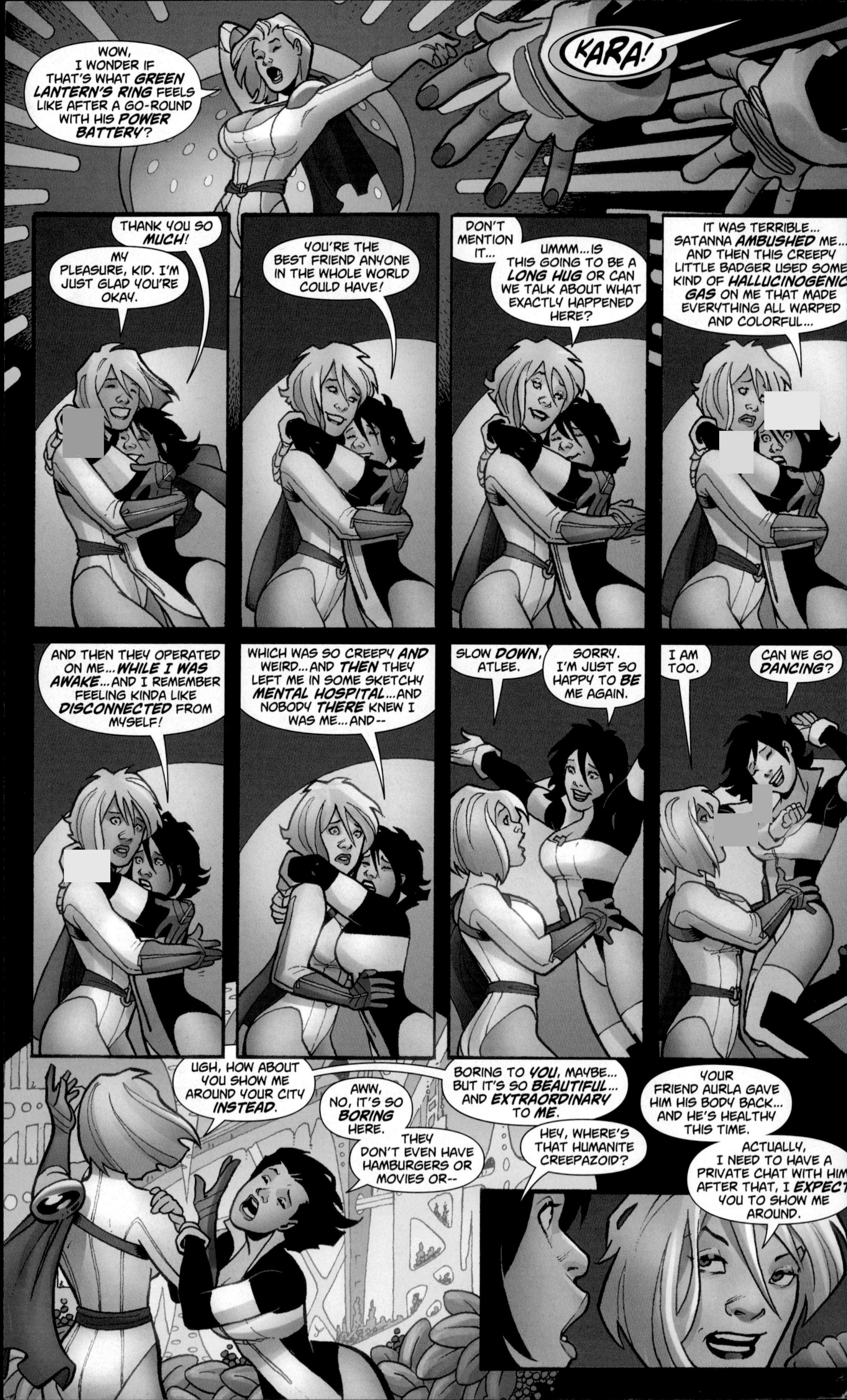
WOW, I WONDER IF THAT'S WHAT GREEN LANTERN'S RING FEELS LIKE AFTER A GO-ROUND WITH HIS POWER BATTERY?
KARA!
THANK YOU SO MUCH!
MY PLEASURE, KID. I'M JUST GLAD YOU'RE OKAY.
YOU'RE THE BEST FRIEND ANYONE IN THE WHOLE WORLD COULD HAVE!
DON'T MENTION IT...
UMMM...IS THIS GOING TO BE A LONG HUG OR CAN WE TALK ABOUT WHAT EXACTLY HAPPENED HERE?
IT WAS TERRIBLE... SATANNA AMBUSHED ME... AND THEN THIS CREEPY LITTLE BADGER USED SOME KIND OF HALLUCINOGENIC GAS ON ME THAT MADE EVERYTHING ALL WARPED AND COLORFUL...
AND THEN THEY OPERATED ON ME... WHILE I WAS AWAKE... AND I REMEMBER FEELING KINDA LIKE DISCONNECTED FROM MYSELF!
WHICH WAS SO CREEPY AND WEIRD... AND THEN THEY LEFT ME IN SOME SKETCHY MENTAL HOSPITAL... AND NOBODY THERE KNEW I WAS ME... AND--
SLOW DOWN, ATLEE.
SORRY. I'M JUST SO HAPPY TO BE ME AGAIN.
I AM TOO.
CAN WE GO DANCING?
UGH, HOW ABOUT YOU SHOW ME AROUND YOUR CITY INSTEAD.
AWW, NO, IT'S SO BORING HERE.
THEY DON'T EVEN HAVE HAMBURGERS OR MOVIES OR--
BORING TO YOU, MAYBE... BUT IT'S SO BEAUTIFUL... AND EXTRAORDINARY TO ME.
HEY, WHERE'S THAT HUMANITE CREEPAZOID?
YOUR FRIEND AURLA GAVE HIM HIS BODY BACK... AND HE'S HEALTHY THIS TIME.
ACTUALLY, I NEED TO HAVE A PRIVATE CHAT WITH HIM. AFTER THAT, I EXPECT YOU TO SHOW ME AROUND.

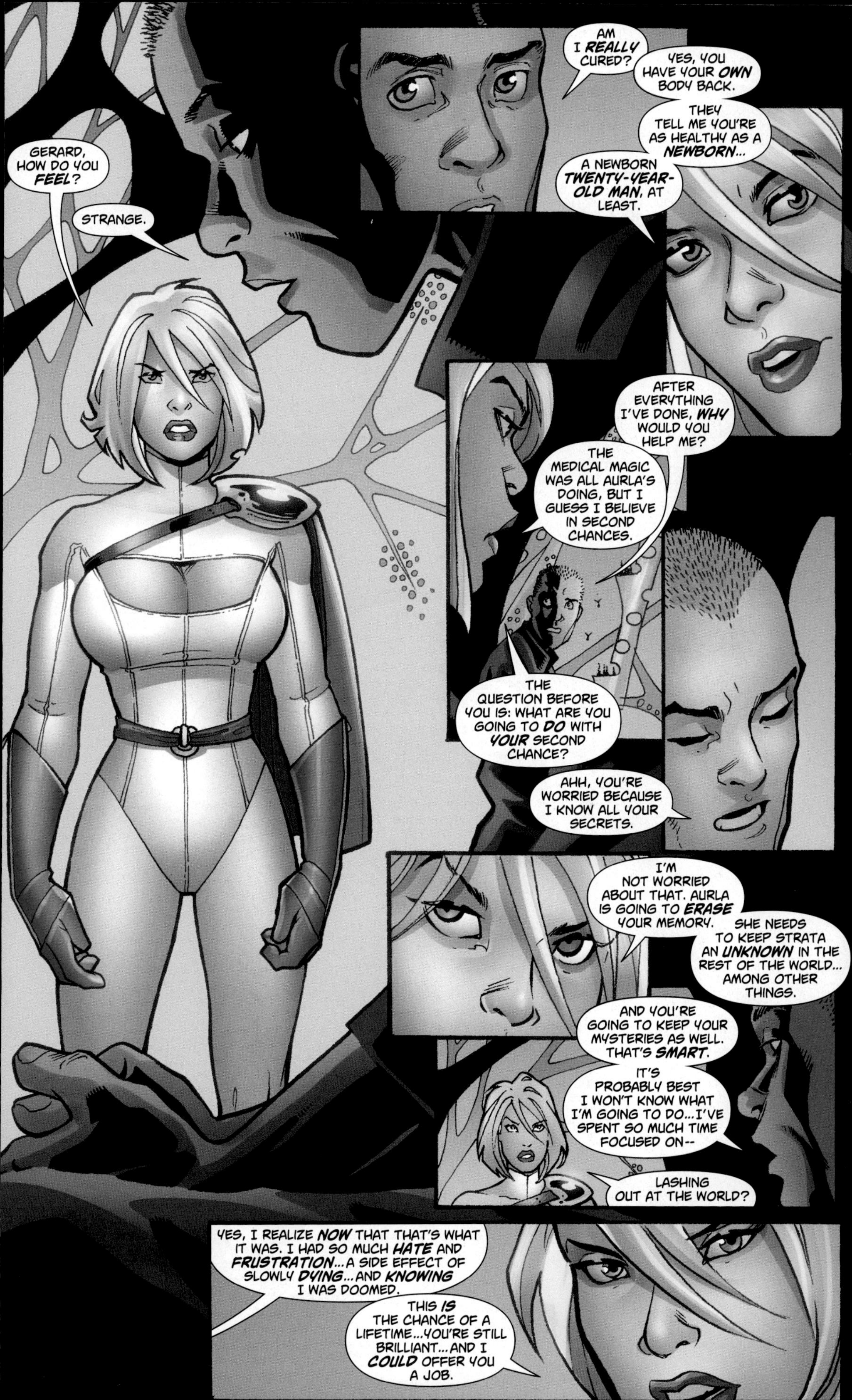
GERARD, HOW DO YOU FEEL?
STRANGE.
AM I REALLY CURED?
YES, YOU HAVE YOUR OWN BODY BACK.
THEY TELL ME YOU'RE AS HEALTHY AS A NEWBORN...
A NEWBORN TWENTY-YEAR-OLD MAN, AT LEAST.
AFTER EVERYTHING I'VE DONE, WHY WOULD YOU HELP ME?
THE MEDICAL MAGIC WAS ALL AURLA'S DOING, BUT I GUESS I BELIEVE IN SECOND CHANCES.
THE QUESTION BEFORE YOU IS: WHAT ARE YOU GOING TO DO WITH YOUR SECOND CHANCE?
AHH, YOU'RE WORRIED BECAUSE I KNOW ALL YOUR SECRETS.
I'M NOT WORRIED ABOUT THAT. AURLA IS GOING TO ERASE YOUR MEMORY.
SHE NEEDS TO KEEP STRATA AN UNKNOWN IN THE REST OF THE WORLD... AMONG OTHER THINGS.
AND YOU'RE GOING TO KEEP YOUR MYSTERIES AS WELL. THAT'S SMART.
IT'S PROBABLY BEST I WON'T KNOW WHAT I'M GOING TO DO... I'VE SPENT SO MUCH TIME FOCUSED ON--
LASHING OUT AT THE WORLD?
YES, I REALIZE NOW THAT THAT'S WHAT IT WAS. I HAD SO MUCH HATE AND FRUSTRATION... A SIDE EFFECT OF SLOWLY DYING... AND KNOWING I WAS DOOMED.
THIS IS THE CHANCE OF A LIFETIME... YOU'RE STILL BRILLIANT... AND I COULD OFFER YOU A JOB.

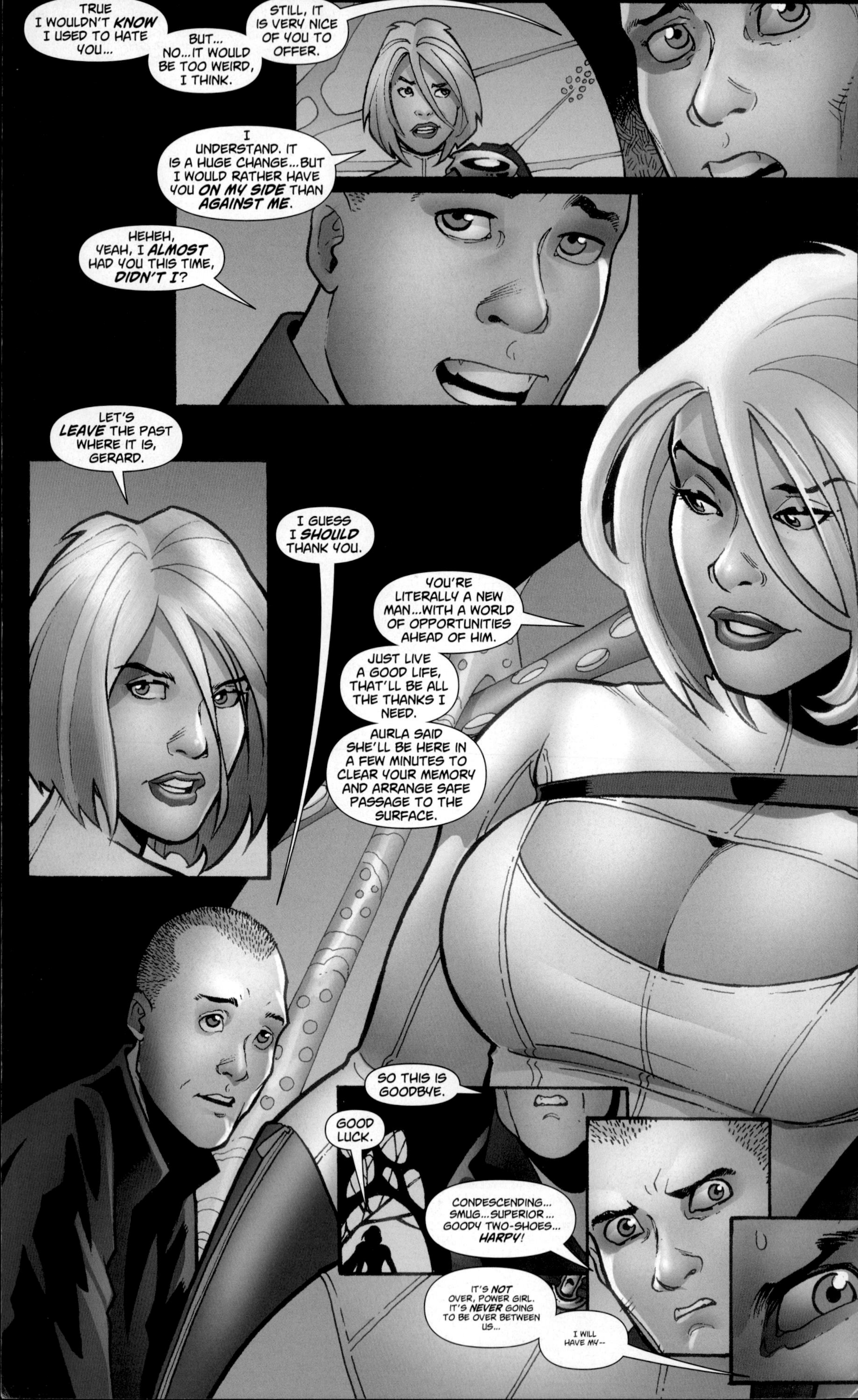
TRUE I WOULDN'T KNOW I USED TO HATE YOU...
BUT... NO...IT WOULD BE TOO WEIRD, I THINK.
STILL, IT IS VERY NICE OF YOU TO OFFER.
I UNDERSTAND. IT IS A HUGE CHANGE...BUT I WOULD RATHER HAVE YOU ON MY SIDE THAN AGAINST ME.
HEHEH, YEAH, I ALMOST HAD YOU THIS TIME, DIDN'T I?
LET'S LEAVE THE PAST WHERE IT IS, GERARD.
I GUESS I SHOULD THANK YOU.
YOU'RE LITERALLY A NEW MAN...WITH A WORLD OF OPPORTUNITIES AHEAD OF HIM.
JUST LIVE A GOOD LIFE, THAT'LL BE ALL THE THANKS I NEED.
AURLA SAID SHE'LL BE HERE IN A FEW MINUTES TO CLEAR YOUR MEMORY AND ARRANGE SAFE PASSAGE TO THE SURFACE.
SO THIS IS GOODBYE.
GOOD LUCK.
CONDESCENDING... SMUG...SUPERIOR... GOODY TWO-SHOES... HARPY!
IT'S NOT OVER, POWER GIRL. IT'S NEVER GOING TO BE OVER BETWEEN US...
I WILL HAVE MY--

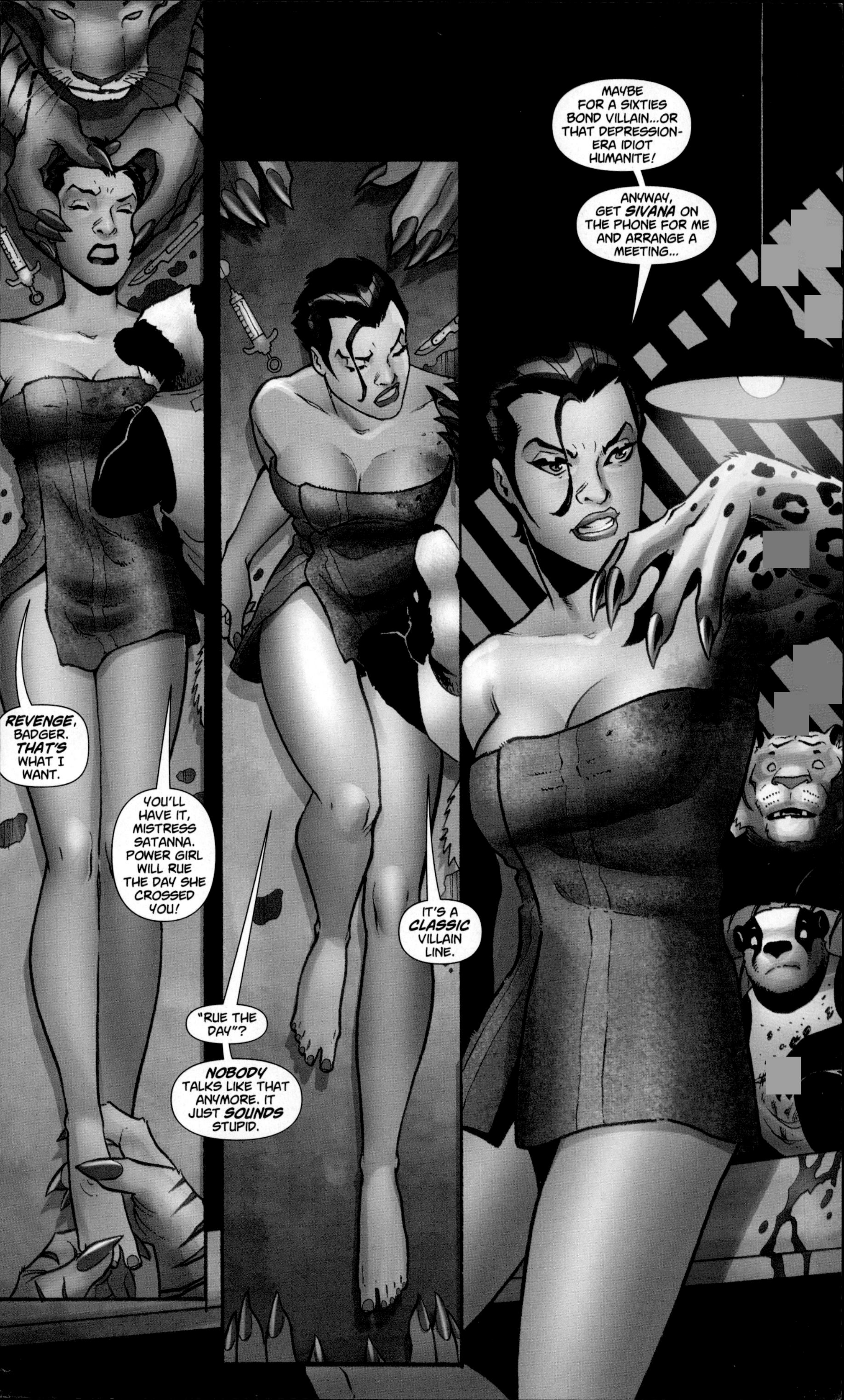
REVENGE, BADGER. THAT'S WHAT I WANT.
YOU'LL HAVE IT, MISTRESS SATANNA. POWER GIRL WILL RUE THE DAY SHE CROSSED YOU!
"RUE THE DAY"?
NOBODY TALKS LIKE THAT ANYMORE. IT JUST SOUNDS STUPID.
IT'S A CLASSIC VILLAIN LINE.
MAYBE FOR A SIXTIES BOND VILLAIN...OR THAT DEPRESSION-ERA IDIOT HUMANITE!
ANYWAY, GET SIVANA ON THE PHONE FOR ME AND ARRANGE A MEETING...

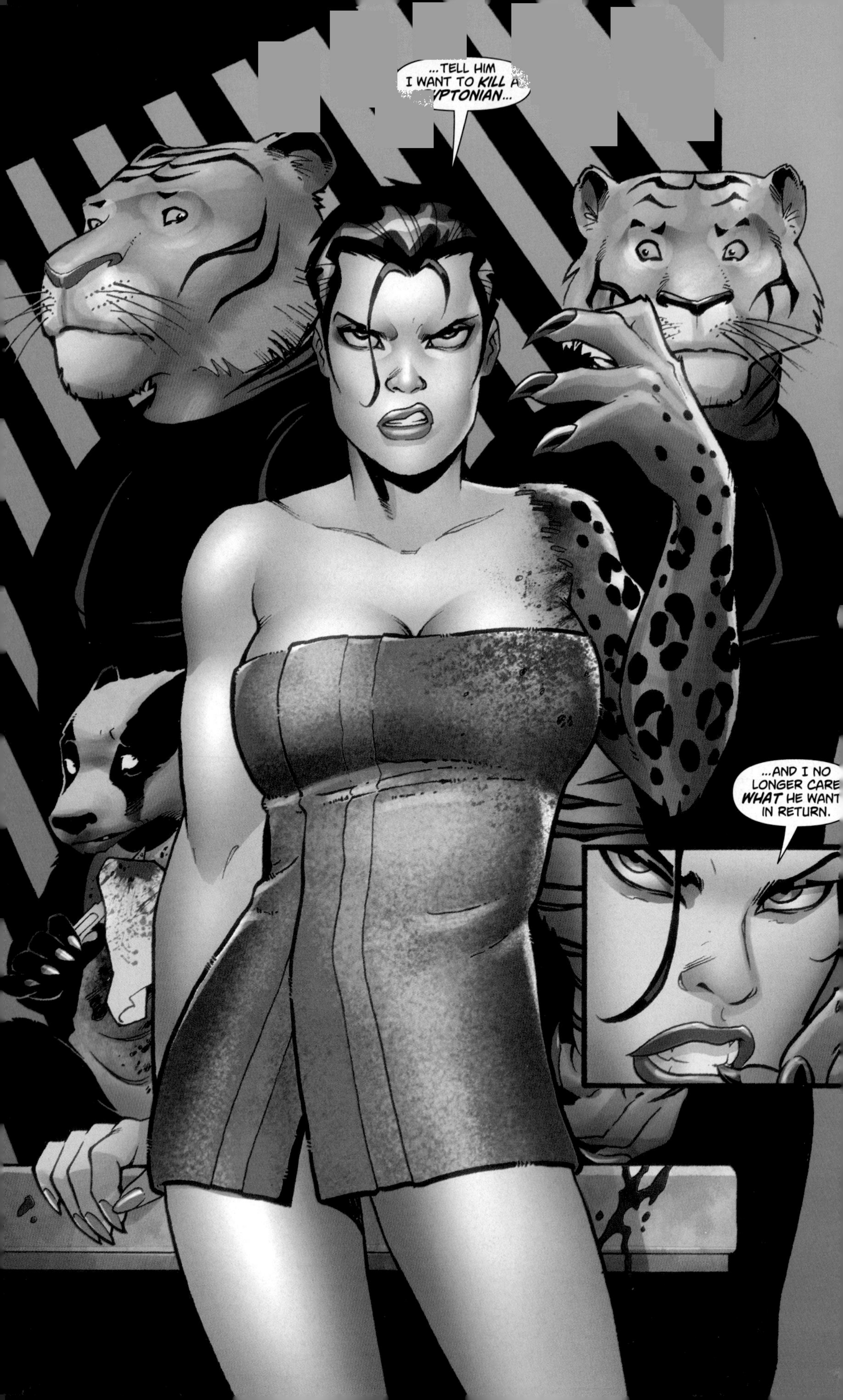
...TELL HIM I WANT TO KILL A
...AND I NO LONGER CARE WHAT HE WANT IN RETURN.

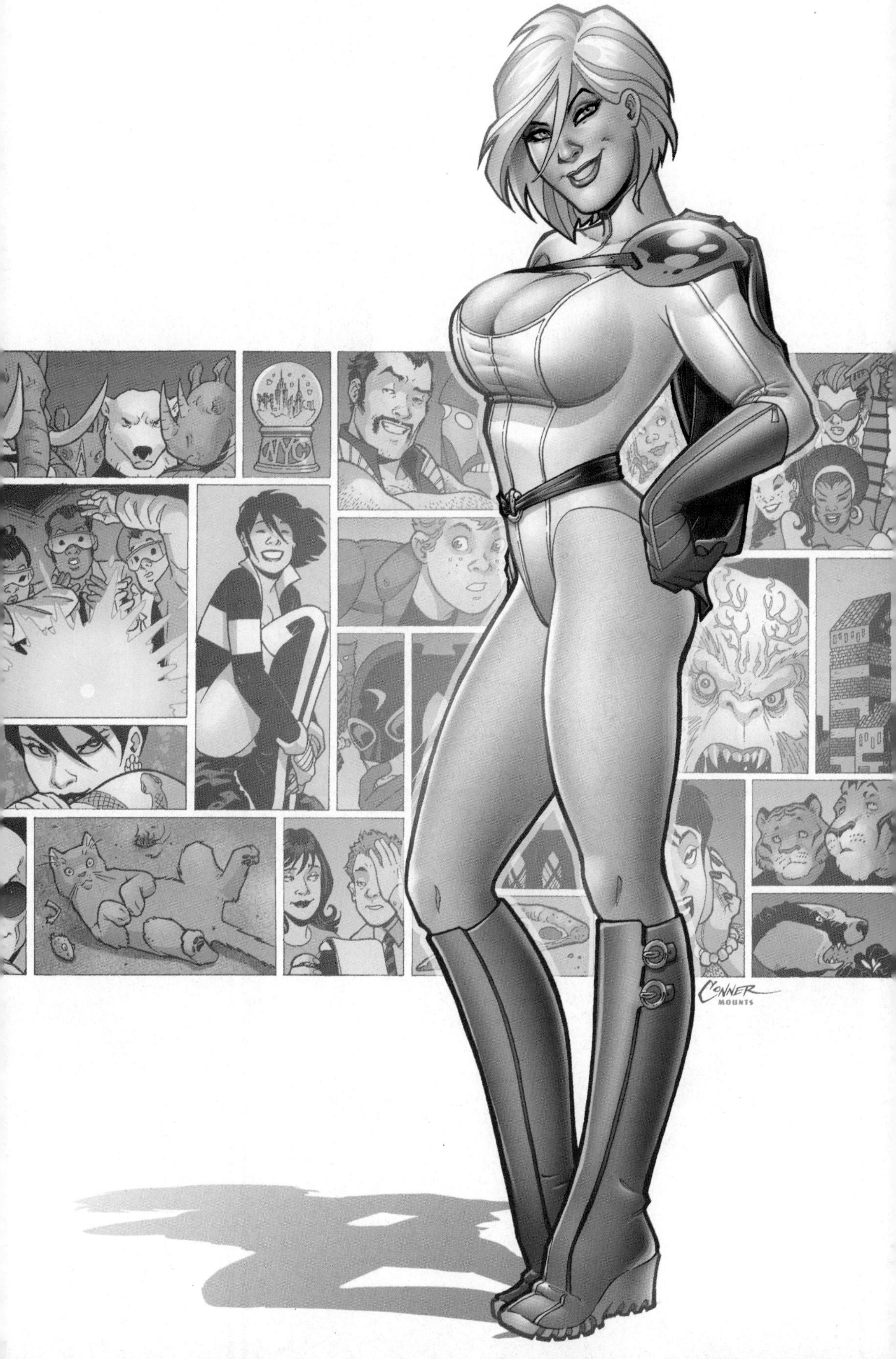
NYC
CONNER
MOUNTS

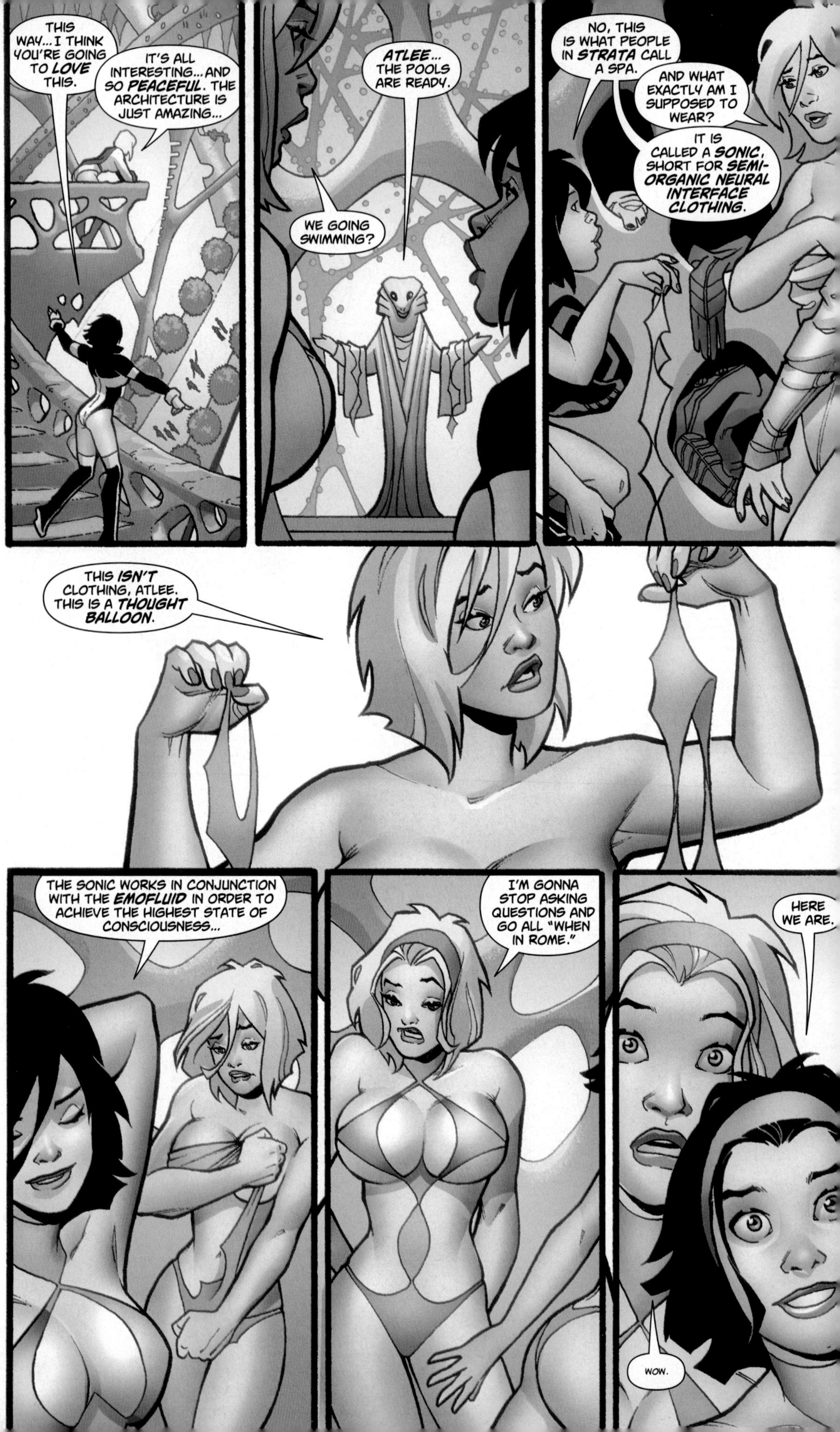
THIS WAY... I THINK YOU'RE GOING TO LOVE THIS.
IT'S ALL INTERESTING... AND SO PEACEFUL. THE ARCHITECTURE IS JUST AMAZING...
ATLEE... THE POOLS ARE READY.
WE GOING SWIMMING?
NO, THIS IS WHAT PEOPLE IN STRATA CALL A SPA.
AND WHAT EXACTLY AM I SUPPOSED TO WEAR?
IT IS CALLED A SONIC, SHORT FOR SEMI-ORGANIC NEURAL INTERFACE CLOTHING.
THIS ISN'T CLOTHING, ATLEE. THIS IS A THOUGHT BALLOON.
THE SONIC WORKS IN CONJUNCTION WITH THE EMOFLUID IN ORDER TO ACHIEVE THE HIGHEST STATE OF CONSCIOUSNESS...
I'M GONNA STOP ASKING QUESTIONS AND GO ALL "WHEN IN ROME."
HERE WE ARE.
WOW.

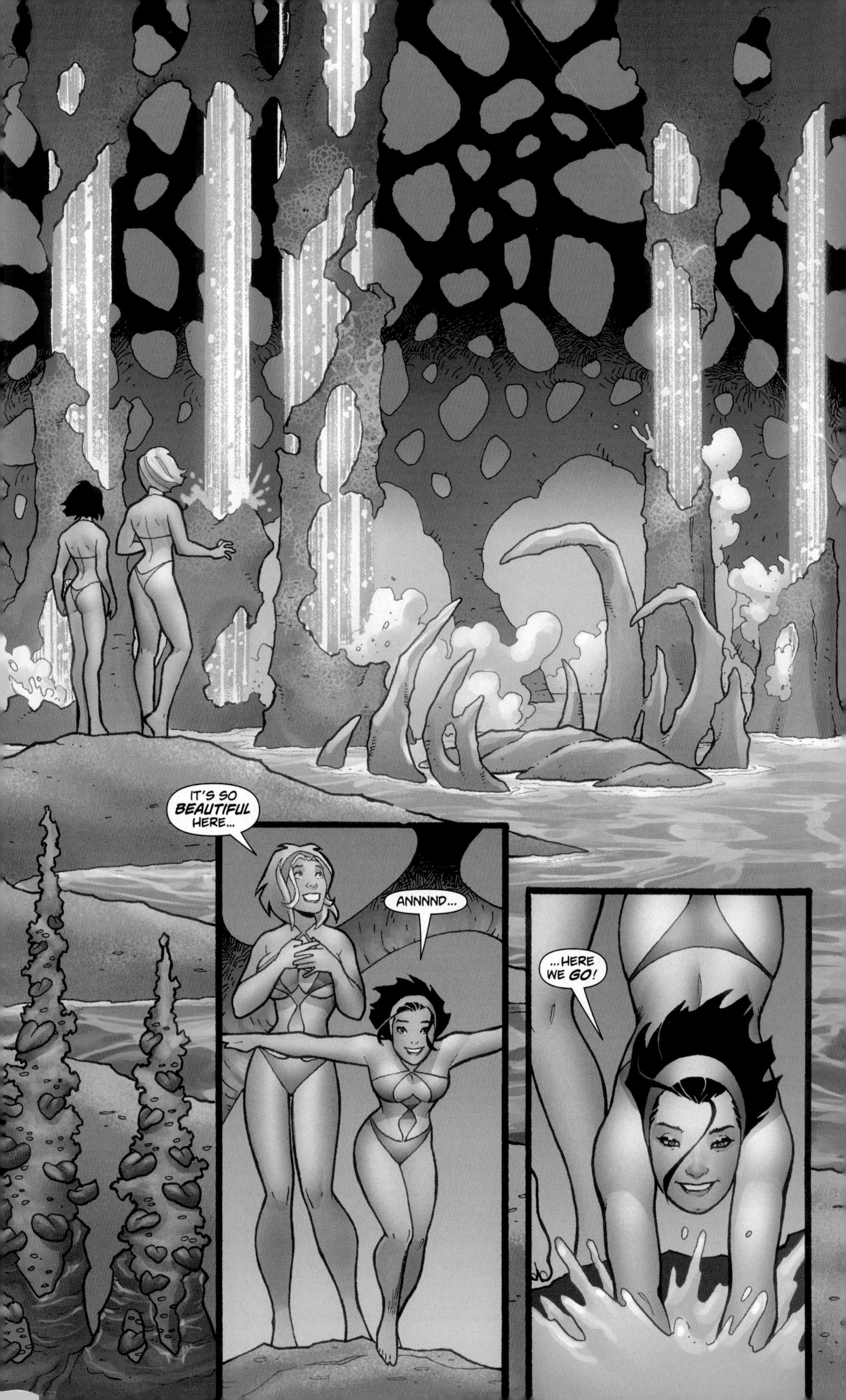
IT'S SO BEAUTIFUL HERE...
ANNNND...
...HERE WE GO!

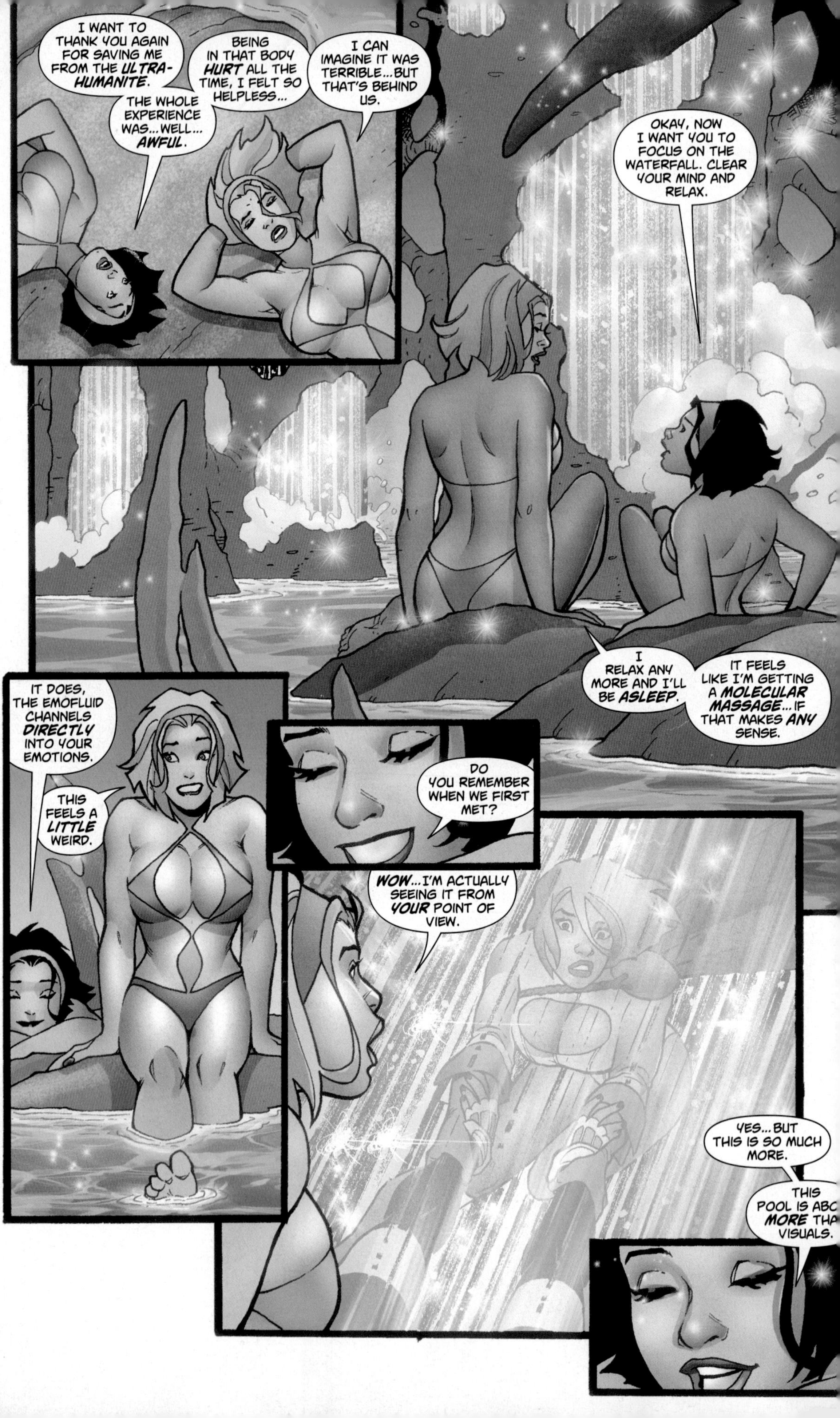
I WANT TO THANK YOU AGAIN FOR SAVING ME FROM THE ULTRA-HUMANITE.
THE WHOLE EXPERIENCE WAS...WELL... AWFUL.
BEING IN THAT BODY HURT ALL THE TIME, I FELT SO HELPLESS...
I CAN IMAGINE IT WAS TERRIBLE...BUT THAT'S BEHIND US.
OKAY, NOW I WANT YOU TO FOCUS ON THE WATERFALL. CLEAR YOUR MIND AND RELAX.
I RELAX ANY MORE AND I'LL BE ASLEEP.
IT FEELS LIKE I'M GETTING A MOLECULAR MASSAGE...IF THAT MAKES ANY SENSE.
IT DOES, THE EMOFLUID CHANNELS DIRECTLY INTO YOUR EMOTIONS.
THIS FEELS A LITTLE WEIRD.
DO YOU REMEMBER WHEN WE FIRST MET?
WOW...I'M ACTUALLY SEEING IT FROM YOUR POINT OF VIEW.
YES...BUT THIS IS SO MUCH MORE.
THIS POOL IS ABO MORE THA VISUALS.

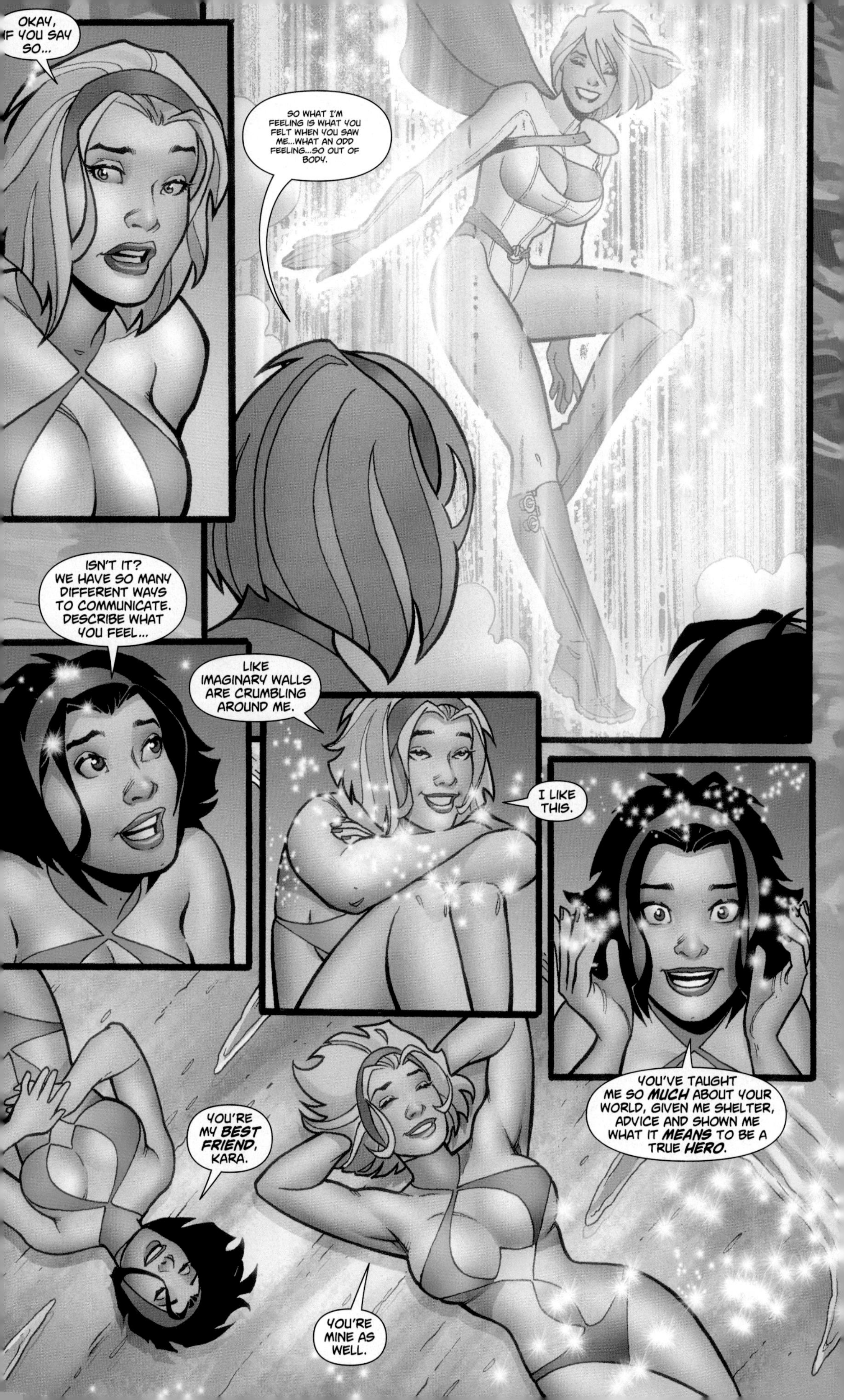
OKAY, IF YOU SAY SO...
SO WHAT I'M FEELING IS WHAT YOU FELT WHEN YOU SAW ME...WHAT AN ODD FEELING...SO OUT OF BODY.
ISN'T IT? WE HAVE SO MANY DIFFERENT WAYS TO COMMUNICATE. DESCRIBE WHAT YOU FEEL...
LIKE IMAGINARY WALLS ARE CRUMBLING AROUND ME.
I LIKE THIS.
YOU'VE TAUGHT ME SO MUCH ABOUT YOUR WORLD, GIVEN ME SHELTER, ADVICE AND SHOWN ME WHAT IT MEANS TO BE A TRUE HERO.
YOU'RE MY BEST FRIEND, KARA.
YOU'RE MINE AS WELL.

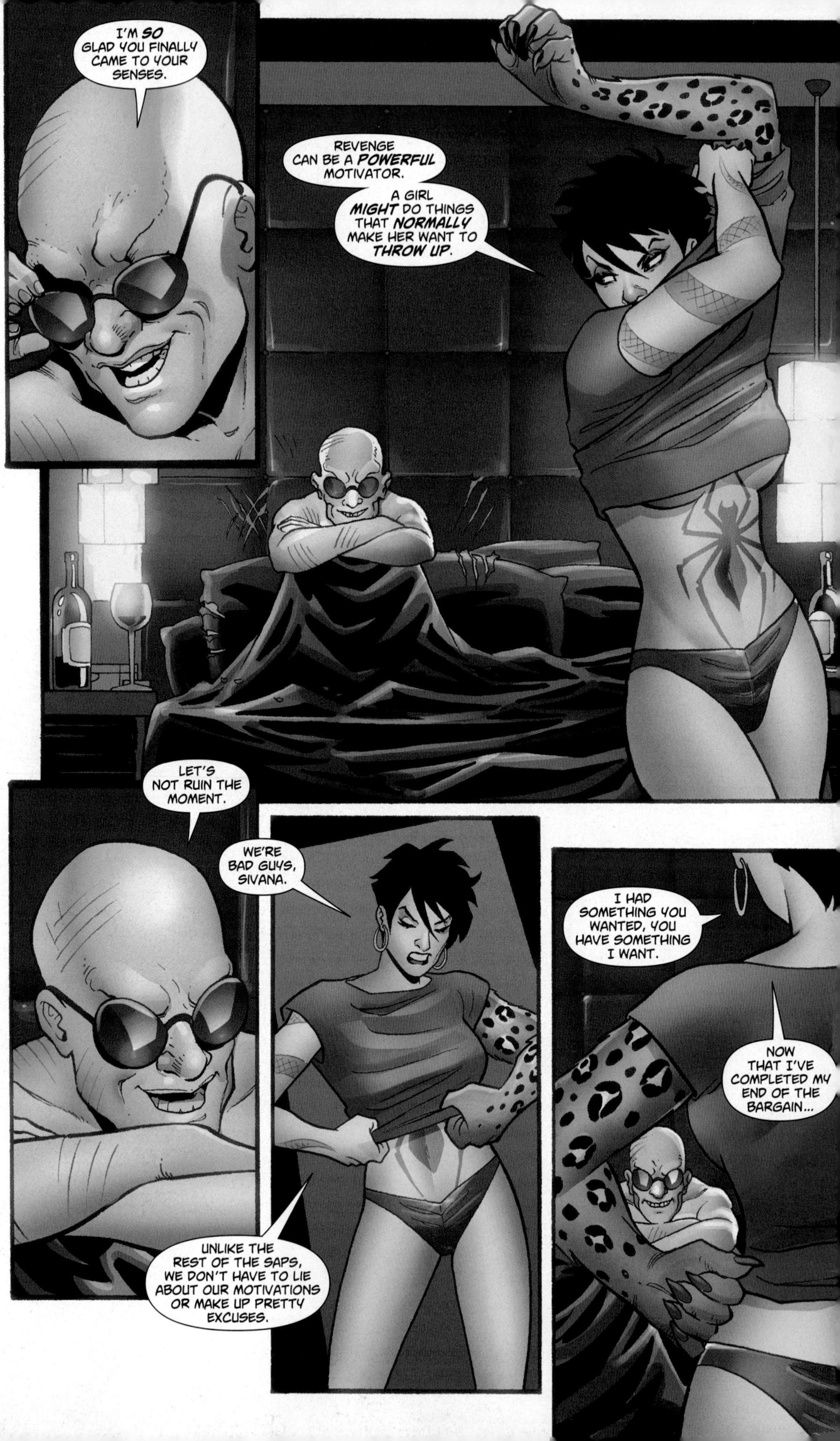

I'M SO GLAD YOU FINALLY CAME TO YOUR SENSES.
REVENGE CAN BE A POWERFUL MOTIVATOR.
A GIRL MIGHT DO THINGS THAT NORMALLY MAKE HER WANT TO THROW UP.
LET'S NOT RUIN THE MOMENT.
WE'RE BAD GUYS, SIVANA.
UNLIKE THE REST OF THE SAPS, WE DON'T HAVE TO LIE ABOUT OUR MOTIVATIONS OR MAKE UP PRETTY EXCUSES.
I HAD SOMETHING YOU WANTED, YOU HAVE SOMETHING I WANT.
NOW THAT I'VE COMPLETED MY END OF THE BARGAIN...

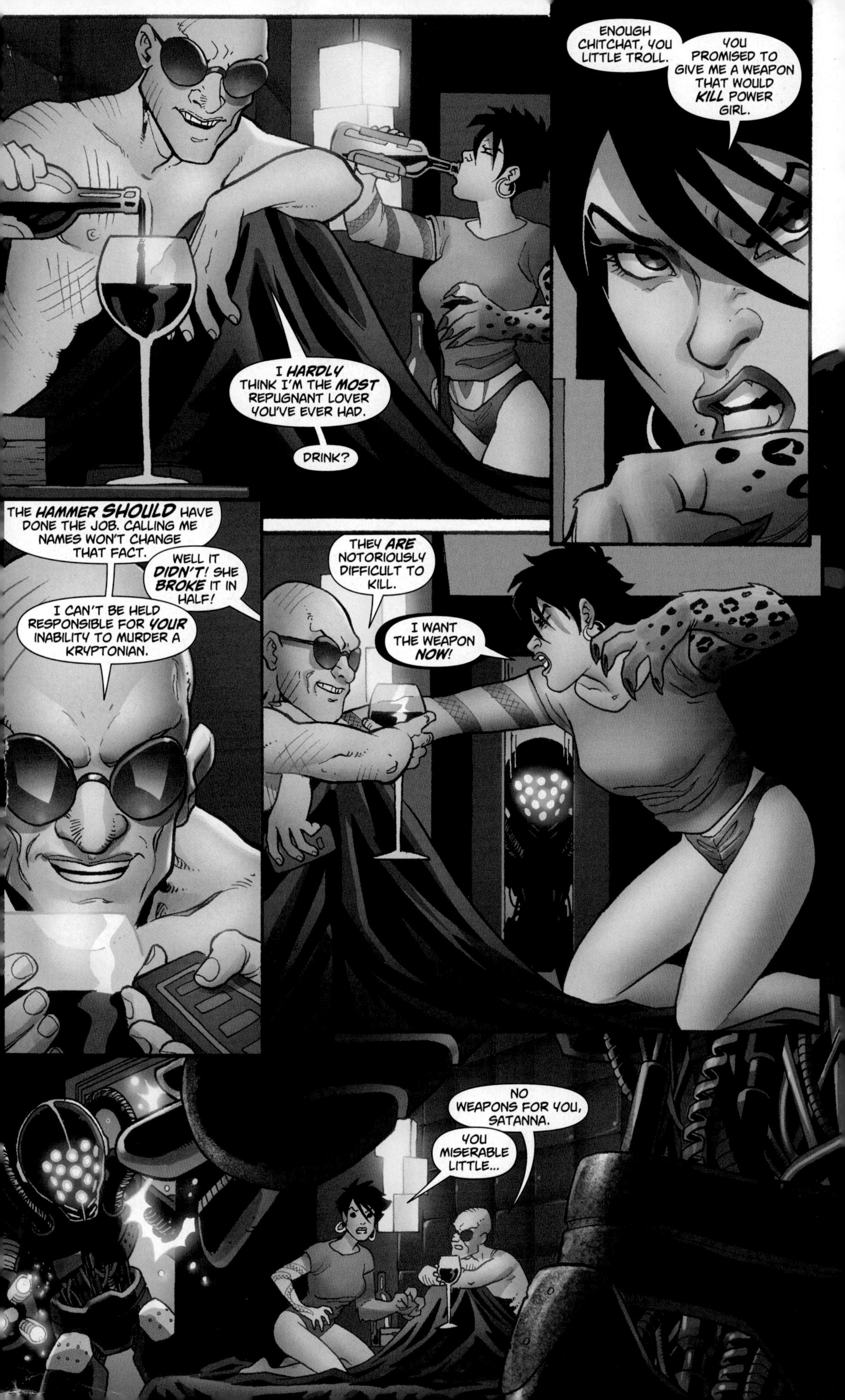
I HARDLY THINK I'M THE MOST REPUGNANT LOVER YOU'VE EVER HAD.
DRINK?
ENOUGH CHITCHAT, YOU LITTLE TROLL.
YOU PROMISED TO GIVE ME A WEAPON THAT WOULD KILL POWER GIRL.
THE HAMMER SHOULD HAVE DONE THE JOB. CALLING ME NAMES WON'T CHANGE THAT FACT.
WELL IT DIDN'T! SHE BROKE IT IN HALF!
I CAN'T BE HELD RESPONSIBLE FOR YOUR INABILITY TO MURDER A KRYPTONIAN.
THEY ARE NOTORIOUSLY DIFFICULT TO KILL.
I WANT THE WEAPON NOW!
NO WEAPONS FOR YOU, SATANNA.
YOU MISERABLE LITTLE...

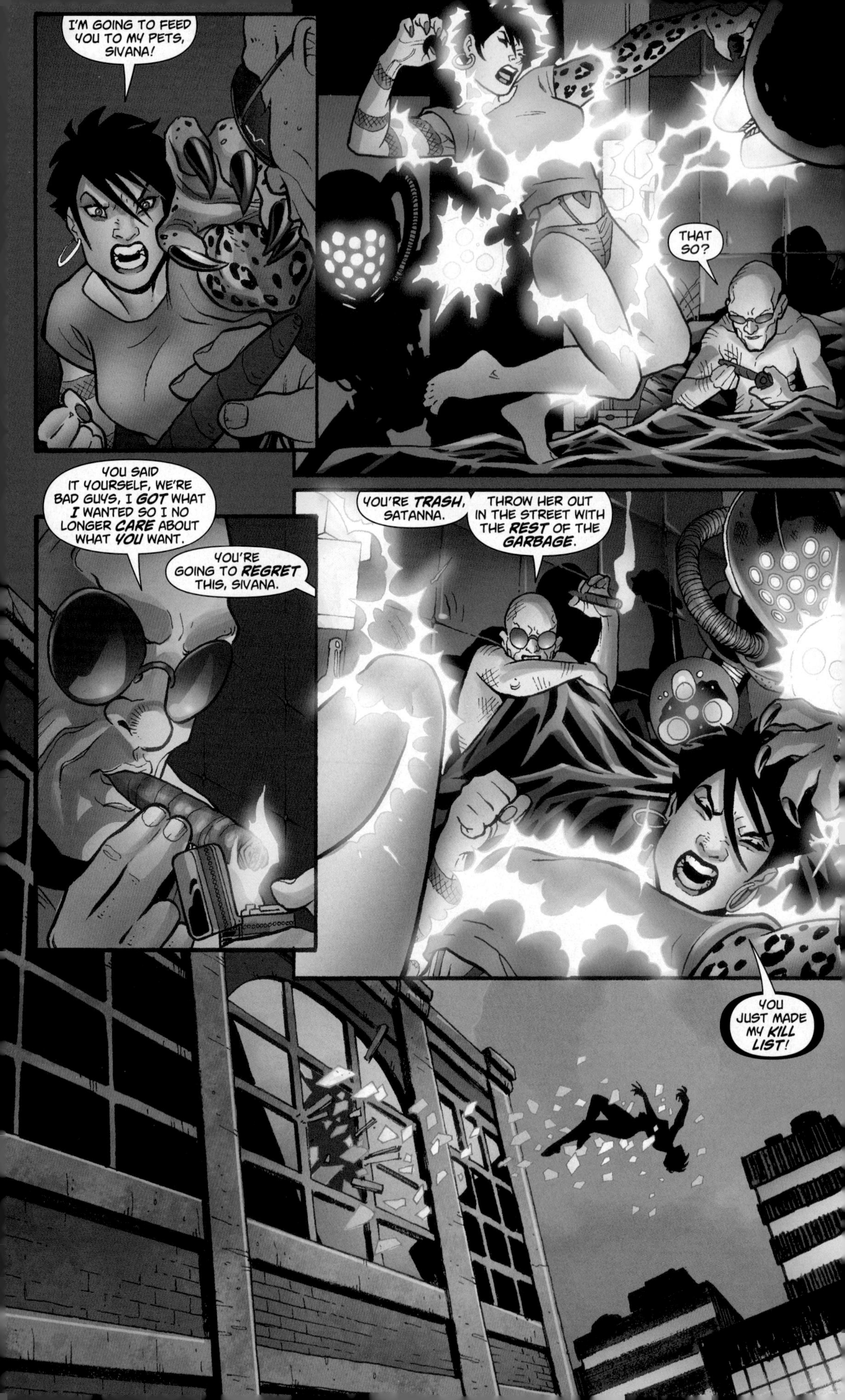
I'M GOING TO FEED YOU TO MY PETS, SIVANA!
THAT SO?
YOU SAID IT YOURSELF, WE'RE BAD GUYS, I GOT WHAT I WANTED SO I NO LONGER CARE ABOUT WHAT YOU WANT.
YOU'RE GOING TO REGRET THIS, SIVANA.
YOU'RE TRASH, SATANNA.
THROW HER OUT IN THE STREET WITH THE REST OF THE GARBAGE.
YOU JUST MADE MY KILL LIST!

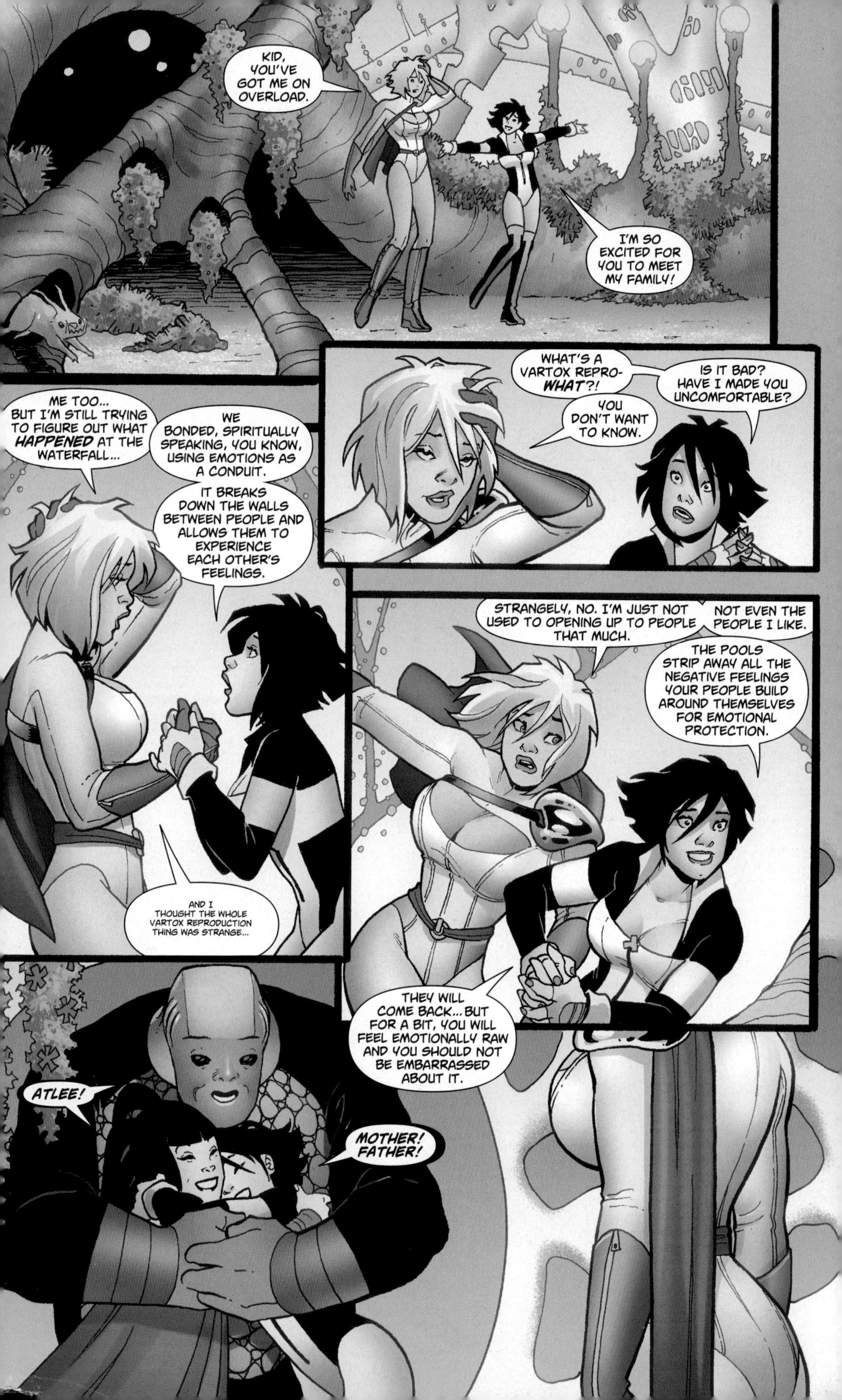
KID, YOU'VE GOT ME ON OVERLOAD.
I'M SO EXCITED FOR YOU TO MEET MY FAMILY!
WHAT'S A VARTOX REPRO-*WHAT*?!
YOU DON'T WANT TO KNOW.
IS IT BAD? HAVE I MADE YOU UNCOMFORTABLE?
ME TOO... BUT I'M STILL TRYING TO FIGURE OUT WHAT *HAPPENED* AT THE WATERFALL...
WE BONDED, SPIRITUALLY SPEAKING, YOU KNOW, USING EMOTIONS AS A CONDUIT.
IT BREAKS DOWN THE WALLS BETWEEN PEOPLE AND ALLOWS THEM TO EXPERIENCE EACH OTHER'S FEELINGS.
AND I THOUGHT THE WHOLE VARTOX REPRODUCTION THING WAS STRANGE...
STRANGELY, NO. I'M JUST NOT USED TO OPENING UP TO PEOPLE THAT MUCH.
NOT EVEN THE PEOPLE I LIKE.
THE POOLS STRIP AWAY ALL THE NEGATIVE FEELINGS YOUR PEOPLE BUILD AROUND THEMSELVES FOR EMOTIONAL PROTECTION.
THEY WILL COME BACK... BUT FOR A BIT, YOU WILL FEEL EMOTIONALLY RAW AND YOU SHOULD NOT BE EMBARRASSED ABOUT IT.
ATLEE!
MOTHER! FATHER!

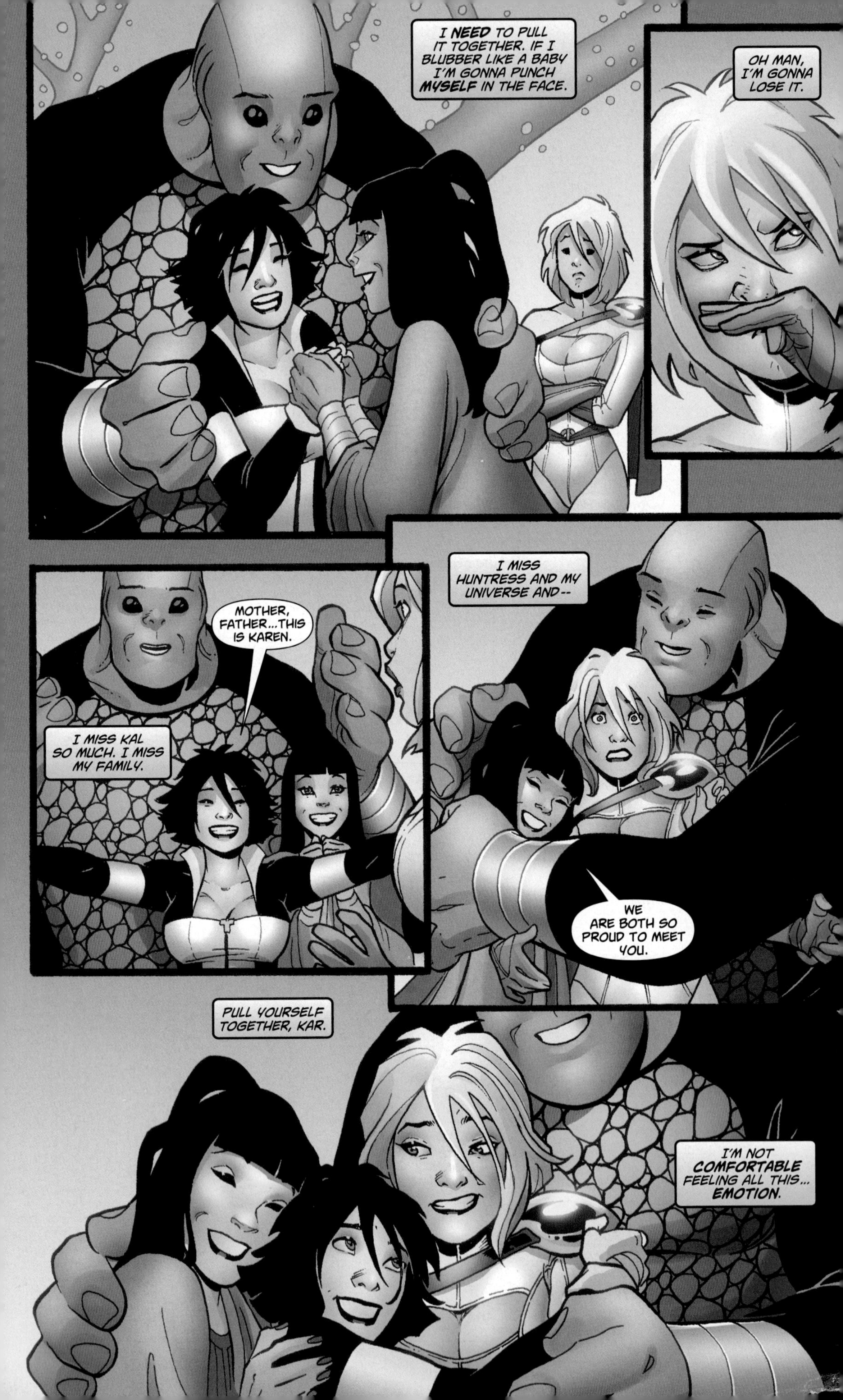

I NEED TO PULL IT TOGETHER. IF I BLUBBER LIKE A BABY I'M GONNA PUNCH MYSELF IN THE FACE.
OH MAN, I'M GONNA LOSE IT.
MOTHER, FATHER...THIS IS KAREN.
I MISS KAL SO MUCH. I MISS MY FAMILY.
I MISS HUNTRESS AND MY UNIVERSE AND--
WE ARE BOTH SO PROUD TO MEET YOU.
PULL YOURSELF TOGETHER, KAR.
I'M NOT COMFORTABLE FEELING ALL THIS... EMOTION.

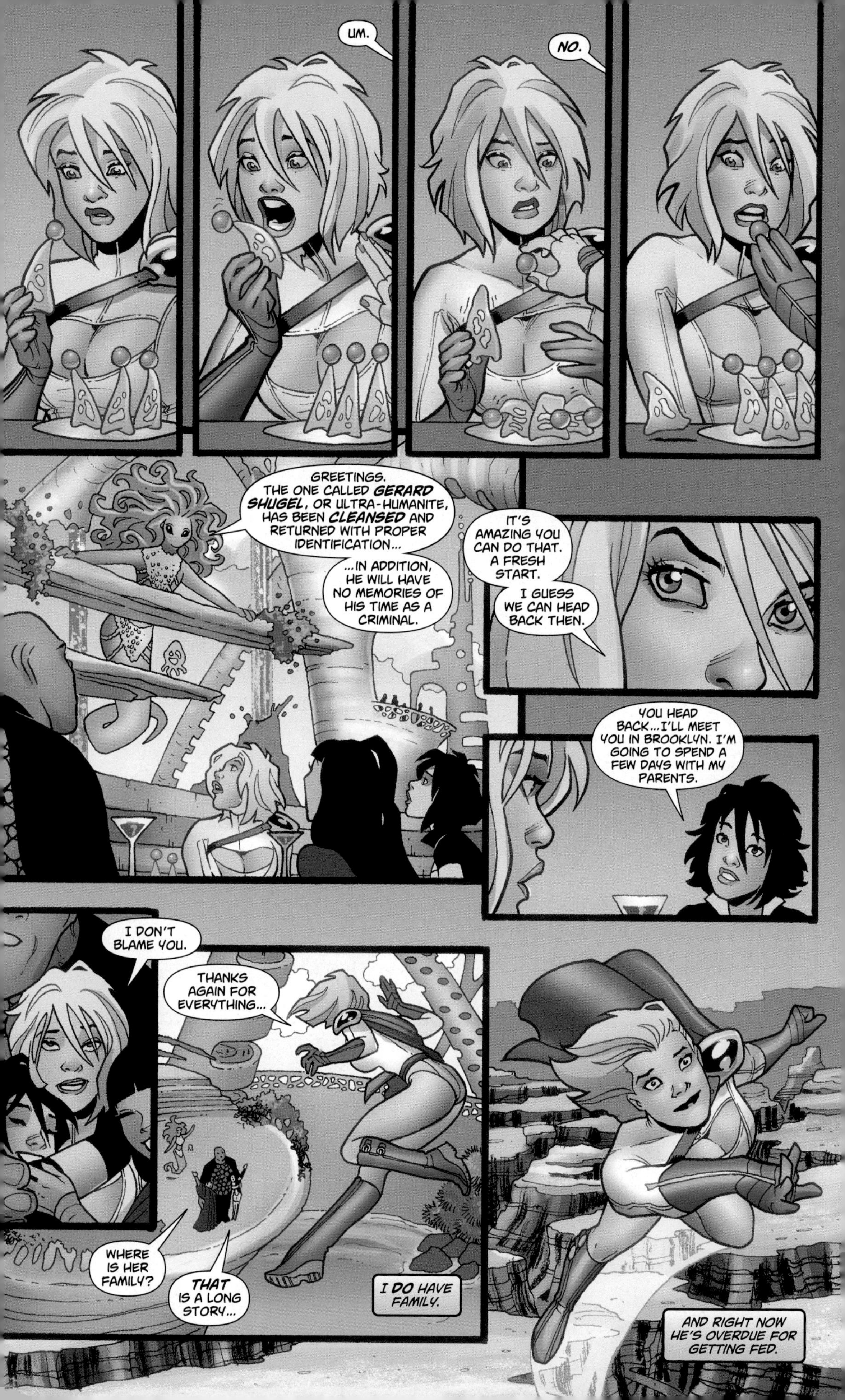

UM.
NO.
GREETINGS. THE ONE CALLED GERARD SHUGEL, OR ULTRA-HUMANITE, HAS BEEN CLEANSED AND RETURNED WITH PROPER IDENTIFICATION...
...IN ADDITION, HE WILL HAVE NO MEMORIES OF HIS TIME AS A CRIMINAL.
IT'S AMAZING YOU CAN DO THAT. A FRESH START.
I GUESS WE CAN HEAD BACK THEN.
YOU HEAD BACK...I'LL MEET YOU IN BROOKLYN. I'M GOING TO SPEND A FEW DAYS WITH MY PARENTS.
I DON'T BLAME YOU.
THANKS AGAIN FOR EVERYTHING...
WHERE IS HER FAMILY?
THAT IS A LONG STORY...
I DO HAVE FAMILY.
AND RIGHT NOW HE'S OVERDUE FOR GETTING FED.

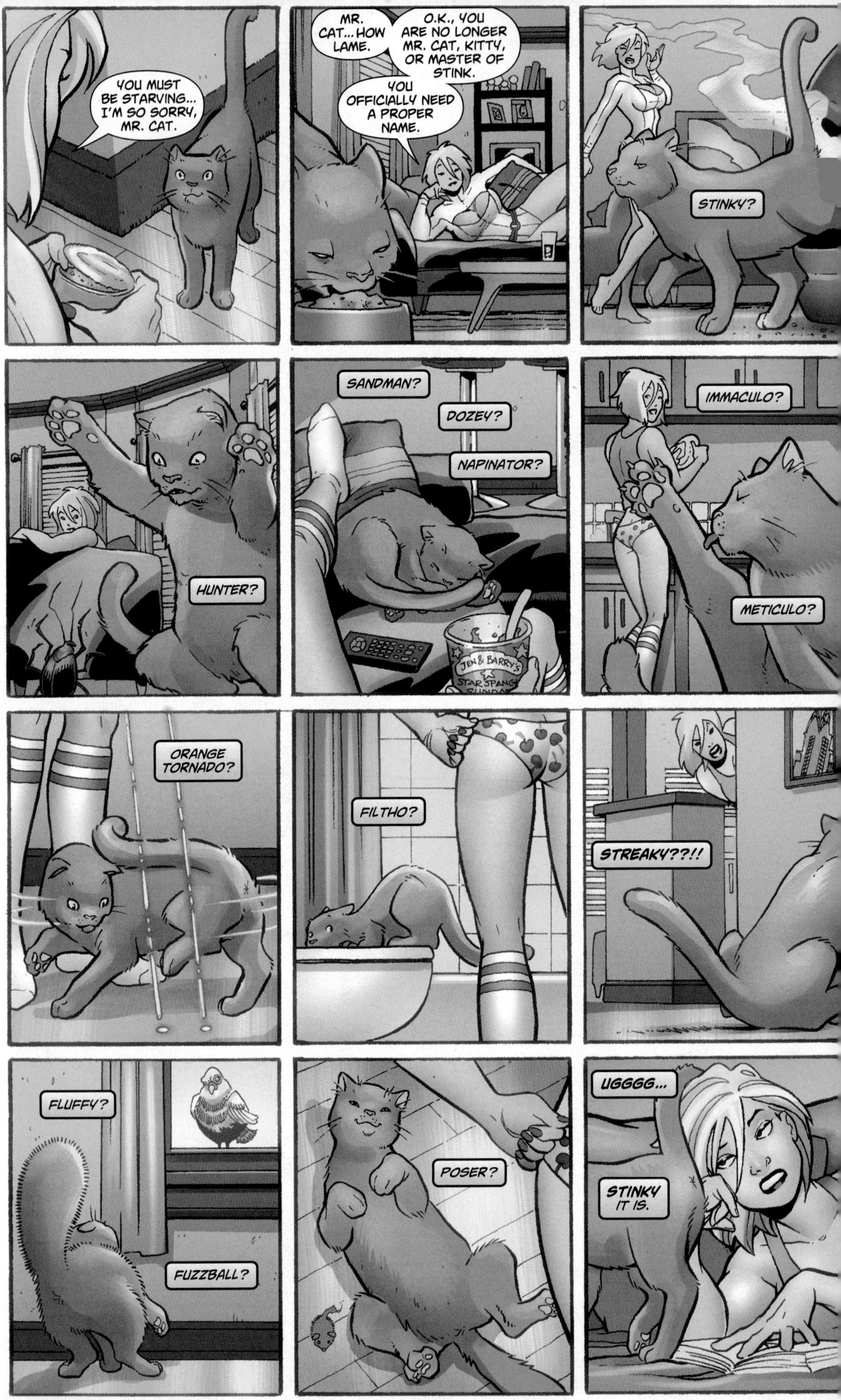
YOU MUST BE STARVING... I'M SO SORRY, MR. CAT.
MR. CAT... HOW LAME.
O.K., YOU ARE NO LONGER MR. CAT, KITTY, OR MASTER OF STINK.
YOU OFFICIALLY NEED A PROPER NAME.
STINKY?
HUNTER?
SANDMAN?
DOZEY?
NAPINATOR?
JEN & BARRY'S
IMMACULO?
METICULO?
ORANGE TORNADO?
FILTHO?
STREAKY??!!
FLUFFY?
FUZZBALL?
POSER?
UGGGG...
STINKY IT IS.

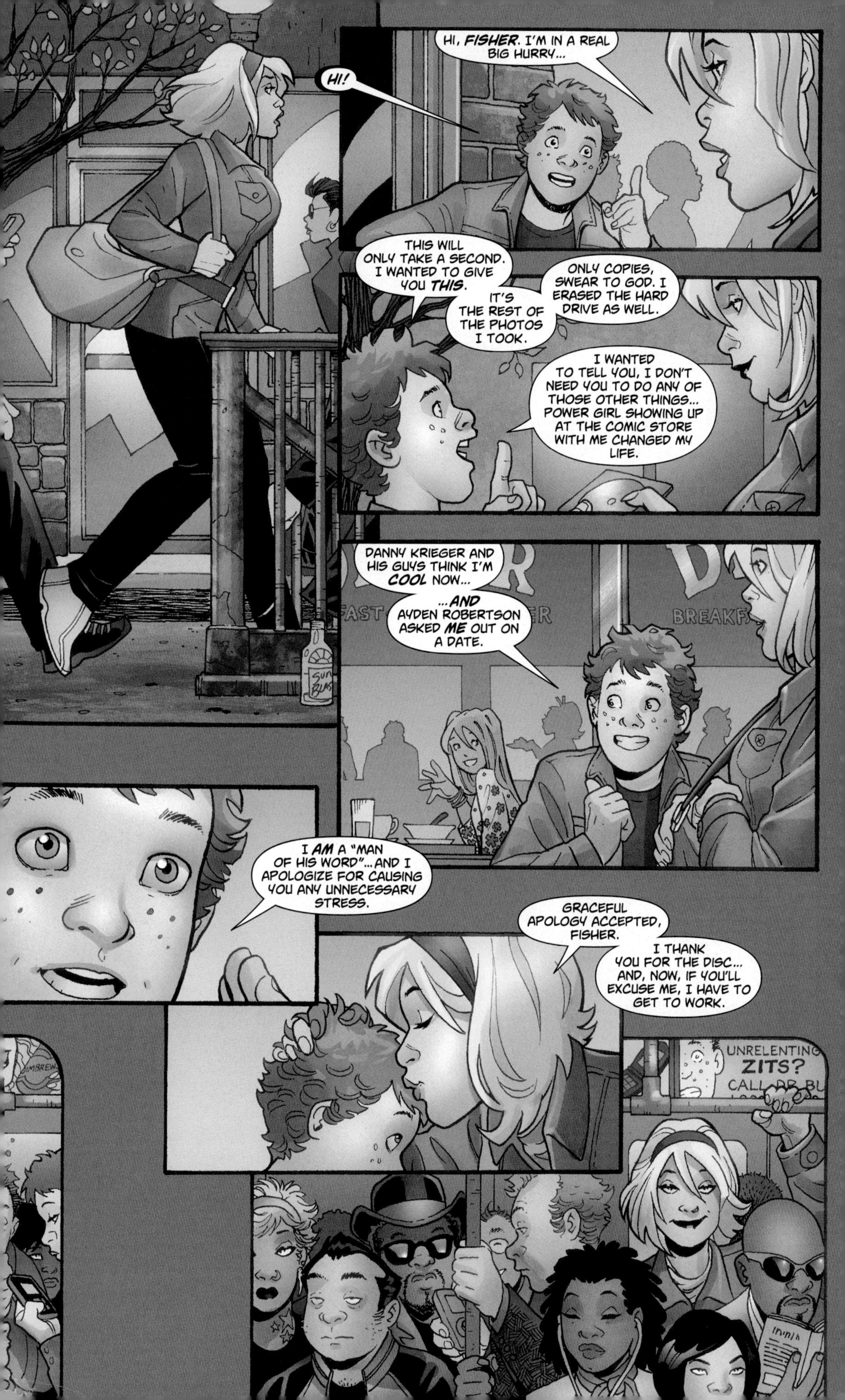
HI!
HI, FISHER. I'M IN A REAL BIG HURRY...
THIS WILL ONLY TAKE A SECOND. I WANTED TO GIVE YOU THIS.
IT'S THE REST OF THE PHOTOS I TOOK.
ONLY COPIES, SWEAR TO GOD. I ERASED THE HARD DRIVE AS WELL.
I WANTED TO TELL YOU, I DON'T NEED YOU TO DO ANY OF THOSE OTHER THINGS... POWER GIRL SHOWING UP AT THE COMIC STORE WITH ME CHANGED MY LIFE.
DANNY KRIEGER AND HIS GUYS THINK I'M COOL NOW...
...AND AYDEN ROBERTSON ASKED ME OUT ON A DATE.
BREAKF
I AM A "MAN OF HIS WORD"...AND I APOLOGIZE FOR CAUSING YOU ANY UNNECESSARY STRESS.
GRACEFUL APOLOGY ACCEPTED, FISHER.
I THANK YOU FOR THE DISC... AND, NOW, IF YOU'LL EXCUSE ME, I HAVE TO GET TO WORK.
UNRELENTING ZITS?

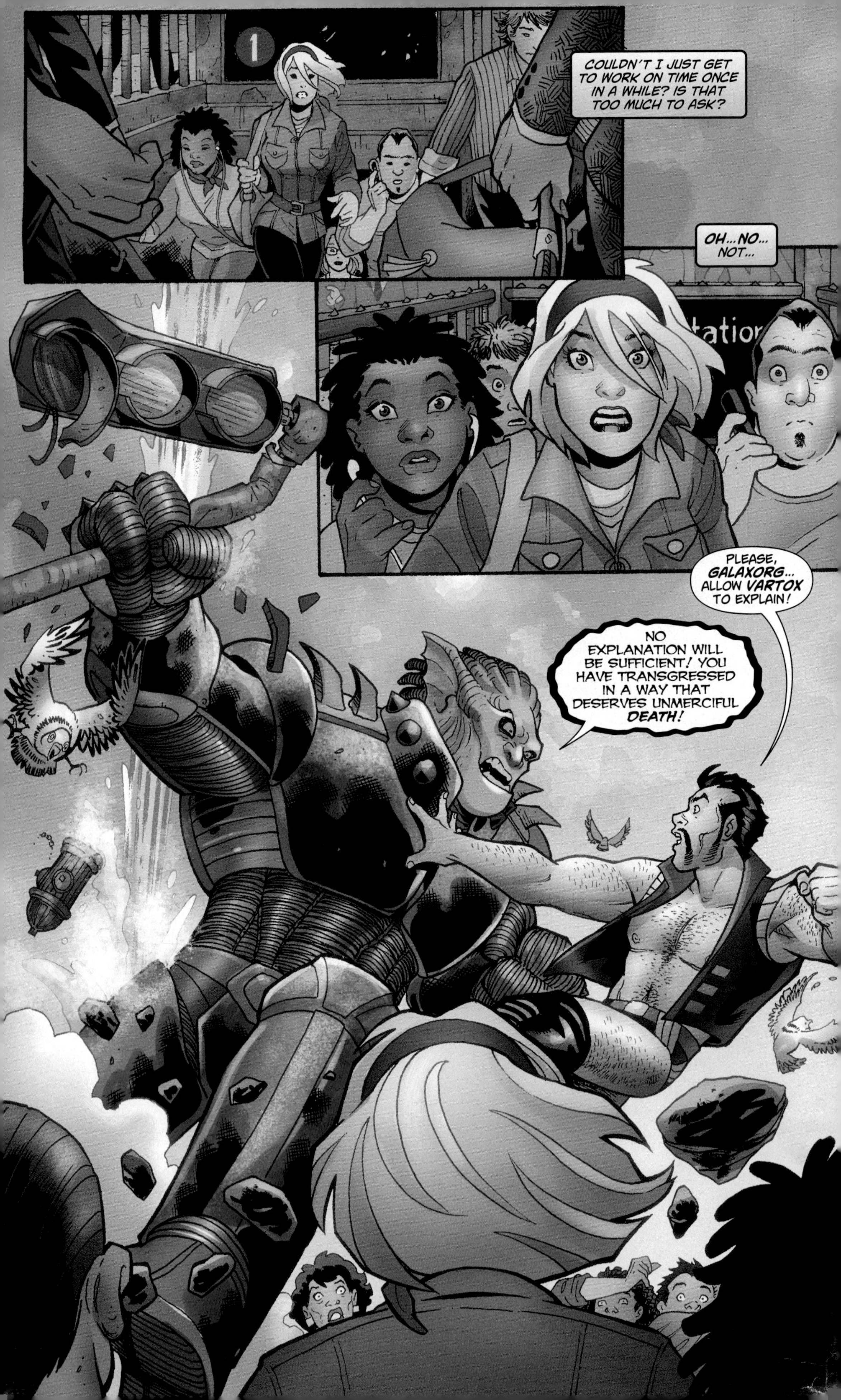
COULDN'T I JUST GET TO WORK ON TIME ONCE IN A WHILE? IS THAT TOO MUCH TO ASK?
OH... NO... NOT...
PLEASE, GALAXORG... ALLOW VARTOX TO EXPLAIN!
NO EXPLANATION WILL BE SUFFICIENT! YOU HAVE TRANSGRESSED IN A WAY THAT DESERVES UNMERCIFUL DEATH!

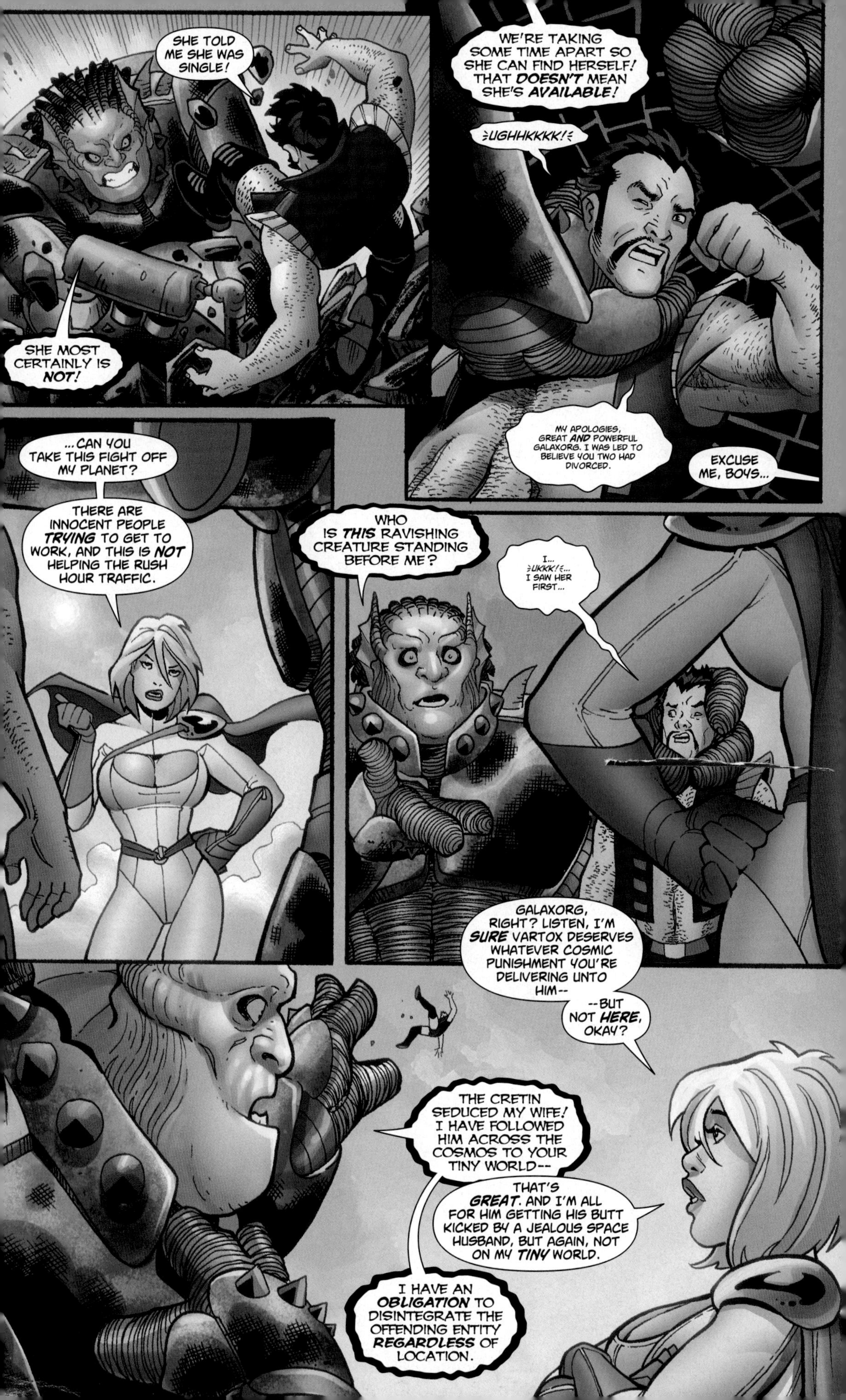
SHE TOLD ME SHE WAS SINGLE!
SHE MOST CERTAINLY IS NOT!
WE'RE TAKING SOME TIME APART SO SHE CAN FIND HERSELF! THAT DOESN'T MEAN SHE'S AVAILABLE!
UGHHKKKK!
MY APOLOGIES, GREAT AND POWERFUL GALAXORG. I WAS LED TO BELIEVE YOU TWO HAD DIVORCED.
EXCUSE ME, BOYS...
...CAN YOU TAKE THIS FIGHT OFF MY PLANET?
THERE ARE INNOCENT PEOPLE TRYING TO GET TO WORK, AND THIS IS NOT HELPING THE RUSH HOUR TRAFFIC.
WHO IS THIS RAVISHING CREATURE STANDING BEFORE ME?
I... UKKK!... I SAW HER FIRST...
GALAXORG, RIGHT? LISTEN, I'M SURE VARTOX DESERVES WHATEVER COSMIC PUNISHMENT YOU'RE DELIVERING UNTO HIM--
--BUT NOT HERE, OKAY?
THE CRETIN SEDUCED MY WIFE! I HAVE FOLLOWED HIM ACROSS THE COSMOS TO YOUR TINY WORLD--
THAT'S GREAT. AND I'M ALL FOR HIM GETTING HIS BUTT KICKED BY A JEALOUS SPACE HUSBAND, BUT AGAIN, NOT ON MY TINY WORLD.
I HAVE AN OBLIGATION TO DISINTEGRATE THE OFFENDING ENTITY REGARDLESS OF LOCATION.

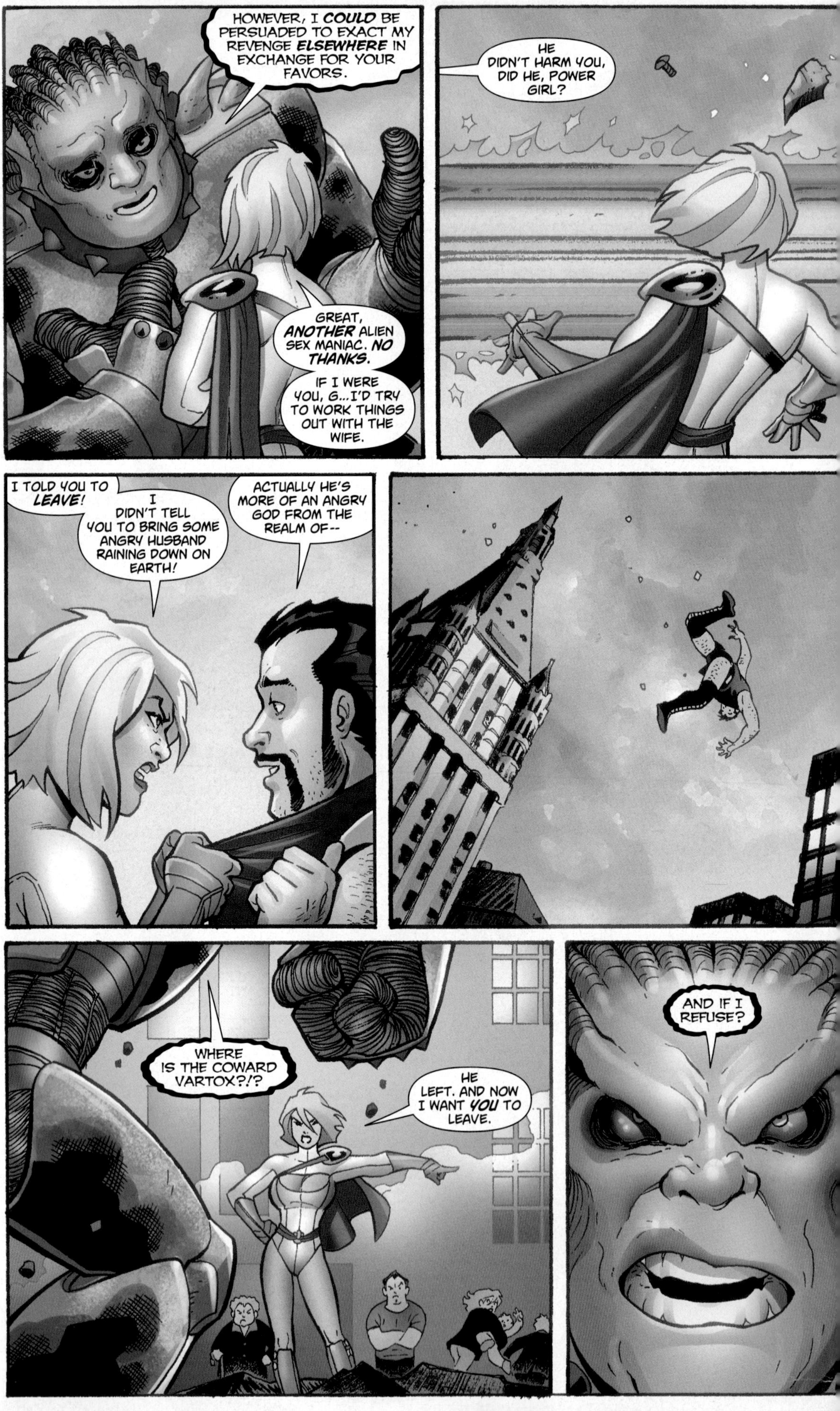
HOWEVER, I COULD BE PERSUADED TO EXACT MY REVENGE ELSEWHERE IN EXCHANGE FOR YOUR FAVORS.
GREAT, ANOTHER ALIEN SEX MANIAC. NO THANKS.
IF I WERE YOU, G...I'D TRY TO WORK THINGS OUT WITH THE WIFE.
HE DIDN'T HARM YOU, DID HE, POWER GIRL?
I TOLD YOU TO LEAVE!
I DIDN'T TELL YOU TO BRING SOME ANGRY HUSBAND RAINING DOWN ON EARTH!
ACTUALLY HE'S MORE OF AN ANGRY GOD FROM THE REALM OF--
WHERE IS THE COWARD VARTOX?!?
HE LEFT. AND NOW I WANT YOU TO LEAVE.
AND IF I REFUSE?

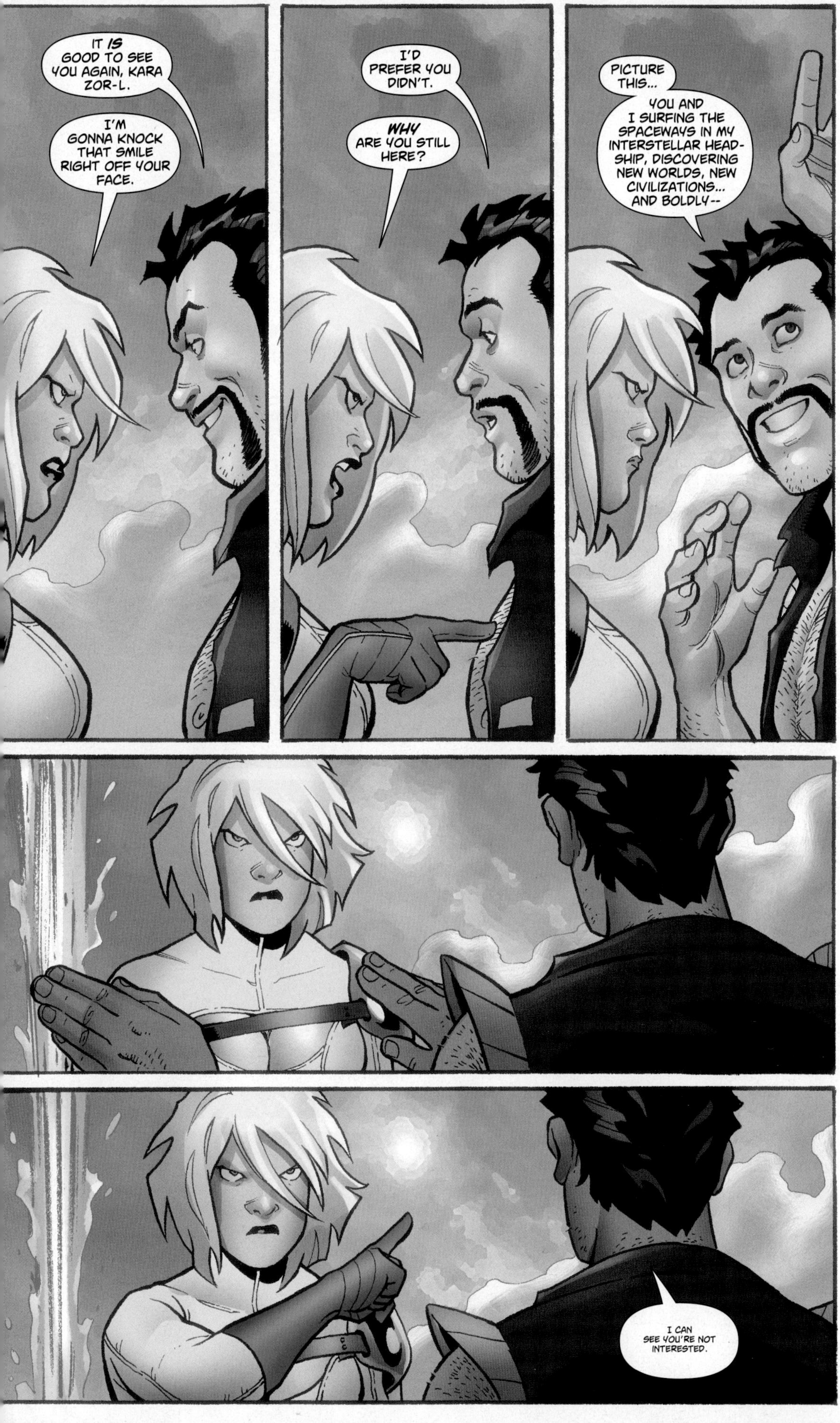
IT IS GOOD TO SEE YOU AGAIN, KARA ZOR-L.
I'M GONNA KNOCK THAT SMILE RIGHT OFF YOUR FACE.
I'D PREFER YOU DIDN'T.
WHY ARE YOU STILL HERE?
PICTURE THIS...
YOU AND I SURFING THE SPACEWAYS IN MY INTERSTELLAR HEAD-SHIP, DISCOVERING NEW WORLDS, NEW CIVILIZATIONS... AND BOLDLY--
I CAN SEE YOU'RE NOT INTERESTED.

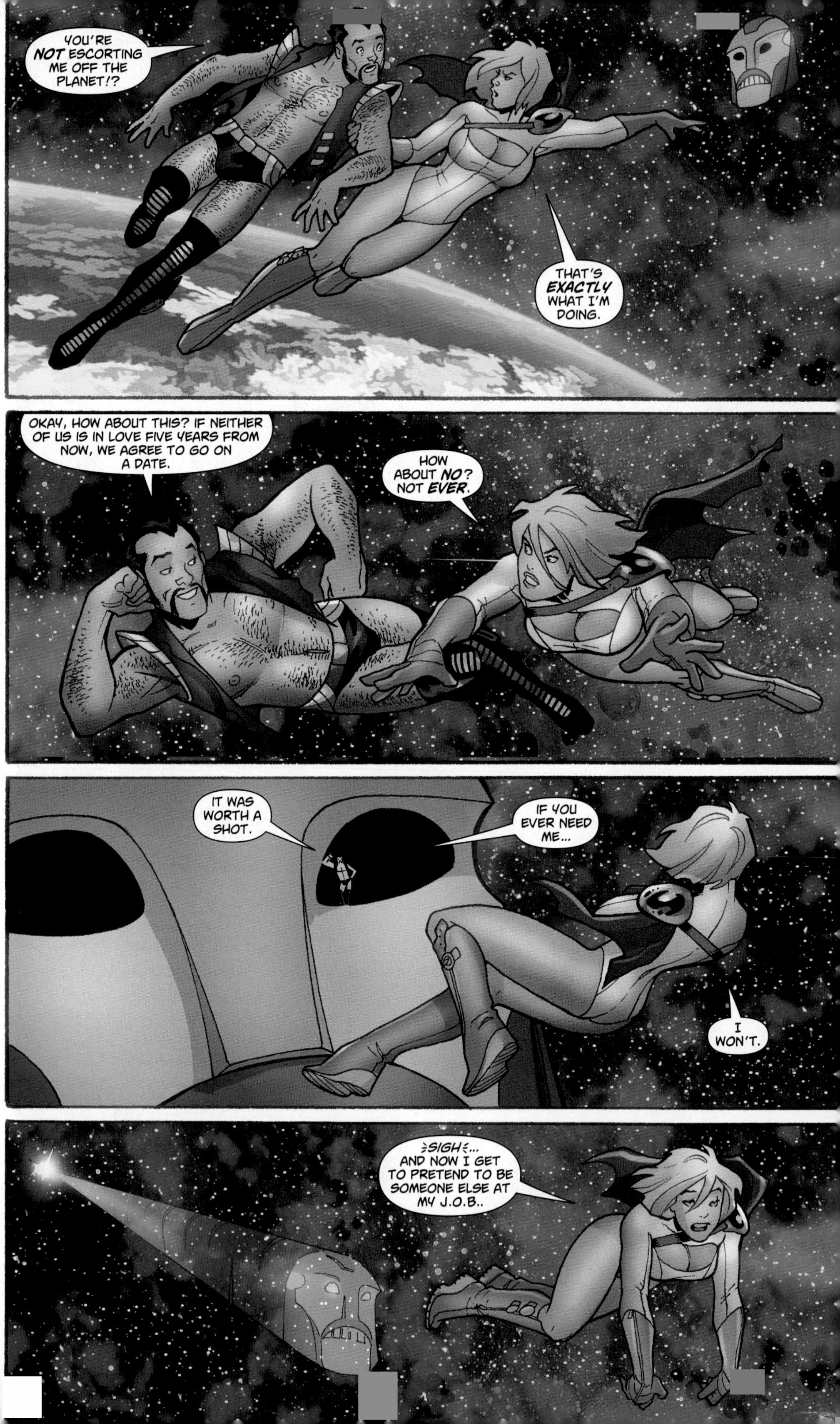
YOU'RE NOT ESCORTING ME OFF THE PLANET!?
THAT'S EXACTLY WHAT I'M DOING.
OKAY, HOW ABOUT THIS? IF NEITHER OF US IS IN LOVE FIVE YEARS FROM NOW, WE AGREE TO GO ON A DATE.
HOW ABOUT NO? NOT EVER.
IT WAS WORTH A SHOT.
IF YOU EVER NEED ME...
I WON'T.
≥SIGH≤... AND NOW I GET TO PRETEND TO BE SOMEONE ELSE AT MY J.O.B..

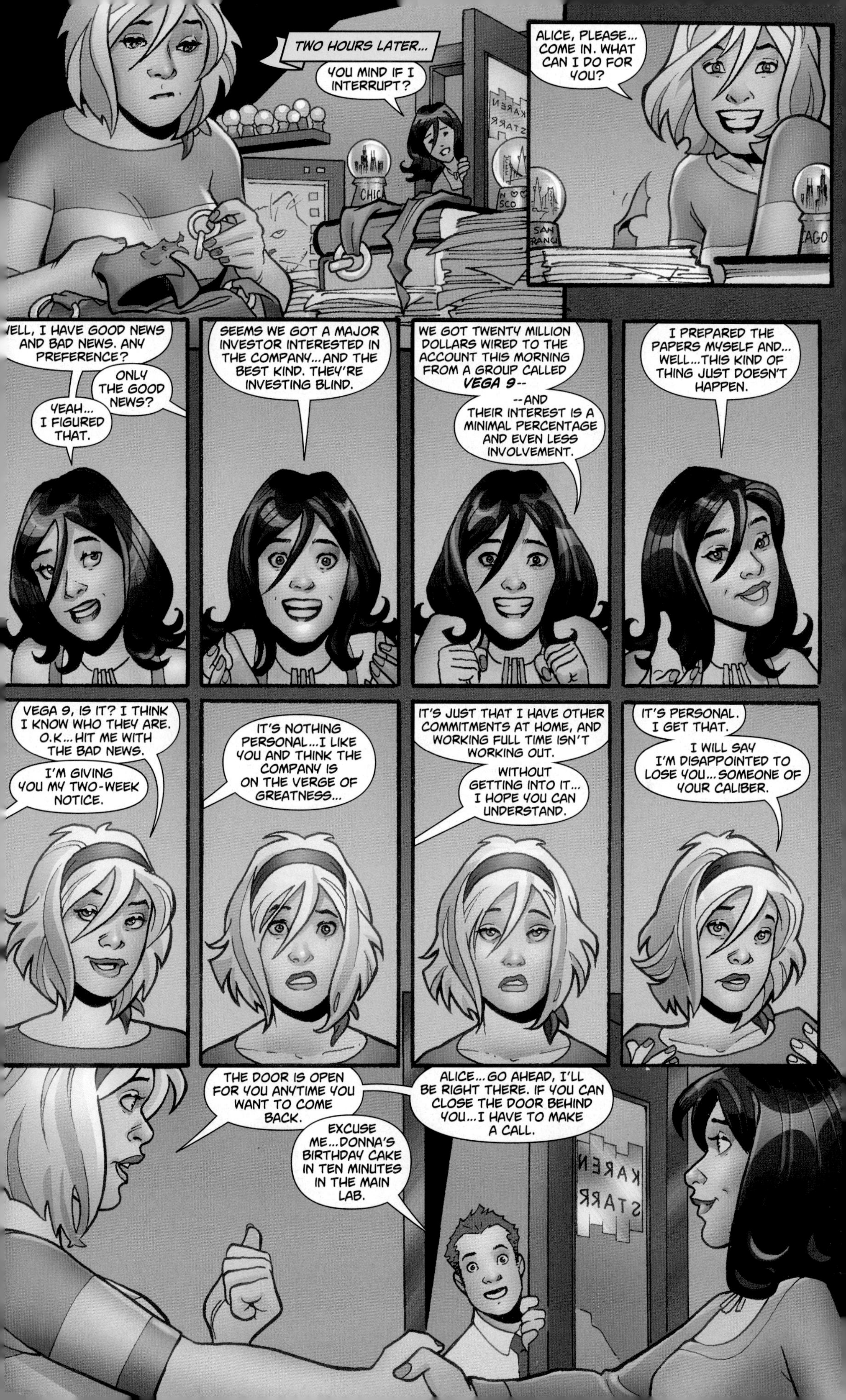
TWO HOURS LATER...
YOU MIND IF I INTERRUPT?
ALICE, PLEASE... COME IN. WHAT CAN I DO FOR YOU?
KAREN STARR
WELL, I HAVE GOOD NEWS AND BAD NEWS. ANY PREFERENCE?
ONLY THE GOOD NEWS?
YEAH... I FIGURED THAT.
SEEMS WE GOT A MAJOR INVESTOR INTERESTED IN THE COMPANY...AND THE BEST KIND. THEY'RE INVESTING BLIND.
WE GOT TWENTY MILLION DOLLARS WIRED TO THE ACCOUNT THIS MORNING FROM A GROUP CALLED VEGA 9--
--AND THEIR INTEREST IS A MINIMAL PERCENTAGE AND EVEN LESS INVOLVEMENT.
I PREPARED THE PAPERS MYSELF AND... WELL...THIS KIND OF THING JUST DOESN'T HAPPEN.
VEGA 9, IS IT? I THINK I KNOW WHO THEY ARE. O.K...HIT ME WITH THE BAD NEWS.
I'M GIVING YOU MY TWO-WEEK NOTICE.
IT'S NOTHING PERSONAL...I LIKE YOU AND THINK THE COMPANY IS ON THE VERGE OF GREATNESS...
IT'S JUST THAT I HAVE OTHER COMMITMENTS AT HOME, AND WORKING FULL TIME ISN'T WORKING OUT.
WITHOUT GETTING INTO IT... I HOPE YOU CAN UNDERSTAND.
IT'S PERSONAL. I GET THAT.
I WILL SAY I'M DISAPPOINTED TO LOSE YOU...SOMEONE OF YOUR CALIBER.
THE DOOR IS OPEN FOR YOU ANYTIME YOU WANT TO COME BACK.
EXCUSE ME...DONNA'S BIRTHDAY CAKE IN TEN MINUTES IN THE MAIN LAB.
ALICE...GO AHEAD, I'LL BE RIGHT THERE. IF YOU CAN CLOSE THE DOOR BEHIND YOU...I HAVE TO MAKE A CALL.
KAREN STARR

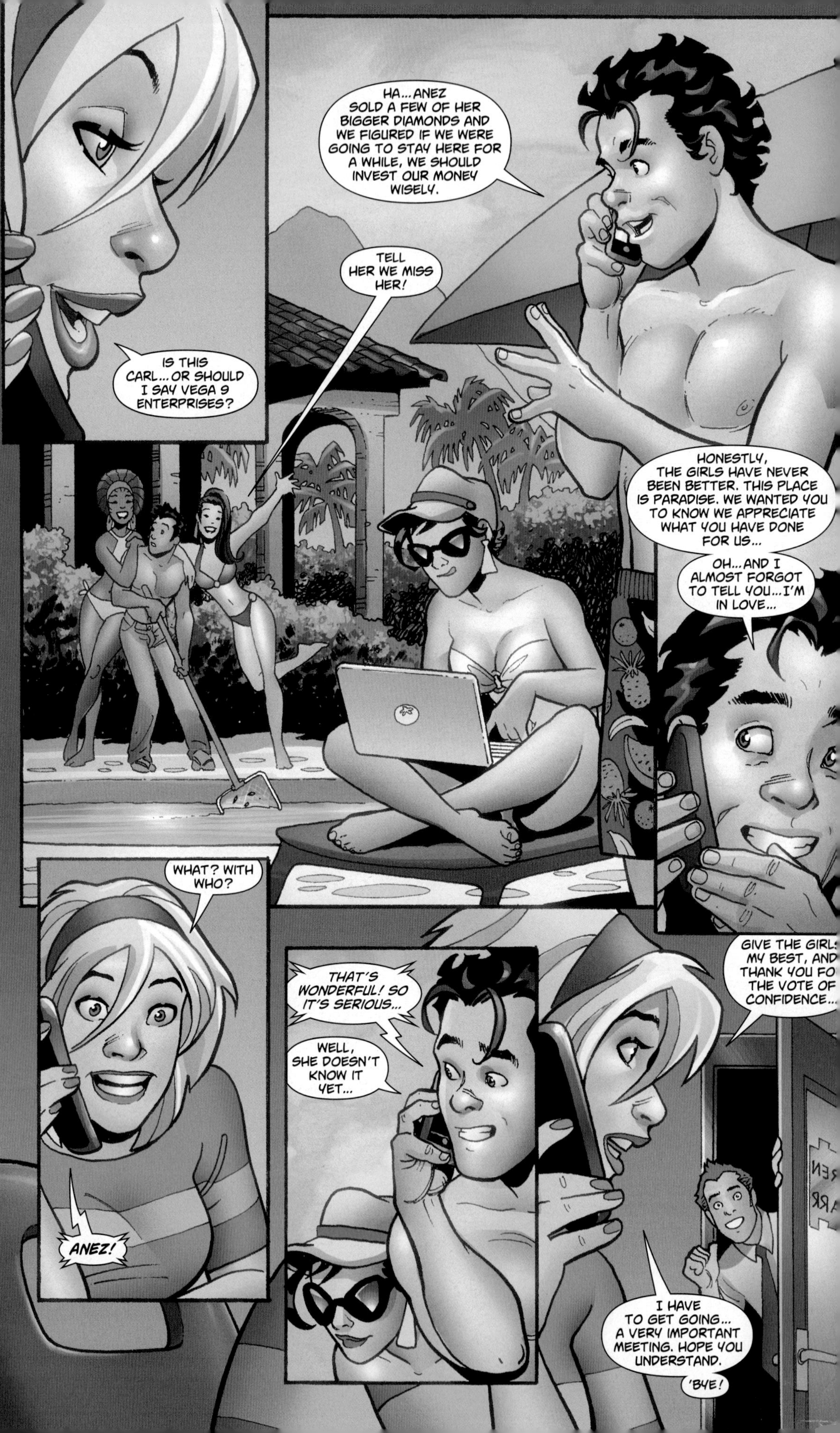
IS THIS CARL...OR SHOULD I SAY VEGA 9 ENTERPRISES?
HA...ANEZ SOLD A FEW OF HER BIGGER DIAMONDS AND WE FIGURED IF WE WERE GOING TO STAY HERE FOR A WHILE, WE SHOULD INVEST OUR MONEY WISELY.
TELL HER WE MISS HER!
HONESTLY, THE GIRLS HAVE NEVER BEEN BETTER. THIS PLACE IS PARADISE. WE WANTED YOU TO KNOW WE APPRECIATE WHAT YOU HAVE DONE FOR US...
OH...AND I ALMOST FORGOT TO TELL YOU...I'M IN LOVE...
WHAT? WITH WHO?
ANEZ!
THAT'S WONDERFUL! SO IT'S SERIOUS...
WELL, SHE DOESN'T KNOW IT YET...
GIVE THE GIRLS MY BEST, AND THANK YOU FO THE VOTE OF CONFIDENCE...
I HAVE TO GET GOING... A VERY IMPORTANT MEETING. HOPE YOU UNDERSTAND.
'BYE!

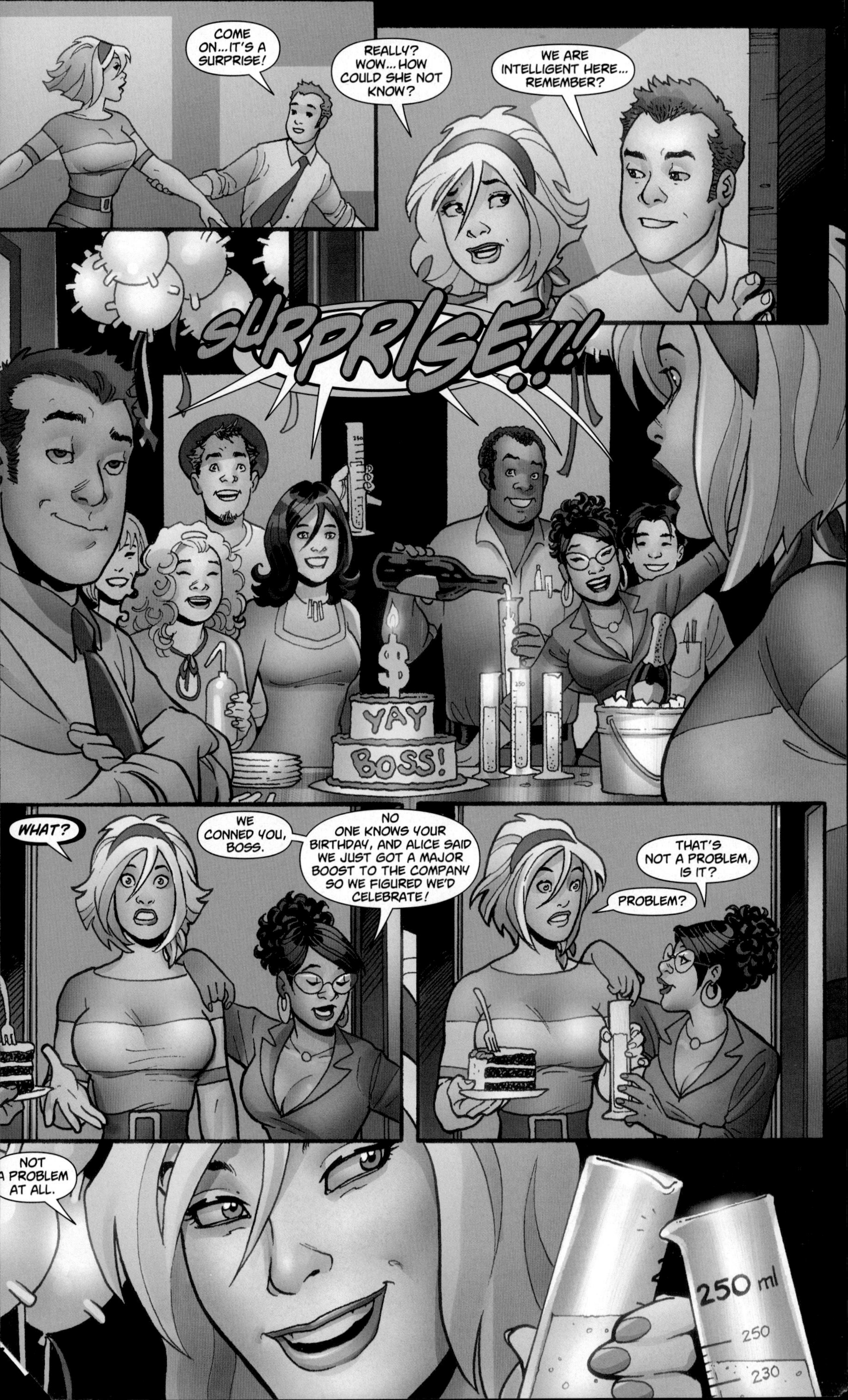
COME ON...IT'S A SURPRISE!
REALLY? WOW...HOW COULD SHE NOT KNOW?
WE ARE INTELLIGENT HERE... REMEMBER?
SURPRISE!!!
YAY BOSS!
WHAT?
WE CONNED YOU, BOSS.
NO ONE KNOWS YOUR BIRTHDAY, AND ALICE SAID WE JUST GOT A MAJOR BOOST TO THE COMPANY SO WE FIGURED WE'D CELEBRATE!
THAT'S NOT A PROBLEM, IS IT?
PROBLEM?
NOT A PROBLEM AT ALL.
250 ml

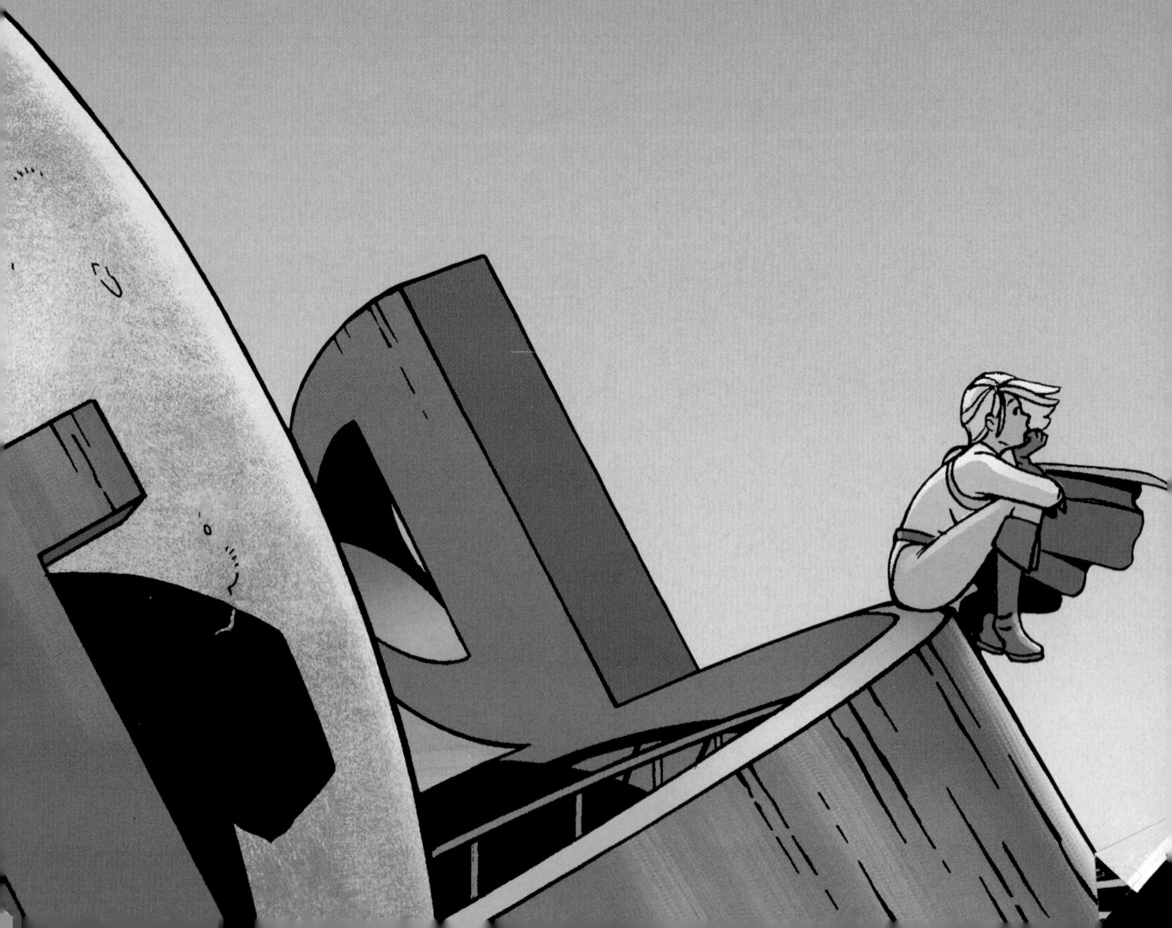

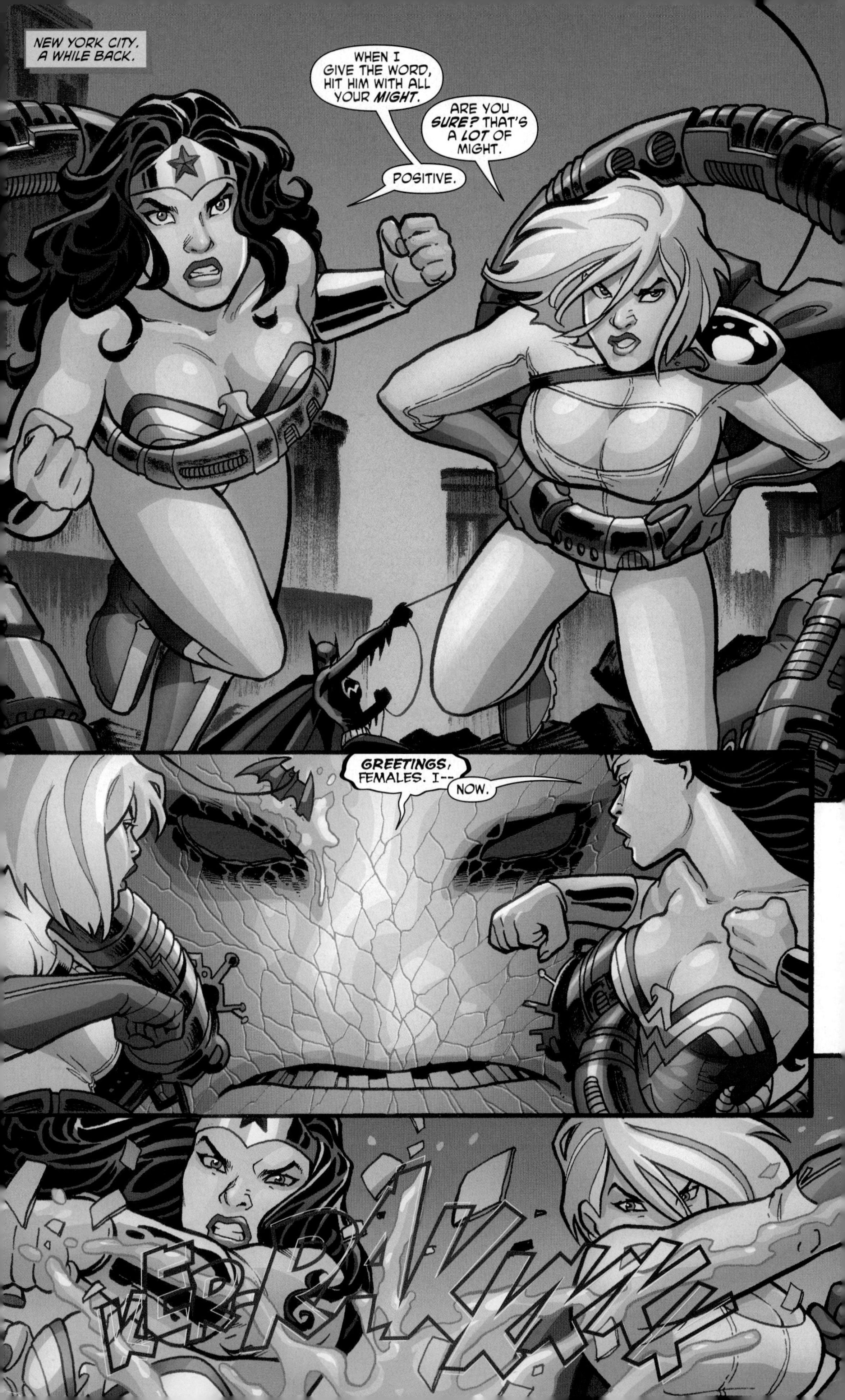
NEW YORK CITY. A WHILE BACK.
WHEN I GIVE THE WORD, HIT HIM WITH ALL YOUR MIGHT.
ARE YOU SURE? THAT'S A LOT OF MIGHT.
POSITIVE.
GREETINGS, FEMALES. I--
NOW.

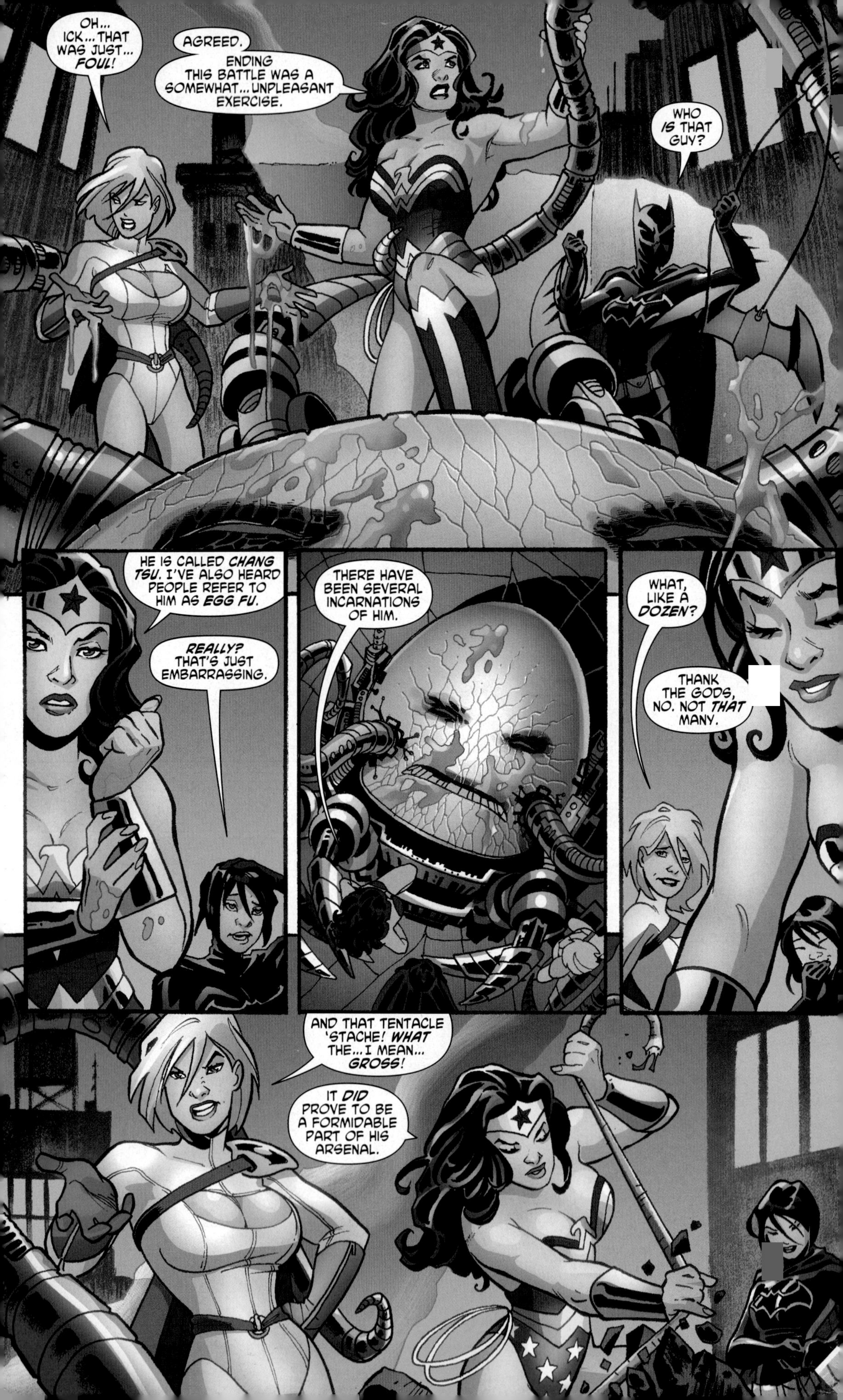
OH... ICK...THAT WAS JUST... FOUL!
AGREED. ENDING THIS BATTLE WAS A SOMEWHAT...UNPLEASANT EXERCISE.
WHO IS THAT GUY?
HE IS CALLED CHANG TSU. I'VE ALSO HEARD PEOPLE REFER TO HIM AS EGG FU.
REALLY? THAT'S JUST EMBARRASSING.
THERE HAVE BEEN SEVERAL INCARNATIONS OF HIM.
WHAT, LIKE A DOZEN?
THANK THE GODS, NO. NOT THAT MANY.
AND THAT TENTACLE 'STACHE! WHAT THE... I MEAN... GROSS!
IT DID PROVE TO BE A FORMIDABLE PART OF HIS ARSENAL.

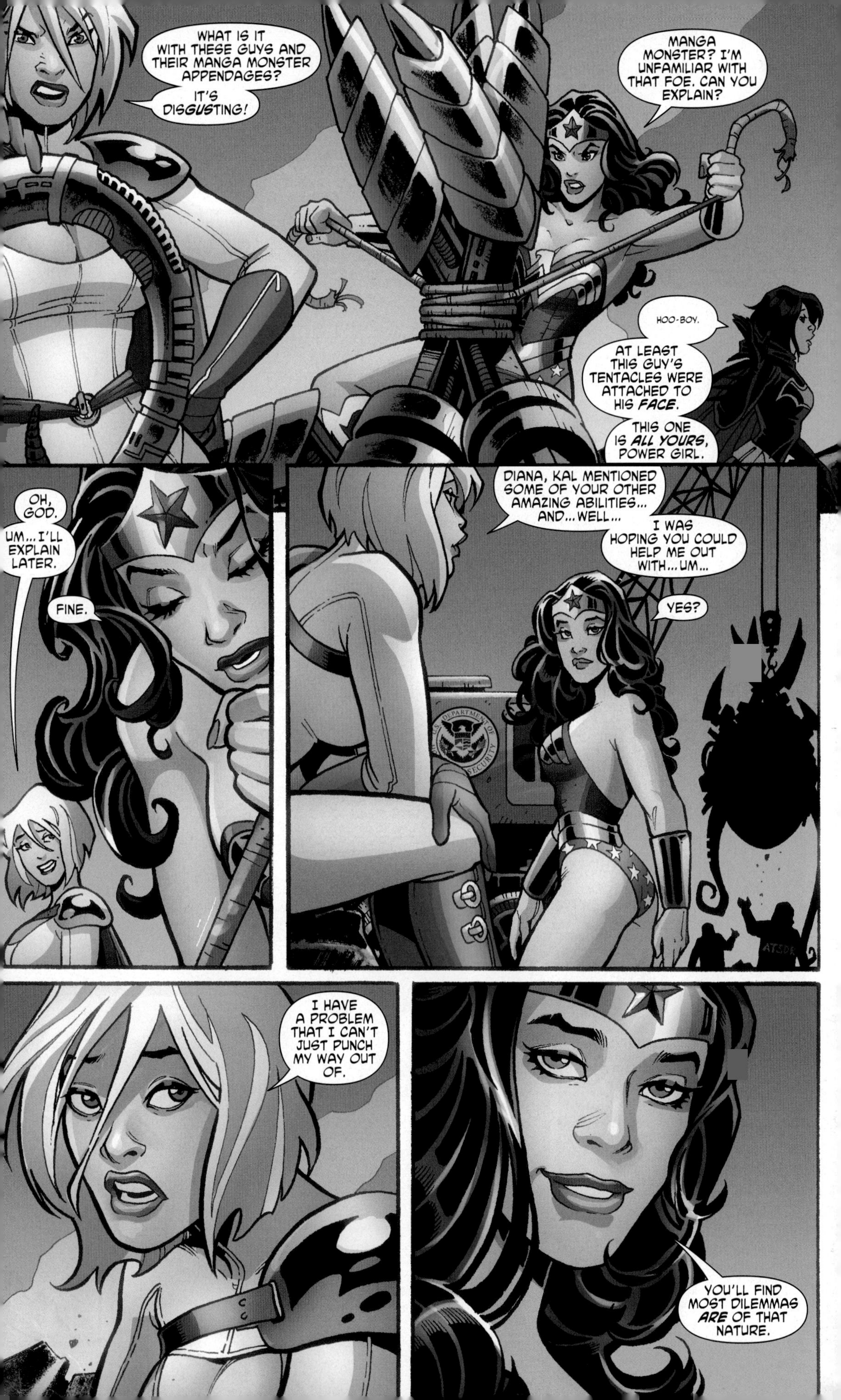
WHAT IS IT WITH THESE GUYS AND THEIR MANGA MONSTER APPENDAGES?
IT'S DISGUSTING!
MANGA MONSTER? I'M UNFAMILIAR WITH THAT FOE. CAN YOU EXPLAIN?
HOO-BOY.
AT LEAST THIS GUY'S TENTACLES WERE ATTACHED TO HIS FACE.
THIS ONE IS ALL YOURS, POWER GIRL.
OH, GOD.
UM... I'LL EXPLAIN LATER.
FINE.
DIANA, KAL MENTIONED SOME OF YOUR OTHER AMAZING ABILITIES... AND... WELL...
I WAS HOPING YOU COULD HELP ME OUT WITH... UM...
YES?
I HAVE A PROBLEM THAT I CAN'T JUST PUNCH MY WAY OUT OF.
YOU'LL FIND MOST DILEMMAS ARE OF THAT NATURE.

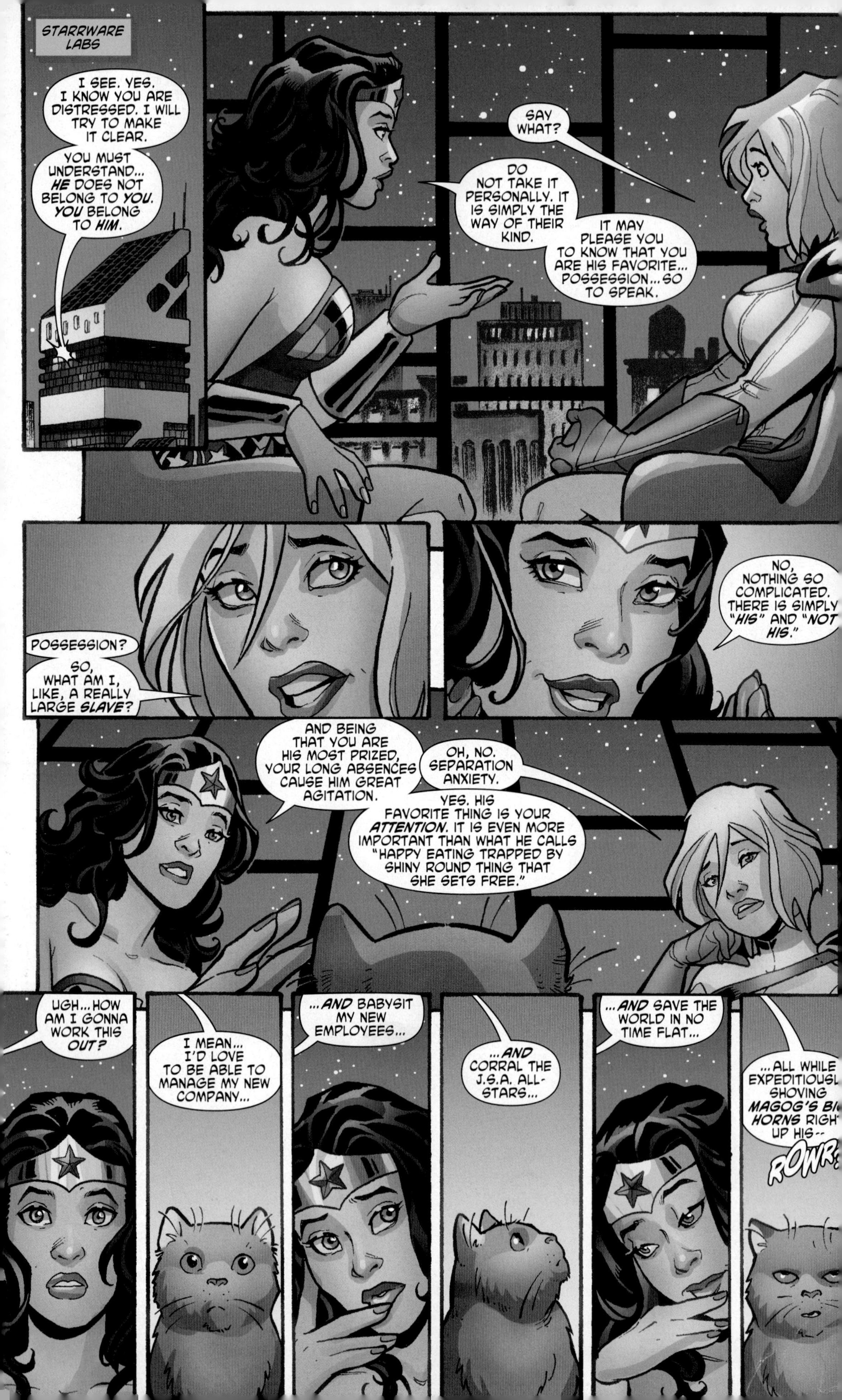

STARRWARE LABS
I SEE. YES. I KNOW YOU ARE DISTRESSED. I WILL TRY TO MAKE IT CLEAR.
YOU MUST UNDERSTAND... HE DOES NOT BELONG TO YOU. YOU BELONG TO HIM.
SAY WHAT?
DO NOT TAKE IT PERSONALLY. IT IS SIMPLY THE WAY OF THEIR KIND.
IT MAY PLEASE YOU TO KNOW THAT YOU ARE HIS FAVORITE... POSSESSION... SO TO SPEAK.
POSSESSION?
SO, WHAT AM I, LIKE, A REALLY LARGE SLAVE?
NO, NOTHING SO COMPLICATED. THERE IS SIMPLY "HIS" AND "NOT HIS."
AND BEING THAT YOU ARE HIS MOST PRIZED, YOUR LONG ABSENCES CAUSE HIM GREAT AGITATION.
OH, NO. SEPARATION ANXIETY.
YES. HIS FAVORITE THING IS YOUR ATTENTION. IT IS EVEN MORE IMPORTANT THAN WHAT HE CALLS "HAPPY EATING TRAPPED BY SHINY ROUND THING THAT SHE SETS FREE."
UGH... HOW AM I GONNA WORK THIS OUT?
I MEAN... I'D LOVE TO BE ABLE TO MANAGE MY NEW COMPANY...
...AND BABYSIT MY NEW EMPLOYEES...
...AND CORRAL THE J.S.A. ALL-STARS...
...AND SAVE THE WORLD IN NO TIME FLAT...
...ALL WHILE EXPEDITIOUSL SHOVING MAGOG'S BI HORNS RIGH UP HIS--
ROWR

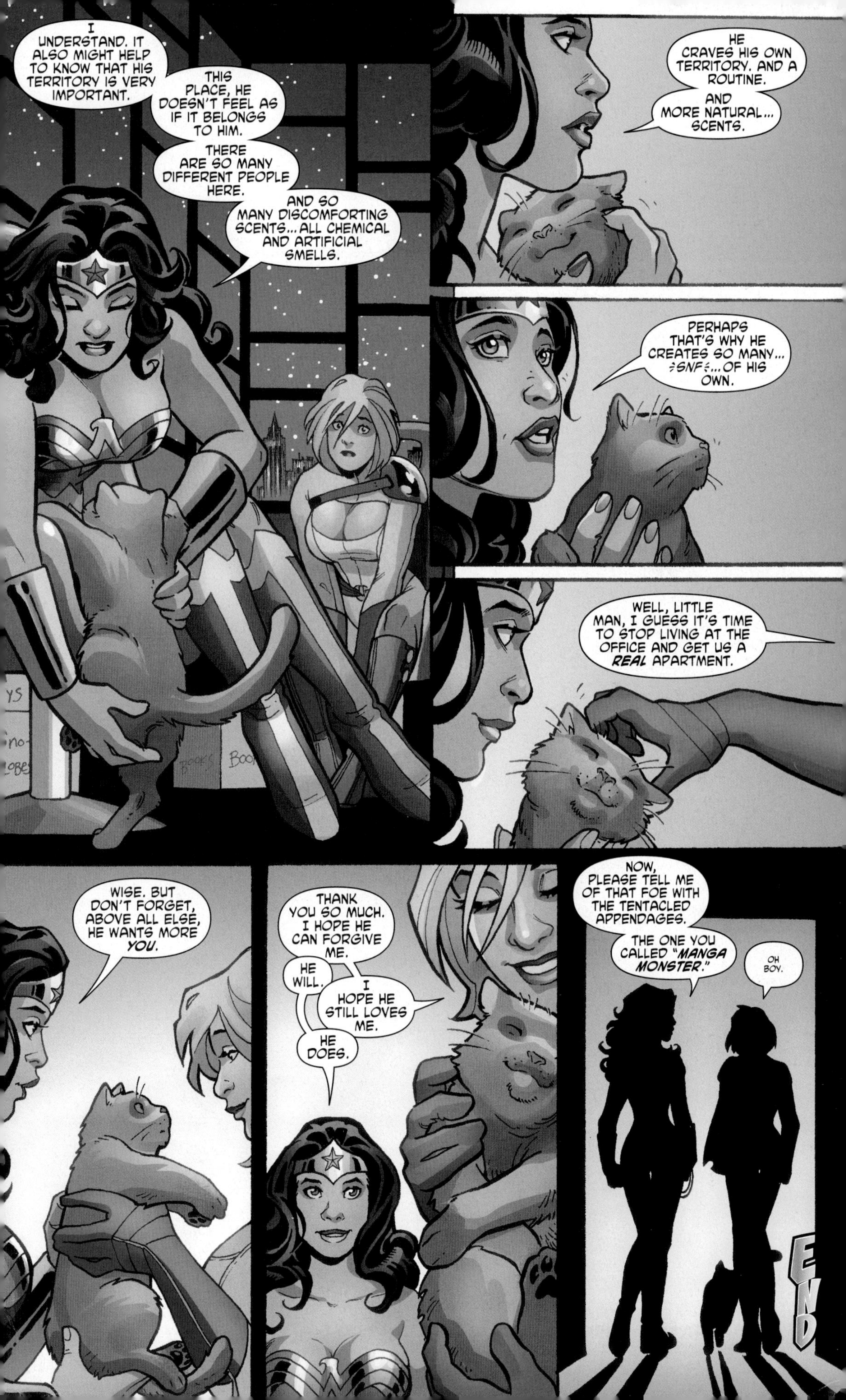
I UNDERSTAND. IT ALSO MIGHT HELP TO KNOW THAT HIS TERRITORY IS VERY IMPORTANT.
THIS PLACE, HE DOESN'T FEEL AS IF IT BELONGS TO HIM.
THERE ARE SO MANY DIFFERENT PEOPLE HERE.
AND SO MANY DISCOMFORTING SCENTS... ALL CHEMICAL AND ARTIFICIAL SMELLS.
HE CRAVES HIS OWN TERRITORY. AND A ROUTINE.
AND MORE NATURAL... SCENTS.
PERHAPS THAT'S WHY HE CREATES SO MANY... SNF... OF HIS OWN.
WELL, LITTLE MAN, I GUESS IT'S TIME TO STOP LIVING AT THE OFFICE AND GET US A REAL APARTMENT.
WISE. BUT DON'T FORGET, ABOVE ALL ELSE, HE WANTS MORE YOU.
THANK YOU SO MUCH. I HOPE HE CAN FORGIVE ME.
HE WILL.
I HOPE HE STILL LOVES ME.
HE DOES.
NOW, PLEASE TELL ME OF THAT FOE WITH THE TENTACLED APPENDAGES.
THE ONE YOU CALLED "MANGA MONSTER."
OH BOY.
END

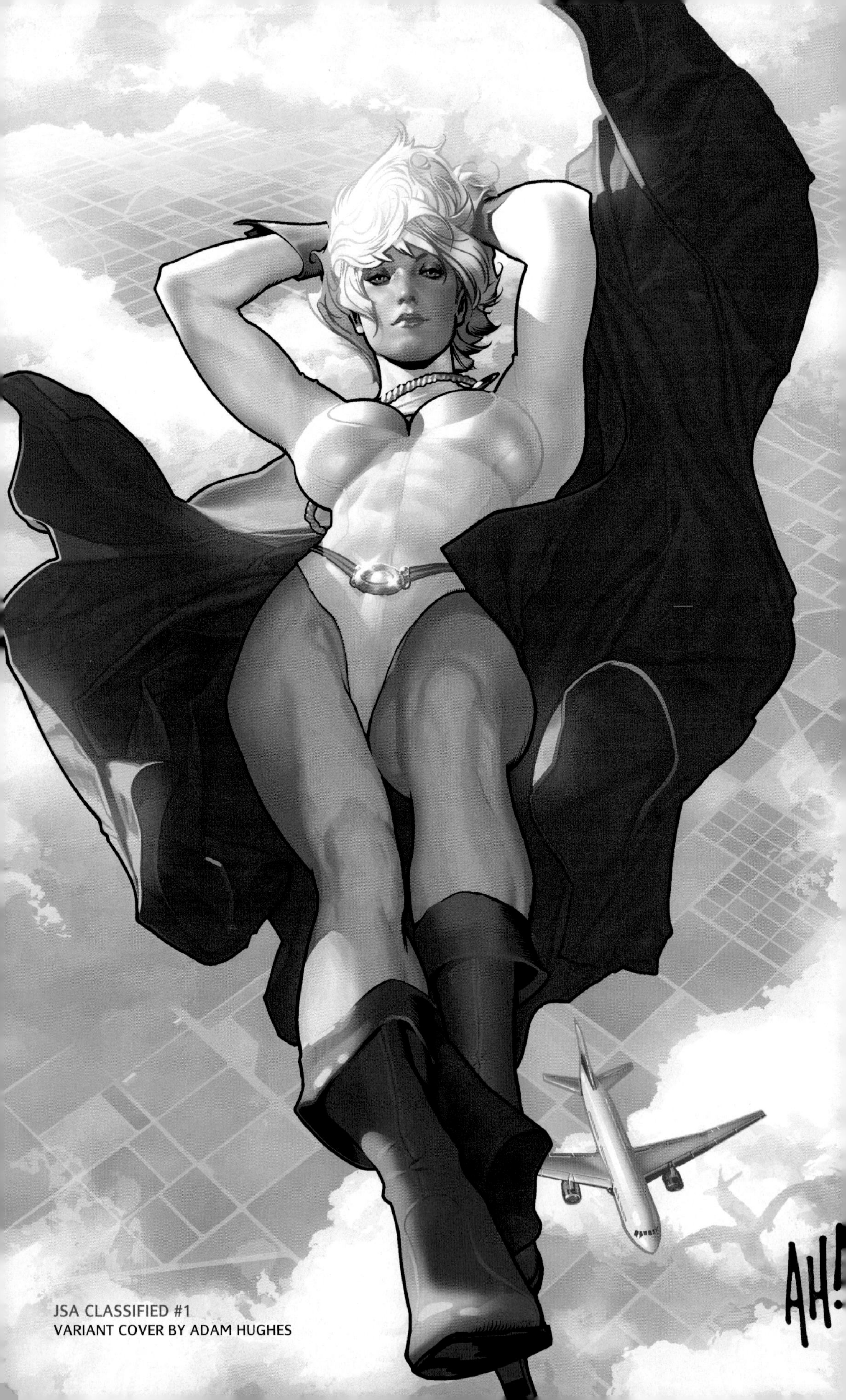
AH!

JSA CLASSIFIED #1
VARIANT COVER BY ADAM HUGHES

JSA CLASSIFIED #2
SECOND-PRINTING COVER BY ADAM HUGHES

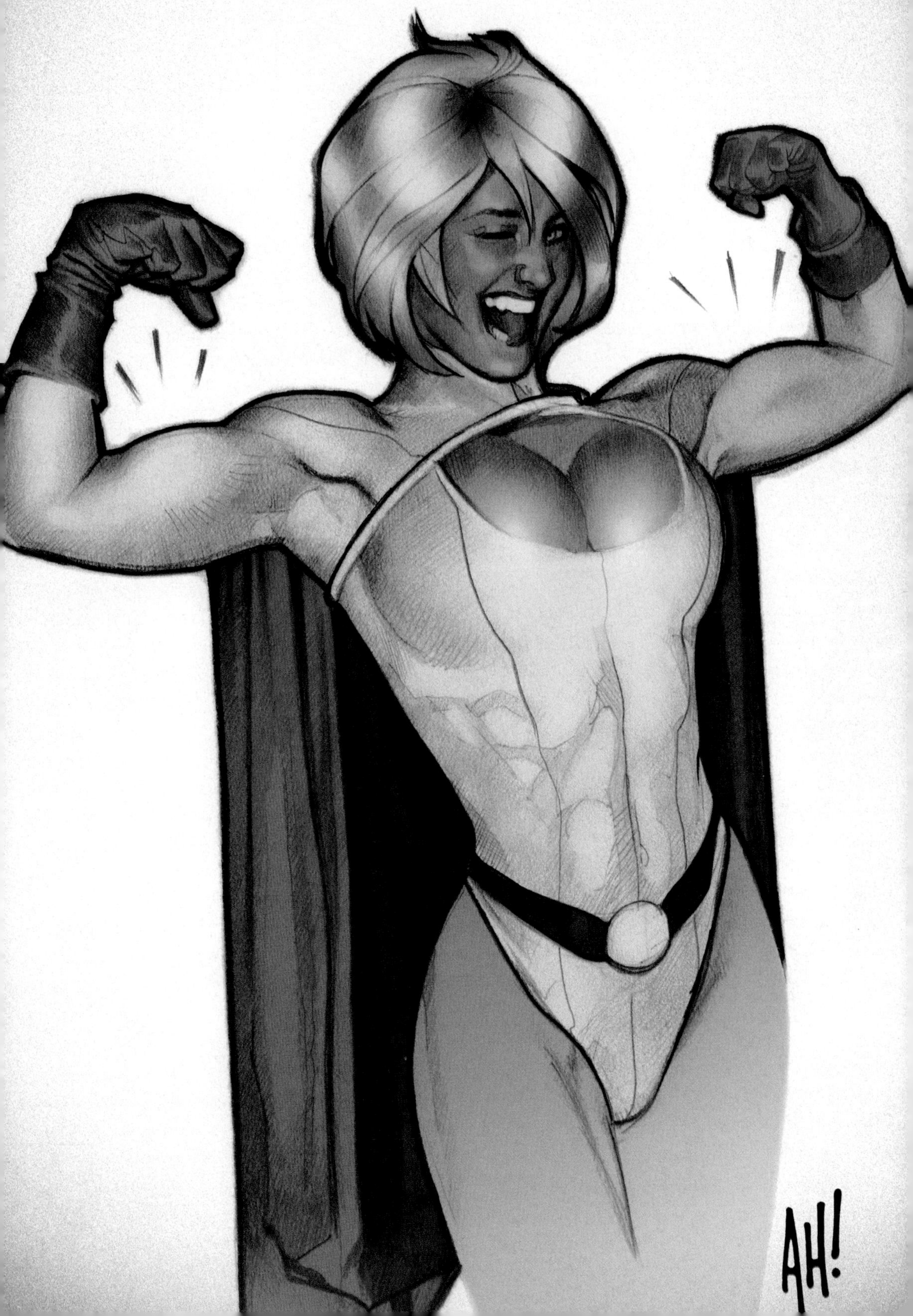
AH!

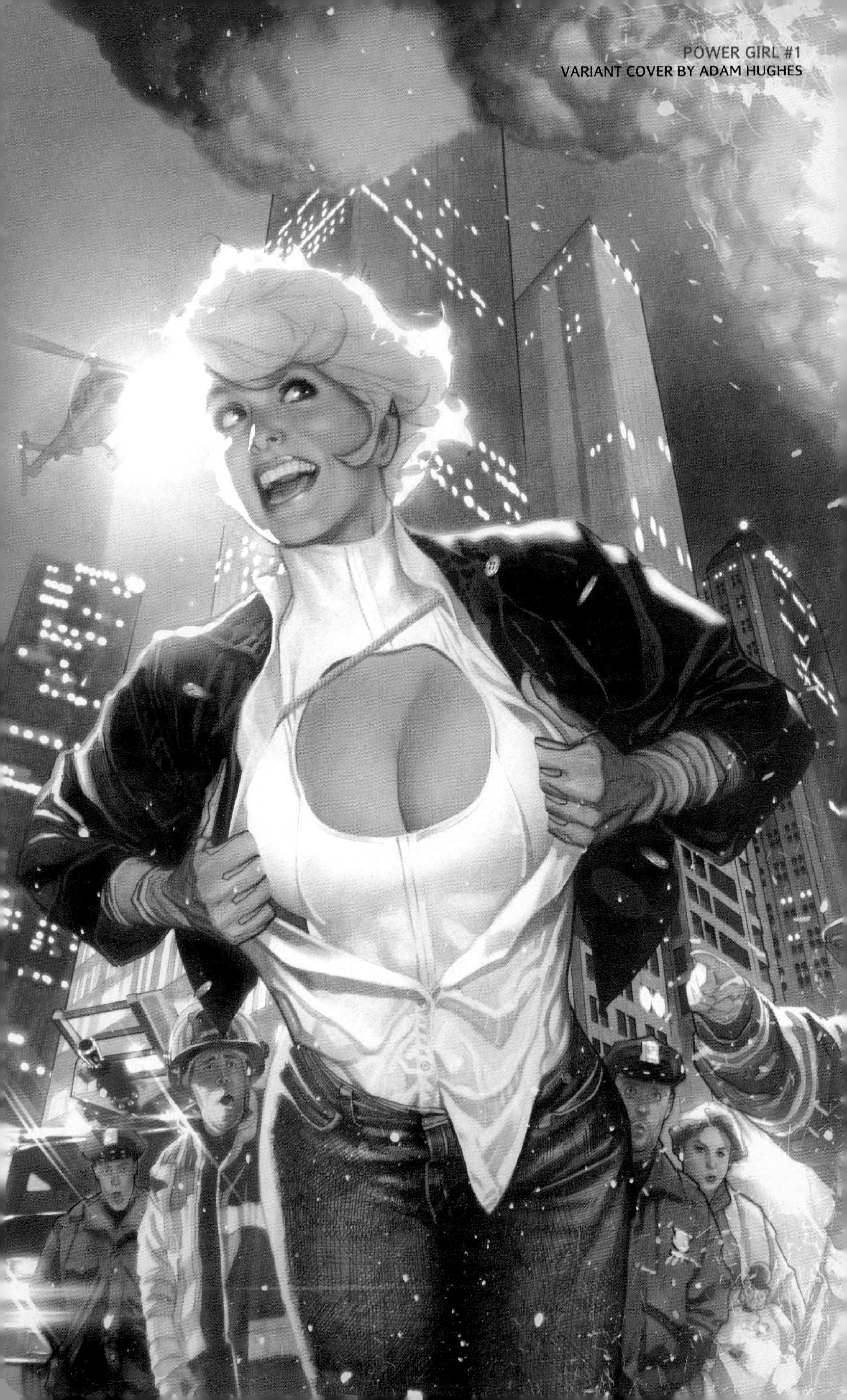

POWER GIRL #1
VARIANT COVER BY ADAM HUGHES

POWER GIRL #2
VARIANT COVER BY ADAM HUGHES

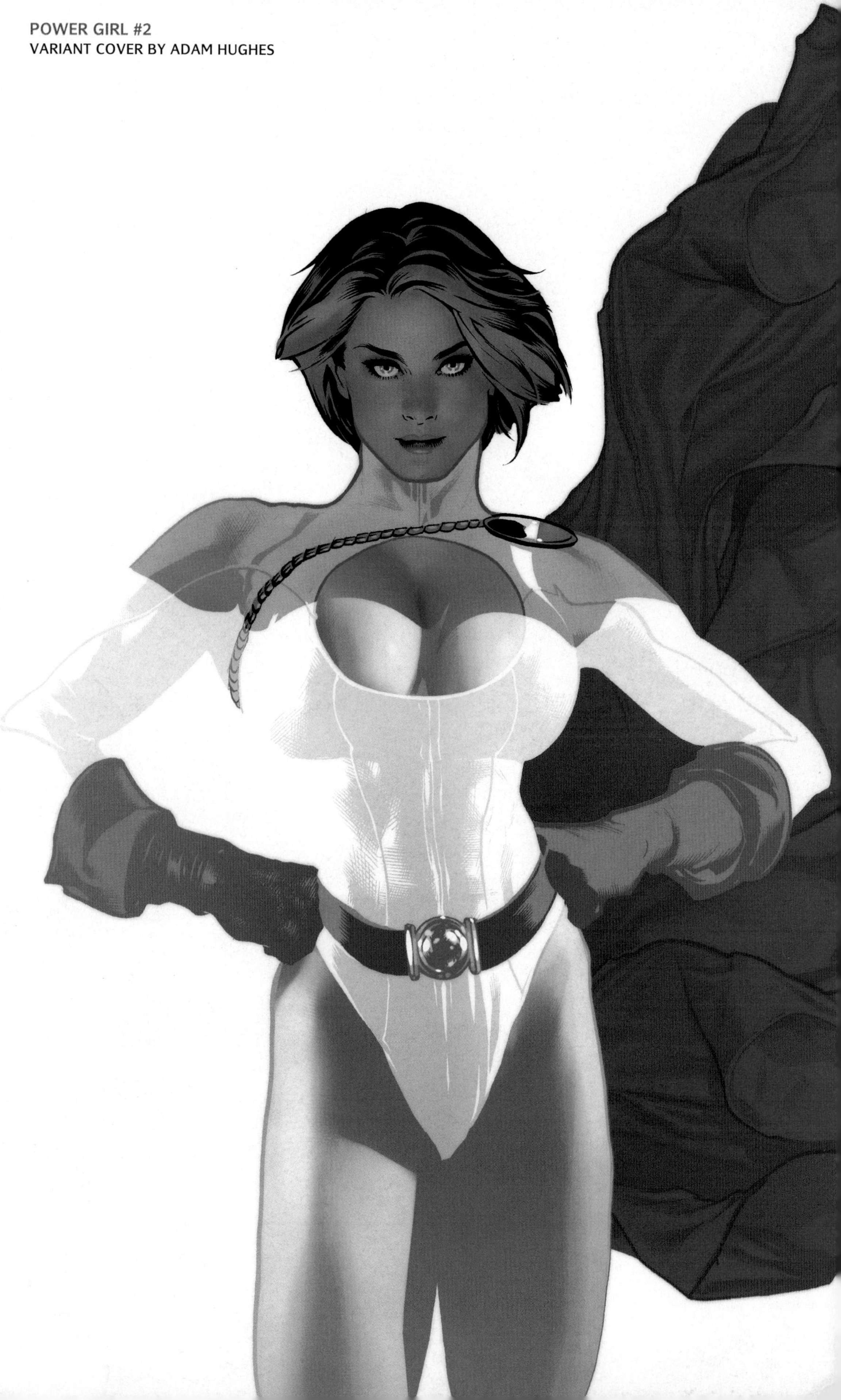

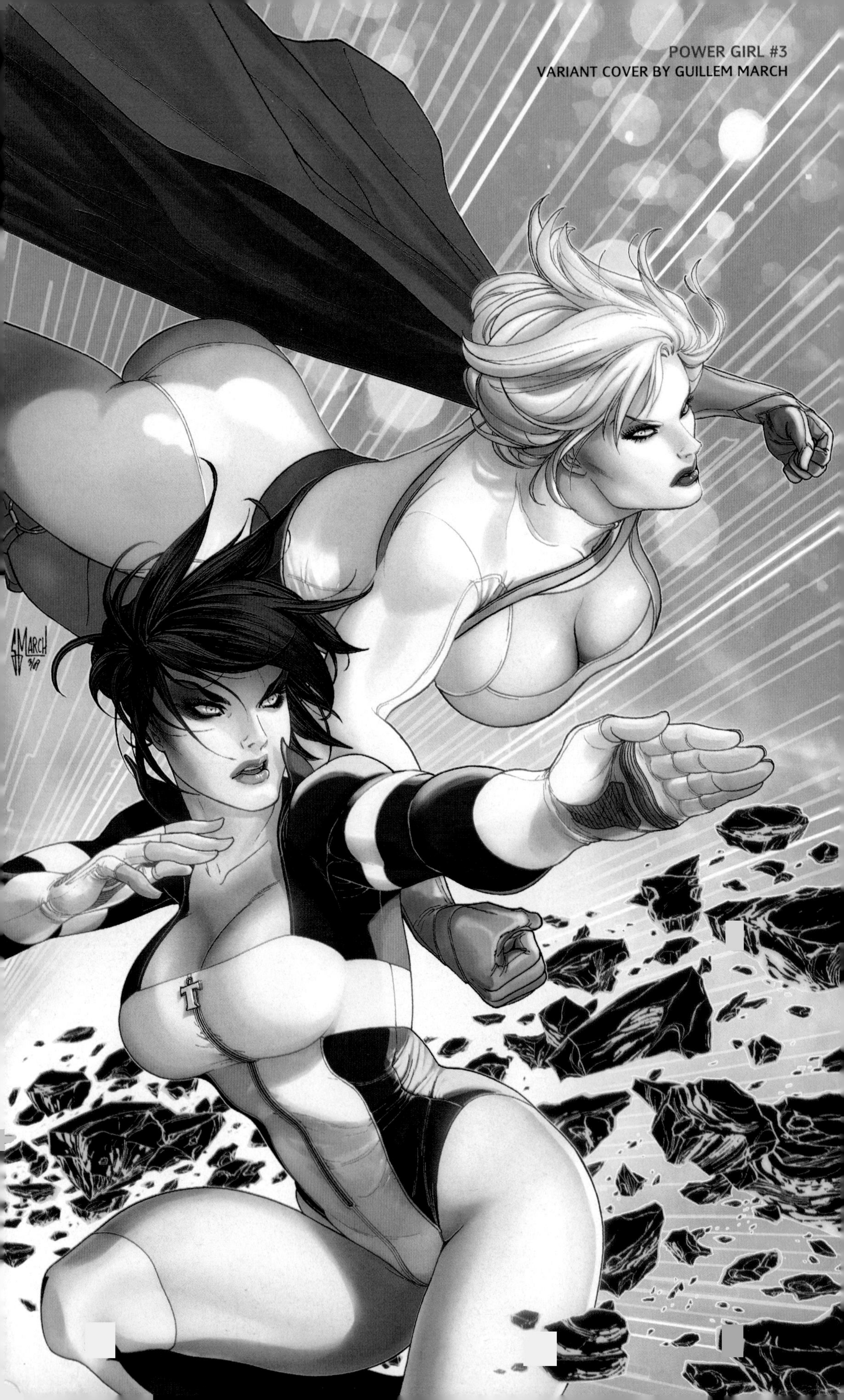

POWER GIRL #3
VARIANT COVER BY GUILLEM MARCH

POWER GIRL #4
VARIANT COVER BY GUILLEM MARCH

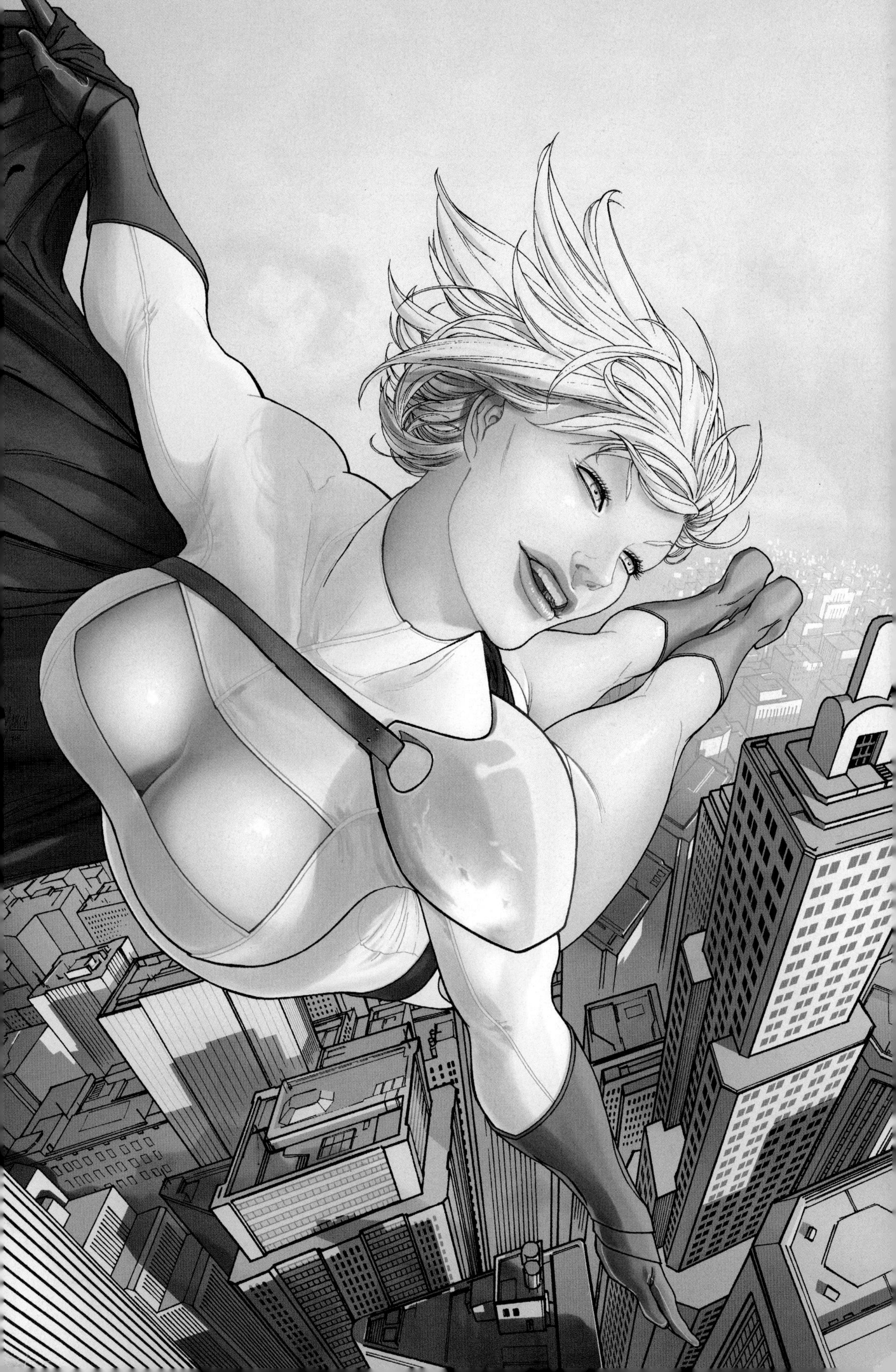

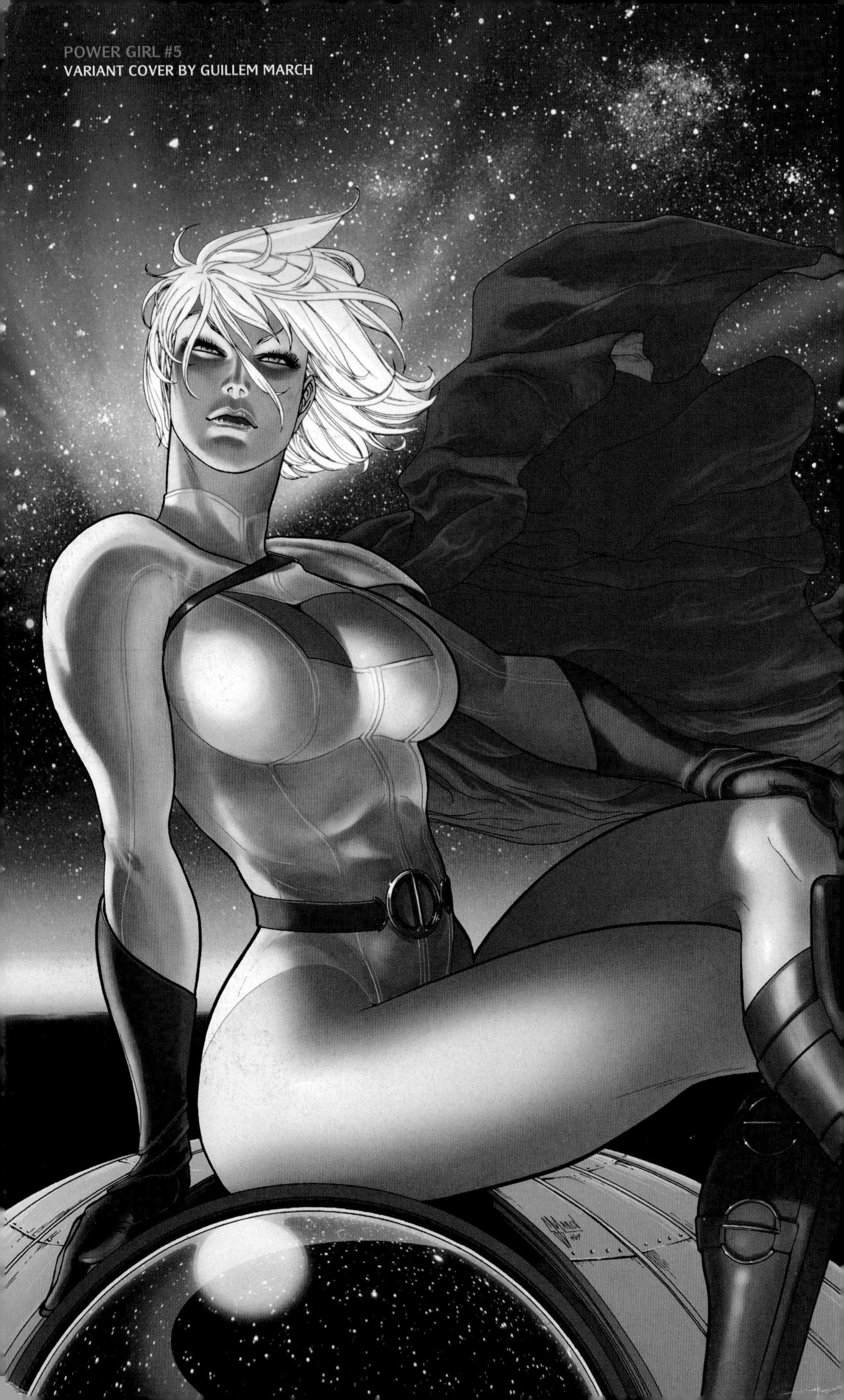

POWER GIRL #5
VARIANT COVER BY GUILLEM MARCH

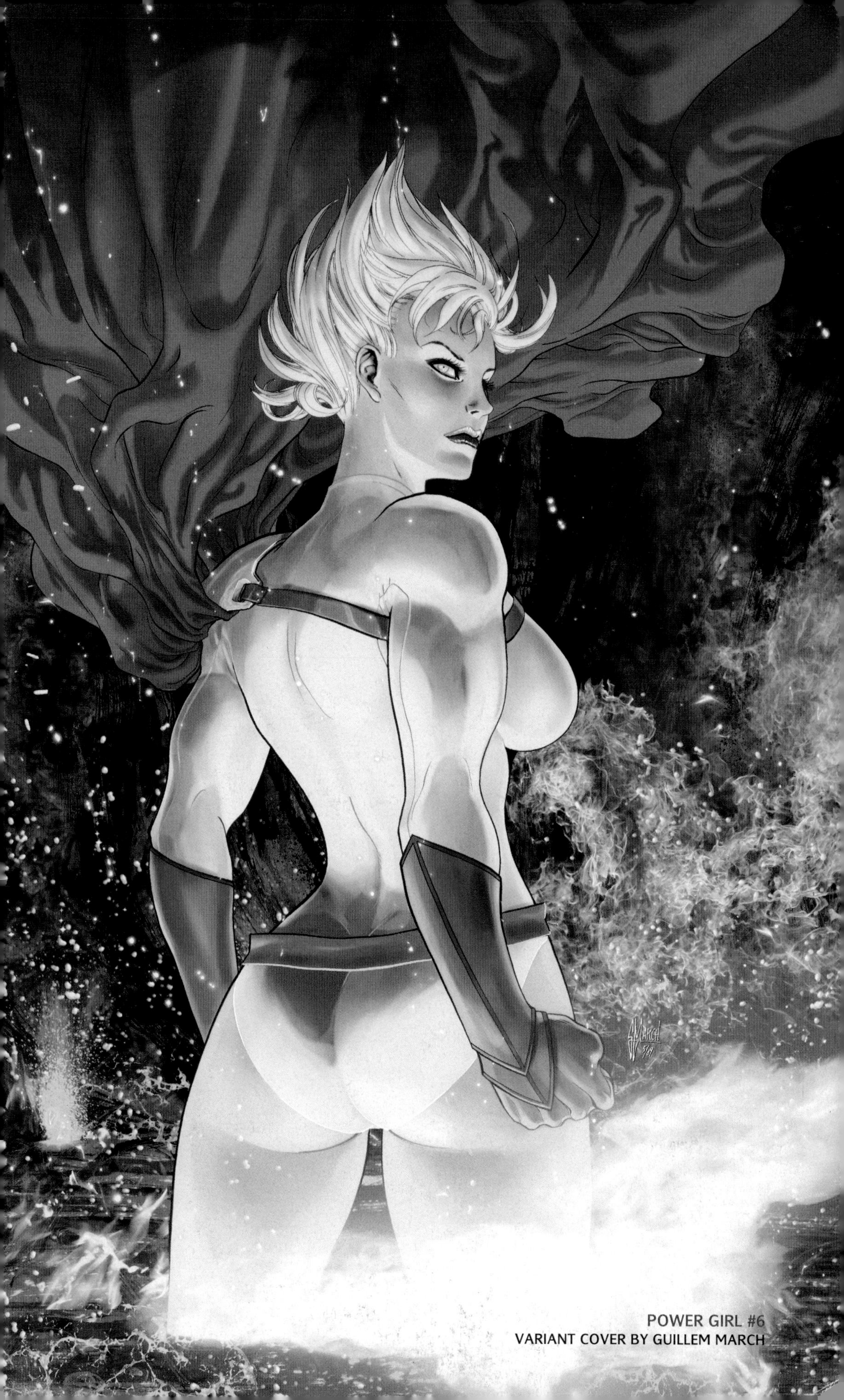

POWER GIRL #6
VARIANT COVER BY GUILLEM MARCH

POWER GIRL SKETCHBOOK BY AMANDA CONNER

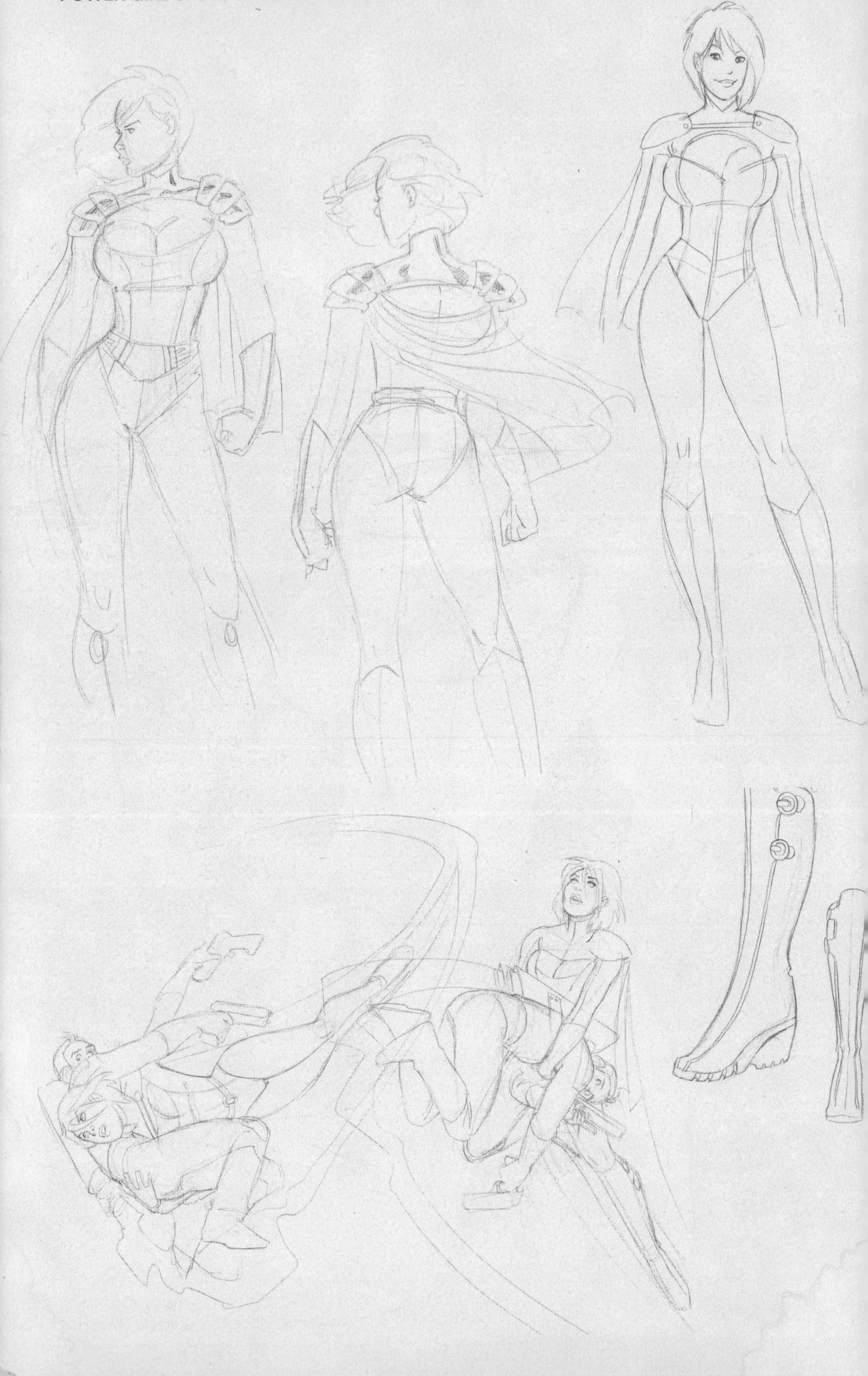

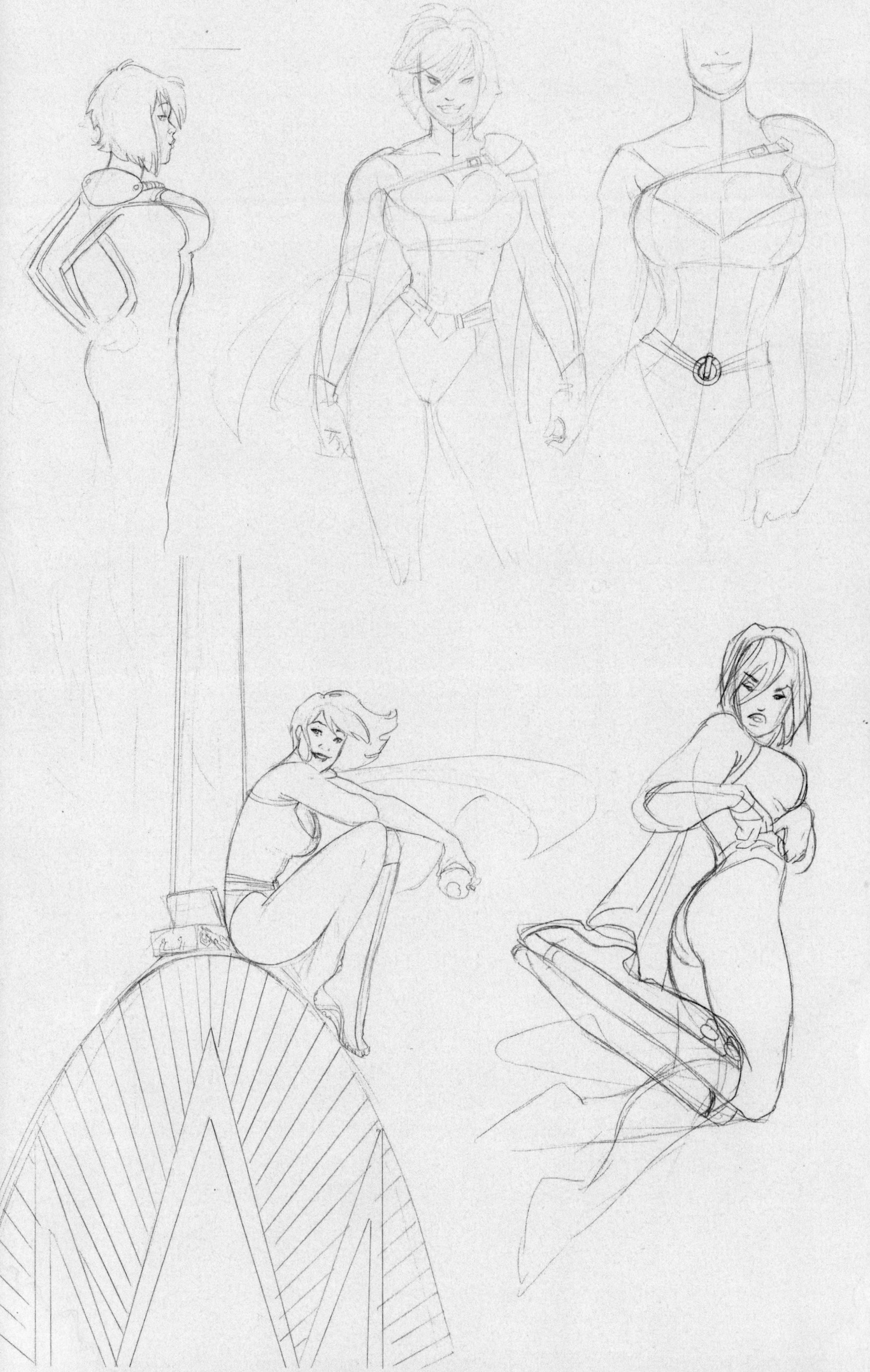

POWER GIRL #2 COVER SKETCH

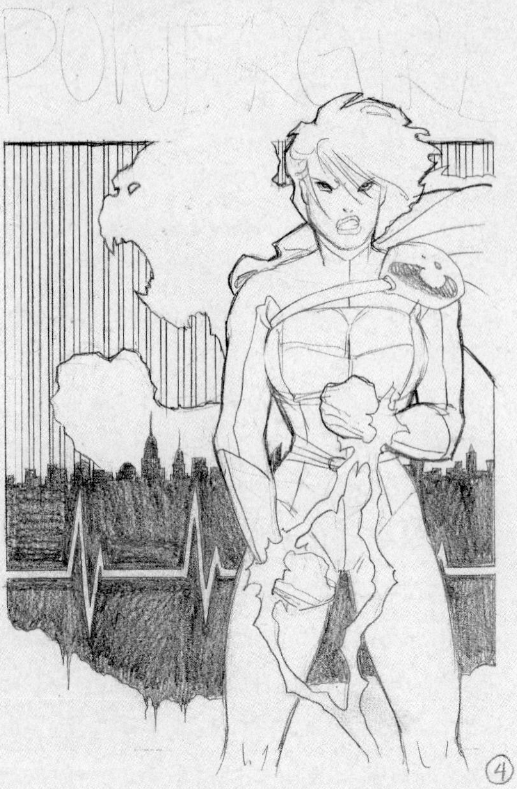

POWER GIRL #6 COVER SKETC

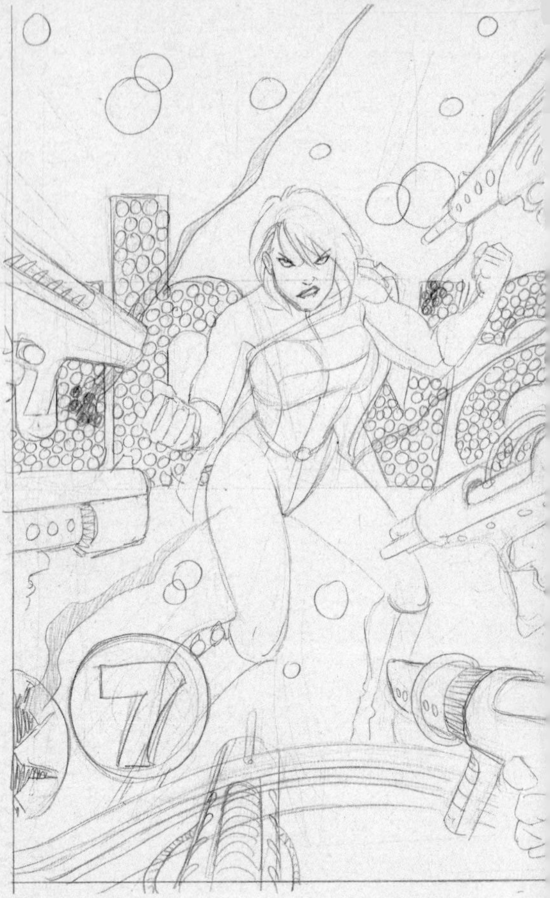

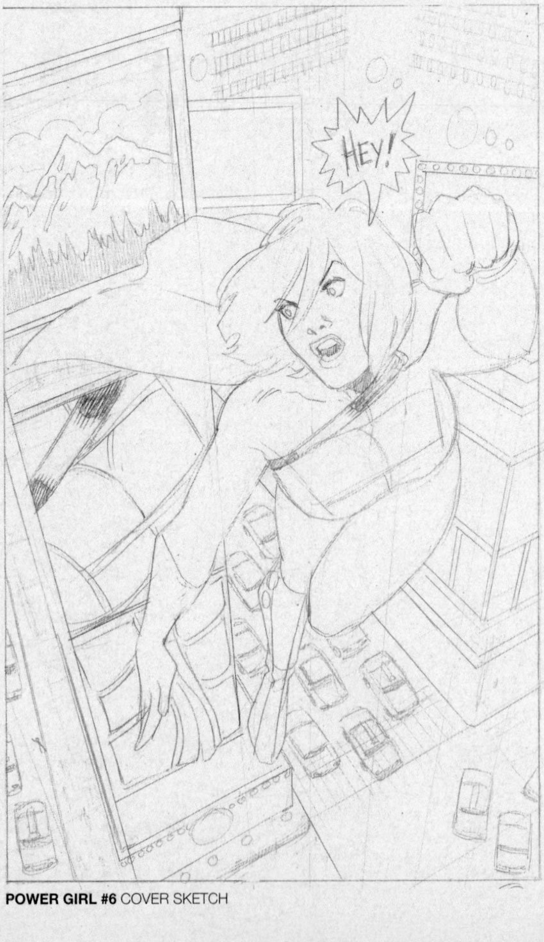
HEY!

POWER GIRL #6 COVER SKETCH